23rd Edition

Deskbook Encyclopedia of
Employment Law

- Employee Benefits
- Sexual Harassment
- Workers' Compensation

- Drug Testing
- Race Discrimination
- Employee Handbooks

- FLSA Issues
- Unemployment
- Hiring Practices

CEEL *Center for*
Education & Employment Law

Center for Education & Employment Law
P.O. Box 3008
Malvern, Pennsylvania 19355
www.employmentlawreport.net

The Library of Congress has catalogued this book as follows:

Employment - 23rd ed.

      p.   cm.

    Includes bibliographical references and index.

    ISBN 978-1-933043-86-9

      1. Labor laws and legislation—United States—Digests.

        I. Center for Education & Employment Law

KF3314.D47   2005

344.73'01—dc20

[347.3041]   94-441

                                        CIP

Library of Congress Catalog Card Number: 94-441
ISBN 978-1-933043-86-9

Cover Design by Patricia Jacoby
    Cover photo ©iStock.com/Feverpitched (gavel)
    Cover photo ©iStock.com/KatarzynaBialasiewicz (disabled man)
    Cover photo ©iStock.com/paolo81 (packed box)
    Cover photo ©mediabakery.com/Jack Hollingsworth (business meeting)

Other Titles Published by Center for Education & Employment Law:

Deskbook Encyclopedia of Public Employment Law
Deskbook Encyclopedia of American School Law
Higher Education Law in America
Keeping Your School Safe & Secure: A Practical Guide
Legal Update for Teachers: The Complete Principal's Guide
Private School Law in America
Students with Disabilities and Special Education

CHAPTER ONE
Discrimination

TABLE OF CONTENTS

CHAPTER TWO
Employer Liability

TABLE OF CONTENTS

CHAPTER THREE
Discipline, Suspension and Termination

CHAPTER FOUR
Employee Benefits

TABLE OF CONTENTS

CHAPTER FIVE
Labor Relations

TABLE OF CONTENTS

CHAPTER SIX
Employment Practices

TABLE OF CONTENTS

CHAPTER SEVEN
Workers' Compensation

TABLE OF CONTENTS

CHAPTER EIGHT
Unemployment Compensation

TABLE OF CONTENTS

INTRODUCTION

The *Deskbook Encyclopedia of Employment Law* provides a comprehensive selection of state and federal court decisions that impact employment. It covers a wide range of important topics including discrimination, employer liability, discipline and termination, employee benefits, and labor relations. Our editorial staff reviews court decisions from the past year for inclusion in the deskbook and arranges them topically so you can locate them easily. Within each chapter, the subsections contain explanatory passages to help you develop an overall understanding of the legal issues in that particular area. More importantly, each case summary has been written in everyday language with important facts, issues, and holdings highlighted in boldface type.

For your convenience, we have also included relevant provisions of the U.S. Constitution and compiled a topical list of U.S. Supreme Court decisions, separated into specific topics to allow you to gather more information on areas of particular interest to you.

We have designed the *Deskbook Encyclopedia of Employment Law* to provide professionals involved in all areas of employment law with access to important cases in the field. Our aim has been to make the law accessible to you regardless of your level of understanding of the legal system.

Thomas D'Agostino, Esq.
Managing Editor
Center for Education & Employment Law

ABOUT THE EDITORS

Curt J. Brown is the editorial director of the Center for Education & Employment Law. Prior to assuming his present position, he gained extensive experience in business-to-business publishing, including management of well-known publications such as *What's Working in Human Resources*, *What's New in Benefits & Compensation*, *Keep Up to Date with Payroll*, *Supervisors Legal Update*, and *Facility Manager's Alert*. Mr. Brown graduated from Villanova University School of Law and graduated *magna cum laude* from Bloomsburg University with a B.S. in Business Administration. He is admitted to the Pennsylvania bar.

Thomas D'Agostino is a managing editor at the Center for Education & Employment Law and is the editor of *Higher Education Legal Alert*. He graduated from the Duquesne University School of Law and received his undergraduate degree from Ramapo College of New Jersey. He is a past member of the American Bar Association's Section of Individual Rights and Responsibilities as well as the Pennsylvania Bar Association's Legal Services to Persons with Disabilities Committee. Mr. D'Agostino is admitted to the Pennsylvania bar.

Laurel Kalser is the editor of the monthly newsletters *Employment Law Report* and *Public Employment Law Report*. Ms. Kalser graduated *cum laude* from the University of Pennsylvania, and received her law degree from the University of Miami in Coral Gables, Florida, where she was a member of the Moot Court Board for outstanding appellate advocacy. Ms. Kalser is admitted to the Florida Bar.

HOW TO USE YOUR DESKBOOK

We have designed your *Deskbook Encyclopedia of Employment Law* in an accessible format for both attorneys and non-attorneys to use as a research and reference tool toward prevention of legal problems.

Using Your Deskbook to Conduct Research

As a research tool, our deskbook allows you to conduct your research on two different levels by topics or by cases.

➤ *Researching a Topic*

If you have a general interest in a particular **topic** area, our **table of contents** provides descriptive section headings with detailed subheadings for each chapter.

✓ For your convenience, we also include the chapter table of contents at the beginning of each chapter.

> **Example:**
> For information on notice under the FMLA, the table of contents indicates that a discussion of that subject takes place in Chapter Six under the section heading, The Family and Medical Leave Act, and begins on page 407.
>

If you have a specific interest in a particular **issue**, our comprehensive **index** collects all of the relevant page references to particular issues.

> **Example:**
> For cases involving breach of contract, the index refers you to the page numbers where that issue is discussed.

 Breach of contract, 164-174
    Oral contracts, 168-174
    Oral representations, 169-171
    Written contracts, 165-168

➢ *Researching a Case*

If you know the **name** of a particular case, our **table of cases** will allow you to quickly reference the location of the case.

> **Example:**
> If you wanted to look up the case *Hoffman Plastic Compounds, Inc. v. NLRB*, you would look in the table of cases, which has been arranged alphabetically, under H.
>
> **H**
>
> Hodgkins v. New England Telephone Co., 406
> Hoffman Plastic Compounds, Inc. v. NLRB, 296
> Hoffman v. Professional Med Team, 417
> Hoffman v. Solis, 345
> Hogue v. Blue Bell Creameries, L.P., 492
> Holbrook v. Harman Automotive, Inc., 122

✓ Each of the cases summarized in the deskbook also contains the case citation that will allow you to access the full text of the case from a law library. *See How to Read a Case Citation, p. 559.*

If your interest lies in cases from a **particular state**, our **table of cases by state** will identify the cases from your state and direct you to the page numbers where they are located.

Example:

If cases from Texas are of interest, the table of cases by state, arranged alphabetically, lists all of the cases from Texas that have been summarized in the book.

TEXAS

Administaff Companies, Inc. v. New York
   Joint Board, 360
Aetna Health Care v. Davila, 234
Air Line Pilots Ass'n Int'l v. O'Neill, 338
Alaniz v. Zamora-Quezada, 43
Arnett v. Sears, Roebuck and Co,, 284
Baham v. McLane Foodservice, Inc., 415
Barnes v. United Parcel Service, Inc., 450

✓ Remember, the judicial system has two court systems – state and federal – which generally function independently of each other. *See The Judicial System, p. 555.* We have included the federal court cases in the table of cases by state according to the state in which the court resides. However, federal court decisions often impact other federal courts within that particular circuit. Therefore, it may be helpful to review cases from all of the states contained in a particular circuit.

Reference Tool

As a reference tool, the deskbook includes information of a general nature that can be helpful in determining legal rights and responsibilities. For example:

Appendix A contains provisions of the **U.S. Constitution** that are relevant to employment law. The Commerce Clause, for instance, located on page 539, grants Congress the right to regulate commerce and is the source of power for most of the laws enacted by the legislature.

Appendix B contains a list of recent and important **U.S. Supreme Court employment cases**. The cases are arranged by subject matter and have been placed in reverse chronological order (from newest to oldest).

We hope you benefit from the use of your *Deskbook Encyclopedia of Employment Law*. If you have any questions about how to use the book, please contact Thomas D'Agostino at tdagostino@pbp.com.

TABLE OF ABBREVIATIONS

The following abbreviations are used in your *Deskbook Encyclopedia of Employment Law*.

ADA – Americans with Disabilities Act

ADEA – Age Discrimination in Employment Act

ALJ – administrative law judge

CBA – collective bargaining agreement

CEO – chief executive officer

CFO – chief financial officer

CGL – comprehensive general liability

COBRA – Consolidated Omnibus Budget Reconciliation Act of 1985

COO – chief operating officer

DOT – Department of Transportation

DUI – driving under the influence

EEO – equal employment opportunity

EEOC – Equal Employment Opportunity Commission

EPPA – Employee Polygraph Protection Act

ERISA – Employee Retirement Income Security Act

FAA – Federal Aviation Administration

FCA – False Claims Act

FELA – Federal Employers' Liability Act

FLSA – Fair Labor Standards Act

FMLA – Family and Medical Leave Act

FRA – Federal Railroad Administration

TABLE OF ABBREVIATIONS

HMO – health maintenance organization

HR – human resources

HSA – Hours of Service Act

INS – Immigration and Naturalization Service

IRCA – Immigration Reform and Control Act

IRS – Internal Revenue Service

IT – information technology

LHWCA – Longshore and Harbor Workers' Compensation Act

LMRA – Labor Management Relations Act

LMRDA – Labor Management Reporting and Disclosure Act

MPPA – Multi-employer Pension Plan Amendments Act of 1980

NLRA – National Labor Relations Act

NLRB – National Labor Relations Board

OSHA – Occupational Safety and Health Administration

OSH Act – Occupational Safety and Health Act

OWBPA – Older Workers Benefit Protection Act

PTO– paid time off

RICO – Racketeer Influenced and Corrupt Organizations Act

RIF – reduction in force

RLA – Railway Labor Act

STAA – Surface Transportation Assistance Act

Title VII – Title VII of the Civil Rights Act of 1964

UPS – United Parcel Service

USERRA – Uniformed Services Employment and Reemployment Rights Act

WARN Act – Worker Adjustment and Retraining Notification Act

TABLE OF CASES

TABLE OF CASES

TABLE OF CASES

TABLE OF CASES

TABLE OF CASES

TABLE OF CASES

TABLE OF CASES

TABLE OF CASES

TABLE OF CASES

TABLE OF CASES

TABLE OF CASES

TABLE OF CASES

TABLE OF CASES

TABLE OF CASES

TABLE OF CASES

TABLE OF CASES BY STATE

TABLE OF CASES BY STATE

TABLE OF CASES BY STATE

TABLE OF CASES BY STATE

TABLE OF CASES BY STATE

WYOMING

CHAPTER ONE

Discrimination

I.   RACE AND NATIONAL ORIGIN DISCRIMINATION

Title VII of the Civil Rights Act of 1964 and 42 U.S.C. § 1981 protect against employment discrimination on the basis of race, and Title VII (but not Section 1981) protects against national origin discrimination. State laws also protect workers from race and national origin discrimination.

Under both state and federal law, employers cannot discriminate on the basis of race or national origin in hiring, promotions, benefits, firing, discipline, transfers, etc. In other words: **Never** take race into account when making any employment decision.

Note that with respect to race and national origin claims as well as other claims of unlawful bias filed under Title VII, employers may be held liable for the discriminatory intent of a supervisor who is not directly involved in taking adverse action against an employee. In these cases, a supervisor with discriminatory intent influences the decision of the person who takes the adverse action. The Supreme Court validated this "cat's paw" theory of liability in *Staub v. Proctor Hospital*, 131 S.Ct. 1186, 179 L.Ed.2d 144 (U.S. 2011).

You may take national origin into account where you can show that having an employee of a particular national origin is a <u>bona fide occupational qualification</u> for a specific position. However, such situations will be extremely rare.

Even if you don't take race or national origin into account in your employment decision-making, you still could become liable if you make decisions that are designed to be neutral but have a negative impact on persons of certain races or ethnic backgrounds. This is known as <u>disparate impact discrimination</u>.

A. Federal Statutes and Supreme Court Interpretations

Title VII applies to any entity engaged in an industry affecting commerce that has 15 or more employees. Its coverage is limited to employment discrimination based upon race, color, sex, religion or national origin.

The U.S. Equal Employment Opportunity Commission (EEOC) is empowered to enforce Title VII through investigation and administrative complaint procedures or federal court lawsuits. Indeed, a private individual alleging discrimination must pursue administrative remedies within the EEOC before the individual will be allowed to sue an employer under Title VII.

Plaintiffs who prevail in an employment discrimination lawsuit will be entitled, where appropriate, to back pay, front pay, accumulated seniority and other benefits, and attorneys' fees. Further, Title VII allows the recovery of monetary damages for intentional discrimination except for cases of race discrimination where monetary damages are already available under 42 U.S.C. § 1981. Title VII is found at 42 U.S.C. § 2000e *et seq.*

§ 2000e-2. Unlawful employment practices

(a) Employer practices

It shall be an unlawful employment practice for an employer –
(1) to fail or refuse to hire or to discharge any individual, or otherwise to discriminate against any individual with respect to his compensation, terms, conditions, or privileges of employment, because of such individual's race, color, religion, sex, or national origin; or
(2) to limit, segregate, or classify his employees or applicants for employment in any way which would deprive or tend to deprive any individual of employment opportunities or otherwise adversely affect his status as an employee, because of such individual's race, color, religion, sex, or national origin.

* * *

42 U.S.C. § 1981
Equal rights under the law

(a) All persons within the jurisdiction of the United States shall have the same right in every State and Territory to make and enforce contracts, to sue, be parties, give evidence, and to the full and equal benefit of all laws and proceedings for the security of persons and property as is enjoyed by white citizens, and shall be subject to like punishment, pains, penalties, taxes, licenses, and exactions of every kind, and to no other.
(b) For purposes of this section, the term 'make and enforce contracts' includes the making, performance, modification, and termination of contracts, and the enjoyment of all benefits, privileges, terms, and conditions of the contractual relationship.
(c) The rights protected by this section are protected against impairment by nongovernmental discrimination and impairment under color of State law.

* * *

♦   One of the most important Supreme Court cases in the area of civil rights is *Griggs v. Duke Power Co.*, where the Court held that **Title VII forbids not only practices adopted with a discriminatory motive, but also those that have a discriminatory effect**. In *Griggs,* a group of black employees at a North Carolina power plant sued under Title VII, challenging their employer's requirement that employees possess a high school diploma or pass an intelligence test as a condition of employment. Section 703 of the act authorized the use of an ability test, so long as it was not intended or used to discriminate. The district court held that the employer's prior policy of racial discrimination had ended, and the Court of Appeals upheld that determination. The U.S. Supreme Court then held that if a practice excludes minorities and that practice cannot be shown to be related to job performance, it is prohibited, even if the employer lacked discriminatory intent. Title VII does not preclude the use of testing or measuring procedures, so long as they are demonstrably a reasonable measure of job performance. In this case, the procedures were not related to job performance. Therefore, they violated Title VII. *Griggs v. Duke Power Co.*, 401 U.S. 424, 91 S.Ct. 849, 28 L.Ed.2d 158 (1971).

◆   The Supreme Court created a shifting burden of proof standard for Title VII discrimination lawsuits in a case where a black civil rights activist engaged in disruptive and illegal activity, asserting that his discharge and the employer's hiring practices were racially motivated. Soon after, the employer advertised for qualified personnel but rejected the activist's reemployment application on the grounds of his illegal conduct. The activist filed a complaint with the EEOC and claimed a Title VII violation. The EEOC found that there was reasonable cause to believe that the decision violated Title VII, which forbids discrimination against applicants or employees for protesting discriminatory employment conditions. The activist then filed suit against the employer, and a Missouri federal district court ruled that the activist's illegal activity was not protected.

The case reached the U.S. Supreme Court, which held that in a private, non-class-action complaint under Title VII, the complaining party has the burden of establishing a *prima facie* **case** of employment discrimination. Therefore, the activist had to show that:

1) he belonged to a racial minority
2) he applied and was qualified for a job the employer was trying to fill
3) he was rejected, and
4) the employer continued to seek applicants with his qualifications.

Even though the activist had done this, the employer had responded to the activist's *prima facie* case by showing that it had a reason for rejecting him. The Court remanded the case with instructions to provide the activist an opportunity to establish his ultimate burden to show that the employer's reason for refusal was simply a pretext for a racially discriminatory decision. *McDonnell Douglas Corp. v. Green*, 411 U.S. 792, 93 S.Ct. 1817, 36 L.Ed.2d 668 (1973).

◆   A Tennessee school district employee answered questions about discrimination as part of an investigation into a sexual harassment complaint. Shortly thereafter, she was fired. She sued for retaliation under Title VII, but a federal court granted pretrial judgment to the county. After the Sixth Circuit affirmed, the U.S. Supreme Court reversed, holding that the employee could pursue her claim under **the "opposition" clause of Title VII**, which prohibits an employer from retaliating against an employee who opposes discrimination. *Crawford v. Metropolitan Government of Nashville and Davidson County*, 555 U.S. 271, 129 S.Ct. 846, 172 L.Ed.2d 650 (2009).

◆ A black assistant manager at an Illinois restaurant claimed he was fired because he complained that a white colleague fired a black subordinate for race-based reasons. He sued the restaurant for retaliation under 42 U.S.C. § 1981, which prohibits race discrimination in the making and enforcement of contracts. The case reached the U.S. Supreme Court, which held that **Section 1981 also prohibits employers from retaliating against employees who complain of race discrimination**. The right to "make and enforce contracts" also includes the right to complain of race discrimination without being retaliated against for doing so. *CBOCS West, Inc. v. Humphries*, 553 U.S. 442, 128 S.Ct. 1951, 170 L.Ed.2d 864 (2008).

◆ Two African-American employees in Alabama sued under Title VII when they were passed over for promotions in favor of two white employees. The plant manager called them "boy" when talking to them. A jury ruled in their favor, but the Eleventh Circuit held that the use of the word "boy" by itself was not evidence of discrimination. The U.S. Supreme Court held that **the use of the word "boy" by itself could evidence racial animus**, given the context of the remark, inflection or tone of voice, local custom and historical usage. Also, the employees did not have to prove that their qualifications were so superior to the white employees' that the difference virtually jumped off the page and slapped the court in the face. A better test was needed for determining pretext in the qualifications context – e.g., were the plaintiff's qualifications "clearly superior"? Or could no reasonable person have chosen the selected candidate over the plaintiff? The Court remanded the case. *Ash v. Tyson Foods, Inc.*, 546 U.S. 454, 126 S.Ct. 1195, 163 L.Ed.2d 1053 (2006).

◆ A Missouri halfway house demoted and ultimately discharged an African-American correctional officer, who sued for race discrimination under Title VII. A federal court found that the employer's stated reasons for its actions were pretextual. However, the court held that the officer had failed to carry his ultimate burden of proving that the adverse actions were racially motivated. The case reached the U.S. Supreme Court, which agreed that **even if an employer's asserted reasons for its actions are pretextual, a plaintiff is not necessarily entitled to judgment as a matter of law**. Once the officer established a *prima facie* case of discrimination, a presumption arose that the employer unlawfully discriminated against him. This presumption placed upon the employer the burden of proving that the adverse actions were taken for legitimate, nondiscriminatory reasons. However, the ultimate burden of persuasion remained at all times with the employee. The case was remanded to determine whether the employer intentionally discriminated against the officer. *St. Mary's Honor Center v. Hicks*, 509 U.S. 502, 113 S.Ct. 2742, 125 L.Ed.2d 407 (1993).

◆ A federal court ordered a union to end its discriminatory practices, establishing a 29% nonwhite membership goal (based on the percentage of nonwhites in the relevant labor pool in New York City). After the union failed to comply, the court imposed a fine to be placed in a special fund so as to increase nonwhite membership in the union. The U.S. Supreme Court noted that **Title VII allowed the kind of affirmative, race-conscious relief the district**

court had ordered. A court need not order relief only for actual victims of past discrimination, but can also order relief of a broader scope to satisfy the purposes of Title VII. *Local 28 of Sheet Metal Workers v. EEOC,* 478 U.S. 421, 106 S.Ct. 3019, 92 L.Ed.2d 344 (1986).

◆   A union and a Louisiana company entered into a collective bargaining agreement. The agreement included an affirmative action plan designed to raise the percentage of black craftworkers in the company's plants to the percentage of blacks in the local labor force. After some junior black employees were selected for in-plant craft training programs over some senior white employees, a lawsuit was brought, alleging that the affirmative action program violated Title VII. The U.S. Supreme Court stated that **Title VII's prohibition against racial discrimination did not condemn all private, voluntary, race-conscious affirmative action plans**. To do so would defeat the very purpose of Title VII. The affirmative action plan here was permissible. It opened employment opportunities for blacks in areas that were traditionally closed to them, it did not unnecessarily trammel the interests of white employees, and it did not create an absolute bar. Finally, the plan was a temporary measure, designed only to eliminate a manifest racial imbalance. *United Steelworkers v. Weber,* 443 U.S. 193, 99 S.Ct. 2721, 61 L.Ed.2d 480 (1979).

◆   Two white employees of a transportation company were discharged for misappropriating cargo from one of the company's shipments. However, a black employee, charged with the same offense, was not fired. When they sued under Title VII, the U.S. Supreme Court held that **Title VII and Section 1981 apply to whites as much as to nonwhites in the private employment context**. A discipline policy that is applied more harshly to whites than nonwhites violates Title VII. *McDonald v. Santa Fe Trail Transportation Co.,* 427 U.S. 273, 96 S.Ct. 2574, 49 L.Ed.2d 493 (1976).

B. Race Discrimination

Most cases of race discrimination get filed under Title VII (intentional and unintentional discrimination) or 42 U.S.C. § 1981 (intentional discrimination only). Under Title VII, employees must first avail themselves of administrative remedies before suing, whereas under Section 1981, employees can proceed to court directly.

Since most employers ensure that intentional race discrimination does not occur, the greater danger often lies in unintentional discrimination – for example, where an employer requires a college degree for a job that does not necessitate such an education. Even though this policy is neutral on its face, it could be construed as discriminatory where more whites than minorities graduate from college.

Affirmative Action: While affirmative action may be permissible in very limited circumstances – for example, where there has been historic discrimination or where a current imbalance is due to past discriminatory practices – you should not assume that an affirmative action policy will comply with Title VII.

◆   An African-American sales manager in Pennsylvania sued her employer under 42 U.S.C. § 1981, claiming her supervisor mistreated her based on her race, such as by trying to change her sales territory, delaying processing of her expense reports, assigning a product launch to a white manager, and giving her negative and unfair feedback on projects. But **the sales manager did not produce enough evidence to show that she suffered an adverse job action** or that the supervisor's treatment of her was based on her race. Her sales territory never changed; the negative feedback did not adversely affect her pay or benefits; and the delayed expense reports and assignment of a project to a white manager did not tangibly alter her working conditions. The court ruled for the employer. *Walker v. Centocor Ortho Biotech*, 558 Fed.Appx. 216 (3d Cir. 2014) (Unpublished).

◆   An African-American HR manager in Florida sued his employer for race discrimination under Title VII after **the employer outsourced the job functions he performed**. An appeals court rejected his claim. The HR manager wasn't replaced, and the employer explained that it outsourced his job functions for three legitimate reasons: the company had recently lost business and had to lay people off; the outsourcing saved the company $8,000; and the company was concerned about the manager's job performance. *Taylor v. Teakdecking Systems, Inc.*, 571 Fed.Appx. 767 (11th Cir. 2014) (Unpublished).

◆   An African-American salesman in Ohio received awards for outstanding performance. When his employer acquired another company, it decided to reduce a nine-person unit to four. The salesman was laid off, purportedly based on a low recent performance review and interviews conducted by his supervisor. He sued for race discrimination under Title VII, and a district court ruled against him. But the Sixth Circuit reversed. It determined that **a jury could find the salesman was unlawfully singled out for layoff** because the performance review ratings were suspiciously low, he was treated differently in the layoff interview, and evidence suggested managers were hostile toward minorities. *Rachells v. Cingular Wireless Employees Services, LLC*, 732 F.3d 652 (6th Cir. 2013).

◆   Security footage showed an African-American cashier taking money from a register on four different days. Her Alabama employer terminated her after an investigation. She said the money was hers, and she sued the employer for race bias under Title VII. **The court rejected her claim that she showed race discrimination because a white cashier came up short and was not disciplined.** She did not support her claim that the other cashier came up short or did so because she took money. The termination was upheld. *Austin v. Compass Group*, No. 2:12-CV-02564, 2014 WL 37738 (N.D. Ala. 1/6/14).

◆   An African-American administrative assistant for a Texas company had difficulty getting along with co-workers. The employee and white co-workers kept accusing each other of threatening and harassing behavior. The employer investigated and determined the employee was the instigator. It issued her a final warning, and she was later fired after a manager saw her provoke a co-worker in the office parking lot. The employee sued for race discrimination, noting that the white employees were merely placed on a performance improvement plan while she was fired. **She lost because the white co-workers were not similarly situated.** Whereas they demonstrated job performance issues such as failing to meet deadlines, the employee engaged in combative behavior. *Gudger v. Citgo Petroleum Corp.*, N. 4:12-CV-02145, 2013 WL 5526993 (S.D. Tex. 10/4/13).

◆   An African-American shipping manager at a Tennessee plant engaged in some horseplay with a co-worker, who got hurt and filed for workers' compensation. A biased HR director misrepresented to the head of HR that two supervisors had agreed that the shipping manager should be fired. The company issued the shipping manager a final warning, which prevented him from getting a promotion. He sued for discrimination. A federal court granted pretrial judgment to the company, but the Sixth Circuit reversed, finding issues of fact that required a trial. **Evidence showed that the company relied on information from the biased HR director.** *Chattman v. Toho Tenax America, Inc.*, 686 F.3d 339 (6th Cir. 2012).

◆   An African-American husband and wife worked for the same company in Arkansas. They were in their 50s when the company refused to train the wife for a higher-level position and fired the husband. When they sued for discrimination, they lost. The Eighth Circuit noted that the husband had accumulated five written warnings – thus allowing for his discharge – and the wife had three disciplinary warnings on file, making her ineligible for the transfer. *Gibson v. American Greetings Corp.*, 670 F.3d 844 (8th Cir. 2012).

◆   A black warehouse clerk in Tennessee married her area manager. Because spouses could not supervise each other, the company tried to find her another position but couldn't. It then told her either she or her husband would have to resign. She quit and sued the company for race discrimination, asserting that white couples weren't forced to leave their jobs. However, she lost because **she failed to show that race played a part in the forced resignation**. The white couples she cited as examples were able to find jobs within the company that didn't result in one supervising the other. *Ayers-Jennings v. Fred's Inc.*, 461 Fed.Appx. 472 (6th Cir. 2012).

◆   Following workplace shootings by a white supremacist, a company instituted "zero tolerance" policies on race discrimination. It later fired seven white employees, including one supervisor, for forwarding emails that were derogatory to African-Americans. The company subsequently discovered that two African-American employees had forwarded an email that insulted whites. It suspended the two employees. When the white supervisor sued for race discrimination, a Georgia federal court granted pretrial judgment to the company. However, the Eleventh Circuit reversed, noting that **a jury might decide that the company fired the white employees because of their race**. *Smith v. Lockheed Martin Corp.*, 644 F.3d 1321 (11th Cir. 2011).

◆ An African-American employee in Colorado was disciplined on 23 occasions over a seven-year period for sexual harassment and other problems. An HR representative wrote a memo recommending his discharge and warning that the company faced potential liability if the women he had been accused of harassing were to sue. The memo also warned that the company could be sued for reverse discrimination by white employees treated more harshly. After the company fired the employee, he sued for race discrimination. The Tenth Circuit ruled against him, noting that **the HR rep's memo was made without regard to race**. The multiple disciplinary incidents justified his discharge. *Crowe v. ADT Security Services, Inc.*, 649 F.3d 1189 (10th Cir. 2011).

◆ An African-American vision center manager at a Minnesota Wal-Mart called an employee at home during non-working hours (at the employee's request) to discuss the manager's difficulty getting along with subordinates. Two days later, the manager complained to a district manager about race discrimination, and a few days after that, the employee told the district manager about the off-duty phone call. The district manager fired the manager for violating Wal-Mart's working-off-the-clock policy. The manager sued for race discrimination. A federal court and the Eighth Circuit ruled against her, noting that **engaging in protected activity did not insulate her from being disciplined for violating company rules**. *Chivers v. Wal-Mart Stores, Inc.*, 641 F.3d 927 (8th Cir. 2011).

◆ A black salesman for a company in Illinois complained to HR about race discrimination. Ten days later, he was fired. He filed a charge with the EEOC, which then sought information on the company's hiring records for the city of Chicago because **only six of the company's 120 Chicago employees were black and they all worked at an office in an African-American neighborhood**. Further, the sales people at that office were divided into two teams, primarily along racial lines. The company fought the subpoena, but the Seventh Circuit ruled that it had to comply with the request for information on its hiring practices. *EEOC v. Konica Minolta Business Solutions U.S.A., Inc.*, 639 F.3d 366 (7th Cir. 2011).

◆ A black cable company employee in Wisconsin received a call from a customer who wanted to have the cable connection in his building moved to another spot. The employee determined that this was a "transfer" request and not a "relocate" order – making him eligible for a $25 commission. He negotiated a new service agreement with the customer and logged in the $25 commission. After his actions were questioned, he was fired. However, the HR manager decided she needed to investigate further. She spoke with the customer, who supported the employee's position, and realized that the situation was not as clear-cut as previously thought. The company reinstated the employee. He nevertheless sued for race discrimination and lost. The Seventh Circuit found **no evidence he was disciplined because of his race**. *Davis v. Time Warner Cable of Southeastern Wisconsin, LP*, 651 F.3d 664 (7th Cir. 2011).

◆   A black Missouri applicant met with a company's branch service manager to discuss possible employment. She disclosed that she had two shoplifting convictions on her application. Nevertheless, the branch manager told her he wanted to hire her and sent her for a drug test. In a second interview, he told her that the regional manager warned him not to hire her because she was black. The applicant didn't get the job and contacted the EEOC, which sued on her behalf. A federal court and the Eighth Circuit ruled for the company, noting that **its policy of refusing to hire anyone with a theft-related conviction automatically disqualified her from the job regardless of any racial bias**. *EEOC v. Con-Way Freight*, 622 F.3d 933 (8th Cir. 2010).

◆   An Indiana car salesman was fired by the dealer's new Pakistani Muslim manager for failing to meet production goals. He was later rehired to work at a different dealership. He then filed EEOC charges relating to his earlier termination. When the manager at the new dealership discovered the charges, he threatened to fire the employee unless he withdrew the charges. The employee agreed to drop the charges but never did so. He stayed away from work even though his manager called several times to inform him that he still had a job. When he sued for race discrimination and retaliation, a jury awarded him $1.1 million, but the Seventh Circuit reversed, noting that **even though the manager got angry with the employee and threatened him, the company repeatedly informed him that he wasn't fired**. *Chapin v. Fort-Rohr Motors, Inc.*, 621 F.3d 673 (7th Cir. 2010).

◆   An African-American store manager in Pennsylvania received a final warning for performance problems. She received a second final warning for missing a mandatory meeting and bringing her grandson to work with her. Later, she asked her district manager if she could close her store early because her son was having a medical emergency. The district manager apparently gave a vague answer that she took for permission to close. When she was fired, she sued for race discrimination, but a federal court and the Third Circuit ruled against her. Here, **the company followed the progressive discipline in the handbook, which also clearly stated that employment was at will**. And a white manager who was not fired for closing his store early had no prior disciplinary incidents. *Coleman v. Blockbuster, Inc.*, 352 Fed.Appx. 676 (3d Cir. 2009).

◆   A company in Pennsylvania invited an African-American to attend a training session for an independent contractor traveling sales job. The invitee attended the training and signed an agreement at the end of the session. However, she refused to shake the recruiter's hand, and he then said, "You ain't nothing but the N word." When she asked if he was calling her a "nigga," he allegedly smirked. The company then made the decision not to retain the independent contractor as a sales rep. She sued under 42 U.S.C. § 1981. A federal court granted pretrial judgment to the company, but the Third Circuit reversed. **It joined the First, Seventh and Eleventh Circuits in holding that independent contractors are protected by Section 1981**, and it also held that fact issues required a trial over whether race was involved in the decision. *Brown v. J. Kaz, Inc.*, 581 F.3d 175 (3d Cir. 2009).

◆   An African-American applicant for a position in Ohio interviewed for the job but was not hired. She claimed race discrimination, asserting that she had been asked different questions than two white applicants, one of whom already worked for the company in a different position. When she sued under Title VII she lost. A federal court and the Sixth Circuit held that **the company could ask different follow-up questions** based on how interviewees responded to questions about experience and familiarity with the company's hands-off management style. *Alexander v. CareSource*, 576 F.3d 551 (6th Cir. 2009).

◆   An African-American truck driver complained of race discrimination when he learned that a white driver received a raise. Because he made more money than the other drivers, the black driver did not receive a raise himself. He filed a charge with the EEOC. Seven months later, a customer complained that he was harassing its employees. The driver received a warning letter and then sued, claiming race discrimination and retaliation. An Arkansas federal court ruled against him, and the Eighth Circuit affirmed. Here, even though he claimed a discriminatory motive, **his employer was allowed to believe the customer and issue the disciplinary warning**. *Littleton v. Pilot Travel Centers, LLC*, 568 F.3d 641 (8th Cir. 2009).

◆   A black manager at a UPS facility in Indiana dated and then married a white employee who worked in another department. This was in violation of the company's anti-fraternization policy. After UPS fired the manager, he sued under Title VII, **claiming that he was fired because the company didn't want him associating with a white woman**. A federal court granted pretrial judgment for UPS, and the Seventh Circuit affirmed. Here, the manager was warned to "rectify" the situation and failed to do so. Also, he failed to show that similarly situated white couples were treated differently. Another white manager who refused to end a relationship with an employee was fired too. *Ellis v. United Parcel Service*, 523 F.3d 823 (7th Cir. 2008).

◆   A white assistant coach for a New York university married a black woman and was fired four years later, when the team's performance slipped. The university also fired a black assistant coach, but retained the most junior assistant coach, who was white. When the coach sued under Title VII, **claiming he had been discriminated against because of his association with a black woman**, the Second Circuit held that there were fact issues for a jury as to whether the reason offered by the university was a pretext for discrimination. The coach offered evidence that a vice president was biased against blacks and that there was pressure to fire him to appeal to the university's mostly white alumni. *Holcomb v. Iona College*, 521 F.3d 130 (2d Cir. 2008).

◆   A black assistant store manager at a Walgreen store in Illinois was twice offered the manager position at a predominantly black, low-income store. He turned down both offers. **When a manager position opened up in a predominantly white, affluent neighborhood, he sought that promotion.** His supervisor told him that the store "was possibly not ready to have a black manager." A white candidate was selected, and the assistant manager was given differing reasons for why he didn't get the job. He sued. After a federal court granted pretrial judgment to the company, the Seventh Circuit reversed, finding that a jury could conclude that the real reason for the non-promotion was racial bias. *Simple v. Walgreen Co.*, 511 F.3d 668 (7th Cir. 2007).

C. Racial Harassment

Like sexual harassment, racial harassment is prohibited by Title VII and state law. Every employer should have a policy banning all harassment. The policy should include a means for employees to report the harassment without fear of retaliation.

✦   A female sales consultant for a North Carolina tile and stone manufacturer/distributor did business with a salesman for a home and remodeling center. The sales consultant, who was African-American, said the salesman referred to two women in a photograph as "black b----es." She also said he talked about bringing "beautiful, black girls" home with him and made a comment that after a night of partying he was "f---ed up as a n----r's checkbook." In addition, he called the sales consultant a "black b---h" on the phone. The consultant complained to management, which continued to allow the salesman on the premises but barred him from communicating with the sales consultant. **The sales consultant resigned and sued her employer for race harassment** under Title VII. A federal appeals court decided that factual questions existed as to whether the employer was liable for harassment. It said a jury would have to decide. *Freeman v. Dal-Tile Corp.*, 750 F.3d 413 (4th Cir. 2014).

✦   An African-American UPS driver in Alabama found banana peels on his truck four times over a period of several months. He also encountered two workers wearing shirts and hats with a confederate flag. He complained of racial harassment and, at night, the workers confronted him about that in the truck yard. Eventually he quit and sued under Title VII. A federal court granted pretrial judgment to UPS, but the Eleventh Circuit reversed, noting that the incidents with **the bananas, together with the confederate flag shirts** and the confrontation, raised a factual question about whether he was subjected to a racially hostile environment. A jury would have to decide. *Jones v. UPS Ground Freight*, 683 F.3d 1283 (11th Cir. 2012).

✦   An African-American employee of a company in Maine complained to the owner that a co-worker was racially harassing him. The owner demanded that the co-worker stop harassing him and threatened to fire the co-worker if the harassment continued. He also told the employee to let him know if it did. The harassment did continue, but the employee never told the owner about it. He later took disability leave and then sued the company for a racially hostile work environment under Title VII. A federal court and the First Circuit ruled against him, noting that the company did all it needed to do. **The employee had many opportunities to tell the owner about the continuing harassment, but he never did it.** *Wilson v. Moulison North Corp.*, 639 F.3d 1 (1st Cir. 2011).

◆   An African-American airline employee in Illinois worked as a probationary ground mechanic in the airline's auto shop before transferring back to his fleet service job. Four months later, he complained of harassment in the auto shop, but wasn't clear about the racial harassment he suffered until after he had met twice with an HR rep. At that point, his complaints were investigated, but no evidence of racial harassment was uncovered. When he later sued under Title VII, a federal court and the Seventh Circuit ruled against him. **The employer distributed an anti-harassment policy and immediately followed up on his complaint** when he finally lodged it. But he failed to follow the airline's reporting procedure until after he'd transferred to his old job. *Montgomery v. American Airlines*, 626 F.3d 382 (7th Cir. 2010).

◆   A black employee in Arkansas claimed that she was subjected to a racially hostile environment by her white co-workers. She was told not to answer the phone because she sounded black, a supervisor made "gorilla" gestures behind her and a former supervisor told her to "hang in there" when she complained to him. Eventually the company fired the worst harasser, but the employee quit anyway and sued under Title VII. A jury awarded her $65,000 in damages, and the Eighth Circuit upheld the award. Here, **although the company had a harassment policy in place, it did not show that the employee unreasonably failed to follow it**. She complained to the supervisor and a former supervisor, but it took too long for the company to act. *Fuller v. Fiber Glass System, LP*, 618 F.3d 858 (8th Cir. 2010).

◆   A black certified nurse's aide at a long-term healthcare facility in Indiana claimed that she was subjected to a hostile work environment. The facility allowed its patients to request no black aides as part of their care. It claimed that it had to honor resident's requests under state patient privacy laws. After the aide was fired on what she thought were trumped up charges, she sued under Title VII. A federal court granted pretrial judgment to the facility, but the Seventh Circuit Court of Appeals reversed that decision, noting that a jury could find a racially charged atmosphere where **the facility's assignment sheets reminded employees every day that certain patients wanted nothing to do with black aides**. And even if the facility had to account for state patient privacy laws, Title VII takes precedence over those laws. *Chaney v. Plainfield Healthcare Center*, 612 F.3d 908 (7th Cir. 2010).

◆   Two black employees in Missouri complained of racial harassment and were told to "tough it out" by their supervisor. They asserted that co-workers used the "N" word, scrawled racial graffiti on workbenches and falsely accused them of safety violations that could get them fired. When they sued under Title VII, a federal court found the instances of harassment too isolated to amount to a racially hostile work environment and granted pretrial judgment to the company. But the Eighth Circuit reversed, finding issues of fact that required a trial. A jury would have to decide if the company's response was inadequate and if the co-workers' actions were severe or pervasive enough to amount to actionable harassment. *Watson v. CEVA Logistics U.S., Inc.*, 619 F.3d 936 (8th Cir. 2010).

◆   A black female welder at a Michigan rail yard complained to her supervisor after a male co-worker called her a "black bitch." The co-worker was admonished not to use offensive language. After a seasonal furlough, the welder returned to work. Two weeks later she filed an injury report, claiming that the co-worker moved a truck while she was standing on its bed, causing her to fall and hurt her back. Other employees confirmed the co-worker's denial of that incident. The welder was fired for filing a false injury report and she sued under Title VII. A federal court and the Sixth Circuit ruled against her, noting that **the single slur did not amount to a hostile work environment** and that the company legitimately believed she filed a false report. *Ladd v. Grand Trunk Western Railroad*, 552 F.3d 495 (6th Cir. 2009).

◆   Three white employees of a company in Tennessee brought a lawsuit alleging that they had been **harassed by their co-workers because of their friendships with black employees**. They asserted that the company knew or should have known about the harassment, and that it did nothing to stop it. One of the plaintiffs also claimed that she was told she could not apply for a better job because of her friendships, and that a co-worker threatened to hurt her if she reported his racist comments. The Sixth Circuit held that the Title VII claims for two of the employees failed because they could not show the harassment was severe or pervasive enough to alter their working conditions. However, the third employee was allowed to proceed with her lawsuit. *Barrett v. Whirlpool Corp.*, 556 F.3d 502 (6th Cir. 2009).

◆   A driver for a trucking company in Iowa was married to a black woman. He was subjected to a number of pranks by a co-worker, who also made a number of racially derogatory comments. However, all but one of the comments were made outside his hearing. He only learned of them later from co-workers. When he complained to his supervisor, the supervisor said that if he didn't like the way things were run, he could leave his keys on the supervisor's desk. He quit and sued under Title VII. A federal court and the Eighth Circuit ruled against him. **The comments he did not hear did not rise to the level of a hostile work environment**, and the pranks pulled on him were also pulled on other drivers, even if not to the same extent. *Carpenter v. Con-Way Cent. Express, Inc.*, 481 F.3d 611 (8th Cir. 2007).

◆   An African-American Boeing employee in Maryland was told by his team leader to refer to him as "Massah Dave." He reported the comment to a supervisor and the human resources (HR) department, and requested a written apology. The team leader signed a written apology drafted by HR, and the employee signed a statement indicating that he accepted the apology. No further incidents arose. The employee nevertheless sued Boeing under Title VII. A federal court and the Fourth Circuit ruled against him. **The single comment was not severe or pervasive enough to create Title VII liability.** And the employee had accepted the apology as being a sufficient response. *Lamb v. The Boeing Co.*, 213 Fed.Appx. 175 (4th Cir. 2007).

D. National Origin Discrimination

Title VII prohibits discrimination on the basis of national origin by employers, but discrimination against noncitizens on the basis of alienage has been upheld by the U.S. Supreme Court.

National origin discrimination claims are very similar to race discrimination claims but are a bit broader in scope and don't offer all the protections of race discrimination claims.

For example, although race can never be a bona fide occupational qualification for a job, national origin can, in very limited circumstances. Still, as a general rule, **never** make employment-related decisions on the basis of national origin.

* A citizen of Mexico, who resided lawfully in the United States, sought employment as a seamstress with a manufacturing company. Her application was rejected due to a longstanding policy against the employment of aliens. She sued the company in a Texas federal court, asserting discrimination on the basis of national origin in violation of Title VII. The case came before the U.S. Supreme Court, which held that the company's refusal to hire the woman because of her citizenship was not national origin discrimination in violation of Title VII. Even though it protects aliens against discrimination because of race, color, religion, sex, or national origin, **Title VII does not prohibit discrimination against aliens on the basis of alienage**. Here, the company had not refused to hire the applicant because of her Mexican ancestry, but because she was not a United States citizen. This was not forbidden by Title VII. *Espinoza v. Farah Manufacturing Co.*, 414 U.S. 86, 94 S.Ct. 334, 38 L.Ed.2d 287 (1973).

* A bank worker from Cambodia consistently received job evaluations indicating a need for improvement. These evaluations were received before and after a co-worker who allegedly said she should "go back ... where she came from" and had "slanty eyes" became her supervisor. After the co-worker became her supervisor, the worker received a written warning. **She then resigned and sued for national origin discrimination under Title VII.** A trial court ruled for the bank, and the Eighth Circuit affirmed. The worker had a well-documented history of performance problems, and the alleged slurs were made approximately two years before the co-worker became her supervisor and evaluated her – too long to suggest the evaluations were based on bias. *Muor v. U.S. Bank Nat'l Ass'n*, 716 F.3d 1072 (8th Cir. 2013).

* A native Brazilian worked for a company in Minnesota under an H-1B visa. She received above-average performance reviews until she got a new position and a new supervisor, at which point her supervisor began asking her to do tasks she believed the supervisor ought to be doing. The supervisor told her she needed to do more in the reorganized job. Later, the supervisor put her on a performance plan. She lost her job when the company eliminated a number of positions (because she was on the performance plan). She claimed, and a co-

worker testified, that the supervisor told her she didn't want the employee to obtain permanent resident status. However, when she sued for national origin discrimination, she lost. A federal court and the Eighth Circuit ruled that **discrimination on the basis of immigration status wasn't the same as national origin discrimination**. *Guimaraes v. SuperValu, Inc.*, 674 F.3d 962 (8th Cir. 2012).

♦   A company with a location in Minnesota fired a Hispanic branch manager after an investigation revealed that he was routinely harsh with his employees. He claimed that he was really fired because of his national origin. When he sued under Title VII and state law, he lost. The Eighth Circuit held that the company's asserted reason for the termination – his refusal to "take ownership" of the problem – was not a pretext for discrimination. *Martinez v. W.W. Grainger, Inc.*, 664 F.3d 225 (8th Cir. 2011).

♦   Four Hispanic Illinois employees signed up for a senior technician position. No white employees signed up for the job. The company decided to wait to fill the slot until after an outsourcing plan became known. It then allowed the department head to create a list of interested employees and hire from it rather than use the sign-up sheet. **Two of the Hispanic employees were not allowed to compete for the job.** They sued for discrimination. A federal court granted pretrial judgment to the company, but the Seventh Circuit ruled that a trial was required. Even though the department head had treated one Hispanic employee well, there was enough evidence that he treated the two plaintiffs poorly to justify a trial. *Diaz v. Kraft Foods Global, Inc.*, 653 F.3d 582 (7th Cir. 2011).

♦   Three white Illinois employees went to breakfast at a restaurant with a Filipino and a Hispanic on a Saturday while working an overtime shift. The following Monday, the white employees and the Filipino told their group leader that they had not taken a lunch break. They were paid for a full shift. The Hispanic employee did not work that Monday. About a month later, a supervisor asked the Hispanic employee about that day and he told the supervisor that they had gone to breakfast. After an investigation, the three white employees and the Filipino were fired. The three white employees sued for discrimination and lost. A federal court and the Seventh Circuit held that **they were not similarly situated to the Hispanic employee because they had lied about their hours**, asserting they had not taken a break that day. *Antonetti v. Abbott Laboratories*, 563 F.3d 587 (7th Cir. 2009).

♦   An engineer of Indian ethnicity was fired after numerous complaints about his performance and reports from colleagues about insubordination. He sued under Title VII, claiming that his supervisor made a handful of slurs about people of Asian origin. He claimed national origin harassment and wrongful discharge. An Illinois federal court and the Seventh Circuit ruled for the company, noting that **the engineer never complained about the slurs** and that they weren't pervasive enough to amount to harassment anyway. Further, the numerous complaints about his performance justified his termination. *Andonissamy v. Hewlett-Packard Co.*, 547 F.3d 841 (7th Cir. 2008).

* A Muslim car salesman in Texas endured a number of harassing comments from his supervisor and co-workers. **His supervisor called him Taliban and Arab, even though he was from India**, and also mocked his religious dietary restrictions and his need to pray during the workday. After September 11, his co-workers suggested that he was involved in the terrorist attacks, and one told him he should go back to where he came from because of his beliefs. The supervisor also issued him a written warning for acting like a "Muslim extremist," and banged on his office partition to startle the salesman every time he walked by. When the salesman complained, he was fired. He filed a complaint with the EEOC, which sued for national origin discrimination on his behalf. A federal court granted pretrial judgment to the dealership, but the Fifth Circuit reversed, noting that all these incidents, when added together, could amount to a hostile work environment under Title VII. A trial was required. *EEOC v. WC & M Enterprises*, 496 F.3d 393 (5th Cir. 2007).

* An Egyptian-born Muslim worked as a manager trainee at a Minnesota convenience store. After the busy holiday season, he was demoted to assistant trainee based on reports of insubordination. His hours were also cut back. He walked off the job after being accused of harassment, then sued under Title VII, claiming discrimination on the basis of his Arabic race. A federal court and the Eighth Circuit ruled against him. The company had **a legitimate reason for demoting him** and for cutting back his hours. Also, derogatory comments by an assistant manager could not be attributed to the company because the assistant manager was not involved in the decision to demote him. *Elnashar v. Speedway SuperAmerica, LLC*, 484 F.3d 1046 (8th Cir. 2007).

* An Iraqi supervisor at an Ohio manufacturing plant was fired because of numerous complaints about the demeaning way he communicated with his subordinates and because his superiors saw him ignore potential safety problems. He sued under Title VII, asserting that the real reason was national origin discrimination. He pointed out that employees discussed the Iraq war over lunch, and that, at his termination meeting, the operations manager said, "Maybe it's the people of Northwest Ohio who have a problem with you." A federal court and the Sixth Circuit held that the company provided ample evidence to support its decision to fire the supervisor. **The single comment, in the context of a discussion about his personality and management conflicts, could be construed as a statement about Midwestern congeniality.** The termination was upheld. *Abdulnour v. Campbell Soup Supply Co., LLC*, 502 F.3d 496 (6th Cir. 2007).

* A Kansas company learned that the Immigration and Naturalization Service was going to inspect its facility and became concerned because it had hired 300 people in a short time and knew it might not have completed I-9 forms for them. A Hispanic employee who had been hired under a more careful screening process was **suspended until he provided documentation of his eligibility to work**. After providing the documentation, he demanded a written apology and a complete explanation of why he had been suspended. The HR manager believed the demand amounted to a voluntary resignation and told the employee

to leave the office. The employee, believing he had been fired, sued under Title VII. The case reached the Tenth Circuit Court of Appeals, which ruled in favor of the company. Here, the suspension was legitimate. Further, the HR manager's belief that the employee would not return to work without a written apology justified the termination decision. And the employee failed to show that this reason was actually a pretext for national origin discrimination. *Zamora v. Elite Logistics*, 478 F.3d 1160 (10th Cir. 2007).

♦   An employee of a security company in Pennsylvania was fired when he refused to remove or cover Confederate flag stickers on his lunch box and pickup truck. He sued the company under Title VII, asserting discrimination on the basis of religion and national origin, based on his claim as a "Confederate Southern-American." A federal court dismissed his case, and the Third Circuit affirmed. Although national origin usually refers to a country of origin, it could be expanded to include a region. However, **even if "Confederate Southern-American" was a valid national origin, the employee's claim still failed**. The Confederate flag sends out a message that stigmatizes African-Americans by representing the belief that white men have the right to own black slaves. And the employee was not fired because of his status or beliefs, but because he refused to remove or cover the stickers. *Storey v. Burns Int'l Security Services*, 390 F.3d 760 (3d Cir. 2004).

II. GENDER DISCRIMINATION

Gender discrimination, like race discrimination, violates Title VII of the Civil Rights Act of 1964. Where an employee proves under Title VII that his or her employer has engaged in unlawful intentional discrimination on the basis of sex, the employee will be entitled to recover money damages in addition to equitable relief.

Where the discrimination is unintentional, money damages are not available (except for equitable relief like back pay).

Plaintiffs who are unable to produce direct evidence of gender bias may attempt to establish unlawful discrimination by relying on the burden-shifting framework of *McDonnell Douglas Corp. v. Green*, 411 U.S. 792, 93 S.Ct. 1817, 36 L.Ed.2d 668 (1973). This framework may also be used in Title VII cases involving alleged discrimination based on other protected characteristics.

Where an employer shows that sex is a bona fide occupational qualification for a position, it will be able to legally discriminate against members of one sex. However, such instances will be rare. As a general rule, **never** take gender into account in hiring and promotion decisions.

A. Title VII

♦   A group of current and former female employees of Wal-Mart sued the company in a California federal court for sex discrimination under Title VII.

They sought class action certification on behalf of 1.5 million women nationwide. The case reached the U.S. Supreme Court, which ruled against them. The Supreme Court noted that **the women could not show that their individual claims were sufficiently tied together by a common practice of discrimination** by the company. Wal-Mart gave local supervisors discretion over employment matters, and in a company of that size, it was unlikely that all the managers exercised their discretion in the same way. The employees would have to pursue their claims individually. *Wal-Mart Stores, Inc. v. Dukes*, 131 S.Ct. 2541, 180 L.Ed.2d 374 (U.S. 2011).

◆ One of the few female area managers for an Alabama plant worked for the company from 1979 until 1998. For most of that time, she and all other salaried employees received or were denied raises based on their supervisors' evaluations of their job performance. Initially, her salary was in line with the salaries of male area managers, but over time her pay slipped in comparison. She alleged that the pay disparity began in the 1980s as retaliation because she rejected a supervisor's sexual advances. She also claimed that another supervisor gave her a poor evaluation because of her gender. However, she didn't complain to the EEOC until March 1998. When she finally sued under Title VII, the case reached the U.S. Supreme Court. Over a vigorous dissent, the Court held that she waited too long to sue. **She could not prove that the most current raises she received were the result of any discriminatory intent.** She should have filed an EEOC charge within 180 days after each of the earlier poor evaluations. *Ledbetter v. Goodyear Tire & Rubber Co., Inc.*, 550 U.S. 618, 127 S.Ct. 2162, 167 L.Ed.2d 982 (2007). The federal Congress later negated the Court's ruling in *Ledbetter* by passing the Lilly Ledbetter Fair Pay Act, which established that the 180-day filing period restarts with each new paycheck received after an allegedly discriminatory action.

◆ A Caesars Palace (Las Vegas) employee claimed she was disciplined and finally fired because of her gender. She was the only woman who worked in the hotel and casino's warehouse. Although her work was regarded as "excellent," she had a number of problems with her co-workers and supervisors. When she complained about being singled out because she was a woman, the human resources (HR) department refused to intervene. At trial, she recounted several incidents of discrimination where she was formally reprimanded for rules infractions while similarly situated male employees were not. Caesars maintained that she was fired because of the disciplinary problems. She countered that, although she was not a perfect employee, her gender was the "real" reason or motivating factor for her discharge. The jury awarded $264,000 to the employee. The Ninth Circuit and the Supreme Court affirmed. **A plaintiff in a discrimination case need not have direct proof of bias to qualify for a "mixed motive" jury instruction.** Title VII provides that "a plaintiff need only 'demonstrate' that an employer used a forbidden consideration with respect to 'any employment practice.'" *Desert Palace Inc. d/b/a Caesars Palace Hotel & Casino v. Costa*, 539 U.S. 90, 123 S.Ct. 2148, 156 L.Ed.2d 84 (2003).

◆   A female director of the American Dental Association sought a promotion to the position of legislative director. She competed for the position with a male; both had received "distinguished" performance ratings. After she was rejected, she sued for gender discrimination, claiming that the male candidate had been pre-selected. A jury found discrimination and awarded her $52,718 in back pay. However, the district court judge refused to allow the jury to consider punitive damages. The case reached the U.S. Supreme Court, which clarified that punitive damages are available when employers act with **malice or reckless indifference** to the plaintiff's federally protected rights. In other words, the terms "malice" and "reckless indifference" pertain to "the employer's knowledge that it may be acting in violation of federal law." **Punitive damages** are not warranted where the employer is unaware of the relevant federal prohibition, or where the employer discriminates with the distinct belief the discrimination is lawful, such as where it reasonably believes a bona fide occupational qualification is satisfied. *Kolstad v. American Dental Ass'n*, 527 U.S. 526, 119 S.Ct. 2118, 144 L.Ed.2d 494 (1999).

◆   An employee of an Illinois educational materials company filed a sex discrimination complaint against her employer with the Equal Employment Opportunity Commission (EEOC) asserting that she should have received a promotion. The employer then fired her. The EEOC sued the employer on her behalf for retaliation under Title VII. The employer sought to dismiss the case, stating that it did not have 15 employees during 20 weeks in the past two years and therefore did not come within the coverage of the act. The case reached the U.S. Supreme Court, which held that the appropriate test is whether the parties have an employment relationship on the day in question. **Since the employer had employment relationships with 15 or more employees for 38 weeks of the calendar year in question, it was an "employer" under Title VII.** *Walters v. Metropolitan Educ. Enterprises, Inc.*, 519 U.S. 202, 117 S.Ct. 660, 136 L.Ed.2d 644 (1997).

◆   A senior manager at a nationwide professional accounting firm was refused admission as a partner. She sued the firm under Title VII, charging that it had discriminated against her on the basis of sex in its partnership decisions. The district court found that the firm had discriminated against the manager, but held that it could avoid equitable relief if it could prove by clear and convincing evidence that it would have made the same decision absent a discriminatory motive. The U.S. Court of Appeals, D.C. Circuit, affirmed. The U.S. Supreme Court held that under Title VII, the employer could avoid liability if it showed by a mere preponderance of the evidence that it would have made the same decision even if it had not taken the manager's gender into account. This preserved the employer's right to freedom of choice. The court then reversed and remanded the case for a determination of whether the same decision would have been made absent the discrimination. *Price Waterhouse v. Hopkins*, 490 U.S. 228, 109 S.Ct. 1775, 104 L.Ed.2d 268 (1989).

Under the Civil Rights Act of 1991, if it is shown that **discrimination is a contributing factor in the employment decision**, then (assuming that the employer can show that it would have made the same decision absent the discrimination) courts will be prohibited from ordering certain injunctive relief – like reinstatement. However, money damages may still be available.

◆   A regional general manager for a Puerto Rico employer had a flirtatious relationship with an HR representative. He said the HR representative successfully campaigned to have him fired after he rebuffed her advances. **He sued under Title VII, alleging sex discrimination.** A federal appeals court vacated a lower court's decision to reject the sex bias claim. It said the regional general manager had a valid sex discrimination claim based on his discharge. *Velazquez-Perez v. Developer Diversified Realty Corp. (DDR)*, 753 F.3d 265 (1st Cir. 2014).

◆   A male employee in Utah claimed a male supervisor favored a female co-worker in violation of Title VII, such as by paying her higher bonuses and granting her excessive amounts of leave. He believed the supervisor and the co-worker may have had an affair and said the two "acted like they were married." He also claimed the supervisor's relationship with the co-worker created a hostile work environment, and he accused his employer of conducting a biased investigation into his complaints. The court rejected his claims. At most, the employee presented evidence that one female co-worker received preferential treatment. This evidence did not support the Title VII claim, and it is well-settled that **favoritism based on a consensual romantic relationship between a supervisor and a subordinate cannot support a claim of gender-based discrimination.** *Clark v. Cache Valley Electric Co.*, 577 Fed.Appx. 693 (10th Cir. 2014).

◆   A lot checker for an Illinois company dated a co-worker whose girlfriend also worked for the company. The girlfriend threatened the lot checker, who complained to her supervisor about the girlfriend's behavior. The company later asked the lot checker to take a drug test based on her behavior during a safety inspection of her work vehicle. The company said the lot checker responded slowly, had difficulty following the conversation and had constricted pupils. The lot checker refused to take the drug test, and she was fired. **She sued under Title VII, claiming she was fired because she complained about the girlfriend.** But her claim failed because it was not based on a trait protected under Title VII, such as race or gender. *Northington v. H&M Int'l*, 712 F.3d 1062 (7th Cir. 2013).

◆   An investor analyst in Missouri claimed that his supervisor subjected him to humiliating and undeserved criticism, forcing him to resign. He said she made the workplace so intolerable that he had no choice but to leave. When he sued for sex discrimination under Title VII, he lost. The Eighth Circuit Court of Appeals held that he presented **no evidence that he was singled out because of his gender**. *Hawks v. J.P. Morgan Chase Bank*, 591 F.3d 1043 (8th Cir. 2010).

◆   A temporary employee for a company in Pennsylvania applied for a permanent position but did not get it. The company ended her temporary assignment and she found another job eight months later that paid less. When she sued for gender discrimination, a jury ruled in her favor and a trial court awarded her over $164,000 in compensatory damages ($63,000 in back pay and $101,000 in front pay). However, the Third Circuit vacated the award, finding that it had been improperly calculated. The lower court should not have relied on her testimony as to what sort of raises she would have gotten had she been hired. On remand, she would get the chance to receive both back pay and front pay if she could show that her new pay was not substantially equivalent to her old pay. *Donlin v. Philips Lighting North America Corp.*, 581 F.3d 73 (3d Cir. 2009).

✦ A UPS driver in Arkansas used her seniority to obtain a higher-paying "feeder driver" position. However, on her second day on the new job, she caused an accident. She was told that she was no longer qualified for the feeder job and that she should report to her old job as a regular driver. She filed a grievance with her union, and a week later filed a complaint with the EEOC, claiming race and gender discrimination. Meanwhile, another supervisor determined that she should not have been disqualified from the feeder job because of the accident. Upon learning of the EEOC charge, UPS postponed reinstating her to the feeder job. Two months later, UPS and the union reached a settlement reinstating her to the feeder job with full back pay, seniority and all benefits. She nevertheless sued under Title VII and lost. The Eighth Circuit held that **the demotion was not an adverse action because UPS corrected it in a timely manner**. *Jackson v. United Parcel Service, Inc.*, 548 F.3d 1137 (8th Cir. 2008).

✦ An employee in Maine applied for a promotion to a managerial position. She was already performing many of the job's tasks, had stellar performance reviews, and had been encouraged to apply for the job by superiors. However, her immediate supervisor told her that she decided not to promote her, saying it was nothing she did or didn't do; it was just that she had a lot on her plate with her kids. The employee had an 11-year-old son and triplets in kindergarten. When she sued under Title VII, a federal court granted pretrial judgment to the company. The First Circuit reversed, finding issues of fact that required a trial. Here, **a jury could find that she was denied a promotion because she was a woman with young children**. *Chadwick v. WellPoint, Inc.*, 561 F.3d 38 (1st Cir. 2009).

✦ A Colorado woman applied for a job at a power plant and reached the interview stage. An all-male panel interviewed her, and she did not get the job. She sued for discrimination under Title VII and lost because the subjective interview process was not discriminatory. **The panel asked the same questions of every applicant** and ranked them using predetermined criteria from an HR interview guide. The questions were meant to elicit information about job competencies, technical knowledge, initiative and comfort taking risks, adaptability, communication skills and ability to work on a team. Also, another female interviewee scored second highest and was offered a job. *Turner v. Public Service Co. of Colorado*, 563 F.3d 1136 (10th Cir. 2009).

✦ A casino sales manager in Nevada claimed that she was reprimanded for making two phone calls to her children, while a male employee who also called his children was not reprimanded. Also, **her supervisor allegedly said that**

mothers can't perform as well as men or women without children and that they should stay at home. After she complained about him, she was fired. She sued for discrimination and retaliation under Title VII. The casino claimed it had a valid reason for her termination – poor performance – and a federal court granted it pretrial judgment. However, the Ninth Circuit reversed, finding issues of fact that required a trial. *Gerving v. Opbiz, LLC d/b/a Aladdin Resort and Casino*, 324 Fed.Appx. 692 (9th Cir. 2009).

◆   An Ohio moving and storage **company decided to lay off people in departments staffed predominantly by women**. Of the 13 employees laid off, only one was male. Four of the laid-off women sued for discrimination, alleging that the company's reduction in force had a disparate impact (or discriminatory effect) on female employees. A federal court and the Sixth Circuit ruled in the company's favor, noting that the employees failed to prove that the company's asserted reasons for laying people off from the heavily female departments were pretextual. Those departments were more strongly affected by declining business. *Shollenbarger v. Planes Moving & Storage*, 297 Fed.Appx. 483 (6th Cir. 2008).

◆   A company told a South Dakota employee it was eliminating her position around the same time she informed it she was pregnant. The company then moved up her evaluation and told her she would have to relocate or leave the company. Two weeks later she had a miscarriage. When she refused the transfer, she was fired. She sued for sex discrimination under Title VII and lost because **the transfer offer was not an adverse action**. Further, the Eighth Circuit held that the company had no liability for causing her miscarriage through the stress of the relocation situation. *Reynolds v. Ethicon Endo-Surgery, Inc.*, 454 F.3d 868 (8th Cir. 2006).

◆   A New Mexico car dealership disciplined a female manager for unsatisfactory performance because she was chronically late for work, made personal phone calls and frequently wasn't in the office such that the dealership had to assign someone else as her backup. However, the dealership didn't discipline a male manager who was also often tardy. When the EEOC sued on her behalf, the Tenth Circuit ruled in favor of the dealership. Here, the two employees were not similarly situated because **the female's problems affected productivity while the male's did not**. No one had to do extra work for him. Thus, the dealership did not violate Title VII. *EEOC v. PVNF, LLC*, 487 F.3d 790 (10th Cir. 2007).

◆   The CEO of the Wisconsin Health Fund became romantically interested in a dentist who worked for the fund and decided to promote her to the position of director of the dental clinic. To do so, he had to fire the current director of the clinic – a male with an MBA as well as a dental degree. After being fired, the male clinic director sued the health fund for sex discrimination under Title VII. A federal district court and the Seventh Circuit Court of Appeals ruled against him. **Favoring a woman because of romantic interest is not sex discrimination** even when the male is more qualified for the job. Here, the decision to fire the male and hire the female was purely personal and not based on a belief that women were superior workers. *Preston v. Wisconsin Health Fund*, 397 F.3d 539 (7th Cir. 2005).

♦   A Colorado employee worked as a meat wrapper for a company's retail stores. Subsequently, she was given the opportunity to work as a temporary project employee. The assignment was not considered a promotion, and she was not given higher pay or better benefits. She stayed in temporary assignments for nearly two years. Her supervisor then told her he did not need her anymore, and she was returned to her meat-wrapping position, again with no change in salary or benefits. She sued for sex discrimination under Title VII, alleging that two male employees with less experience were kept in the temporary assignment to complete the work she had been told was done. A federal court dismissed her lawsuit on the grounds that the company had not taken "adverse action" against her, but the Tenth Circuit reversed. **The reassignment could be an adverse action because it resulted in a reduction in responsibility.** A trial was required. *Stinnett v. Safeway, Inc.*, 337 F.3d 1213 (10th Cir. 2003).

♦   After a lawsuit by the EEOC, a Florida federal court found that a restaurant intentionally discriminated against four women even though they did not apply for jobs during the period covered by the lawsuit. The restaurant appealed to the Eleventh Circuit, which affirmed in part. The Eleventh Circuit held when **a plaintiff has not actually applied and been rejected for a job**, a case of discrimination can be established by showing 1) a real and present interest in the job, and 2) that she was effectively deterred from applying by the employer's discriminatory practices. Here, two of the women were unable to show that they had a real and present interest in applying for the jobs during the applicable time period. The other two women showed that they had a real and present interest that was effectively deterred by the restaurant's male-servers-only policy. Those two plaintiffs were entitled to back pay and prejudgment interest. *EEOC v. Joe's Stone Crabs, Inc.*, 296 F.3d 1265 (11th Cir. 2002).

B. The Equal Pay Act

Enacted by Congress in 1963, the Equal Pay Act requires that employers pay males and females the same wages for the same work. As such, the act applies only to sex discrimination in pay. Race-based equal pay claims must be litigated under the more general provisions of Title VII.

Because the Equal Pay Act is part of the Fair Labor Standards Act, employees are protected by the act as long as the employer is engaged in an industry affecting interstate commerce (in contrast to Title VII's 15-employee minimum for triggering coverage). In other words, most employers are covered.

The employee's burden of proof under the act has been interpreted to require only that the jobs under comparison be substantially equal. Strict equality of the jobs under comparison is not required. Thus, if two jobs are basically the same, male and female workers generally must be paid the same.

The Equal Pay Act does allow different pay pursuant to a valid seniority system, a merit system, a system that measures earnings by quantity or quality of production, or a differential based on any other factor other than sex.

◆   A female applications engineer in Michigan alleged that she was paid much less than males who held the same position, in violation of the EPA. The court rejected her claim because **although her job was comparable, her skills and background were not**. Two of the males had between 15 and 25 years of experience, while the female was new to the job. Other males dealt with higher-level decision-makers and were more skilled with respect to high-stakes negotiations. The female lacked the skills, experience and qualifications of the men who held the positions. *Foco v. Freudenberg-NOK General Partnership*, 549 Fed.Appx. 340 (6th Cir. 2013) (Unpublished).

◆   A female business manager brokered sales of manufacturers' products to supermarkets. She was one of the company's most successful business managers, on a par with the top male business manager, but she earned three times less than he did. She sued under Title VII and the Equal Pay Act, presenting evidence that **male managers made twice what she and the other female managers made despite the fact that they all did the same work**. The company claimed that the difference was due to education and experience. An Illinois federal court granted pretrial judgment to the company, but the Seventh Circuit reversed, finding issues of fact that required a trial. Although the education issue explained why males' starting salaries were greater, the company failed to explain why their raises were so much greater than the females'. *King v. Acosta Sales and Marketing, Inc.*, 678 F.3d 470 (7th Cir. 2012).

◆   A Missouri company promoted a female HR manager making $41,548 to another position with a salary of $45,600. It replaced her in the old position with a male candidate at a starting salary of $62,500 and asserted that its new hiring policy allowed it to pay market rate for his services. The female employee sued under the Equal Pay Act, and the company claimed the difference in pay was justified by a factor "other than sex." A federal court granted pretrial judgment to the company, but the Eighth Circuit reversed. **The company could not just claim that the new hiring policy justified the higher salary for the man.** It also had to provide information about the respective employees' education, experience and other qualifications. *Drum v. Leeson Electric Corp.*, 565 F.3d 1071 (8th Cir. 2009).

◆   An employee of GE worked in the collections department and received high evaluations. Although she had been with the company for 25 years, she earned less than some male collectors who had been transferred in or been demoted from other positions. At age 60, she was discharged as part of a reduction in force. She sued GE under the Equal Pay Act and the ADEA. A Georgia federal court ruled against her, and the Eleventh Circuit Court of Appeals affirmed. Here, **she could not show an Equal Pay Act violation because the company had a salary retention policy** (under which demoted employees earned the same salaries) that had been uniformly applied to both men and women for decades. This policy bolstered employee morale and saved GE the cost of training new employees. Also, she failed to prove an ADEA violation because GE showed that it would have made the same decision absent any discrimination. She was laid off on the basis of a "comparison matrix" score that was not related to her age. *Steger v. General Electric Co.*, 318 F.3d 1066 (11th Cir. 2003).

◆   A saleswoman for a transportation company was appointed to the position of trade show specialist. She was paid her same wage of $756 a week and had to relinquish her company car, but she was allowed to reduce some of her outside accounts. After she resigned, the company appointed a man to the position, paying him $900 a week and allowing him to use a company car. Four months into the job, he was also given an assistant. The saleswoman sued the company for violating the Equal Pay Act (EPA) and state law. A jury found the company violated the EPA, and a federal court awarded her nearly $10,000 in lost wages, the same amount in liquidated damages, emotional distress damages of $30,000 and punitive damages of $200,000. The Eighth Circuit upheld all but the punitive damages award. The job responsibilities for both employees were substantially similar, and **the evidence supported the jury's finding that gender was the reason she had been paid less**. Even though the man had 100 accounts to the woman's 85, he also had an assistant to help him. *Lawrence v. CNF Transportation, Inc.*, 340 F.3d 486 (8th Cir. 2003).

◆   A female human resources coordinator at an Indiana manufacturer's plant was responsible for handling matters for the plant's 50 salaried research and development employees. She was paid less than the human resources (HR) managers at two larger plants (127 and 268 workers: some salaried and some hourly). One of the larger plants was also unionized. When the manufacturer eventually closed the plant, the HR coordinator sued under the Equal Pay Act, asserting that she had been improperly paid less than the male HR managers at the other two plants. A federal court ruled for the manufacturer, and the Seventh Circuit affirmed. Here, **the female HR coordinator did not perform responsibilities that required the same skill and effort as the male HR managers** in the larger plants. They had more employees to train, union grievances to resolve, hourly wages to track, and a greater number of personnel records to monitor and maintain. *Howard v. Lear Corp. EEDS & Interiors*, 234 F.3d 1002 (7th Cir. 2000).

C. Pregnancy Discrimination

The Pregnancy Discrimination Act (42 U.S.C. § 2000e(k)) amended Title VII of the Civil Rights Act in 1978 to include pregnancy discrimination.

The act prohibits less favorable treatment of pregnancy-related conditions than that afforded to other medical conditions and disabilities. In other words, if you provide paid leave for other kinds of medical conditions, you cannot refuse to provide paid leave for a pregnancy-related condition.

Employers need not provide greater benefits for pregnant employees than they provide for other employees who have non-work-related disabilities. So if you don't provide paid leave for employees who suffer illness or injury outside the workplace, you don't have to provide paid leave for pregnant employees.

◆   AT&T based pension calculations on a seniority system that gave less retirement credit for pregnancy absences than it did for medical leave generally. After the Pregnancy Discrimination Act took effect, the company changed its policy prospectively, but did not make any retroactive adjustments. A group of female employees and their union sued the company under Title VII, alleging sex and pregnancy discrimination. A California federal court ruled for the employees, but the U.S. Supreme Court ultimately reversed. **The Pregnancy Discrimination Act did not apply retroactively, and the company could calculate retirement benefits in part by using the prior system.** *AT&T Corp. v. Hulteen*, 556 U.S. 701, 129 S.Ct. 1962, 173 L.Ed.2d 898 (2009).

◆   A company manufactured batteries made primarily from lead. In 1982, the company began a policy of excluding pregnant women and women capable of bearing children from jobs involving lead exposure. In 1984, a group of affected employees initiated a class action suit against the company, challenging its fetal protection policy as sex discrimination that violated Title VII. A Wisconsin federal court granted pretrial judgment to the company, finding that it had established a business necessity defense. The U.S. Court of Appeals, Seventh Circuit, affirmed, and the case reached the U.S. Supreme Court.

The Court noted that **there was a clear bias in the company's policy allowing fertile men but not women the choice of risking their reproductive health**. Thus, there was clear sex discrimination involved. Even though there was no malevolent motive involved, the policy could not be termed "neutral." Accordingly, the only way for the company to justify the discrimination was by establishing that gender was a bona fide occupational qualification, which it could not do. Decisions about the welfare of future children must be left to parents rather than employers. Since the company complied with the lead standard developed by the Occupational Safety and Health Administration and issued warnings to its female employees about the dangers of lead exposure, it was not negligent, and a future court would have difficulty finding it liable. The Court reversed the lower court decisions and struck down the company's fetal protection policy. *Int'l Union, UAW v. Johnson Controls, Inc.*, 499 U.S. 187, 111 S.Ct. 1196, 113 L.Ed.2d 158 (1991).

◆   After a Michigan nursing home employee became pregnant, her employer asked her to get a statement from her doctor confirming her ability to work without restrictions. The doctor said the employer should not lift more than 50 pounds, and the employer told the employee she could no longer work due to the restriction **even though she passed several "essential functions" tests**. The employee sued the employer under the Pregnancy Discrimination Act, and a federal appeals court reversed a ruling in favor of the employer. A jury could find that the employer relied on its policy of accommodating only work-related conditions as a pretext for pregnancy discrimination. *Latowski v. North Woods Nursing Center*, 549 Fed.Appx. 478 (6th Cir. 2013) (Unpublished).

◆   A Texas employee took maternity leave and gave birth by caesarean section. Later, the incision became infected, delaying her return to work. Three months later, she contacted a vice president and asked if she could pump breast milk in a back room when she returned to work. The vice president told her the company had filled her spot because they hadn't heard from her and assumed she had abandoned her job. She filed EEOC charges, and it sued on her behalf under the Pregnancy Discrimination Act (PDA), claiming that she had been fired for asking to pump breast milk at work. A federal court dismissed the claim, finding that there was no right to pump breast milk under the PDA, so even if that was the real reason she was fired, she couldn't prevail. But a federal appeals court vacated that ruling, concluding that **sex discrimination under Title VII can include taking an adverse employment action against a female employee because she is lactating or expressing milk**. *EEOC v. Houston Funding II, Ltd.*, 717 F.3d 425 (5th Cir. 2013).

◆   A client services employee for an Indiana home care company became pregnant, and she claimed that **a supervisor asked her if she was going to quit after she gave birth**. About a month later, she was fired. She sued the employer for pregnancy discrimination under the Pregnancy Discrimination Act, and a district court ruled against her. But the Seventh Circuit reversed, finding that the employer's shifting explanations for the discharge could justify a jury finding of unlawful discrimination. *Hitchcock v. Angel Corps, Inc.*, 718 F.3d 733 (7th Cir. 2013).

◆   An Illinois law firm's marketing director was fired while on maternity leave. She sued, claiming **the firm's HR director told her that the reason she was fired was because she took leave**, and that the firm discriminated against people who took medical or maternity leave. She sought to present the statements as evidence that she was fired for illegal reasons. The law firm claimed that the statements were hearsay and shouldn't be admitted. However, the Seventh Circuit ruled that the statements were admissible under an exception to the hearsay rule because they were made by an agent of the firm acting within the scope of her employment. *Makowski v. SmithAmundsen LLC*, 662 F.3d 818 (7th Cir. 2011).

◆   A South Dakota bank employee became pregnant. She wasn't eligible for FMLA leave because her due date was less than a year after she started working for the bank. Her supervisors allowed her to reserve five PTO days to bridge the gap until she became eligible for short-term disability leave six days into her maternity leave. Meanwhile, she used 120 of her 160 hours of PTO for non-pregnancy reasons. Her supervisors warned her that she could be disciplined for missing any more work. She then took a day off to care for a sick child, and later took a day off to visit a doctor for cramping. **Her supervisors issued her a formal warning for her previous absences unrelated to her pregnancy.** She believed she had been fired and sued under the Pregnancy Discrimination Act. A federal court and the Eighth Circuit ruled against her, noting that she had not been constructively discharged or even subjected to an adverse action. *Trierweiler v. Wells Fargo Bank*, 639 F.3d 456 (8th Cir. 2011).

* A nursing home in Indiana had a policy allowing light-duty work only for employees injured on the job or those who were disabled and needed it as a reasonable accommodation. When the activities director suffered complications from her pregnancy, she requested light-duty work. The nursing home refused to grant her request and fired her when she couldn't perform her job duties. She sued under the Pregnancy Discrimination Act and the ADA, but lost. The Seventh Circuit ruled that **the policy didn't violate the Pregnancy Discrimination Act because it treated pregnant and non-pregnant employees the same**. Also, it didn't violate the ADA because it allowed disabled employees to work light-duty positions. *Serednyj v. Beverly Healthcare, LLC*, 656 F.3d 540 (7th Cir. 2011).

* An Iowa bank hired a pregnant teller, who rushed to the bathroom with nausea four to eleven times each morning after arriving at work. She rejected the bank's offer of a later start time. The bank then fired her and she sued for pregnancy discrimination, but she lost when the Eighth Circuit held that **the bank did not need to treat her more favorably than its non-pregnant employees**. Since the bank did not tolerate any teller leaving her station that many times – including once while in the middle of a transaction with a customer – it could fire her without violating Title VII. *Elam v. Regions Financial Corp.*, 601 F.3d 873 (8th Cir. 2010).

* A South Dakota medical clinic fired an employee after the managing partner found out she was pregnant. It also refused to hire a pregnant applicant. It claimed that the reason it took both actions was because both women's absences would coincide with its busy season (a legitimate reason). Both women contacted the EEOC, which sued on their behalf. A jury awarded the employee $15,341 in back pay and gave the applicant $5,757. The Eighth Circuit upheld the awards and also ruled that the jury should have been allowed to consider awarding punitive damages because there was evidence that the clinic's managers knew they were violating the law and acted in reckless disregard of it. *EEOC v. Siouxland Oral Maxillofacial Surgery Associates, LLP*, 578 F.3d 921 (8th Cir. 2009).

* A pregnant insurance company employee in Pennsylvania asked about time off for doctor's appointments and was told by a vice president (and part owner) that they would "play it by ear." The company required her to call in every day she was going to be absent. She later learned that her baby had deformities and decided to terminate the pregnancy. Her husband called the vice president and allegedly was told that she could take time off for the abortion and the funeral. However, when she called in after the funeral, she was told she was fired. She sued under the Pregnancy Discrimination Act (PDA). A federal court granted pretrial judgment to the company, but the Third Circuit reversed. It held that **the PDA protects a woman who decides to terminate a pregnancy**, and that there was evidence the employee was treated more harshly than male employees who needed time off for medical reasons. *Doe v. C.A.R.S. Protection Plus, Inc.*, 527 F.3d 358 (3d Cir. 2008).

◆   A Michigan fire safety officer claimed that she was promised the supervisor position at Chrysler's Auburn Hills facility. However, when she filled out forms explaining that she was pregnant and needed a new uniform that would fit, she was offered a promotion that was significantly inferior to the one at Auburn Hills. She began a three-month maternity leave several weeks later and did not return to work. Instead, she sued for sex discrimination under state law. A jury found that she was discriminated against because she was pregnant, but it rejected her claim of constructive discharge. The Sixth Circuit affirmed the ruling in her favor, but modified the award, noting that **she was only entitled to pay for the time between when she was offered the inferior position and when she quit**. *Lulaj v. The Wackenhut Corp.*, 512 F.3d 760 (6th Cir. 2008).

◆   A railroad offered a healthcare plan that excluded coverage for all male and female contraceptive methods, both prescription and non-prescription, when those methods were used solely for contraception. The plan allowed coverage for contraception when it was medically necessary for a non-contraceptive purpose. A number of female employees sued for sex discrimination under the Pregnancy Discrimination Act, and a Nebraska federal court ruled in their favor. The Eighth Circuit reversed. Here, **the plan was gender-neutral, excluding all contraception methods**. Further, since contraception prevents pregnancy, it is not "related to pregnancy" as meant by the act so the plan couldn't discriminate on the basis of pregnancy. *In re Union Pacific Railroad Co.*, 479 F.3d 936 (8th Cir. 2007).

◆   A New York employee sued her employer seeking benefits for her infertility treatments. She alleged violations of Title VII, the Pregnancy Discrimination Act and state law based on the employer's refusal to cover certain infertility procedures under its health benefits plan. Although the plan covered some treatments, it expressly excluded surgical impregnation procedures. A federal court ruled in favor of the employer, and the Second Circuit affirmed. **The employer limited coverage equally between men and women**, so there was no violation of Title VII or the Pregnancy Discrimination Act. Despite the fact that surgical implantation procedures would be performed only on women, both male and female employees were denied coverage for such a procedure. *Saks v. Franklin Covey Co.*, 316 F.3d 337 (2d Cir. 2003).

D. Sexual Harassment

Three U.S. Supreme Court cases establish important rules relating to sexual harassment. The first, *Oncale*, states that employers can be held liable for same-sex harassment against employees. This means, for example, that if male employees harass another male employee, the employer can be held liable.

The other two cases, *Ellerth* and *Faragher*, state that when a claim is based on supervisor conduct and no adverse action is taken against an employee, an employer can successfully defend itself by showing:

that it exercised reasonable care to prevent and promptly correct any sexual harassment and that the employee unreasonably failed to use the employer's remedies or otherwise avoid harm.

This defense is not available if the employee was subjected to an adverse job action such as a firing or demotion.

An employer is liable for a co-worker's harassment if it was negligent in controlling workplace conditions.

Note that harassment because of race, national origin, religion, age or disability will be examined the same way as sexual harassment. The same analysis is used to determine whether a hostile work environment exists and to determine whether the employer has made a good-faith effort to prevent the harassment.

1. Supreme Court Cases

◆ An African-American catering assistant for a university in Indiana alleged that a white caterer intimidated and harassed her based on her race. The caterer did not have the power to hire, fire, promote, transfer or discipline the assistant. The assistant sued under Title VII, claiming that the caterer was her supervisor and that the university was therefore responsible for the discriminatory treatment. A district court ruled for the university on the basis that the caterer was not the assistant's supervisor. A federal appeals court agreed, and the U.S. Supreme Court affirmed. It held that for purposes of Title VII, **an employee is a supervisor only if his employer empowers him to take tangible employment actions** against the alleged victim. *Vance v. Ball State Univ.*, 133 S.Ct. 2434, 186 L.Ed.2d 565 (U.S. 2013).

◆ An employee at a Louisiana café quit after 10 months, claiming she had been sexually harassed and forced to quit because of that. She sued under Title VII, and a jury awarded her $40,000. Two weeks later, the café sought to have the action dismissed because it did not have 15 employees. It claimed the federal court thus had no jurisdiction to hear the case. A federal court and the Fifth Circuit agreed, but the U.S. Supreme Court reversed. It ruled that **the 15-employee requirement was not jurisdictional**. In other words, the café had a duty to raise that defense at or before trial. Having failed to do so, it could not later try to assert the defense. *Arbaugh v. Y&H Corp.*, 546 U.S. 500, 126 S.Ct. 1235, 163 L.Ed.2d 1097 (2006).

◆ When a Tennessee worker sued her employer under Title VII for subjecting her to a hostile work environment, a federal court found that her co-workers' conduct amounted to sexual harassment, that her supervisors were aware of the harassment, that she was forced to take a medical leave of absence, and that she was fired for refusing to return to the hostile work environment. It awarded her over $107,000 in back pay and benefits as well as $300,000 in compensatory damages – the maximum permitted by 42 U.S.C. § 1981a(b)(3). The court determined that the award was insufficient to compensate the employee, but that it was bound by a previous case, which held that front pay was subject to the statutory cap. The Sixth Circuit affirmed. However, the U.S. Supreme Court reversed, holding that **front pay was not an element of compensatory**

damages within the meaning of the Civil Rights Act of 1991. As a result, the worker could be awarded $300,000 in compensatory damages as well as an additional amount in front pay (money awarded for lost pay between the time of the judgment and when the employee is reinstated, or as here, money awarded in lieu of reinstatement). *Pollard v. E.I. du Pont de Nemours & Co.*, 532 U.S. 843, 121 S.Ct. 1946, 150 L.Ed.2d 62 (2001).

✦   An Illinois employee alleged that she was subjected to constant *quid pro quo* sexual harassment from one of her supervisors, a mid-level manager who had the authority to hire and promote, subject to higher approval. The employee refused all of the supervisor's advances, but she suffered no tangible retaliation and was even promoted once. Despite her knowledge of the employer's sexual harassment policy, she never complained to upper-level management about the supervisor's behavior. Instead, she resigned and sued for sexual harassment and constructive discharge in violation of Title VII.

The U.S. Supreme Court held that Title VII imposes vicarious liability on an employer for actionable discrimination caused by a supervisor with authority over an employee. When a supervisor discriminates in the terms and conditions of a subordinate's employment, his actions draw upon his superior position over the subordinate. However, **where no tangible employment action is taken against the employee, the employer may assert a two-pronged affirmative defense**. First, the employer must prove that it exercised reasonable care to prevent and promptly correct any sexual harassment. Second, it must prove that the employee unreasonably failed to avail herself of any employer remedies or failed to avoid harm otherwise. However, the affirmative defense is not available when the supervisor's harassment culminates in a tangible employment act such as discharge or demotion. The Court remanded the case for trial. *Burlington Industries, Inc. v. Ellerth*, 524 U.S. 742, 118 S.Ct. 2257, 141 L.Ed.2d 633 (1998).

✦   A former lifeguard for a city in Florida sued the city, alleging she was sexually harassed by supervisors. A district court entered judgment for the lifeguard, but a federal appeals court partially reversed that decision. The U.S. Supreme Court held that employers are subject to vicarious liability under Title VII for a supervisor's sexual harassment. However, it also held that in such cases **employers can raise an affirmative defense that focuses on whether the employer acted reasonably to prevent and correct harassment as well as the employee's conduct in seeking to avoid harassment**. Applying those rules, the court held the city was liable because it did not exercise reasonable care to prevent harassing behavior. *Faragher v. City of Boca Raton*, 524 U.S. 775, 118 S.Ct. 2275, 141 L.Ed.2d 662 (1998).

✦   A Louisiana offshore service employed a roustabout to work on oil platforms in the Gulf of Mexico. He claimed that he was forcibly subjected to sex-related humiliating actions, assault and threats of rape by co-workers, including two employees with supervisory authority. When he complained to the employer's safety compliance clerk, the clerk did nothing and stated that he had also been subjected to abuse by the co-workers. Eventually, the roustabout quit and sued the employer for sex discrimination under Title VII. The case reached the U.S. Supreme Court, which stated that sex discrimination in the form of **same-sex harassment that is so objectively offensive that it alters the conditions of employment** is actionable under Title VII. The Court found no language in Title VII that bars a sex discrimination claim when the complaining party and alleged perpetrators are of the same sex, and it rejected the employer's assertion that allowing the claim would transform Title VII into a general code of workplace civility. The Court noted that not all verbal or physical harassment in the workplace is prohibited by Title VII, since it does not cover conduct that is not severe or pervasive enough to create an objectively hostile or abusive work environment. *Oncale v. Sundowner Offshore Services, Inc.*, 523 U.S. 75, 118 S.Ct. 998, 140 L.Ed.2d 201 (1998).

✦   A woman worked for a District of Columbia bank in various capacities over a four-year period. Her supervisor allegedly harassed her, demanding sexual favors, and she accused him of forcibly raping her on several occasions. When she took an indefinite sick leave, the bank discharged her. She then sued the bank, claiming that she had been subjected to sexual harassment in violation of Title VII. A federal court ruled for the bank, finding that it did not have notice of any harassment, and that its policies forbade such behavior. The U.S. Court of Appeals reversed. The U.S. Supreme Court stated that **sexual harassment is clearly a form of sex discrimination prohibited by Title VII**. While absence of notice of harassment will not necessarily shield an employer from liability, employers are not always automatically liable for sexual harassment by their supervisory employees. Congress intended agency principles to apply to some extent. The Court affirmed the court of appeals' holding and remanded the case. *Meritor Savings Bank, FSB v. Vinson*, 477 U.S. 57, 106 S.Ct. 2399, 91 L.Ed.2d 49 (1986).

✦   A Tennessee woman worked as a manager of a rental equipment company. The company president often insulted her because of her gender and frequently made her the target of unwanted sexual innuendoes. The employee quit and sued for sexual harassment. A federal court found that the president's conduct did not violate Title VII because it was not so severe as to seriously affect the manager's psychological well-being. The Sixth Circuit affirmed. The U.S. Supreme Court reiterated the standard set forth in *Meritor Savings Bank, FSB v. Vinson*, above. "Title VII is violated when the workplace is permeated with discriminatory behavior that is **sufficiently severe or pervasive to create a hostile environment**." This standard required showing only an objectively hostile environment – one that a reasonable person would find hostile – as well as the victim's subjective perception that the environment was abusive. The Court reversed and remanded the case so the trial court could consider the psychological harm to the victim as just one factor. *Harris v. Forklift Systems, Inc.*, 510 U.S. 17, 114 S.Ct. 367, 126 L.Ed.2d 295 (1993).

2. The *Faragher/Ellerth* Defense

When an employee alleges sexual harassment by a supervisor and the harassment did not result in an adverse employment action, an employer can avoid liability by showing two things: It acted reasonably to prevent and promptly remediate any such harassment, and the employee unreasonably failed to take advantage of preventive or corrective opportunities provided by the employer or otherwise unreasonably failed to avoid harm. This defense, known as the *Faragher/Ellerth* defense, only comes into play when the alleged harassment is committed by a supervisor. If harassment is allegedly suffered at the hands of a co-worker, the employer can defend a claim against it by showing it took reasonable steps to control workplace conditions.

Having and distributing to every employee a sexual harassment policy is only the first step in avoiding liability. Employers must also ensure that the policy can be implemented effectively. For example, a policy that requires employees to report harassment to their supervisors will not be effective if the supervisors are doing the harassing.

◆   The vice president of a family-owned business in New York (who was also the owner's husband) was accused of sexual harassment by an employee. The company's HR director told the vice president to work at home and then spoke about the problem with a management consultant. When the owner of the company learned about the contact with an outsider, she fired the HR director for disclosing confidential information. She then allowed her husband to return to the office. The harassed employee quit. She and the HR director sued under Title VII. A federal court and the Second Circuit dismissed the HR director's claim, but the employee was awarded more than $30,000 by a jury. The Second Circuit upheld the award, determining that **the *Faragher/Ellerth* defense didn't apply because the vice president was essentially an alter ego of the company**. *Townsend v. Benjamin Enterprises, Inc.*, 679 F.3d 41 (2d Cir. 2012).

◆   Four mid-level supervisors at a railway facility in Nebraska claimed that their manager sexually harassed them on a daily basis. However, even though the supervisors had been trained on the company's sexual harassment policy, they waited months to report it. They claimed they feared retaliation and believed that an anonymous hotline never yielded results. When they eventually reported it, the company investigated and informed the manager that it planned to fire him. He quit instead. The supervisors later sued under Title VII, but **lost because they had unreasonably delayed reporting the problem to the company**. *Crawford v. BNSF Railway Co.*, 665 F.3d 978 (8th Cir. 2012).

◆   An Arizona employee claimed that her store manager sexually harassed her, but the district manager and the regional HR manager who conducted the investigation didn't check the store's loss-prevention videos (which showed the harassing behavior), didn't interview certain employees, didn't inform corporate HR about the complaint and didn't inform the employee about the outcome of the investigation (letting the manager resign with no mention of the misconduct). When the EEOC sued on her behalf, the Ninth Circuit upheld an award of $15,000 in compensatory damages and $50,000 in punitive damages. **The employer could not claim the *Ellerth/Faragher* defense because its shoddy investigation didn't comply with the law.** *AutoZone, Inc. v. EEOC*, 421 Fed.Appx. 740 (9th Cir. 2011).

◆   An Oklahoma pharmacy technician waited several months to complain that her supervisor had sexually harassed her. Later that day, she tried to retract her complaint. She also failed to give HR a written statement detailing the harassment. The employer investigated but couldn't substantiate the allegations. It nevertheless counseled the supervisor that harassment would not be tolerated. After HR notified the technician that it was unable to substantiate her complaint and considered the investigation closed, she went on a pre-approved medical leave and then offered details. When the employer refused to reopen the investigation, she sued. The Tenth Circuit ruled against her, noting that **the company had taken the steps outlined in *Ellerth/Faragher* and she had acted unreasonably.** *Christian v. AHS Tulsa Regional Medical Center, LLC*, 430 Fed.Appx. 694 (10th Cir. 2011).

◆   An Alabama mine worker told his union steward that he was being harassed by his same-sex supervisor. He also told the steward not to process a grievance because he was afraid of retaliation. Later, he complained to the company's general manager, who immediately instructed the supervisor to avoid harassing conduct and placed the worker with a different crew and a different supervisor. When the worker sued under Title VII, a federal court and the Eleventh Circuit ruled against him. **The employer promptly addressed and corrected the supervisor's conduct, and the worker unreasonably delayed reporting it** to the manager for fear of reprisal. *Speigner v. Shoal Creek Drummond Mine*, 402 Fed.Appx. 428 (11th Cir. 2010).

◆   A customer service supervisor for an airline in New York complained to her manager about his sexually harassing behavior toward female passengers and employees. She did not complain to her manager's boss because the one time she did complain to him about unfair treatment, he placed her on probation for 60 days on the grounds that she had ill-treated a male subordinate. After the airline later fired her, she sued for sexual harassment. A federal court granted pretrial judgment to the airline because the supervisor failed to complain to her manager's boss about the harassment. However, the Second Circuit reversed, finding **an issue of fact over whether failing to complain to the manager's boss was unreasonable, given that he seemed hostile to employee complaints**. A trial was needed. *Gorzynski v. JetBlue Airways Corp.*, 596 F.3d 93 (2d Cir. 2010).

◆   An Illinois cashier complained that a service shop supervisor was sexually harassing her. The company disciplined the supervisor and then adjusted schedules to make certain that another manager was always on duty when the cashier and service shop supervisor worked the same shifts. However, the cashier wanted the company to guarantee that she would never have to work the same shift as the supervisor. She quit and sued under Title VII, but the Seventh Circuit ruled against her. The employer's corrective actions had been swift, reasonable and appropriate in light of the small size of the business. Further, **there was no evidence that the cashier was forced to work in close proximity to the supervisor after she complained**. *Roby v. CWI, Inc.*, 579 F.3d 779 (7th Cir. 2009).

3. Individual Supervisor Liability

As a general rule, supervisors will not be held individually liable for sexual harassment under Title VII. However, they might incur liability under state civil rights laws or under other tort laws (torts are civil wrongs other than breach of contract).

Because employers can be held liable for their supervisors' harassing conduct, employers need to make sure that their supervisors are aware that harassment of any sort will not be tolerated.

◆   After being fired, a Georgia employee claimed that she had been sexually harassed by the owner of the company. She sued him and the company under Title VII, asserting that he should be held individually liable because even though the company was her official employer, it was in reality the alter ego of the owner. A federal court ruled for the owner, and the Eleventh Circuit affirmed. Here, it would not matter if the company was the owner's alter ego because **Title VII did not allow for individual liability**. In addition, the company was not liable because the employee never availed herself of the *Ellerth/Faragher* defense. Even though the company had a harassment policy in place, she never claimed harassment until she was fired. *Dearth v. Collins*, 441 F.3d 931 (11th Cir. 2006).

◆   An employee sued her employer, a manufacturer with facilities in Rhode Island, for sexual harassment and retaliation in violation of Title VII and state law. She named her immediate supervisor and his supervisor as individual defendants because of their alleged participation in the harassment and their failure to investigate other incidents reported to them. A Rhode Island federal court denied the supervisors' motion to be dismissed from the case. It followed its earlier holding that **supervisors could be personally liable for violations of Title VII** and state law. Because Title VII defines "employer" as a person with 15 or more employees or "any agent of such a person," under traditional agency principles, the employer and the employer's agent could be held jointly and severally liable under Title VII, the court reasoned. The majority of federal appeals courts have ruled that supervisors cannot be personally liable for violations of Title VII, but the First Circuit has not yet ruled on the issue. *Wyss v. General Dynamics Corp.*, 24 F.Supp.2d 202 (D.R.I. 1998).

◆   A Florida employee alleged that the president of the company for which she worked repeatedly made sexual comments and told explicit jokes in her presence. On two occasions, he touched her in an offensive manner. She was allegedly fired for confronting him about his behavior. She sued him and the company, claiming violations of Title VII and the Florida Civil Rights Act. The court dismissed the Title VII and state civil rights act complaints against the president in his individual capacity. **Neither act provided for individual liability.** However, the employee presented evidence that the president had been acting in his capacity as a supervisor when the alleged incidents occurred. If this was proven, the company might be held liable for his conduct. The court denied the company's dismissal motion. *Blount v. Sterling Healthcare Group, Inc.*, 934 F.Supp. 1365 (S.D. Fla. 1996).

4. Low-Level Employees and Third Parties

Although employers generally can escape liability for the harassing acts of low-level employees or third parties where the employers do not know of the harassment, they can be held liable where they have allowed a culture of harassment to exist. For this reason, it is important to make clear to all employees that harassing behavior will not be tolerated under any circumstances.

♦   A Pennsylvania employee claimed that a male co-worker exposed himself to her and several co-workers in front of their team leader. Several weeks later, she reported the incident to a senior-level manager and an HR manager. An investigation resulted in discipline for the entire team because of vulgar language, which the company was trying to eliminate. Shortly after that, the employee was fired for fabricating data. She sued for sexual harassment and retaliation, but lost. The Third Circuit held that **the team leader could not be considered a management-level employee whose knowledge could be imputed to the company**. Thus, any delay in disciplining over the incident was not sufficient to create liability for the company. The retaliation claim also failed because the company had a legitimate reason for firing the employee. *Huston v. The Proctor & Gamble Paper Products Corp.*, 568 F.3d 100 (3d Cir. 2009).

♦   A Wisconsin employee complained to a more senior co-worker about harassment by several male employees. The co-worker allegedly informed the plant manager, who told her to notify the company's vice president. Nothing was done. A year later the employee complained to the HR department, which investigated and fired two male employees. The employee believed that she was being ostracized for reporting the harassment and quit. When she sued under Title VII, a federal court granted pretrial judgment to the company. The Seventh Circuit reversed, finding issues of fact that required a trial. Here, **if the plant manager was informed of the harassment, he was negligent in not following up on the complaint**. *Bombaci v. Journal Community Publishing Group, Inc.*, 482 F.3d 979 (7th Cir. 2007).

♦   A restaurant company owned by two Alabama men obtained a franchise to operate a Western Sizzlin restaurant. After one of the men allegedly harassed female employees, charges were filed with the EEOC. Lawsuits were filed against Western Sizzlin, the restaurant company, and the harassing owner. A state court granted pretrial judgment to Western Sizzlin, and the plaintiffs appealed. They asserted that Western Sizzlin was vicariously liable for the harassing acts of the owner. The Alabama Supreme Court disagreed, noting that **Western Sizzlin was not vicariously liable for the harassment** because the control it retained over the restaurant's operations was limited to ensuring that the restaurant company was complying with the franchise agreement. However, the court reversed the dismissal of the direct negligence claims against Western Sizzlin, finding that issues of fact existed as to whether it had breached a duty of care to the employees. *Kennedy v. Western Sizzlin Corp.*, 857 So.2d 71 (Ala. 2003).

◆   An Illinois bank employee experienced a series of unsolicited incidents instigated by a co-worker over two-and-a-half years. Finally, the employee complained to bank managers. The bank investigated, but the co-worker denied the allegations, and the bank could not corroborate her story. Nevertheless, the bank took steps to address her concerns. However, in the meantime, her work deteriorated. The bank fired her almost a year-and-a-half after the harassment complaints were brought to its attention. The Seventh Circuit held that as soon as it became aware of the employee's complaint, **the bank acted promptly and took appropriate steps** to end the harassment. Nor was the bank's action in firing the employee retaliatory. First, the lapse of 15 months between her complaint and her discharge was simply too long to raise an inference of retaliation. In addition, the record contained ample evidence of the employee's substandard performance during those 15 months, including that she was unable to follow instructions and that other employees had to redo her work. *Caudillo v. Continental Bank/Bank of America*, 191 F.3d 455 (7th Cir. 1999).

5. Damage Awards

Where employers are found liable for harassment under Title VII, money damages can be awarded under 42 U.S.C. § 1981a – an amendment to Title VII. Section 1981a sets damages caps that vary depending on the size of the employer.

◆   An employee at an Arkansas manufacturing facility complained to the plant manager that his female supervisor had made sexual advances toward him, including at a bar after work. The company began a thorough investigation but was unable to verify his most serious assertions. However, it determined that the supervisor acted inappropriately by socializing with employees in bars after work. When she returned from leave, the employee claimed that she retaliated against him by criticizing him in public and giving him too much work. Again the company could not substantiate his claims. He resigned, then sued under Title VII and state law. A jury awarded him compensatory and punitive damages, but the Eighth Circuit **vacated the punitive damages award because the company did not act with reckless indifference** to the law when it refused to fire the supervisor or transfer the employee. *Dominic v. DeVilbiss Air Power Co.*, 493 F.3d 968 (8th Cir. 2007).

◆   A female Chicago bank manager sued the bank, two shareholders and the bank president for sex discrimination and harassment under Title VII, alleging a steady stream of inappropriate behavior from the three men. She also sued them for assault and battery, and intentional infliction of emotional distress. A jury awarded her $200,000 against the bank, which the court **reduced to $50,000 under 42 U.S.C. § 1981a**. The jury also awarded her $200,000 for the assault and battery and $100,000 in punitive damages. The Seventh Circuit upheld the awards, finding they were not excessive, and that the jury properly considered testimony by a lay-witness friend about her emotional state. *Farfaras v. Citizens Bank and Trust of Chicago*, 433 F.3d 558 (7th Cir. 2006).

◆   An Arizona employee sued under Title VII, alleging that she was subjected to a sexually hostile work environment. The jury agreed and awarded her $100,000 in damages for pain and suffering, mental anguish, shock and discomfort, and $1 million in punitive damages. The court applied **the statutory cap of 42 U.S.C. § 1981a** and reduced the damages award to $200,000. The employee appealed, asserting that the cap on damages violated the Fourteenth Amendment's Equal Protection Clause. The Ninth Circuit upheld the cap as constitutional. Congress legitimately restricted the amount of damages available for public policy reasons. *Lansdale v. Hi-Health Supermart Corp.*, 314 F.3d 355 (9th Cir. 2002).

◆   An employee of a debt collection company in Kansas was subjected to continuing harassment by a number of co-workers and supervisors. She reported the incidents to the office general manager, who had the power to discipline employees and who was responsible for implementing human resource policies, including an anti-harassment policy. He brushed her complaints aside, telling her that the men were revenue producers while she was not and that **she would just have to tolerate their behavior**. When she sued for sexual harassment, a jury awarded her $5,000 in compensatory damages and $1 million in punitive damages. The court reduced the punitive damages award to $295,000 under 42 U.S.C. § 1981a(b)(3), and the company appealed. The Tenth Circuit affirmed, noting that under *Kolstad v. American Dental Ass'n*, 527 U.S. 526 (1999), the standard for punitive damages was not how egregious the employer's conduct was, but rather the employer's knowledge that it might be acting in violation of federal law. Here, the general manager's actions were not merely inadequate; they were reckless and malicious. *Deters v. Equifax Credit Information Services, Inc.*, 202 F.3d 1262 (10th Cir. 2000).

◆   A New York employee claimed that she was subjected to repeated, unwelcome sexual advances and comments from her supervisor and that the company took no action despite her complaints. When she sued the company under Title VII, a jury awarded her $100,000 in punitive damages, but no compensatory (actual) damages. The company appealed to the Second Circuit, asserting that since no compensatory damages were awarded, no punitive damages should have been awarded. The court of appeals joined the Seventh Circuit in holding that **punitive damages could be awarded in a Title VII case even where there is no award of actual or compensatory damages**. The statutory caps imposed by the Civil Rights Act of 1991 eliminated the need for actual damages as a precondition for punitive damages under Title VII. *Cush-Crawford v. Adchem Corp.*, 271 F.3d 352 (2d Cir. 2001).

6.   Same-Sex Harassment Cases

In the *Oncale* case, (this chapter), the Supreme Court held that same-sex harassment can be actionable under Title VII.

◆   A lesbian HR director at an Iowa medical practice claimed the practice's female CEO barraged her with improper emails, texts and face-to-face remarks about being gay. She further alleged that the CEO talked to her about gay relationships and having gay sex. The director sued under Title VII, claiming she was discriminated against and harassed based on her sex and/or sexual orientation. The court decided that while Title VII does not ban bias based on sexual orientation, **the HR director stated a plausible claim of bias or harassment because of sex**. A retaliation claim was also allowed to proceed. *Robertson v. Siouxland Community Health Center*, 938 F.Supp.2d 831 (N.D. Iowa 2013).

◆   A male iron worker in Louisiana claimed that his supervisor called him names like "faggot" and "princess," and simulated sexual intercourse while he was bent over at his job. Neither he nor his supervisor was gay. The EEOC sued on his behalf, and a jury awarded him $450,000 for same-sex harassment. A Fifth Circuit panel vacated the award on the basis that the supervisor was an equal opportunity offender who harassed others in the same way. On rehearing, the full Fifth Circuit decided that the EEOC could rely on gender-stereotyping evidence to prove unlawful same-sex discrimination under Title VII and that the EEOC produced enough evidence to support its sex-stereotyping theory. It concluded that punitive damages were not warranted, though it further found that injunctive relief was appropriate. *EEOC v. Boh Brothers Construction Co., LLC*, 731 F.3d 444 (5th Cir. 2013).

◆   An employee on a four-man crew that serviced oil rigs claimed that he was tormented by a co-worker who was either gay or bisexual. The tormenter grabbed and poked his bottom and made comments about his pretty lips. When he complained to a supervisor, he was told to kick the harasser's ass and to duke it out with him. Instead he walked off the job and sued for sexual harassment under state and federal law. A Michigan federal court and the Sixth Circuit ruled against him because **he failed to prove that his tormenter was gay or bisexual, so he couldn't show that the harassment was because of his gender**. *Wasek v. Arrow Energy Services, Inc.*, 682 F.3d 463 (6th Cir. 2012).

◆   An Illinois nurse was subjected to sexual comments and offensive touching by the facility's executive director. **She complained to three different supervisors, per company policy, but the company did not take any action.** Despite her complaints, the nurse was on relatively friendly terms with the director, allowing the director's lesbian lover to baby-sit her daughter and providing medical assistance to the director's mother. She was later fired for unrelated reasons, then sued for sexual harassment. The company sought pretrial judgment, which the Seventh Circuit Court of Appeals denied. Here, there were questions of fact as to whether the company exercised reasonable care to prevent and correct the director's behavior. A trial was required. *Kampmier v. Emeritus Corp.*, 472 F.3d 930 (7th Cir. 2006).

◆   A female team leader at a manufacturing plant in Missouri repeatedly blew kisses at another female team leader, attempted to kiss her on the mouth and made suggestive comments to her like "I want you, honey." The second team leader resigned, then sued for same-sex harassment under Title VII. A federal court and the Eighth Circuit ruled against her. This was not sexual harassment because the aggressor was just a sarcastic person who was not motivated by sexual desire or hostility to women. **While her behavior was boorish and vulgar, it was not harassment "because of sex."** There was simply not enough evidence of motivation by homosexual desire. *Pedroza v. Cintas Corp.*, 397 F.3d 1063 (8th Cir. 2005).

♦ A male security guard, while acting as a supervisor, disciplined two other male guards, who reacted by launching a campaign of retaliation against him. They slashed his tires, taunted him after he was demoted to a non-supervisory position, and made lewd gestures and obscene remarks. The guard complained, and an investigation revealed that there was no corroborating evidence. Nevertheless, the guard and one of the "harassers" were reassigned. The other "harasser" was fired for unrelated reasons. When the guard sued under Title VII, a federal court ruled for the company. The U.S. Court of Appeals, D.C. Circuit, affirmed. Here, **the guard failed to show that the harassers acted the way they did because of his gender**. They did not treat him differently than women; they treated him differently than all other company employees. This was nothing more than a workplace grudge that could not be classified as same-sex sexual harassment. *Davis v. Coastal Int'l Security, Inc.*, 275 F.3d 1119 (D.C. Cir. 2002).

7. Other Sexual Harassment Cases

Sexual harassment is the single largest problem area for most employers. As the following cases show, liability for sexual harassment can arise in a wide variety of situations. The lesson to take away is this:

—have and distribute a sexual harassment policy
—make your intolerance of harassing behavior known
—provide a good avenue for employees to report inappropriate behavior
—investigate any claims of harassment promptly and thoroughly, and
—take decisive and meaningful action to eliminate future harassment without punishing the person who reports the harassment.

♦ Two female restaurant employees in Wisconsin complained about sexually abusive treatment by managers, but the company's district manager and general manager did nothing about the problem. The employees contacted the EEOC, which sued on their behalf. The company asserted that its sexual harassment policy protected it, but a jury disagreed. On appeal, the Seventh Circuit largely affirmed. **The sexual harassment policy was kept locked in a cabinet**, employees were never told how to report complaints, and the policy indicated that they could get in trouble for making frivolous complaints. *EEOC v. Management Hospitality of Racine, Inc.*, 666 F.3d 422 (7th Cir. 2012).

♦ For close to two weeks, **a supervisor in New Jersey kept apologizing to an employee for telling her he wanted to date her**. She found his actions troubling and took leave for two months, at which point the company deemed her to have quit. She then sued for sexual harassment under state law. A federal court granted pretrial judgment to the company, and the Third Circuit affirmed. Here, the supervisor's apologies were at worst an annoying attempt to restore their professional relationship; they could not be construed as creating a sexually hostile work environment. *Anastasia v. Cushman Wakefield*, 455 Fed.Appx. 236 (3d Cir. 2011).

◆   A butcher at a Sam's Club in Puerto Rico claimed that his team leader pursued him romantically and when she learned that he wasn't interested, she punished him with undesirable tasks, threatened him with a negative evaluation and publicly humiliated him. **He complained to management on three occasions, but they allegedly did little.** And she retaliated against him after he reported her behavior. After he complained to Puerto Rico's labor department, Wal-Mart finally transferred the team leader to a different location. When he sued for sexual harassment under Title VII, a federal court granted Wal-Mart pretrial judgment, but the U.S Court of Appeals, First Circuit, reversed that decision, finding that the lawsuit could continue. He presented sufficient evidence that management didn't take his complaints seriously. *Perez-Cordero v. Wal-Mart Puerto Rico, Inc.*, 656 F.3d 19 (1st Cir. 2011).

◆   An employee of a Hy-Vee store in Missouri claimed that **a cake decorator shaped dough into penises and other body parts**, and that she also smacked employees' buttocks and engaged in other sexually charged behavior with men and women. After the employee was fired for performance issues, she sued under state law for sexual harassment and retaliation. A federal court and the Eighth Circuit ruled against her, noting that the decorator's alleged misconduct was directed at men and women equally and not motivated by sexual desire for the employee. *Smith v. Hy-Vee, Inc.*, 622 F.3d 904 (8th Cir. 2010).

◆   An Alabama sales rep was the only female in her office. She claimed she was subjected to sexually offensive language on a daily basis and that the male sales reps kept the radio tuned to a station that aired pornographic talk and advertisements. When she complained, little was done. If she changed the channel, the male sales reps changed it back. And the manager used the word "bitch" to refer to other women, including female customers. She finally quit and sued under Title VII. A federal court granted pretrial judgment to the company because the sexually offensive language wasn't directed at her. The Eleventh Circuit reversed, noting that while the record was filled with evidence of general, indiscriminate vulgarity, **there was also ample evidence of gender-specific, derogatory comments made about women** on account of their sex. Thus, there was enough evidence to require a trial. *Reeves v. C.H. Robinson Worldwide, Inc.*, 594 F.3d 798 (11th Cir. 2010).

◆   A doctor who owned a North Carolina medical practice made shocking and obscene statements to his employees. **He made these comments to men and women, but also made highly personal and sexually graphic remarks to one particular female employee**, who quit after her complaints failed to correct his behavior. She sued for sexual harassment. A federal court granted pretrial judgment to the clinic, but the Fourth Circuit reversed, finding issues of fact that required a trial. Here, a jury could conclude that the owner's conduct was bad enough to constitute illegal sexual harassment under Title VII. *EEOC v. Fairbrook Medical Clinic, P.A.*, 609 F.3d 320 (4th Cir. 2010).

◆   Four female employees of two arthritis clinics owned by a Texas doctor sued him for sexual harassment and retaliation. They all rejected his advances. Three were fired, while the fourth quit after being told she might be fired. A jury awarded compensatory and punitive damages to all four women, but the Fifth Circuit reversed as to the one employee who quit. **Resigning in anticipation of being fired does not rise to the level of a "tangible employment action."** *Alaniz v. Zamora-Quezada*, 591 F.3d 761 (5th Cir. 2009).

◆   A research technician at an Indiana facility endured derogatory names by her supervisor. He called her "dumb," "pushy," "aggressive," a "redneck," "made for the back seat of a car," and said she looked like a "dyke" at various times over a four-year period. After the facility was acquired by a new company, the researcher lost her job. She then sued for sexual harassment under Title VII. A federal court and the Seventh Circuit ruled against her, noting that **the harassment she endured was not objectively severe or pervasive**. Further, a male researcher had also complained about the supervisor calling him fat. *Scruggs v. Garst Seed Co.*, 587 F.3d 832 (7th Cir. 2009).

◆   A new manager at an Arkansas store asserted that the district manager sexually harassed her by rubbing her shoulders and asking about her marital status, then fired her when she wouldn't sleep with him. When she sued, a federal court and the Eighth Circuit ruled against her. Although the manager's comment (over the phone) that she ought to be in bed with him drinking a Mai Tai was inappropriate, **the comment combined with his behavior was not severe or pervasive enough to amount to harassment** under Title VII. *Anderson v. Family Dollar Stores of Arkansas Inc.*, 579 F.3d 858 (8th Cir. 2009).

◆   A female employee for a transportation company in Ohio was subjected to a work environment where the mostly male employees regularly denigrated women, calling them sluts, whores, bitches and dykes. Her co-workers also viewed sexually explicit pictures on their computers and left pornographic magazines on their desks. When she tried to complain to her manager, he made her do so in the open area rather than in his office. He then yelled out over the open workplace to tell the offending worker (in that instance) to stop. The poor treatment of women continued, however, and she did not call the company hotline because someone told her an employee had been fired for doing so. When she quit and sued under Title VII, a federal court granted pretrial judgment to the company, but the Sixth Circuit reversed. It noted that **the harassment didn't have to specifically target her**, and she didn't have to show that her work productivity declined. *Gallagher v. C.H. Robinson Worldwide, Inc.*, 567 F.3d 263 (6th Cir. 2009).

◆   An Illinois Ford employee claimed that she was harassed by co-workers on the chassis line. Ford couldn't corroborate the claim, but it shifted her to a motor line where she no longer experienced harassment. She nevertheless filed an EEOC complaint. The following year, while the complaint was pending, she agreed to a one-time buyout offered to eligible employees. She signed a waiver releasing Ford from any and all claims she might have against it, and then received $100,000. When she later sued for the harassment, a federal court and the Seventh Circuit ruled against her. **She knowingly and voluntarily signed the waiver as part of a valid reduction in force**, and she could have bargained for more money to cover her pending EEOC complaint. *Hampton v. Ford Motor Co.*, 561 F.3d 709 (7th Cir. 2009).

◆   A Kentucky restaurant manager rejected sexual advances from his two supervisors. Shortly thereafter, he was fired without warning on the grounds that he was not "supporting" his general manager. He called his former district manager and was told that he could maintain his position if he agreed to transfer to another location 120 miles away. After a month of commuting, he quit to take another job, then sued for sexual harassment. The company claimed that no adverse action was taken against him, but a jury disagreed. The Sixth Circuit upheld the jury's award, noting that although a lateral transfer is not normally an adverse action, the jury permissibly found that **the 120-mile transfer made the action adverse**. *Keeton v. Flying J, Inc.*, 429 F.3d 259 (6th Cir. 2005).

◆   A supervisor for a Missouri company cut a peephole in the women's bathroom wall so he could spy on a female employee. Eventually he was caught when another female employee noticed something wrong. The targeted employee then sued the company for sexual harassment under Title VII. A federal court and the Eighth Circuit ruled against her because she was not aware of the peeping at the time it was going on. **Title VII requires sexual harassment to be both subjectively and objectively offensive**, which it could not be if the harassed party did not know she was being harassed. *Cottrill v. MFA, Inc.*, 443 F.3d 629 (8th Cir. 2006).

E.   Sexual Orientation and Identity Issues

Title VII does not protect against sexual orientation discrimination, nor does it protect against gender identity discrimination. However, many state laws provide protections in these areas. There may also be protection for gender identity disorders under disability discrimination laws.

◆   An employee in Illinois claimed co-workers made offensive remarks about his sexual orientation and race. He alleged that graffiti on bathroom walls at work made vulgar references to sexual acts and accused him of having AIDS. The employer had the graffiti covered with paint. The employee was later suspended after a verbal disagreement with a supervisor. He was then laid off and then recalled. He sued, claiming he was harassed in violation of Title VII when co-workers mistreated him **because he did not act the way they believed**

a male should act. The court rejected his claim, finding it was based on speculation. The employer took prompt remedial steps in response to the harassing conduct. *Muhammad v. Caterpillar, Inc.*, 767 F.3d 694 (7th Cir. 2014).

◆ A pre-operative female-to-male transgender applied for a job as a part-time package handler at UPS in Minnesota, binding his breasts, cutting his hair short and wearing men's clothes. He used his given name and never told the interviewer he was a pre-operative transgender. Still, he didn't get the job. UPS claimed it was because he had a poor job history, but he thought it was because of discrimination. He asserted that at the end of his interview, someone came into the room and whispered in the interviewer's ear, after which the interviewer stated that UPS wasn't hiring and that the applicant gave poor interview answers. When he sued, he lost. The Eighth Circuit held that **there was no evidence UPS knew he was transgender** and that it had a legitimate reason for not hiring him – his poor job history. *Hunter v. United Parcel Service, Inc.*, 697 F.3d 697 (8th Cir. 2012).

◆ A front desk clerk at an Iowa hotel wore men's button-down shirts and had a masculine, "Ellen DeGeneres kind of look." She received praise and raises, but when the director of operations saw her at the front desk during the day shift, **he decided she didn't have that "Midwestern girl look" and sought to transfer her to the night shift**. Her manager refused to transfer her and was then asked to resign. The director then told the clerk she would have to interview with him to keep her shift, but three days later, he fired her. She sued for gender discrimination under Title VII, and the Eighth Circuit held that she deserved a trial. Here, the hotel did not claim poor performance until after it fired her, and she had no history of discipline. Also, the hotel didn't follow its written termination procedures. *Lewis v. Heartland Inns of America, LLC*, 591 F.3d 1033 (8th Cir. 2010).

◆ A self-described effeminate gay man worked at a Pennsylvania plant that produced business forms. He endured anti-gay slurs from both men and women, as well as graffiti in the restroom. Co-workers also called him "Rosebud" and "Princess." After he was laid off, he sued for discrimination under Title VII. The Third Circuit ruled that **he could pursue his claim that he was discriminated against based on gender stereotypes**. He could also pursue a retaliation claim that he was laid off for complaining about the stereotype-based harassment. *Prowel v. Wise Business Forms, Inc.*, 579 F.3d 285 (3d Cir. 2009).

◆ A salon in New York **fired an openly gay assistant stylist** because she got an "extremely unprofessional-looking haircut at a barbershop," which amounted to insubordination. She claimed that she was really fired because she did not conform to gender stereotypes of how a woman should look. When she sued the salon under Title VII, she lost. A federal court and the Second Circuit held that the salon did not violate Title VII. The salon could require her to have her hair cut by its stylists as a means of advertising its techniques. Title VII does not protect against sexual orientation discrimination, and this was not gender stereotyping. *Dawson v. Bumble & Bumble*, 398 F.3d 211 (2d Cir. 2005).

✦   While working for a Georgia car dealership, a service technician transitioned from male to female. She violated company rules by wearing skirts and heels in a service area and by using a unisex customer restroom instead of an employee restroom to change into and out of her uniform. Her employment was terminated after she was caught sleeping in a car in the service center when she was supposed to be working. She sued for sex discrimination under Title VII, but the court rejected her claim. **The evidence showed the technician was fired for sleeping on the job.** The company granted her a generous amount of leave so she would undergo reassignment surgeries, and this fact further undercut the claim of unlawful discrimination. *Chavez v. Credit Nation Auto Sales*, No. 13-cv-00312, 2014 WL 4585452 (N.D. Ga. 9/12/14).

F. State Law

State laws generally track the language of Title VII and the Equal Pay Act, and the analyses used to determine whether discrimination has occurred are generally the same as in cases involving the federal statutes.

Sometimes there is more protection under state law – for example, a number of states bar discrimination on the basis of <u>sexual orientation</u> and <u>marital status</u>. Since there is no protection under federal law for these kinds of discrimination, employees in states that protect against this type of discrimination will sue under state law. There also may be individual supervisor liability under state law.

✦   A male dentist fired his female assistant because he had personal feelings for her and because **his wife viewed her as a threat to their marriage and demanded that he do so**. The assistant sued the dentist for sex discrimination under Iowa law. The state's highest court rejected her claim. The assistant was not fired because she was female; she was fired because the dentist had personal feelings for her and his wife got jealous. *Nelson v. Knight*, 834 N.W.2d 64 (Iowa 2013).

✦   After a female applicant was rejected for a warehouse position six times, she sued the employer for gender discrimination under a West Virginia law. The employer said its policy required all interested candidates to submit a resume and fill out an online application before they could be hired for a warehouse job. However, there was evidence that a supervisor hired a male temporary worker who did not even apply for a permanent position. **Also, the supervisor assigned a male applicant higher scores for experience and computer knowledge, even though the female had more experience and had received more computer training.** Based on this evidence, a jury could find the employer manipulated its process to avoid hiring women. The court refused to grant pretrial judgment to the employer. *Blankenship v. Caterpillar Global Mining, LLC*, 964 F.Supp.2d 578 (S.D. W.Va. 2013).

✦   The new president and CEO of the Alliance of Automobile Manufacturers hired the assistant who had worked for the interim president. Problems quickly developed between the two, and the HR manager met with the assistant regularly to tell her that the CEO was frustrated with her performance. The CEO fired her about a year later, and she sued for age and gender discrimination under the D.C. Human Rights Act. However, she lost because **she couldn't prove that his reason for firing her – that they had incompatible work styles – was a pretext for discrimination**. And if he really was biased against her, why would he hire her and then begin the process of firing her shortly thereafter? *Vatel v. Alliance of Automobile Manufacturers*, 627 F.3d 1245 (D.C. Cir. 2011).

◆ A student at a private college in New York worked in the college's computer center during her sophomore year. She claimed that her supervisor sent her sexually harassing emails and monitored her Internet use after she complained. When she sued the college under New York City's Human Rights Law, the college claimed that it exercised reasonable care to prevent or correct the discrimination. Thus, it was entitled to use the *Ellerth/Faragher* defense. However, the New York Court of Appeals disagreed, ruling that the *Ellerth/Faragher* affirmative defense doesn't apply to the Human Rights Law. So **the college could be liable even if it exercised reasonable care to prevent or correct the harassment**. *Zakrzewska v. New School*, 928 N.E.2d 1035 (N.Y. 2010).

◆ A Wal-Mart pharmacist left her work area to get a soda at a nearby counter. While she was away, a pharmacy technician wrote and filled a fraudulent prescription. When Wal-Mart discovered the fraud 18 months later, after the technician wrote another fraudulent prescription, it fired both the technician and the pharmacist. However, it didn't fire the male pharmacist who not only was on duty during the second incident, but also initialed the fraudulent prescription. The fired pharmacist then learned that she had been paid significantly less than Wal-Mart's male pharmacists. She sued for sex discrimination under state law, and a jury awarded her $972,000 in compensatory damages and $1 million in punitive damages. The Supreme Judicial Court of Massachusetts upheld the award, noting that **male pharmacists were not punished for leaving their work area** and that Wal-Mart failed to follow its progressive discipline policy. *Haddad v. Wal-Mart Stores, Inc.*, 914 N.E.2d 59 (Mass. 2009).

◆ A retail employee in Tennessee was fired after the company determined that she had used her computer ID to sell herself merchandise and modify her special order to obtain a partial refund. The company had a strict "no self-service" policy to deter theft and dishonesty. She sued under Title VII and state law, claiming that the real reason for the termination was gender bias. The Sixth Circuit disagreed. The company had a reasonable belief that she violated its "no self-service" policy, and it consistently discharged employees who violated that policy. *Sybrandt v. Home Depot*, 560 F.3d 553 (6th Cir. 2009).

III. AGE DISCRIMINATION

The Age Discrimination in Employment Act forbids discrimination against individuals <u>at least 40 years old</u>. This includes not only hiring and firing decisions, but also the provision of benefits. For example, healthcare benefits for older employees are generally more expensive than the same level of benefits for younger employees.

Thus, employers can provide fewer benefits to older employees than to younger workers, as long as the amount of payment made or cost incurred on behalf of the older employees is equal to or greater than the amount paid or cost incurred on behalf of the younger workers.

Where age is a bona fide occupational qualification, it may be used as a factor in employment decisions. However, for most jobs, age will not be a valid consideration. As a general rule, **never** take age into account in employment decisions.

Like the Equal Pay Act, the Age Discrimination in Employment Act of 1967 (ADEA) (29 U.S.C. § 621 *et seq.*) is part of the Fair Labor Standards Act. It applies to institutions that have 20 or more employees and that affect interstate commerce. The ADEA extends its protections to any individual 40 years old or older.

A. Supreme Court Cases

One of the Supreme Court's most important decisions came in the *O'Connor* case, (this chapter), where it held that employees can sue under the Age Discrimination in Employment Act (ADEA) even when they are not replaced by persons outside the protected class. Another key Supreme Court ruling in this area is the *Gross* case (this chapter), which set the standard of proof in federal age discrimination cases.

As long as the reason for an adverse decision is age-based, the decision will subject the employer to potential liability.

The Supreme Court also held, in the *Oubre* case, that waivers and releases must comply with the Older Workers Benefit Protection Act (OWBPA) (an amendment to the ADEA) in order to be valid. Thus, if you offer an employee a severance package in exchange for a promise not to sue, it must comply with the OWBPA.

◆   New York night watchmen sued under the ADEA after they were removed from their positions and assigned less desirable jobs as night porters and light-duty cleaners. The employer asserted that they should have arbitrated their claims under a collective bargaining agreement in place. The case reached the U.S. Supreme Court, which agreed with the employer that **the watchmen had to arbitrate their claims under the ADEA**. The union and the employer bargained in good faith and agreed that employment-related discrimination claims would be subject to arbitration. And the ADEA does not preclude the arbitration of such claims. As a result, the employees had to arbitrate their claims. They still retained the option of suing their union for breach of the duty of fair representation; they could also sue the union directly under the ADEA;

and they could still bring individual claims to the EEOC or the NLRB. *14 Penn Plaza LLC v. Pyett*, 556 U.S. 247, 129 S.Ct. 1456, 173 L.Ed.2d 398 (2009).

♦   A 54-year-old claims administration director for a financial services company in Iowa was reassigned to a job as a claims project coordinator. The employer transferred many of his duties to a newly created position and gave the job to a woman in her early 40s whom the coordinator had previously supervised. He sued under the ADEA, presenting evidence that he was reassigned in part because of his age. The company claimed the reassignment was part of corporate restructuring. The U.S. Supreme Court held that **an employee can win an ADEA claim by only proving that age was the sole motivating factor for the adverse action**. *Gross v. FBL Financial Services, Inc.*, 557 U.S. 167, 129 S.Ct. 2343, 174 L.Ed.2d 119 (2009).

♦   An atomic power laboratory in New York was ordered to reduce its work force and had to cut 31 jobs. It did so in part by ranking employees on job performance, flexibility and criticality. The flexibility factor assessed whether the employees' skills were transferable to other assignments. The criticality factor assessed the importance of the employees' skills to the lab. When 30 of the 31 people laid off were age 40 or older, an ADEA lawsuit ensued. A jury ruled that the layoff process had a disparate impact on older employees, but the Second Circuit reversed, finding the employees should have been required to prove that the selection process was unreasonable. The Supreme Court vacated and remanded the case. Here, **the burden should have been on the employer to prove that its layoff process used reasonable factors other than age**. *Meacham v. Knolls Atomic Power Laboratory*, 554 U.S. 84, 128 S.Ct. 2395, 171 L.Ed.2d 283 (2008).

♦   After an older employee in Kansas was fired as part of a reduction in force, she sued for age discrimination. When she sought to introduce testimony from five other employees who claimed that their supervisors discriminated against them because of age, the court refused to allow the "me too" testimony. The Tenth Circuit reversed, but the Supreme Court reversed the court of appeals. It held that such **"me too" testimony can be admitted if it is relevant and not unduly prejudicial**. This is a fact-based inquiry that is best left to the trial court to ascertain. *Sprint/United Management Co. v. Mendelsohn*, 552 U.S. 379, 128 S.Ct. 1140, 170 L.Ed.2d 1 (2008).

♦   A group of senior, longtime police officers with a Mississippi city challenged the city's revised pay policy because it gave proportionately higher raises to officers with less than five years' tenure. They claimed that the revised policy had a disparate (discriminatory) impact on them. The U.S. Supreme Court held that **the officers could sue for disparate impact discrimination under the ADEA**. To win, the officers would have to identify a "specific test, requirement, or practice with the pay plan that ha[d] an adverse impact on older workers." The city claimed that the differential was justified by the need to make junior officers' salaries competitive with comparable positions in the market. Here, the Court determined that the policy was based on reasonable factors other than age and therefore did not violate the ADEA. *Smith v. City of Jackson*, 544 U.S. 228, 125 S.Ct. 1536, 161 L.Ed.2d 410 (2005).

◆　A company and a union entered into a collective bargaining agreement, which eliminated the company's obligation to provide health benefits to subsequently retired employees, except for current workers at least 50 years old. Employees aged 40 to 49 filed charges with the EEOC, claiming that the bargaining agreement violated the ADEA. When the company and union refused to settle, the employees sued in an Ohio federal court, which dismissed the action on the grounds that the ADEA did not cover "reverse age discrimination." The case reached the U.S. Supreme Court, which held that the ADEA was never intended to prevent an employer from favoring an older worker over a younger one. Rather, Congress was concerned with discrimination against older workers. **Reverse age discrimination is not barred by the ADEA.** *General Dynamics Land Systems, Inc. v. Cline*, 540 U.S. 581, 124 S.Ct. 1236, 157 L.Ed.2d 1094 (2004).

◆　The Supreme Court held that in a lawsuit brought under the ADEA, once the employee presented a *prima facie* case of discrimination and showed that the employer's asserted nondiscriminatory reason for its adverse action was false, **intentional discrimination could be inferred** without further evidence of discrimination. This reaffirmed the holding of *St. Mary's Honor Center v. Hicks*, 509 U.S. 502 (1993), a Title VII case that set forth the same standard. The case involved a supervisor in the "hinge room" of a manufacturer of toilet seats and covers. After he was fired for failing to keep accurate records, he sued under the ADEA and presented evidence that his record keeping had been proper. The district court had properly let the case go to the jury without further evidence of discrimination, and the jury's award of $98,000 should not have been overturned by the court of appeals. *Reeves v. Sanderson Plumbing Products*, 530 U.S. 133, 120 S.Ct. 2097, 147 L.Ed.2d 105 (2000).

◆　The OWBPA imposes specific requirements on employers who discharge employees and seek **a waiver or release of potential claims** against them under the ADEA. The requirements apply where an employee is offered a severance package. A valid OWBPA waiver must provide at least 20 days' notice to the employee to consider the waiver, written advice to consult an attorney prior to executing the waiver, a seven-day period after signing the waiver to revoke consent, and specifically refer to rights or claims arising under the ADEA. A Louisiana employer presented an employee with a severance agreement and waiver after she received a poor performance rating. The employer gave her only 14 days to consider the waiver, failed to allow seven days after signing the release during which to change her mind, and made no reference to ADEA claims. The employee signed the release, waiving all claims against the employer in return for $6,258. She then sued the employer for constructive discharge in violation of the ADEA. The court granted the employer pretrial judgment, ruling that she had ratified the defective release by retaining the severance pay.

The Fifth Circuit affirmed the district court judgment, but the U.S. Supreme Court found that the employee's **retention of the severance pay did not effectively waive the ADEA claim**. The OWBPA amended the ADEA with specific statutory commands forbidding the waiver of an ADEA claim unless the statutory requirements are met. The Court reversed and remanded the case, since the release did not comply with OWBPA standards and was unenforceable. The failure to tender back the severance pay award did not excuse the employer's failure to comply with the OWBPA. *Oubre v. Entergy Operations, Inc.*, 522 U.S. 422, 118 S.Ct. 838, 139 L.Ed.2d 849 (1998).

◆   A 56-year-old North Carolina employee was fired by his employer after 12 years of work and replaced by a 40-year-old man. The discharged employee sued under the ADEA. The U.S. Supreme Court agreed to review the question of whether the employee was barred from proving age discrimination under the ADEA solely because he had been replaced by a worker who was 40 years old and also within the class of persons protected by the ADEA. It stated that, in age discrimination cases, it was **not necessary that the employee be replaced by someone outside the protected class**. Under that logic, a 40-year-old worker replaced by a 39-year-old worker would be entitled to ADEA protection while the 56-year-old employee in this case would gain no relief despite being replaced by an individual who was 16 years younger. Because the ADEA prohibits discrimination on the basis of age, the replacement of an employee by a substantially younger employee was a far more reliable indicator of age discrimination. *O'Connor v. Consolidated Coin Caterers Corp.*, 517 U.S. 308, 116 S.Ct. 1307, 134 L.Ed.2d 433 (1996).

◆   A 62-year-old secretary at a Tennessee publishing company had access to company financial records and made copies of documents when she became concerned that the company would fire her because of her age. The company dismissed the secretary under a work force reduction plan. She sued under the ADEA, seeking back pay and other relief. When the company learned that she had copied financial documents, it filed a motion for pretrial judgment, which the court granted on the basis of the secretary's misconduct. The Sixth Circuit affirmed, but the U.S. Supreme Court reversed. It rejected the reasoning of the lower courts that the secretary's misconduct constituted proper grounds for termination based on the **after-acquired evidence**. Employee wrongdoing remained relevant and would preclude reinstatement or front pay as an appropriate remedy in this case. However, the district court could not impose an absolute rule barring the secretary's recovery of back pay. The remedy should calculate back pay from the date of the unlawful discharge to the date the company discovered the wrongdoing. *McKennon v. Nashville Banner Publishing Co.*, 513 U.S. 352, 115 S.Ct. 879, 130 L.Ed.2d 852 (1995).

◆   A Massachusetts manufacturing employee was fired at age 62, a few weeks before his pension benefits were due to vest. He sued under the ADEA and the Employee Retirement Income Security Act. The case reached the U.S. Supreme Court, which noted that when **an employer's decision is wholly motivated by factors other than age**, no ADEA violation occurs. This was true even when the motivating factor was correlated with age (such as pension status). Because age and years of service may be analytically distinct, an employer could take account of one while ignoring the other. The Court remanded the case to the court of appeals to determine if the jury had sufficient evidence to find a violation of the ADEA. *Hazen Paper Co. v. Biggins*, 507 U.S. 604, 113 S.Ct. 1701, 123 L.Ed.2d 338 (1993).

◆   An airline company required all cockpit crew members (pilots, copilots and flight engineers) to retire at the age of 60. A Federal Aviation Administration regulation prohibited persons from serving as pilots or copilots after turning 60, but there was no similar provision for flight engineers. A group of flight engineers and pilots who wished to become flight engineers sued the airline in a California federal court, contending that the mandatory retirement provision violated the ADEA. The airline argued that the **age 60 limit was a bona fide occupational qualification** (BFOQ) reasonably necessary to the safe operation of the airline. A jury held for the employees, and the Ninth Circuit affirmed. The U.S. Supreme Court stated that even if it was "rational" for the airline to set age 60 as the limit for flight engineers, the airline still had to show that it had reasonable cause to believe that all or substantially all flight engineers over 60 would be unable to safely perform their job duties, or that it would be highly impractical to deal with older employees on an individual basis to determine whether they had the necessary qualifications. Because the airline had not shown this, the Court affirmed the decisions for the employees. *Western Air Lines, Inc. v. Criswell*, 472 U.S. 400, 105 S.Ct. 2743, 86 L.Ed.2d 321 (1985).

B. Layoffs for Economic Reasons

Layoffs and discharges for financial reasons have become common in today's business environment. Generally, such actions do not violate the Age Discrimination in Employment Act (ADEA). However, where they are used to create a younger work force or eliminate higher-paid employees, they can result in liability.

Employers should carefully ascertain whether any layoff or reduction in force is going to result in the release of more older workers than younger workers. The failure to consider age (or race, national origin, religion and sex) can result in liability.

◆   An electrical and instrumentation designer in Kentucky said that his site project manager made comments about how the design group was getting too old. The employer then assigned a 41-year-old designer to the team. Two years later, the older designer was laid off at age 52 after the employer suffered a downturn in business and he received a low rating from the site manager. He sued for age discrimination under state law, claiming the site manager told him the younger designer was being groomed for a lead designer job because he was younger. He also claimed the site manager was concerned that the older designer would be retiring soon. A district court ruled for the employer, but the Sixth Circuit reversed. **There was direct evidence, in the form of the site**

manager's alleged comments, that the employer used potential length of future tenure as a proxy for age. *Sharp v. Aker Plant Services Group, Inc.*, 726 F.3d 789 (6th Cir. 2013).

◆ A supervisor at a Michigan company decided, for budgetary reasons, to lay off two of three bindery workers on the third shift. He laid off a 65-year-old and a 58-year-old while keeping a 29-year-old, whom he decided was more productive and more of a team player. The 58-year-old sued under the ADEA, but lost. The Sixth Circuit held that even though the supervisor was unaware of the company's layoff policy, he still essentially followed the guidelines by considering productivity, performance, attendance and other factors. *Schoonmaker v. Spartan Graphics Leasing, LLC*, 595 F.3d 261 (6th Cir. 2010).

◆ After merging with Verizon, MCI decided to implement a reduction in force (RIF) to eliminate duplicate jobs. A 56-year-old Illinois employee selected for the RIF sued for age discrimination, asserting that his direct supervisor had referred to him as an "old timer." However, because the company had laid off some younger employees too, and had stated that the reason for laying him off was because his skills were obsolete, he lost. A federal court and the U.S. Court of Appeals, Seventh Circuit, noted that **a company may permissibly discharge employees who can't perform the upgraded and more complicated tasks required after a merger.** *Martino v. MCI Communications, Inc.*, 574 F.3d 447 (7th Cir. 2009).

◆ Southwestern Bell implemented a reduction in force for 22 first-line managers and one area manager. It grouped the managers by job title and location, determined which locations could be handled by fewer managers, rated the managers into A, B or C categories, and then ranked the C-rated managers against one another. Three of the laid-off managers sued for age and gender discrimination under Title VII. An Oklahoma federal court granted pretrial judgment to Southwestern Bell, and the Tenth Circuit largely affirmed. However, it allowed one manager's claim to go to trial because her supervisor allegedly told her she was being laid off because of her age. As for the other claims, the company implemented the RIF process consistently and without pretext. *Sanders v. Southwestern Bell Telephone*, 544 F.3d 1101 (10th Cir. 2008).

◆ A custodian at a private school near Philadelphia also performed security guard responsibilities until the day he closed the school's theater before students were finished and forced them to wait for their rides home in the rain. He was sent home early because his supervisor wanted to motivate him to improve his performance. Later, he was laid off as part of the outsourcing of the entire custodial department. When he sued for age discrimination, he lost. The Third Circuit found no evidence of age bias. **The school had a legitimate reason for disciplining him (poor performance)** and for laying him off (financial concerns). Plus, six of the eight employees who lost their jobs were under age 40. *Abraham v. Abington Friends School*, 215 Fed.Appx. 83 (3d Cir. 2006).

♦   A 51-year-old engineer with a company in New Mexico was laid off in a reduction in force. He was selected because even though he had good technical skills, he repeatedly second-guessed managers and did not get along well with co-workers. He sued for discrimination under the ADEA and lost. A federal court and the Tenth Circuit held that **the reason for the layoff – that he was a poor team player – was legitimate**, even if the company relied on subjective observations to reach its decision. *Pippin v. Burlington Resources Oil and Gas Co.*, 440 F.3d 1186 (10th Cir. 2006).

♦   A 49-year-old Indiana employee who had received satisfactory evaluations was laid off as part of a reduction in force. She sued under the ADEA, citing her overall satisfactory ratings. The company cited the negative comments in her review relating to her rapport with co-workers and her duplicative business practices. It also asserted that a new computer program handled most of her duties. A federal court and the Seventh Circuit ruled for the company. **Even though the employee would have been retained under normal circumstances**, she could be laid off as part of the reduction in force without violating the ADEA. *Merillat v. Metal Spinners, Inc.*, 470 F.3d 685 (7th Cir. 2006).

♦   A cab company in Oregon purchased a new insurance policy that did not cover drivers over age 70. However, it was not aware of that fact until the day before it had to provide proof of insurance to city officials or lose its business license. It then temporarily fired a 72-year-old driver until it could resolve the insurance issue. In the meantime it found a job for the driver with a competitor, and the insurer agreed to cover the driver if he passed a physical. He refused to take the physical, instead suing the company for age discrimination. A federal court granted pretrial judgment to the company, but the Ninth Circuit reversed, finding that factual questions existed regarding **whether the company harbored discriminatory motives**. A jury would have to decide the case. *Enlow v. Salem-Keizer Yellow Cab*, 389 F.3d 802 (9th Cir. 2004).

C. Constructive Discharge

Sometimes, employers are reluctant to fire employees and, as a result, they create difficult working conditions in the hope that the employees will quit. But if an employer forces an employee to quit, and a judge or jury determines that a reasonable person in the same situation would also have quit, the resignation is treated like a discharge and the employer becomes liable.

♦   A company in Alabama instituted a voluntary severance program as part of a two-stage program to reduce its work force. It scored employees on work-related skills. A 52-year-old employee was ranked last in his group and was offered early retirement, the possibility of seeking a transfer or staying put and hoping his job would not be eliminated in the future. He chose the early retirement, then sued under the Age Discrimination in Employment Act (ADEA) when he learned that his job would not have been eliminated. A federal court and the Eleventh Circuit ruled against him. **The voluntary severance program was not a constructive discharge** because his choice was never "quit or be fired." Thus, no adverse action had been taken against him. *Rowell v. BellSouth Corp.*, 433 F.3d 794 (11th Cir. 2005).

◆   An executive with a Puerto Rico advertising company was told to hire new creative talent. When he resisted, many of the employees in his office were transferred to another location and he was given new responsibilities. He was told that his proposals looked tired and that the company needed new blood. He was also ordered to complete a three-page report by the next morning. He became depressed and took sick leave for a year. He then requested an additional five weeks of paid vacation. When his request was denied, he stayed away from work anyway and was fired. In his ADEA lawsuit, the First Circuit ruled against him. He did not show the company had taken **an adverse action against him** that could be construed as age bias. He was not constructively discharged. *Suárez v. Pueblo Int'l, Inc.*, 229 F.3d 49 (1st Cir. 2000).

◆   A 59-year-old employee of a paper mill in Arkansas was responsible for three machines. While preparing a machine for repair, he failed to follow the proper safety procedures, and a younger employee under his supervision filed a union grievance against him. The paper mill's labor relations manager recommended that he be fired, but the mill manager decided instead to suspend him for 120 days. He quit and sued for age discrimination under the ADEA, asserting that the mill had constructively discharged him. A jury awarded him $670,000, which the court doubled to $1.3 million, finding that the ADEA violation was willful. The Eighth Circuit U.S. Court of Appeals reversed, holding that **the employee had not shown that the mill intended to force his resignation by suspending him**. In fact, it chose suspension over termination. As a result, the mill did not violate the ADEA. *Tatom v. Georgia-Pacific Corp.*, 228 F.3d 926 (8th Cir. 2000).

◆   A corporation employed a 60-year-old Texas man as the vice president of one of its divisions. When the new division president and the president of the corporation decided they wanted a younger management team, the employee was given three options, the least offensive of which appeared to be a job as warehouse supervisor at the same salary but with a reduction in benefits. He accepted that position. When he reported for work, however, he was placed in charge of maintenance at the warehouse and spent 75% of his working time sweeping floors and cleaning up the employees' cafeteria. He sued the company under the ADEA. He was awarded $3.4 million. The Fifth Circuit affirmed, noting that there was substantial evidence to support the jury's ADEA verdict. The court also noted that the degrading and humiliating way in which the vice president had been stripped of his duties and demoted to a menial position took the case out of the realm of an ordinary employment dispute. Here, **the corporation sought to humiliate the vice president in the hopes that he would quit**. *Wilson v. Monarch Paper Co.*, 939 F.2d 1138 (5th Cir. 1991).

D. OWBPA

The Older Workers Benefit Protection Act (OWBPA) is an amendment to the Age Discrimination in Employment Act (ADEA) that prohibits discrimination against older workers in all employee benefits "except when age-based reductions in employee benefit plans are justified by significant cost considerations." This is the equal benefits/equal cost defense.

Specifically, the regulations state that a benefit plan will be considered in compliance with the ADEA where the actual amount of payment made, or cost incurred, on behalf of an older worker is equal to that made or incurred on behalf of a younger worker, even though the older worker receives a lesser amount of benefits or insurance coverage.

Many employers attempt to head off age discrimination lawsuits through the use of waivers that discharged employees sign in exchange for a cash payment. Such waivers are valid only if they are "knowing and voluntary."

♦   A group of employees over the age of 40 signed a severance agreement provided by IBM when they were laid off in a reduction in force. The agreement stated that it was a release of all claims against IBM, including claims under the ADEA, and later stated that the covenant not to sue did not apply to actions based solely on the ADEA. It used the terms "release" and "covenant not to sue" interchangeably. When **the employees sued, challenging the agreement under the OWBPA** (part of the ADEA), a California federal court dismissed their action, finding the agreement was written in a manner calculated to be understood by an average individual selected for layoff. The Ninth Circuit disagreed, ruling that the language was not clear. The employees could continue their lawsuit. *Syverson v. IBM Corp.*, 472 F.3d 1072 (9th Cir. 2007).

♦   A 55-year-old Iowa manager was laid off after company officials determined that a new system allowed a coordinator to do his job. He was offered two severance options, consulted with an attorney, and signed one. He then sued for discrimination under the ADEA, claiming that the waiver he'd signed did not comply with the OWBPA because it was not written in a manner calculated to be understood by the individual signing it. A federal court and the Eighth Circuit ruled against him. **The provisions in question complied with Department of Labor regulations** that made certain exceptions for ADEA claims. *Parsons v. Pioneer Seed Hi-Bred Int'l, Inc.*, 447 F.3d 1102 (8th Cir. 2006).

♦   An engineer for a company in Minnesota received a waiver agreement in which he agreed not to sue the company for any claims, including under the ADEA, in exchange for a sum of money. The waiver also contained a covenant not to sue in which he was informed that he would not be liable for the company's attorney fees if he sued it under the ADEA. He did not understand the language and asked for a clarification, but the company did not provide one. When he later sued under the ADEA, a federal court granted pretrial judgment to the company, but the Eighth Circuit reversed. The waiver used unexplained legal terms of art (General Release and Covenant Not to Sue). This ambiguity meant that **the waiver was not "knowing and voluntary" under the OWBPA**. *Thomforde v. IBM Corp.*, 406 F.3d 500 (8th Cir. 2005).

◆   The 57-year-old chief administrator of the psychiatric department of a Pennsylvania health network was fired for improperly handling lease negotiations for a new office. He signed a separation and release agreement in which he agreed not to file a charge, complaint or lawsuit against the company. In return, he received a guarantee of 36 weeks of salary. If he accepted a lower-paying job during that time, the company would make up the salary difference until the 36 weeks ended. Later, he learned that a 44-year-old had replaced him. He filed EEOC charges that were dismissed as untimely and then sued under the ADEA. A federal court ruled for the company, and the Third Circuit affirmed. **The waiver barred the administrator from pursuing his claim.** Its language was clearly written so that he could understand it; he was given 21 days to sign the waiver and was advised to consult an attorney; and the waiver was supported by adequate consideration. It complied with the OWBPA. *Wastak v. Lehigh Valley Health Network*, 342 F.3d 281 (3d Cir. 2003).

E. Procedural Issues

In many cases, whether an employer will be held liable for age discrimination depends on evidentiary issues like hearsay statements from supervisors. Comments like: "We need new blood around here" and "You're 10 years behind the times" can be real trouble, especially if they're made by a decisionmaker.

◆   A 59-year-old Nielsen Media Research employee violated company policy by inputting the wrong address for a homeowner who was participating in market research. She had previously violated a company policy by leaving gifts at unoccupied households. She was placed on a developmental improvement plan (less severe than a performance improvement plan) for the earlier violations and was fired for making the address error. She sued for age discrimination, claiming that two younger employees were not fired for making similar address errors and other mistakes. A federal court granted pretrial judgment to the company, but the Ninth Circuit reversed, finding issues of fact that required a trial. **Even though the other employees had different supervisors, they might all be similarly situated because the company required uniform discipline.** *Earl v. Nielsen Media Research, Inc.*, 658 F.3d 1108 (9th Cir. 2011).

◆   Three female Seton Hall professors in their 60s learned that younger male and female employees were earning more than they were. They asked to be paid more, but the university denied their request, causing them to sue. The case reached the Supreme Court of New Jersey, which held that the state's Law Against Discrimination treats each pay period offense as an unlawful act. As a result, **even though the discriminatory pay decisions went back more than two years, the**

professors could still sue. However, they could only recover wages going back two years. *Alexander v. Seton Hall Univ.*, 8 A.3d 198 (N.J. 2010).

♦   A Sprint manager in Kansas was laid off in a company-wide reduction in force. She sued under the ADEA, seeking to introduce testimony from five former employees who claimed that their managers had discriminated against them because of their age. A federal court refused to admit the testimony because the other employees had different supervisors who were not involved in the decision to lay off the manager in this case. And the manager here did not allege that Sprint had a pattern or practice of discriminating against older workers; she claimed only that she had been discriminated against. *Mendelsohn v. Sprint/United Management Co.*, 402 Fed.Appx. 337 (10th Cir. 2010).

♦   A 69-year-old senior vice president at Kmart was demoted to vice president after a 41-year-old became the new chairman of the board. The chairman made several ageist comments, criticizing the vice president for being the old guy and for being around too long. The chairman also allegedly told the vice president to look for a new job after he hired a consultant to take over the vice president's former position. The vice president resigned and then sued for age discrimination. A Michigan federal court granted pretrial judgment to Kmart, but the Sixth Circuit reversed, finding issues of fact that required a trial. **The chairman's comments may have indicated a discriminatory animus.** *Marsico v. Sears Holding Corp.*, 370 Fed.Appx. 658 (6th Cir. 2010).

♦   An Ohio insurance company manager was fired after he received falling performance ratings for a few years. He sued the company, claiming that the real reason for his termination was his age. A jury agreed and **awarded him $6 million in compensatory damages as well as $10 million in punitive damages**. The Sixth Circuit upheld the compensatory damages award, but it reversed and remanded on the punitive damages issue. There was evidence that the manager's supervisors treated him less favorably than younger managers, lowering his ratings despite circumstances beyond his control. However, there was no company-wide policy of discrimination against the elderly, so the punitive damages award should not have exceeded the award of compensatory damages. *Morgan v. New York Life Insurance Co.*, 559 F.3d 425 (6th Cir. 2009).

♦   JP Morgan Chase fired a 56-year-old sales team leader in New York and replaced him with a 40-year-old who had no supervisory experience. The company claimed morale under the older employee had declined, though a vice president had praised the employee as "the best in the world at what he does" shortly before his termination. Later the company said the employee didn't cover sales accounts, but he claimed he was ordered not to. Further, he claimed that the company failed to follow its own termination procedures by not consulting his past supervisors or co-workers. When he sued under the ADEA, the Second Circuit held that he raised issues of fact for a jury. *Weiss v. JP Morgan Chase & Co.*, 332 Fed.Appx. 659 (2d Cir. 2009).

♦   The EEOC issued a proposed rule that would allow employers to reduce retirees' health benefits when the retirees became eligible for Medicare. The proposed rule **exempted from the ADEA employer efforts to coordinate retirees' healthcare benefits when the retirees reach 65**. The AARP sued, challenging the proposed rule, and a Pennsylvania federal court found the rule valid. The Third Circuit Court of Appeals agreed, noting that the ADEA grants the EEOC the authority to provide narrow exemptions that are reasonable and necessary and "proper in the public interest." Here, the EEOC issued the rule in response to the fact that employer-sponsored retiree health benefits were decreasing. The proposed rule would permit employers to offer retirees benefits to the greatest extent possible. *AARP v. EEOC*, 489 F.3d 558 (3d Cir. 2007).

F. Other Age Discrimination Cases

Age discrimination claims tend to increase when the economy worsens and employers engage in downsizing. Thus, age should always be considered before any final action is taken to lay off or discharge employees.

Also, state laws are sometimes more protective than the Age Discrimination in Employment Act (ADEA). For example, some states bar discrimination on the basis of age without setting a minimum age. Thus, a 25-year-old employee who is not promoted because she is deemed to be too young might be able to sue for age discrimination under state law.

◆   A technical assistance employee in Oklahoma said managers talked about his "shelf life" and whether he was about to "hit the bench" when deciding whether to eliminate his job. The manager was fired, and he sued for age discrimination under the ADEA. A district court ruled against him, and the Tenth Circuit affirmed. **Use of the term "shelf life" did not prove unlawful age discrimination.** Instead, it was used to refer to how much more billable work the employee's client needed to have done. Also, the evidence indicated that poor performance reviews were motivated by the employee's poor performance and not age bias. *Roberts v. Int'l Business Machines Corp.*, 733 F.3d 1306 (10th Cir. 2013).

◆   A 55-year-old chef for a university in Mississippi claimed that a new general manager waged a campaign to get him fired because **she wanted a younger person to have his job**. He claimed she called the HR department with false allegations, forced him to order too much food, refused to let him conduct inventory and kept him in the dark about catered events. The district manager fired the chef, and the chef filed a lawsuit that alleged violation of the ADEA. A federal district court ruled against him, but the Fifth Circuit reversed as to the age bias claim. It held a jury could infer that the general manager sabotaged the chef based on his age and influenced the firing decision. *Chambers v. Sodexo, Inc.*, 510 Fed.Appx. 336 (5th Cir. 2013).

◆   A supervisor at a pork processing plant in Iowa was terminated after 41 years on the job. At the time, he was 62 years old. The employer said the firing was motivated by insubordination and declining performance. The employee sued under the ADEA. A trial court ruled against him, but the Eighth Circuit reversed. **The employer never explained what it meant by "declining performance,"** and the employee was never disciplined before the discharge. A question existed as to whether the reason of "declining performance" was really just a pretext for unlawful age bias. *Ridout v. JBS USA, LLC*, 716 F.3d 1079 (8th Cir. 2013).

✦   A Kentucky auto parts supplier fired a 58-year-old manager and replaced him with a 48-year-old. The employer acknowledged that the fired manager had a good attitude and sound technical skills, but said it fired him because he could not lead his department in the way that it preferred. The manager sued under the ADEA, but the Sixth Circuit upheld a ruling against him. **Evidence, including employee surveys, showed he lacked leadership skills.** There was insufficient evidence that the employer's explanation was a pretext for unlawful age bias. *Carter v. Toyota Tsusho America*, 529 Fed. Appx. 601 (6th Cir. 2013).

✦   An Indiana sales associate was fired at age 56. At about the same time, the employer hired a 24-year-old and a 29-year-old to work in sales. In the year before he was released, the salesman generated more than half of the employer's profits. The sales associate sued for age discrimination under the ADEA. A district court ruled for the employer, but the Seventh Circuit said a trial was needed. **The timing of the termination was suspicious in light of the hirings, and the new hires had no experience.** Also, the employer said it let the salesman go because he earned too much, but it paid his replacements more. *Mullin v. Temco Machinery, Inc.*, 732 F.3d 772 (7th Cir. 2013).

✦   A salesman in Hawaii wrote a letter to the head of sales, accusing sales managers of giving the best sales opportunities to another salesperson. He resigned, but he was later contacted by the former employer and asked if he was interested in returning as a sales manager. The salesman said that at a meeting held to discuss the possibility, three managers he had complained about in the letter "battered" him about it. He was 67 years old at the time, and a new vice president gave the job to someone who was much younger. **The salesman sued for age discrimination under the ADEA**, and the court refused to grant pretrial judgment to the employer. It was possible that the managers tainted the new vice president's hiring decision and were biased against him based on his age. They had allegedly called him an "old fart," told him he was "too old" for attractive women, and complained to him that another salesperson was an "old timer." *Beecham v. Wyndham Vacation Resorts, Inc.*, No. 11-00129, 2013 WL 6730755 (D. Haw. 12/18/13) (Unpublished).

✦   A property management company in Oklahoma fired a 53-year-old property manager and promoted a 23-year-old clerical worker to property manager. The EEOC sued the employer on the fired employee's behalf, alleging violation of the ADEA. A co-worker testified that the company CEO told him the employee was fired because she was older. **Two other co-workers testified that the CEO told them the employee was fired because she was old and ugly.** The district court refused to grant pretrial judgment to the employer, finding that the "old and ugly" comment was a code phrase for age bias. It said a jury could find there was illegal age discrimination. *EEOC v. Kanbar Property Management, LLC*, No. 12-CV-00422, 2013 WL 4512671 (N.D. Okla. 8/23/13).

◆   A Georgia pharmaceutical sales employee who was fired at age 49 sued her former employer for age discrimination under the ADEA. A company vice president said the employee was fired because she gave – or appeared to give – special perks to a physician. **However, the physician said the vice president told him that the employee did nothing wrong.** The physician further said the vice president indicated that the employee should not have been fired. A federal district court ruled for the company, but the Eleventh Circuit reversed. The vice president's alleged statements could be viewed as an admission that the stated reason for the termination was pretextual. *Kragor v. Takeda Pharmaceuticals America, Inc.*, 702 F.3d 1304 (11th Cir. 2012).

◆   A Massachusetts publishing company raised the performance standard for its advertising salespeople and, as a result, fired four salesmen between the ages of 47 and 51. It raised the standards because it wasn't able to eliminate the weakest performers under the old system. The salesmen, who were a few years away from having their pensions vest, sued for age discrimination and also claimed ERISA violations, but lost. A federal court and the First Circuit held that **the company's desire to eliminate weak performers gave it a legitimate reason** for the increased performance standards. *Cameron v. Idearc Media Corp.*, 685 F.3d 44 (1st Cir. 2012).

◆   A Pennsylvania company fired four over-50 supervisors for sending and/or receiving pornographic emails, but it didn't fire other employees who had done the same. The supervisors sued under the ADEA, but the Third Circuit ruled against them. **The company didn't have to fire younger workers whose infractions hadn't been as serious** or who were not supervisors. *Hodczak v. Latrobe Specialty Steel Co.*, 451 Fed.Appx. 238 (3d Cir. 2011).

◆   A 57-year-old Indiana sales manager claimed that his director belittled him and took away most of his duties because the director thought he was too old. After he complained, the company learned that the director belittled everyone in the department. It fired the director. A new director took over and assigned the manager to revamp a training class. He believed he wasn't qualified to do this, but tried, then had a breakdown and took disability leave after the new director criticized the class as being too similar to the old one. He accepted early retirement, then sued for discrimination under the ADEA. A federal court and the Seventh Circuit ruled against him, noting that **his injury – the anxiety that left him unable to work – wasn't related to the discrimination**. *Barton v. Zimmer, Inc.*, 662 F.3d 448 (7th Cir. 2011).

◆   A 65-year-old used car salesman in Louisiana claimed that the used car sales manager referred to him as an "old motherf----r" on many occasions, refused to let him transfer to the new car sales division and threatened to beat him up numerous times. He finally quit and sued for a hostile work environment under the ADEA, also bringing claims for religious-based harassment under

Title VII and constructive discharge. A federal court granted pretrial judgment to the dealership, but the Fifth Circuit reversed, holding that **the salesman could sue for a hostile work environment under the ADEA**. He also presented sufficient evidence of religious harassment and constructive discharge to move ahead with those claims. *Dediol v. Best Chevrolet, Inc.*, 655 F.3d 435 (5th Cir. 2011).

◆   A mold-maker in Minnesota wanted to **move from manual mold-making to computer-controlled mold-making** with a machine. It laid off three class A mold-makers who were over 40 and the most skilled at manual mold-making. It then hired five younger employees who were less skilled, but who either had a better grasp of the machine or took positions requiring less skill. The three laid-off employees sued for age discrimination, but a federal court and the Eighth Circuit ruled against them, noting that the company offered a legitimate, nondiscriminatory reason for its actions. *Rahlf v. Mo-Tech Corp., Inc.*, 642 F.3d 633 (8th Cir. 2011).

◆   A company in Iowa hired a 60-year-old engineer, who performed various tasks for two different supervisors over the next six years. He received evaluations indicating that both supervisors found deficiencies in his work, including his communication and interpersonal skills. After he was fired, he sued for age discrimination but lost. The Eighth Circuit held that the company offered a legitimate reason for firing him. And it hired him when he was 60 years old, which tended to show it did not discriminate based on age. *Haigh v. Gileta USA*, 632 F.3d 464 (8th Cir. 2011).

◆   An over-50 engineering technician in Tennessee sought to miss a mandatory training session so he could attend the Daytona 500. His request was denied. He then sent an email to all the employees in his group, as well as to his manager, asking to be reimbursed $1,600 for the money he'd already spent to go to Daytona. The manager warned him this was insubordinate and could get him fired. On the Thursday and Friday before training, the technician took the days off without logging them into the computer calendar. After his suspension for that misconduct, he was fired because his GPS indicated he was near his home when his daily log said he was elsewhere. When he sued for age discrimination, he lost. A federal court and the Sixth Circuit held that he could only succeed if he could show that age was the sole reason he was fired. Instead, **the company had legitimate reasons for discharging him**. *Love v. Electric Power Board*, 392 Fed.Appx. 405 (6th Cir. 2010).

◆   Boeing sold a Kansas plant to a newly formed company, which had no employees. The new company relied on recommendations from Boeing supervisors for its hiring decisions. When a 55-year-old employee wasn't recommended, he sued for age discrimination, noting that **his prior evaluation showed him as meeting all expectations**. The Tenth Circuit held that his case required a trial. His supervisor's non-recommendation because of "limited skills/low quality/low productivity/marginal teaming abilities" contradicted his earlier evaluation. *Woods v. The Boeing Co.*, 355 Fed.Appx. 206 (10th Cir. 2009).

✦   An over-50 sales manager in Illinois with a history of tardiness and complaints against him from his team members received commissions on two huge deals with which he was only tangentially involved. As a result, he achieved 186% of his sales quota for the year. Without those two deals, he wouldn't have made his quota. The following year, he was given 60 days to improve his deal-closing performance and then was fired when he failed to do so. He sued for age discrimination and lost. The Seventh Circuit held that the evidence showed that **his status as a top earner was misleading**. *Senske v. Sybase, Inc.*, 588 F.3d 501 (7th Cir. 2009).

✦   A 45-year-old employee of a Tennessee manufacturer got into an argument with a 25-year-old co-worker in the restroom. There were conflicting reports of the scuffle, but the 45-year-old employee admitted to touching the younger employee's arm. The company fired her but only suspended the younger employee. She sued for age discrimination and lost. The Sixth Circuit ruled that **the company's anti-violence policy, coupled with its practice of treating physical contact more seriously than other incidents, justified the difference in how the employees were disciplined**. *Johnson v. Interstate Brands Corp.*, 351 Fed.Appx. 36 (6th Cir. 2009).

✦   A newly hired employee in Texas received a password and user ID. He also received a copy of the company's policy on information security, which informed him that he was responsible for safeguarding them and that he was responsible for all transactions made with his password. The company later discovered that someone using his password had accessed pornographic websites on the break-room computer. It fired him, and he sued for age discrimination. A federal court and the Fifth Circuit ruled against him. **It didn't matter if he hadn't actually accessed the porn websites. What mattered was that the company reasonably believed he had.** *Cervantez v. KMGP Services Co. Inc.*, 349 Fed.Appx. 4 (5th Cir. 2009).

✦   A 71-year-old purchasing manager for a hotel in Arkansas accepted free samples from vendors and failed to report them to the hotel in violation of company policy. Subsequently, a third party called the hotel to report what she believed was stolen hotel property in the manager's possession. A hotel investigator examined the property and believed it was stolen, whereupon the manager was fired. He sued for discrimination under the ADEA and lost. The Eighth Circuit noted that **the hotel legitimately believed he had stolen the property**, and the manager failed to present any evidence of age bias. *Roeben v. BG Excelsio Limited Partnership*, 545 F.3d 639 (8th Cir. 2008).

✦   A 48-year-old information services program manager at a Best Buy location in Minnesota asked if he could help out on a new project the company was working on – a store-within-a-store for home theater products. He helped develop and launch the new project, then was informed that he would no longer be needed once the development phase ended and the rollout began. He was given 60 days to find another job within the company. His old job had been eliminated, and he failed to find anything else. After his termination, he sued under the ADEA. A federal court and the Eighth Circuit ruled against him. Here, his managers thought he wouldn't be interested in the nuts-and-bolts phase of implementing the project, and also believed he didn't have the skills necessary for it. **The youthful culture – starting each morning with a huddle and cheer – did not suggest a pretext for age discrimination.** *Loeb v. Best Buy Co.*, 537 F.3d 867 (8th Cir. 2008).

IV. DISABILITY DISCRIMINATION

The Americans with Disabilities Act (ADA), 42 U.S.C. § 12101 *et seq.*, prohibits discrimination against qualified individuals with disabilities with respect to job application procedures, hiring, advancement, discharge, compensation, training, and other terms and conditions of employment.

The language of the ADA is based on Section 504 of the Rehabilitation Act of 1973, which applies only to programs or activities receiving federal funds. The ADA expands Section 504's limited scope to most employers with at least 15 employees. Many states have enacted similar legislation on behalf of individuals with disabilities. These laws generally are based on the language of the ADA and Section 504.

The ADA Amendments Act, effective January 1, 2009, expands the definition of "disability" under the ADA, rejecting the holdings in several Supreme Court decisions and portions of the EEOC's regulations. It states that mitigating measures, other than ordinary eyeglasses or contacts, can't be considered in determining whether an individual is disabled.

The ADA Amendments Act also expands the definition of "major life activities" to include such activities as bending, reading and communicating and adds in "major bodily functions" like normal cell growth, digestive and reproductive functions.

Under the Amendments, the focus in ADA lawsuits shifts from whether the plaintiff has a disability to whether the plaintiff was discriminated against because of a disability. The Amendments streamline the process of examining if a disability exists and make it easier for individuals to qualify for coverage.

A. The ADA and the Rehabilitation Act

The ADA requires employers to make reasonable accommodations for employees (and applicants) with disabilities. However, employers need not make the specific accommodation requested by the employee. As long as they offer an accommodation that is reasonable, they can avoid liability.

Note that the employee who is disabled must be able to perform the essential functions of the job (either with or without a reasonable accommodation). If the employee cannot meet that standard, he will not qualify for ADA protection.

Also, to be disabled under the ADA, the employee must have more than an impairment – he must have an impairment that <u>substantially limits</u> one or more major life activities. In other words, the impairment must substantially limit the individual's ability to perform tasks of central importance to most people's daily lives. The inability to perform one particular job generally will not be sufficient to demonstrate that an individual is disabled under the ADA.

Drug and alcohol users have some protections under the ADA. However, they can be held to the same standards of conduct as other employees. Homosexuality, transvestism and transsexuality are not considered impairments under the ADA.

Section 504 of the Rehabilitation Act (29 U.S.C. § 794) provides that no otherwise qualified individual with a disability shall, solely by reason of his or her disabilities, be excluded from the participation in, be denied the benefit of, or be subjected to discrimination under any program or activity receiving <u>federal financial assistance</u>.

Since most employers do not receive federal financial assistance, most cases of disability discrimination will be brought under the ADA or state law rather than the Rehabilitation Act.

1. Supreme Court Cases

♦   An Arizona employee tested positive for cocaine during a drug test at work and was allowed to resign rather than face termination. Two years later, the employee sought to be rehired to the same position. He attached to his application glowing reference letters from his pastor and his Alcoholics Anonymous counselor. The company refused to rehire him, and he sued under the ADA. He asserted that the no-rehire policy violated the ADA by discriminating against him **because of a record of a disability or because he was regarded as disabled**. A federal court granted pretrial judgment to the company, but the Ninth Circuit reversed. It stated that the no-rehire policy violated the ADA as applied to former employees whose only work-related offense was testing positive because of their addiction. On further appeal, the U.S. Supreme Court held that the employer could legitimately refuse to rehire an employee who was discharged for violating workplace conduct rules. The employer's neutral no-rehire policy satisfied its obligation under *McDonnell Douglas* to provide a legitimate, nondiscriminatory reason for refusing to rehire the employee. The only remaining question was whether the stated reason for the refusal to rehire was in fact the real reason. The Court remanded the case. *Raytheon Co. v. Hernandez*, 540 U.S. 44, 124 S.Ct. 513, 157 L.Ed.2d 357 (2003).

On remand, the Ninth Circuit Court of Appeals held that a trial was required because the company gave inconsistent reasons for why it refused to rehire the employee. *Hernandez v. Hughes Missile Systems Co. (Raytheon)*, 362 F.3d 564 (9th Cir. 2004).

* A bookkeeper at a medical clinic in Oregon sued the clinic under the ADA after she was fired. The clinic sought to have the case dismissed, alleging that it did not have **the necessary 15 employees to qualify it as a covered employer under the ADA** because the four physician-shareholders who owned the clinic could not be counted as employees. A federal court agreed with the clinic and dismissed the case, but the Ninth Circuit reversed. The case reached the U.S. Supreme Court, which adopted the Equal Employment Opportunity Commission's standard for determining when a director-shareholder should be counted as an employee under the ADA. The standard provides six factors for ascertaining whether the organization has control over the individual. The Court reversed and remanded the case for a determination of whether the doctor-shareholders should be counted as employees. *Clackamas Gastroenterology Associates, P.C. v. Wells*, 538 U.S. 440, 123 S.Ct. 1673, 155 L.Ed.2d 615 (2003).

* The U.S. Supreme Court held that a gas company could reject an applicant for a position in a California refinery where the applicant suffered from hepatitis C and could die from prolonged exposure to chemicals in the refinery. Here, the gas company made an offer of employment, then conducted a medical exam that found the hepatitis. When it revoked the offer, the applicant sued under the ADA, claiming that since he was not a direct threat to anyone else in the workplace, the company could not refuse to hire him. The Supreme Court stated that **the "direct threat" defense could be applied to prevent harm to the individual seeking a job**. It was not limited to preventing harm to "others" in the workplace. If a person's disability would create a direct threat of harm to himself in the workplace, the employer need not hire the person, even if the individual is willing to take the risk. *Chevron U.S.A. v. Echazabal*, 536 U.S. 73, 122 S.Ct. 2045, 153 L.Ed.2d 82 (2002).

* A 10-year customer service employee for an airline was placed in a mail room position after he injured his back handling cargo. He obtained the position by invoking his seniority rights. A few years later, he learned that two senior employees were going to bid on the mail room position. He asked the airline to make an exception to its seniority policy to accommodate his back injury by allowing him to stay in the mail room. After allowing the employee to stay in the mail room for five months, the airline decided not to make an exception to its seniority policy, and the employee lost his job. He sued the airline under the ADA, and a California federal court ruled that requiring the airline to accommodate the employee would cause an undue hardship. The Ninth Circuit reversed, and the airline appealed. The U.S. Supreme Court held that as a general rule, an accommodation under the ADA is not reasonable if it conflicts with an employer's **seniority rules**. However, employees may present evidence of special circumstances that make a "seniority rule exception" reasonable in a particular case. The Court remanded the case. *US Airways, Inc. v. Barnett*, 535 U.S. 391, 122 S.Ct. 1516, 152 L.Ed.2d 589 (2002).

◆   An employee at a Kentucky manufacturing plant had a severe case of carpal tunnel syndrome and tendonitis that prevented her from gripping tools and raising her arms over her head for extended time periods. She was assigned to modified-duty positions for two years, but she eventually became unable to perform two essential job functions. She began missing work and was eventually fired for poor attendance. When she sued under the ADA, a federal court found that she was not disabled under the statute. The Sixth Circuit reversed, but the U.S. Supreme Court reversed the court of appeals. It held that the ADA requires a person to be substantially limited in a "major" life activity, and that **the employee's inability to perform a manufacturing job did not qualify her as disabled under the act**. If the employee was substantially limited in the ability to perform the types of tasks that are centrally important to people's daily lives (like household chores, bathing and brushing her teeth), then she would be disabled under the ADA. The Court remanded the case. *Toyota Motor Manufacturing v. Williams*, 534 U.S. 184, 122 S.Ct. 681, 151 L.Ed.2d 615 (2002). Congress invalidated the *Williams* decision when it passed the ADA Amendments Act of 2008, in which it stated that the ruling interpreted the term "substantially limits" too narrowly.

◆   Twin sisters with uncorrected vision of 20/200 or worse, but corrected vision of 20/20 or better, applied to United Air Lines for positions as global airline pilots. United rejected them because they did not meet its minimum requirement of at least 20/100 uncorrected vision. They sued under the ADA. A Colorado federal court dismissed their lawsuit, and the case reached the U.S. Supreme Court, which found that the sisters had not shown they were disabled under the ADA. First, because the ADA defines a disability as an impairment that "substantially limits" a major life activity, and because the sisters, with glasses or contacts, had 20/20 vision, **they were not presently substantially limited**. The sisters also failed to show that they were regarded as disabled by United. Even though it regarded them as unable to perform in the particular position of global airline pilot, it did not regard them as substantially limited in the major life activity of working. Other jobs were still available to them, including jobs such as regional pilots or pilot instructors. *Sutton v. United Air Lines, Inc.*, 527 U.S. 471, 119 S.Ct. 2139, 144 L.Ed.2d 450 (1999). The ruling in *Sutton* was invalidated by the ADA Amendments Act of 2008, in which Congress concluded that the Court interpreted the ADA's definition of disability too narrowly in the *Sutton* case.

◆   The U.S. Supreme Court held that a mechanic with high blood pressure that was controllable with medication was not disabled under the ADA, because **his high blood pressure did not substantially limit him in the major life activity of working**. Further, he was not regarded as disabled. Rather, he was regarded as unqualified to work in the single position of United Parcel Service mechanic because he could not obtain a Department of Transportation health certification. *Murphy v. United Parcel Service*, 527 U.S. 516, 119 S.Ct. 2133, 144 L.Ed.2d 484 (1999).

◆   An Oregon truck driver with monocular vision was fired because he did not meet the visual acuity standards of the Federal Motor Carrier Safety

Regulations. The U.S. Supreme Court noted that the driver was not necessarily disabled within the meaning of the ADA. Even though he had monocular vision, his brain had developed subconscious mechanisms for coping with his visual impairment. This was a mitigating measure (like glasses or medication) that had to be taken into account when determining whether he was substantially limited in one or more major life activities. An employer who requires as a job qualification that an employee **meet a federal safety regulation** does not have to justify enforcing the regulation simply because the government has waived the safety standard experimentally in an individual case. *Albertsons, Inc. v. Kirkingburg*, 527 U.S. 555, 119 S.Ct. 2162, 144 L.Ed.2d 518 (1999).

◆   A Texas employee suffered a stroke and applied for Social Security benefits, alleging that she was disabled and unable to work. When her condition improved, she returned to work. However, her employer fired her less than a week later. She sued in a Texas federal court under the ADA asserting that a reasonable accommodation would allow her to perform her job. The court ruled that she could not assert she was disabled in her application for and receipt of Social Security benefits, and later claim that she could perform the essential functions of her job. The case reached the U.S. Supreme Court, which held that **the pursuit and receipt of Social Security Disability Insurance benefits does not automatically bar a person from litigating a claim under the ADA**. However, to survive a motion to dismiss, the person must present a sufficient explanation of the seeming contradiction that she is disabled under the Social Security Act (SSA) while not disabled under the ADA. Because the SSA does not take into account a reasonable accommodation when it determines whether a person is disabled for Social Security purposes, qualifying for such benefits might not bar an ADA claim. *Cleveland v. Policy Management Systems Corp.*, 526 U.S. 795, 119 S.Ct. 1597, 143 L.Ed.2d 966 (1999).

◆   A Florida school board fired an elementary school teacher after she suffered three relapses of tuberculosis within two years. She sued for discrimination on the basis of disability under Section 504 of the Rehabilitation Act. The court held that contagious diseases such as tuberculosis were not disabilities within the meaning of Section 504 and determined that the teacher was not a qualified individual with a disability who was entitled to hold her former position. The U.S. Court of Appeals, Eleventh Circuit, reversed the lower court's ruling, and the U.S. Supreme Court agreed to review the case. On appeal, the Court stated that **contagion cannot remove a person from Section 504 coverage**. *School Board of Nassau County v. Arline*, 480 U.S. 273, 107 S.Ct. 1123, 94 L.Ed.2d 307 (1987). The Supreme court later decided, in *Bragdon v. Abbott*, 524 U.S. 624 (1998), that asymptomatic HIV was a covered disability under the ADA.

2. Reasonable Accommodation

Reasonable accommodation may include making facilities readily accessible to individuals with disabilities, job restructuring, job-sharing, reassignment to vacant positions, the acquisition or modification of equipment, provision of readers and interpreters, and the modification of employment tests.

Employers seeking to show that a proposed accommodation is not reasonable must show that providing the accommodation would create an <u>undue hardship</u>.

♦   A night-shift inspector in Indiana was warned to stay alert. When she was found sleeping in a restroom, she said that medicine she was taking was causing her to fall asleep. The employee's doctor recommended that the employee be given additional rest periods. But she was fired, and a month later she was diagnosed as having narcolepsy. She sued under the ADA, alleging failure to accommodate her disability. A federal appeals court reversed a decision for the employer, finding that **the employer did not engage in the interactive process that the ADA requires**. Instead, it simply rejected the doctor's recommendation. *Spurling v. C&M Fine Pack, Inc.*, 739 F.3d 1055 (7th Cir. 2014).

♦   An employee with legal blindness worked for an Indiana ice cream franchise in a position that typically required rotation between a number of duty stations. Because he had difficulty performing some tasks, a store manager assigned him exclusively to a work station where minimal accommodation was required. The employee refused to follow an order to put away his cellphone, and he shoved a trash can at a manager who asked him to take out the garbage. He was suspended for 10 days, and his hours were cut when he returned. **He quit and sued, alleging an unlawful failure to accommodate under the ADA.** The court rejected his claim, finding that the employer met its duty to accommodate. Also, there was no evidence that the employee was suspended or deprived of hours on the basis of his disability. *Bunn v. Khoury Enterprises, Inc.*, 753 F.3d 676 (7th Cir. 2014).

♦   After undergoing surgery to repair her bladder, a hairdresser at a nursing home in Illinois was medically restricted from lifting more than 50 pounds and pushing residents in wheelchairs. The hairdresser claimed that an administrator told her she could not work with restrictions and refused to let someone help her transport residents who used wheelchairs. She alleged an unlawful failure to accommodate under the ADA. A federal appeals court reversed a decision against her. It found that **a question existed as to whether wheeling patients to the facility's beauty salon was an essential function**, especially since the hairdresser said she performed the function for only about two hours a day on two days per week. The administrator should have talked to the hairdresser about how much time she spent performing the function, the court said. *Kauffman v. Petersen Health Care VII, LLC*, 769 F.3d 958 (7th Cir. 2014).

♦   A claims adjuster in Colorado injured his knee and back while investigating a roof claim. He was assigned to desk work and then to field claims that did not involve roofs or ladders. After more than a year, the adjuster was still not able to perform roof inspections. He was fired because he could not do so. He sued under the ADA, and he lost. Handling roof claims was an essential job function, and **the employer was not required to accommodate the adjuster's limitations indefinitely**. Also, the fact that it accommodated him for a time and then fired him did not mean the termination was discriminatory. *Wehrley v. American Family Insurance Co.*, 513 Fed.Appx. 733 (10th Cir. 2013).

❖   A New York merchandise handler with autism asked to talk to a supervisor. The supervisor said the merchandise handler, who had a knife that was used to cut tape and open boxes, blocked her from leaving the cubicle where they met. He was fired the next day. **He sued the employer, saying it violated the ADA by failing to provide him the accommodation of a job coach.** He said he would have requested a job coach but was told by the employer that he was not allowed to have one. The court found factual issues existed as to whether the employer illegally denied the employee a job coach. *Glaser v. Gap Inc.*, 994 F.Supp.2d 569 (S.D.N.Y. 2014).

❖   A Washington customer service associate had high customer dissatisfaction ratings. She was placed on a series of performance improvement plans but was ultimately terminated. She sued under the ADA, saying the employer should have sat down with her to explore how her migraines and pain due to endometriosis affected how she related to customers. **She also said the employer should have lowered its customer satisfaction standards to accommodate her pain.** The court rejected her claims. It was the employee's responsibility to begin a discussion about possible accommodations, and the ADA did not require the employer to allow higher customer dissatisfaction rates as a job accommodation. *Kelley v. Amazon.com, Inc.*, No. 12-cv-5132, 2013 WL 6119229 (E.D. Wash. 11/21/13).

❖   A computer technician for a New York employer had diabetes. He was assigned to work the 9:00 a.m. to 5:30 p.m. shift. Without authorization, he began coming in to work at 8:30 a.m. because the earlier start time enabled him to better manage his condition. When the employer asked for a doctor's note explaining the need for the earlier start time, the employee provided only a vague letter from his doctor. The employer refused to allow the earlier start time. **The employee said he had no choice but to stop working**, and he was terminated for job abandonment. When he sued for failure to accommodate under the ADA, he lost. He did not provide the employer with enough information to show he needed the schedule change to accommodate his diabetes. *Reyes v. Krasdale Foods, Inc.*, 945 F.Supp.2d 486 (S.D.N.Y. 2013).

❖   A church secretary in Illinois asked for weekends off so she could care for her daughter, who had a mental disability. The church denied the request, and she sued under the ADA. A federal district court ruled for the church, and the Seventh Circuit affirmed. **The duty to accommodate under the ADA does not extend so far as to require employers to accommodate employees based on their relationship or association with an individual who has a disability.** *Magnus v. St. Mark United Methodist Church*, 688 F.3d 331 (7th Cir. 2012).

❖   An Illinois plant worker with fibromyalgia and sleep apnea worked a day shift with no overtime as per his doctor's advice until the company decided to change to rotating shifts. He tried the new schedule but found it too painful and asked to go back to his old shift. He presented a note from his doctor supporting his need to do so. Instead, the company laid him off for seven months until a day-shift position became available. He sued under the ADA. A federal court granted pretrial judgment to the company, but the Seventh Circuit reversed, finding issues of fact that required a trial. There was a question as to whether he was disabled and **whether overtime and rotating shifts were essential job functions**. *Feldman v. Olin Corp.*, 692 F.3d 748 (7th Cir. 2012).

✦   The EEOC claimed that an airline violated the ADA by **refusing to automatically assign a disabled Illinois employee to a vacant position upon her request** because she was minimally qualified for it. The airline claimed it could give the job to a better-qualified, non-disabled person. The issue came before the Seventh Circuit, which ruled that the airline had to give the job to the disabled person because there was no bona fide seniority system in place to prevent the reassignment. *EEOC v. United Airlines, Inc.*, 693 F.3d 760 (7th Cir. 2012).

✦   A UPS employee in California, deaf since birth, **asked for a sign-language interpreter for weekly staff meetings**, but was told that the company only needed to provide him with notes of the meetings afterward. Eventually the EEOC sued on his behalf, asserting that in addition to interpreters for the meetings, the company ought to provide interpreters for its harassment policy and its online computer training. A federal court granted pretrial judgment to UPS, but the Ninth Circuit reversed, finding issues of fact that required a trial. Here, the employee couldn't ask questions at meetings or understand co-workers' questions, and his repeated assertions that he didn't understand parts of the trainings he received should have informed the company that its accommodations were not effective. *EEOC v. UPS Supply Chain Solutions*, 620 F.3d 1103 (9th Cir. 2010).

✦   A Rite Aid employee in Pennsylvania became blind in one eye due to glaucoma, making it difficult for her to drive at night. She obtained a doctor's note to that effect and requested a shift change so that she wouldn't have to drive in the dark. The company refused the request on the grounds that it might be viewed as unfair by other workers. Eventually she quit and sued under the ADA and state law. A federal court granted pretrial judgment to the company, but the Third Circuit reversed, noting that **a change in shift might be a reasonable accommodation** that the company had refused to consider. The case required a trial. *Colwell v. Rite Aid Corp.*, 602 F.3d 495 (3d Cir. 2010).

✦   An Iowa production employee was diagnosed with a form of multiple sclerosis that caused extreme fatigue, numbness and problems standing, sitting and walking. The HR manager told her to take extra breaks if needed, and to let the company know if she needed other accommodations. Although the company required all production employees to work overtime, it did not require the employee to do so for a time after her doctor restricted her hours. Later it fired the employee because she could not work overtime. She sued under the ADA, but a federal court and the Eighth Circuit ruled against her. **The employee could not be reasonably accommodated because there was no position available that did not require overtime.** Also, the company did not violate the ADA by asking the doctor to clarify his report. *Tjernagel v. The Gates Corp.*, 533 F.3d 666 (8th Cir. 2008).

◆   An insurance company employee in Rhode Island suffered from ulcerative colitis. A week before she was to give a presentation, she told her supervisor she needed time off because some of her symptoms might be returning. He told her to take time off after the presentation. She gave the presentation, but failed to shorten it as her supervisor's boss had instructed, then took two weeks at home rather than the one she had agreed upon with her supervisor. He told her she was being reassigned to a less prestigious project. A short time later she was hospitalized and did not return to work. When she sued under the ADA, the First Circuit ruled for the company. **Her vague comments about feeling ill did not put the company on notice that she needed the time off immediately.** And the demotion was justified by her refusal to shorten the presentation as ordered. *Freadman v. Metropolitan Property and Casualty Insurance Co.*, 484 F.3d 91 (1st Cir. 2007).

◆   An Arkansas route sales manager for a company that delivered frozen foods to customers' houses injured his arm when he fell off a customer's porch. Following surgery, he was restricted to carrying no more than 10 pounds and restricted from driving his route because of the heaviness of the truck doors. The company fired him after it was unable to find light-duty assignments for him. When he sued under the ADA, he lost. The Eighth Circuit held that the manager was not disabled under the ADA because he was not substantially limited in his ability to care for himself. Also, **the company had no duty to assign another employee to travel with him** for the purpose of opening and closing doors. *Didier v. Schwan Food Co.*, 465 F.3d 838 (8th Cir. 2006).

3.   Regarded As Disabled

Not only does the ADA bar discrimination on the basis of disability, it also bars discrimination on the basis of a perceived disability. Further, it bars discrimination against individuals who have a record of a disability.

◆   A driver of hazardous material in Wyoming learned that he had hepatitis C and told his supervisor, also mentioning that he was depressed and that his treatment might cause suicidal thoughts. **The company gave him three months of paid leave, partly so he could obtain documentation that he was fit to work, but also so it could research his condition.** He filed a charge of discrimination with the EEOC and obtained a doctor's opinion that he could return to work. However, he hurt his back at home and since the company had no light-duty positions available, he collected short-term disability benefits until they expired, at which time he quit. When he sued, alleging that the company regarded him as disabled, the Tenth Circuit ruled against him, finding no ADA violation. *Fryer v. Coil Tubing Services, LLC*, 415 Fed.Appx. 37 (10th Cir. 2011).

◆   A Nebraska employee had a miscarriage and missed work off and on for the next three years due to complications. She later took long-term disability (LTD) leave for irritable bowel syndrome. Shortly afterward, the company questioned whether her condition was caused by a mental illness and it required her to undergo an independent psychiatric exam. She underwent the exam, but the company didn't contact her about her status for a year. When her LTD ran out, she was informed that if she wished to return to work, she needed to submit a doctor's release. She failed to do so and was fired. When she sued for disability discrimination, asserting that the company regarded her as disabled by a mental illness, she lost because **even though the company illegally regarded her as disabled, her failure to submit the doctor's release gave the company a legitimate reason to fire her**. *Norman v. Union Pacific Railroad Co.*, 606 F.3d 455 (8th Cir. 2010).

◆   The doctor of a Wisconsin assembly-line employee restricted her to sedentary work and a lifting restriction of 10 pounds. Later, the doctor lifted the sedentary restriction and authorized her to lift up to 20 pounds. Her employer eventually discharged her after deciding it didn't have enough work to keep her busy. She sued under the ADA, claiming the employer perceived her to have a disability, but the Seventh Circuit ultimately ruled against her. Although a jury found that perceived disability was one of the reasons for the discharge, it also found that **the employer would have fired her anyway**. The Seventh Circuit held that the ADA did not permit "mixed motive" claims, and since the employer offered a legitimate reason for the termination, the employee could not win her claim. *Serwatka v. Rockwell Automation Inc.*, 591 F.3d 957 (7th Cir. 2010).

◆   A driver for a home-delivery food service in Indiana learned that he might have MS and was placed on disability leave. He later returned to work, but the day before he was to go to the Mayo Clinic for additional tests and treatment, his supervisor wrote him up for depositing a post-dated check too soon and for not adhering to the company's dress code. While he was at the clinic, his supervisor drove his route and allegedly discovered that he'd falsified records. **The supervisor fired him, but back-dated the termination to the day he left for the clinic.** When he sued for disability discrimination, the Seventh Circuit reversed pretrial judgment for the company, finding issues of fact that required a trial. The company may have illegally regarded him as disabled. *Brunker v. Schwan's Home Delivery Service, Inc.*, 583 F.3d 1004 (7th Cir. 2009).

◆   A Nebraska bank employee began to lose his voice as a result of a neurological condition. However, the problem didn't affect his job performance, even though he worked with the public. After experiencing financial pressures, **the bank decided to raise his quota (and only his quota)** on loan volume to a level that would require him to outperform the entire branch's mortgage volume – a level never achieved either before or after his discharge. The bank fired him when he failed to reach that level, but it did not fire a co-worker who was performing worse than he was. When he sued under the ADA, the Eighth Circuit held that he was entitled to a trial. A jury could find that the real reason for his firing was discrimination. *Willnerd v. First National Nebraska, Inc.*, 558 F.3d 770 (8th Cir. 2009).

◆   A supervisor for a manufacturer in Pennsylvania underwent chemotherapy for breast cancer and began to suffer from short-term memory loss, a condition known as "chemo brain." To compensate, she took extra notes and excelled at her job, receiving promotions, raises and bonuses. However, **when the company instituted a reduction in force, it lowered her performance rating** and laid her off after she expressed concern about commuting to a new location and learning new skills. When she sued under the ADA, a jury awarded her $170,000 in back pay and $30,000 in compensatory damages. The Third Circuit upheld the award, finding sufficient evidence that the manufacturer regarded her as disabled or that it discriminated against her because of her "record of" disability. *Eshelman v. Agere Systems, Inc.*, 554 F.3d 426 (3d Cir. 2009).

◆   A pharmacy assistant in New York applied for a job with Wal-Mart. He did not disclose that he had cerebral palsy, nor did he ask for any accommodation to do the job. The pharmacy manager told him to stock merchandise and dispense prescriptions, but she feared that he was mismatching prescriptions and customer names. She refused to schedule him for a second week, and he was transferred to a position collecting shopping carts. He was then offered a job in the food department stocking shelves. He quit and sued under the ADA, alleging that the company perceived him as disabled. A jury agreed and awarded him $600,000 in compensatory damages and $300,000 in punitive damages. The Second Circuit upheld the awards. Here, **the employee's disability was obvious, and the company failed to engage in the interactive process** with the employee to determine if a reasonable accommodation was possible. *Brady v. Wal-Mart Stores, Inc.*, 531 F.3d 127 (2d Cir. 2008).

◆   A Utah administrative assistant worked for a regional vice president who became concerned when he couldn't reach her by phone while he was on business trips. He had a surveillance camera placed in her work area and fired her when she was not there during the time she was supposed to be. She sued under the ADA, claiming that she was perceived as having a disability because an HR rep gave her a workers' compensation form for a work-related injury. A federal court and the Tenth Circuit held that this was not enough to show the company regarded her as disabled. **She could have a work-related injury without being perceived as disabled.** *Bartunek v. Fred Meyer, Inc.*, 271 Fed.Appx. 815 (10th Cir. 2008).

◆   An Iowa applicant with arthritis and a history of heart problems took a physical and was cleared for driving a forklift, an essential job function. However, the doctor reported that a functional capacity exam would be needed if the job required heavy lifting. After initially informing the applicant that he'd passed the exam, the company told him he'd failed. At trial, the company changed its reason for not hiring him, asserting that it had eliminated the shift he'd applied for. A jury awarded the applicant $60,000 in back pay and $100,000 in punitive damages under the ADA and state law. The Eighth Circuit upheld the awards. Here, the company didn't eliminate the shift until weeks after it rejected the applicant. Also, **its assertion that heavy lifting was a job requirement was suspect because it didn't include the task of heavy lifting in its job description**. The company wrongly regarded the applicant as disabled. *Chalfant v. Titan Distribution*, 475 F.3d 982 (8th Cir. 2007).

* A boiler operator with a company in Iowa underwent shoulder surgery and then experienced pain while removing obstructions from the stoker. When he complained of the pain, the plant manager reassigned him to a position that did not require any lifting or repetitive use of his left arm. However, he believed the new position was demeaning because it required him to clean floors and paint pipes. He was later fired for secretly videotaping the inside of the plant. He sued under the ADA, asserting that the company regarded him as disabled. A jury awarded him back pay and punitive damages, but the Eighth Circuit vacated the award. **The company could reassign him to a less desirable job at the same location and same pay** if it regarded him as unable to perform one aspect of a particular job. This did not violate the ADA. *Knutson v. Ag Processing, Inc.*, 394 F.3d 1047 (8th Cir. 2005).

* A senior bridge inspector in New York sued his former employer under the ADA, claiming he was fired based on his perceived disability of lack of agility. The employer said he was fired because he did not perform the job duties of walking on rebar mats, bending down to measure concrete, climbing ladders to inspect work, and turning in reports. The court decided that employer **statements about the employee's lack of agility and inability to do the job** were enough to send the question of unlawful discrimination based on perceived disability to a jury. *Sacks v. Gandhi Engineering, Inc.*, 999 F.Supp.2d 629 (S.D.N.Y. 2014).

4. Temporary Impairments

Generally, temporary impairments do not count as disabilities under the ADA. However, if the temporary condition is severe enough and lasts long enough, it might be deemed a disability under the act.

* A research analyst for a Virginia company injured his legs while exiting a commuter train. Doctors told him not to put any weight on his left leg for six weeks, and told him he would not be able to walk normally for seven months. While in the hospital, the employee asked his employer about working part time remotely and eventually returning on a full-time basis. The employer did not respond and later terminated his employment. The employee sued for disability discrimination and failure to accommodate under the ADA. **A federal appeals court reversed a decision against him**, finding he sufficiently alleged that he had a disability and that it was reasonable for the EEOC to include temporary impairments under the definition of disability. *Summers v. Altarum Institute*, 740 F.3d 325 (4th Cir. 2014).

* A Texas flight attendant had psoriasis-related arthritis that flared up three or four times a month. He took intermittent leave under the FMLA until the airline determined that he had not worked enough hours in the preceding 12 months to warrant further leave. It then fired him for exceeding 12 absences when he continued to miss work. He sued under the ADA, and a jury awarded him $80,000. The court vacated the award, however, finding that he was not disabled under the law because he couldn't meet the airline's attendance requirements. On appeal, the Fifth Circuit reinstated the jury's verdict and stated that **a disability**

that is episodic is still a disability if it substantially limits a major life activity when it flares up. Also, since the airline had allowed non-disabled flight attendants to accumulate more than 12 absences without being fired, the jury permissibly inferred that discrimination was the real reason for the discharge. *Carmona v. Southwest Airlines Co.*, 604 F.3d 848 (5th Cir. 2010).

◆   A New York employee injured her Achilles tendon on her way to work and went out on sick leave for approximately 25 weeks. After surveillance indicated that she was more mobile than she had led the company to believe, she was fired. She sued under the ADA, the FMLA and other laws. A federal district court ruled against her, noting that **her temporary condition did not qualify as a disability** under the ADA, and that she failed to prove a causal connection between her FMLA leave and her firing. Her misuse of sick leave and misrepresentation of her limitations justified her discharge. *O'Reilly v. Consolidated Edison Co. of New York, Inc.*, 374 F.Supp.2d 278 (E.D.N.Y. 2005).

◆   After a corporate takeover, a successful Ohio sales rep was left out of sales meetings, as were other female employees. The sales rep then broke her ankle. She could not travel, but she could conduct business by phone, a common practice for the sales staff. Her supervisor, however, constantly raised her broken ankle as an issue, became verbally abusive, and berated her for not being on the road. He stopped giving her any work, citing her broken ankle as the reason. He would also not allow her to work by phone. The sales rep was then fired because of an alleged drop in business and customers. No other employees were laid off, despite a large drop in business at other plants. She sued for sex discrimination under Title VII and disability discrimination under the ADA. An Ohio federal court held that ordinarily a temporary impairment does not qualify as a disability, but in this case, **the employer regarded it as an impairment that substantially limited major life activities**. The supervisor believed that the rep could not adequately perform her job with a broken ankle. Also, he refused to accommodate her by allowing her to work by phone, even though other salespeople often worked by phone out of their homes. The lawsuit could proceed. *Spath v. Berry Plastics Corp.*, 900 F.Supp. 893 (N.D. Ohio 1995).

5. Undue Hardship and Direct Threat

An undue hardship is "an action requiring significant difficulty or expense." Thus, an accommodation that costs a lot of money or negatively impacts a large number of employees generally will be considered an undue hardship.

A direct threat is a threat to either the worker or others that arises as a result of the worker's disability. If hiring a worker will result in a direct threat of harm to the worker or others (even with an accommodation), the employer need not hire the worker. See the *Chevron* case, this chapter.

◆   After 20 years with Walgreens, a store manager slipped on some ice and injured her knee. She took medical leave and had surgery on the knee. She then requested to return to work with "reasonable accommodations." Walgreens offered her another store manager position, but she and her doctor informed Walgreens management that she should permanently refrain from bending, stooping, squatting, kneeling, climbing stairs and using ladders. Her doctor also said that **she should spend no more than five hours each day standing**. Walgreens fired her, and she sued under the ADA. She lost. A Massachusetts federal court and the First Circuit held that she could not perform the essential functions of the job. *Jones v. Walgreen Co.*, 679 F.3d 9 (1st Cir. 2012).

◆   A photography studio in Colorado hired a deaf woman. Her job duties were to convince customers to have a portrait taken, take the photo, convince the customers to buy a photo package, and work in the photo lab developing pictures. Eventually the studio fired her because she had trouble communicating with customers. The EEOC sued on her behalf, claiming an ADA violation, but a federal court and the Tenth Circuit ruled for the studio. **The employee couldn't perform an essential function of the job – effectively communicating with customers.** *EEOC v. The Picture People, Inc.*, 684 F.3d 981 (10th Cir. 2012).

◆   A neonatal nurse in Oregon had attendance issues before she developed fibromyalgia. Her attendance only got worse thereafter. The hospital met with her and allowed her to call in when she was having a bad day so that she could move her shift to another day in the week without having to find a replacement. Despite that accommodation and others – like not making her work two days in a row – she continued to have unplanned absences. Eventually she was fired. When she sued under the ADA, she lost. The Ninth Circuit held that **the hospital could make attendance and punctuality an essential job function**. Here, apparently, the only thing that would satisfy the nurse was an open schedule that allowed her to come and go as she pleased. *Samper v. Providence St. Vincent Medical Center*, 675 F.3d 1233 (9th Cir. 2012).

◆   An employee of a company with offices in New York and Puerto Rico had a bad back, which made it difficult for her to drive. The company allowed her to work at home a few days a week. After an audit, her job responsibilities were changed. She then suffered from depression and took several months of leave. When she sought to return to work, she indicated that her back had worsened and asked to be allowed to work at home four days a week. The company rejected her proposed accommodation and later fired her for overstepping her authority. She sued for discrimination under the ADA but lost. A Puerto Rico federal court and the First Circuit held that the company had legitimate reasons for firing her. And **her proposed accommodation wasn't reasonable**. *Gomez v. Rural Opportunities, Inc.*, 626 F.3d 654 (1st Cir. 2010).

◆   While in residency at a hospital, an Ohio doctor was diagnosed with Asperger's syndrome. His supervisors saw that he could not relay instructions between healthcare professionals, and he also had difficulty making diagnoses, answering questions and communicating on the phone. After the hospital fired him, he sued under the ADA for failure to accommodate his condition, alleging that with understanding by his supervisors, he could manage his Asperger's.

The Sixth Circuit disagreed. **Diagnosis and communication was an essential element of the job, and his proposed accommodation was unworkable.** *Jakubowski v. The Christ Hospital*, 627 F.3d 195 (6th Cir. 2010).

♦   A patient care technician in Minnesota who suffered from depression, after being repeatedly disciplined for unpredictable absences, told her supervisors that she was having problems with her medication, and that she might miss a day here and there because of it. She was fired after she failed to show up for work one day, and she sued under the ADA and state law. A federal court and the Eighth Circuit ruled against her, noting that she was not a qualified individual with a disability because **she was unable to perform an essential function of her job – regular and reliable attendance**. She never specifically identified how her depression limited her job or her life so as to allow the employer to engage in the interactive process to find an accommodation. *Rask v. Fresenius Medical Care North America*, 509 F.3d 466 (8th Cir. 2007).

♦   A paraplegic worked as a mold polisher in a Florida plant and was frequently late by about a minute because the time clock was located in a small room and was often blocked by storage boxes or tables he had to navigate his wheelchair around. Whenever he punched in late, he stayed after his normal shift time. He sometimes worked 60 hours a week, and he was considered an excellent performer. However, a new company president instituted a no-fault attendance policy, and he was fired for his lateness. When he sued under the ADA, a federal court granted pretrial judgment to the company on the grounds that punctuality was an essential job function. The Eleventh Circuit reversed, finding issues of fact as to whether punctuality was really essential to the job. **The company had failed to show that his tardiness harmed its operations.** *Holly v. Clairson Industries*, 492 F.3d 1247 (11th Cir. 2007).

♦   UPS required all its package car driver applicants to pass a hearing test before being considered for the job, even though some of the applicants would be driving vehicles that were not covered by Department of Transportation regulations. A class of hearing-impaired individuals challenged the test in a California federal court, which required UPS to show that passing the test was a bona fide occupational qualification. On appeal, the Ninth Circuit held that the lower court applied too stringent a standard. Instead, **UPS only had to prove that there was a significant correlation between the hearing requirement and the performance of the job's essential qualifications**. It also had to prove that an accommodation would pose an undue hardship. This "business necessity" defense more closely tracks the language of the ADA. *Bates v. United Parcel Service, Inc.*, 511 F.3d 974 (9th Cir. 2007).

♦   A trucking company in Wisconsin fired an excellent driver after he was diagnosed with neurocardiogenic syncope – a disorder of the nervous system that causes fainting. Even though the driver took medication to help control his condition, fainting spells were still possible. An employee with the same condition had driven off a bridge to his death two years earlier. Thus, the company adopted a zero-tolerance policy for the condition. The EEOC sued on the driver's behalf, but the Seventh Circuit ruled for the company. Here, the risk of another serious injury was not zero, and the company had a right to decide it didn't want to take that risk. It did not regard the driver as unable to perform the job, but rather **decided to implement safety standards higher than the minimum required by the federal government.** *EEOC v. Schneider National, Inc.*, 481 F.3d 507 (7th Cir. 2007).

♦   **Exxon could establish a policy that imposed across-the-board safety qualification standards.** The standards permanently removed employees who had undergone treatment for substance abuse from safety-sensitive positions. This resulted in the demotions of several employees who had undergone such treatment many years before. When the EEOC sued on their behalf under the ADA, a Texas federal court sent the case to the Fifth Circuit, which held that Exxon could defend the standard as a business necessity. It did not have to show that such employees were a direct threat to the health or safety of others in the workplace. The direct threat standard focuses on the individual employee and examines the specific risk posed by the employee's disability. Business necessity, on the other hand, addresses whether a standard can be justified across the board. Here, the standard was a proper requirement for all safety-sensitive employees. *EEOC v. Exxon Corp.*, 203 F.3d 871 (5th Cir. 2000).

6. Other ADA Cases

The ADA, by its very nature, requires an individualized examination of the employee's disability and any proposed accommodations in order to determine whether the ADA was violated. As a result, litigation under the ADA is often harder to avoid than litigation under other anti-discrimination statutes. So if you know an employee has a disability (and sometimes you won't), try to accommodate.

However, employees with disabilities do not have to be given special consideration; they merely have to be given the same consideration as non-disabled employees. Thus, an employee with a disability who is less productive than one without disabilities can be considered for layoff in a reduction in force under the ADA.

♦   A Tennessee manufacturer instituted a policy banning employees from being impaired at work by alcohol or any drug, including any prescription or over-the-counter drug. It ordered plant-wide drug testing, which was conducted by a third-party company. Six employees who tested positive for medications sued, claiming a violation of the ADA. Five of the six had been fired, while one kept her job because she stopped taking her medication. The court said **it was up to a jury to decide** whether the employee's testing program constituted an improper medical examination or disability-related inquiry under the statute. *Bates v. Dura Automotive Systems, Inc.*, 767 F.3d 566 (6th Cir. 2014).

♦   A freight driver in Pennsylvania took a leave of absence to be treated for alcoholism. He then signed a return-to-work agreement that barred him from drinking – on or off the job – for as long as he stayed employed with his employer. After he returned, he relapsed and was terminated. He sued under the ADA, but he lost. The Third Circuit affirmed a ruling for the employer, finding that **the return-to-work agreement was lawful** and the employee could be fired for violating it. *Ostrowski v. Con-Way Freight*, 543 Fed.Appx. 128 (3d Cir. 2013).

❖   A facility manager for an Ohio employer had multiple sclerosis. He told his supervisor that he was sick, that he was being treated by several doctors, and that he had an MRI. However, he did not tell the supervisor of his multiple sclerosis diagnosis. When he was terminated, he sued for disability discrimination under the ADA. **He lost because there was no evidence showing the supervisor knew or should have known of the diagnosis.** Therefore, there was not enough evidence to show the termination was motivated by the employee's disability. *Nilles v. Givaudan Flavors Corp.*, 521 Fed.Appx. 364 (6th Cir. 2013).

❖   A quality assurance specialist for a Georgia employer became agitated during a work meeting. He banged his hand on a table and said someone "was going to pay" for the alleged harassment he had been subjected to because he was from Ghana. He was interviewed by a psychologist, who indicated concern about the employee's emotional and psychological stability. The employer placed the employee on leave. **The employer then told the employee he needed to be evaluated by a psychiatrist if he wanted to keep working for the employer.** The employee met with the psychiatrist, who concluded the employee could return to work. The employee sued the employer under the ADA, claiming it unlawfully subjected him to the psychiatric examination. A trial court ruled against him, and the Eleventh Circuit affirmed. The examination was job-related because the essential functions of any job require an ability to handle stress and work well with others, and it was consistent with business necessity because the employer had information suggesting the employee might be dangerous. *Owusu-Ansah v. The Coca-Cola Co.*, 715 F.3d 1306 (11th Cir. 2013).

❖   After an Indiana employee injured his shoulder at work, a company officer discussed the injury on a Facebook page that was maintained for the company's benefit. The post suggested that the employee missed too much time from work due to the injury, and it referred to him as a "loser." **The employee sued the company under the ADA, asserting a violation of the law's confidentiality provision.** The employer defended the claim by arguing that the employee voluntarily disclosed his injury to the public in a lawsuit he filed against the company before the Facebook post was made. It also argued that he was not sufficiently harmed to maintain the claim under the ADA. The court refused to dismiss the case, finding that a fact question existed as to whether the employer learned of the employee's condition within the context of a medical examination. It also determined that the employee sufficiently alleged that he was injured by the post. *Shoun v. Best Formed Plastics, Inc.*, No. 3:14-cv-463, 2014 WL 2815483 (N.D. Ind. 6/23/14).

◆ A distribution center employee in Kentucky injured his wrist while unloading a trailer. The ability to lift 60 pounds was an essential function of his job. After the injury, the employer placed the employee on temporary light duty. He took leave and had surgery, but **18 months later he could still not lift 60 pounds**. When the employer terminated his employment, he alleged an unlawful failure to accommodate under the ADA. The court ruled against him, finding that the accommodations he suggested – having a co-worker help him with heavier lifting and letting him keep the light-duty job – were not legally required because they would excuse him from performing an essential job function. *Wilhite v. Wal-Mart Stores East, LP*, No. 13-CV-0056, 2014 WL 4684009 (W.D. Ky. 9/19/14).

◆ A technology consulting company in Wisconsin assigned an employee to a client. When the employee failed to show up for work at the client location one day, the employer emailed the employee to find out what was going on. The employee responded with an email saying he had a migraine headache. After the employee quit, the client told prospective employers that the employee "gets migraines." The EEOC sued the client under the ADA, accusing it of violating a statutory provision barring disclosure of information obtained in response to a medical examination or inquiry. A federal district court ruled against it, and the Seventh Circuit affirmed. **The employer's email was not a medical inquiry**, so there was no statutory violation. *EEOC v. Thrivent Financial for Lutherans*, 700 F.3d 1044 (7th Cir. 2012).

◆ A mildly retarded construction worker in Nebraska was fired for violating the company's "no fighting" policy. His foreman had yelled at him. When he yelled back, the foreman grabbed him by the coat, and he tried to slug the foreman, knocking off the foreman's respirator mask. The foreman walked away, and the incident ended. But the worker was fired, while the foreman was only suspended and demoted. When the worker sued under the ADA, he lost. The Eighth Circuit said that **although the foreman started it, he escalated the incident by hitting the foreman**. And there was no evidence that the company used the "no fighting" rule to fire him because of his disability. *Ryan v. Capital Contractors, Inc.*, 679 F.3d 772 (8th Cir. 2012).

◆ A Virginia employee suffered from leukemia that restricted him to working eight hours a day and 40 hours a week. However, his job as a maintenance engineer required him to work 12-hour shifts. He sought to be allowed to work eight-hour shifts, but the company deemed him not disabled because he could work 40 hours a week, so it denied his request. He ultimately obtained an eight-hour shift job with the company, but nevertheless sued under the ADA. He lost. The Fourth Circuit held that **his inability to work overtime did not make him substantially limited in the major life activity of working**. *Boitnott v. Corning, Inc.*, 669 F.3d 172 (4th Cir. 2012).

◆ A medical assistant in Oklahoma suffered from stress-related migraines that forced her to submit her resignation. She later sought to rescind her resignation, but the hospital decided not to allow that. A few months later she stopped having migraines and sued the hospital for violating the ADA. The Tenth Circuit Court of Appeals held that she failed to meet the ADA's definition of disabled because she couldn't show she was substantially limited in the major life activity of working. Even under the stricter guidelines of the new EEOC regulations, **she could only show that she couldn't work that particular job**. *Allen v. Southcrest Hospital*, 455 Fed.Appx. 827 (10th Cir. 2011).

◆   A diabetic twilight hub manager for UPS began to experience unusual numbness and pain, and took a medical leave of absence. When he returned to work three months later, he was assigned to the midnight hub position. He later informed the HR manager that he needed daytime hours to accommodate his diabetes. But neither he nor his doctor provided any medical documentation, so UPS denied his shift change request. He retired and later sued under the ADA. A Louisiana federal court and the Fifth Circuit ruled against him. His **failure to provide medical information backing up his shift change request** and his early retirement doomed his lawsuit. *Griffin v. United Parcel Service*, 661 F.3d 216 (5th Cir. 2011).

◆   After a Michigan emergency medical technician (EMT) had an affair with a married co-worker, fellow employees became concerned about her mental health and voiced concerns to her superiors. The office manager looked into getting her counseling and informed the EMT of her counseling options. Around that same time, the EMT screamed at a male acquaintance while driving the ambulance in an emergency situation. The company director then told her she had to get counseling to continue working. She quit instead because she had no money for counseling. When she sued under the ADA, the Sixth Circuit held that while some counseling isn't a medical exam, **being ordered to see a healthcare professional qualifies as a medical exam**. A court would have to decide if the counseling was job-related and justified by a business necessity. *Kroll v. White Lake Ambulance Authority*, 691 F.3d 809 (6th Cir. 2012).

◆   An airline's operations manager at a Michigan airport had a wife who was suffering from a rare autoimmune disease. She received treatment under his group health insurance plan. Shortly after her condition worsened, six of the manager's subordinates violated several airport security rules. He never reported the violations to the airline. It found out about them as part of a Transportation Security Administration investigation. The airline then fired the manager. He sued under the ADA, **claiming that he was fired because of his association with a disabled person**, but a federal court and the Sixth Circuit ruled against him, noting that the airline had a legitimate reason for discharging him. *Stansberry v. Air Wisconsin Airlines Corp.*, 651 F.3d 482 (6th Cir. 2011).

◆   A Utah employee voluntarily disclosed to his HR manager that he was HIV positive. The following month, the employee became an independent contractor and a driver-trainer. With his consent, the company drew up a form that would inform a potential trainee that his trainer was HIV-positive. A trainee signed the form, and the driver-trainer took him out on the road. However, the driver-trainer grew stressed by a series of events and called in, insisting that he needed to see his doctor. The company terminated his contract two days later. When the EEOC sued on his behalf under the ADA, it lost because it couldn't show that he had suffered an adverse action due to his HIV. Instead, **his contract was terminated because he left during the job and didn't say he needed the leave for HIV-related reasons.** Further, he had voluntarily disclosed his HIV status and so could not complain about the form. *EEOC v. C.R. England, Inc.*, 644 F.3d 1028 (10th Cir. 2011).

◆   A manager who was employed by an automotive services store in Illinois had a history of soft-tissue injury to his back. As a result of his back condition, the manager experienced intermittent flare-ups. He took several medical leaves of absence. The leaves of absence ranged from one week to three weeks in duration. In addition, the manager was subjected to restrictions on twisting, standing for long periods of time and lifting. The company placed the manager on involuntary medical leave, and it later fired him. Following his termination from employment, the manager proceeded to file administrative charges of unlawful discrimination with the EEOC. After conducting an investigation into the charges, the EEOC filed a lawsuit on the manager's behalf. A federal court granted pretrial judgment to the company. However, the Seventh Circuit appeals court issued a decision reversing the lower court's ruling. The appeals court determined that **issues of fact existed regarding whether the intermittent back flare-ups were a disability under the ADA.** A trial was required to resolve the manager's claim, the appeals court said. *EEOC v. AutoZone, Inc.*, 630 F.3d 635 (7th Cir. 2010).

◆   An Alabama worker was employed on a temporary basis. He was subsequently offered a full-time job, although the offer of full-time employment was contingent on his ability to pass a pre-offer drug test. Because the worker took barbiturates to treat his epilepsy, the drug test he took for the company came back positive. In a telephone conversation, a medical review officer asked the worker a number of questions about his epilepsy. The medical review officer asked the worker what he took to control his epilepsy and what his dosages were. His supervisor was allegedly in the room at the time. Although the medical review officer cleared his drug test and the HR department cleared him for employment, the supervisor refused to hire him. The EEOC subsequently found he did not have a disability as defined by the ADA. **The worker filed a lawsuit against the company, alleging a violation of the ADA's prohibition against pre-offer medical inquiries.** A federal district court granted pretrial judgment to the company, but the Eleventh Circuit reversed. Even without a disability, he could sue the company for violating the medical inquiries provision. *Harrison v. Benchmark Electronics Huntsville, Inc.*, 593 F.3d 1206 (11th Cir. 2010).

◆   A 68-year-old restaurant employee in Arizona called the company hotline to complain about ageist comments made by his supervisor, who then gave him a series of written warnings. He called the hotline again to complain of retaliation and to inform the company of hand pain he suffered from working in the walk-in cooler. He was then fired. When he sued for retaliation and discrimination under the ADA, the Ninth Circuit held that **since he had failed to show he was disabled, he was limited to equitable relief like reinstatement and back pay** for the retaliation. *Alvarado v. Cajun Operating Co.*, 588 F.3d 1261 (9th Cir. 2009).

♦   A mill operator in Oregon took leave to undergo surgery for job-related and non-job-related injuries. Over a year later her doctor authorized her to return to work with certain restrictions. The company, pursuant to its policy, **required her to undergo a physical capacity exam before returning to work**. During the physical, the employee's blood pressure and heart rate were taken, and her pain level and use of medication were ascertained. The physical found her unable to lift 65 pounds, so the company refused to let her return to work. She sued the company for violating the ADA. A federal court found that the physical wasn't a medical exam, but the Ninth Circuit ruled that it was, and remanded the case for a determination of whether the exam was justified by business necessity and job-relatedness. *Indergard v. Georgia-Pacific Corp.*, 582 F.3d 1049 (9th Cir. 2009).

♦   A Texas employee who suffered from chronic fatigue syndrome – a medical condition that can't be diagnosed by a lab test and has no known causes – was fired for failing to disclose that she had the medical condition upon her hiring. She tried to explain that she had been symptom-free for 13 years and believed she no longer had the condition, but the employer fired her anyway. The EEOC sued on her behalf, but a federal court granted pretrial judgment to the employer. The Fifth Circuit reversed, finding **a factual question over whether her condition qualified as a disability under the ADA**. Also, it appeared that the employer failed to attempt to accommodate her, instead searching for a reason to fire her. The case required a trial. *EEOC v. Chevron Phillips Chemical Co.*, 570 F.3d 606 (5th Cir. 2009).

♦   A safety supervisor in Wyoming, whose job required her to travel to customers' worksites, was diagnosed with epilepsy and restricted from driving. As a result, the company fired her, maintaining that she could not hold a safety-sensitive position unless she obtained a full release from her doctor. She never obtained the release. After her firing, she sued for discrimination under the ADA and also sought overtime wages under the FLSA. A jury ruled in her favor on both claims, but the Tenth Circuit vacated the ADA award. It held that **driving was not a major life activity** under the statute. However, the employee might still prevail if she could show that she was regarded as disabled. *Kellogg v. Energy Safety Services, Inc.*, 544 F.3d 1121 (10th Cir. 2008).

♦   A Florida phone company technician had diabetes, hypertension and some other disorders that prevented him from losing weight. He weighed 325 pounds and was thus too heavy to work on ladders or buckets because of manufacturer safety policies. Although the company accommodated him for a while by ensuring he was not assigned any jobs that required climbing, eventually he was told to lose weight or apply for another job within the company. He rejected a job offer and failed to lose weight, then was fired. When he sued under the

ADA, a federal court and the Eleventh Circuit ruled against him. **His obesity did not amount to a disability under the ADA.** *Greenberg v. BellSouth Telecommunications, Inc.*, 498 F.3d 1258 (11th Cir. 2007).

♦   An Arkansas Wal-Mart order filler sustained a permanent injury to her right arm and hand that prevented her from performing the essential functions of her job. She sought reassignment to a router position, which was a vacant and equivalent position under the ADA. However, Wal-Mart required her to compete for the job with other candidates and eventually hired a more qualified non-disabled candidate for the job. It reassigned her to a janitorial position making about half her previous wages. She sued under the ADA and lost. The Eighth Circuit held that **Wal-Mart was not required to hire her over the more qualified candidate just because she was disabled.** *Huber v. Wal-Mart Stores, Inc.*, 486 F.3d 480 (8th Cir. 2007).

B. State Laws

State laws generally follow the wording of the federal laws, and the analysis of state statutes tends to be very similar to that used in deciding cases under Section 504 and the ADA. However, state laws might be more inclusive – that is, they might apply to all employers in the state, regardless of size, and they might cover conditions that are not covered by the ADA (like gender dysphoria).

♦   A technologist in Ohio alleged that her employer violated a state law by refusing to accommodate her back injury. The employer asserted that the claim was preempted by the Labor Management Relations Act because it would necessitate an interpretation of rights under an applicable CBA. A federal district court agreed, but the Sixth Circuit reversed. **The disability bias claim could be resolved without interpreting the CBA.** *Paul v. Kaiser Foundation Health Plan of Ohio*, 701 F.3d 514 (6th Cir. 2012).

♦   After a 549-pound blackjack dealer was fired, he sued his employer for disability discrimination under West Virginia law. The employer said the dealer was fired because he failed to tuck in his shirt as required and took work breaks in public areas. **The dealer said he could not find clothes that fit, and he claimed he became short of breath trying to walk to and from a break room.** The employee did not show he was substantially limited or was regarded as disabled. Also, the fact that the same person hired and fired the dealer was evidence that the employer's decision was not motivated by unlawful discrimination. *Andrew O. v. Racing Corp. of West Virginia*, No. 12-1255, 2013 WL 3184641 (W. Va. 6/24/13).

♦   A Massachusetts employee obtained medical insurance for his family through his employer. After his wife began receiving treatment for cancer and incurred medical expenses, he was fired. **The employer said it fired the employee because he left work without punching out, but the employee said his supervisor knew he wasn't punching out and never questioned him**

about it. The employee claimed disability discrimination under state law. A trial court rejected his claim, but an appeals court reinstated it. It decided that the state law was to be construed liberally, and it said that when an employer takes an adverse action against an employee based on hostility toward his spouse's disability, it treats him as if he were disabled himself. *Flagg v. AliMed, Inc.*, 992 N.E.2d. 354 (Mass. 2013).

◆   An Oregon drill press operator applied for a job and, knowing that a drug test would be required, disclosed that he was using marijuana for anxiety and nausea under the state's medical marijuana law. The company refused to hire him, and he sued for discrimination. The case reached the Oregon Supreme Court, which ruled for the company. **Federal law made marijuana illegal and trumped state law to the contrary.** In addition, state discrimination law did not protect people who use illegal drugs. *Emerald Steel Fabricators, Inc. v. Bureau of Labor and Industries*, 348 Or. 159 (Or. 2010).

◆   A Massachusetts restaurant employee with multiple sclerosis suffered a flare-up, causing numbness and loss of muscular control, and affecting her ability to walk, grasp and balance. While she was at home, her manager called her and told her not to return to work. When she later tried to report for work, he only allowed her to work a part-time, light-duty job, telling her that she could fall and cost the restaurant $200,000 to $300,000 if she returned to her regular job. She sued for discrimination under state law, which is similar to the ADA. A federal court granted pretrial judgment to the restaurant, but the First Circuit reversed, finding enough evidence of **"regarded as"** discrimination to warrant a trial. *Sensing v. Outback Steakhouse*, 575 F.3d 145 (1st Cir. 2009).

◆   A Connecticut liquor company truck driver injured his back lifting a case of liquor and was placed on a light-duty assignment for 60 days. He sought a permanent transfer from his truck driver job to one in the warehouse, which would allow him to avoid lifting cases of liquor. The company refused to consider his bid even though the job was open. Instead, it terminated him based on its policy requiring injured employees to be fully healed to return to their original jobs. When he sued under state law, a court granted pretrial judgment to the company because Connecticut law did not specify that employers had to reasonably accommodate disabled employees. However, the Connecticut Supreme Court reversed and remanded the case, noting that **even though the statute did not mention reasonable accommodation, the employer still had to accommodate** unless it would cause an undue hardship. *Curry v. Allan S. Goodman, Inc.*, 944 A.2d 925 (Conn. 2008).

◆   The president of a clothing division reported to the CEO of the company's western region – a short-tempered manager who yelled and cursed often. **After the president took a leave for breast cancer, she claimed the CEO became even more abusive.** Eventually, because of poor performance by her division, she was demoted as part of a restructuring. She sued for disability discrimination and lost. Even though she suffered a tangible employment action – demotion and salary reduction – the company proffered a legitimate reason for its action: poor sales by her division. Also, she never told anyone at the company that she was being harassed until after she left. *Ferraro v. Kellwood Co.*, 440 F.3d 96 (2d Cir. 2006).

◆   An Oregon millwright took marijuana under the state's medical marijuana program to calm muscle spasms in his legs so he could sleep at night. He was fired after testing positive for marijuana. When he sued for disability discrimination, he lost. The Supreme Court of Oregon held that he was not a disabled person because even though he had spasms that otherwise would have substantially limited his ability to sleep, **the marijuana mitigated his impairment so that it was no longer a substantial limitation** on a major life activity. *Washburn v. Columbia Forest Products, Inc.*, 134 P.3d 161 (Or. 2006).

◆   An engineer who worked for a large Washington airplane manufacturer was a biological male at the time of hire. After a number of years, the engineer determined that he was a transsexual. Transsexualism is known as gender dysphoria. The engineer then began treatment by a physician to undergo sex reassignment surgery. To qualify, he had to live full time for a year in the social role of a female. He approached his employer with his intentions and was informed that he could not use the female restrooms or wear feminine attire while he was still an anatomical male. The manufacturer allowed him to wear unisex clothing but required him to report daily to his manager – who would monitor his attire. The manufacturer fired the engineer for wearing an outfit that included pink pearls. He sued for handicap discrimination. The Supreme Court of Washington stated that although gender dysphoria qualified as an abnormal condition, the employer **discharged the employee for violating the employer's directives on acceptable attire, not for being gender dysphoric**. *Doe v. Boeing Co.*, 846 P.2d 531 (Wash. 1993).

V. RELIGIOUS DISCRIMINATION

Religious discrimination in employment is prohibited by Title VII. Employers who violate the act by intentionally discriminating against employees because of their religion or religious practices may be liable for compensatory and punitive damages, as well as equitable relief.

There are, however, some exceptions, such as the one in Section 702 of the Civil Rights Act for <u>religious organizations</u>. The U.S. Supreme Court has held that an employer must make reasonable accommodations for the religious beliefs of employees. However, Title VII does not require accommodations that impose an <u>undue hardship</u> on the employer.

Also, religion (like sex, national origin and age) might be a <u>bona fide occupational qualification</u> for a particular job. For example, a Lutheran school can legitimately hire only Lutheran teachers, though it probably cannot hire only Lutheran janitors.

In 2014, the EEOC released guidance relating to the duty of employers to accommodate religious garb and grooming in the workplace. It explained that Title VII applies to all aspects of religious practices or beliefs.

◆   An airline employee belonged to a religion known as the Worldwide Church of God. It proscribed work from sunset Friday to sunset Saturday. Because of the employee's seniority, the airline was able to accommodate his religious beliefs until he transferred to a new position. The airline agreed to permit the union to seek a change of work assignments, but it was **unwilling to violate the seniority system**. The airline rejected a proposal that the employee work only four days a week, stating that this would impair critical functions. Eventually, the employee was discharged for refusing to work on Saturdays. He sued both the union and the airline under Title VII, claiming religious discrimination. A Missouri federal court ruled in favor of the defendants, and the U.S. Court of Appeals affirmed in part. However, it did hold that the airline failed to satisfy its duty to accommodate the employee's religious needs. On appeal to the U.S. Supreme Court, it was held that the airline made reasonable efforts to accommodate the religious beliefs of others. The Court reversed the court of appeals' decision and held in favor of the airline. *Trans World Airlines v. Hardison*, 432 U.S. 63, 97 S.Ct. 2264, 53 L.Ed.2d 113 (1977).

◆   An employee of a chain of New England retail stores managed a clothing department at a location in Connecticut. When the store began to keep Sunday hours, the employee worked occasional Sundays for two years. He then notified his employer that he would no longer work on that day because it was his Sabbath. A Connecticut law stated that employers could not require their employees to work on their Sabbath days, and refusal to work on the Sabbath was not grounds for dismissal. The employer demoted the employee to a clerical position. The employee then resigned and filed a grievance administratively. He was found to have been discharged in violation of the statute, and a state trial court upheld that decision. The Connecticut Supreme Court reversed, and the case came before the U.S. Supreme Court, which held that the Connecticut law violated the Establishment Clause of the First Amendment. Essentially, it **imposed on employers an absolute duty to conform their business practices to the particular religious practices of their employees**. Under this law, Sabbath religious concerns automatically controlled all secular interests at the workplace. The primary effect of this law, then, was the advancement of religion, which is forbidden by the Establishment Clause. The Court affirmed the state supreme court's decision. *Estate of Thornton v. Caldor, Inc.*, 472 U.S. 703, 105 S.Ct. 2914, 86 L.Ed.2d 557 (1985).

◆   Two Jehovah's Witnesses worked as part-time couriers for FedEx in Florida. The employees' religion prevented them from working on Saturdays, so the employer offered them a job that allowed them to have Saturdays off. But the jobs would mean a large pay cut, so the employees did not take them. The employer then gave the employees 90 days to find another job in the company. Several positions became available, but the employees did not apply for them. The employer then determined that the employees had resigned. They sued under state law, claiming the employer forced them to resign and unlawfully failed to accommodate their religious beliefs. A federal appeals court upheld a ruling for the employer. **The employer offered accommodations that were reasonable**, even though changing positions may have meant less pay, a longer commute and potential loss of seniority. *Telfair v. Federal Express Corp.*, 567 Fed.Appx. 681 (11th Cir. 2014) (Unpublished).

◆   Two Catholic nuns in Ohio began volunteering with the Red Cross, and Red Cross supervisors formally evaluated their performance. Supervisors recommended "promotions" that would have led to additional responsibilities, but the promotions were not granted. The nuns separately also volunteered at a county emergency management agency, but they were asked not to return after they expressed disappointment with regard to how the agency was managed. The nuns sued the Red Cross and the agency for religious discrimination and harassment under Title VII. The nuns said the executive director of the Red Cross was biased against them because they were not Roman Catholic. A federal appeals court upheld a lower court's determination that the nuns could not pursue their claims because **they were not employees**. They were not paid or provided with health benefits, and they created their own schedules. *Marie v. American Red Cross*, 771 F.3d 344 (6th Cir. 2014).

◆   The director of a family business sued the business, claiming he was subjected to religious discrimination and a hostile work environment. Shareholders terminated the director from a sales job he held after he included comments about his faith during a eulogy. A district court ruled against him on his Title VII claim because **he was not an employee of the company**, and the Third Circuit agreed. The director had the right to control the business, so he was not an employee and could not sue under Title VII. *Mariotti v. Mariotti Building Products, Inc.*, 714 F.3d 761 (3d Cir. 2013), *cert. denied*, 134 S.Ct. 437 (U.S. 2013).

◆   A Muslim wore a religious head scarf known as a hijab. She wore the hijab to a job interview at an Oklahoma clothes store. At the interview, the employer described the dress code, and **the applicant did not say the code conflicted with her religious need to wear the hijab**. When the store decided not to hire the applicant, the EEOC sued it for religious discrimination under Title VII. A district court ruled in the EEOC's favor, but the Tenth Circuit reversed. The employer did not unlawfully fail to accommodate the applicant because it was never placed on notice that an accommodation was needed. *EEOC v. Abercrombie & Fitch Stores, Inc.*, 731 F.3d 1106 (10th Cir. 2013).

◆   A material handler for an Indiana employer asked for a month off so he could return to his native Nigeria to bury his father and participate in traditional burial rituals. **Two letters that he wrote to the company explained the rituals and said his family would suffer spiritual consequences if he did not participate.** The employer denied his request. He went anyway, and he was fired. When he sued for religious bias under Title VII, a district court ruled against him. But the Seventh Circuit reversed, finding that a jury could decide he had requested a religious accommodation and acted out of a sincerely held religious belief. *Adeyeye v. Heartland Sweeteners, LLC*, 721 F.3d 444 (7th Cir. 2013).

◆ An applicant for a job as a car salesman for a New Jersey dealership was a practicing Sikh whose religion prohibited him from shaving his beard or cutting his hair. He claimed he was denied the job because he would not shave his beard. The EEOC sued on his behalf under Title VII, claiming unlawful failure to accommodate and unlawful failure to hire. The court denied the dealership's motion for pretrial judgment. Though the dealership claimed it would have accommodated the applicant if it knew he needed a religious accommodation, the applicant's garb, which included a turban, made it clear he was a person of faith. **At the very least, the dealership was on notice to inquire further.** *EEOC v. United Galaxy, Inc.*, No. 10-4987 (ES), 2013 WL 3223626 (D.N.J. 6/25/13).

◆ A New Jersey truck driver claimed that his two direct supervisors harassed him because they thought he was Jewish. They called him names like "Jew Bag" and "Jew Bastard," and told him that if he were German, they'd burn him in an oven. When he complained to the head of the facility where he worked, he was told to laugh it off and the slurs would stop. Instead he sued under the state's Law Against Discrimination. The company asserted that it couldn't be liable because the driver wasn't Jewish, but the Superior Court, Appellate Division, disagreed. **The law allowed employees to sue for harassment because they are perceived as being members of a protected class.** *Cowher v. Carson & Roberts*, 40 A.3d 1171 (N.J. Super. Ct. App. Div. 2012).

◆ A sales employee in Puerto Rico became a Seventh-Day Adventist and asked for Saturdays off. The company instead **offered to transfer him to one of two positions that didn't require rotating Saturday work**. The salary was only slightly less, but without commissions, he would earn a lot less money. He declined that option but was unable to find employees to swap Saturday shifts with him (another option offered by the company). After resigning, he sued for discrimination under Title VII. The First Circuit ruled against him, noting that the company did all it had to under the law. *Sanchez-Rodriguez v. AT&T Mobility Puerto Rico, Inc.*, 673 F.3d 1 (1st Cir. 2012).

◆ A temporary placement agency refused to refer a Muslim woman to a client that ran a commercial printing operation because the woman wore a khimar (a scarf that covers the head and can extend to the waist) and the client's dress code policy prohibited workers from wearing headwear or loose clothing that could get caught in the machines. The woman filed a religious discrimination complaint with the EEOC, which sued the temp agency for violating Title VII. A Minnesota federal court and the Eighth Circuit ruled for the temp agency, noting that **the client's legitimate and facially neutral safety policy** justified the refusal to refer the woman for employment. *EEOC v. Kelly Services, Inc.*, 598 F.3d 1022 (8th Cir. 2010).

◆ Two editorial writers for an Indiana paper claimed that they were **fired or forced to resign because of their religious belief that homosexuality is a sin**. When they sued under Title VII, a federal court and the Seventh Circuit ruled against them. The court noted that one of the writers repeatedly violated the newspaper's overtime policy, continuing to work overtime without obtaining permission first. And the other writer made numerous spelling and reporting errors that required retractions or apologies to involved parties. The newspaper put forth legitimate, nondiscriminatory reasons for its decisions and thus was not liable under Title VII. *Patterson v. Indiana Newspapers, Inc.*, 589 F.3d 357 (7th Cir. 2009).

◆   A Jiffy Lube technician in Massachusetts practiced Rastafarianism, which prohibited him from cutting his hair or shaving. When a new grooming policy took effect, requiring employees who had customer contact to be clean-shaven and to keep their hair neatly trimmed, he asked for an accommodation so he could continue to work with customers rather than simply working in the lower bay. The company's vice president refused to discuss the matter and assigned him to the lower bay. He quit and then sued for religious discrimination. A state court granted pretrial judgment to the company, but the Supreme Judicial Court of Massachusetts reversed. Here, because **the company failed to engage in the interactive process**, it could not show that exempting the technician from the policy was the only possible accommodation and that doing so would impose an undue hardship on its business. The case required a trial. *Brown v. F.L. Roberts & Co., Inc.*, 896 N.E.2d 1279 (Mass. 2008).

◆   A North Carolina employee observed the Sabbath from sundown Friday to sundown Saturday. He also observed 20 religious days during the year, 14 of which did not coincide with his Sabbath. He met with HR to discuss possible accommodations, including transferring to a different shift or job, leaving his shift uncovered during his Sabbath, and being excused from the part of his shift that conflicted with his Sabbath. Ultimately, the HR manager decided that those accommodations wouldn't work because he lacked the seniority to transfer. He was allowed to use vacation, holiday and 60 hours of unpaid leave under the company's no-fault attendance policy. However, after exhausting all his leave options, he missed 11 days of work and was fired. When he sued for religious discrimination, he lost. The Fourth Circuit Court of Appeals held that **Title VII's obligation to reasonably accommodate doesn't require a company to "totally" accommodate a religious request**. *EEOC v. Firestone Fibers & Textiles Co.*, 515 F.3d 307 (4th Cir. 2008).

◆   A secretary for an Alabama medical center was required to work alternate weekends. However, as a Seventh-Day Adventist, she could not work her Friday or Saturday shifts from 3:00 p.m. to 11:00 p.m. With the center's approval, she managed to swap all her Saturday shifts with co-workers. However, she failed to show up for her scheduled Friday shifts for three months and was placed on an involuntary leave of absence. Rather than immediately firing her, the center offered her a flexible certified nursing assistant position, which would allow her to work on Sundays instead of Fridays and Saturdays. **It offered her the transfer even though she had not been employed for at least 12 months – a requirement the center was willing to waive** in her case. When she never responded to the offers, the center deemed her to have voluntarily resigned. She sued for religious discrimination under Title VII, but a federal court and the

Eleventh Circuit ruled against her. The center met Title VII's reasonable accommodation requirement. *Morrissette-Brown v. Mobile Infirmary Medical Center*, 506 F.3d 1317 (11th Cir. 2007).

♦   A software developer for a company in California claimed that she was **passed over for promotion because she did not belong to the same religion** (the Fellowship of Friends) as the hiring manager, who allegedly exercised his decision-making authority in favor of members of the same religion. When she sued for discrimination under Title VII, a federal court granted pretrial judgment to the company, noting that it offered legitimate nondiscriminatory reasons for the non-promotion. However, the Ninth Circuit reversed, finding issues of fact that required a trial. Here, she presented evidence that she was more qualified, that she was paid less than a Fellowship member in the same job and that the hiring manager told other managers she wasn't interested in the job. *Noyes v. Kelly Services*, 488 F.3d 1163 (9th Cir. 2007).

♦   A Home Depot employee in New York could not work Sundays because of his religion. His managers accommodated him for a year until a new store manager took over. She told him he needed to be "fully flexible" and offered him afternoon or evening shifts so he could attend church in the morning. He refused, explaining that he couldn't work on Sundays at all. After he was fired for missing a Sunday shift, he sued for religious discrimination under Title VII. A federal court granted pretrial judgment for Home Depot, but the Second Circuit reversed, finding an issue of fact that required a trial. **The offer to let the employee have Sunday mornings off was no accommodation at all.** *Baker v. The Home Depot*, 445 F.3d 541 (2d Cir. 2006).

♦   An Iowa employee alleged that the woman in the next cubicle propositioned her and then, after becoming religious, sought to convert her. The day before a mediation session to work out these and other problems, the employee took FMLA leave. She was fired when she failed to return to work, and sued under Title VII and state law. A federal court and the Eighth Circuit ruled against her. The claimed sexual harassment was not severe or pervasive enough to alter her working conditions, and the religious harassment stopped when she asked the co-worker to stop proselytizing. **The only continued "offensive" conduct was the posting of religious material in the next cubicle, which management determined did not violate company policy.** *Powell v. Yellow Book USA, Inc.*, 445 F.3d 1074 (8th Cir. 2006).

♦   A Muslim from Afghanistan claimed that he was subjected to continuing harassment by co-workers at the Maine meat plant where he worked. He sued for race, national origin and religious harassment under Title VII, citing a number of incidents. A jury agreed that the company knew or should have known about the harassment, but refused to award damages, finding **no evidence that the employee sought medical treatment for counseling or lost work as a result of the harassment**. The First Circuit Court of Appeals upheld the jury's findings. Although the jury could have awarded damages, it was not compelled to do so. *Azimi v. Jordan's Meats, Inc.*, 456 F.3d 228 (1st Cir. 2006).

◆   An evangelical Christian quality assurance manager in Arizona counseled an openly gay female employee to stop dating other women. She also brought up the employee's sexual orientation at the employee's performance review. Subsequently, she was fired for violating the company's harassment policy, which prohibited harassment on the basis of sexual orientation. The policy also subjected the harasser to immediate termination for coercing, intimidating or threatening a co-worker. When she sued the company for religious discrimination under Title VII, a federal court and the Ninth Circuit ruled against her. The termination was not religious discrimination in violation of Title VII. **Her harassment of her subordinate made her discharge legitimate and nondiscriminatory.** *Bodett v. CoxCom, Inc.*, 366 F.3d 736 (9th Cir. 2004).

VI. RETALIATION

Retaliation (disciplining an employee for engaging in activity protected by law) is forbidden by Title VII and other federal statutes, as well as by most state statutes. However, to succeed on a claim of retaliation, the employee must show a connection between the protected activity and the discipline.

Firing an employee is clearly an adverse employment action; so is demoting him. But many actions can be less clear-cut. For example, giving an employee "the silent treatment" probably won't be considered actionable retaliation. However, it still might lead to litigation, and even if you were to win such a lawsuit, it would cost you to defend it. Therefore, **never** retaliate against an employee for action that might be construed as protected under the law.

◆   A physician who was of Middle Eastern descent held a university faculty position in Texas. He filed a Title VII action claiming that a superior harassed him based on his race and religion. He alleged that he was constructively discharged as a result. In addition, he alleged that the university retaliated against him for complaining about the alleged harassment. A trial court ruled for the physician, and a federal appeals court affirmed as to the retaliation claim but vacated the lower court's ruling with respect to the constructive discharge claim. On the retaliation claim, it said the jury could have found the employer was motivated, at least in part, by a desire to retaliate. But the U.S. Supreme Court ruled that this "mixed motive" standard does not apply to Title VII retaliation claims. Instead, **plaintiffs must show the employer would not have taken the retaliatory action "but for" the fact that they engaged in protected activity**. The case was remanded. *Univ. of Texas Southwestern Medical Center v. Nassar*, 133 S.Ct. 2517, 186 L.Ed.2d 503 (U.S. 2013).

◆   A Kentucky man and his fiancée worked for the same company. After the fiancée filed a sex discrimination charge against the company, it fired her fiancé. He then filed retaliation charges against the company, but a federal court held that he couldn't sue because Title VII doesn't protect against third-party retaliation. After the Sixth Circuit affirmed, however, the Supreme Court reversed, holding that **the employee could pursue a claim for retaliation after**

the company fired him following his fiancée's bias complaint. *Thompson v. North American Stainless, LP*, 131 S.Ct. 863, 178 L.Ed.2d 694 (U.S. 2011).

◆   After a Tennessee female rail worker complained to company officials that her supervisor had repeatedly told her that women shouldn't be working in the yard and made insulting remarks to her in front of co-workers, she was reassigned to a less favorable position. She filed a retaliation charge with the EEOC and was shortly thereafter suspended for insubordination. After she filed a grievance with her union, the company found she had not been insubordinate and reinstated her with back pay. When she sued for retaliation, a jury awarded her $46,750. The U.S. Supreme Court upheld the award, noting that **reassignment of job duties can be retaliation if it is "materially adverse" to an employee**. It defined materially adverse as a harmful action that could dissuade a reasonable worker from making a charge of discrimination. The suspension was also materially adverse even though she was reinstated with back pay because a reasonable employee might choose not to file a discrimination charge knowing she could be out of work indefinitely. *Burlington Northern and Santa Fe Railway Co. v. White*, 548 U.S. 53, 126 S.Ct. 2405, 165 L.Ed.2d 345 (2006).

◆   An oil corporation fired an African-American employee, who then filed a complaint against it with the EEOC. While the charge was pending, the former employee applied for work with another company. When the company contacted the oil corporation for a reference, the corporation gave him a negative reference, which he believed was in retaliation for having filed the EEOC charge. The former employee sued the corporation for retaliatory discrimination under Title VII. A Maryland federal court dismissed the case, ruling that Section 704(a) of Title VII does not protect the rights of former employees. The Fourth Circuit affirmed. The U.S. Supreme Court reversed, finding that Section 704(a) **protects former employees from retaliatory action**. It agreed with the EEOC that to exclude former employees from Section 704(a) protection would undermine Title VII by allowing retaliation against victims of discrimination. This might give an incentive to employers to fire employees who brought EEOC complaints. *Robinson v. Shell Oil Co.*, 519 U.S. 337, 117 S.Ct. 843, 136 L.Ed.2d 808 (1997).

◆   A merchandise assembler in Pennsylvania had an affair with a store manager. The manager ended the affair and told the merchandise assembler's live-in girlfriend about it. There was a confrontation between the merchandise assembler and the manager at work, and three witnesses said the merchandise assembler threatened the manager during the confrontation. The merchandise assembler then told a store manager that the manager had been sexually harassing him at work. After the merchandise assembler was terminated, he sued and claimed he was fired in retaliation for his complaint of sexual harassment and other discrimination complaints he had filed two years earlier. The court rejected the retaliation claim. The two-year period was too long to show retaliation. Though the 11-day period between the sexual harassment complaint and the termination was not, **the overall circumstances indicated that the discharge was not retaliatory** – especially since the merchandise assembler did not complain of sexual harassment until just after his confrontation with the manager. *Motto v. Wal-Mart Stores East, LP*, 563 Fed.Appx. 160 (3d Cir. 2014).

◆   After he had been written up twice for poor job performance, an employee of a pet-food manufacturing company in Alabama twisted his ankle at work and filed a workers' compensation claim. He subsequently was written up two more times and was terminated. The employee then settled his workers' compensation claim, **signing an agreement that said the settlement was a "compromise of all claims" he had or would have in the future**. He subsequently sued the employer, claiming it terminated his employment because he filed the workers' compensation claim. A federal appeals court found the release was broad enough to bar the retaliation claim. *Sparks v. Sunshine Mills, Inc.*, 580 Fed. Appx. 759 (11th Cir. 2014) (Unpublished).

◆   An employee of an Arkansas warehouse was laid off after he verified co-workers' complaints that a supervisor repeatedly made racial slurs. He sued for retaliation under Title VII and 42 U.S.C. § 1981. A federal appeals court upheld a jury verdict in his favor, finding **there was sufficient evidence** to support the finding that he was terminated because he verified the harassment claims. *Sayger v. Riceland Foods*, 735 F.3d 1025 (11th Cir. 2013).

◆   A radiology technician in Kansas made a series of Facebook postings in which she said her supervisor overpaid people he liked, including her. She also called him a snake and added that he needed to keep his "creepy hands to himself." She was fired because the employer thought she lied about being overpaid and because she disrupted the employer's investigation into the claim. **She sued, claiming she was illegally fired in retaliation for the Facebook posts.** A federal appeals court ruled against her, finding she was fired because she falsely accused the supervisor of wrongdoing and sent texts to her co-workers about the investigation while it was ongoing. *Debord v. Mercy Health System of Kansas, Inc.*, 737 F.3d 642 (10th Cir. 2013).

◆   A female employee worked with her brothers in a family business. She said that when she tried to talk one of her brothers out of having an affair with an employee, he gave her duties to the employee, ignoring her and letting the employee berate her. She quit and sued under Title VII, claiming unlawful retaliation. A trial court dismissed her complaint, and the Second Circuit affirmed. **Title VII does not cover claims based on a supervisor's decision to extend special treatment to a paramour.** *Kelly v. Howard I. Shapiro & Associates Consulting Engineers, PC*, 716 F.3d 10 (2d Cir. 2013).

◆   A New Orleans airline employee complained to HR that a co-worker had posted a photo of her on Facebook, depicting her leaning over a table with a portion of her underwear visible. The HR manager investigated and found that three employees were responsible. The three employees were disciplined but not suspended or fired. She filed harassment charges with the EEOC. Later, she was accused of texting a photo of a tattooed penis to one of the three. At a meeting with HR, she allegedly became belligerent and uncooperative. She was suspended for 12 days and was paid after the suspension ended. Shortly thereafter, she was fired in a reduction in force (RIF) because of her lack of seniority. When she sued for retaliation under Title VII, she lost. A federal court and the Fifth Circuit held that **the manager who selected her for the RIF had no knowledge of her complaint** or EEOC charges. *Yancy v. U.S. Airways*, 469 Fed.Appx. 339 (5th Cir. 2012).

♦   A security officer at a New York nuclear power plant complained that he was sexually harassed by the instructor at a firing range. The instructor denied the charge but was removed from his position. Later, the security officer was the subject of three "fact-finders" – non-disciplinary investigations into suspected performance problems. They came about because of a missing gas mask, because he allegedly let a drunk officer into the work site and because he allowed a suspicious truck to stay parked in the yard on his shift. He quit and sued for retaliation. A federal court and the Second Circuit ruled against him. **The power plant had good reason to conduct the "fact-finders," and they were not sufficiently adverse** to be considered unlawful under Title VII. *Tepperwien v. Entergy Nuclear Operations, Inc.*, 663 F.3d 556 (2d Cir. 2011).

♦   A vice president at an Illinois bank rejected the advances of one of the bank's board of directors. She complained to HR, but the board member resigned before he was interviewed in the subsequent investigation. A new president then took over the bank and fired the vice president two months later. He claimed that the bank was losing money and that other employees could do the same work she did. She sued for retaliation under Title VII, and a federal court granted pretrial judgment to the bank. However, the Seventh Circuit reversed, finding issues of fact that required a trial. Here, **the vice president's job was the only one eliminated, and the bank hired four new vice presidents at around that same time**. *Egan v. Freedom Bank*, 659 F.3d 639 (7th Cir. 2011).

♦   The Cuban-American controller of a family-owned company in Florida wrote a letter to the CEO, complaining of national origin discrimination by the CEO's sister, the CFO. The brother and sister fired the controller the next day on the grounds that it would be awkward to keep her around. She sued for retaliation, but a federal court granted pretrial judgment to the company. However, the Eleventh Circuit reversed, finding issues of fact that required a trial. **The letter to the CEO was not threatening**, so the family's assertion that they thought she was trying to blackmail them into a large severance or somehow sabotage the company was questionable. *Alvarez v. Royal Atlantic Developers, Inc.*, 610 F.3d 1253 (11th Cir. 2010).

♦   A black customer service agent for an airline in Ohio complained to HR about racial bias by his supervisor. A month later, he received a final warning letter citing insubordination. He claimed that the discrimination continued and that his supervisor's boss told him she was tired of his complaints. She then recommended that he be fired. After his termination, he sued for retaliation under Title VII. A federal court granted pretrial judgment to the airline, but the Sixth Circuit reversed, finding issues of fact that required a trial. **The supervisor's boss's statement, coupled with the timing of the firing, suggested that the discharge may have been retaliatory.** *Hill v. Air Tran Airways*, 416 Fed.Appx. 494 (6th Cir. 2011).

◆   An Oregon employee claimed that two co-workers and his supervisor taunted him for being gay. About a month into the job, he took a day off because of stress. But when he called in to report that he was taking the day off, he failed to speak with his supervisor, which violated the company's call-in policy. He visited HR the next day to file a complaint, but was fired two days later. When he sued for harassment and retaliation, a federal court granted pretrial judgment for the company, but the Ninth Circuit Court of Appeals reversed. It found an issue of fact as to whether he was fired for filing a complaint of harassment. Even though the company gave a legitimate reason for firing him – his violation of the call-in policy – **the timing of the firing was suspicious**. A trial was required to determine the real reason the company fired him. *Dawson v. Entek Int'l*, 630 F.3d 928 (9th Cir. 2011).

◆   An inventory accounting employee for a company that made rail and tank cars had a history of making errors and other performance problems, like tardiness. She was reprimanded and threatened with termination for repeated errors. She complained to HR that her boss sent out pornographic emails, after which the company suspended him for five days and cut off his Internet access. The offensive emails stopped after that. More than 180 days later, she filed a complaint with the EEOC. Shortly thereafter, the company found her largest error yet, resulting in a loss of thousands of dollars. It fired her, and she sued. An Arkansas federal court and the Eighth Circuit ruled against her. Her sexual harassment claim failed because she waited more than 180 days after the last email to file charges with the EEOC, and her retaliation claim failed because **the company had a legitimate reason for firing her – repeated costly errors**. *Burkhart v. American Railcar Industries*, 603 F.3d 472 (8th Cir. 2010).

◆   An Oklahoma call center employee grew frustrated over not being promoted to a supervisory position, and complained to his superiors that women and minorities were getting favorable treatment. A few weeks later, he was fired for inappropriate behavior, including insulting employees on the call center floor. He sued for retaliation, but lost. The Tenth Circuit held that **apart from the timing of the discharge, there was nothing to suggest it was retaliatory**. And he admitted to much of the improper conduct, including the insults and his inability to give subordinates coaching and feedback. *Anderson v. AOL, LLC*, 363 Fed.Appx. 581 (10th Cir. 2010).

◆   A Colorado employee investigated payroll problems for an airline. When she discovered that the airline was improperly paying shift differential to male ramp managers, her supervisor allegedly told her to look the other way. She found other instances of males receiving more money than female employees. Her supervisor continued to criticize her performance to her and to others, so she sent him a series of emails accusing him of making false accusations against her. Her supervisor then told her she could either resign or accept a transfer and demotion. After she resigned, she sued for discrimination and retaliation under Title VII. A federal court granted pretrial judgment to the airline, but the Tenth Circuit reversed. **The ultimatum could be construed as an adverse action, and it might have been a pretext.** *Barone v. United Airlines, Inc.*, 355 Fed.Appx. 169 (10th Cir. 2009).

◆   A New Hampshire employee testified in a harassment case against his employer. The next day, the company began an investigation into a complaint filed against him a few weeks earlier. That investigation led to his termination during a reduction in force, when his supervisor had to choose between firing the employee or a high-achieving manager. When he sued the company for retaliation under state law, a federal court and the First Circuit ruled against him. **He failed to prove his supervisor even knew of his testimony in the harassment case.** *Dennis v. Osram Sylvania, Inc.*, 549 F.3d 851 (1st Cir. 2008).

◆   An Indiana employee allegedly had a consensual sexual relationship with his supervisor until he got married. After he tried to end the relationship, his supervisor reported that he was being insubordinate and he was fired. He sued for retaliation under Title VII, claiming he was fired for rejecting his supervisor's advances, and a jury found the company liable. However, the Seventh Circuit reversed, noting that **he did not engage in any protected activity under Title VII**. He failed to show that he believed his supervisor's actions were illegal or that he was sexually harassed. *Tate v. Executive Management Services, Inc.*, 546 F.3d 528 (7th Cir. 2008).

VII. DISCRIMINATION AGAINST VETERANS

The Uniformed Services Employment and Reemployment Rights Act (USERRA) guarantees the right of military reservists to return to their jobs with their rights of seniority, status, pay and other benefits as if they had not been absent due to reserve obligations. It also prohibits denials of hiring, retention and promotion because of reserve obligations.

◆   A technician at a Chicago hospital claimed that his supervisors didn't like the fact that he was a member of the Army Reserves and missed work two to three weeks a year as well as one weekend per month for training. He asserted that they falsely accused him of misconduct to get him fired. He claimed that his supervisor exaggerated one incident and lied about another. When he sued under USERRA, a jury ruled in his favor. However, the Seventh Circuit reversed, noting that there was no evidence that the HR vice president who fired him was "singularly influenced" by his supervisors' anti-military bias. On further appeal, the Supreme Court reversed the Seventh Circuit, noting that **the discharge wasn't insulated from the supervisors' bias because they wrote the reports the HR vice president relied on to finalize the decision to fire him.** *Staub v. Proctor Hospital*, 131 S.Ct. 1186, 179 L.Ed.2d 144 (U.S. 2011).

♦ An Army Reserves member who worked for United Parcel Service in Alabama suffered a combat injury to his knee after being deployed to Iraq. When he returned, he told the employer the injury prevented him from returning to his job as a package car driver. The employer told him no other full-time jobs met his medical restrictions. It offered him a part-time job, but he rejected the offer and later sued under the USERRA. The court rejected his claim, saying there was no evidence that the employer was hostile to employees because they served in the military. *Ward v. United Parcel Service*, 580 Fed.Appx. 735 (11th Cir. 2014).

♦ A Minnesota bank employee also served as a member of the National Guard. He got sick while at a Fort Benning in Georgia and continued to feel ill after returning home. He missed more than two weeks of work and was fired because he didn't call his supervisor to report his absence as company policy required. Although he called in sick the first two weeks, he didn't call in when he missed the next three days. When he sued under USERRA, he lost because the bank had reasonable grounds for firing him. A federal court and the Eighth Circuit ruled that **the employee knew or should have known of the bank's policies for calling in sick** and that he could be fired for violating them. *To v. U.S. Bancorp*, 651 F.3d 888 (8th Cir. 2011).

♦ A pilot for a corporate jet service in Missouri signed up for the Air Force reserve. When the company's CEO found out about it, he became angry and told the pilot that the reserve duties had better not inconvenience him. However, the pilot was granted military leave once a month for three years without incident. The CEO then learned that the pilot was planning to quit and move to Texas, where his wife had found another job. The CEO fired the pilot, who sued under USERRA. A federal court and the Eighth Circuit ruled against him, noting that **the CEO had a legitimate reason for firing him – the fact that he was about to quit**. *Rademacher v. HBE Corp.*, 645 F.3d 1005 (8th Cir. 2011).

♦ A Tennessee employee complained that his company improperly denied him military leave pay under USERRA. Shortly thereafter, the company investigated him for email abuse. It discovered that his personal email usage was much more than "incidental" and fired him. It cited more than 3,200 emails and more than 240 folders he created to store them. It also noted that he had written many long, multi-paragraph replies to many emails, demonstrating that he was spending an inordinate amount of time on personal and Naval Reserve business rather than on work. He sued for retaliation under USERRA, but lost. The Sixth Circuit held that **his email abuse was far worse than that of another employee who was fired for the same reason**. And he failed to show that his military status was a factor in his termination. *Escher v. BWXT Y-12, LLC*, 627 F.3d 1020 (6th Cir. 2010).

♦ A Puerto Rico employee told his supervisor that he planned to return to active duty in the near future. He then applied for a promotion but didn't get it. About the time he returned to active status, he received a poor job evaluation. He was placed on a 90-day performance improvement plan (PIP), which he completed before being mobilized to Iraq and Afghanistan. The company nevertheless extended the PIP for three months after his military leave. When he sued under USERRA, the First Circuit held that he had raised a question for trial over whether the extension of the PIP was retaliation for his military service. However, the failure-to-promote and the poor-evaluation claims failed. *Vega-Colon v. Wyeth Pharmaceuticals*, 625 F.3d 22 (1st Cir. 2010).

◆   A computer technician for a Virginia company was formally reprimanded several times prior to her call-up for active military duty. When she returned to work six months later, some of her job duties changed because of the company's contract with an outside federal agency. The change affected all similar employees. Four months later, after being warned again about her performance and attitude, she was fired when she left the office without authorization to attend to a customer at an off-site location. She sued under USERRA, but a federal court and the Fourth Circuit ruled against her. **The employee's refusal to correct her misconduct justified the firing.** *Francis v. Booz, Allen & Hamilton, Inc.*, 452 F.3d 299 (4th Cir. 2006).

◆   An employee of Circuit City in Texas claimed that he was fired solely because of his status as a Marine Reserve officer. He sued the company under USERRA, and the company sought to compel arbitration. A federal court ruled that USERRA superseded the arbitration agreement, but the Fifth Circuit reversed. It noted that nothing in USERRA prevented a court from enforcing an arbitration agreement (which dealt with procedural, not substantive rights). **The employee had to arbitrate his USERRA claim.** *Garrett v. Circuit City Stores, Inc.*, 449 F.3d 672 (5th Cir. 2006).

◆   A customer support technician for a company in North Dakota took a military leave of 14 months to go overseas. While he was gone, the company lost the account he had been working on, and it sent him a layoff notice. When he returned from overseas, he filled out a job application, indicating that he would not be available to work until May 4, 2004. A human resources manager told him there were no jobs available and that he was not the only one looking for work. The technician's attorney then faxed a letter to the head of the company's compliance office demanding the technician's immediate rehire. Within 48 hours the company notified the technician that he should report to work on May 4. He sued the company for violating USERRA, but a federal court ruled against him. **His reemployment occurred "promptly" under USERRA, which does not require immediate reinstatement following military leave in excess of one year.** *Vander Wal v. Sykes Enterprises, Inc.*, 377 F.Supp.2d 738 (D.N.D. 2005).

CHAPTER TWO

Employer Liability

I. EMPLOYEE INJURIES

An employer may be liable for the tortious (wrongful) acts of its employees to fellow employees. However, state workers' compensation laws, designed to provide an employee's <u>exclusive remedy</u> for job-related injuries, preempt many such claims. See Chapter Seven, Section I.

Where the injury is not within the course and scope of employment, and workers' compensation is not available, an employer may be held liable for its negligence in hiring or supervising the employee(s) who caused the injury.

Allowing employees to engage in horseplay, for example, might result in liability if an employee becomes injured. If the injury is deemed not to have arisen out of and in the course of the employment, workers' compensation will not be available. However, the employee could sue for negligent supervision or negligent hiring and might obtain a much larger award than would otherwise be available under workers' compensation.

Even if the employee cannot recover under tort law and has to settle for workers' compensation benefits, the employer will face increased costs as a result (like higher premiums and lost productivity). Thus, it is important to keep tight control over the workplace to minimize the chance for employee injury.

A. Intentional Conduct

Generally, employers will be held liable for their intentional harmful conduct toward their employees. Some actions are deemed to be intentionally harmful despite the lack of any malicious intent. For example, removing safety mechanisms on certain machines to increase productivity might, if an injury results, lead to a ruling that the injury was intentionally inflicted and move the case outside the workers' compensation system.

Employers may also be held liable for the intentional harmful conduct of their employees where the employees act within the scope of their employment or act with apparent authority on behalf of the employer.

Further, employers can be held liable even for the intentional harmful conduct of third parties, where they create an atmosphere that allows for such conduct. For example, telling a female employee to put up with the harassing behavior of an important client can lead to liability, as can refusing to install safety lighting in the parking lot of a workplace that is known to be in a bad area.

◆   The business manager for a Minnesota car dealership complained to the owner's father that the general manager was sexually harassing her. Ten days later she was fired. She sued not only the car dealership, but the owner and his father (who had financed the dealership's acquisition) under state law. A court entered a default judgment against the dealership, but it refused to find liability against the owner and his father. The Minnesota Court of Appeals affirmed. Although the owner could theoretically be held liable for aiding and abetting sexual harassment under state law, **the business manager failed to show that the owner knew about the harassment**. And the owner's father had no legal relationship with the dealership. *Matthews v. Eichorn Motors, Inc.*, 800 N.W.2d 823 (Minn. Ct. App. 2011).

◆   A District of Columbia court dismissed an "aiding and abetting" sexual harassment claim against the owner of a hair salon over the unwanted advances of a male co-worker because **the employee failed to show how the owner knew about the harassment**. She complained to the store manager once a week and eventually quit after the co-worker showed her a picture of his genitals. When she sued both the salon and its owner, the court said that she could only proceed with her lawsuit against the salon. *King v. Triser Salons*, 815 F.Supp.2d 328 (D.D.C. 2011).

✦   While working with another apprentice to install wiring at an apartment complex, an apprentice with an electrical company in Connecticut lost the tip of his forefinger when the other apprentice drilled a hole from the floor above while he was running his fingers through another hole trying to find some wires. He collected workers' compensation benefits and then sued the company for intentionally creating a dangerous working environment by failing to properly train him and the other apprentice. The case reached the Supreme Court of Connecticut, which ruled against him. **He failed to prove that the company knew its conduct was substantially certain to cause his injury.** At worst, the company was negligent. *Motzer v. Haberli*, 15 A.3d 1084 (Conn. 2011).

✦   An Ohio manufacturing employee was injured when an 800-pound metal coil fell on her legs while she and a co-worker were balancing it, trying to load it onto her press with a forklift. She sued the employer, alleging that it acted with the intent of causing her injury by making her participate in a dangerous activity without proper safety systems in place. She also asserted that the state's employment intentional tort statute was unconstitutional. A court granted pretrial judgment to the employer, but the Court of Appeals of Ohio reversed. It held that the employment intentional tort statute exceeded the legislature's constitutional authority and that a trial on the facts was required. On further appeal, the Supreme Court of Ohio held that the statute was constitutional and that it **prevented the employee from recovering for her injuries because she never showed that the employer committed a tortious act with the intent to injure her**. *Kaminski v. Metal & Wire Products Co.*, 927 N.E.2d 1066 (Ohio 2010).

✦   A Sears employee in Illinois who developed software and compiled data (to determine which customers should be extended credit and how much) received a performance review he deemed unwarranted. He claimed he was disabled and took medical leave, but **returned to the office on a number of occasions and allegedly deleted files from his computer before quitting**. Sears was able to restore much of the data, but still lost between $40,000 and $50,000 in labor and computer time. The company notified the police, and the employee was later charged with tampering with computer files. He was found in Massachusetts and arrested, but when a witness failed to appear, the prosecutor decided not to pursue the case. He then sued Sears for malicious prosecution and lost. The Seventh Circuit said that Sears had probable cause to believe he maliciously deleted the files. *Deng v. Sears, Roebuck and Co.*, 552 F.3d 574 (7th Cir. 2009).

✦   An Arkansas employee endured requests for sex, grabbing of her private parts and cell phone messages from one of the owners of the company for whom she worked. When she complained to the other owner, he told her not to flirt with his partner. He later threatened to fire her if she didn't sign a memo indicating that any inappropriate behavior between her and his partner was consensual. She refused to sign the memo and left work, then sued under Title VII. A jury found one partner liable for harassment and the other for retaliation. It awarded her $50,000 in compensatory damages, $60,000 in lost wages and $150,000 in punitive damages. The partner who had retaliated against her then filed for bankruptcy and sought to be relieved of the debt. A bankruptcy judge and the Eighth Circuit Bankruptcy Panel ruled that **he could not be discharged of a debt caused by his "willful and malicious" conduct**. *In re Porter*, 375 B.R. 822 (8th Cir. 2007).

◆   An employee of Lockheed-Martin harbored extreme racial hatred toward his African-American co-workers. While attending a mandatory training course on company grounds, he retrieved two weapons from his truck, then gunned down a number of co-workers before taking his own life. One employee's estate sued the company for $5 million in compensatory damages (as well as unspecified punitive damages), asserting that the company intentionally failed to provide a safe work environment. The estate claimed the company knew the killer hated blacks and also knew of his violent nature. The company sought pretrial judgment on the grounds that workers' compensation was the estate's exclusive remedy for the loss. A Mississippi federal court held that the estate could pursue its lawsuit against the company. The U.S. Court of Appeals, Fifth Circuit, then ruled that workers' compensation was the exclusive remedy for the estate. Here, the shooter was acting outside the scope of his employment, but **he shot the co-worker because of the co-worker's employment** while the co-worker was on the job. *Tanks v. Lockheed Martin Corp.*, 417 F.3d 456 (5th Cir. 2005).

◆   While cutting metal bands to wrap around stacks of wood, a lumber company employee was struck in the left eye by a piece of metal banding, which caused a deep laceration. Despite five surgeries, he became blind in that eye. He sued the company, seeking damages for his injury, and the company asserted that his sole remedy was workers' compensation. A court agreed, granting pretrial judgment to the company, but the Supreme Court of Appeals of West Virginia reversed and remanded the case. Here, the company failed to comply with an OSHA regulation requiring it to perform a hazard evaluation of the worksite to determine if personal protective equipment was necessary. As a result, **the company could not claim it did not know of the hazards of band cutting** and the necessity of safety glasses. *Ryan v. Clonch Industries, Inc.*, 219 W.Va. 664, 639 S.E.2d 756 (W.Va. 2006).

◆   After an employee was apparently too slow in performing a task, a co-worker yelled at him. Profanities were exchanged, and the co-worker grabbed the employee by the neck, causing the employee to fall to the floor. He sustained minor injuries. The company fired both men for fighting, and the employee sued the company, seeking recovery for his physical and mental injuries, and past and future lost wages. He asserted that the company was vicariously liable for the co-worker's assault on him. A jury ruled in his favor, and the court awarded him $145,275. The Louisiana Supreme Court noted that the exclusivity provisions of workers' compensation did not bar the employee's suit because the co-worker intentionally attacked the employee. Also, since **the co-worker was acting in the course and scope of his employment when he attacked the employee**, the company was responsible for the damages that resulted. However, the company was not responsible for damages that resulted from the firing. Because the employee had been hired "at will," he could be fired at any time so long as the reason for the discharge did not violate public policy. The court remanded the case for a redetermination of the damages owed. *Quebedeaux v. Dow Chemical Co.*, 820 So.2d 542 (La. 2002).

◆   To detect drug use by employees, a trucking company in California installed **video cameras and listening devices behind two-way mirrors in its employee restrooms**. When the equipment was discovered, a group of employees sued the company for invasion of privacy. The company maintained that it was allowed to install the equipment by the collective bargaining agreement, (CBA) and that the employees' lawsuit was therefore preempted by Section 301 of the Labor Management Relations Act. A federal court ruled for the company, but the Ninth Circuit Court of Appeals reversed.

The court of appeals noted that a state law claim is not preempted under Section 301 of the LMRA unless it "necessarily requires the court to interpret an existing provision of a CBA that can reasonably be said to be relevant to the resolution of the dispute." Here, the claims were based entirely on California constitutional and statutory rights of privacy guaranteed to all persons regardless of whether they were subject to a CBA. Also, even if the CBA allowed for the surveillance equipment, that provision would be void because Section 301 did not permit parties to a bargaining agreement to contract for what is illegal under state law. *Cramer v. Consolidated Freightways, Inc.*, 255 F.3d 683 (9th Cir. 2001).

B. Emotional Distress

Claims for intentional infliction of emotional distress require extreme and outrageous conduct. For negligent infliction of emotional distress, the conduct need not be as severe, but there must be a physical injury that accompanies the emotional distress in order for a recovery to be made.

The possibility of recovery for negligent infliction of emotional distress is much lower than it is for intentional infliction of emotional distress because workers' compensation will often bar recovery for such claims. Thus, most of the cases that follow involve claims for intentional infliction of emotional distress.

◆   A New Jersey employee kept pictures and ballet slippers that belonged to her deceased daughter in her cubicle at work. She told co-workers about her daughter's tragic passing on numerous occasions. Eventually, an HR manager spoke with her superior, pointing out that a number of co-workers had gotten to the point where they avoided contact with her and took work or questions elsewhere. Her superior then informed her that she had to remove the pictures and ballet slippers from her cubicle and that she could no longer speak to co-workers about her daughter because it was causing a disruption in the workplace. She became distraught and eventually resigned. Then she sued for intentional infliction of emotional distress as well as constructive discharge. A court granted pretrial judgment to the company, and the Superior Court, Appellate Division, affirmed. **The superior's statements, although insensitive, were not so extreme and outrageous as to go beyond all possible bounds of decency.** Further, the superior's statements were not made with the intent to cause emotional distress. *Ingraham v. Ortho-McNeil Pharmaceutical,* 25 A.3d 1191 (N.J. Super. Ct. App. Div. 2011).

◆   Over a 10-year period, an unknown individual placed a series of hoax calls to McDonald's and other fast-food restaurants, convincing managers there to strip-search various employees. **McDonald's knew about the calls but didn't train its managers or even notify them of the potential for such hoax calls.** When a call came in to a Kentucky McDonald's, with the caller falsely identifying himself as a police officer and implicating a female employee in an investigation, a manager agreed to strip-search the employee, who also agreed to the search in lieu of being arrested and searched at the police station. Even the employee's fiancé was brought in to search her body cavities. During that search (with the manager out of the room) the fiancé sexually assaulted the employee. McDonald's fired the manager, the fiancé went to prison, and both the employee and the manager sued. A jury awarded the employee more than $6 million in compensatory and punitive damages on her multiple claims, and awarded the manager over $1 million in damages for intentional infliction of emotional distress as a result of McDonald's failure to inform the manager about the hoax calls. The Kentucky Court of Appeals largely upheld the awards, though it reduced the manager's award to $500,000. *McDonald's Corp. v. Ogborn,* 309 S.W.3d 274 (Ky. Ct. App. 2009).

◆   A manager and an HR representative allegedly lied to an employee, telling him that a co-worker had accused him of sexual harassment, and implied that the person who made the complaint was a man. The employee became upset and was given a few days' paid leave to compose himself. The company also provided him with counseling services. He nevertheless began to suffer panic attacks and quit working eight months later. He then sued the company for intentional infliction of emotional distress. A Missouri federal court and the Eighth Circuit ruled against him, noting that **even if the manager and HR rep falsely accused him of making homosexual advances, he could not show that this rose to the level of outrage necessary** to support his claim. Also, the company offered him paid time off and counseling services. *Bailey v. Bayer CropScience, L.P.,* 563 F.3d 302 (8th Cir. 2009).

◆   Four California insurance agents alleged that they were forced to use certain practices to place customers into higher band ratings that were, unbeknownst to them, illegal. Later, the California Department of Insurance got involved and the agents informed corporate security that they had moved customers from lower to higher mileage bands using the practices endorsed by the company. The company then fired them for violating company policy regarding mileage bands. The agents sued the company for wrongful termination and intentional infliction of emotional distress. The company sought to dismiss the claims, but a federal court refused to do so. Here, the agents alleged that the company knew the mileage band practices were illegal but advised them that these practices were legitimate. They also alleged that the company told them **they would be fired if they did not engage in these practices,** and after they did so, the company fired them as "scapegoats." *Maffei v. Allstate California Insurance Co.*, 412 F.Supp.2d 1049 (E.D. Cal. 2006).

◆   A loss prevention officer for a store in Connecticut was fired after he stopped a customer for shoplifting when the customer had in fact stolen nothing. He claimed that he was ordered to turn over his keys and that the phone in his office was ripped from his hand, with a company official telling him it was for employees only. He sued for assault and battery and false imprisonment, among other claims, and the company sought to dismiss the lawsuit. A Connecticut federal court held that **the assault and battery and false imprisonment claims could proceed to the extent that they were alleging only emotional distress injuries**. *Rosario v. J.C. Penney*, 463 F.Supp.2d 228 (D. Conn. 2006).

◆   A security guard in Maryland was threatened by her boyfriend and obtained a protective order against him, which she showed to her project manager. Despite the project manager's orders to her supervisor to assign her only to indoor, locked posts, the supervisor assigned the guard to an unsecured post outside the building. The former boyfriend tracked her down at work, kidnapped her, then assaulted and raped her, releasing her after six hours. The guard sued her employer for intentional infliction of emotional distress. A federal court granted pretrial judgment to the employer, but the U.S. Court of Appeals, Fourth Circuit, reversed, finding issues of fact that required a trial. It stated that workers' compensation did not bar the lawsuit. **A jury could infer that the supervisor intended to inflict emotional distress on the guard** by ignoring managers' instructions to assign the guard to an indoor post. *Gantt v. Security USA*, 356 F.3d 547 (4th Cir. 2004).

C. Negligence

Negligence refers to acts or omissions demonstrating a failure to use reasonable or ordinary care. In particular, a claim of negligence requires:

—the existence of a duty (duty of care, duty to supervise, duty of confidentiality, etc.),

—a breach of that duty, and

—a resulting injury which is caused by that breach.

Although many negligence claims brought by employees will be barred by workers' compensation, there are situations where such claims will survive. And even where those lawsuits are ultimately unsuccessful, the costs of litigation are high.

Negligence claims are more likely to succeed when they do not arise exclusively from the employer/employee relationship. In other words, if the employer's negligence causes an injury to an employee, and the injury occurs outside the work environment or because of factors not associated with the employment, the lawsuit is more likely to be allowed to proceed.

1. Negligence Generally

♦   Starbucks kept unencrypted personnel information (including employees' names, addresses and Social Security numbers) on a laptop computer that was stolen from a Starbucks restaurant. The company sent a letter to affected employees, alerting them of the theft and offering free credit monitoring services for a year. Three employees nevertheless sued the company for negligently failing to protect their personal data. A Washington federal court dismissed their action, holding that they failed to show they suffered a cognizable injury, but the Ninth Circuit Court of Appeals reversed. **The three employees alleged a credible threat of real and immediate harm from the stolen laptop.** Their lawsuit could proceed. *Krottner v. Starbucks Corp.*, 628 F.3d 1139 (9th Cir. 2010).

♦   A Texas waitress was harassed by a cook, who became physical with her on several occasions. Her complaints to management resulted in his being moved to a new shift, but there was overlap, and he continued his harassment of her. Further complaints resolved nothing. She quit, then sued under the state's human rights act and also asserted claims of negligence. A jury found that she had been assaulted and forced to quit, and it awarded her $850,000 in damages on the negligence claim, which allowed for greater damages than the human rights act. On appeal, the Texas Supreme Court ruled that **the human rights claim preempted the negligence claim** and that she was limited to the recovery available under that act – no more than $300,000. It remanded the case for action under only the human rights act. *Waffle House, Inc. v. Williams*, 313 S.W.3d 796 (Tex. 2010).

♦   A Florida bank manager sued the bank for negligence and an intentional tort after she was shot during a robbery. She asserted that the bank knew of the danger she faced because of previous aggravated assaults at the bank and a prior robbery during which an employee was pistol-whipped. In fact, the bank had hired a security guard after the earlier robbery but had eliminated that position for economic reasons. The bank sought to dismiss her lawsuit, claiming that workers' compensation was her exclusive remedy. A federal court and the Eleventh Circuit agreed with the bank that the manager was bound by the exclusivity of workers' compensation. **The bank's alleged misconduct was not "substantially certain" to result in the manager's injury or death.** *Locke v. SunTrust Bank*, 484 F.3d 1343 (11th Cir. 2007).

♦   A temporary worker was assigned to work as a press operator for a manufacturer in Rhode Island. **He injured his finger after returning from a coffee break when the press came down on his hand.** After collecting workers' compensation benefits from the temp agency, he sued the manufacturer for negligence. The case reached the Supreme Court of Rhode Island, which ruled that the manufacturer was a "special employer" under state law, and that it was immune to a lawsuit because the temp worker was entitled to workers' compensation benefits from the temp agency. Also, the coffee break did not count as an employer-sponsored social activity such that workers' compensation exclusivity could be avoided. *Urena v. Theta Products, d/b/a Sprague Industries*, 899 A.2d 449 (R.I. 2006).

◆   An employee of a family-owned business in New Jersey managed the customer service department until she left the company for a new job. Later, her new employer questioned the professional experiences she had listed on her résumé and called the former employer's customer service supervisor. He stated that the former employee had never been a manager there. She was fired a few days later. She sued the former company for negligent representation, and a trial court dismissed the case. The Superior Court, Appellate Division, reinstated the lawsuit. It noted that **employers can be held liable for providing false information about a former employee's work history** to a prospective or current employer who calls for references. However, there were questions of fact that required a trial here. *Singer v. Beach Trading, Inc.*, 876 A.2d 885 (N.J. Super. Ct. App. Div. 2005).

◆   An employee of a supermarket in Massachusetts had a conversation with a co-worker in which he mentioned "guns, revenge, life and politics." The co-worker reported the conversation to a manager, allegedly distorting the employee's comments. The supermarket, aware that the employee suffered from depression, immediately suspended him for three days, then fired him pursuant to its "zero tolerance" to workplace violence policy. It also contacted the police to report the threats. Two police officers were waiting outside the building as the employee left on his last day, and they allegedly forced him to go to a hospital for evaluation. After he was released, he sued the supermarket under the state civil rights law. A federal court ruled against him, and the First Circuit Court of Appeals affirmed that decision. The civil rights claim failed because the supermarket had a legal privilege to report the threats to the police. Even if the co-worker distorted the conversation, **the supermarket did not violate the employee's civil rights by reporting the alleged threats**. *Andresen v. Diorio*, 349 F.3d 8 (1st Cir. 2003).

◆   A bartender at a club in Indiana suffered injuries when she tried to assist a patron who was attacked by several other patrons in the VIP area. She sued the club for **negligently failing to provide security**, and the club sought to have the case dismissed on the grounds that workers' compensation was the bartender's sole remedy. A trial court refused to dismiss the case and later found in favor of the bartender. The Court of Appeals of Indiana affirmed. Here, the club failed to prove the bartender was engaged in an activity that was at least incidental to her employment. Further, the club failed to provide a security officer in the VIP area like it was supposed to do, and it allowed the assailant patrons to enter the club even though they did not comply with its dress code. The lower court properly awarded damages to the bartender. *Eagledale Enterprises, LLC v. Cox*, 816 N.E.2d 917 (Ind. Ct. App. 2004).

◆   When a corporation decided to spin off a subsidiary, the subsidiary's CEO told employees at a facility about the transaction's probable impact. He reported that the facility was profitable, would not close, and that employees would not lose their jobs. Four months later, employees at the facility were informed that the facility would be closing in a couple of months. A number of employees sued the company and the CEO for negligent misrepresentation, but a trial court ruled against them. The North Carolina Court of Appeals affirmed. Here, **the CEO did not have a duty to the employees; he only owed a duty of care to the company**. Further, the employees failed to show that the CEO knew the plant would be closing at the time he made the statement, and they failed to show that they relied on the CEO's statement to their financial detriment (e.g., they did not show that they turned down any job offers as a result). *Jordan v. Earthgrains Co.*, 576 S.E.2d 336 (N.C. Ct. App. 2003).

◆   A Utah retail store employee was assaulted and raped in an employee parking lot after leaving work. She sued the employer and shopping center for negligence. The court used the state's comparative negligence statute to apportion damages by comparing the relative fault among multiple parties and apportioning liability according to each party's fault. Since the unknown assailant was liable for a large portion of the damage award, the employer's and center's liability was substantially reduced. The employee appealed to the Supreme Court of Utah, which held that under the comparative negligence statute, **fault could not be attributed to an unknown wrongdoing party**. It had to be apportioned only among known defendants, plaintiffs, and persons immune from suit. The trial court had erroneously ruled that the comparative fault of the assailant had to be included. The court reversed and remanded the case. *Field v. Boyer Co., L.C.*, 952 P.2d 1078 (Utah 1998).

◆   The Nevada Supreme Court refused to impose liability on an employer based on claims of fraudulent or negligent misrepresentation, among other claims, where a former employee alleged that his supervisor violated a company confidentiality policy when he **revealed the employee's participation in a chemical dependency program to co-workers**. After the employee was discharged for circulating rumors that two co-workers were having an affair, he sued for negligence, wrongful termination, misrepresentation and emotional distress, among other claims. The Supreme Court of Nevada held that the employee failed to show that the employer had fraudulently induced him into accepting employment or seeking treatment for alcoholism. There was a similar failure of proof in his claims for emotional distress. The negligent misrepresentation claim was inapplicable to the supervisor's alleged breach of the confidentiality policy, since the cause of action is available only in the context of business transactions. *Barmettler v. Reno Air, Inc.*, 956 P.2d 1382 (Nev. 1998).

◆   An oil company worker abused drugs and was hospitalized a number of times for paranoid schizophrenia. He occasionally failed to take his medication and skipped meetings with his psychologist. The company's physician examined the employee and determined that he was disturbed and depressed. His wife later testified that she was assured by the employee's supervisor that she would be advised if termination was imminent. After the company fired him for poor job performance without any warning, the employee committed suicide within two weeks. His wife sued the employer under the Texas Wrongful Death Statute, claiming negligent and wrongful discharge, intentional and negligent infliction of emotional distress and gross negligence. A jury returned a verdict against the employer for gross negligence and awarded the wife $700,000. The employer appealed to the Court of Appeals of Texas, which determined that **a primary factor in determining employer liability was the foreseeability of the risk of danger to the employee**. An employer generally owes no duty of care to employees based on termination decisions. The employer was not negligent in failing to warn the wife of the imminent termination, and it had no duty to undertake his medical care. The suicide was not reasonably foreseeable. The court reversed and remanded the case. *Shell Oil Co. v. Humphrey*, 880 S.W.2d 170 (Tex. Ct. App. 1994).

2. FELA Actions

The Federal Employers' Liability Act (FELA) establishes a cause of action for railroad workers to recover damages for injuries resulting from employer negligence.

The act differs from workers' compensation in that it does not make the railroad "the insurer" for all employee injuries the way workers' compensation does. In other words, where the railroad is not negligent, it will not be liable for the employee's injuries.

♦   A pipefitter employed by a railroad was exposed to asbestos while removing insulation from pipes over a three-year period. He attended an "asbestos awareness" seminar and began to fear that he would develop cancer or another asbestos-related disease. He filed a FELA action against the employer in a New York federal court, seeking damages for emotional distress and his expenses for expected future medical checkups. The employer admitted negligence but denied that the employee had suffered emotional distress or physical harm. The court agreed with the employer and dismissed the action, but the Second Circuit reversed. The case reached the U.S. Supreme Court, which discussed the physical impact rule it had previously set forth in FELA decisions, permitting emotional distress claims where the distress accompanies a physical injury. Employees injured as a result of a physical impact due to employer negligence may also recover damages for negligent infliction of emotional distress. However, the Court **refused to extend the physical impact rule to cover simple physical contact with a substance** such as asbestos that threatens some future risk of disease. The Court characterized the employee's contact with asbestos as an exposure, not a physical impact, and it reversed the court of appeals' decision. The employee had advanced no evidence of an emotional injury, and the Court dismissed the claim for the cost of extra medical checkups. *Metro-North Commuter Railroad Co. v. Buckley*, 521 U.S. 424, 117 S.Ct. 2113, 138 L.Ed.2d 560 (1997).

✦   A long-time locomotive engineer in West Virginia received documents explaining a voluntary separation or early retirement program. The papers included a release of any claims of any kind against the railroad. He signed the release and accepted a buyout of $35,000. Nineteen years later, he died of mesothelioma. His widow sued the railroad under FELA, but a state court granted pretrial judgment to the railroad. The Supreme Court of Appeals of West Virginia reversed, finding issues of fact that required a trial. It held that **the release signed by the engineer as part of the voluntary separation program did not release his mesothelioma claim absent evidence that the release was executed as part of a settlement for mesothelioma**. *Ratliff v. Norfolk Southern Railway Co.*, 680 S.E.2d 28 (W. Va. 2009).

✦   A New York railroad employee was killed by a train in the railway yard. His widow sued for wrongful death under FELA, and a jury found the railroad 75% negligent, making the employee 25% negligent. She was awarded $825,000 after his 25% liability was taken into account. She appealed to the Supreme Court, Appellate Division, which found that **the jury permissibly assessed 25% fault against the employee**. However, the widow should have been granted a slightly higher award for cost of living increases, as well as salary increases. *Sneddon v. CSX Transportation*, 848 N.Y.S.2d 502 (N.Y. App. Div. 2007).

✦   A track laborer and backhoe operator for a railroad in Indiana died of lung cancer. His estate sued the railroad under the FELA, alleging that the cancer was caused by workplace exposure to asbestos fibers, diesel fumes and exhaust, and herbicides. The employee also had a long history of smoking cigarettes. The estate's **expert testified that the employee's exposure to diesel fumes and asbestos played a significant role in his development of cancer**. He also testified that he could not state to any degree of medical certainty that the employee would not have developed lung cancer if he had not been exposed to asbestos and diesel fumes. The railroad sought to exclude the deposition testimony and asked for pretrial judgment. The court denied its requests, and the Indiana Court of Appeals affirmed. A jury would have to determine how much liability, if any, to attach to the railroad. *Norfolk Southern Railway Co. v. Estate of Wagers*, 833 N.E.2d 93 (Ind. Ct. App. 2005).

✦   A railroad company arranged an influenza vaccination program for company employees who worked at a Texas office. The program was voluntary and took place on the employer's premises during work hours. One employee who participated in the program received a flu shot, then collapsed and struck his head upon returning to his office. He filed a FELA action against the employer, asserting that he had suffered a permanently disabling injury. The court granted pretrial judgment to the railroad, but the Fifth Circuit reversed. Was the employee injured in the scope of his employment? Previous decisions by federal courts applied a broad standard when interpreting the scope of employment under FELA. If a jury could reasonably find that the employer's motivation toward the program was a self-interested desire to reduce absenteeism, **the employee might have felt compelled to accept a flu shot for the employer's benefit**. The employer had planned, administered, paid for and promoted the flu shot program, creating factual issues about its motivation that made pretrial judgment inappropriate. The case required a trial. *Smith v. Medical and Surgical Clinic Ass'n*, 118 F.3d 416 (5th Cir. 1997).

D. Independent Contractors

Whether an employer may be held liable for injuries sustained by an independent contractor requires a determination of the worker's status. If the employer exerts a significant amount of *control* over the worker, the worker's status may change from independent contractor to employee.

In addition to control over the worker, courts look to other factors, such as the skill required, the type of occupation, supplying of tools, length of time employed, and method of payment.

If the worker retains his/her status as an independent contractor, then workers' compensation will not be available and the worker will likely sue for any injuries sustained under the principles of negligence (duty, breach of duty and harm caused by that breach).

*   A California driver sued his former employer, alleging that it improperly classified him and other drivers as independent contractors. He said that as a result, he and the others were unlawfully denied sick leave, vacation and severance wages. A federal appeals court found **the drivers were employees even though they signed agreements that explicitly said they were independent contractors**. The actual relationship between the parties was determinative, and it showed the drivers were employees: The employer controlled their pay; decided which days they worked; controlled their appearance; closely monitored and supervised them; and supplied trucks that could not be used for any other purpose. *Ruiz v. Affinity Logistics Corp.*, 754 F.3d 1093 (9th Cir. 2014).

*   Home Depot hired IBM to provide computer installation, wiring and networking products and services at several stores, including one in Pennsylvania. IBM subcontracted some of the installation work to another company. While working on a wooden plank near the ceiling, one of that company's electricians fell approximately 14 feet and suffered permanent injuries. He sued Home Depot and IBM for negligence. A Pennsylvania federal court held that **Home Depot and IBM did not retain control over the methods of work used by the subcontractor or the electrician** such that they could be liable for the injuries. They also were not liable under the "peculiar risk" exception because the work was not particularly risky and did not pose a special danger to the electrician. Working on an unsecured board high above the ground presented open and obvious risks to the electrician and his employer. *Warnick v. Home Depot U.S.A., Inc.*, 516 F.Supp.2d 459 (E.D. Pa. 2007).

• A nurse who worked at a home for mentally disabled adult males was injured when she was attacked by a patient. At the time of the attack, she was performing services as a "consulting nurse" under a contract she signed with the home. When she brought a tort action against the home to recover for her injuries, the home first asserted that she was an employee and thus limited to the exclusive remedy of workers' compensation. It also claimed it was not negligent and that the nurse failed to inform officials that the resident required more care than the home could provide. A court granted pretrial judgment to the home, but the Louisiana Court of Appeal reversed. **The nurse was an independent contractor and not an employee, so she was not limited to the exclusive remedy of workers' compensation.** However, questions of fact existed as to whether the home was negligent. That issue required a trial. *Mouton v. We Care Homes, Inc.*, 915 So.2d 971 (La. Ct. App. 2005).

• A staffing agency that provided nurses to a Missouri hospital contracted with a male nurse to operate the hospital's acute-care dialysis unit. The nurse accepted employment with the agency on the condition that he be assigned exclusively to the hospital. The agency agreed. After a female patient accused the nurse of raping her while she was receiving dialysis, investigators found nothing conclusive to support the allegation. However, they did find that the nurse had used inappropriate language in violation of hospital policy. Because he had been warned about his language earlier, the hospital told the agency not to assign the nurse to its facility. **The nurse then sued the hospital for tortious interference with his employment relationship**, and his wife sued for loss of consortium. A jury awarded the nurse $250,000 and his wife $50,000. The Missouri Court of Appeals upheld the award. Here, the nurse had a valid business expectancy with respect to his assignment at the hospital. Also, his admission to having conversations about sexual matters was not an admission to sexual harassment. Thus, the hospital did not have an absolute legal justification for taking action against him. *Hensen v. Truman Medical Center*, 62 S.W.3d 549 (Mo. Ct. App. 2001).

• An employee of a contractor working on a California housing development was injured when a wall that he and his co-workers were attempting to raise collapsed on him. The employee sought recovery against the contractor under the state workers' compensation act. He also sued the project owner, alleging that raising the wall created a peculiar risk of injury to him. The court entered pretrial judgment for the owner, and this decision was affirmed by the court of appeal. The California Supreme Court held that a general contractor that hired an independent contractor to do inherently dangerous work **could not be held liable for negligence to an employee of the independent contractor**. Although the peculiar risk doctrine allows innocent bystanders and neighbors to be compensated for independent contractor negligence, employees of the contractor are not entitled to the same protections. Since there was no duty by the owner to protect the contractor's employees in this case, the court affirmed the judgment for the owner. *Toland v. Sunland Housing Group, Inc.*, 74 Cal.Rptr.2d 878, 955 P.2d 504 (Cal. 1998).

♦ A Nebraska taxi company entered into lease agreements with its drivers, wherein the company rented cabs to drivers and a lessor-lessee relationship existed between the parties. The agreements also contained terms that limited driver control, including limitations on work hours, contribution to a company self-insurance fund and cab-calling procedures. Drivers were prohibited from subleasing vehicles and were not permitted to use phones or beepers in vehicles. They kept their fares, and the company did not withhold taxes. When an injured driver submitted a claim for workers' compensation benefits, the state workers' compensation court held that he was an independent contractor who was not entitled to benefits. The Supreme Court of Nebraska reversed, stating that **he was an employee because of the employer's exercise of control over his work**. Other factors such as the skill required, the type of occupation, supplying of tools, length of time employed, and method of payment also indicated that the driver was an employee. *Hemmerling v. Happy Cab Co.*, 247 Neb. 919, 530 N.W.2d 916 (Neb. 1995).

♦ A Wyoming natural gas processing company hired a well service to rework some oil wells. The parties had an unwritten working agreement and they assumed that the well service was an independent contractor. Nonetheless, gas company employees routinely exercised control and direction of work performed by employees of the well service. A well service employee was severely injured in an accident resulting, in part, from violation of OSHA safety regulations. He sued the gas processing company and obtained a damage award of over $1.6 million. The company appealed to the Supreme Court of Wyoming, which stated that the gas company had performed an active role in supervising and inspecting the well service's work. Therefore, **the well service lost its independent contractor status**, because it no longer had the ability to manage its own operations and direct its own employees. This resulted in abandonment of the protection of the independent contractor rule, and the gas company became liable for the well service employee's injuries. The court affirmed the trial court's decision. *Natural Gas Processing Co. v. Hull*, 886 P.2d 1181 (Wyo. 1994).

II. DEFAMATION

Employers enjoy a limited privilege to communicate necessary information about their employees to the police and prospective employers who require employee information. They may also communicate within the company to ensure that managers who need to know about certain employees are made aware of any necessary accommodations or potential problems.

Courts employ a balancing of interests analysis in determining what information must remain confidential. An employer loses its privilege to communicate information and may become liable for defamation where it communicates false information that damages the employee.

<u>Excessive publication</u> may also expose an employer to liability. For example, if you only need to tell one manager about an allegation of sexual harassment, and you tell other managers about it, you could be liable for defamation.

A. Intra-Company

1. Generally

♦   A Minnesota insurance company told a managing director about subordinates' complaints and warned her to improve her behavior. Her subordinates described the workplace as dysfunctional and called her management style "blame and shame." They also said that team morale was low. She denied the problems and was later fired for falsifying her expense account. She sued, claiming that the company defamed her by telling her about the subordinates' complaints. The Eighth Circuit ruled against her, noting that the statements by the subordinates were subject to a qualified privilege. **They were made as part of an investigation into employee misconduct.** Thus, the company was not liable for making them. *Chambers v. The Travelers Companies, Inc.*, 668 F.3d 559 (8th Cir. 2012).

♦   A site director for a telemarketing company in Texas was investigated for participating in an inappropriate lap dance with a female employee toward whom he was allegedly showing favoritism. He admitted to the inappropriate lap dance, and the investigator reported the admission to the vice president of employee relations. The vice president held a conference call with the investigator and another employee relations worker and recommended termination, writing up a report detailing the lap-dancing as a violation of company policy and forwarding it on to a senior vice president. After he was fired, he sued for discrimination and defamation. A jury awarded him over $1 million in damages for libel, but the court awarded judgment as a matter of law to the company and the Fifth Circuit affirmed. It **found no evidence of actual malice in the vice president's report**. Even if the lap-dancing didn't violate company policy, the vice president testified that she believed it did. The director failed to prove that the vice president acted with malice. *Stoddard v. West Telemarketing, L.P.*, 316 Fed.Appx. 350 (5th Cir. 2009).

♦   A vice president of a Virginia company received a job evaluation stating that: 1) she and her team were "significantly off plan" on certain financial targets; 2) she was responsible for certain losses that adversely affected the company; 3) her frequent verbosity and vocal opinions led others to stop participating in open dialogue; 4) she seemed unwilling to accept feedback; and 5) she engaged in inappropriate criticisms of others. After she was fired, she sued for defamation, among other claims. **A jury awarded her $1.5 million in compensatory damages and $2 million in punitive damages.** The Supreme Court of Virginia reversed and remanded the case. Here, the first two statements were actionable as factual statements that could be proved true or false. However, the latter three were essentially opinion and not actionable. Thus, since the jury did not delineate which statements it found defamatory, a new trial had to be conducted. *Raytheon Technical Services Co. v. Hyland*, 641 S.E.2d 84 (Va. 2007).

+ A sales manager at an Indiana radio station was fired while he was on paternity leave for failing to meet certain work goals. The station's general manager then learned that pornographic material had been posted on a website the station had been trying to procure (with the same call letters). After a meeting, he inaccurately accused the former sales manager of posting the pornography on the site. The sales manager then lost his next two jobs and sued for defamation. A federal court and the Seventh Circuit ruled for the radio station. Here, **the false statements about the sales manager did not relate to his ability to do his job** even though they suggested that he lacked certain qualities desirable in an employee. Conversely, attacking a teacher's integrity would be defamatory because part of a teacher's job is to serve as a role model for students. *Cody v. Harris*, 409 F.3d 853 (7th Cir. 2005).

+ A service manager in Amtrak's product line division had his performance evaluated as part of a company-wide decision to lay off the lowest-rated 10% of mid-level managers. His supervisor gave him four sevens and three threes on the one-to-seven scale, but the general manager lowered his score to five threes (meets expectations) and two twos (rarely meets expectations). She also lowered the ratings of four other employees. The lowered rating put the employee in the bottom 10%, and he was fired. He sued Amtrak for defamation in a Minnesota federal court, which ruled in favor of the company. The Eighth Circuit affirmed. Here, the "meets expectations" ratings could not form the basis of a defamation suit. Only the two twos could be considered. Further, Amtrak had implemented a review process to make sure the ratings were consistently applied, and the general manager had reasonable cause to lower the employee's rating. Even if she was wrong in doing so, **the employee could not prove that her statements about his performance were made with "actual malice,"** the standard required to prove defamation here. *Landers v. National Railroad Passenger Corp.*, 345 F.3d 669 (8th Cir. 2003).

+ A pharmaceutical company employee alleged that she was subjected to a hostile work environment and that her performance evaluations declined as she continued to reject her supervisor's advances. She also claimed that when she told her supervisor that she intended to file a sexual harassment complaint against him, he drafted a warning letter detailing her alleged professional shortcomings and threatening probation. The letter was approved by the supervisor's superior and the human resources director and was placed in her file. She was fired when she refused to return to work following a leave she took after she was denied a promotion (allegedly because of the warning letter in her file). She sued, **asserting that the company defamed her by retaining the warning letter**. When the company sought to dismiss the lawsuit, the court denied the motion. Issues of fact required a trial. Here, even if the letter was written outside the scope of the supervisor's employment, the company ratified the alleged misconduct by retaining the letter. There was also evidence that the supervisor and his superior knew the letter contained untruths but published it anyway. *Lewis v. Forest Pharmaceuticals, Inc.*, 217 F.Supp.2d 638 (D. Md. 2002).

◆   A production associate at a North Carolina company was **fired for allegedly using a work computer to access pornographic Internet sites**. The allegation arose after a student worker saw several employees, including a "big, tall muscular woman" viewing sexual material on the Internet on a Wednesday and Thursday night shift. The associate maintained that she wasn't even at work on Thursday night and that she didn't normally work in the area where the student saw the employees using the terminal. The associate was fired after a meeting with other managers at which she was accused of the conduct. She sued for slander and tortious interference with her contractual rights, and a state court dismissed her case. The North Carolina Court of Appeals reversed, noting that the associate had raised material questions of fact over her claims. She had certain contractual rights by virtue of her 11-year tenure with the company and its "open door" policy, and there were questions about whether the company had met its duty to conduct a fair and thorough investigation. *Barker v. Kimberly-Clark Corp.*, 524 S.E.2d 821 (N.C. Ct. App. 2000).

◆   The union steward of a telephone crew at an Oregon telecommunications facility suspected that his immediate supervisor abused alcohol. The steward communicated his suspicions to higher-level supervisors during a training seminar. Within a month, the company discharged the supervisor and offered him another position in California. The supervisor rejected the offer and filed a defamation complaint against the steward and his union. The union filed a third-party complaint against the employer for contribution and indemnity. The case reached the Supreme Court of Oregon, which considered arguments by the steward, union and employer that the steward's statements could not constitute defamation based on the common law rule that intra-corporate communications are shielded from liability. The court determined that **the intra-corporate non-publication rule should not apply to the steward's statements**. Allowing defamation suits to be filed in cases involving intra-corporate communications protected individual interests in personal reputation. *Wallulis v. Dymowski*, 323 Or. 337, 918 P.2d 755 (Or. 1996).

◆   A Massachusetts car rental manager experienced difficulty with her supervisor during a training conference. On the final day of the conference, she was escorted to a small room and interrogated concerning the theft of an agency automobile. She became hysterical and cried when another employee accused her of lying. The interrogator also stated that the company had strong evidence that she was involved in the theft. She sued the rental company for slander and violation of the Massachusetts Civil Rights Act. The court held that the only slanderous statement was the one in which the co-worker stated that the company had strong evidence that the manager had been involved in the theft. Also, the civil rights act did not allow employees to sue employers for the actions of other employees. The First Circuit determined that many of the other statements made by the interrogating employee were slanderous, including the accusation that the manager was a liar. **There was no requirement that the defamatory statement be communicated to a large group of people in order to create liability.** However, the district court had properly held that the civil rights act did not impose liability on the employer based upon its employee's reckless conduct. The court affirmed in part. *Lyons v. National Car Rental Systems, Inc.*, 30 F.3d 240 (1st Cir. 1994).

2. Publication to Co-Workers

Memos, computer bulletin boards and presentations are all potential pitfalls that should be carefully considered before passing on information that could lead to a defamation lawsuit. For example, telling employees that a worker was fired for theft might result in a lawsuit that, even if you win, will be expensive.

Use only facts and not conclusions when addressing sensitive topics (for example, "Joe was fired for removing company property from the premises," not, "Joe was fired for stealing"). Also, remember that you often need not say anything about a sensitive situation. The grapevine will usually take care of getting the information out.

◆   An assistant vice president at an insurance agency in New Jersey was terminated. In connection with the termination, a termination form was completed. The form said the employee was fired for falsifying financial records and intimidating subordinates to cover it up. The form was distributed to several company departments. In addition, a senior vice president told an HR employee and a higher-level official that the employee stole from the company. The employee sued, claiming defamation. The court rejected the claim because **the people who made the communications had a duty or interest in doing so**. The statements were made to people within the company who had a legitimate interest in knowing about them. *Christensen v. Weichert Insurance Agency, Inc.*, No. 4953-11T2, 2013 WL 6122593 (N.J. Super. Ct. App. Div. 11/22/13).

◆   An insurance company employee in Michigan was fired after he instructed a claims adjuster to delay payment on a claim of more than $100,000. He asserted that it was common practice to regulate payments each month and that his superiors had told him to delay the payment. He also claimed that his superiors defamed him by accusing him of a breach of ethics. When he sued, a federal court and the Sixth Circuit ruled against him. It noted that **the company had a qualified privilege to defame him by making statements to other employees who had an interest in his conduct on the job**, and their positions required them to investigate whether he ought to be fired. *Whiting v. Allstate Insurance Co.*, 433 Fed.Appx. 395 (6th Cir. 2011).

◆   A vice president at Staples, headquartered in Massachusetts, sent a mass email to 1,500 employees referencing the company's code of ethics and informing the recipients that a sales director was fired for violating its travel and expense policies. The sales director sued for defamation, but a federal court granted pretrial judgment to the company, noting that everything in the email was substantially true. The First Circuit reversed. Under Massachusetts law, **the truth or falsity of the email was irrelevant if the sales director could show that the company acted with "actual malice" in sending out the email**. Here, there were questions of fact as to whether the email was sent to humiliate the sales director, particularly because the same vice president fired another employee for embezzlement and never sent out an email concerning that event or identifying that person. *Noonan v. Staples, Inc.*, 556 F.3d 20 (1st Cir. 2009).

◆   The niece of a healthcare patient in Connecticut told an employee she could have the patient's furniture after the patient died. The employee told a supervisor about the gift, and the supervisor asked for the patient's dresser, which the employee gave her. The rest of the furniture went to the facility where they worked. However, the facility prohibited accepting gifts from patients and their families, so the employee gave back the pieces she had taken. After an investigation, the facility fired her for theft, even though it knew she had the niece's permission to take the furniture. She sued for wrongful discharge and defamation. The wrongful discharge claim was dismissed, but she prevailed on the defamation claim, winning an award of $224,000. The Connecticut Supreme Court upheld the award, noting that **the company acted with malice because it knew she didn't steal when it fired her and broadcast that information to people within the company**, who then spread rumors about her. *Gambardella v. Apple Health Care, Inc.*, 969 A.2d 736 (Conn. 2009).

◆   A financial company in Illinois fired an in-house attorney for improper conduct after the attorney's supervisor wrote a memo to his superior claiming that the attorney had used profanity during his performance evaluation. The superior also sent a memo to a vice president, who initiated the termination process. The attorney then sued the company for defamation, asserting that he never used profanity, that the memos were unprivileged communications to third parties (the superior and the vice president), and that he was fired as a result. A jury ruled in favor of the attorney, and the company appealed. The Appellate Court of Illinois upheld the verdict. The internal memos constituted publication of the defamatory statement, and the jury properly determined that **publication was not privileged**. *Popko v. Continental Casualty Co. and CNA Financial Corp.*, 823 N.E.2d 184 (Ill. App. Ct. 2005).

◆   A supervisor at a company was accused of sexual harassment by a subordinate, who quit and filed a charge with the Ohio Civil Rights Commission (OCRC). The company conducted an investigation, then stated to the OCRC that there was no evidence of a hostile environment. When the former subordinate sued, the company conducted another more detailed investigation, after which it believed there were some grounds for the charge of harassment. It settled the lawsuit and fired the supervisor, then conducted a series of meetings with employees to explain that it fired the supervisor for sexual harassment. He sued the company for defamation, and a jury returned a verdict in his favor for $100,000 in compensatory damages and $500,000 in punitive damages. The Ohio Court of Appeals affirmed, noting that the jury could conclude that the company defamed the supervisor with actual malice. After stating to the OCRC that no evidence of harassment existed, the company conducted a series of meetings at which it named the supervisor and asserted that he committed sexual harassment. *Blatnik v. Avery Dennison Corp.*, 774 N.E.2d 282 (Ohio Ct. App. 2002).

◆   A female pilot brought a sexual harassment lawsuit against an airline, and a federal jury awarded her $875,000. Before the trial, however, the pilot also filed a lawsuit against the airline and seven individual male pilots for retaliatory harassment, infliction of emotional distress and defamation as a result of derogatory comments about her and the sexual harassment lawsuit on the employees' computer bulletin board. Users could only access the bulletin board through the airline's electronic crew management system, which provided pilots and flight attendants with information on schedules, pay and flight pairings. However, management employees were not allowed to use the bulletin board; no airline department was responsible for monitoring its content, and all computer operations were outsourced to another company. The court dismissed the defamation action, and the appellate division affirmed. On further appeal, the New Jersey Supreme Court reversed. It noted that the male pilots could be sued for defamation in New Jersey if they knew their defamatory messages would be published in the state. Also, if the airline had knowledge that the male pilots were engaging in retaliatory harassment, then it had a duty to remedy that harassment. The court remanded the case for further proceedings. *Blakey v. Continental Airlines*, 751 A.2d 538 (N.J. 2000).

◆   A Nevada employee sued her former employer and two supervisors for defamation. A federal court ruled against the employee, finding that she had failed to establish that defamatory information had been conveyed to individuals outside the company, which was a necessary part of a defamation claim under existing Nevada law. The former employee appealed to the U.S. Court of Appeals, Ninth Circuit, which affirmed. The sharing of allegedly defamatory information with a co-worker did not satisfy the publication requirement of Nevada defamation law. *Crowe v. Wiltel Communications Systems*, 103 F.3d 897 (9th Cir. 1996).

◆   Several days after the Ninth Circuit's decision in *Crowe*, above, the Supreme Court of Nevada announced a new standard for employment defamation cases in a case involving an employee who was fired for sexually harassing a female co-worker. The employee sued for wrongful discharge and defamation, among other claims. The supreme court disregarded the notion that intra-corporate communications could never form the basis for a defamation claim. **Intra-corporate communication would only be a defense under which the employer bore the burden of showing that a communication was privileged.** *Simpson v. Mars Inc.*, 929 P.2d 966 (Nev. 1997).

◆   A Tennessee automotive parts worker supported the unionization of the plant where he worked. Management employees learned that defective parts were being produced at the plant, and the pro-union employee was fired for sabotaging the production line. In an alleged attempt to limit further sabotage, the plant manager circulated a memo to employees that criticized the union for its unfair tactics and for exploiting the pro-union employee's firing. The discharged employee sued the company for defamation. The court ruled for the employer, and the Sixth Circuit affirmed. The discharged employee failed to show that the memo had been published with actual malice – a standard that required the complaining party to show that the defamatory communication was made with reckless disregard for its truth or falsity. Because there was evidence that the manager believed that the employee had engaged in sabotage, the district court had properly ruled for the company. *Holbrook v. Harman Automotive, Inc.*, 58 F.3d 222 (6th Cir. 1995).

◆   An Indiana employer fired six employees for dishonesty after an investigation of theft. Because rumors about other terminations persisted after the firings, the company made a slide presentation at a staff meeting that included the names of the discharged employees and the reasons for dismissal. The slide presentation also reaffirmed "core values" of the company, including trust and honesty. Five terminated employees sued for defamation. The case reached the Supreme Court of Indiana, which held that **intracompany communications concerning employee performance were protected by a qualified privilege**. In order to invoke the privilege, the communication must be made in good faith, limited in scope to its purpose, and published to appropriate parties only. A communication motivated by ill will that is excessively published, or published with disregard for the truth, is not privileged. Here, although the statements were made to a large group of employees and were later posted in a place where non-employees could read them, the company had not excessively published the information. The communication was made to quash rumors within the company and to reaffirm core values. *Schrader v. Eli Lilly and Co.*, 639 N.E.2d 258 (Ind. 1994).

B. Prospective Employers

Talking with prospective employers is a recognized exception under the laws of defamation. However, it still pays to be careful about what you say. Don't make conclusory statements like: "Sally was fired for harassing her assistant." Instead, use more neutral language: "Sally was discharged for touching her assistant inappropriately and for making statements he found offensive."

◆   A New Jersey medical center gave a negative reference to a fired employee's prospective employer. The reference mentioned why he was fired and some of his performance deficiencies, and it also stated that he wasn't eligible for rehire. The employee sued for defamation, but he lost. An appellate court noted that the employee had signed an authorization that released the medical center from liability for individuals who provided information in good faith about his competence and qualifications. Further, **the reference was taken from factual information found in his personnel file**. As a result, the employee couldn't show that the medical center acted with ill will or reckless disregard for the truth. Finally, state law required the medical center to provide information to other healthcare entities about a former or current employee's suitability for work. *Senisch v. Carlino*, 32 A.3d 217 (N.J. Super. Ct. App. Div. 2011).

◆   A Rhode Island nurse at a rehabilitation center was suspended for three days because her director believed she failed to dispense necessary medication to patients. She disputed the allegation and resigned to avoid working under that shadow. Two years later, she contacted a placement agency, which asked the center for a reference. The director **wrote that she would not rehire the nurse because of "unacceptable work practice habits."** After she discovered the contents of the reference, the nurse sued the director for defamation. The case reached the Rhode Island Supreme Court, which ruled for the director. Here, the statement wasn't defamatory, and even if it was, the director had a qualified privilege because she acted in good faith. *Kevorkian v. Glass*, 913 A.2d 1043 (R.I. 2007).

♦   A former National Security Agency employee took a job as CEO of a technology services company in Virginia, then learned that the company's financial situation was significantly worse than he had been led to believe. The company had lost nearly $3 million before his hiring, partly due to accounting problems and inventory discrepancies. Shortly after discovering the losses, he was fired. He applied for a job with another company, but **the chairman of his old company told hiring officials that the employee had mismanaged the company, losing $3 million**. When the employee failed to get the job, he sued for defamation. A jury awarded him $5 million in compensatory damages and $1 million in punitive damages. The Supreme Court of Virginia upheld the award, finding sufficient evidence that the chairman made the false statement with the intent to defame. Also, the statement was not protected as opinion. *Government Micro Resources, Inc. v. Jackson*, 624 S.E.2d 63 (Va. 2006).

♦   A nurse was diagnosed with panic disorder and agoraphobia, which caused her to fear leaving her home and traveling. Although medication would treat her condition, she refused to take it out of a fear of addiction. Her accommodation requests were ignored, and she filed a disability discrimination claim. Her employer then fired her for "disobeying a direct order and abandoning a vulnerable client," even though her supervisor later testified that she was merely asked if she "would be around for a while" before she left. It informed her that the matter would be reported to the state board of nursing, but it never reported the incident. The nurse felt compelled to disclose the reason for her termination. She sued the employer for discrimination and defamation and was awarded $23,000. The Minnesota Court of Appeals upheld the award, noting that the nurse qualified as disabled under state and federal law and that she was **compelled to self-publish the employer's defamatory statements** because she believed potential employers knew or could find out the reasons for her firing. *Kuechle v. Life's Companion P.C.A. Inc.*, 653 N.W.2d 214 (Minn. Ct. App. 2002).

♦   A stock room clerk with limited English language skills worked for a New York employer. He was administered a polygraph test to determine if he was stealing from the company. The test did not reveal that the employee was lying, but he resigned and went to work for a Maryland bank as a teller trainee. The bank then **solicited a reference** from the New York employer, which responded that the employee had been discharged for pilferage. The company later corrected itself, stating that the bad reference was due to human error. The bank nevertheless fired the employee, and he sued the New York employer for defamation. A court awarded him $100,000 in damages, including $75,000 in punitive damages. A state court of special appeals reversed the punitive damage award, and a new trial resulted in an award of $700,000 for the former employee. The Court of Appeals of Maryland reversed and remanded the case for a new trial. An employer can be forced to pay **punitive damages** in a defamation case only when the complaining employee establishes that it had actual knowledge that a defamatory statement was false. *Le Marc's Management Corp. v. Valentin*, 349 Md. 645, 709 A.2d 1222 (Md. 1998).

C. Third Parties

There are some limited privileges available for making statements about employees to third parties. For example, statements made in judicial proceedings cannot be used in defamation lawsuits. However, unless necessary, negative statements about employees should *never* be made to third parties.

◆   An employee of a Nevada company sued for wrongful discharge following his termination. While the case was going on, the employer's CEO responded to an online article about the case by emailing the newspaper to say the employee's claims were "delusional" and that the employee used "outright lies and fabrications" to excuse his termination. The employee then added a defamation claim to the suit. The state's highest court reversed a decision that the CEO had an absolute privilege to make the statements. It said **the CEO may have had a conditional right to reply** to the initial online article. *Jacobs v. Adelson*, 325 P.3d 1282 (Nev. 2014).

◆   A sales representative in Indiana was discharge because he did not produce documentation showing he was authorized to work in the United States. He told the employer he had a Social Security card but could not find it. Pursuant to its policy, the employer informed the state's insurance department in writing that the employee was terminated because he failed to provide employment eligibility verification documents. The employee sued the employer, accusing it of defaming him by sending the notice to the insurance department. He said that since state law required such reporting only in cases involving specific crimes and misdeeds, the employer's report implied that his discharge resulted from one of them. A trial court rejected the claim, and the Seventh Circuit affirmed. **Nothing in the employer's report was false**, and the employer was simply following policy when it submitted the report. Also, though state law did not require the report, it did not forbid it. *Martino v. Western & Southern Financial Group*, 715 F.3d 195 (7th Cir. 2013).

◆   A retail employee in Missouri entered information on a sabotaged register, which generated a receipt with a racial slur appearing next to the phone number. The employee didn't catch the slur when she handed the receipt to the customer. When the customer returned to the store to complain about the slur the next day, the store fired the employee and issued a statement saying that it was "shocked and sickened" that an employee could do something "so out of keeping with [its] values." The media reported the incident and quoted the statement. A week later, **the store learned that the slur had been put into the database by a different fired employee**. The employee then sued for defamation. A federal court granted pretrial judgment to the store, but the Eighth Circuit reversed, finding issues of fact that required a trial. The case was allowed to proceed. *Cockram v. Genesco, Inc.*, 680 F.3d 1046 (8th Cir. 2012).

◆   After the IRS notified a California company that 231 of its employees were using invalid Social Security numbers, the company required the employees with the invalid numbers to either provide valid ones or be fired. One employee showed that the supposedly invalid number was an error, but the other employees were all fired after being unable to prove they were authorized to work in the United States. A number of them, along with a community activist, protested outside the company's plants and a customer's place of business, claiming that the firings were discriminatory. The company sued the protestors for defamation and interference with contractual relations. The protestors sought to strike the lawsuit as a "strategic lawsuit against public participation" but, except for an unfair competition claim, a court allowed the lawsuit to continue. The Court of Appeal affirmed that ruling, noting that **the company had made a *prima facie* showing that the protestors made provably false statements that they knew were false** and that they interfered with the company's contractual relations with its customer. *Overhill Farms, Inc. v. Lopez*, 119 Cal.Rptr.3d 127 (Cal. Ct. App. 2010).

◆   After an Illinois account executive was fired, he sued his former employer for defamation, alleging that one of his supervisors contacted one of his clients to inform the client that the executive had threatened two superiors. He asserted that he never threatened them. He also claimed that an HR representative told his wife, his sister and a friend that he had threatened his superiors, and finally that the company contacted the police to inform them of the threats and have them attend his grandfather's funeral. The former employer sought to dismiss the case. An Illinois federal court refused to do so. It noted that the account executive's claims were not barred by the workers' compensation act, which provides the exclusive remedy for accidental injuries in the workplace. **He put forth a valid claim for defamation and intentional infliction of emotional distress** that could not be dismissed at this stage. *Graves v. Man Group USA, Inc.*, 479 F.Supp.2d 850 (N.D. Ill. 2007).

◆   Officials of an insurance company fired a Texas branch manager after an agent at the branch fraudulently altered the policy value of a life insurance application. The agent claimed that the branch manager was aware of this and other fraudulent practices that were common at the branch. Because the manager was a registered agent of the **National Association of Securities Dealers** (NASD), the company filed a required NASD Form U-5, which explained the cause of employment termination as failure to follow company rules and procedures. The insurer filed an amended Form U-5 stating that the branch manager had been the subject of a customer complaint for condoning forgery. It later amended the forms twice to reflect a settlement with two other customers and the filing of another lawsuit arising from the same agent's fraudulent behavior. The branch manager sued the insurer for defamation, alleging that company officials had made statements referring to him that were later republished by videotape. He obtained an award of $1.3 million in compensatory damages and $5 million in punitive damages. The insurer appealed to the Seventh Circuit, which held that **an employer enjoys a qualified privilege to tell the NASD its reasons for terminating an agent**. The district court had failed to inform the jury how to define reckless disregard for the manager's rights. Jury instructions concerning NASD rules were also improper, resulting in prejudice to the insurer. The judgment was vacated. *Dawson v. New York Life Insurance Co.*, 135 F.3d 1158 (7th Cir. 1998).

◆   A Pennsylvania laborer filed a complaint with a local human rights commission, alleging that co-workers used racial slurs against him. The following day, he was fired for tardiness, absenteeism and drug use. The state Department of Labor and Industry found that he had been fired for filing the human rights complaint and awarded him benefits. During unemployment compensation proceedings, the employer sent the department a copy of two documents detailing its reasons for the termination. The employee claimed the documents falsely stated that he sold and used illegal drugs, was on parole and was repeatedly late or absent from work without excuse. He sued for defamation, but the court dismissed the case, holding that the documentary evidence submitted for unemployment compensation purposes was absolutely privileged. An appeals court affirmed, holding that **all communications made in the course of a judicial proceeding are accorded an absolute privilege** for which there can be no civil liability. *Milliner v. Enck*, 709 A.2d 417 (Pa. Super. Ct. 1998).

III. AUTOMOBILE INCIDENTS

Generally, when an employee is involved in an automobile accident, an employer will be held vicariously liable only if the employee was acting in furtherance of the employer's business or if the employee's actions were authorized by the employer.

A. Intoxicated Employees

Obviously, employers never want employees to drive while intoxicated, but liability can arise where employers knowingly allow employees to do so. Holiday parties and summer picnics are potential problems if employees are expected to attend and the employer serves alcohol.

Problems may also arise where supervisors and their employees go out for a few drinks after work, though employers are unlikely to be held liable in such situations.

◆   An Indiana employee consumed alcohol at a business meeting with his supervisor and a client. He left the meeting to drive home, and he struck and killed another driver. **After the accident, he registered .12 on an alcohol**

breath test machine. The dead driver's estate sued the employee's employer for wrongful death and negligence. The court rejected the claim because at the time of the accident, he was not "engaged in a task incidental to his everyday employment." *Dodson v. Carlson*, 1 N.E.3d 781 (Ind. Ct. App. 2014).

◆   A hotel bartender in California attended his employer's holiday party. He consumed alcohol before and during the party. About 20 minutes after he arrived at home after leaving the party, he decided to drive a drunk co-worker home. While doing so, he struck another vehicle and killed its driver. **After the accident, he had a .16 blood alcohol level.** The deceased driver's parents sued the bartender, his employer and others for wrongful death. A trial court ruled against them, but a state appeals court reversed. A factual issue existed as to whether the employee became intoxicated at the party. If he did, a factual issue existed as to whether he was acting within the scope of his employment when he did so. If he was, the employer could be liable. *Purton v. Marriott Int'l. Inc.*, 218 Cal.App. 4th 499 (Cal. Ct. App. 2013).

◆   Near the end of a workday, a chef for a rehab facility in Massachusetts met his supervisor at a restaurant to discuss work issues. While there, he ordered two drinks. On his way home, he struck a pedestrian, who suffered severe injuries and sued the facility for vicarious liability. The case reached the Supreme Judicial Court of Massachusetts, which ruled in favor of the facility, finding that the chef was not acting within the scope of his employment at the time he struck the pedestrian. The chef paid for his own drinks, and there was no special relationship between the chef and the facility such that a duty of care arose to protect the pedestrian. **The facility's alcohol and substance-abuse policy was not designed to protect the public at large** but rather residents, visitors and co-workers. Thus, the facility was not liable for the pedestrian's injuries. *Lev v. Beverly Enterprises-Massachusetts, Inc.*, 929 N.E.2d 303 (Mass. 2010).

◆   A railroad company employee in New Mexico who had a history of alcohol problems left a job site near Los Lunas on a Friday afternoon. He was expected at a job site near Grants the following morning. He left for Grants, but then headed to Gallup, where he had family and where he became intoxicated. Later that night, he headed back toward Grant and struck another vehicle, killing both himself and the other driver. The other driver's family sued his employer, asserting that it was negligent and that the employee was acting in the scope and course of his employment at the time of the crash. The Court of Appeals of New Mexico disagreed. **The employee was not acting in the scope and course of his employment, and the company could not be held vicariously liable for the death.** The job did not require him to drive or place him at the scene of the accident, and there was no indication the employee had been drinking on the job. *Ovecka v. Burlington Northern Santa Fe Railway Co.*, 194 P.3d 728 (N.M. Ct. App. 2008).

◆   While driving home from her shift, a New York pub employee struck a construction employee working on an interstate highway. He sued the pub to recover for his injuries, and a court granted pretrial judgment to the pub. He appealed, claiming that the employee was acting in the scope of her employment at the time of the accident because the pub encouraged its employees to drink alcohol with customers to help promote social good will and business for the bar. Thus, it was foreseeable that an employee might become impaired in her ability to operate her vehicle upon leaving the pub. An appellate court found the pub not liable. **Even if the pub encouraged its employees to drink, the employee was driving home from work** and was not acting within the scope of her employment at the time of the accident. *Cunningham v. Petrilla*, 30 A.D.3d 996, 817 N.Y.S.2d 468 (N.Y. App. Div. 2006).

✦ An employee of a tower service company in Texas got in an accident while driving one of his employer's trucks. He was intoxicated at the time. The man he hit sued the company for vicarious liability and negligently entrusting the vehicle to the employee. The company maintained that the employee did not have permission to drive the truck at the time of the accident, did not have permission to drive while intoxicated, and was not acting in the course and scope of his employment at the time of the accident. The Texas Court of Appeals held that the employee was not acting in the course and scope of his employment, so the company was not vicariously liable. **Company policy did not allow for the use of company vehicles where alcoholic beverages were consumed.** However, the negligent entrustment claim required a trial. *Green v. Ransor, Inc.*, 175 S.W.3d 513 (Tex. Ct. App. 2005).

✦ A Washington employee left a company awards banquet where she had consumed alcohol. She caused a traffic accident that injured the driver of another vehicle. A Breathalyzer test revealed a blood-alcohol level of .17, and a lawsuit resulted against the company. The employee then stated that she had attended a restaurant immediately after leaving the banquet where she had three drinks prior to the accident. The court granted pretrial judgment to the employer based on insufficient evidence that the employee had become intoxicated at the banquet. The Supreme Court of Washington reversed, noting that there was an issue of fact as to whether the employee had been observed to be intoxicated at the banquet. **An employer may be vicariously liable for an intoxicated employee's actions** where the employee attends an event at which attendance is mandatory and becomes intoxicated under circumstances where the employee has knowledge that she will operate a motor vehicle. An employer may also be liable for negligently furnishing alcohol to an employee who is obviously intoxicated. *Fairbanks v. J.B. McLoughlin Co., Inc.*, 929 P.2d 433 (Wash. 1997).

✦ An Arizona radiology technician had a history of drug abuse that was known to her employer. She arrived at work while under the influence of cocaine and ingested more cocaine during the workday. Her supervisor observed her intoxicated condition and ordered her to leave the premises prior to the end of her shift. The technician left work in her car and collided head-on with another vehicle, seriously injuring the other driver. The driver filed a negligence lawsuit against the employer. The court dismissed the lawsuit, and the Court of Appeals of Arizona affirmed. **Employers are not liable for the**

negligent acts of intoxicated employees occurring off the employer's property, even though the employer may be aware of the intoxication. The employer was not liable simply because it had ordered the technician to leave the premises. The employer had not directed her to drive a vehicle and had no duty to prevent her from doing so. *Riddle v. Arizona Oncology Services, Inc.*, 924 P.2d 468 (Ariz. Ct. App. 1996).

◆   A North Carolina publishing company held a retirement party for an editor at the home of a company officer. Employees were not required to attend the party and did not receive compensation for spending time there. An employee who attended the party had three or four drinks and left the party after almost three hours. Shortly after leaving, he became involved in an automobile accident in which the driver of another vehicle was seriously injured and later died. The estate sued the employer. A state court ruled for the employer, and the Supreme Court of North Carolina affirmed. Evidence indicated that the employee was not intoxicated upon leaving the party and that the employer lacked knowledge concerning his potentially intoxicated state. There was also insufficient evidence to establish that the employee had been acting within the scope of his employment when he caused the injury. The employer could not be held liable because the party was held at a private home, **attendance was not required, and employees were not compensated for being there**. *Camalier v. Jeffries*, 460 S.E.2d 133 (N.C. 1995).

◆   A major oil company sponsored a Christmas party for its Alaska employees. The company contracted with a hotel to provide all the services associated with the party, including alcohol service. Shortly after midnight, a few employees decided to go to a local tavern. An intoxicated employee was driven to the tavern and back home again by a concerned co-employee. After he arrived home, he left his residence and drove out of town, where he was involved in an accident. The personal representatives of the accident victims sued the oil company and the co-employee who had driven the intoxicated employee home. The court ruled for the oil company and the co-employee. The Supreme Court of Alaska affirmed. Since the oil company did not hold a liquor license, it was not liable as a social host for the injuries resulting from the employee's intoxication. The court **refused to impose a duty on the employer** not only of getting the employee safely home, but of securing the keys or setting up an all-night vigil to make sure the employee did not leave again. Also, the co-employee had conscientiously discharged his duty by driving the employee home. *Mulvihill v. Union Oil Co.*, 859 P.2d 1310 (Alaska 1993).

B. Other Accidents

Where employees are running *errands* for their employers or are combining personal and business errands, a potential for liability exists. With respect to injuries sustained by employees, workers' compensation will generally be available.

However, where third parties are injured, employers can be vicariously liable for the negligence of their employees.

◆   A Texas truck driver hit a pedestrian at a rest stop. The pedestrian sued, claiming the driver was negligent and his employer negligently hired him. The court said a jury would have to decide if the driver was negligent, especially since he admitted he did not look around before accelerating. In addition, the employer might be liable for negligent hiring because **the driver had eight accidents on his record when he applied for the job** but was not asked about his driving history. *Ramirez v. Colonial Freight Warehouse Co., Inc.*, 434 S.W.3d 244 (Tex. Ct. App. 2014).

◆   A driller for an energy company in California was given a company pickup truck that he was allowed to use for his commute. He could also make stops with the truck during his commute, as long as they were on the way. The employee went 140 miles out of his way with the truck to help his wife buy a car. On the way back, he was involved in a motor vehicle accident. People in the other vehicle sued the driller's employer for negligence, but the court rejected the claim because the driller **was acting outside the scope of his employment** when the accident happened. *Halliburton Energy Services v. Dep't of Transportation*, 162 Cal.Rptr.3d 752 (Cal. Ct. App. 2013).

◆   An employee traveled to Yuma, Arizona, so that he could commute daily to Mexico to work on a natural gas compressor. His employer paid for his rental car, his hotel room and his meals, as well as for his travel time because he had to cross an international border every day and there were often delays. One day after work, on his way back to the hotel after going out to dinner, he made an improper left turn and hit a motorcyclist, who sued the company for his injuries. The Arizona Supreme Court upheld rulings for the company. **The employee was not subject to the company's control at the time of the accident.** He could eat wherever and whenever he wanted after his workday ended. *Engler v. Gulf Interstate Engineering, Inc.*, 280 P.3d 599 (Ariz. 2012).

◆   A Maryland longshoreman decided to work on Martin Luther King Day so he could get extra pay. He reported to work at 8 a.m. and checked out the next morning at 6 a.m. While driving home after his 22-hour shift, he fell asleep at the wheel, crossed the center line and crashed head-on into a police officer who was driving to work. He died in the accident, and the officer suffered catastrophic injuries. The officer sued the company, but the Maryland Court of Appeals ruled against him because **the company had no influence over how the longshoreman operated his car**. It had no duty to the general public to ensure that the longshoreman didn't work excessive hours or drive home while fatigued. *Barclay v. Briscoe*, 47 A.3d 560 (Md. Ct. App. 2012).

◆   An employee of a framing subcontractor ran over an employee of a concrete subcontractor while moving his truck at a construction site. The injured employee sued the framing subcontractor for vicarious liability. A trial court granted pretrial judgment to the framing subcontractor, finding that its employee wasn't acting in the course and scope of his employment while moving his truck; therefore, the framing subcontractor couldn't be vicariously liable. However, the California Court of Appeal reversed. **A jury could find**

that the employee was furthering the framing subcontractor's interest while moving his truck. If the employee was performing actions necessary for his "comfort, convenience, health or welfare" on the job, then he would be acting within the scope of his employment. A trial was required. *Vogt v. Herron Construction, Inc.*, 200 Cal.App.4th 643 (Cal. Ct. App. 2011).

♦   While on her way home after delivering papers, a newspaper delivery driver in Arizona collided with a bicyclist, who died from injuries sustained in the accident. The bicyclist's widow sued the newspaper, claiming that it was vicariously liable for the delivery driver's negligence. A trial court ruled for the newspaper, and the Arizona Court of Appeals affirmed. **The delivery driver was not acting in the scope of her employment at the time of the accident**, so the newspaper couldn't be vicariously liable for her negligence. Further, the court refused to apply the "employee's own conveyance rule" – a workers' compensation rule – to this tort action. So even though the employee would have been covered by the rule under workers' compensation had she suffered an injury, the widow couldn't use the rule to recover in a vicarious liability action against the employer for negligence. *Carnes v. Phoenix Newspapers, Inc.*, 251 P.3d 411 (Ariz. Ct. App. 2011).

♦   While driving home from work, a project superintendent for a commercial construction company in Ohio failed to stop at a red light and rear-ended the vehicle in front of him. The injured occupants of that vehicle sued him and his employer for negligence. The company sought pretrial judgment, asserting that the superintendent was a fixed-situs employee not acting within the scope of his employment at the time of the accident, which meant that it could not be liable for his negligence. A trial court and the Court of Appeals of Ohio agreed. The superintendent performed no duties or actions on behalf of the company after leaving the job site and did not have an after-hours, on-call requirement of any kind. **He was simply driving home. As a result, the company could not be liable for his negligence.** *Davis v. Galla*, No. L-08-1149, 2009 WL 580459 (Ohio Ct. App. 3/6/09).

♦   On the way home after a 12-hour shift, a Texas oil-drilling company employee collided with another vehicle, killing four people. The families of the victims sued the company, alleging that it had a duty to prevent fatigued employees from driving home and endangering others. The case reached the Texas Supreme Court, which held that the company had no such duty. There are no quantitative ways to determine whether a particular employee is incapacitated by fatigue. Further, **there was no evidence that the company knew the employee was too tired to drive**. And even if it had known, it could only have a duty to protect others if it exercised some control over his decision to drive home or required him to drive home. *Nabors Drilling, U.S.A., Inc. v. Escoto*, 288 S.W.3d 401 (Tex. 2009).

IV. DANGEROUS CONDITIONS

Liability for dangerous workplace conditions and equipment often involves consideration of whether an employer-employee relationship exists between the parties, and may depend upon an employer's ownership of equipment or property. Independent contractors have greater rights to sue for injuries suffered on the job.

Where an employer fails to provide a safe working environment, liability may also depend on state and federal labor laws, such as the Occupational Safety and Health Act (discussed in Chapter Five, Section IV), which requires employers to provide a safe working environment.

Employer liability is generally foreclosed by the exclusive remedy doctrine of workers' compensation laws. See Chapter Seven, Section I. However, liability can arise for intentional injuries to workers. Moreover, if the employer is also a landlord, or a seller of products or services, liability can arise outside of the employer-employee relationship.

A. Dangerous Premises

Where dangerous conditions exist in the workplace, employers can be liable outside of workers' compensation in limited circumstances – for example, where the employer knows that injury is substantially certain to arise as a result of those dangerous conditions.

An exception in workers' compensation law allows workers to sue their employers for intentionally causing injuries. Dangerous conditions (like defective machinery or hazardous chemicals) can be deemed to be intentionally injurious so as to allow for tort liability.

◆   A company in Ohio fired an employee for having a .22 caliber pistol under the front seat of his car. The company had a policy prohibiting employees from using or possessing a firearm on its property – including company parking lots – while conducting official company business. He sued, claiming the company violated his constitutional right to carry a gun. The case reached the Sixth Circuit, which noted that **Ohio had limited the right to bear arms by allowing employers to ban guns on their private property**. *Plona v. UPS*, 558 F.3d 478 (6th Cir. 2009).

◆   A group of business owners in Oklahoma brought a lawsuit arguing that the state's "weapons in the workplace" law violated the Occupational Safety and Health (OSH) Act. The law penalized employers for taking action against employees who kept firearms in locked cars on company property. The case reached the Tenth Circuit, which held that the law did not violate the OSH Act. OSHA has no specific standards on workplace violence, and **it specifically declined to set a standard banning firearms from the workplace**. The court upheld the "weapons in the workplace" law. *Ramsey Winch, Inc. v. Henry*, 555 F.3d 1199 (10th Cir. 2009).

◆   A Missouri hotel employee, being driven to work, was struck by a valet driver coming out of the hotel driveway, which did not have a stop sign. The employee sued the valet and the hotel for his injuries, claiming premises liability based on the lack of a stop sign. A trial court dismissed the lawsuit because of the question of workers' compensation, but the Supreme Court of Missouri reversed. Here, **the employee was not covered by workers' compensation because he was not yet on the job.** He was on a public street outside the hotel when the valet hit him, not on hotel property or its extended premises. Going to or returning from work is a personal act, so the employee could not be said to have been acting in the course of his employment at the time of the accident. The employee's lawsuit was reinstated. *Harris v. Westin Management Co. East*, 230 S.W.3d 1 (Mo. 2007).

◆   A North Carolina deli and bakery manager **tripped on an extension cord that was stretched across a hallway**. She fell, sustaining injuries to her knee, shoulder and back. When she sought a 10% increase in workers' compensation benefits due to the employer's willful failure to comply with a statutory requirement, the employer claimed that no statute specifically disallowed the stretching of an extension cord across a hallway so as to allow for the 10% increase. The Workers' Compensation Commission awarded the 10% increase, and the North Carolina Court of Appeals upheld that ruling. A federal OSHA regulation prohibited obstructions in aisles that could create a hazard, and an OSHA regulation was considered a statutory requirement. *Brown v. Kroger Co.*, 610 S.E.2d 447 (N.C. Ct. App. 2005).

◆   When a New York City modeling agency hired a sales director with asthma, it allegedly promised to do something about secondhand smoke in the office. The director complained that the smoke caused shortness of breath, sinusitis and nausea. The agency allegedly ignored her complaints and fired her only six weeks into the job for incompetence. She sued the agency for violating the city's Smoke-Free Air Act. The agency sought to exclude her expert witness testimony that she was **harmed by secondhand smoke after only six weeks**. A state trial court refused to prohibit the testimony, noting that there was sufficient scientific support for the expert's theory and that whether the length of time of exposure was enough to cause injury was for the jury to decide. *Gallegos v. Elite Model Management Corp.*, 758 N.Y.S.2d 777 (N.Y. Sup. Ct. 2003).

◆   A Texas manufacturing plant used machines that leaked coolant onto the floor. To lessen the risk of employee injury, the employer instructed machine operators to stand on wooden pallets while working and to occasionally take time to clean off dripping coolant with rags. An absorbent material was also made available for employees to throw on the floor to absorb excess coolant. A machine operator fell or slipped between the wooden pallets near her machine and injured her back. She required surgery and sued the employer for negligence. The employer did not subscribe to the state workers' compensation system and was prohibited from asserting the common law defenses of contributory negligence, assumption of the risk, and fellow servant negligence. After a trial, the court awarded the employee more than $291,000. The employer appealed to the Court of Appeals of Texas. On appeal, the employer argued that it could not be held liable for the employee's injuries where it had provided at least one safe way for her to perform her assigned tasks. It also alleged that the injuries were not foreseeable. The court held that there was sufficient evidence that an employee could be injured even by following the employer's prescribed safety methods. The employer had established an hourly quota of pieces and did not hold routine safety meetings or give specific safety instructions to employees. **An employer has a non-delegable duty to provide safety rules and instructions to its employees**, and the employer failed to show that it had met this duty. It also failed to show that the injury was unforeseeable. Judgment affirmed. *Woodlawn Manufacturing, Inc. v. Robinson*, 937 S.W.2d 544 (Tex. Ct. App. 1996).

♦   An Alabama hospital employee was robbed and shot in her employer's parking lot after leaving work. A co-worker observed the armed assailant after the shooting. The injured employee filed a claim for workers' compensation benefits and received disability and medical payments. She joined the co-worker in a lawsuit against the employer in which they asserted that the employer had negligently failed to provide them with security. A jury found in favor of the employees. The employer appealed to the Supreme Court of Alabama, which held that the injured employee's negligence claim was barred by the exclusivity provision of the state workers' compensation act. The claims based on failure to provide adequate security required proof that injury was foreseeable. The only basis for this finding would be evidence of similar criminal acts in the area that placed the employer on notice of a potential danger to employees. While there were 57 reports of crime in the area during the previous five years, 48 of these involved motor vehicle thefts and none involved an armed assault. This was **insufficient to place the employer on notice of a danger of criminal activity**. Therefore, the injuries had been unforeseeable. The court reversed and remanded the case. *Baptist Memorial Hospital v. Gosa*, 686 So.2d 1147 (Ala. 1996).

♦   An Idaho employee who was exposed to dangerous chemicals on the job experienced six miscarriages in a five-year period. When she became pregnant a seventh time, she requested her employer's permission to change work locations and later delivered a child without complications. She sued the employer for wrongful death, failure to warn her of dangerous working conditions and battery. A court granted the employer's motion to dismiss the lawsuit, and the U.S. Court of Appeals, Ninth Circuit, affirmed. It observed that **Idaho does not recognize a cause of action for wrongful death involving a nonviable fetus** and that none of the fetuses had been viable at the time of death. *Santana v. Zilog, Inc.*, 95 F.3d 780 (9th Cir. 1996).

B. Defective Equipment

If an employer knows that equipment is defective and likely to cause injury, it can be held liable for the harm that results despite workers' compensation. Courts may treat such conditions as an exception to the exclusivity rule of workers' compensation and allow employees to sue for additional money.

◆   An employee in Kentucky was working as a laser cutter operator for a company that contracted with the temporary staffing agency that employed him. He was caught in the laser cutter machine and suffered significant injuries to his ribs, chest, lungs, liver, and head. The temp agency paid his workers' compensation benefits, but he sought enhanced benefits, alleging that the client company intentionally disabled the automatic shut-off function of the machine. An administrative law judge awarded enhanced benefits, but the Kentucky Court of Appeals reversed, finding that even though the client company intentionally violated its duty to provide a safe workplace by disabling the automatic shut-off on the laser cutting machine, **there was no evidence that the temp agency participated in disabling the shut-off switch or knew that the switch had been disabled**. The temp agency did not have a duty to become familiar with all the equipment in all the facilities where it placed employees. *Jones v. Aerotek Staffing*, 303 S.W.3d 488 (Ky. Ct. App. 2010).

◆   An Ohio refinery employee noticed a fire while driving behind a plant and informed the dispatcher of the blaze. She then stopped her truck to help another employee attach a hose to a hydrant, rather than return to the shipping department as required by company policy. **She was not wearing protective equipment, which was also a company requirement.** A secondary explosion occurred and she suffered second- and third-degree burns, making her unable to work. She sued the refinery for her injuries, asserting that she was not bound by the exclusivity of workers' compensation, but a federal court and the Sixth Circuit ruled against her. The employee failed to show that she was required to engage in the activity that ultimately injured her without the proper equipment. Rather, she voluntarily placed herself in harm's way. *Harris v. Sunoco, Inc.*, 137 Fed.Appx. 785 (6th Cir. 2005).

◆   A Kentucky employee sustained a closed head injury and died as a result of a 30-foot fall off a roof where he was working. His estate asserted that it was entitled to a 30% increase in death benefits because of safety violations. Specifically, **the employer did not provide fall protection gear** or fall protection training. The Workers' Compensation Board determined that the estate was entitled to the 30% increase, and the employer appealed. The court of appeals and the Supreme Court of Kentucky affirmed the ruling in favor of the estate. Because the death resulted from the employer's intentional safety violation, the estate was entitled to the increase. *Realty Improvement Co., Inc. v. Raley*, 194 S.W.3d 818 (Ky. 2006).

◆   After a machine operator was severely burned while steam-cleaning a machine, he sued the company, claiming that his injuries were a direct result of the company's "intentionally tortious conduct" because the equipment had failed in the past and the company knew that someone was substantially certain to be injured if working on it. The trial court dismissed the case because he failed to show intentional wrongdoing under the Ohio "employment intentional tort" statute, but the court of appeals found the statute unconstitutional and reversed. The Ohio Supreme Court affirmed, holding that the legislature had no power to eliminate **the common law right to sue an employer for intentional**

misconduct. The statute held employers liable only for any act that deliberately and intentionally injured, caused an occupational disease in, or caused the death of an employee. The statute also required clear and convincing proof that the employer had committed the intentional tort. By establishing these standards, the court said, the legislature created requirements so unreasonable and excessive that the chance of recovery of damages was virtually zero. *Johnson v. BP Chemicals*, 707 N.E.2d 1107 (Ohio 1999).

♦   A temporary laborer operated a winch while working for a North Carolina subcontractor on a sewer line project. He attempted to manually adjust the cable as it was reeled into the winch and suffered severe injuries when his glove caught on the cable and he was pulled into the winch. He filed a personal injury lawsuit against the temporary service, subcontractor, general contractor and other entities, asserting that they had intentionally engaged in misconduct that was substantially certain to cause serious injury or death, thereby avoiding the exclusivity provision of the state workers' compensation act. The court ruled against him, and he appealed to the Court of Appeals of North Carolina, arguing that the equipment lacked safety guards in violation of state and federal safety regulations, creating a substantial certainty of serious injury or death. The court found that many of the regulations cited by the employee did not apply to winch operation and that **violation of the regulations alone would not entitle him to a finding of employer knowledge of substantial certainty to cause serious injury or death**. He could have unplugged the winch before touching the cable but decided not to take this precaution. The employer had used winches for over 25,000 employee days without any injuries or safety violations prior to the employee's injury. The court affirmed the ruling against him. *Tinch v. Video Industrial Services, Inc.*, 497 S.E.2d 295 (N.C. Ct. App. 1998).

♦   A Missouri worker was killed while operating a machine at a wire rope factory. The worker's survivors sued employees of the company, including its vice president, managers, foremen and engineers. The survivors claimed that the employees had failed to respond to requests for safety systems and switches on the machine. A court dismissed the lawsuit against the employees, and the Missouri Court of Appeals affirmed. An employer has a duty to provide a safe work environment, and the state workers' compensation act gives employers immunity from common law liability for breaches of the duty. Employer immunity under the workers' compensation act extended to employees carrying out company duties, and **a co-worker's failure to perform a delegated duty does not create liability** unless the co-worker took some affirmative action that increased the risk of injury. That was not the case here, so the employees were immune. *Felling v. Ritter*, 876 S.W.2d 2 (Mo. Ct. App. 1994).

♦   An employee of a Michigan manufacturing company witnessed the death of a co-worker from a few feet away. The co-worker was struck by a metal bar from a defective machine. The employee alleged that he was struck by the victim's flesh and a piece of metal. However, he did not allege that he had been cut or bruised. Even though the employee was unrelated to the victim and not a close friend, he alleged that the incident caused him emotional distress with physical injuries, including aggravation of his asthma and high blood pressure. He stated that the emotional shock of the incident caused him to suffer a stroke more than one year later. He sued the manufacturer of the machine in a Michigan federal court, which noted that the law did not provide a remedy for third-party bystanders who were not immediate family members. It granted pretrial judgment to the employer. The Sixth Circuit reversed and remanded the case. Even though **the employee was precluded from recovering as a bystander because he was not related to the co-worker**, a fact issue existed as to whether the employee's injuries were caused, at least in part, by his fear for his own safety at the time of the accident. If so, he would be entitled to a recovery. There were also fact issues as to whether the employee suffered objective physical injury as a result of that fear and as to whether the manufacturer's actions caused his injuries. *Maldonado v. National Acme Co.*, 73 F.3d 642 (6th Cir. 1995).

◆ A Wisconsin woman was injured when her hand was drawn into a box-making machine. The president and primary owner of the plant had purchased the box-making machine and leased it to the plant. The employee sued the president. A court entered pretrial judgment in favor of the president, but the Court of Appeals of Wisconsin reversed. Although the exclusive remedy provision of the Worker's Compensation Act provides that the right to the recovery of compensation shall be the exclusive remedy against the employer, under the **doctrine of dual capacity**, an employer may be liable to an employee where the employer acts as a third person rather than as an employer. Here, the president, as the owner and lessor of the machine as well as the president and owner of the corporation, constituted two separate legal persons. Personally purchasing and leasing the machine did not allow him to escape potential tort liability because he created a separate legal entity and accepted the personal advantages derived from such an arrangement. *Rauch v. Officine Curioni, S.P.A.*, 508 N.W.2d 12 (Wis. Ct. App. 1993).

C. Other Dangerous Conditions

Most often, liability in cases involving dangerous conditions arises where employers know of conditions that are *unsafe* and allow workers to continue encountering those conditions – for example, where a safety device is turned off to allow for greater productivity.

As long as the employer knows (or should know) about the dangerous condition, the potential for liability exists. Thus, you should patrol the workplace often and ensure that potentially dangerous conditions are eliminated to the greatest extent possible.

◆ A foreman for a Georgia utility company violated an OSHA regulation by digging himself into an 11-foot wall of dirt while looking for a utility cable. The Department of Labor fined the employer, but the Eleventh Circuit reversed that determination. **The supervisor's knowledge of his malfeasance could not be imputed to the employer.** *ComTran Group, Inc. v. U.S. Dep't of Labor*, 722 F.3d 1304 (11th Cir. 2013).

◆   An employee of a New Jersey paving company was injured when he was struck by a vehicle while acting as a flagger during a job. The employer did not utilize available safety measures, such as a fluorescent jacket, warning signs, cones and flags. **The employee sued the employer in tort, but a state appeals court rejected the claim.** The lack of safety precautions did not overcome the exclusive remedy provision of the state's workers' compensation law. *Fendt v. Abrahams*, 2013 WL 1405096 (N.J. Super. Ct. App. Div. 4/9/13).

◆   OSHA cited a crane company in Ohio because a company employee did not properly barricade a rotating part of a crane at a construction site. The company challenged the citation on the basis that no one was exposed to the hazard. The court rejected the company's argument. For the citation to be justified, **it was not necessary to show employees were actually exposed to the hazardous condition**; it was only necessary to show that it was reasonably predictable that employees would be within the zone of danger. *All Erection & Crane Rental Corp. v. Occupational Safety and Health Review Comm'n*, 507 Fed.Appx. 511 (6th Cir. 2012).

◆   A corporation operated a sewage treatment facility in Arizona. After one employee died and another was injured when they were overcome by toxic sewage gas in an underground tank, the state prosecuted the company for negligent homicide as well as endangerment and violating a safety regulation which caused the death of an employee. **The company was convicted and ordered to pay fines and penalties of $1.77 million.** The Arizona Court of Appeals affirmed the conviction and the fines, noting that the savings clause of the Occupational Safety and Health Act did not preclude prosecution under state law. The court rejected the company's argument that the trial court had improperly created a new criminal law by ruling that it could be prosecuted for failing to fulfill its duty to provide a safe workplace because that duty was not codified in any criminal statute. A state statute that abolished all common-law offenses did not abolish the use of common-law duties as a basis for criminal liability. *State v. Far West Water & Sewer, Inc.*, 228 P.3d 909 (Ariz. Ct. App. 2010).

◆   A paper mill in Oklahoma had a policy barring employees from possessing firearms on company property. The mill became concerned about substance abuse and called the county sheriff about using dogs to sniff for drugs/firearms. As a part of that search, guns were discovered in a number of vehicles belonging to employees and contractors. The employees and contractors were fired, and they sued, **alleging that their right to bear arms was violated by the company's policy.** The case reached the Tenth Circuit, which ruled that the company was within its rights to act as it did. Also, an amendment to state law prohibiting companies from banning guns locked in trunks had not yet taken effect at the time of the firings and so was not applicable. *Bastible v. Weyerhauser Co.*, 437 F.3d 999 (10th Cir. 2006).

◆   An employee of a Texas drive-in attempted to pick up a freezer cover from the floor. It was there because the manager was repairing the freezer. The cover was "razor sharp" and sliced open the employee's hand. She claimed that she lost the use of her hand and that after she returned to work, she was belittled and forced to try to hold a french-fry scooper in her injured hand. She sued for premises liability, assault and emotional distress. A court granted pretrial judgment to the company, but the Texas Court of Appeals reversed. **There was a question about whether the cover posed an unreasonable risk of harm.** Further, the employee did not have to show an intent to injure her to prove the assault claim. Finally, she could proceed with her emotional distress claim. A trial was required. *Hall v. Sonic Drive-In of Angleton, Inc.*, 177 S.W.3d 636 (Tex. Ct. App. 2005).

♦   An Oregon grocery store maintenance clerk, while off duty, was standing outside the front entrance talking to his roommate, who was also an off-duty store employee. The head clerk ran out of the store chasing a shoplifter who had stolen a bottle of wine. He yelled to the employees to assist him, and the clerk did so, running in the direction the head clerk indicated even though he did not see the shoplifter. He left store property and headed into a dark parking lot, where he ran off a small ledge and tore the ACL in his left knee. After the Workers' Compensation Board determined that his injuries were not compensable because they had not occurred in the course of his employment, he sued the store for negligence. A jury ruled in his favor, and the Oregon Court of Appeals upheld the verdict. **There was sufficient evidence that the injury to the maintenance clerk was reasonable and that the head clerk acted unreasonably in asking him to pursue the shoplifter.** *Najjar v. Safeway, Inc.*, 125 P.3d 807 (Or. Ct. App. 2005).

♦   A Louisiana nurse tested positive for HIV after being splashed with blood from an HIV-positive patient who was being shaved for surgery. She claimed that a co-worker and supervisor either negligently or intentionally failed to advise her of the patient's condition, causing her injury. A Louisiana trial court denied her claim under state law and the Court of Appeal of Louisiana, Third Circuit, reviewed her appeal. The court determined that genuine issues of fact existed concerning the actual notice given to the nurse by her supervisor on the **hazards presented by the patient** and the need to take adequate protective measures. The motives and intent of the supervising employee were also in dispute, making the pretrial judgment inappropriate. The case was reversed and remanded. *Juneau v. Humana, Inc.*, 657 So.2d 457 (La. Ct. App. 1995).

♦   An Ohio industrial employee's position required him to periodically test a sulfuric acid solution and to add the correct amount of concentrated sulfuric acid when necessary. After a number of years, the plant decided to install a meter in the sulfuric supply line. The plant supervisor called an equipment supplier and asked for a meter suitable for use with sulfuric acid. After he was told that no such meter existed he asked for a water meter. The supplier warned the supervisor that the meter wasn't intended for use with sulfuric acid. The supervisor installed the meter. When the employee used the sulfuric acid line, it burst – drenching him with concentrated sulfuric acid. He sued his employer for an intentional tort. The case reached the Court of Appeals of Ohio. An action brought by an employee for an intentional tort requires proof that the employer either specifically desired to injure the employee or **knew that injury to the employee was substantially certain to result** from the employer's act. Here, the employer had been warned that the meter was unsuitable for its intended use in a process that was already known to be dangerous. The employer installed the device despite this knowledge. Therefore, the employer could be treated as if it desired the harm that resulted from its conduct. The employee had alleged facts that could convince reasonable minds that the defendant knew that injury was substantially certain to occur. The case was allowed to proceed. *Howard v. Columbus Products Co.*, 611 N.E.2d 480 (Ohio Ct. App. 1992).

♦ A North Carolina construction company was hired to perform services at a manufacturing plant. It delivered a welding machine to the job site to be used by its employees. The standard practice was for the construction company to deliver the welding machine without a male-end plug. At the site, the plug was then wired and grounded by an employee of the manufacturer. The manufacturing employees used the welding machine for projects totally unrelated to the construction project. A manufacturing employee was electrocuted when he touched both the welding machine and another piece of grounded equipment. A safety compliance officer issued the construction company a citation for failure to train employees and properly inspect equipment, but the Safety Health and Review Board dismissed the citation. A court reinstated the citation, and the Court of Appeals of North Carolina affirmed. **The construction company was aware that the welding machine utilized high voltages of electricity.** It also knew that if improperly grounded, the welding machine was dangerous. The company had a non-delegable duty to inspect the grounding of its welding machine and properly train all employees. *Brooks v. BCF Piping, Inc.*, 426 S.E.2d 282 (N.C. Ct. App. 1993).

V. EMPLOYEE INJURY OF THIRD PARTY

Where an employee injures a third party, workers' compensation law does not bar recovery in a lawsuit against the employer. However, if the employee was not acting in furtherance of the employer's business, the injured party will not be able to recover from the employer on a theory of <u>vicarious liability</u> (also known as *respondeat superior*).

A. Sexual Assaults

Sexual assaults are never in the furtherance of an employer's business. However, employers can still be liable where they are negligent in investigating potential employees, especially where those employees come into regular contact with customers.

The more employees will come into contact with customers and members of the public, the more they should be investigated. For example, you wouldn't want to hire a convicted rapist to deliver furniture to customers' homes.

+ A FedEx Kinko's employee also had his own computer-repair business. He struck up a conversation with a customer, gave her his card and visited her home to repair her computer. After repeated visits over six months, during which he earned her trust, the customer left him alone with her youngest son and he raped the boy, who then sued FedEx for negligent hiring and supervision, among other claims. The employee had admitted to a conviction for statutory rape when he was 18 and his girlfriend was 17, but a background check failed to reveal that he had felony convictions for sexually abusing boys in another state. Nevertheless, FedEx was found not liable by a Connecticut federal court because **it could not have reasonably foreseen that the employee would gain access to a customer's home and sexually abuse a child while off duty**. *Doe v. Federal Express Corp.*, 571 F.Supp.2d 330 (D. Conn. 2008).

+ A steel plant foreman made numerous vulgar comments to a female security guard assigned to provide security at the plant. She complained to the plant manager at least three times. One night, while she was making her rounds, the foreman followed her into an office, then forced her into a restroom and raped her. After his arrest, the security guard sued the plant for negligence, claiming that it failed to take reasonable steps to prevent the rape. The case reached the Michigan Supreme Court, which ruled in favor of the plant. Here, **the rape was not a foreseeable result** of the foreman's comments. Further, he had no prior criminal record and had never touched her or physically threatened her. Accordingly, the plant could not be liable for negligence. *Brown v. Brown*, 478 Mich. 545, 739 N.W.2d 313 (Mich. 2007).

+ The general manager of a dry cleaning business in Colorado was accused of sexual harassment by three employees, but the owner of the business did not discipline him after he denied the accusations. Later, the manager took a friend's 12-year-old daughter to the business while it was closed and sexually assaulted her. Her family sued the owner for negligent supervision and lost when the Colorado Supreme Court determined that even though the manager had a propensity for sexual harassment, **his assault of the girl was not foreseeable**. Had the manager assaulted a customer or employee during business hours, the owner likely would have been liable. *Keller v. Koca*, 111 P.3d 445 (Colo. 2005).

+ A staffing services company in Virginia hired a man three different times between 1998 and 2001 to perform janitorial services at a university. Each time it **failed to perform a criminal background check** on him even though its contract with the university required it to conduct such checks on any employee assigned to work there. A university student claimed that the janitor assaulted her and sued the company for negligent hiring and retention. She claimed that the company would have discovered a protective order issued against the janitor for assaulting a woman in a restaurant if it had performed the criminal background check. A federal court granted pretrial judgment to the company, but the Fourth Circuit reversed, finding a triable issue of fact about whether the company would have discovered the protective order. *Blair v. Defender Services, Inc.*, 386 F.3d 623 (4th Cir. 2004).

◆   A Texas company sponsored a banquet that a non-employee attended as a guest. The next night, the non-employee attended a dinner party thrown by a regional sales manager, at which she passed out – possibly due to a date rape drug. She was sexually assaulted by the host and a company vice president. The company investigated and fired the two perpetrators. Later, she sued the company for negligence with respect to its sexual harassment policies. She also asserted that the event at which she was assaulted was sufficiently business related to impose a duty on the company to protect her from harm. A jury found that although she was raped, **the perpetrators were not acting within the scope of their employment at the time of the assault**. Thus, the company was not liable. The Texas Court of Appeals affirmed. Even though the dinner party was held the day after the company-sponsored event, the company did not have a duty to protect the non-employee. Also, the plaintiff failed to show that the company should have known of the danger the executives presented to her. Their behavior was not foreseeable. *Capece v. NaviSite Inc.*, No. 03-02-00113-CV, 2002 WL 31769032 (Tex. Ct. App. 2002).

◆   A customer of a Chicago cable company sued the company for negligent hiring after one of its installers pointed a gun at her and sexually assaulted her during a business trip to her home. Employees were required to have a valid driver's license, and the installer lied on his job application that his license was valid when, in fact, it had been suspended. The cable company did not conduct a criminal background or reference check on the installer. Had it done so, it would have learned about the suspended license and several other speeding violations. A state court ruled for the cable company. Because the customer was not able to show that the **failure to investigate the installer's background** was the proximate cause of her injury, the court of appeals affirmed. Here, the company would not have discovered any "unfitness" other than the installer's traffic problems, and that would not have put it on notice of the installer's danger to customers. *Strickland v. Communications and Cable of Chicago, Inc.*, 710 N.E.2d 55 (Ill. App. Ct. 1999).

◆   An employee of an Indiana phone company (with a 27-year unblemished employment record) entered the home of a customer and engaged in unwanted sexual touching. The customer sued the phone company for negligent hiring, misrepresentation, vicarious liability for its employee's assault, and intentional infliction of emotional distress. The state trial court rejected the customer's argument that the phone company negligently hired the employee and engaged in any misrepresentation to the public. However, it refused to grant pretrial judgment in the company's favor on the issue of whether it could be held accountable for the employee's assault. The Indiana Court of Appeals reversed, finding that the company was entitled to pretrial judgment on the issue of vicarious liability because it **had no duty to foresee the employee's sexual assault**. Even though company employees had committed similar acts in the past, the court rejected the argument that "improper conduct by a few implies the foreseeability of improper conduct by all." *Indiana Bell Telephone Co. v. Maynard*, 705 N.E.2d 513 (Ind. Ct. App. 1999).

✦   A Kentucky maintenance company employed a worker with an extensive criminal record. The worker's brother-in-law, who was a regional manager for the company, was responsible for hiring him. The worker sexually assaulted a department store employee at a store where he was assigned. The victim sued the maintenance company. The court granted the maintenance company pretrial judgment, and the victim appealed to the Court of Appeals of Kentucky, asserting that the maintenance company could be held directly liable for negligent hiring. The court found that an employer can be held liable when its **failure to exercise ordinary care in the hiring or retention of an employee** creates a foreseeable risk of harm to a third person. There was evidence that the maintenance company knew or should have known of the employee's criminal background and should have conducted a criminal check under both its own established policy and its agreement with the department store. Because of the employer's knowledge that the employee would be locked inside the store with a single store employee, the court reversed and remanded the case for further proceedings. *Oakley v. Flor-Shin, Inc.*, 964 S.W.2d 438 (Ky. Ct. App. 1998).

✦   A Texas trucking company hired a long-haul driver without confirming a statement on his employment application that he had no prior criminal record. The employer also failed to contact the employee's last employer, but it checked his driving record as required by federal regulations. The employee had a history of sexual misconduct that would have been available in military, criminal and previous employment records. While driving through Austin, the employee left his vehicle and sexually assaulted a college student. The student sued the employer, asserting that it was liable for negligent hiring, supervision and retention of the employee. The court ruled for the employer. The Court of Appeals of Texas affirmed, noting that although federal regulations impose a duty on transportation employers to promote highway safety and prevent accidents by requiring them to confirm the competency of drivers, **verification of criminal background information is not required of all job applicants** and is mandatory only where the wrongdoing party is in a special relationship of trust with a vulnerable group of potential victims. The employer had no expectation that hiring the employee created a risk of sexual assault, and thus had no duty to investigate the employee's criminal background. *Guidry v. National Freight, Inc.*, 944 S.W.2d 807 (Tex. Ct. App. 1997).

✦   The same court held that a vacuum cleaner manufacturer could be held liable for failing to warn or require its distributors to perform a background check of prospective **employees who sold products at the homes of customers**. The case could be distinguished from *Guidry*, above, because the door-to-door sales employment situation created a heightened obligation to an employer where a particular risk of harm was foreseeable. *Scott Fetzer Co. v. Read*, 945 S.W.2d 854 (Tex. Ct. App. 1997).

✦   In 1964, a real estate partnership hired an ex-convict who had been convicted of manslaughter nine years earlier. The employee worked as a porter and lived in the building for over 20 years. During that time, he developed a relationship with a woman in the building and became the godfather of her daughter. The woman then discovered that the employee was sexually molesting her daughter. She sued the real estate partnership and its successor for negligent hiring. The New York Supreme Court, Appellate Division, held that the real estate partnership's hiring of the employee could not be considered the proximate cause of an injury years later. His development of a close relationship with the family was an **independent and unforeseeable intervening event** that severed any connection between the hiring and the molestation. The family's claim was based on a theory that would violate an important public policy of the state, which was to encourage employment of ex-convicts. *Ford v. Gildin*, 613 N.Y.S.2d 139 (N.Y. App. Div. 1994).

◆   After experiencing back pain and bladder problems, a Washington man went to a clinic, where the doctor told him that certain tests were necessary because of irregularities in the prostate exam. He was also told that a sperm sample was required and that the normal procedure was for the doctor to manually obtain it. The doctor stimulated the patient to ejaculation. Approximately two and a half years later, another patient complained to the director of the clinic about inappropriate sexual behavior by the doctor. The clinic determined that the doctor had engaged in improper sexual conduct with more than 100 patients during a period of two and a half years.

The patient then sued the clinic. The trial court ruled for the clinic, and the Court of Appeals of Washington affirmed. In order to hold an employer vicariously liable for the acts of its employees, it must be established that the employee was acting in furtherance of the employer's business and that he was acting within the scope of employment. The patient argued that the doctor's sexual assault happened in conjunction with an authorized examination and therefore, the clinic should be held liable. The court disagreed and determined that the tortious sexual assault should not be attributable to the clinic. The **assault emanated from the doctor's personal motives for sexual gratification**. There was no evidence that the act was done in furtherance of the clinic's business. *Thompson v. Everett Clinic*, 860 P.2d 1054 (Wash. Ct. App. 1993).

B. Other Injuries

Courts will sometimes hold employers liable for injuries caused by employees even though the employees are not furthering their employers' interests. Usually, this occurs when employers are negligent in hiring or supervising their employees. More commonly, the employee is doing something that is partly for the employer's benefit and partly for his own.

◆   For six months, an Illinois employee emailed death threats to his wife from his work computer. He then killed her and their two sons. **The wife's estate sued the employer for wrongful death, claiming that it voluntarily undertook a duty** to monitor and address the employee's emails by instituting a policy banning electronic transmission of inappropriate, obscene, harassing or abusive communications using its systems. A state appeals court held that the suit adequately stated the elements of a wrongful death suit based on the voluntary undertaking theory. *Regions Bank v. Joyce Meyer Ministries, Inc.*, 15 N.E.3d 545 (Ill. App. Ct. 2014).

♦   A construction worker in Illinois was hired for two days to help complete a home construction project. **Six weeks later, he broke into the home and assaulted the owner.** The owner sued the construction company for negligent hiring and retention, noting the worker's past criminal record. But the court rejected her claim because at the time of the assault, the home was no longer a worksite and the construction company had no right to control the worker's actions. *O'Rourke v. McIlvaine*, 19 N.E.3d 714 (Ill. App. Ct. 2014).

♦   A pharmacist in Michigan pulled out his gun and fired at would-be robbers. No one was hurt, but the employer terminated the pharmacist for violating its "no-escalation" policy. He sued the employer, **alleging he was terminated in violation of public policy because he had lawfully exercised his right of self-defense**. The court upheld the termination. The employee worked on an at-will basis for a private employer. No explicit legislative statement barred him from being fired for exercising his right to self-defense, and he was not fired for refusing to violate the law. He did not have a well-established and unlimited right to exercise self-defense at work. *Hoven v. Walgreen Co.* 751 F.3d 778 (6th Cir. 2014).

♦   A bar/restaurant patron claimed he was injured when security guards removed him from the premises. He sued the bar/restaurant for his alleged injuries. A Utah appeals court rejected his claim because **the bar/restaurant did not directly employ the guards** or control how they provided security. Instead, security was provided by an independent contractor that had entered into an agreement to provide security services with the bar/restaurant. The fact that the bar/restaurant set the hours worked by the security guards did not mean it was liable. *Castellanos v. Tommy John LLC*, 321 P.3d 218 (Utah Ct. App. 2014.)

♦   A long-haul trucker in Kentucky assaulted his girlfriend's ex-husband during a haul. The victim sued the trucker's employer for negligent hiring, training and supervision. **A state appeals court ruled against him.** When it hired the trucker, the employer verified his past employment as he reported it and checked his driving history. Those results did not reveal a propensity for violence or make the assault foreseeable. Therefore, the employer was not liable. *Carberry v. Golden Hawk Transportation, Inc.*, 402 S.W.3d 556 (Ky. Ct. App. 2013).

♦   An African-American customer at a Massachusetts department store alleged that a store clerk made racist comments to her. She sued the store for race discrimination under 42 U.S.C. § 1981, which bars discrimination in the making and enforcement of contracts. A federal district court ruled for the store, and the First Circuit affirmed. **Even if the clerk made the comments, they did not prevent the customer from completing her transaction.** *Hammond v. Kmart Corp.*, 733 F.3d 360 (1st Cir. 2013).

♦   A restaurant cook deliberately placed a human hair in a customer's steak. The customer sued the restaurant for negligent hiring and supervision, vicarious liability and breach of implied warranty. A jury found the restaurant did not properly supervise the cook, but it also found the failure did not cause the customer's injuries. It also found the restaurant breached an implied warranty that the food would be fit for consumption. The trial court allowed a damages award based on the theory that the jury must have believed the restaurant was negligent. **An appeals court decided that the negligent supervision claim failed as a matter of law** because the jury found that no act or omission on the part of the restaurant caused the employee's offensive conduct. Also, there was no evidence that the allegedly negligent hiring was causally connected to the contamination of the steak. Further, the trial court erred by entering a judgment for compensatory and punitive damages based on an implied finding of negligence by the employer. *Hansen v. Texas Roadhouse, Inc.*, 827 N.W.2d 99 (Wis. Ct. App. 2012).

♦   KFC conducted criminal background checks on managers, but not cashiers. When a customer at a Philadelphia KFC hesitated on what sort of side orders he wanted, a cashier told him to hurry up and then got into an argument with him. Eventually, the cashier pulled out a gun and struck the customer in the face with it. The customer sued KFC for his injuries, alleging negligence and asserting that the company should have known about the cashier's propensity for violence. However, a federal court ruled for KFC. It noted that **a background check wouldn't have made KFC aware of the cashier's propensity for violence** because his prior convictions were for nonviolent crimes. Further, no one had reported the cashier for suspicious behavior. *Harris v. KFC U.S. Properties, Inc.*, No. 10-3198, 2012 WL 2327748 (E.D. Pa. 6/18/12).

♦   A South Dakota Pizza Hut hired an employee to prepare food, do dishes and cut pizza. He told management that he was on parole for a felony conviction based on a gang-related incident that resulted in serious injury. He never displayed violent tendencies at work until seven months later when an ex-employee, who had been friends with him, showed up at the restaurant to return a borrowed CD. The employee claimed the ex-employee owed him money and punched him in the face, breaking his jaw in three places. The ex-employee sued Pizza Hut for negligent hiring and supervision, but the Supreme Court of South Dakota ruled against him, noting that **the assault was not foreseeable**. Further, the restaurant didn't have a duty to conduct a pre-employment background investigation because the employee had limited contact with the public. *Iverson v. NPC Int'l, Inc.*, 801 N.W.2d 275 (S.D. 2011).

♦   A Wal-Mart customer in Missouri who had received four suspicious money orders presented them to the customer service counter to determine if they were in fact valid. The employee behind the counter called a manager, who called the police, who arrested the customer for attempting to cash fake money orders. Wal-Mart refused to press charges, and the case against her failed. She then sued the store for false imprisonment but lost because **she couldn't show that the company's employees called the police for illegitimate purposes** or that they knowingly made false statements to the police. Her malicious prosecution claim also failed. *Fisher v. Wal-Mart Stores, Inc.*, 619 F.3d 811 (8th Cir. 2010).

♦   A worker at an Arizona smelter fell into a gap created when two temporary employees removed access ramps and placed caution tape around the opening.

He thought a handrail was in place, leaned on the caution tape and fell. When he sued the temporary employees' employer, the employer asserted that it could not be vicariously liable for his injuries because **the temporary employees were under the actual control of the smelter at the time of the accident**. A court granted pretrial judgment to the worker on that issue, and a jury awarded him $1.5 million in damages. The court of appeals reversed and remanded the case, and the Supreme Court of Arizona affirmed that decision. There was a fact issue as to whether the temporary employees' employer ceded its right to control the actions of its employees to the smelter. This issue required a trial. *Tarron v. Bowen Machine & Fabricating, Inc.*, 235 P.3d 1030 (Ariz. 2010).

◆   A Wisconsin employee became upset after a neighbor yelled at him for letting his son urinate in the neighbor's yard. The employee **used a work computer to obtain information on the neighbors and then harass them**, signing them up for various subscriptions, placing false and anonymous ads about them over the Internet, and calling them at work from his company cell phone. The police finally tracked the harassment to the employee, and the neighbors eventually sued the employer for negligence and negligent supervision. The Wisconsin Court of Appeals ruled for the company, noting that it was not reasonably foreseeable that giving an employee unsupervised access to a computer would create a risk of harm to a third party. Employers are not guarantors of their employees' conduct. *Sigler v. Kobinsky*, 762 N.W.2d 706 (Wis. Ct. App. 2008).

◆   A Mississippi restaurant worker thought a customer was hitting on his girlfriend. He clocked out, then tried to provoke the customer into a fight. The manager heard the commotion and ordered the two to take it outside. A group of employees and customers followed the two out to the parking lot, where another employee struck the customer, who fell from the second-floor parking lot to a concrete surface, severing his spine and becoming a quadriplegic. He sued the restaurant for his injuries, and a jury awarded him $20 million for pain and suffering, medical expenses and lost earnings. The Fifth Circuit upheld the award, noting the manager's failure to intervene to break up the fight. The court of appeals also stated that **the restaurant had a duty to control its off-duty employees to protect its patrons from a foreseeable, unreasonable risk of harm**. *Foradori v. Harris*, 523 F.3d 477 (5th Cir. 2008).

◆   The president of a company in Kentucky owned his own plane and often flew it for business purposes. He invited his pastor along on a trip to Indianapolis so the pastor could visit family while the president worked. On the way back, the plane struck a cell phone tower and both men were killed. The pastor's estate sued the company for vicarious liability, but the Supreme Court of Kentucky held that the estate could not recover for the pastor's death. Even if the president acted within the scope of his authority in inviting the pastor along, **the pastor did not join the president on the trip for the purpose of accomplishing work for the company**. *Mid-States Plastics, Inc. v. Estate of Bryant*, 245 S.W.3d 728 (Ky. 2008).

◆   A California employee sent anonymous threats over the Internet using a company computer. Eventually, the messages were traced back to him. He was arrested and fired. The two people he had threatened sued the company for negligence, and the company asserted that it was immune under Section 230 of the Communications Decency Act of 1996 (CDA). The case reached the California Court of Appeal, which ruled for the company. Here, the company was a "provider of interactive computer service" under the CDA's definition; **because it was only the publisher of information provided by the employee and had no knowledge of the threats, it had immunity** under Section 230. *Delfino v. Agilent Technologies, Inc.*, 52 Cal.Rptr.3d 376 (Cal. Ct. App. 2006).

◆   After discovering his wife was having an affair with one of her co-workers, a man divorced his wife and sued her employer for alienation of affection. He asserted that the company negligently and recklessly allowed the illicit relationship to be carried on in its offices and elsewhere. The company sought to dismiss the lawsuit, but the Mississippi Supreme Court refused to do so. However slim, **there was a possibility the husband could prove that the company intentionally interfered with his marital relationship**. The court allowed the lawsuit to continue to the next stage. *Children's Medical Group v. Phillips*, 940 So.2d 931 (Miss. 2006).

◆   While a clerk at a bookstore was stooped down to retrieve a book from a bottom shelf, a customer touched her or her shirt. He claimed he was trying to help her tuck her shirt in; she claimed he inappropriately touched her buttocks. Her managers and a security guard detained the customer for over an hour, questioning and photographing him, and calling the police. When he later sued for false imprisonment, a Florida federal jury awarded him $117,000. The Eleventh Circuit upheld the award, noting that **the company did not have in place a policy that would have prevented employees from unlawfully detaining customers**. *Johnson v. Barnes & Noble Booksellers, Inc.*, 437 F.3d 1112 (11th Cir. 2006).

◆   An employee of a New Jersey company used his work computer to access pornography in violation of company policy. For two years, several employees, including his supervisor and the company's finance director, knew about his activity. Yet the company made no real efforts to stop him, only warning him to do so without taking any other action. He transmitted nude photos of his wife's 10-year-old daughter to child porn sites and was arrested. His wife sued the company for negligence. A court granted pretrial judgment to the company, but the Superior Court of New Jersey, Appellate Division, reversed. Here, **the employer breached its duty to report and/or take effective action to stop the employee's activities**. However, there was an issue of fact as to whether the company's breach of duty resulted in harm to the daughter. A trial was required. *Doe v. XYZ Corp.*, 887 A.2d 1156 (N.J. Super. Ct. App. Div. 2005).

◆   The California Supreme Court held that the owner of a restaurant could be held liable for the stabbing of a man in the restaurant's parking lot where **restaurant employees failed to call 911 even though they saw the assault**. The victim was a regular patron of the restaurant but was not eating there that night. The attacker ran into the restaurant yelling for a knife, grabbed one, then ran back outside and stabbed the victim. The court said that if the employees failed to call 911 because their illegal immigrant status would be discovered, the owner would be liable. However, if they failed to call because they feared the attacker would hurt them, or that they would be retaliated against later, the owner would not be liable. Since the victim was an invitee of the restaurant, its employees had a duty to take reasonable and minimally burdensome measures to aid him. The case required a trial. *Morris v. De La Torre*, 113 P.3d 1182 (Cal. 2005).

◆   A disgruntled phone services company customer received an email calling him pathetic and "a grumpy, horrible man." The email purported to come from an employee in the Kentucky Attorney General's (AG's) office but, in fact, was sent by several customer service employees of the company who forged the origin of the email. The AG employee sued the company and the customer service employees for defamation, negligent supervision and emotional distress. The company sought to dismiss all claims against it, and a federal court granted the request. Here, **the company was not vicariously liable for the employees' conduct** because even though it was in response to a customer complaint and sent on company equipment during working hours, it did not further the company's interest and could not have been expected in view of the employees' duties. Further, the AG employee failed to show that the company knew or should have known that the employees would do what they did. *Booker v. GTE.net LLC*, 214 F.Supp.2d 746 (E.D. Ky. 2002).

◆   A bellman at a resort in South Carolina also performed delivery services for the company on his day off. He picked up accounting and payroll documents from two affiliated corporate entities and delivered them to the company. One day, he was speeding on a road adjacent to one of the entities when he lost control of the car and hit another vehicle. He died, and a passenger in the other car was severely burned. When she sued the company and the two affiliated entities in a Georgia state court, they asserted that the bellman was acting as an independent contractor at the time of the accident. The court agreed and granted pretrial judgment to the defendants. However, the Georgia Court of Appeals reversed as to the company. Here, there were **questions of material fact as to whether the bellman was acting as an employee on his day off**. Several items might lead a jury to so find: 1) he simply took over delivery responsibilities that the manager of one of the entities had previously performed; 2) the company exercised control over the time, manner and method in which he performed his delivery services; and 3) the delivery of the documents furthered the company's business. There would have to be a trial on this issue. *Thompson v. Club Group Ltd.*, 553 S.E.2d 842 (Ga. Ct. App. 2001).

VI. CONTINUING VIOLATION DOCTRINE

The continuing violation doctrine can cause an employer to be liable for conduct occurring outside the statute of limitations where it or its supervisory employees have engaged in a continuing course of conduct against an employee, or where the company has knowingly allowed an employee to engage in a continuing course of conduct against a third party.

As long as at least one of the unlawful acts occurs within the statute of limitations, and as long as the acts are related to one another, the continuing violation doctrine allows the whole series of acts to be taken into account when determining liability.

◆   A black Amtrak worker alleged that he was harassed and disciplined more harshly than other employees because of his race. A California federal court dismissed his action, holding that Amtrak could not be liable for conduct occurring outside the 300-day limitations period of Title VII. The U.S. Supreme Court held that a Title VII plaintiff alleging discrete or retaliatory acts must file his charge within the appropriate 180- or 300-day limitations period. However, a charge of a **hostile work environment** (a series of acts that may not be actionable on their own, occurring over a period of time) will not be time-barred if all acts constituting the claim are part of the same unlawful practice and at least one act falls within the filing period. *National Railroad Passenger Corp. v. Morgan*, 536 U.S. 101, 122 S.Ct. 2061, 153 L.Ed.2d 106 (2002).

◆   A UPS manager in California suspected that supervisors were falsifying employees' time cards to hide violations of wage-and-hour laws. She sought an audit, but her manager became upset with her and criticized her performance. She was then transferred to another division and given only a 1% raise. After she wasn't recommended for a bonus award, she was placed on a performance improvement plan. During this time, she also received a "Manager of the Quarter" award. Later she was demoted. She then sued for discrimination and retaliation as well as negligent hiring and supervision, claiming that she faced a chain of adverse employment actions going back more than a year. However, **the court refused to allow her to use the continuing violation doctrine to tie together all the adverse actions she claimed**. The supervisor who transferred her had no input into the later decision not to award her a bonus. Thus, UPS could not be liable for events occurring before March 30, 2008. *Muniz v. United Parcel Service, Inc.*, 731 F.Supp.2d 961 (N.D. Cal. 2010).

◆   A female employee at an Indiana company claimed that she endured hostile working conditions, including having to look at pornographic images on male team leaders' computer screens. The company maintained that the pornographic images were the sole problem. It suspended 11 men for two weeks and transferred the woman to another team. She claimed that the company's actions had little effect, that the male team leaders continued to view pornography and that they blamed her and other women for their suspensions. When she ultimately sued, the company claimed that no harassment had occurred in the previous 300 days. The court instructed the jury to consider only the working conditions for the past 300 days, and the jury ruled for the company. However, the Seventh Circuit reversed. **The employee should have been allowed to present evidence of the working conditions for all of her time at the company.** *Bright v. Hill's Pet Nutrition, Inc.*, 510 F.3d 766 (7th Cir. 2007).

◆   A female repair technician worked at a garage in Staten Island for nine years. For the last seven years, she was the only female there. When she quit, she asserted that she had endured disparaging treatment every day. She also claimed that her supervisors were non-responsive to her complaints, and that the company's ethics hotline was not effective in eliminating the harassment. A New York federal court granted pretrial judgment to the company, but the Second Circuit reversed. Here, a reasonable jury could find that she was subjected to a sexually hostile work environment during her nine years with the company. Also, under the continuing violation doctrine, **all the harassing acts of the prior nine years could be used in determining whether the work environment was hostile** (despite the 300-day statute of limitations normally imposed by Title VII). *Petrosino v. Bell Atlantic*, 385 F.3d 210 (2d Cir. 2004).

◆   An engineer with a California company was diagnosed with multiple sclerosis and allegedly began to experience disability discrimination and harassment. Five years later, she resigned and sued, asserting that the unlawful behavior was part of a pattern of continuing wrongdoing such that all the acts of the past five years should be considered. A court agreed, and a jury awarded her $925,000 in emotional distress damages and $476,000 in economic damages. The court of appeal held that the jury should only have considered improper behavior from the past year. The California Supreme Court reversed, finding that neither court had applied the proper standard for determining a continuing violation. To succeed on a continuing violation claim, the employee must show that **the actions before and after the limitations period are sufficiently similar in kind**, that they occur with sufficient frequency, and that they have not acquired a degree of permanence that would put the employee on notice that additional efforts to resolve the problem would be futile. Thus, when a reasonable employee realizes that further efforts to obtain an accommodation or end harassment will be futile, the statute of limitations begins to run. The court remanded the case for further proceedings. *Richards v. CH2M Hill, Inc.*, 111 Cal.Rptr.2d 87 (Cal. 2001).

◆   A Massachusetts employee was subjected to both verbal and physical sexual harassment by her supervisor and co-workers. However, she did not report it because they acted the same "to everybody." After a number of years, she reported the harassment and the men were disciplined. They then began retaliating against her. She sued the company under state law, and a trial court ruled that she could only assert hostile environment incidents that occurred within the past six months. The Supreme Judicial Court of Massachusetts held that **she might be entitled to the benefit of the continuing violation doctrine**. Unless she knew or reasonably should have known that she was in a pervasively hostile environment that was unlikely to improve (such that she should have filed a timely complaint with the Commission Against Discrimination), she could assert otherwise untimely claims under the continuing violation doctrine. The court remanded the case for further proceedings. *Cuddyer v. Stop & Shop Supermarket Co.*, 750 N.E.2d 928 (Mass. 2001).

CHAPTER THREE

Discipline, Suspension and Termination

I. AT-WILL EMPLOYMENT

At-will employment is what most of us toil under. As at-will employees, we can quit at any time, but we can also be fired at any time for any reason or no reason at all. The at-will presumption has some exceptions, including an employee discharge that violates an important <u>public policy</u> or forces an employee to choose between employment and personal legal rights.

<u>Just-cause employment</u> offers more protections against firing, and it is more common in union workplaces and in the public employment sector. In these relationships, employees can only be fired for just cause (like insubordination or incompetence). However, they can still quit at any time.

•   Store managers for a New Jersey supermarket chain sued for breach of contract following their termination from employment, claiming upper management created an implied employment contract when they told the store managers at meetings that they would maintain their employment as long as they stayed out of trouble. The court rejected their claims, finding that **the alleged statements did not alter their at-will employment status**. Nor did an employee handbook's failure to specifically designate them as at-will employees create an employment contract. *McCrone v. Acme Markets*, 561 Fed.Appx. 169 (3d Cir. 2014) (Unpublished).

•   A Maryland pharmaceutical sales representative was fired after she raised ethical concerns about her supervisor. She sued her employer, claiming breach of contract. She claimed that statements in the employer's code of conduct and a policy statement issued by the employer's ethics office transformed her from an at-will employee to an employee who worked under a contract. The statements expressed the employer's policy against retaliation. The court held that the **policy statements did not change the nature of the worker's employment** from at will to contract. *Scott v. Merck & Co., Inc.*, 497 Fed.Appx. 331 (4th Cir. 2012).

•   An Idaho cashier and receptionist was promoted until she reached the position of safety and loss facility director. She was fired more than a year later without cause. She claimed it was because she recommended various safety and compliance measures, which the company didn't want to take. The company asserted that it was part of a larger reduction in force. She sued for breach of an express and implied contract, bad faith and violation of public policy. However, she had received an email informing her that her employment was at will, and she never expressed an intent to report any safety issues to OSHA or any other regulatory agency. The case reached the Supreme Court of Idaho, which ruled against her. **She was an at-will employee at the time of her discharge**, and she could not prove retaliation because she failed to show she was engaged in protected activity. *Bollinger v. Fall River Rural Elec. Co-op., Inc.*, 152 Idaho 632, 272 P.3d 1263 (Idaho 2012).

•   An at-will New Jersey employee asked for and received maternity leave nine times. She became pregnant again, and she again sought a six-month maternity leave. Her employer guaranteed her reinstatement unless her job was declared surplus by a reduction in force. Before her maternity leave expired, she asked for another six months off, which the employer granted. When she sought to return to work after that period, the employer decided it no longer had work for her and fired her. She sued for breach of contract and interference with her leave rights under the FMLA and state law. A court granted pretrial judgment to the employer, but the Superior Court, Appellate Division, ruled that a trial was required on the breach of contract claim. **Even though she was an at-will employee, the maternity leaves the employer granted her may have altered the nature of the employment relationship.** *Lapidoth v. Telcordia Technologies, Inc.*, 22 A.3d 11 (N.J. Super. Ct. App. Div. 2011).

♦   An Indiana employee had difficulty getting along with her office mate. She complained to the owner about the office mate's use of the office's single phone for personal calls. The company owners ordered the office mate to use her cell phone or the lobby phone for such calls, but the office mate soon reverted to using the office phone again. The employee complained again and wrote up a list of complaints against the office mate. During a lengthy meeting with all the parties, the employee rolled her eyes and talked back to the owners. They fired her for insubordination, and she sued. A federal court and the Seventh Circuit ruled against her, finding that **she was justifiably discharged for insubordination.** *Everroad v. Scott Truck Systems, Inc.*, 604 F.3d 471 (7th Cir. 2010).

♦   A company in North Carolina hired a vice president of marketing. The vice president's father was the chairman of the board of directors. A month later, the board voted to remove the chairman and sent the vice president a letter stating that it would not retaliate against him as a result of his father's separation from the company. A year later, the company restructured various jobs and eliminated the vice president of marketing's position. He sued for wrongful discharge and breach of contract, claiming that the letter constituted a contract of employment and that he had been wrongfully fired. The North Carolina Court of Appeals disagreed. Here, **the non-retaliation letter he received was not supported by consideration so as to form a contract of employment**. He was already employed at the time he received the letter, and the letter did not increase or diminish his pay, duties, responsibilities or anything else. As a result, he was an at-will employee who could be fired in the reorganization. *Franco v. Liposcience, Inc.*, 676 S.E.2d 500 (N.C. Ct. App. 2009).

♦   A Connecticut employee also operated a plumbing business on the side with her husband. After a fire destroyed one of the company's facilities, its Connecticut facility had to take up more of the workload. The employee began to feel stressed out and called in sick for two weeks. She continued to work with her husband in the plumbing business. The company ordered her to submit to a medical examination at a hospital, but she never showed up or told anyone at the company that she didn't intend to do so. As a result, the company fired her for insubordination for failing to comply with a direct order, as well as for her noncompliance with the employee handbook's provisions on physical exams. She sued for wrongful discharge and breach of an implied contract. The Appellate Court of Connecticut ruled against her, finding the company properly fired her for refusing to submit to a medical exam. **Her vague assertion of illness justified the company's demand that she undergo a medical exam as**

set forth in the employee handbook. *Joyner v. Simkins Industries, Inc.*, 957 A.2d 882 (Conn. App. Ct. 2008).

♦   A Connecticut employee received a written offer to become regional sales manager for another company. The offer was for five days hence and stated that employment would be at will, meaning the employee could quit or be fired at any time. He signed and returned the offer, then was asked to provide job references, which he did. He quit his old job and showed up for work at the new company on the designated day. However, due to a problem with his references, he was asked to provide additional references and was sent home. That evening, he was informed that he would not be hired due to a problem with the references. He sued for breach of contract, claiming that he could not be fired until after he began working for the company. The Connecticut Court of Appeals disagreed. It noted that **the at-will doctrine extends to all aspects of the employment relationship, including the job offer**. *Petitte v. DSL.net, Inc.*, 925 A.2d 457 (Conn. App. Ct. 2007).

♦   An America Online employee was fired from her job in New Mexico as a "coach" for the company's consultants. She sued, claiming AOL breached an implied contract to fire her only for cause. A federal court granted pretrial judgment to AOL, and the Tenth Circuit affirmed. Comments from the employee's supervisors (that employees were not fired without cause) did not countermand the **four written documents she received, each of which expressly stated that her employment was at will**. The application, the job offer letter, a "business and personal conduct" form and the employee handbook all stated that her employment was at will and that she could be fired at any time, with or without cause. As a result, she was entitled to no relief. *Sullivan v. America Online, Inc.*, 219 Fed.Appx. 720 (10th Cir. 2007).

♦   A doctor worked as the associate medical director of the medical department of the *New York Times*. She claimed she was fired after she refused, on ethical grounds, to provide management with confidential medical records of employees without their knowledge or consent, and also asserted that she was told to misinform employees regarding whether their illnesses and injuries were work related, in order to cut down on workers' compensation claims. The doctor was fired in a restructuring, and she sued for breach of contract. A state court ruled in her favor, and an appellate court affirmed. However, the New York Court of Appeals reversed. It refused to apply a narrow exception to the employment-at-will doctrine involving the ethical obligations of attorneys. Unlike a situation where an attorney is acting only on behalf of her clients, the doctor here was also acting on behalf of the *Times*. Thus, she was **an at-will employee who could be fired for refusing to breach her ethical obligations**. *Horn v. New York Times*, 760 N.Y.S.2d 378 (N.Y. 2003).

♦   An employer enforced an anti-nepotism policy precluding any store manager from supervising a family member. One of the company's Texas stores hired the brother of an employee. It trained and promoted him to store manager. The company's management was aware of the family relationship, but no attempt was made to enforce the anti-nepotism policy. Approximately 17 years after the brother was employed at his sister's store as her supervisor, the company determined that the arrangement violated the anti-nepotism policy. After the sister declined to accept a transfer and was, fired, she sued the company for wrongful termination. The Supreme Court of Texas noted that although Texas law presumes employment to be at will, **the at-will doctrine is subject to agreements to the contrary**. In this case, the company had fired the employee for the only reason it could not lawfully fire her. It had expressly waived the anti-nepotism policy as it applied to the sister. *Goodyear Tire & Rubber Co. v. Portilla*, 879 S.W.2d 47 (Tex. 1994).

II. EMPLOYEE HANDBOOKS

Employee handbooks and manuals are usually intended only as a guide for both employer and employee. Yet, these documents can modify at-will employment if they do not clearly state that they are nothing more than a guide.

Courts generally require an employer to conspicuously state that the handbook does not create an employment contract to avoid having the handbook construed as a contract. This means that the typeface must be in **bold letters** or CAPITAL LETTERS

> or in a separate paragraph

or in some way <u>stand out</u> from the rest of the text of the manual.

Where the handbook is deemed to be a contract, any rights or procedures listed therein become "written" into the contract with the employee. Thus, if the handbook mentions progressive discipline, the employer might be forced to issue warnings and suspensions before firing an employee for misconduct.

A. Layoffs and Seniority

When seniority is addressed in employee handbooks, it should be discussed as a preference and not an entitlement. In other words, don't state that employees will be laid off in reverse order of seniority. Instead, state that seniority will be taken into account and a preference will be granted for senior employees.

♦   After 28 years, and two years shy of qualifying for a "Class C" pension, a West Virginia employee was fired. He claimed that the firing was for financial reasons and that it **violated the company's well-established policy of making major employment decisions on the basis of seniority** (because several less-senior employees continued working for the company in jobs that he could perform). He also asserted that the company's handbook created an implied contract. A federal court ruled against him, finding that the handbook did not alter the at-will nature of the relationship. Thus, even if the company violated its own internal policy regarding seniority, the employment remained at will, and the court refused to enforce the internal policy. The employee also failed to show that there was a substantial public policy against firing employees to save on pension obligations so as to override the at-will doctrine. *Veltri v. Graybar Electric Co., Inc.*, No. 5:09CV101, 2010 WL 2365446 (N.D. W.Va. 6/9/10).

◆   After 16 years as a driver for a company in Illinois, an employee was informed that his position was being eliminated due to budgetary issues. The employee sued for breach of contract, alleging he was wrongfully discharged because a less-senior employee was retained. **He asserted that the employee manual's seniority provisions required the company to terminate the other employee first.** The Appellate Court of Illinois disagreed. The manual did not constitute a contract between the parties. It contained a disclaimer stating that the manual was intended to serve as a general outline of company policy, and that it did not create a contract, express or implied. Thus, the seniority provisions of the manual did not require the company to terminate the other employee first. *Ivory v. Specialized Assistance Services, Inc.*, 365 Ill.App.3d 544, 850 N.E.2d 230 (Ill. App. Ct. 2006).

◆   A Massachusetts investment company employee was recruited to be a sales rep for the company, making him eligible for incentive compensation. Company policy at that time did not provide for the loss of incentive compensation upon termination. Later, the company issued a new handbook, which changed that policy, eliminating incentive compensation upon termination. The employee was then let go in a sales group restructuring. He received severance pay of $137,933, including a bonus of over $58,000. He nevertheless sued, claiming he was due incentive compensation after his discharge. The Appeals Court of Massachusetts disagreed. **The new handbook modified the incentive compensation agreement between the parties**, and the company properly fired him as part of a cost-cutting measure because he remained an at-will employee. *York v. Zurich Scudder Investments, Inc.*, 849 N.E.2d 892 (Mass. App. Ct. 2006).

◆   An airline in North Carolina hired a pilot and gave him a handbook addressing seniority, progressive discipline, and other terms and conditions of employment. It provided a three-step warning process for most offenses. When the pilot became unavailable for an assignment, he was not given progressive discipline, but was instead sent a termination letter. He sued the airline for breach of contract, alleging that it should have taken the seniority and progressive discipline provisions of the handbook into account. A federal court ruled for the airline, deciding that the handbook did not modify the at-will employment relationship. The **seniority and progressive discipline provisions did not imply that the airline could not fire the pilot** for an unspecified major infraction. Further, the pilot signed a document acknowledging that the employment was at will. He had been properly fired. *Norman v. Tradewinds Airlines, Inc.*, 286 F.Supp.2d 575 (M.D.N.C. 2003).

◆   A Michigan employer maintained an employment handbook declaring that employees would not be discharged without good cause. The employer later added disclaimer language to the handbook, stating that it did not constitute a contract of employment and that the employment relationship was at will. One longtime human resources employee, who had been hired prior to adoption of the handbook, claimed that her supervisor gave her a poor work evaluation after she refused to wear a dress to a company function. She was eventually laid off in a reduction in force while her male supervisor and several other younger, less senior males were retained. She sued the employer and supervisor for breach of contract and employment discrimination. The case reached the Supreme Court of Michigan, which noted that **the handbook policy did not overcome the presumption of employment at will**. It contained a specific disclaimer that no just-cause employment contract existed. The employee's discrimination claims also failed because she failed to prove that discrimination was a motivating factor in her layoff. The reduction in force had been based on economic factors. *Lytle v. Malady*, 579 N.W.2d 906 (Mich. 1998).

♦   A Wyoming mining company distributed employee handbooks to four supervisors, which stated that they could be terminated only for cause. The handbooks established 90-day probationary periods, after which an employee became "permanent," and stated that layoffs would generally be made in the reverse order of seniority. The employer later issued a series of handbooks that qualified these provisions by specifying that employment remained at will. It laid off the four supervisory employees while retaining some less experienced employees with better performance ratings. The supervisors sued for breach of contract, breach of an implied covenant of good faith and fair dealing and reliance upon the earlier handbooks. A federal court granted pretrial judgment to the employer, and the supervisors appealed. The Tenth Circuit observed that the handbooks were sufficiently ambiguous to prevent pretrial judgment on the issue of whether they reasonably created an expectation that there would be no dismissals without cause and that the company would perform layoffs by seniority. The case required a trial. *McIlravy v. Kerr-McGee Corp.*, 119 F.3d 876 (10th Cir. 1997).

B. Progressive Disciplinary Policies

Progressive discipline should be addressed as an option that the employer reserves. It should not be the only possible way to discipline an employee. Thus, the handbook could state that:

> the employer reserves the right to discipline any employee for violating company rules and policies, and can take disciplinary action up to and including employment termination for any such violation.

♦   A New Jersey manager was terminated after an audit showed **his subordinates had tampered with time sheets**. He sued, claiming breach of an implied contract to apply a progressive discipline policy. The court rejected his claim, finding he was employed on an at-will basis and the employer was not obligated to discipline the employee progressively. *Horan v. Verizon New Jersey, Inc.*, No. L-7635-10, 2014 WL 1672366 (N.J. Super Ct. App. Div. 4/29/14) (Unpublished).

◆   After he was fired, a bank employee brought a wrongful termination lawsuit. He claimed that the handbook and a letter of employment he received created a contract even though both documents stated that the employment was to be at will and the handbook stated that it was not a contract. He cited to language in the letter that seemed to contradict the at-will language. However, the Wyoming Supreme Court noted that nothing in the letter indicated a term of employment so as to modify the express language later in the document, which stated that the employment was to be at will. Further, **the handbook contained disclaimer language and stated that he could be fired without undergoing progressive discipline** if the bank felt that was appropriate. Accordingly, the lawsuit failed. *Kuhl v. Wells Fargo Bank, N.A.*, 281 P.3d 716 (Wyo. 2012).

◆   Five managerial employees of a company in Connecticut were fired. They sued the company, claiming that it should have used progressive discipline against them, and they cited a management training course that they attended for the company, in which they were told that they should provide progressive discipline before firing other employees. **They asserted that the training course created a contractually binding agreement that they would not be fired without progressive discipline** or an opportunity for improvement. A trial court ruled for the company, and the Appellate Court of Connecticut affirmed. The representations made during the training course were not promissory in nature and thus did not create a binding contract not to fire employees without progressive discipline. They merely offered principles that managers ought to follow. *Brule v. Nerac, Inc.*, 13 A.3d 723 (Conn. App. Ct. 2011).

◆   A company in Vermont had a personnel manual that described progressive discipline and just cause termination policies for employee misconduct. It stated that two written warnings would be given before termination. When the company experienced an economic slowdown, it attempted to reorganize, and one employee resisted changes a new manager tried to institute. She received a letter of reprimand from the company's president, but the letter stated that it was not a disciplinary warning. A month later she was fired. She sued, claiming breach of an implied contract that she would only be fired for just cause after progressive discipline. The Vermont Supreme Court held that **the letter of reprimand established the company's intent to abide by its progressive discipline policy**. Even though the employee could have been laid off for economic reasons without progressive discipline, she was fired for insubordination. *Havill v. Woodstock Soapstone Co.*, 865 A.2d 335 (Vt. 2004).

◆   A 55-year-old manager of a company in Massachusetts claimed that he was improperly fired. He asserted that he should have been progressively disciplined under the employee handbook and the "Guide to Corporate Conduct." He claimed that the real reason for the termination was age discrimination. The company argued that the manager attempted to misuse company property for his personal benefit; that he retaliated against another employee who refused to cooperate in that misuse; and that he had an abusive management style. The First Circuit Court of Appeals held that **the manager was not entitled to progressive discipline**. Nothing in the handbook or the guide promised progressive discipline. And even if the company generally applied progressive discipline to its employees, there was never any such policy for management. *Joyal v. Hasbro, Inc.*, 380 F.3d 14 (1st Cir. 2004).

✦   A Michigan hospital fired an ICU nurse for putting other staff in life-threatening danger. It believed she was trying to discharge the current on a defibrillator before telling other members of the hospital's ICU department to stand clear. An arbitrator found that the nurse was not going to discharge the current, but was just attempting to turn the defibrillator on. As such, the arbitrator concluded **her mistake, although negligent, was not "gross neglect,"** as the hospital claimed. The collective bargaining agreement in place identified two levels of discipline, the first warranting suspension for careless conduct and the second warranting discharge for gross neglect or abuse of a patient. In light of a previous reprimand, the arbitrator ordered the nurse to be reinstated with a six-month suspension. The Sixth Circuit held that the arbitrator did not exceed his authority. Nor did the arbitrator's order violate Michigan's public policy of ensuring safe and competent nursing care. The arbitrator did not order the hospital to reinstate her to the same department but gave it the flexibility of placing her in a less dangerous position and providing whatever training it deemed appropriate. *MidMichigan Regional Medical Center v. Professional Employees Local 79*, 183 F.3d 497 (6th Cir. 1999).

C. Handbook Terms

Disclaimers need to be clearly stated. If you want to ensure that your handbook is not a contract, plainly state that in bold or larger type on the first page of the handbook. Or consider distributing a separate sheet for employees to sign, indicating that they received a copy of the handbook and agreeing that it does not change the at-will nature of the job.

The optimal handbook contains language that is clear and understandable to employees, yet provides the flexibility the employer needs to run the business without constraints on seniority, discipline, etc.

The NLRB has taken the position that handbooks may not ban employees from making disparaging comments about the employer online, require employees to obtain authorization before talking about the employer to the media or at a public meeting, or require employees to inform the employer about any work-related correspondence received from the government.

✦   A Boeing engineer was demoted out of management for exerting influence to get two relatives hired. He sued for breach of an implied contract and wrongful demotion, but he lost. The Washington Court of Appeals noted that an employer can be bound by written materials that create an implied contract (like a handbook that modifies the at-will nature of the employment) or by providing written materials that create an atmosphere of job security and fair treatment with promises of specific treatment in specific situations. Here, however, **the code of conduct and other documents that the employee relied on did not**

amount to an implied contract. They did not promise specific treatment for specific situations and, in fact, contained disclaimers of any promises. *Quedado v. Boeing Co.*, 168 Wash.App. 363, 276 P.3d 365 (Wash. Ct. App. 2012).

♦   A Texas employer had **an employee handbook stating that it could unilaterally modify any policy including its mandatory arbitration policy**. It also stated that the handbook was not a contract of employment. After an employee who signed an arbitration agreement was fired, she sued for discrimination, and the employer sought to compel arbitration. The case reached the Supreme Court of Texas, which ruled that the employee had to arbitrate her claim. The arbitration agreement was not illusory as the employee argued because it did not reference the handbook. It was a stand-alone contract that could not be construed as non-binding on the employer. Accordingly, the handbook provision allowing the employer to unilaterally modify any policy didn't apply to the arbitration agreement because the handbook was not a contract. *In re 24R, Inc.*, 324 S.W.3d 564 (Tex. 2010).

♦   A South Dakota FedEx driver complained that he experienced offensive and harassing conduct. Shortly thereafter, his supervisors investigated his delivery records due to suspicious delays and gaps in delivery times and found that he had scanned at least one package as delivered prior to delivery in order to meet scheduled delivery times. He was fired and sued for wrongful discharge. The company asserted that its **handbook expressly identified him as an at-will employee and** that **there was no public policy exception allowing him to succeed in his lawsuit**. The case reached the Eighth Circuit, which agreed that his discharge was permissible. The handbook clearly made his employment at will, and any harassment he endured was not actionable under Title VII or state law. The termination did not violate a substantial public policy. *Semple v. Federal Express Corp.*, 566 F.3d 788 (8th Cir. 2009).

♦   A company in Indiana created an employee handbook with a chapter on family and medical care leave even though it did not have enough employees to be eligible for coverage under the FMLA. The handbook offered similar benefits to those available under the FMLA. When an employee took unpaid leave and was replaced by another employee, he sued the company for violating the FMLA as well as for promissory estoppel (alleging that he reasonably relied, to his detriment, on a promise to provide benefits). A federal court granted pretrial judgment to the company, but the Seventh Circuit reversed. It found questions of fact over whether the handbook created a binding contract, and also determined that **the handbook gave rise to a cause of action for promissory estoppel**. It remanded the case for further proceedings. *Peters v. Gilead Sciences, Inc.*, 533 F.3d 594 (7th Cir. 2008).

♦   A Texas nurse fell while moving a patient. A month later she spoke with a co-worker about receiving medical treatment. The co-worker told her she would have to undergo a drug screening as part of any treatment at the company's facilities. She chose not to undergo the drug screen, which raised suspicions and resulted in the company requesting a for-cause drug screen. She eventually agreed to the drug screen, but resigned before the results came back (positive for marijuana and a narcotic). She then sued the company for negligence, and also asserted that it owed her $2,458 for the cash value of her accrued time off pursuant to the employee handbook. The Texas Court of Appeals held that the company was not negligent and noted that **the handbook clearly identified itself as a "guide" rather than a contract. Thus, the paid time-off policy was voluntary and could be changed at any time.** *Drake v. Wilson N. Jones Medical Center*, 259 S.W.3d 386 (Tex. Ct. App. 2008).

◆   A Hispanic field supervisor for a company with an office in Wyoming lost out on a promotion and had a new manager remove from the office some of the equipment he used to provide oilfield services. He suspected his days were numbered and quit, then sued for racial harassment and breach of contract, among other claims. He asserted that the employee manual created a contract that promised continued employment and **cited the job security provision of the manual**, wherein the company stated that it made "every effort to provide continuous employment." It also stated: "An individual employee can increase his job security by increasing his knowledge and skills. The more knowledge and skill you acquire, the more productive you are likely to be, and naturally the more productive, the better your chance for stable employment." However, the Tenth Circuit noted that those provisions did not <u>promise</u> continued employment. The court allowed the racial harassment claim to proceed but not the breach of contract action. *Herrera v. Lufkin Industries, Inc.*, 474 F.3d 675 (10th Cir. 2007).

◆   The director of a shelter for battered women in South Carolina called the executive director to inform her that no one was operating the hotline but refused to tell the executive director who had given her that information. The executive director suspended her for insubordination, doubled her duties, then fired her when she refused to accept them. She sued for breach of contract, claiming the employee handbook altered the at-will nature of the employment and that she had been fired in violation of its nondiscrimination provision. The handbook stated that the shelter reserved the right to terminate an employee at any time if the executive director believed it was in the shelter's best interests. The Supreme Court of South Carolina ruled that **the handbook did not create contractual rights because of the disclaimer**. The director was not fired in violation of the nondiscrimination provision. *Hessenthaler v. Tri-County Sister Help, Inc.*, 616 S.E.2d 694 (S.C. 2005).

◆   An Indiana employee of United Parcel Service (UPS) was demoted. He sued for breach of contract, maintaining that the employee handbook stated that company policy was that employees would not be demoted without just cause. The company asserted that a handbook disclaimer stated that the handbook did not create a contract. The disclaimer further stated that the handbook gave the employee no rights. The Seventh Circuit Court of Appeals held in favor of UPS. It rejected the notion (adopted by Oklahoma and Alaska) that in addition to stating that the handbook did not create a contract, it also had to state that the employee could be terminated at the will of the employer. Here, **the disclaimer was sufficient to inform the employee that the**

handbook did not create a contract. Nor could the employee use the doctrine of promissory estoppel (detrimental reliance) because it was not reasonable for him to rely on the statement that he would not be demoted without cause. *Workman v. United Parcel Service*, 234 F.3d 998 (7th Cir. 2000).

◆   A nurse who worked in the intensive care unit of a Wisconsin hospital was discharged after telling a supervisor that she was not going to return to work following a lunch-time doctor's appointment. Prior to the appointment, the nurse had received five disciplinary warnings. She sued for wrongful discharge/breach of contract in a state court, which dismissed her claims. The Court of Appeals of Wisconsin affirmed, noting that although the handbook in place at the time the nurse was hired provided that discipline could only be for just cause upon completion of the probationary period, the updated handbook contained a specific disclaimer that it did not create any employment contractual rights. Here, the nurse had signed an acknowledgement form for the earlier handbook, which stated that she understood it to be "a working guide of policies, rights and responsibilities for [hospital] employees." The form also stated that the handbook did not "replace or supercede original hospital policies," and that hospital **policies, practices and procedures were subject to change at the sole discretion of management**. This language did not alter the at-will relationship. Moreover, the updated handbook clearly reserved the hospital's right to amend or delete any provisions at any time, without advance notice. *Helland v. Froedtert Memorial Lutheran Hospital*, 601 N.W.2d 318 (Wis. Ct. App. 1999).

◆   A hospital implemented a new employee handbook that changed the discipline procedure. Under the old handbook, discharge could only be for cause, and the third reprimand an employee received would result in automatic dismissal. Under the new handbook, a "flexible" progressive disciplinary procedure was established. Shortly after the new handbook was in place, a nurse's supervisor filled out three performance reports based on three different complaints from patients' family members. She then recommended termination, stating that "the third reprimand results in automatic dismissal." The nurse sued for wrongful discharge. The Vermont Supreme Court ruled for the nurse. **Because the supervisor's report recommending termination mirrored language used in the old handbook, there was an ambiguity as to which handbook ought to be used.** Further, the new handbook was unclear as to what the progressive disciplinary procedure was. Finally, the new handbook had been in effect only four months when the nurse was fired. *Trombley v. Southwestern Vermont Medical Center*, 738 A.2d 103 (Vt. 1999).

III. BREACH OF CONTRACT

Breach of contract complaints arise under both oral and written employment contracts, often where the employee claims that an oral promise or language contained in an employee handbook has modified the presumption of employment at will. Resolution of these cases involves an examination of the agreement between the parties.

A. Written Contracts

When a straightforward written employment contract exists, any dispute is generally resolved by looking at the language it contains. However:

—some written contracts are modified by oral agreement,
—some employee handbooks modify the terms of at-will employment, and
—some employment relationships are governed by a writing only in part.

For example, there may be a drug-testing agreement or a non-compete agreement but no other writings to memorialize the employment relationship. In such a case, the writing generally modifies the at-will relationship only to the extent that the situation pertains to the writing.

✦   A global commodity manager was transferred from New York to Texas. He signed a relocation expense and reimbursement agreement that required him to repay his relocation expenses if he resigned less than a year after the move. When he resigned within a year, the employer sued to get the money back. The employee argued that the agreement was not enforceable because he was fraudulently induced to move to Texas on the promise of a promotion. The court rejected his claim. **The agreement explicitly excluded any prior written or oral promises**, and it did not promise a promotion. It also indicated that the manager had read and understood the agreement and had assented to it knowingly and voluntarily. *Dresser-Rand Co. v. Bolick*, No. 14-12-00192, 2013 WL 3770950 (Tex. Ct. App. 7/9/13).

✦   An Illinois investment analyst worked under an employment agreement, under which he would forfeit a substantial contingent payment if he was fired for cause. He became upset when a friend of his was fired for refusing to accept a lower-paying job with a subsidiary. He interrupted an executive meeting, pulled down his pants and "mooned" his bosses. Initially, he received a formal warning, but when the CEO returned from a vacation, he was fired for cause, thus forfeiting close to $2 million. He sued, claiming he should not have been fired for cause because he was a valuable employee with an exemplary record and he'd already received the formal warning. The case reached the Appellate Court of Illinois, which held that **the "mooning" caused injury to the company and satisfied the "for cause" requirement**. *Selch v. Columbia Management*, 977 N.E.2d 287 (Ill. App. Ct. 2012).

✦   The founder of an IT company sought to hire a scientist as the company's director of research and sent him an engagement letter, formally offering him the position. In the letter, the scientist was offered a 3% ownership stake. If he left in the first year, the company could buy back all his stock. If he left in the second year, the company could buy back one-third of his stock. And if he left before the end of his third year, the company could buy back two-thirds of his stock. He accepted the offer and moved to Washington, D.C. There, he signed an agreement informing him that he was an at-will employee and requiring the company to re-purchase his shares on a pro rata basis if he left within his first three years. A little over a year later, he was fired. He sued for breach of contract and lost. A federal court held that **the engagement letter detailing the stock re-purchase did not amount to a written three-year contract of employment**. *Yung v. Institutional Trading Co.*, 693 F.Supp.2d 70 (D.D.C. 2010).

◆   A South Carolina account executive agreed to an email offer of employment for two years. He quit his old job and showed up for work at the new company, where he was informed that there were new conditions attached to the offer. He objected to the new conditions and to the reduced salary but continued working. At the start of year two, he rejected a severance offer that was lower than set by the contract terms and was fired. He sued for breach of contract. The case reached the Supreme Court of South Carolina, which held that **the company breached the two-year contract as laid out in the email**. Also, the employee did not consent to the reduction in pay by continuing to work for the company after it reduced his salary because he objected to the change and showed his superior the email stating the contract terms. The company also violated the state Payment of Wages Act by reducing the executive's salary in contravention of the contract. *Mathis v. Brown & Brown of South Carolina, Inc.*, 698 S.E.2d 773 (S.C. 2010).

◆   A New York employee worked as the administrative director for two nursing facilities under a two-year employment contract. The contract provided that if the parties wanted to renew the contract, they would have to enter into "good faith negotiations" no more than nine months before its expiration. Neither party ever discussed renewing the contract, and when it expired, the employee continued to work for the company. When the company was sold, the new owner fired the employee a few months later. The employee sued for breach of contract, and a trial court ruled that her continued employment past the contract's expiration date gave rise to the presumption that the parties intended to renew the contract. The New York Court of Appeals disagreed. Here, the contract expressly provided against automatic renewal. Thus, **the employment became at will after the contract expired**, and the employee was properly fired. *Goldman v. White Plains Center for Nursing Care, LLC*, 896 N.E.2d 662 (N.Y. 2008).

◆   An Arkansas employee signed an employment agreement that guaranteed her 36 months of employment. If the company fired her without just cause as set out in the handbook before that time, she would be entitled to $5,000. If she quit before the 36 months, she would have to pay $5,000. The company fired her two months later, and she sued it for wrongful discharge. A trial court found no just cause for the termination because the term "insubordination" was not defined in the handbook. He awarded her $5,000, but the Court of Appeals of Arkansas reversed. The employee angrily confronted the president after he asked her to go to the office, get a key out of the safe and put it on her desk for another employee to pick up. A few days later, she grew belligerent when he talked to her and other employees about a form that was supposed to be placed in files. This was **insubordination justifying the discharge**. *Magic Touch Corp. v. Hicks*, 260 S.W.3d 322 (Ark. Ct. App. 2007).

❖   A Mississippi hospital hired an emergency room doctor under a one-year employment contract. The contract contained a provision allowing either party to terminate the employment without cause upon 60 days' notice. It also allowed the hospital to terminate the doctor's employment at any time for cause (as defined by the hospital). When the hospital fired the doctor because of patient complaints about rude and obnoxious behavior and insensitivity, the doctor sued for wrongful termination and breach of contract. The Court of Appeals of Mississippi held that **the contract between the doctor and hospital, although ostensibly for one year, actually created an at-will employment relationship**. Thus, the breach of contract action failed. *Miranda v. Wesley Health System, LLC*, 949 So.2d 63 (Miss. Ct. App. 2006).

❖   A regional account director for an advertising agency was offered a management supervisor position in the company's Los Angeles office and received a three-page letter stating the terms of the offer. The letter also explained the 90-day assessment period and explained that the employment was at will, meaning the company could terminate his employment "at any time," just as he could quit at any time. He signed and returned the letter, then was fired two years later. He sued for breach of contract, claiming that by oral representations, conduct and documents, the company had led him to understand that although he could be fired at any time, he could only be fired for cause. The case reached the Supreme Court of California, which held that **even though the letter did not state that the employee could be fired "without cause," it was not ambiguous**. It did not have to state whether cause was required for termination. The breach of contract claim failed. *Dore v. Arnold Worldwide, Inc.*, 39 Cal.4th 384, 139 P.3d 56 (Cal. 2006).

❖   An applicant for a sales position in Missouri took detailed notes about salary and bonuses for the next three years at a meeting with the company president and a branch manager. After the meeting, at the top of the page, he and the branch manager wrote the words, "contract with [company]," and they both signed it. The president did not sign the page. When the salesman was fired during the first year of his employment, he sued for breach of contract. A federal court granted pretrial judgment to the company, but the Eighth Circuit Court of Appeal reversed, finding **issues of fact over whether the notes amounted to an enforceable contract**. Here, there was enough ambiguity in the notes (as to whether the company intended to offer three years of employment) such that a jury would have to consider them. *Baum v. Helget Gas Products, Inc.*, 440 F.3d 1019 (8th Cir. 2006).

❖   A doctor in Vermont entered into a written contract with a physicians' group. The contract allowed for termination "with or without cause" 180 days after written notice was provided. The doctor refused to refer patients to certain specialists in the group because he believed they provided substandard or unnecessary care. When the group decided to close the office where the doctor worked, it gave him notice. It ultimately kept the office open, retaining a less senior doctor. He sued for breach of contract based on the implied covenant of good faith and fair dealing, as well as wrongful discharge in violation of public policy. The Vermont Supreme Court held that the doctor could proceed with his wrongful discharge claim despite the "with or without cause" provision of the contract. **Public policy could supersede the written termination provision.** *LoPresti v. Rutland Regional Health Services, Inc.*, 865 A.2d 1102 (Vt. 2004).

◆   An Oklahoma supervisor was reprimanded for sexually harassing a secretary. He was also instructed to apologize and participate in an alcohol treatment program. When he later made sexual comments to the secretary, she sued the employer for sexual harassment and creation of a hostile work environment. The employer further disciplined the supervisor and later fired him. He began working as an independent contractor and obtained a work assignment involving his former employer. The secretary complained when she learned of the assignment, and he was then removed from the project. He responded by suing his former employer for breach of contract and negligent investigation of the sexual harassment claim.

The court ruled for the employer, and the Tenth Circuit affirmed. According to the court, the presumption of employment at will cannot be overcome unless an employee demonstrates that the **employer's representations place substantive restrictions on its power to discharge**. The former supervisor was unable to show that certain employment documents, including the disciplinary letter he received, constituted a contract of employment that placed substantive restrictions on the employer's ability to discharge him. The breach of contract claim therefore failed. The court also held for the employer on the claim of negligent investigation of sexual harassment. Negligent investigation is not a recognized legal cause of action in Oklahoma. There also was insufficient evidence that the employer had interfered with his employment as an independent contractor. *Vice v. Conoco, Inc.*, 150 F.3d 1286 (10th Cir. 1998).

B.   Oral Contracts

In the absence of a written employment contract, the employment relationship is governed by statutory and common law principles, including the presumption of employment at will. Oral statements are less likely to be construed as creating a contract than writings, but where they are sufficiently definite, they can alter the at-will nature of employment.

One problem with oral contracts is the statute of frauds, which states that no oral contract is enforceable if, by its terms, it is not capable of being performed <u>within a year</u>. So an oral contract for three years is not enforceable under the statute of frauds.

Another problem is the likelihood of confusion or disagreement as to the contract's terms. Without a sufficiently clear writing, the contract is subject to the parties' memories. For example, what one party perceives as a guarantee of employment might be perceived by the other side as a mere statement of intent.

◆   A company unilaterally instituted a management security (no-layoff) policy. Four years later, the company notified its managers that industry conditions could force it to discontinue the program. After nearly another two years, the company announced that it was going to discontinue the program in six months. It offered a severance package to managers affected by the new layoff policy. Sixty former managers sued the company for breach of contract, claiming that it could not end the no-layoff policy unless it could show that there had been a change materially affecting its business plan. The California Supreme Court ruled that **because the company had unilaterally instituted the program, it could unilaterally end the program** so long as the termination occurred after a reasonable period of time and the company provided reasonable notice of the change. Here, after the change, the managers continued to work for the company, signifying their acceptance of the change. No further consideration was needed to support the modified contract. *Asmus v. Pacific Bell*, 999 P.2d 71 (Cal. 2000).

1. Oral Representations

Employers often make statements to employees about an intent to keep the employees around for a long period of time, either to reassure the employees or to motivate them. The statements are seldom meant to be construed as enforceable promises. Yet, employees often take them that way.

So if you're going to make those kinds of statements, keep them as vague as possible and make sure your employees know that they continue to be at-will employees.

◆   A salesman at an Oregon car dealership told his general manager that he was planning to take another job at a newspaper. In reliance on the general manager's alleged promise of a corporate job with the dealership, the salesman declined to take the job at the newspaper. When the dealership gave the corporate job to someone else, **the salesman sued it for promissory estoppel and fraudulent misrepresentation**. The state's highest court said a jury could find in his favor, even though the alleged promise was one of at-will employment. *Cocchiara v. Lithia Motors, Inc.*, 297 P.3d 1277 (Or. 2013).

◆   A prospective employee of Honeywell sued the company after she was not offered a job. She asserted that the company misrepresented that it would hire her once she passed a background check and that it then failed to do so. However, when she sued for negligent misrepresentation, an Arizona federal court granted pretrial judgment to the company, noting that such a claim requires the plaintiff to show that the defendant misrepresented present facts. **Negligent misrepresentation cannot be based on a promise of future conduct.** The Ninth Circuit affirmed. The employment offer letter expressly stated that her employment was subject to her passing the background check, which was a promise of future employment. As such, she could not succeed in her negligent misrepresentation claim. *Bowman v. Honeywell Int'l, Inc.*, 438 Fed.Appx. 613 (9th Cir. 2011).

♦   An employee of a company was solicited by a childhood friend to leave his job and begin working for the friend's business in Nevada. He decided to take the new job under a contract that specified his contract for the first five years, reaching a maximum salary of $100,000 per year. After 15 years, he would own 10% of the new parent company. However, the friend never actually started the new company, instead transferring ownership of the business to a living trust. And the employee was never paid the salary he had been promised. He was fired after bringing the breaches to the friend's attention, and he sued for breach of contract, negligent misrepresentation, fraud and luring under false pretenses. A Nevada federal district court held that the contract's language established that it was at-will employment because it extended for an indefinite term rather than a specific amount of time. Also, the negligent misrepresentation claim could not proceed because the representations made were either honest or intentionally false – they were not negligent. However, **the employee might be able to prove that he was lured under false pretenses and that the friend committed fraud**. Those claims were allowed to proceed. *Cundiff v. Dollar Loan Center LLC*, 726 F.Supp.2d 1232 (D. Nev. 2010).

♦   The principals of a real estate company interviewed a candidate for its presidency and asked if he would be willing to make a long-term commitment to the company. He agreed to make a 10-year commitment, and they allegedly agreed to employ him for 10 years. They gave him an offer letter with his salary, starting date and benefits, but which was silent as to the term of employment. He sold his townhouse in Florida and moved to Washington, D.C., where he bought a $1.9 million penthouse to serve as a residence and facility for entertaining clients. Within a year the relationship soured, and the president was fired. He sued for breach of contract. A federal court refused to grant pretrial judgment to the company. Although the 10-year oral contract was ostensibly barred by the statute of frauds, the company might be equitably estopped from asserting the statute of frauds as a defense. Here, **the president presented evidence that he reasonably relied on the principals' oral representations to his detriment** by selling his home and purchasing a penthouse. A jury would have to decide the outcome. *Morris v. Buvermo Properties, Inc.*, 510 F.Supp.2d 112 (D.D.C. 2007).

♦   A financial director for a company was contacted by a headhunter for another company and agreed to head up a division devoted to computer fraud and forensic investigation. He was told that he would be employed for as long as it took to build the department and as long as he desired. He took the job and was fired two months later. When he sued for breach of an oral contract, his lawsuit was dismissed. The Appellate Court of Illinois affirmed the ruling for the company. Here, **the promise of employment was not sufficiently clear and definite to overcome the presumption that the employment was at will**. Further, the promises were not unambiguous offers of permanent employment such that the employee could claim promissory estoppel (detrimental reliance on a promise by another). *Robinson v. BDO Seidman, LLP*, 854 N.E.2d 767 (Ill. App. Ct. 2006).

◆   A Connecticut company employed a husband and wife in high-level positions, then underwent a reorganization and fired the husband. The wife expressed concern to an executive vice president (VP) regarding how her employment would be affected if her husband accepted a job with a competitor. **The VP promised that the company would take no adverse action against her if her husband got a job with a competitor.** When the husband landed such a job, the company reduced her duties, limited her client contact, and asked her to agree to restrictive obligations in relation to her husband's job. When she refused, she was fired. She sued, and a jury ruled in her favor, awarding her $850,000. The Connecticut Supreme Court affirmed. Even though the company had not contractually agreed not to take adverse action, it had promised not to do so, and the wife had justifiably relied on that promise. Thus, her promissory estoppel claim was actionable. *Stewart v. Cendant Mobility Services Corp.*, 837 A.2d 736 (Conn. 2003).

◆   The president of an Ohio electronics company told one of his account executives that he was going to be the president's "right-hand guy" for a long, long time. He also indicated that they were going to have many other ventures together and asked the executive to "look at this five, ten years from now." Subsequently, he fired the executive and a colleague following accusations of sexual harassment. They sued for breach of contract, asserting that either an implied or an express contract of employment existed to prevent the firing. The Ohio Court of Appeals found that **the president's statements did not modify the at-will nature of the employment**. The statements he had made were not specific promises but rather sweeping comments about the future. He never represented that the executive and his colleague were secure in their jobs regardless of their workplace conduct, and there was no dispute that misconduct had occurred. Since their employment had been at will, their breach of contract lawsuit failed. *Daup v. Tower Cellular, Inc.*, 737 N.E.2d 128 (Ohio Ct. App. 2000).

◆   A South Carolina telephone company employee was suspended for improperly disposing of company property. He asserted that he had disposed of the property according to the instructions of a company official, but the company fired him for lying. The employee appealed the decision through the company's progressive appeal process until the company's general manager affirmed the discharge. He then sued for breach of contract based on the employee handbook and alleged **statements by company officials that he would be discharged only for good cause such as misconduct**. The Supreme Court of South Carolina held that the employer's alleged offer stating that the employee would have his job as long as he kept his nose clean and did his job was not sufficiently explicit to constitute an offer to limit termination to just cause. Thus, his at-will employment status was not altered. *Prescott v. Farmers Telephone Co-op., Inc.*, 516 S.E.2d 923 (S.C. 1999).

2. Covenant of Good Faith and Fair Dealing

In every employment relationship, there is a duty of good faith and fair dealing – even in at-will employment relationships. Employees have a duty of loyalty to the company, and employers have a duty to comply with the terms of the employment contract in good faith.

◆   A company in Georgia fired an employee after discovering that he was involved in a competing business. It learned this information from emails a manager discovered on his personal computer, which he used for work. He sued for computer theft, computer trespass and computer invasion of privacy, and the company countersued him for breach of the duty of loyalty. A trial court awarded the company over $39,000. He appealed. The Georgia Court of Appeals affirmed, noting that the company had offered him a work computer but that he had chosen to use his own computer at work. Thus, his privacy rights were diminished. The manager's actions in checking the emails were not taken with the intention of stealing or interfering with the employee's property or examining his personal data. As for the breach of duty, had the employee simply been making plans to compete after leaving the company, he would have been justified in doing so. But instead **he solicited customers for a rival business while still employed**, in violation of the employment manual. Thus, he breached his duty of loyalty to the company. *Sitton v. Print Direction, Inc.*, 312 Ga.App. 365, 718 S.E.2d 532 (Ga. Ct. App. 2011).

◆   A lighting products company in Virginia had an employee handbook that notified employees they were not allowed outside employment that conflicted with the company's interests. The handbook also addressed confidential information, although the company did not require employees to sign confidentiality or noncompete agreements. While working for the company, a manager created a competing business and used a company computer to seek legal advice. When he quit, he deleted emails, spreadsheets and files from his computer. A forensic computer expert recovered the material on the hard drive. The manager also encouraged two sales reps who were independent contractors to send business to his new company. The old company sued the former manager and two former sales reps for breach of fiduciary duty. A jury awarded the company $1.5 million in compensatory damages and $56,700 in punitive damages. The Supreme Court of Virginia upheld the award for the company, finding that the manager and sales reps breached their duty of loyalty to the company. **Even though the sales reps were independent contractors, they received exclusive territories in exchange for an expectation of loyalty.** *Banks v. Mario Industries of Virginia, Inc.*, 650 S.E.2d 687 (Va. 2007).

◆   An employee of an Illinois-based commercial real estate developer used a company laptop to identify properties to acquire and assist with acquisitions. When he quit to start his own business, he deleted all the data he had collected and also downloaded a secure-erasure program to write over the deleted files to prevent anyone else from recovering them. The company sued him for breach of contract and for violating the Computer Fraud and Abuse Act (CFAA). A federal court dismissed the lawsuit, but the Seventh Circuit reinstated it. **The CFAA prohibits knowingly transmitting a program or command to intentionally damage a protected computer without authorization.** Here, the allegation in the lawsuit was that he had done just that. *Int'l Airport Centers, LLC v. Citrin*, 440 F.3d 418 (7th Cir. 2006).

♦   A food products company employed a salaried traffic manager to arrange for transportation of its products to stores. During the course of his employment, the manager and his wife formed a company through which they arranged for the transportation of goods for various companies, including two of the company's competitors. Although the manager's wife ran the business out of their home, the manager spent about 15 minutes during each workday on his business. The company fired the manager three years later for failing to conduct inspections of its off-site warehouses and negotiate lower freight rates. It then learned of his home business and sued him in state court for conversion (similar to theft) and breach of his duty of loyalty. The trial court dismissed the complaint. The Appellate Division reversed and remanded for a new trial on the breach of duty claim. The New Jersey Supreme Court then held that **the manager's actions in spending 15 minutes a day on his home business might amount to a breach of the duty of loyalty he owed the company**. On remand, the court would have to determine whether the manager's assistance to the company's competitors was substantial. If so, the company would be entitled to relief. *Cameco, Inc. v. Gedicke*, 724 A.2d 783 (N.J. 1999).

♦   A Colorado employer fired a route supervisor for falsifying time cards. The supervisor sued for failing to follow progressive disciplinary policy, breach of an express covenant of good faith and fair dealing, and other claims. The court awarded damages for breach of contract, plus punitive and noneconomic damages. The case reached the Supreme Court of Colorado, which **refused to recognize a tort claim for breach of the covenant of good faith and fair dealing in employment** but found that the breach of contract action was viable due to the employer's misconduct. Thus, economic and noneconomic damages were available, but punitive damages were not. *Decker v. Browning-Ferris Industries of Colorado, Inc.*, 947 P.2d 937 (Colo. 1997).

♦   A medical imaging technologist employed by a Delaware chemical corporation became aware of his supervisor's potential conflict of interest with the employer because of the supervisor's involvement in another company's medical imaging technology business. After he met with his supervisor to express his concern, the supervisor became angry and prohibited him from visiting other corporate locations or having visitors without permission. The supervisor gave him negative performance evaluations, and the technologist soon quit. He sued the corporation and supervisor for breach of the employment contract and breach of the covenant of good faith and fair dealing in employment relationships. A jury awarded the technologist over $500,000 in damages. The employer appealed to the Supreme Court of Delaware, arguing that the trial court had given the jury improper instructions by allowing them to find liability based on the supervisor's hatred, ill will or intent to injure. The court agreed, finding that the employment relationship of the parties was at will and that in order **to create an exception for breach of the covenant of good faith, there must be a showing of employer malice**, intent to injure, and causation of termination based on falsified grounds. The trial court decision was reversed. *E.I. DuPont de Nemours and Co. v. Pressman*, 679 A.2d 436 (Del. 1996).

IV. WRONGFUL DISCHARGE

Employers may not discharge employees for engaging in <u>protected activity</u> or asserting rights to which they are legally entitled, such as the filing of a workers' compensation claim. Even if the employment relationship is at will, actions that violate an important public policy may create liability.

Thus, even though at-will employees can be fired at any time for any reason or no reason at all, they cannot be fired for a reason that violates public policy (like discrimination or retaliation for whistleblowing).

A. Public Policy Protections

When an employee engages in activity that is beneficial to society (like jury duty) or is otherwise protected (e.g., as a minority, a disabled person, a person 40 or older), firing that employee is likely to result in a wrongful discharge or discrimination lawsuit. This does not mean you can't fire such employees, but it does mean you should document the reasons for doing so very carefully to protect yourself from litigation.

Of course, you should always <u>document the reasons for firing</u> any employee, even when the employment is at will. Suppose that the reason for the firing is that the employee dyes her hair green and you hate green hair. You should still document this. It may seem stupid to a court, but it is not a reason that violates public policy.

1. Criminal Activities

Employees cannot be fired for refusing to participate in illegal activities. Nor should they be fired for refusing to participate in activities that they, in good faith, believe are illegal.

♦   The regional sales manager for a company in South Carolina was supposed to be paid straight commissions from two office locations. The manager became concerned that she wasn't being paid for the commissions from one of the offices. She did not file a written complaint with the Department of Labor, but instead met with her superior and showed him a copy of the compensation agreement. The superior then contacted the owner, who admitted that, due to an oversight, he had forgotten to pay the manager the commissions from the second office. The company fired the manager the next day, paying her more than what she was owed for the commissions. **When she sued for wrongful discharge for violating the Payment of Wages Act, she lost.** The Supreme Court of South Carolina held that she would have had to file a written complaint with the Department of Labor or at least indicated to the employer that she intended to file such a complaint to get the protections of the act. *Barron v. Labor Finders of South Carolina*, 713 S.E.2d 634 (S.C. 2011).

♦   A newly hired telecommunications employee with muscle spasms and chronic pain used marijuana on his doctor's recommendation pursuant to California's Compassionate Use Act of 1996, which provides a defense to criminal drug charges. He was fired after flunking the company's preemployment drug test and sued for wrongful discharge in violation of public policy as well as disability discrimination under state law. The case reached the California Supreme Court, which held that **the employer did not have to accommodate the employee's use of marijuana at home** despite the Compassionate Use Act. Nor did the termination violate public policy because marijuana remains an illegal drug under federal law. *Ross v. RagingWire Telecommunications, Inc.*, 42 Cal.4th 920, 174 P.3d 200 (Cal. 2008).

♦   A Tennessee truck driver refused to drive a truck that had only a copy of the original "cab card" showing registration of the vehicle. The next day he was fired. He sued for retaliatory discharge, claiming that he had been fired for refusing to participate in an illegal activity (a Tennessee Department of Safety regulation required the truck to carry an original "cab card" showing registration). A jury ruled for the truck driver, but the Court of Appeals of Tennessee reversed. It held that the employee's refusal to perform the assigned work based on the regulation requiring the original cab card, as opposed to a photocopy, did not further important public policy concerns, and therefore would not support a claim of retaliatory discharge. **The illegal activity the employee chooses not to engage in must implicate important public policy concerns for the employee to be able to claim protection** against retaliatory discharge. *Franklin v. Swift Transportation Co., Inc.*, 210 S.W.3d 521 (Tenn. Ct. App. 2006).

♦   A national childcare company discharged a regional director after she refused to fire employees who had threatened to sue over their workers' compensation claims. The Washington Court of Appeals held that the order to fire the employees was unlawful. The regional director had received good performance reviews until about two months after she and five other employees were in a work-related car accident. All of them, including the regional director, filed workers' compensation claims. But a week after the accident, the company's operations director ordered the regional director to fire the other five employees. The operations director had heard that two of them were contemplating a lawsuit against the company and "didn't trust either of them not to sue." The operations director also told the regional director that it would be in the company's best interest to dismiss them to avoid any more problems. The regional director refused to do so and received her first poor performance review several days later. She was fired a month later for neglecting her duties and sued. She won because **her refusal to unlawfully fire the other employees was a substantial factor in her own termination**. *Lins v. Children's Discovery Center of America, Inc.*, 976 P.2d 168 (Wash. Ct. App. 1999).

♦   A Virginia woman alleged that her employer violated state criminal laws when he groped her, demanded that she have sex with him and fired her after she rejected him. She sued for wrongful termination, but the court dismissed her case, finding that she was not covered by either federal or state law because the employer had fewer than five employees. Also, Virginia's Human Rights Act was the only state law that could create a public policy allowing her to sue for wrongful termination. Since she was an at-will employee, she could not sue unless there was a public policy allowing her to do so. The Supreme Court of Virginia held that **she could use the state's criminal laws to state a public policy argument that her termination had been wrongful**. It reversed and remanded the case. *Mitchem v. Counts*, 523 S.E.2d 246 (Va. 2000).

♦   The director of security, safety and occupational health for a Colorado brewery engaged in a series of covert drug purchases under the direction and approval of his supervisors to discover whether some employees were using illicit drugs. He was later fired for misusing company funds and engaging in sexual improprieties with a co-worker. He appealed his discharge to an internal appeals panel, asserting that the supervisors had **conspired to discharge him by making the illegal drug purchases appear to be his idea**. The panel affirmed the discharge action, and he sued the employer for wrongful discharge in violation of public policy and intentional infliction of emotional distress. The Colorado Supreme Court held that even if the employee's claims were true, the conduct alleged by the employee (using him as a scapegoat in a criminal conspiracy involving illegal drugs and money laundering) did not rise to the level of outrageousness necessary to sustain a claim of intentional infliction of emotional distress. The court also held that the employee could not succeed on his wrongful discharge claim because he was not fired in retaliation for whistleblowing or for refusing to commit criminal acts. He had already been fired when he blew the whistle on the employer. *Coors Brewing Co. v. Floyd*, 978 P.2d 663 (Colo. 1999).

♦   A supervisor working for a Texas construction company learned that some of his co-workers were involved in a workplace conspiracy including theft, fraud and violations of state and federal regulations involving the construction of a nuclear power plant. He found discrepancies in recordkeeping, including falsified claims for hours worked. He refused to participate in the fraudulent activity and received negative performance ratings. When he took a vacation, the company fired him as part of a work force reduction. He sued the company, and a jury awarded him $150,000 for wrongful termination. The employer appealed to the Court of Appeals of Texas, which found substantial evidence in the record of a criminal conspiracy among the employee's co-workers. Here, **the conspiracy involved falsification of records in violation of federal and state law**. Accordingly, although the employment relationship was at will, the wrongful termination action was permissible. *Ebasco Constructors, Inc. v. Rex*, 923 S.W.2d 694 (Tex. Ct. App. 1996).

2. Unsafe Working Conditions

Employees cannot be fired for reporting unsafe working conditions. Nor should they be fired for refusing, in good faith, to work in such conditions. Employers occasionally win such lawsuits, but the cost of litigating a wrongful discharge lawsuit is high.

Moreover, if the workplace is in fact unsafe, there is a potential for liability (either tort liability or workers' compensation). Thus, when an employee complains of unsafe working conditions, an investigation should be undertaken to ascertain whether a safety threat exists.

♦   A supervisor for a company in Ohio claimed that he was fired because he had expressed concerns about the safety of the workplace to outside parties, including a fire captain and an insurance adjuster. The company asserted that it fired him for insubordination. When he sued for wrongful discharge, the case reached the Supreme Court of Ohio, which ruled against him. As an at-will employee, he had to show that there was a specific and clear public policy that was violated by his termination. This he failed to do. **His mere assertions that the company jeopardized workplace safety by firing him did not point to a specific public policy that the company violated.** *Dohme v. Eurand America, Inc.*, 956 N.E.2d 825 (Ohio 2011).

♦   A FedEx driver in Massachusetts reported that fumes from his truck were making him sick. He filed a complaint with OSHA, which found that the problem with the fumes had already been investigated and fixed. The driver had a history of problems and had been warned about threatening a customer. He had also been reassigned to a new route. He asked several customers to complain about his changed route and received another warning letter as well as a suspension for disclosing confidential information. After a rancorous meeting with a new senior manager, he resigned. But when he learned that the two disciplinary warnings prevented him from being rehired, he tried to rescind the resignation. FedEx refused to rescind the resignation, and he sued for constructive discharge. A federal court and the First Circuit ruled against him, finding **no evidence that FedEx constructively discharged him for filing the OSHA complaint**. *Meuser v. Federal Express Corp.*, 564 F.3d 507 (1st Cir. 2009).

♦   A safety coordinator for an energy company in Iowa openly disagreed with company policies allowing for a one-man line crew and permitting linemen to use a body belt instead of a body harness. When a new supervisor learned of his failure to support the company's safety policies, she fired him. He sued the company for wrongful discharge, and a federal jury awarded him $920,000 in damages. The company appealed. The Eighth Circuit affirmed the award, finding that even though the employee handbook contained a disclaimer that employment was strictly at will (such that the employee could be fired at any time for any reason or no reason at all), a public policy exception modified the employment-at-will doctrine. Under Iowa's Occupational Safety and Health Act, there was an implied cause of action for wrongful discharge where an **employee is fired for trying to institute new or perfect existing safety policies**. *Korht v. MidAmerican Energy Co.*, 364 F.3d 894 (8th Cir. 2004).

♦   An Indiana production worker claimed that he was protected from retaliatory discharge under Indiana's Occupational Safety and Health Act (IOSHA). The U.S. Court of Appeals for the Seventh Circuit disagreed. The Indiana legislature "created a specific statutory remedy," which forbids the discharge of an employee who files a complaint with state labor department officials within 30 days of the suspected violation. According to the record, the worker **only reported the claimed safety violation to his employer's safety division**. Because he did not pursue the remedy provided by statute, he was not entitled to rely on it for protection. The case arose after the worker engaged in horseplay and insubordinate conduct. He claimed that two co-workers then failed to follow proper safety procedures and deliberately set him up for a "near miss" accident. He reported the incident to the plant's safety department. Ultimately, he was fired for misconduct. In his lawsuit for retaliatory discharge under the IOSHA, the Seventh Circuit found that he had no rights under the act. *Groce v. Eli Lilly & Co.*, 193 F.3d 496 (7th Cir. 1999).

◆   A helicopter manufacturer employed an aircraft maintenance instructor for several years as a member of a nonmilitary project team. However, the employer instructed him to conduct maintenance training at a military base in Bahrain when the U.S. became involved in military action in the Persian Gulf. The instructor refused to travel to Bahrain based on the threat to his personal safety as supported by a U.S. government travel advisory discouraging travel to the area. The employer fired the instructor and removed him from its premises under a security escort. He sued for wrongful discharge and negligent and intentional infliction of emotional distress. The Supreme Court of Connecticut held that there was evidence that **the employer had directed the employee to work in an unsafe location**. As a result, the employee's wrongful discharge claim could continue. He could not be forced to work in conditions that posed a risk of death or serious bodily harm. However, the employer prevailed on the negligent and intentional infliction of emotional distress claims. *Parsons v. United Technologies Corp.*, 243 Conn. 66, 700 A.2d 655 (Conn. 1997).

◆   The Supreme Court of Oklahoma rejected a claim by a discharged private security employee that the Oklahoma Occupational Safety and Health Standards (OSHS) Act provided an underlying public policy that precluded his employer from firing him in retaliation for protesting unsafe working conditions. The case arose when the employee protested a new company security policy by rigging a package with an alarm that sounded during a meeting. The employer fired the employee, who sued for retaliatory discharge. The court observed that the state OSHS Act no longer applied to private employers and could not create a valid public policy exception to the presumption of employment at will for private employers. The federal Occupational Safety and Health Act was also unavailable to provide protection in this case. **No public policy existed under state workplace safety laws that would form the basis for a retaliatory discharge claim** against a private employer. *Griffin v. Mullinix*, 947 P.2d 177 (Okla. 1997).

3.   Other Public Policy Protections

As a way to avoid potential wrongful discharge liability, make certain that the real reason an employee is being fired is not retaliation for some activity or speech that is protected or that in some way advances public policy.

◆   While driving to work, a New Hampshire quality control inspector became involved in a road rage incident. The other driver followed the employee into the employee's parking lot at work, where the employee swatted the other driver's cell phone from her hand and the pair shouted obscenities at each other. The employee was discharged, and he sued. **He claimed he was fired in violation of a public policy that encouraged him to defend himself.** The court rejected his claim, saying he did not articulate a public policy that encouraged him to get into a shouting match on company property. *Leeds v. BAE Systems*, 80 A.3d 366 (N.H. 2013).

◆   A car salesman in Missouri was fired after he bought a car from another dealer without giving his employer a chance to match the price. **He sued, claiming that the employer's price-matching rule offended public policy by restraining consumer trade.** The court rejected his claim because he did not identify a direct and clear legal mandate barring the price-matching rule. *Hedrick v. Jay Wolfe Imports I, LLC*, 404 S.W.3d 454 (Mo. Ct. App. 2013).

◆   A Michigan sales representative sued a former employer, accusing it of violating statutes including a law regarding sales commissions. His new employer fired him. He claimed the new employer discharged him because he sued the former employer, **in violation of a state public policy supporting whistleblowers**. The court ruled that a jury would have to decide whether the termination was legal. *Bailey v. Scoutware, LLC*, No. 12-10281, 2013 WL 3946036 (E.D. Mich. 7/31/13).

◆   A Sears loss prevention manager in Florida investigated allegations of sexual harassment made by an employee. She and a male employee interviewed the harassment victim, but they believed the victim was not completely forthcoming, so the manager interviewed her again by herself. This time, the victim relayed that she had been raped three times but that she didn't want to go to the police or have her husband find out. The manager told Sears it needed to contact police. Instead, it fired the employee accused of rape and later fired the manager. The manager sued for retaliation but lost. A federal court and the Eleventh Circuit ruled that **she wasn't protesting sexual harassment or assault but rather the way Sears investigated the allegations. This wasn't protected activity.** *Brush v. Sears Holding Corp.*, 466 Fed.Appx. 781 (11th Cir. 2012).

◆   An Iowa employee filed a formal complaint with the company's HR representative regarding her supervisor's harassing behavior. A few days later, she met with the plant manager and two others to discuss. The plant manager kept interrupting her. He then wadded up the complaint, threw it in the garbage, pointed to the door and told her he never wanted to see her again. She emailed a company official the next day to say that she'd been pushed out the door. Two days later, the HR director called to tell her she wasn't fired. After an investigation, the HR director told her to return to work. She instead sued for retaliation. A federal court granted pretrial judgment to the company, but the Eighth Circuit reversed, finding that **the company could be liable for the improper firing, even though it was rescinded two days later**. A trial was required. *Young-Losee v. Graphic Packaging Int'l, Inc.*, 631 F.3d 909 (8th Cir. 2011).

♦   A dentist in Colorado implemented a new policy that prevented employees from taking meal or rest breaks or leaving the office, except to use the restroom, even when a patient had cancelled an appointment. An assistant told her husband about the policy; he contacted an attorney who told him the policy was illegal, and he then emailed the dentist to inform him of that fact. The dentist fired the assistant and refused to pay her accrued vacation. He also accused her of stealing $240 from the office, even though it was being remodeled at the time and several people had keys to it. When she couldn't find comparable employment, she started her own business and sued for retaliatory discharge. A judge awarded her back pay up until she started her business, but awarded no punitive damages. The Colorado Court of Appeals went even farther than the trial court, noting that **the dentist fired her for objecting to an unlawful work schedule**. The back pay period didn't end when she started the new job. Also, the judge should have awarded punitive damages against the dentist for his vindictive discharge of the assistant. *Bonidy v. Vail Valley Center for Aesthetic Dentistry, P.C.*, 232 P.3d 277 (Colo. Ct. App. 2010).

♦   A Wal-Mart employee signed a "Global Assignment Letter" as part of his transfer to Costa Rica as a Global Services Manager. The letter detailed his starting salary and benefits. It stated that his anticipated employment would last three years, but also provided that it was not a contract of employment. After he moved to Costa Rica, his superiors became unhappy with his work. He reported inhumane working conditions at the factories. He also had an inappropriate relationship with a subordinate. After he was fired for violating the company's anti-fraternization policy, he sued for wrongful discharge and breach of contract. He claimed he was fired in violation of public policy for reporting the inhumane working conditions. He also asserted that the letter amounted to an enforceable contract. The Arkansas Court of Appeals ruled against him, noting that the letter did not amount to an employment contract because it clearly stated that it didn't. Also, his discharge did not violate public policy because **he failed to show that Wal-Mart's failure to prohibit inhumane working conditions in its foreign factories implicated a well-established public policy** as set forth by statute or the state's constitution. *Lynn v. Wal-Mart Stores, Inc.*, 280 S.W.3d 574 (Ark. Ct. App. 2008).

♦   A nursing home employee reported suspected patient abuse to the Nebraska Department of Health and Human Services. A few days later, her supervisor yelled at her for going over her head, then fired her when she refused to resign. **She sued for retaliatory discharge in contravention of public policy, and a jury awarded her $79,000 for emotional distress.** The nursing home appealed, and the Supreme Court of Nebraska upheld the award for the employee. Here, the evidence showed that the employee was fired for making a report of abuse as mandated by the Adult Protective Services Act, and there was sufficient evidence of emotional distress to support the damage award. *Wendeln v. The Beatrice Manor, Inc.*, 712 N.W.2d 226 (Neb. 2006).

♦   A bank teller in Nebraska attended a public meeting and questioned the propriety of a school board action, asking about the potential tax consequences of a proposed merger with another school district. The superintendent and two school board members then told bank officials they would not deal with the teller when they visited the bank to conduct personal business. Two weeks later, the teller was fired. She sued the bank under 42 U.S.C. § 1983 (Section 1983), **alleging that she was fired for speaking at the public meeting** and that the bank had acted under color of state law by conspiring with the school board members to retaliate against her for her public speech. Although the bank claimed it could not be held liable under Section 1983 because it was not a public entity, the Eighth Circuit held that if a conspiracy was shown, the teller could win. The teller was entitled to a trial on the issue. *Dossett v. First State Bank*, 399 F.3d 940 (8th Cir. 2005).

❖ A security guard for a company that provided security services to an oil refinery in Illinois went on television and talked about a fellow security officer who bragged about being a felon. The guard stated that convicted felons should not be trusted to provide security at oil refineries, which are potential terrorist targets. He was then placed on indefinite suspension, and 11 months later sued for wrongful discharge. The company sought to dismiss the lawsuit because he had agreed (as a condition of employment) to take action within six months of the date a cause of action arose. The Seventh Circuit Court of Appeals refused to dismiss the case because **it was not clear that the company actually fired the guard at the time it placed him on indefinite suspension**. *Thomas v. Guardsmark, Inc.*, 381 F.3d 701 (7th Cir. 2004).

❖ An at-will manager at Sears was **fired for correcting an employee's time card**. He sued the store for wrongful discharge, asserting that Sears had violated a public policy requiring employers to keep accurate employee records. The Ohio Court of Appeals ruled against him, finding that he failed to demonstrate that his discharge jeopardized the public policy of keeping accurate employment records. Through regulatory oversight (including inspections) and civil and criminal penalties, the state and federal government have adequate means to enforce the public policy here. The discharge was not wrongful. *White v. Sears, Roebuck & Co.*, 837 N.E.2d 1275 (Ohio Ct. App. 2005).

❖ A transportation company in Texas required its truck drivers to submit to random drug testing pursuant to Department of Transportation (DOT) regulations. A driver submitted to urinalysis and tested positive for marijuana. However, the company failed to comply with the DOT procedures for collecting a sample. For example, the collection container was unsealed, and it was out of the driver's sight for over a minute after he provided the sample while he was washing his hands. After he was fired, he sued the company for failing to use ordinary care in collecting his urine sample, which he alleged resulted in the positive reading. A jury awarded him over $800,000 in lost wages and mental anguish, as well as $100,000 in exemplary damages. The court of appeals affirmed the award, but the Supreme Court of Texas reversed. It held that **the company did not owe the driver a common-law duty of care when collecting the urine sample** for drug testing pursuant to DOT regulations. *Mission Petroleum Carriers, Inc. v. Solomon*, 106 S.W.3d 705 (Tex. 2003).

✦   An administrative assistant for a senior care facility in Maryland initially received an "above average" performance evaluation. However, she was later reprimanded for complaining about her shortened workweek, for failing to conform to a new recruiting policy and for refusing assistance in improving her performance. After receiving an employee warning report, she informed her supervisor she would be late in returning it to the company because she wanted to talk with an attorney before formally responding. She thought some of the statements in the report were libelous. The company fired her the same day. She sued for wrongful termination, asserting that the company violated public policy by firing her for expressing an intent to seek legal counsel. The case reached the Maryland Court of Appeals, which dismissed the action. Although Maryland public policy favors access to attorneys, **it does not require employers to retain at-will employees who attempt to seek legal advice on a work-related matter**. The exceptions to the at-will doctrine are few and narrow, and consulting an attorney is not one of them. *Porterfield v. Mascari II, Inc.*, 823 A.2d 590 (Md. 2003).

✦   When a Nevada hospital employee incurred large medical expenses, he tried to negotiate repayment with the hospital. The negotiations failed, and the employee informed the hospital that he intended to file for bankruptcy protection. Before he could file, the hospital fired him. The trustee in bankruptcy sued the hospital under Section 525(b) of the Bankruptcy Code, which prohibits the termination of an employee solely because the employee is or has been a debtor in bankruptcy. The Bankruptcy Court dismissed the claim against the hospital, finding that **the statute did not protect people who had not yet filed for bankruptcy protection**. The Ninth Circuit affirmed. Because the employee had not yet filed for bankruptcy protection, the hospital did not violate the Bankruptcy Code's prohibition against retaliation. *In re Majewski*, 310 F.3d 653 (9th Cir. 2002).

✦   A provider of electricity in Tennessee had **an exogamy rule, which required that when two permanent-status employees married, one of them had to quit**. When two employees decided to get married, they were informed that one of them would have to quit, but that whichever one did could continue on in a temporary capacity until he or she found a new job. The employees married and returned to work without deciding which one would leave. The husband was then called in to his supervisor's office, where he indicated that he did not agree with the policy. He was fired, and he sued under the First Amendment, alleging that the policy violated his constitutional right to marry (freedom of association). He also asserted that he was fired in retaliation for speaking out against the policy. A federal court granted pretrial judgment to the provider, and the Sixth Circuit affirmed in part. The policy did not significantly restrict his ability to marry. However, there was a question of fact as to whether he had been fired for speaking out against the policy. That issue required a trial. *Vaughn v. Lawrenceburg Power System*, 269 F.3d 703 (6th Cir. 2001).

✦   An employee in the photo processing department at a Nebraska Wal-Mart saw pictures of a child lying on a newspaper, apparently covered with marijuana leaves and $100 bills. Under store policy, she was supposed to take "questionable pictures of minors" to the store manager. She instead showed the pictures to the department manager but was dissatisfied with the response she received. She took copies of the pictures to the police. She was then fired for violating the store's customer confidentiality policy and for showing an unwillingness to adhere to company policies in the future. When she sued under the Nebraska Fair Employment Practices Act, a jury found that Wal-Mart did not have a practice of preventing the reporting of child abuse. It also found that **she failed to prove her report to the police was the sole factor in Wal-Mart's decision to fire her**. It returned a verdict for the store. The Eighth Circuit Court of Appeals affirmed. *Gasper v. Wal-Mart Stores,* 270 F.3d 1196 (8th Cir. 2001).

◆   A California convenience store employee thought employees could help themselves to free soft drinks and coffee at any time. He agreed to testify at a former employee's unemployment compensation hearing. On the way there, he stopped at the store and helped himself to a soft drink. A regional manager who appeared at the unemployment compensation hearing fired him, allegedly for stealing the soft drink. The employee sued for wrongful discharge in violation of public policy, breach of contract, breach of an implied covenant of good faith and fair dealing, slander and intentional infliction of emotional distress. A court awarded the employee $42,000 in damages plus $300,000 in punitive damages for discharge in violation of public policy. The California Court of Appeal noted that employers may not discharge an employee for a reason that violates a fundamental public policy. **Discharge in retaliation for testifying before an unemployment compensation hearing violates a fundamental policy** deemed by the legislature to be vital to the state's economic interests. Thus, the wrongful discharge award was affirmed. The punitive damages award was also affirmed, since the employee had been discharged by a "managing agent" in a policymaking position with immediate control over the decision to fire the employee. The California Supreme Court affirmed the award of punitive damages. *White v. Ultramar, Inc.*, 981 P.2d 944 (Cal. 1999).

B. Jury Duty

Employees who miss work for jury duty cannot be fired for that reason.

◆   While serving on a grand jury, a closing officer for a Louisiana real estate company was fired after making two offensive remarks to the company's business partner. **She sued, claiming she was fired because of her jury service in violation of the Jury System Improvement Act.** The court rejected her claim, finding she did not show her jury service played any role in the decision to terminate her employment. *Rogers v. Bromac Title Services, LLC*, 755 F.3d 347 (5th Cir. 2014).

◆   An on-air traffic manager for a local New York television and radio station was fired after he missed a day of work because of jury duty. He had mentioned to his supervisor and some co-workers that he might be out for jury duty but did not submit any written notice. On the day he was directed to report for jury duty, he tried unsuccessfully to contact his supervisor. In his wrongful discharge lawsuit, the trial court held that the judiciary laws did not allow him to sue for damages. An appellate division court agreed. The applicable section of the judiciary law, although prohibiting an employer from discharging or penalizing an employee for complying with a jury duty directive, provides only that employers will be subject to criminal sanctions for violating the law. It does not provide for any civil cause of action against the employer for wrongful discharge, and at the time the law was passed, the governor vetoed such a remedy. Even though the station's actions violated public policy, **the court had no power to fashion a remedy for wrongful discharge**. *DiBlasi v. Traffax Traffic Network*, 681 N.Y.S.2d 147 (N.Y. App. Div. 1998).

◆   A New York employer maintained an employee handbook encouraging its employees to fulfill their jury duty obligations. An employee accepted jury duty but was soon fired. He sued the employer for breach of contract and violation of **a state law making the dismissal of an employee for serving on a jury a misdemeanor**. The court dismissed the case, and the Appellate Division affirmed. The misdemeanor statute did not create a civil cause of action against an employer for wrongful discharge. Also, even though the employee handbook encouraged employees to fulfill their jury duty obligations, it did not alter the at-will relationship because it contained a prominent disclaimer that it did not create an employment contract. *Gomariz v. Foote, Cone & Belding Communications, Inc.*, 644 N.Y.S.2d 224 (N.Y. App. Div. 1996).

◆   A secretary at a Texas company was selected as a juror and served on a jury for six days. Three days after her selection, she was fired. She sued. A federal court awarded her six months' compensation, which was the maximum amount allowed under the Texas Juror Reemployment Statute (TJRS). She appealed to the U.S. Court of Appeals, Fifth Circuit, asserting that she should have received punitive damages also. The court noted that the TJRS did not seem to contemplate punitive damages. However, by analogizing the statute to the Texas Workers' Compensation Retaliation Statute, the court found that the term "damages" **allowed punitive damages** according to the Texas Supreme Court. Nevertheless, even though punitive damages could be recovered, the maximum amount recoverable was six months' compensation. *Fuchs v. Lifetime Doors, Inc.*, 939 F.2d 1275 (5th Cir. 1991).

C. Workers' Compensation

Employees injured on the job who file claims for workers' compensation and then are discharged often file lawsuits for retaliatory discharge, alleging that their employers have discharged them for filing the workers' compensation claims.

Employees who return to work after filing workers' compensation claims may be required to pass a fitness-for-duty exam to ensure that they can perform the job safely.

For cases dealing with workers' compensation generally, refer to Chapter Seven.

◆   An Illinois woman was allegedly injured on the job. She notified her employer and requested compensation for her medical expenses under the Illinois Workers' Compensation Act. Shortly thereafter, her employer fired her for filing a "false" workers' compensation claim. Her union filed a grievance, and an arbitrator found in the employee's favor and ordered her reinstated with full back pay. Meanwhile, she brought a retaliatory discharge claim against her employer. The case reached the U.S. Supreme Court, which examined whether the employee's claim was preempted by Section 301 of the Labor Management Relations Act. The Supreme Court held that it was not. Therefore, **if the employee could show that she had been discharged to deter her from exercising her rights under the workers' compensation act, she could win her suit**. No interpretation of the parties' collective bargaining agreement would have to be made. Since the inquiries were purely factual, the claim was independent of the agreement and Section 301 did not preempt it. The employee could continue with her claim. *Lingle v. Norge Division of Magic Chef, Inc.*, 486 U.S. 399, 108 S.Ct. 1877, 100 L.Ed.2d 410 (1988).

◆   An Illinois company's policy allowed it to fire any employee seeking worker's compensation benefits if the employee refused to be tested for alcohol and drugs. An injured employee who wanted to file a workers' compensation claim was fired after he refused to take a drug test. He sued, claiming the company illegally retaliated against him for filing a workers' compensation claim. The court rejected the claim, reasoning that **the employee was fired because he refused to take the test** and not because he filed a workers' compensation claim. *Phillips v. Continental Tire The Americas, LLC*, 743 F.3d 475 (7th Cir. 2014).

◆   A Missouri employee slipped and fell after work in an icy parking lot next to his office. The employer fought his claim for workers' compensation benefits, arguing that he was going home when he got hurt and the hazard that caused the injury was not specifically related to his job. The court rejected the argument and decided **the employee could collect workers' compensation benefits under the state's "extended premises" doctrine**, which allows employees to receive workers' compensation benefits for injuries sustained as a result of accidents on property they customarily use to get to and from work if the property is owned or controlled by the employer. *Scholastic, Inc. v. Viley*, No. WD 77546, 2014 WL 5462306 (Mo. Ct. App. 10/28/14).

◆   A property manager in Texas injured his back at work, and an office manager helped him file a workers' compensation claim. The employee took a medical leave of absence. He was later discharged after a leave of two months, and **he said the owner told him he was let go because the owner didn't know how long he would be on workers' compensation**. The property manager sued for retaliation, but he lost. There was no evidence that the employer had any animosity toward the employee because he filed a workers' compensation claim. *McClendon v. Deep East Texas Property Management, LLC*, No. 12012-00331-CV, 2014 WL 13088618 (Tex. Ct. App. 3/31/14).

✦   A manager for a Georgia Wal-Mart was abducted from the store parking lot while walking toward the store to begin her shift. The manager was driven to a wooded area and raped for approximately 90 minutes. The manager later sued Wal-Mart for negligence, claiming the attack lasted longer because Wal-Mart did not provide police with store surveillance video in a timely manner. A state appeals court rejected the claim, finding that workers' compensation was the manager's exclusive remedy because **the attack arose out of her job**. *Dawson v. Wal-Mart Stores*, 751 S.E.2d 426 (Ga. Ct. App. 2013).

✦   An Indiana worker severed the tip of his finger while moving a piece of machinery. While he was waiting for an ambulance, his supervisor told him it was company policy to submit to post-accident drug testing. He told his supervisor he was at a party the week before and that people there had been smoking pot, so his test result might be inconclusive. He passed the drug test. The company filed a workers' compensation claim on his behalf, but the plant manager remained suspicious and ordered him to undergo drug counseling as well as random testing. He refused, was fired and then sued, claiming the real reason was retaliation for the workers' compensation claim. However, a federal court and the Seventh Circuit disagreed, noting that **the real reason was his statement to his supervisor that he might not pass a drug test** and his refusal to undergo drug counseling and random testing. *Smeigh v. Johns Manville, Inc.*, 643 F.3d 554 (7th Cir. 2011).

✦   An Airline employee at O'Hare in Chicago injured his left arm while lifting golf clubs, but he waited three days to report the injury. And though he claimed he was in too much pain to participate in the airport's standard post-injury inquiry, he was then seen using his left arm to drive and make phone calls. **He refused to answer the airline's questions about the injury and lied about using his injured arm afterward.** When the airline fired him, he sued for retaliation, asserting that he had been fired for filing a workers' compensation claim. A jury awarded him over $1 million, but the Seventh Circuit reversed, finding that the case never should have gone to trial. The airline had a legitimate reason for firing him. *Casanova v. American Airlines, Inc.*, 616 F.3d 695 (7th Cir. 2010).

✦   A hotel maintenance employee in Iowa filed three workers' compensation claims in three years. The first claim was for a neck injury from lifting wet carpet; the second claim was made three days after a supervisor criticized him for not finishing his work. He asserted that he had hurt his back while moving a TV. On the third claim, he asserted that he slipped and fell near the loading dock, then changed his story to aver that he hurt his back on a stairway. However, videotapes from a security camera showed that he was not on the stairs at all on the morning he claimed the injury occurred. The hotel fired him, and he sued for wrongful discharge. The Eighth Circuit ruled against him, noting that **he had no public policy right to file a false workers' compensation claim**. *Napreljac v. John Q. Hammons Hotels, Inc.*, 505 F.3d 800 (8th Cir. 2007).

- The owner of a Pennsylvania car dealership fired his brother, who was also the body shop manager, after the brother refused to convince a mechanic to waive his workers' compensation claim against the company. The mechanic had injured himself while unloading heavy computer equipment for the dealership. The brother sued the dealership for wrongful discharge, and a jury awarded him compensatory damages in the amount of $192,000. The case reached the Supreme Court of Pennsylvania, which upheld the award. The same public policy that prohibits firing an employee for seeking workers' compensation applies to situations where an **employee is fired for refusing to force a subordinate not to seek workers' compensation**. *Rothrock v. Rothrock Motor Sales, Inc.*, 883 A.2d 511 (Pa. 2005).

- A Wal-Mart employee in Indiana got into a fight with a co-worker and suffered injuries that required him to go to the hospital. While Wal-Mart conducted an investigation into the fight, he inquired about workers' compensation benefits. Five days later, he and the co-worker were fired for fighting. He sued for retaliation, claiming that he had been fired for asking about workers' compensation. A federal court and the Seventh Circuit Court of Appeals ruled against him. **Wal-Mart had a legitimate reason for firing him: he violated its workplace violence policy.** *Hudson v. Wal-Mart Stores*, 412 F.3d 781 (7th Cir. 2005).

- An employee of a lawn and landscaping services company in Florida injured his shoulder and got treatment at a workers' compensation clinic. He was put on lifting restrictions and was fired a month later. He sued to recover workers' compensation benefits and for retaliatory discharge. The company settled the workers' compensation claim by paying him $8,300 and having him sign a general release waiving "any and all rights" to past, present or future benefits as well as to any claims, demands or causes of action he might have against the company. It then sought to dismiss the retaliatory discharge claim because of the waiver. The Eleventh Circuit held that **he could pursue his retaliatory discharge claim because it was not clear from the language of the general release that he was waiving his right to do so**. *Borque v. Trugreen, Inc.*, 389 F.3d 1354 (11th Cir. 2004).

- A maintenance worker at a school district in Illinois injured his back and obtained workers' compensation benefits for chiropractic treatments. While receiving benefits, he applied for a job with a manufacturer and lied about ever having a work-related back injury on the health history questionnaire that was part of the application process. He agreed that any misrepresentation would be cause for termination. He then injured his back again and sought further chiropractic treatment. The manufacturer fired him after its insurer denied the workers' compensation claim, and he sued for wrongful discharge. An Illinois federal court and the Seventh Circuit Court of Appeals ruled against him. Here, **he was not fired for filing a workers' compensation claim, but for falsifying his answers on the health history questionnaire**. *Carter v. Tennant Co.*, 383 F.3d 673 (7th Cir. 2004).

◆   To control workers' compensation costs, a company that operated a Kansas meatpacking plant had an accident-free incentive program and "cost-per-injury" goals. While doing his job, one of the plant workers injured his back and was put on light duty. Never having been disciplined before, the worker began receiving disciplinary notices once he was assigned to light duty. The company's personnel manager, who knew about the worker's injury, eventually fired him. The worker sued, **claiming that he was fired in retaliation for being injured on the job**. A jury found in his favor and awarded him more than $39,000. The company appealed to the U.S. Court of Appeals, Tenth Circuit, arguing that the district court should have thrown out the award because the jury was allowed to hear evidence that the company's personnel director frequently heard complaints from other plant workers that it mistreated injured workers. The Tenth Circuit agreed. The workers' complaints were inadmissible hearsay. A new trial was needed. *Sanjuan v. IBP, Inc.*, 160 F.3d 1291 (10th Cir. 1998).

D. State Whistleblower Statutes

Reporting violations or suspected violations of law to state agencies qualifies employees for protection under state whistleblower acts. However, reporting violations or suspected violations of law to supervisors within the company may not.

◆   A New Jersey sales manager emailed the company president to express concern about a decision to forgive a customer's debt. The sales manager was later fired after he had conflicts with his supervisor. He sued, claiming he was fired for reporting his concern about the debt. He said the firing violated the state whistleblower law. The court rejected his claim. **The company's decision to forgive the debt did not violate the law or public policy.** The employee did not engage in protected whistleblower activity, the court said. *Patterson v. Glory Foods, Inc.*, 555 Fed.Appx. 207 (3d Cir. 2014) (Unpublished).

◆   A director of maintenance of an Idaho helicopter ambulance service believed a company media statement following a crash did not do enough to exonerate the maintenance department. He began reporting pilots for violating safety requirements. The company had pilots wipe down blades and restricted their hours after the director reported concerns. The director then accused the company of blaming pilot errors on maintenance and covering for pilots "at any cost." The director was fired for being disruptive, and he sued under a state whistleblower act. The state's highest court upheld a jury verdict against him, concluding that **whistleblowers do not have a right to cause unnecessary disruption**. There was evidence here that the director caused discord that was unnecessary and unrelated to his whistleblowing activity. *Van v. Portneuf Medical Center, Inc.*, 330 P.3d 1054 (Idaho 2014).

◆   An assistant merchandise manager at a New Jersey retail store observed a customer fail to adequately supervise a young child. When she assisted in reporting the customer to a state child protection agency, **she was fired for violating a company policy that barred employees from providing personal**

customer information to outsiders. She claimed that the termination violated the state's whistleblower law, which protected employees who refused to participate in a company practice that the employee reasonably believed to be in conflict with a clear public policy regarding the public's health, safety or welfare. The court refused to dismiss the claim under the state whistleblower law. *Stapleton v. DSW, Inc.*, 931 F.Supp.2d 635 (D.N.J. 2013).

♦   A human resources assistant raised concerns that making direct deposit a condition of employment was illegal. **She was told that the issue would be addressed by others and was instructed to focus on other work.** When she continued to press the matter in violation of instructions, she was fired. She sued under a state whistleblower act, but she lost. The employer had a legitimate, nondiscriminatory reason for the termination. *Wood v. SatCom Marketing, LLC*, 705 F.3d 823 (8th Cir. 2013).

♦   A nurse at a Minnesota clinic received an unfavorable performance review that, among other things, criticized her failure to follow proper sterile procedures during a surgery. She was placed on probation for 90 days. In response, she wrote a letter to the clinic's owners, addressing many of the concerns in her review and informing them that she refused to comply with the clinic's policy of attaching a previously used syringe with a new needle to a multi-dose vial of medication and then using the vial with other patients because doing so violated Minnesota law. Thirty minutes later, she was forcibly removed from the premises for insubordination.

Although she was not fired, she refused to return to work and sued for retaliation under the state's Whistleblower Act. The Eighth Circuit ruled against her because **she did not write the letter for the purpose of exposing an unknown illegality; the clinic was aware of the alleged violation before she wrote the letter**. Also, she did not raise the issue, before the trial court, of refusing to perform an act she believed violated the law, and she could not do so for the first time on appeal. *Fjelsta v. Zogg Dermatology, PLC*, 488 F.3d 804 (8th Cir. 2007).

♦   The co-CEO of a Minnesota company was suspected by the board of directors of having an affair with a subordinate. He denied having a sexual affair with her. The board began a formal investigation. That same day, the co-CEO told board members their mileage reimbursement policy might be in violation of federal tax laws. Two weeks later, the co-CEO admitted to having a sexual affair with the subordinate and using a company credit card to buy Viagra and personal cell phones so he could continue to carry on the affair. The board fired him, and he sued, claiming whistleblower protection. A federal court and the Eighth Circuit ruled against him. **The only evidence he presented was the short time span between bringing up the mileage problem and his termination**, while the board presented a legitimate reason for firing him. *Freeman v. Ace Telephone Ass'n*, 467 F.3d 695 (8th Cir. 2006).

♦   An engineer at an Ohio facility lost his job in a reduction in force. He sued the company, claiming that the real reason was retaliation for whistle-blowing activity. He had been assigned to look into air quality issues at the facility and had stated to a supervisor that there were still issues to look into even after the air conditioning system had been cleaned and purified. He had also offered to conduct more research into the problem of mold and had suggested that the company buy an air filter that would remove mold spores from the air. The company claimed that he was fired because of excessive absenteeism and belligerence to co-workers. The Sixth Circuit determined that he did not qualify for whistleblower protection because **his statements were not sufficient to put the company on notice that it was violating any governmental policy** concerning workplace safety. *Jermer v. Siemens Energy & Automation, Inc.,* 395 F.3d 655 (6th Cir. 2005).

◆   A company in North Dakota provided respiratory therapy and medical equipment to home-bound patients. The Fargo office manager questioned the regional manager about the company's practice of having technicians set up the equipment and educate customers on it. She believed this violated state law. He maintained that the practice was legal and told her to address personality conflicts and other personnel problems in the office. When she complained to him about the practice again, she was fired. She sued under the state's whistleblower protection law, and a court dismissed the lawsuit. The North Dakota Supreme Court reversed, noting that **she did not have to report the wrongdoing to a law enforcement or government agency** to enjoy the protections of the act. She only had to act in good faith. And even if she was concerned that employees were being "hung out to dry," this did not mean she acted in bad faith. *Heng v. Rotech Medical Corp. d/b/a/ Arrowhealth Medical Supply,* 688 N.W.2d 389 (N.D. 2004).

◆   Xerox had a fixed-price contract with a Tennessee company to implement a software program, but sought additional funds after unauthorized persons at the company broke the software code, necessitating repairs. Xerox shut down the company's computer system during the dispute over additional payments. It also fired an employee for performance problems. He sued Xerox, alleging that the real reason for his termination was his refusal to keep Xerox's misconduct a secret. A federal court ruled against him, and the Sixth Circuit affirmed. Here, Xerox's risking of a breach of contract action did not give rise to a common law whistleblower claim so as to support his allegation of wrongful termination. If Xerox indeed breached the contract by shutting down the computer system, this was not "illegal" activity that jeopardized the public good. Thus, **the employee could not claim that his firing violated a public policy**. *Fleming v. Xerox Connect Inc.,* 50 Fed.Appx. 211 (6th Cir. 2002).

◆   A supervisor at General Motors (GM) was warned on several occasions about time sheet errors, but was not disciplined. Subsequently, he had a run-in with a co-worker who was a member of the union committee. He claimed that the co-worker shoved him when he refused to leave a room where the committee was meeting. He informed plant security of the incident, as well as two superiors. He also filed a police report. Later, he was prohibited from working overtime because of his time sheet errors and, after claiming two hours' overtime that company investigators determined he did not work, he was fired. He sued under the Michigan Whistleblowers' Protection Act. A trial court ruled for GM, and the Supreme Court of Michigan ultimately concurred. **He had to show more than that he was disciplined after he filed the assault report**; he had to show that he was disciplined because of it. He failed to do so because evidence indicated he had repeatedly falsified his time sheets. *West v. General Motors Corp.*, 665 N.W.2d 468 (Mich. 2003).

✦   A longtime private security guard employed by Sears also had a job as a sheriff's deputy. On a number of occasions, he observed the store manager taking merchandise into his office, which violated company rules. As a result, the security guard decided to install a camera in the manager's office. He also reported the manager's suspicious activities to company officials. Two months later, he was fired for a security problem that occurred at the store a month earlier. He sued Sears for wrongful termination, claiming that the real reason for his firing was his report of suspicious activity by the store manager. A jury ruled in his favor, but an appellate court reversed the decision. The Maryland Court of Appeals affirmed, noting that the security guard was **not entitled to whistleblower protection because he did not report suspected criminal activity to the police.** He merely reported it to company officials. This was not enough to invoke the public policy exception to at-will employment. *Wholey v. Sears Roebuck & Co.*, 803 A.2d 482 (Md. 2002).

E. Federal Statutory Protections

1. ERISA

The Employee Retirement Income Security Act (ERISA), at Section 510, prohibits employers from taking adverse action against employees who assert their rights under the act (29 U.S.C. § 1140).

✦   An employee of an Illinois hospital received an evaluation describing her as an outstanding manager. However, the hospital faced financial troubles, and the employee's husband suffered from prostate cancer, which cost the hospital thousands of dollars in insurance payments. The hospital fired the employee, who sued it for discrimination because of her association with a disabled person. The hospital then asserted for the first time that the reason for her firing was insubordination. She sought to amend her lawsuit to claim retaliation under ERISA, but a federal court granted pretrial judgment to the hospital. The Seventh Circuit reversed, finding issues of fact that required a trial. It also held that **she could amend her complaint to allege retaliation under ERISA.** *Dewitt v. Proctor Hospital*, 517 F.3d 944 (7th Cir. 2008).

✦   A New York human resources (HR) director discovered that a payroll discrepancy resulted in the **under-funding of her company's 401(k) plan.** She told the company's chief financial officer, who advised her to drop the matter, and the controller, who refused to address the problem. Finally she contacted the company's outside attorney, who confirmed her findings and set up a meeting with her and the company's president. Afterward, the HR director was demoted. A year later she was fired. She sued the company under Section 510 of ERISA, alleging retaliation. A federal court dismissed the case, but the Second Circuit reinstated it. The HR director did not have to go as far as filing an official complaint with the government to be protected as a whistleblower. She only had to respond to an inquiry about the matter from company officials. *Nicolaou v. Horizon Media, Inc.*, 402 F.3d 325 (2d Cir. 2005).

♦   The manager of the Chicago office of a Georgia-based manufacturer allowed an employee to conduct personal business on the job and let employees take an unauthorized extra week of holiday time without notifying the Georgia office. At about the same time, the company failed to make required 401(k) contributions. The manager contacted the Illinois Department of Labor concerning the failure to make contributions and made a written complaint to the company's chief financial officer and plan trustee. The company then made appropriate distributions with interest. It later confirmed reports of the extra holiday leave and fired the manager for misuse of company property. He sued, and an Illinois federal court ruled for the employer. The U.S. Court of Appeals, Seventh Circuit, affirmed. This was not a case of an employer taking adverse employment action against an employee to interfere with his pension rights. The reasons given by the employer were not pretextual, and there had been no ERISA violation. **The discharge was justified by misuse of company time and property.** *Grottkau v. Sky Climber, Inc.*, 79 F.3d 70 (7th Cir. 1996).

♦   A Massachusetts engineer's supervisor suspected that the engineer was abusing alcohol. The supervisor suggested that the engineer take a medical leave of absence under the company's short-term disability benefits plan. The plan required a physician's certification of disability within 10 days of the commencement of disability leave. The engineer obtained the certification form from the company and stopped going to work. He submitted the form 30 days later and listed hypertension, rather than alcoholism, as the cause of disability. The company notified the engineer that it considered him as having voluntarily quit and rejected the certification of disability. The engineer sued the company, claiming that it had violated Section 510 of ERISA by terminating his employment to deprive him of disability benefits. A federal court dismissed the case, and the engineer appealed. The U.S. Court of Appeals, First Circuit stated that a retaliatory discharge complaint under ERISA requires proof of an employer's specific intent to interfere with employee benefits. Deprivation of employee benefits must be a motivating factor for the employment termination action, not a mere consequence. In this case, the district court had properly dismissed the case because no reasonable employee would have taken 30 days to return the certification form. The court rejected the engineer's argument that the company had discriminated against him because other employees had not been denied plan participation for failure to return a timely certification. **Inconsistent application of the terms of a health plan did not demonstrate a specific intent to interfere with plan benefits.** *Barbour v. Dynamics Research Corp.*, 63 F.3d 32 (1st Cir. 1995).

* A Pennsylvania packaging employee underwent relatively minor foot surgery and received full medical benefits from her employer's short-term disability plan. A year later, she took a second leave of absence for additional surgery and again received full medical benefits. During the second leave of absence, the company's HR manager hired a private investigator to determine whether the employee was disabled and entitled to continue receiving benefits. The investigator prepared a report, which stated that the employee operated a cleaning service during her leave, despite never actually observing her perform these services. In reliance on the report, the employer fired the employee. She sued in a New Jersey federal court, claiming that the discharge violated ERISA. The court granted pretrial judgment to the employer. On appeal, the Third Circuit, rejected the employer's argument that ERISA claims for wrongful discharge were prohibited in cases where benefits were not withheld and were actually paid. **ERISA provides a cause of action to challenge a discharge where the employee presents evidence of retaliation for exercising ERISA rights.** The district court had improperly awarded pretrial judgment to the employer in view of evidence that the company did not have a regular practice of investigating employees on disability leave. *Kowalski v. L & F Products*, 82 F.3d 1283 (3d Cir. 1996).

* An Ohio physician formed a pension plan for which he served as administrator and trustee on behalf of himself and his employees. Some plan funds were invested with a commodities investor who embezzled the funds, resulting in a substantial loss of plan assets. An employee whose lost share of plan funds was almost $20,000 demanded reimbursement and rejected the physician's offer to repay the amount in the form of taxable bonuses. She sued for reimbursement despite the physician's threats of discharge or reduced work hours. Within a month, the physician fired her, stating that he was reducing the extent of his practice. A federal court awarded the employee the entire amount of claimed plan benefits with interest. It also awarded over $100,000 in back pay and front pay for wrongful discharge in violation of ERISA, plus $33,000 in attorneys' fees. The U.S. Court of Appeals, Sixth Circuit, affirmed. Although ERISA prohibits damage awards that are characterized as legal damages, **the award of back pay here was considered an equitable remedy because it was restitutive**. The front pay award was also an equitable remedy that was not prohibited by ERISA. The court rejected the physician's argument that he should not be liable for plan losses that had been suffered long before the employee's discharge. *Schwartz v. Gregori*, 45 F.3d 1017 (6th Cir. 1995).

2. False Claims Act

The False Claims Act prohibits employers from taking adverse action against employees who assert their rights under the act.

* The vice president of nursing for a healthcare provider in Iowa told the president and CEO of the company that he couldn't open a new office as he had hoped because the Medicare paperwork had not been completed yet. The president blamed her for the delay because she was responsible for regulatory

compliance. She filed a grievance with the HR manager, and the company then fired her. She sued for wrongful discharge under the False Claims Act and also asserted that her termination violated public policy. A federal court ruled against her, noting that she did not engage in any protected conduct under the False Claims Act because **she never showed that the employer filed a false claim against the government**. In fact, she was just doing her job by pointing out the regulatory issue and thus wasn't whistleblowing. She also couldn't show that her firing violated public policy because she couldn't show any unlawful act that she refused to engage in. *Mahony v. Universal Pediatric Services, Inc.*, 643 F.3d 1103 (8th Cir. 2011).

◆   The president of a Rhode Island company that did contract work for the government wrote a letter to the owner stating his belief that the owner's nephew was fraudulently collecting two salaries. He also confronted the nephew, who told him to mind his own business or he would be fired. A month later, the president was fired. He brought a False Claims Act lawsuit against the company. The First Circuit ruled against him. Here, his job required him to warn of possible billing violations. Thus, **to be entitled to False Claims Act protections, he would have had to do more than just send a letter to the owner**; he would have had to make clear that he was alerting her to a possible False Claims Act problem. Also, the nephew's threat was not relevant because he never told the owner about the conversation. *Maturi v. McLaughlin Research Corp.*, 413 F.3d 166 (1st Cir. 2005).

◆   The federal False Claims Act (FCA) allows private citizens to bring an action on behalf of the U.S. government against anyone committing a fraud upon the government. A prevailing party in an FCA action may receive up to 30% of the amount recovered, and the FCA protects employees from retaliatory discharge, demotion or other discrimination for reporting fraudulent activities. A longtime Tennessee telephone company dispatcher observed that service reports were being falsified to avoid the necessity of providing refunds to customers, some of which were government agencies. She showed her supervisor a newspaper article describing a similar fraud being perpetrated in Florida. Afterward, the dispatcher alleged that she was harassed and threatened with discharge. She took a permanent disability leave and sued the employer under the FCA. The court dismissed the complaint. The dispatcher appealed to the U.S. Court of Appeals, Sixth Circuit, which held that **an FCA lawsuit must be based upon public disclosure of allegations of fraud**. The complaining party must be the original source of the disclosure. Here, the employee had based part of her allegations on information already reported by the press and made public in two separate lawsuits. She could not prevail, since she was not the original source of the information. The whistleblower portion of her complaint had been properly dismissed, but the court reversed and remanded the retaliatory discharge portion of the claim. *U.S. ex rel. McKenzie v. BellSouth Telecommunications, Inc.*, 123 F.3d 935 (6th Cir. 1997).

◆   The U.S. Court of Appeals, Fourth Circuit, affirmed a pretrial judgment order for a Maryland employer in an action brought by a former employee who claimed he had been discharged in violation of a public policy stated in the federal False Claims Act. The court ruled that the act contains its own remedy for public policy violations, prohibiting an abusive discharge claim on the basis of public policy. The False Claims Act cause of action failed because **the employee had not told the employer during his tenure that he was pursing an action under the False Claims Act**. The employer was entitled to dismissal of the breach of contract claim and to judgment on its counterclaim for breach of certain nondisclosure agreements. *Zahodnick v. IBM Corp.*, 135 F.3d 911 (4th Cir. 1997).

◆   A Pennsylvania woman worked as the bookkeeper-accountant for a home-health service. The service was a nonprofit corporation that provided skilled nursing care, home health aids, and other services to individuals, some of whom were covered by Medicare. The bookkeeper's duties included providing information and documents used to prepare cost reports to be submitted to a Medicare intermediary. In 1991, the service received a letter from the intermediary requesting additional information concerning the 1990 fiscal year cost report. The service asked the bookkeeper to recreate documents to provide a fictitious account of the services provided by the service. After she refused, she was fired. She then sued the employer for violating the federal False Claims Act. A court noted that the act makes it unlawful for an employer to discharge an employee because the employee refuses to participate in submitting false claims under the Medicare program. The court found for the bookkeeper. The act provides for **reinstatement with the same seniority status the employee would have had but for the discrimination**, two times the amount of back pay, and interest on the back pay. Therefore, the bookkeeper was entitled to receive twice her lost wages, reinstatement, and attorneys' fees. *Godwin v. Visiting Nurse Ass'n Home Health Service*, 831 F.Supp. 449 (E.D. Pa. 1993).

3. Surface Transportation Assistance Act

The Surface Transportation Assistance Act prohibits employers from taking adverse retaliatory action against commercial drivers who report safety concerns with their vehicles.

◆   A trucking company discharged one of its drivers, alleging that he had disabled several lights on his assigned truck in order to obtain extra pay while awaiting repairs. The driver filed a complaint with the Department of Labor, alleging that his firing violated Section 405 of the federal Surface Transportation Assistance Act. A field investigator obtained statements substantiating the driver's claim and offered the company the opportunity to submit a written statement detailing the basis for the employee's discharge, but it was not allowed to examine the substance of the investigator's evidence. A preliminary administrative order called for the employee's reinstatement. The company sued in a Georgia federal court, arguing that reinstatement prior to an evidentiary hearing violated its due process rights. The court ruled for the company. The U.S. Supreme Court affirmed in part and reversed in part. **Due process required pre-reinstatement notice of the employee's allegations, notice of the substance of** the relevant supporting evidence, an opportunity to submit a written response, and an opportunity to meet with the investigator and present statements from rebuttal witnesses. Due process did not require employer confrontation and cross-examination before preliminary reinstatement if a prompt post-reinstatement evidentiary hearing was available. *Brock v. Roadway Express, Inc.*, 481 U.S. 252, 107 S.Ct. 1740, 95 L.Ed.2d 239 (1987).

◆ An Illinois truck driver complained to supervisors that his truck had a bad seat, a door that didn't close properly and a steering problem. He was told to drive the truck anyway. When he asked if someone else could take the truck for a test drive, a supervisor told him to wash and wax the truck. Another driver drove the truck and concluded it was safe to drive. The driver operated the truck, and after talking to a mechanic he said in a daily report that the "steering drag-link" was off center. However, **the mechanic said the driver lied about what the mechanic told him**. The employer then cited the driver for filing a false report and fired him. He sued, claiming violation of the Surface Transportation Assistance Act. A federal appeals court said the case required a trial, concluding that a jury could find the driver was fired because he engaged in protected activity. *Gaines v. K-Five Construction Corp.*, 742 F.3d 256 (7th Cir. 2014).

◆ A Texas commercial truck driver was pulled over by a state trooper and cited for violating state and federal regulations, including one that required cargo to be properly secured. The straps the company had provided were worn, with big cuts in them. He showed the citations to his managers and told them about the problems, but was still ordered to drive the truck the next day. He refused because the trooper told him not to drive it until the defects were cured. The company gave him administrative duties until it could bring the truck into compliance. After fixing some of the defects, the company ordered him to drive the truck. He took out a load with the same straps, but felt the cargo shift on the truck and turned around, fearing for his safety. He was told to drive the truck or go home. After going home, he was fired for abandoning his job. He sued for wrongful discharge, and a jury awarded him $7,569 in lost wages and more than $200,000 in punitive damages. The case reached the Supreme Court of Texas, which upheld the lost wages award but reversed the award of punitive damages. **The company improperly fired him for refusing to violate government safety rules, but he failed to show that it intended to harm him.** *Safeshred, Inc. v. Martinez*, 365 S.W.3d 655 (Tex. 2012).

◆ A feeder driver for UPS had a long history of insubordination, and his start-work times were greater than any of his fellow drivers at the Greensboro, North Carolina facility where he worked. He claimed that he was warned, suspended and discharged for engaging in daily vehicle inspections that exceeded the UPS inspection guidelines but that he felt were necessary under the Federal Motor Carrier Safety Regulations (FMCSR). He insisted on checking his equipment his way, which resulted in numerous delays. After he was fired, a Department of Labor administrative review board found that **he could not show that the employer violated the Surface Transportation Assistance Act (STAA)**. The Fourth Circuit upheld the administrative decision against him. It ruled that he did not engage in protected activity under the STAA's "refusal to drive clause" because he never refused to drive the vehicle. He only drove under protest on one occasion and stated concerns about a dolly brake on another occasion. He was also not protected under the act's "complaint clause" because his complaints did not relate to an actual violation of the FMCSR. Further, UPS's decision to fire him for insubordination was legitimate. *Calhoun v. U.S. Dep't of Labor*, 576 F.3d 201 (4th Cir. 2009).

◆   A Florida employee complained of gasoline fumes in his truck at an employee "speak-out session," a periodic meeting of employees to solicit grievances. Later, the employer fired him after he refused to take a scheduled run, first offering to let him use another truck or a portable radio set. He filed an administrative action against the employer for Surface Transportation Assistance Act (STAA) violations. The U.S. Department of Labor found that the employee had no reasonable apprehension of serious injury to himself or the public arising from use of the truck and held that the employer did not violate the STAA. An administrative law judge affirmed, but the U.S. Secretary of Labor remanded the case. The case reached the U.S. Court of Appeals, Second Circuit, which observed that **the employer had attempted to remedy the employee's safety concerns**, yet the employee had refused to perform his assigned task. The STAA does not require portable radios in vehicles. The speak-out session complaint about gas fumes was not reasonably linked to the firing, since the employee had not mentioned it at the time of the incident leading to discharge. Because the employer had offered to correct the situation, the court ruled in its favor. *Brink's Inc. v. Herman*, 148 F.3d 175 (2d Cir. 1998).

◆   An environmental services employer transported, stored, treated and disposed of hazardous waste. It instituted a policy of charging customers for extra time spent by drivers to bring drums of hazardous waste into compliance with federal regulations. A driver in a Connecticut service center was the subject of many customer complaints for taking too much time at their facilities. After receiving numerous complaints, the driver's supervisor told him to leave each customer's premises without extra time regardless of the condition of the drums. The driver responded that accepting improperly sealed and labeled drums was illegal and could result in his own liability. The employer fired him for being rude to customers, but it reinstated him on the condition that he remain under strict supervision and abide by a strict chain of command.

The employer assigned the driver to haul material between company-owned facilities in order to remove him from customer contact. However, it fired him again for his continuing regulatory compliance concerns, which included a report to the Massachusetts Department of Environmental Protection. The driver filed an administrative action with the U.S. Department of Labor, asserting violation of the STAA. An administrative review board ruled for the driver, and the employer appealed. The First Circuit Court of Appeals rejected the employer's claim that STAA protection was unavailable to employees who make only internal complaints and do not commence formal agency or court proceedings. **The driver had effectively communicated his safety and compliance concerns prior to the first discharge**, and the employer had sufficient notice that he believed the company risked regulatory violations. There was a link between the activity and the discharge, and the court upheld the decision reinstating the driver. *Clean Harbors Environmental Services, Inc. v. Herman*, 146 F.3d 12 (1st Cir. 1998).

4. Other Federal Statutes

Most federal statutes that protect employees contain provisions barring employers from retaliating against employees who exercise their rights under the statutes.

◆   The president and CEO of a Florida insurance holding company discovered that other officers and directors of the company were diverting corporate funds for personal use and submitting false financial statements to government regulators, shareholders and creditors. He contacted the regulators about the statements, causing the directors and officers involved in producing them to orchestrate a scheme to remove him from the company. After his termination, he sued them under the Racketeer Influenced and Corrupt Organizations Act (RICO). A federal court dismissed his lawsuit, and the Eleventh Circuit affirmed. The U.S. Supreme Court also affirmed. It stated that because **the termination was not an act of racketeering and was not independently wrongful** under any substantive provision of RICO, the president could not sue under the statute. *Beck v. Prupis*, 529 U.S. 494, 120 S.Ct. 1608, 146 L.Ed.2d 561 (2000).

◆   An at-will employee of a Georgia-based healthcare company cooperated with federal agents investigating the company for Medicare fraud. The employee had been subpoenaed to testify before the grand jury but never did. After the company was indicted, the employee was expected to appear as a witness in a subsequent criminal trial. He was fired and sued under 42 U.S.C. § 1985(2), alleging that three of the company's officers conspired to intimidate him and to retaliate against him for attending the grand jury proceedings and to keep him from testifying at the criminal trial. Section 1985(2) prohibits people from entering into conspiracies to "deter, by force, intimidation or threat," any witness from testifying in court. It provides a cause of action when parties to a conspiracy cause the witness to be "injured in his person or property."

The district court dismissed the lawsuit, finding that an at-will employee has no constitutionally protected property interest in continued employment. The Eleventh Circuit affirmed, but the U.S. Supreme Court reversed. The sort of harm alleged by the employee – essentially third-party interference with at-will employment relationships – stated a claim for relief under Section 1985(2). Even though at-will employment is not "property" for purposes of the Due Process Clause, **an at-will employee who loses his job suffers injury to his "person or property" as contemplated by Section 1985(2)**. *Haddle v. Garrison*, 525 U.S. 121, 119 S.Ct. 489, 142 L.Ed.2d 502 (1998).

◆   A salesman at a BMW dealership in Illinois heard that a 13-year-old had accidentally stepped on the gas pedal at the Land Rover dealership next door and driven a vehicle down an embankment and into water. He ran over to take pictures, which he posted to Facebook that night along with sarcastic comments. When he was fired as a result, he claimed that he was really fired for posting comments about a hot dog cart the dealership brought in for the launch of a new product, and that the posting was protected activity under the NLRA. An administrative law judge ruled against him, finding that **he was fired for mocking a serious accident**. That decision was later affirmed. *Karl Knauz Motors, Inc. and Robert Becker*, 358 NLRB No. 164 (Sept. 28, 2012).

◆   The Sarbanes-Oxley Act protects whistleblowers at publicly traded companies with respect to reporting fraud or securities violations. The act says that the report must be made to a federal regulatory or law enforcement agency, to Congress, or to a supervisor or someone in the company with the authority to investigate misconduct. Two IT employees of Boeing claimed that they were being pressured to provide certain positive results under the act's reporting requirements and they told a reporter about that pressure. After a story was written in the paper, Boeing fired the employees. When they sued under the act for retaliation, they lost. A Washington federal court and the Ninth Circuit held that **Sarbanes-Oxley does not protect leaks to the media**. *Tides v. The Boeing Co.*, 644 F.3d 809 (9th Cir. 2011).

◆   A Kentucky husband and wife worked for the same company. The husband also bought a welding shop, which forced him and his wife to file for bankruptcy protection under Chapter 7 of the Bankruptcy Code. After he lost his car, he approached two company officials and offered to falsify their income tax returns if they would give him a company car. He and his wife were fired the next day. They sued the company for firing them in violation of federal bankruptcy law. The case reached the Sixth Circuit Court of Appeals, which ruled against them. Here, **their bankruptcy was not the sole reason they were fired**. Rather, the company cited sloppy bookkeeping, rudeness to customers and the car issue as additional reasons for the discharge. Since the Bankruptcy Code only prohibits firing employees "solely" because of their bankruptcy, the company did not violate the law. *White v. Kentuckiana Livestock Market, Inc.*, 397 F.3d 420 (6th Cir. 2005).

◆   A Florida carpenter worked for a contractor at a nuclear power plant. He was transferred to a crew working on a temporary project and began experiencing disagreements with his foreman concerning safety procedures for contaminated tools. The foreman learned that the carpenter went over his head to make a complaint concerning the handling of contaminated tools. The carpenter was then laid off before less experienced crew members. Within 30 days, the entire crew was laid off. The carpenter filed an administrative complaint with the U.S. Department of Labor, claiming that the employer had violated the whistleblower protection provision of the Energy Reorganization Act. An administrative law judge held for the carpenter but only awarded back wages for one month and refused to order reinstatement. The secretary affirmed the final administrative decision, and the U.S. Court of Appeals, Eleventh Circuit, agreed with the secretary that the carpenter had made out a valid claim for discrimination. He showed that the Energy Reorganization Act applied and that **he had been engaged in protected activity that adversely affected the terms and conditions of his employment**. The carpenter's initiation of an internal complaint constituted a protected activity. *Bechtel Construction Co. v. Secretary of Labor*, 50 F.3d 926 (11th Cir. 1995).

◆   An Oklahoma personnel director was responsible for monitoring her employer's compliance with state and federal wage and hour laws. She learned that the employer's overtime compensation policies conflicted with these requirements and met with the company attorney and president. The president fired her within a month for releasing confidential information and for misconduct. She filed a wrongful discharge lawsuit against the employer, and also alleged that her discharge violated the Fair Labor Standards Act (FLSA) and state wage and hour laws. The court dismissed the wrongful discharge claim prior to trial, and it granted the employer's post-trial motion to set aside a jury award of over $325,000 in damages for her FLSA claim. The U.S. Court of Appeals, Tenth Circuit, affirmed, finding no clear statement of Oklahoma law that required an employer to pay overtime. Thus, there was no public policy protecting the employee from an at-will discharge. The court disagreed with the district court's justification for dismissing the FLSA complaint. Nevertheless, **the FLSA did not protect the employee's activity here because she failed to assert her own rights under the act**. Her reporting of the company's potential FLSA violations took place in her capacity as a personnel manager and was not an assertion of her own FLSA rights. *McKenzie v. Renberg's Inc.*, 94 F.3d 1478 (10th Cir. 1996).

V.   CONSTRUCTIVE DISCHARGE

Sometimes, employers will seek to get an employee to quit by making <u>work conditions intolerable</u>. Where such actions force an employee to quit, and where a court determines that the employer's action would make a reasonable employee quit, an employer will generally be found to have constructively discharged the employee.

Generally, constructive discharge lawsuits only arise where the employee is protected (e.g., by being a minority or a disabled person or a member of a particular religion).

A constructive discharge will be deemed to be the same as firing the employee. Any damages the employee could recover for wrongful discharge will also be available to the employee who quits under a constructive discharge.

See also Chapter One for cases involving discrimination.

◆   A communications operator for the Pennsylvania State Police claimed that three of her supervisors subjected her to sexually harassing comments and gestures. She told the EEO officer about the harassment but never filed a complaint. Shortly thereafter, she was arrested for theft in the workplace and was interrogated. She was allowed to resign and then sued under Title VII. **The question of constructive discharge reached the U.S. Supreme Court**, which held that if the constructive discharge was not the result of an official act by the police, but instead the misconduct of a rogue supervisor, then the police could assert the *Ellerth/Faragher* defense. However, if the police sanctioned the actions leading to the constructive discharge, then a tangible employment action would have occurred so as to make the defense unavailable. The Court remanded the case for further proceedings. *Pennsylvania State Police v. Suders*, 542 U.S. 129, 124 S.Ct. 2342, 159 L.Ed.2d 204 (2004).

♦   In July, a newly hired California employee told her boss she was pregnant and would be taking leave in December. In August, she changed her mind and said she would be taking leave in November. Her boss told her he thought she'd taken advantage of him and placed an extreme hardship on his business, but he also told her he would honor her rights under the law. She felt he wanted her to quit and did so. When she sued for harassment and constructive discharge, she lost. The California Court of Appeal held that **his frustration at her pregnancy did not amount to harassment**, and he informed her that he would follow the law, so she could not prove a constructive discharge. *Holmes v. Petrovich Development Co.*, 119 Cal.Rptr.3d 878 (Cal. Ct. App. 2011).

♦   A New York employee quit and sued, asserting that the performance improvement plan (PIP) she was put on amounted to constructive discharge. She claimed it was more onerous than the PIPs given to male employees and that it was impossible to fulfill. A federal court ruled for the employer, and the Second Circuit affirmed. **The employee's placement on the PIP did not amount to a constructive discharge.** The male employees were given PIPs with comparable sales quotas. They managed to meet their quotas, while she didn't even try to meet hers, even though the employer adjusted it in response to her objections. *Miller v. Batesville Casket Co., Inc.*, 312 Fed.Appx. 404 (2d Cir. 2009).

♦   A 53-year-old Kansas news photographer **claimed that he was constructively discharged based on his age** when the TV station he worked for began to emphasize live, on-site reporting. He claimed his shift was changed, he was denied necessary training, he was denied vacation time, and he was issued verbal and written reprimands that forced him to quit. The case reached the Tenth Circuit, which ruled against him. Although his working conditions, and particularly the night shifts, were unpleasant, they were not objectively intolerable such that a reasonable person would have had no other choice but to quit. As for the reprimands, they did not indicate that he faced either discipline or termination. Further, the photographer never formally requested that he be allowed to take owed vacation time. Instead, he asked to sit down to discuss his vacation plans, and management never responded to that request. *DeWalt v. Meredith Corp.*, 288 Fed.Appx. 484 (10th Cir. 2008).

♦   During a job interview for a New Hampshire nonprofit, the agency's food services director told a prospective employee that if she encountered anything she disliked about employees, she made it miserable enough for them to quit so she didn't have to fire them. She hired the applicant as an assistant director and had a good working relationship with her until the assistant director refused to submit time sheets for the director's daughters (who also worked there) because she had questions about whether they worked the hours they reported. For the next two weeks, the director then yelled at her for minor things and gave her a less than satisfactory evaluation. The assistant director quit and sued for wrongful termination. The New Hampshire Supreme Court held that her claim deserved a trial and that **she could use the director's statements at the interview to prove she was constructively discharged**. *Lacasse v. Spaulding Youth Center*, 910 A.2d 1262 (N.H. 2006).

◆   An African-American aircraft cleaning supervisor was confronted about being off base during his designated shift. He resigned in lieu of being fired, then sued under Title VII, claiming constructivel discharge because of race-based harassment, asserting that his supervisor had made four derogatory comments about blacks in the past year. An Oklahoma federal court ruled against him, finding that he was not constructively discharged. **His working conditions were not so severe as to force him to quit**, and his decision to resign in lieu of being fired did not meet the conditions for a constructive discharge. *McGriff v. American Airlines, Inc.*, 431 F.Supp.2d 1145 (N.D. Okla. 2006).

◆   A black human resources (HR) director complained to the corporate attorney that the head of recruiting refused to promote African-Americans to senior-level positions. The month before, the company had eliminated the HR director's position when it combined his department with another and created a new position. It offered him a consulting contract with full salary and benefits for two months, followed by a six-month consulting contract, but informed him he would not be hired for the new job. He quit and sued for wrongful termination and retaliation under 42 U.S.C. § 1981, claiming that he had been constructively discharged. A Virginia federal court and the Fourth Circuit ruled against him. Even though he found the **work environment miserable and professionally unfulfilling**, this was not enough to show a constructive discharge. Also, informing him he would not be hired for the new position did not amount to a termination. *Honor v. Booz-Allen & Hamilton, Inc.*, 383 F.3d 180 (4th Cir. 2004).

VI. COLLECTIVE BARGAINING AGREEMENTS

Where a collective bargaining agreement exists, the agreement governs employment termination issues, as permitted or supplemented by federal labor law. Most of these cases fall within the jurisdiction of the National Labor Relations Board. Generally, collective bargaining agreements bestow greater rights on employees, making it harder for companies to fire them. They also provide a grievance process so discharged or disciplined employees can challenge the actions taken against them without having to resort to lawsuits.

For further cases involving union and employer obligations under federal law, see Chapter Five.

◆ A Louisiana man worked for a company as a machine operator on a hazardous machine. Company rules provided that the use or bringing of controlled substances onto the premises would result in discharge. Police officers found the employee in another person's vehicle on company premises where marijuana was present. They also found traces of marijuana in the employee's car. The company learned of the first incident and fired the employee. He filed a grievance seeking arbitration under the collective bargaining agreement. Shortly before the arbitration hearing, the company learned of the marijuana found in the employee's car. However, the arbitrator then held for the employee because there was insufficient proof that the employee had used marijuana on the premises. The company appealed to a federal court, which overturned the arbitrator's decision. The Fifth Circuit affirmed. The case then reached the U.S. Supreme Court, which noted that the lower courts had erred in overturning the arbitrator's decision because of public policy concerns. Here, **the arbitrator's refusal to consider the later evidence was not bad faith or affirmative misconduct**. Further, arbitrators have wide discretion in formulating remedies, and it was error for the courts to overturn the arbitrator's decision because they viewed discharge as the proper remedy. The Court reversed the lower courts' holdings and upheld the arbitrator's decision. *United Paperworkers Int'l Union v. Misco, Inc.*, 484 U.S. 29, 108 S.Ct. 364, 98 L.Ed.2d 286 (1987).

◆ Caterpillar Tractor Company hired a group of employees to work at a California facility under a collective bargaining agreement. These employees all reached managerial or weekly salaried positions, outside the coverage of the agreement. They held their positions for a number of years and alleged that the employer made oral and written representations that "they could look forward to indefinite and lasting employment." The company then downgraded them to unionized positions that were supposedly only temporary. Thereafter, the company notified them that it was closing the California facility and that they would be laid off. The employees sued for breach of contract, and the case was dismissed for failure to state a claim under Section 301 of the Labor Management Relations Act. The Ninth Circuit Court of Appeals reversed, holding that the case must be heard in state court, and the case reached the U.S. Supreme Court.

The Supreme Court agreed that the state law contract claims were not preempted by Section 301. Here, even though the employees could have brought suit under Section 301, they chose to sue under state law on their individual contracts. **No interpretation or application of the collective bargaining agreement was necessary to decide their claims.** Further, even though the employees were covered by the collective bargaining agreement, their individual contracts were not necessarily subsumed into it. The Court affirmed the court of appeals and held that the state law claims should be heard in state court. *Caterpillar, Inc. v. Williams*, 482 U.S. 386, 107 S.Ct. 2425, 96 L.Ed.2d 318 (1987).

✦   The New York City Transit Authority sought to fire a long-time conductor who had been accused of assaulting a member of the public on a subway platform. Apparently there was a heated exchange about the availability of express train service on a particular subway line, and the conductor, not without provocation, forcefully put his hands on the customer. Under the collective bargaining agreement in place, the matter was submitted to an arbitrator, who modified the penalty to reinstatement without back pay for the period of suspension. The Transit Authority appealed, and the New York Court of Appeals eventually ruled that **the arbitrator did not exceed his authority by changing the termination to a suspension**. *New York City Transit Authority v. Transport Workers Union of America, Local 100*, 924 N.E.2d 797 (N.Y. 2010).

✦   A company that owned and maintained billboards in Wisconsin sought to fire a 22-year employee who had served as a crew chief for the previous 10 years. The firing occurred because the employee, while working on a billboard and wearing a full-body safety harness, disconnected the lanyard from the safety cable to step around another employee and then neglected to reattach it. While driving by, a company official noticed the safety violation and watched for eight minutes before calling the company to report it. He never brought the safety violation to the employee's attention.

   After his discharge, the employee and his union filed a grievance, asserting that the company did not have just cause for the firing. An arbitrator agreed, finding that a six-month suspension without pay was an appropriate penalty. He noted that **the collective bargaining agreement said that the company "may" discharge an employee for committing that kind of safety violation**, also noting that the company official did nothing about it and pointing out the employee's unblemished safety record prior to that incident. The company appealed, but a federal court and the Seventh Circuit upheld the arbitrator's award. *Clear Channel Outdoor, Inc. v. Int'l Unions of Painters and Allied Trades*, 558 F.3d 670 (7th Cir. 2009).

✦   A Montana nursing home decided to terminate a union nurse. She filed a grievance under the collective bargaining agreement (CBA), alleging that her termination was not for just cause and that she was not given a written termination notice within 10 days of the incident precipitating her termination, as required by the CBA. The arbitration committee found that the nursing home violated the CBA and ordered the nurse's reinstatement. However, the nursing home refused to comply with that order. The union then sued to enforce the arbitration decision. The case reached the Montana Supreme Court, which held that **the arbitrators did not exceed their authority by reinstating the employee because of the nursing home's violation of the CBA**. Further, the reinstatement of the nurse did not violate public policy. *Teamsters Union Local No. 2 v. C.N.H. Acquisitions, Inc.*, 204 P.3d 733 (Mont. 2009).

✦   A Michigan garbage truck driver, while substituting on another driver's route, hooked a low-hanging overhead wire and pulled it down from a house while backing up on the wrong side of a dead-end residential street. He immediately informed dispatch, and supervisors arrived on the scene. They determined that the driver violated the company's zero-tolerance safety guidelines and safe driving practices. The driver was suspended without pay and was fired the next day. He filed a grievance with his union, which contended on his behalf that he should have been given a warning and should not have been immediately discharged. **An arbitrator examined the collective bargaining agreement and determined that the offense was one demanding a warning prior to termination.** The arbitrator ordered the driver reinstated with back pay, and the company appealed. A federal court ruled for the company, but the Sixth Circuit reversed, finding that the arbitrator did not operate outside the scope of his authority, and that he was arguably construing and applying the collective bargaining agreement when he ordered reinstatement. *Truck Drivers Local No. 164 v. Allied Waste Systems, Inc.*, 512 F.3d 211 (6th Cir. 2008).

◆   A company fired a Pennsylvania employee for attempting to steal meat from the company by using a stolen credit card. When a security guard told the employee he was being fired, the employee allegedly attacked the guard and broke two ribs. The employee's union filed a grievance, and an arbitrator ruled that the company did not have just cause to fire the employee. The arbitrator ordered the employee to be reinstated. The company notified the employee that it would pay him back pay, but also informed him he was fired for attacking the security guard. The union sued and the Third Circuit ruled that **the second firing was proper**. It was for a different offense. Also, the back pay satisfied the arbitrator's order to reinstate the employee. *United Food & Commercial Workers, Local 1776 v. Excel Corp.*, 470 F.3d 143 (3d Cir. 2006).

◆   A bakery employee in Michigan was fired for violating a company's anti-harassment policy when he said, "Relax, Sambo" to an African-American co-worker. He filed a grievance, and an arbitrator determined that he should be suspended and then placed on probation for five years. When the bakery sued, a federal court ruled for the employee and union. The Sixth Circuit affirmed. Here, the employee had no prior disciplinary record, and **the collective bargaining agreement provided for progressive discipline**. The arbitrator did not exceed his authority in finding that the employee should have been afforded progressive discipline based on both the bargaining agreement and the anti-harassment policy. *Way Bakery v. Truck Drivers Local No. 164*, 363 F.3d 590 (6th Cir. 2004).

◆   A manufacturing company in Tennessee fired a union employee for accumulating too many absenteeism points. Three weeks later, it notified him that it had an alternative reason for firing him – that he had falsified his time card. The union filed grievances with respect to both reasons, but the company denied both. The union proceeded to arbitration with respect to the absenteeism reason, and an arbitrator determined that the employee should not have been fired because he had not accumulated enough points to warrant a discharge. The arbitrator ordered the employee reinstated. When the company refused, a lawsuit resulted. The Sixth Circuit ultimately determined that the union's failure to challenge the alternative reason for the discharge prevented the employee from getting his job back. *Int'l Brotherhood of Boilermakers, Local No. S-251 v. Thyssenkrupp Elevator Manufacturing, Inc.*, 365 F.3d 523 (6th Cir. 2004).

◆   A company fired a truck driver for gross insubordination and fighting on the job with his supervisor. Under the collective bargaining agreement, the company had the right to discharge employees for just cause and without warning for either reason. However, when the truck driver's union challenged the discharge, an arbitrator found that **the company had to establish by clear and convincing evidence that the truck driver had started the fight**. He determined that the company failed to meet this standard and ordered it to reinstate the driver. A Massachusetts federal court held that the arbitrator had exceeded his authority, but the First Circuit Court of Appeals reversed, stating that the arbitrator was free to set the standard for the burden of proof where the bargaining agreement was silent on the issue. As a result, the driver had to be reinstated. *Keebler v. Truck Drivers, Local 170*, 247 F.3d 8 (1st Cir. 2001).

◆   Drivers employed by a Denver concrete manufacturer de-certified their union. Several years later, a driver began unionization efforts. The employer suspended and then discharged the employee for failing to report an on-the-job accident, failing to wear his hard hat and having a bad attitude. The driver complained to the National Labor Relations Board (NLRB), which charged the employer with violating federal labor laws. An administrative law judge determined that the firing had been motivated in part by protected union conduct and ordered the driver reinstated with back pay. The NLRB adopted this decision, and the U.S. Court of Appeals, Tenth Circuit, enforced the NLRB order. The court stated that it is an unfair labor practice to interfere with, restrain or coerce an employee's right to form, join or assist a labor organization, or to discourage membership in a labor organization. There was sufficient evidence to support the NLRB finding that the driver had been engaged in union activities at the time of the discharge and that the employer was aware of his activities. There was also evidence that no other employee had been subjected to similar discipline for similar violations of company rules. Because there was evidence of anti-union sentiment by the employer, **the NLRB could have reasonably found that the discharge was improperly motivated**. *Ready Mixed Concrete Co. v. NLRB*, 81 F.3d 1546 (10th Cir. 1996).

VII. PROCEDURAL CONSIDERATIONS

Prior to taking disciplinary action against an employee, you should consider the consequences of doing so. There may be reasons for avoiding such action. First, are you being consistent? In other words, have you disciplined other employees for similar misbehavior?

Second, even if the employee is at will, should you offer him/her due process? That is, should you give notice of the offense committed and an opportunity to respond? You don't need to provide a full-fledged hearing, but you probably want to get the employee's side before disciplining or firing.

Third, is there some protected activity the employee has engaged in that would make disciplining him/her less attractive? Or is there an employment contract that requires you to follow certain steps?

A. Termination Agreements

Employers often agree to a monetary settlement with a fired employee in exchange for a promise not to sue. If executed properly, these agreements (waivers) can minimize liability and the costs of litigation.

◆ A longtime General Motors (GM) employee who worked on fuel line designs frequently testified for GM in product liability cases. In one Georgia case, he testified that a GM truck fuel system was an inferior product. He was then fired, and he sued GM in a Michigan court for wrongful discharge. GM counterclaimed for breach of a fiduciary duty not to disclose privileged and confidential information and for misappropriating documents. The parties reached a settlement agreement under which the former employee received payment in return for a permanent injunction prohibiting him from testifying as an expert witness in other GM product liability cases without prior written consent. However, the order did not affect the still-pending Georgia litigation. A separate agreement permitted the employee to testify in other cases if another tribunal ordered his appearance.
Six years later, the former employee was subpoenaed to testify in a Missouri wrongful death action involving a GM vehicle fire. GM resisted his appearance, asserting that the Michigan court order barred his testimony. A federal court allowed the employee to testify, and a jury awarded the victim's estate over $11 million in damages. The U.S. Court of Appeals, Eighth Circuit, reversed the judgment under the Full Faith and Credit Clause of the Constitution. The U.S. Supreme Court then found no public policy exception permitting a state court to resist the recognition of a foreign state court judgment. However, the Michigan court order could not control the Missouri action and **could not prevent the employee from testifying**. Moreover, the parties' agreement allowed the employee to testify where ordered by another court. The Court reversed and remanded the case. *Baker v. General Motors Corp.*, 522 U.S. 222, 118 S.Ct. 657, 139 L.Ed.2d 580 (1998).

◆ A Wisconsin software engineer signed a waiver and release when she was laid off. The employee later sued the employer for discrimination and retaliation. The court rejected her claims, finding that **the employee knowingly and voluntarily waived her claims**. *Lawson v. J.C. Penney Corp., Inc.*, 580 Fed.Appx. 492 (7th Cir. 2014) (Unpublished).

◆ The president of a Michigan company sent two key employees a letter saying they would get a year of severance pay if their employment was terminated "or ended in any manner in the future." Approximately two years later, a new president rescinded the terms of the letter. The employees later resigned and sued for the severance pay. A state appeals court ruled they were not entitled to the serverance pay. It said **the letter did not create an obligation**

to pay severance benefits because it did not create any obligation on the part of the employees. The letter merely created a policy that could be modified or revoked. *Klein v. HP Pelzer Automotive Systems, Inc.*, 854 N.W.2d 521 (Mich. Ct. App. 2014).

◆   A company laid off a Mississippi employee and offered her severance in exchange for a promise not to sue on any employment-related issue. She later sued the company for overtime under the FLSA. The company claimed that the severance it had paid was greater than the amount of overtime she was seeking, so it sought to have the case dismissed. However, the Fifth Circuit ruled that she could proceed with her lawsuit. **The severance paid by the company was not a wage payment, advance or otherwise.** Rather, it was money paid in return for a release of claims. And setoffs of FLSA claims cannot be made unless the money paid by the employer can be considered a wage payment. *Martin v. PepsiAmericas, Inc.*, 628 F.3d 738 (5th Cir. 2010).

◆   A magazine photo editor was fired at the age of 62. He received a severance package that included 20 weeks' salary, and in exchange signed a release of all claims against the company up to that point. He later sued, claiming that his position had not been terminated as he'd been told but rather that the company had given it to a younger employee. A New York federal court and the Second Circuit ruled against him, noting that **the severance agreement complied with the OWBPA's requirement that it be "knowing and voluntary."** The agreement clearly set forth that he was giving up the right to sue for conduct occurring before he signed the release. *Ridinger v. Dow Jones & Co.*, 651 F.3d 309 (2d Cir. 2011).

◆   A former construction company employee sued the company and its benefits plan administrator under ERISA for unpaid and untimely contributions to its 401(k) plan, in which he was a participant. The company and the administrator asserted that the lawsuit should be dismissed because of a settlement agreement in a related case involving unpaid overtime wages. The agreement indicated that it was a release of all claims between the parties, but the employee asserted that it applied only to the unpaid overtime wages issue. A District of Columbia federal court disagreed, holding that **the clear language of the settlement served as a release of all claims against the company**. However, his lawsuit against the administrator of the 401(k) plan could continue. *Lindell v. Landis Corp. 401(k) Plan*, 640 F.Supp.2d 11 (D.D.C. 2009).

◆   The vice president of a Tennessee company was fired after she was accused of sexually harassing a former hourly employee. She signed an agreement with the company releasing any employment-related claims she might have had against it as of the date the agreement was signed. As of that date, the former hourly employee had filed a lawsuit against her, and she had hired an attorney. After that date, the former hourly employee settled with the company and then dropped his lawsuit against the vice president. When she sought indemnification from the company for the expenses she incurred in defending the lawsuit, a state appeals court ruled in her favor. **Since the indemnification**

claim did not exist when the release was signed, the release did not bar the claim. Also, since her defense of the lawsuit was successful, and since the lawsuit was brought against her because she was a director of the company, the company had to indemnify her under the state law. *Sherman v. American Water Heater Co., Inc.*, 50 S.W.3d 455 (Tenn. Ct. App. 2001).

◆ A Missouri employee resigned from his job of 30 years under a written agreement calling for a retirement benefit package and an assurance that he was "welcome to approach" the company as a vendor or buyer in the future. The agreement also provided monetary benefits in exchange for dismissal of age discrimination and retaliation claims. He then negotiated a $1.7 million sale involving his former employer. After arranging the details of the sale, the former employer canceled it, and he sued for breach of the resignation agreement and other claims. The court granted the former employer's pretrial judgment motion, and he appealed to the Missouri Court of Appeals.

The court held that the settlement agreement foreclosed the employee's claim for an additional $330 per month in further retirement benefits. The lower court had correctly granted pretrial judgment on that claim and on the employee's claim for tortious interference with a business expectancy. However, the court had improperly granted pretrial judgment on the employee's claim for breach of contract and fraud because of evidence in the record that the sale had been rejected in violation of the negotiated agreement. **The "welcome to approach" language was not insufficiently vague and uncertain to be unenforceable**, and the employee should have received an opportunity to show whether the former employer had breached its contract and defrauded him in the process of negotiating the agreement. *Maupin v. Hallmark Cards, Inc.*, 894 S.W.2d 688 (Mo. Ct. App. 1995).

B. After-Acquired Evidence

After-acquired evidence refers to situations where an employee is fired for an improper reason but the employer then learns that it could have legitimately fired the employee for other misconduct.

Some courts will deny all recovery to employees who have, for example, lied on their applications. Others will just limit the recovery available (usually, back pay from the date of the wrongful termination to the date the employer discovered the misconduct).

◆ A controller in New Jersey told her boss she intended to disclose over-billing practices for an audit as part of the company's compliance with the Sarbanes-Oxley Act. Her relationship with her boss became contentious after that, and she was fired shortly thereafter. She sued for retaliation under the Conscientious Employee Protection Act, and the employer presented after-acquired evidence that she had lied on her application about never having been fired. Therefore, it said it should not be liable for retaliation. A jury ruled for the company, and the employee appealed. The Superior Court of New Jersey, Appellate Division, reversed, noting that **the after-acquired evidence**

should only have been presented in the damages phase of the trial, after the jury determined whether the controller had been improperly fired. Only if the jury found that she had been wrongfully fired could the after-acquired evidence be presented. And that evidence was not definitive anyway because her alleged termination by a previous employer had resulted in a lawsuit that had been settled under a nondisclosure agreement. The case had to be retried. *Redvanly v. Automated Data Processing, Inc.*, 971 A.2d 443 (N.J. Super. Ct. App. Div. 2009).

❖   After an outage shut down both nuclear reactor units at a Michigan nuclear plant, a test engineer informed the night-shift engineer that he believed he had reached or exceeded the work hour limitations set by the Nuclear Regulatory Commission and that he planned to take the next day off. However, the next day, he was told to come in for a meeting. He demanded written authorization before going to work. He then left before a fellow engineer completed crucial documentation on tolerance data. He was suspended and then fired. When he sued for wrongful discharge, the Sixth Circuit held that he engaged in protected conduct when he complained about working excessive hours and required written authorization. The nuclear plant maintained that it had found **after-acquired evidence of personal or objectionable emails** in his mailbox and that it should not have to pay the front pay award. The Sixth Circuit disagreed. Other employees had received or forwarded the same or similar emails without being disciplined. Therefore, the nuclear plant could not use that information to deny the front pay award. *Indiana Michigan Power Co. v. U.S. Dep't of Labor*, 278 Fed.Appx. 597 (6th Cir. 2008).

❖   A doctor signed an employment agreement with a Florida hospital and noted that the reason for leaving his previous position was a change in administration. He worked as the chief medical officer for over two years, and was discharged along with other management personnel upon the replacement of the hospital's top management. He sued for breach of contract, seeking severance pay and other accrued benefits. The hospital defended by stating that he had committed prior acts of moral turpitude, including lying about the circumstances of leaving his previous job and the taking of a bonus he did not earn. When he sought pretrial judgment in his favor, a federal court granted it in part, noting that **the hospital could not use the after-acquired evidence to avoid paying severance to the doctor**. Further, the hospital offered no evidence that he had lied about why he left the previous job. However, there were questions about the bonus that required a trial. *Tomasini v. Mount Sinai Medical Center of Florida, Inc.*, 315 F.Supp.2d 1252 (S.D. Fla. 2004).

❖   A clerical worker used a false employment reference on her job application for a Colorado employer and omitted listing a former employer who had fired her. The employer's handbook allowed termination for misrepresentations. When the employee took an unexcused absence from work, the employer fired her. She sued, asserting that her termination had come in retaliation for her prior complaint to a state agency concerning rest breaks. During pretrial activity, the employer learned of the misrepresentations on her employment application and moved for dismissal on that basis. The case reached the Supreme Court of Colorado, which adopted the **after-acquired evidence rule, permitting an employer to retroactively rely on evidence of employee fraud** in a wrongful discharge action if it can prove that the fraud undermines the basis upon which the employee was hired. An employer may justifiably fire an employee who commits résumé fraud since the misrepresentation fraudulently induces the employer to enter into the contract. *Crawford Rehabilitation Services, Inc. v. Weissman*, 938 P.2d 540 (Colo. 1997).

*   A Kansas nursing home employee removed and copied a videotape of a company meeting and later returned the original tape. She was fired for inconsiderate treatment of residents and sued, claiming that the discharge breached an implied employment contract. During pretrial activity, the employer learned that she had taken the videotape and stated that this action justified her firing. The employee responded that she had viewed the tape in the course of her employment and that her actions complied with company policy. The court agreed with the employer and granted its motion for pretrial judgment. The court of appeals reversed, finding issues of fact that required a trial. **If the employer could establish after-acquired evidence sufficient to justify termination, the employee would not be entitled to any relief.** The Supreme Court of Kansas agreed with the lower courts that the after-acquired evidence doctrine should be recognized in a wrongful discharge case based on breach of an implied contract that raises no public policy issues. It also agreed that material issues of fact remained to be resolved. *Gassmann v. Evangelical Lutheran Good Samaritan Society, Inc.*, 933 P.2d 743 (Kan. 1997).

C. Damage Awards

When employees are fired, they have a duty to try to find other work to mitigate their damages. If they do not try to find other work, their claim for damages will suffer. Thus, even if they were wrongfully discharged, any recovery they obtain may be limited.

Damages can be awarded for breach of contract where one party (usually, the employer) terminates the contract early. Generally, with breach of contract, there are no punitive damages or equitable damages awarded.

Equitable damages (like front and back pay) can be awarded where necessary to make one party (usually, the employee) whole. Front pay is often awarded where it would be counterproductive to reinstate the wrongfully fired employee in the job.

Compensatory and punitive damages can be awarded where the employee brings a tort action against the employer. (A tort is a civil wrong other than breach of contract.) Compensatory damages can include money for emotional distress, and pain and suffering. Punitive damages are awarded to punish one party (usually, the employer) for acting inappropriately.

♦   A New York consultant worked under a contract that allowed his termination upon his "absolute failure to perform the contract's specification." Four months after he signed the contract, he was fired. He sued for breach of contract, and the company countersued for breach of contract, negligence and fraud. The case reached the Supreme Court, Appellate Division, which held that no reasonable view of the evidence would establish that the consultant "absolutely" failed to perform under the contract. During his four months with the company, he was paid $33,000 in salary and bonuses, and the company paid out $116,000 in marketing and advertising costs at his direction. Accordingly, the counterclaims were dismissed, and **the consultant was entitled to recoup the base salary he would have earned ($5,000 per month for over 18 months) plus interest** from the date he was fired. However, on remand, the lower court would have to determine whether that amount should be reduced because of questions over whether he mitigated damages. *Mitchell v. Fidelity Borrowing, LLC*, 40 A.D.3d 557, 837 N.Y.S.2d 78 (N.Y. App. Div. 2007).

♦   An Arizona ex-employee sued his former company for wrongful termination and discrimination. The parties reached a settlement agreement, under which the company would pay him $40,000, "less all lawfully required withholdings." The company then issued him a check for $25,140, retaining $14,860 in federal income tax, FICA and state income tax. After he cashed the check, the company sought to dismiss the lawsuit. He opposed the motion, arguing that taxes should not have been withheld, but the court and the Ninth Circuit disagreed with him. **He never claimed that the settlement award was for physical injuries, so as to make it not taxable.** *Rivera v. Baker West*, 430 F.3d 1253 (9th Cir. 2005).

♦   A Colorado hotel distributed an employee manual allowing medical leaves of absence and granting employees preference for a similar position upon return. Failure to advise the hotel of the availability for return to work upon a doctor's release or a continued absence was deemed voluntary termination. A hotel employee was injured in a non-work-related traffic accident and missed several weeks of work. When her medical leave was to expire, she requested more time off. The request was granted, but the employer later fired her, asserting that she had failed to provide a full medical release and that her former position was unavailable. After she sought reinstatement with restrictions, she was offered her former position. She rejected the offer and sued for breach of contract. The court awarded her damages for loss of salary plus interest accrued after the offer of reinstatement.

The Court of Appeals of Colorado ruled that the award was limited to damages incurred before the offer of reinstatement. The employee appealed to the Supreme Court of Colorado, which affirmed, finding that **an employee may be required to accept a reinstatement offer as part of the general duty to mitigate damages**, absent special circumstances. In this case, the employee had identified no special circumstances that would relieve her of her duty to mitigate her damages. The employer was not required to offer her a position with more favorable terms than she had originally enjoyed, and her rejection of the reinstatement offer was a failure to mitigate her damages. *Fair v. Red Lion Inn*, 943 P.2d 431 (Colo. 1997).

CHAPTER FOUR

Employee Benefits

I. RETIREMENT BENEFITS

ERISA, the Employee Retirement Income Security Act of 1974, 29 U.S.C. § 1001 *et seq.*, is a comprehensive federal statute that imposes uniform rules and standards upon private pension and welfare benefit plans. It describes the fiduciary responsibilities of plan administrators and specifies rules for pension participation, funding, vesting and financial reporting.

ERISA preempts all state laws "as they may now or hereafter relate to any employee benefit plan described in section 1003(a) of this title...." Because the question of ERISA applicability frequently determines the outcome of pension litigation, a substantial body of law has developed concerning whether a particular state law "relates to" a plan described by ERISA.

Defined benefit plans consist of a general pool of assets rather than individual dedicated accounts. Under these plans, employees are entitled to a fixed periodic payment upon retirement, and employers generally bear the risk of investment. If there is under-funding of plan assets, the employer must make up the difference. On the other hand, if there is a surplus of plan assets, the employer may reduce or suspend its contributions.

Defined contribution plans are more common. Under these plans, the employer's contribution is fixed, and the employee receives whatever level of benefits the amount contributed on his or her behalf will provide. Each beneficiary is entitled to whatever assets are dedicated to his or her individual account. Employees bear the risk of loss and reap the rewards of high returns.

A. ERISA in General

ERISA requires each pension plan to provide that an employee's right to normal pension benefits is "non-forfeitable" if the employee meets the statutory age and years of service requirements. ERISA does not create the same requirement with respect to welfare benefits (like vacation benefits).

ERISA also sets certain limits on lawsuits for money damages. It permits ERISA plans (but not individual beneficiaries) to bring such lawsuits against fiduciaries in certain circumstances, and it defines as fiduciaries not only those persons named as fiduciaries by a benefit plan, but also anyone else who exercises discretionary control or authority over the plan's management, administration or assets.

Non-fiduciaries cannot be sued for money damages, but they can be sued for equitable relief (like injunctions and restitution).

ERISA fiduciaries have a number of duties and responsibilities, including: "the proper management, administration, and investment of [plan] assets, the maintenance of proper records, the disclosure of specified information, and the avoidance of conflicts of interest."

1. Supreme Court Cases

◆   A public relations manager in Connecticut had fibromyalgia and lupus. She sought long-term disability benefits. Her plan set a three-year limitations period to seek judicial review of a denial of benefits, and the period began when proof of loss was due. When the plan denied the claim, she sued under ERISA. The suit was filed more than three years after proof of loss was due but less than three years after the plan's denial of her claim became final. The U.S. Supreme Court upheld a ruling against the employee, finding that **the limitations period was enforceable**. *Heimeshoff v. Hartford Life & Accident Insurance Co.*, 134 S.Ct. 604 (U.S. 2013).

◆   A Pennsylvania employee who participated in his employer's health and benefits plan was injured in a car accident. The plan paid his medical expenses, and the employee recovered money from the party that caused the accident. Pursuant to a plan provision, the employer then sought reimbursement from the employee for the medical expenses it had paid. The employee refused to reimburse the employer, which then sued under ERISA to enforce the terms of the plan and get the money back. A federal appeals court ruled that the principle of unjust enrichment trumped the plan's reimbursement clause. The U.S. Supreme Court vacated and remanded. It held that **unjust enrichment principles did not override the contract**. However, it further decided that equitable rules could aid in properly construing the reimbursement provision. *U.S. Airways v. McCutchen*, 133 S.Ct. 1537 (U.S. 2013).

◆   Employees of a company sued an employer and its pension plan under ERISA after the company converted its traditional defined benefit pension plan to a "cash balance" retirement plan. A Connecticut federal court granted some of the relief requested, and the Second Circuit affirmed. The case then reached the U.S. Supreme Court, which held that although the lower court had improperly cited a particular ERISA section when granting relief, another ERISA section applied. ERISA Section 502(a)(3) allows equitable relief to address violations of an ERISA plan's terms. **The company failed to give proper notice of the change**, so if the employees could prove they'd been harmed by the defective notice, they would be entitled to relief. However, the lower court should not have changed the plan to conform to the summary plan description. The summary is not part of the plan. *Cigna Corp. v. Amara*, 131 S.Ct. 1866, 179 L.Ed.2d 843 (U.S. 2011).

◆   A former employee sued his ex-employer, alleging that he had asked the company to make certain changes to his 401(k) investments and that it had never made the changes. He asserted that this failure "depleted" his interest in the plan by approximately $150,000 and amounted to a breach of fiduciary duty under ERISA. A South Carolina federal court granted pretrial judgment to the company, and the Fourth Circuit affirmed. The U.S. Supreme Court vacated and remanded the case, holding that although Section 502(a)(2) of ERISA does not provide a remedy for individual injuries distinct from plan injuries, **ERISA does authorize recovery for fiduciary breaches that impair the value of plan assets in a participant's individual account**. Here, the misconduct alleged by the employee fell squarely within the statutory duties imposed by ERISA. This was a different situation than a defined benefit plan, where participants are entitled to a fixed payment (like from a pension). Here, fiduciary misconduct could reduce a participant's benefits below the amount he would otherwise receive. Further proceedings were necessary. *LaRue v. DeWolff, Boberg & Associates, Inc.*, 552 U.S. 248, 128 S.Ct. 1020, 169 L.Ed.2d 847 (2008).

◆   Participants in a multiemployer pension plan in Illinois retired after accruing enough pension credits to qualify for early retirement payments under a "service only" pension scheme that paid them the same monthly benefit they would have received had they retired at the usual age. They were only 39 at the time. The plan prohibited them from taking jobs as construction workers (but not as supervisors) if they wanted to continue receiving pension payments. They took supervisory construction jobs so as to be able to receive pension benefits in addition to their salaries. The plan then expanded its definition of barred employment to include any construction industry job, and stopped payments when the participants did not leave their supervisory jobs. They sued to recover the suspended benefits, claiming that the suspension violated the "anti-cutback" rule of ERISA, which prohibits any pension plan amendment that would reduce a participant's "accrued benefit."

A federal court ruled for the plan, but the Seventh Circuit reversed, holding that imposing new conditions on rights to benefits already accrued violated the anti-cutback rule. The U.S. Supreme Court affirmed, holding that ERISA Section 204(g) prohibits an amendment expanding the categories of barred post-retirement employment so as to suspend payment of early retirement benefits already accrued. Here, the suspension of benefits allowed by **the plan amendment had the effect of reducing an early retirement benefit that had been promised**. *Cent. Laborers' Pension Fund v. Heinz*, 541 U.S. 739, 124 S.Ct. 2230, 159 L.Ed.2d 46 (2004).

◆   A Washington state law automatically revoked, upon divorce, the designation of a spouse as beneficiary to a life insurance policy or employee benefit plan. When a divorced employee died in a car accident, his children sought the proceeds of his life insurance policy and his pension plan, even though his ex-wife was still named on both documents. Also, both documents were governed by ERISA. A question arose as to whether ERISA preempted the state law, making the children the recipients of the proceeds. The U.S. Supreme Court ruled that **ERISA preempted the state law**. To rule otherwise would require plan administrators to familiarize themselves with the statutes of all 50 states. ERISA allowed them to pay out proceeds per the plan documents. Thus, the ex-wife was entitled to the proceeds. *Egelhoff v. Egelhoff*, 532 U.S. 141, 121 S.Ct. 1322, 149 L.Ed.2d 264 (2001).

◆   The Retirement Equity Act of 1984 allows participants in survivor's annuity plans to designate a beneficiary other than their spouse only with the spouse's consent. A Louisiana telecommunications employee with a wife and three sons participated in several ERISA-qualified retirement plans. Following the death of his wife, the employee remarried. When he died several years later, his sons submitted claims against his estate based upon the first wife's will for his undistributed retirement benefits. A federal court held that the sons were entitled to a share of the retirement benefits under Louisiana community property law. The Fifth Circuit affirmed. The U.S. Supreme Court held that ERISA preempted the state law that allowed the first wife to transfer (upon her death) an interest in undistributed pension plan benefits. **The surviving spouse was entitled to receive the survivor's annuity since she had not waived her**

rights or consented to the designation of the sons as beneficiaries. *Boggs v. Boggs*, 520 U.S. 833, 117 S.Ct. 1754, 138 L.Ed.2d 45 (1997).

✦ A class of former employees of the Kaiser Steel Corporation, who participated in the company's ERISA-qualified retirement plan, brought suit for the plan's losses against an actuary employed by the company. They alleged that the actuary had knowingly participated in misfeasance by plan fiduciaries. Kaiser had hired the actuary when it began to phase out its steel-making operations, prompting early retirement by a large number of plan participants. The actuary failed to change the plan's actuarial assumptions to reflect the additional costs imposed by the retirements. As a result, Kaiser did not adequately fund the plan, and its assets became insufficient to satisfy its obligations. When the plan was terminated, the former employees began receiving only the benefits guaranteed by ERISA, which were substantially lower than the fully vested pensions due them under the plan. After a California federal court and the Ninth Circuit dismissed the complaint, the U.S. Supreme Court affirmed. ERISA Section 502(a)(3) permits plan participants to bring civil actions to obtain "appropriate equitable relief" to redress violations of the plan. The Court determined that **requiring the actuary to make the plan whole for the losses it sustained would not constitute "appropriate equitable relief."** What the employees were seeking here was compensatory damages, not "equitable relief." *Mertens v. Hewitt Associates*, 508 U.S. 248, 113 S.Ct. 2063, 124 L.Ed.2d 161 (1993).

✦ One of the trustees of a sheet metal workers' pension fund embezzled over $375,000 from the union. Two pension plans contended that the trustee had forfeited his right to receive benefits as a result. They also asserted that even if he had not forfeited his benefits, those benefits should be paid to the union and not to him. A Colorado federal court held that because there was a judgment against the trustee for $275,000, a constructive trust should be imposed on the trustee's benefits until the judgment was paid off. The Tenth Circuit affirmed. The U.S. Supreme Court held that the constructive trust violated the prohibition on assignment or alienation of pension benefits called for by ERISA. Here, although the trustee had stolen money from the union, he had not stolen money from the pension funds. Even if the Labor-Management Reporting and Disclosure Act authorized the imposition of a constructive trust when a union officer breached his fiduciary duties, that did not override ERISA's anti-alienation provision. ERISA reflected a congressional policy choice to **safeguard a stream of income for pensioners even if that prevented others from obtaining relief for the wrongs done them**. The Court reversed and remanded the case. *Guidry v. Sheet Metal Workers National Pension Fund*, 493 U.S. 365, 110 S.Ct. 680, 107 L.Ed.2d 782 (1990).

On remand, the federal appeals court held that ERISA's provision regarding alienation did not prevent the garnishment of private pension benefits paid to a beneficiary. It also decided that ERISA did not act to preempt a state law that exempted some pension or retirement benefits from garnishment. In addition, it decided that the state exemption applied. *Guidry v. Sheet Metal Workers Local No. 9*, 39 F.3d 1078 (10th Cir. 1994).

◆ A North Carolina insurance agent sold insurance for competitors after his relationship with an insurer was terminated. When the insurer sought to avoid paying his retirement benefits on the grounds that he violated a non-compete clause, he sued. The U.S. Supreme Court noted that the agent's ERISA claim could succeed only if he was an employee. Because ERISA's definition of "employee" as "any individual employed by an employer" was not helpful, the Court suggested **assessing and weighing all the elements of an employment relationship**, including: the location of the work, the duration of the relationship between the parties, the method of payment, and the provision of employee benefits, among others. The Court reversed and remanded the case for a determination of whether the agent qualified as an employee under traditional agency law. *Nationwide Mutual Insurance Co. v. Darden*, 503 U.S. 318, 112 S.Ct. 1344, 117 L.Ed.2d 581 (1992).

2. Preemption

ERISA preempts state laws that affect employee benefit plans. However, if a state law of general applicability has only a minor connection with covered ERISA plans, it will not be expressly preempted.

The preemption issue is important because if a state law and ERISA both address employee benefit plans, courts need to know whether to apply state or federal law to resolve any conflict.

With large companies, there might be employees in several different states, each with its own laws relating to employee benefit plans. The application of ERISA ensures uniformity of enforceability that makes it easier for ERISA fiduciaries to properly administer their plans.

◆ A company in Massachusetts overpaid a retired employee by $29,000 under a lump sum distribution to an IRA account. When it learned of the mistake, it sought to be reimbursed for the $29,000 plus interest at a rate of 4.98%. The retiree offered to return the excess funds, but he wanted the interest placed in an escrow account to offset any expenses he might incur as a result of the company's mistake. The company rejected the proposal and sued under state law, but the Supreme Judicial Court of Massachusetts held that the lawsuit was preempted by ERISA. **The company had to follow ERISA's enforcement procedures to recover the overpayment.** *Hitachi High Technologies America, Inc. v. Bowler*, 916 N.E.2d 322 (Mass. 2009).

◆ A Massachusetts engineer worked for a company and one of its subsidiaries over his career. At one point, his pension benefits from his earlier work with the company were transferred to another pension trust without notification to his then-current employer. As a result, both the company and the subsidiary included his total service time in their respective pension calculations. Relying on the company's estimate of his pension benefit, he retired. Later, the company notified him that it had overstated his pension benefits and that he was actually entitled to less than half of what he had been receiving – although he was entitled to benefits from the other pension trust to cover his earlier time with the company. He sued the company for negligence and misrepresentation, but the First Circuit held that his claims were preempted by ERISA. **They related to a retirement plan and to the company's recordkeeping responsibilities under that plan.** *Zipperer v. Raytheon Co., Inc.,* 493 F.3d 50 (1st Cir. 2007).

• A California employer sponsored a self-funded employee benefit plan covered by ERISA. The employer contracted with a third party to provide administrative services for the plan, but it retained management control as the plan administrator with final discretion over claims decisions. It also contracted with an insurer for excess loss coverage to reimburse it for payments above a specified deductible amount. The third-party administrator failed to timely process and submit a claim by a plan beneficiary to the excess insurer. As a result, the excess insurer failed to reimburse the employer for benefits it paid the beneficiary through the plan. The employer sued the third-party administrator and excess insurer for breach of contract. The administrator and insurer asserted that the case was preempted by ERISA. The court agreed and dismissed the complaint. The U.S. Court of Appeals, Ninth Circuit, reversed, holding that **ERISA does not preempt regulation of the relationships between the plan and its employees, insurers or creditors.** The state laws at issue here did not directly regulate an ERISA plan. They were laws of general application that did not depend upon the interpretation of ERISA. *Geweke Ford v. St. Joseph's Omni Preferred Care, Inc.,* 130 F.3d 1355 (9th Cir. 1997).

3.   Interference With Benefits/New Plan Offers

ERISA prohibits interfering with employees' benefit rights. For example, it is a violation of ERISA for a company to fire employees to prevent them from seeking medical benefits.

Companies also must provide employees with information about new plan offers. For example, where a company has a new pension plan offer under "serious consideration" and employees have been asked to contemplate early retirement, that new plan offer must be made known to the eligible employees.

If the new plan being contemplated is not under serious consideration (that is, if it is just one of several potential offers being discussed and no firm timetable has been put in place for instituting it), then there is no fiduciary duty to divulge that information to eligible employees.

• A company in Nebraska laid off 15 employees, eight of whom were nearly eligible for pension benefits under the company's early retirement plan. The company amended its plan so that they could get benefits as if they had worked the next year-and-a-half, when they would have been eligible under a 50/25 early retirement provision. A number of the laid-off employees who were eligible under the old 50/25 plan would have qualified for a higher 30-year pension had their employment been accelerated like the other employees. They sued for increased benefits, claiming that the amendment to the plan violated

ERISA and the ADEA. A federal court granted pretrial judgment to the company, and the Eighth Circuit affirmed. **The employees suing did not have their pension benefits altered by the amendment.** Further, the different treatment wasn't motivated by age but by pension status, which is allowed. *Schultz v. Windstream Communications, Inc.*, 600 F.3d 948 (8th Cir. 2010).

◆   A Pennsylvania employee began working for a company in 1980. In 1988, the company was purchased by a new corporation. His pension benefits were recalculated and his hiring date was changed from 1980 to 1988, though his vacation and disability benefits were still calculated using the 1980 hiring date. He later received a letter from the company advising him that his hiring date had been adjusted to 1980. Based on that letter, the employee's wife decided to retire. When the employee was later laid off and learned that his hiring date was in fact 1988, he sued under ERISA, claiming a breach of fiduciary duty. A federal court ruled for the company, and the Third Circuit affirmed. **The wife's decision to retire did not affect the husband's pension benefits** or her potential benefits as his beneficiary so as to allow a claim of detrimental reliance against a fiduciary. *Shook v. Avaya, Inc.*, 625 F.3d 69 (3d Cir. 2010).

◆   A company regularly monitored employees' compliance with its expense policies by hiring an independent contractor to conduct a scan for red flags – patterns of irregular or inaccurate reporting. During one of these monitoring sweeps, several employees were identified as having repeatedly violated company policy by submitting false or improper expense account reports. After the company fired them, they sued, alleging that the real reason for the termination was to deprive them of benefits in violation of ERISA. A Pennsylvania federal court ruled against them. Despite their argument that many of their expenses (like visits to gentlemen's clubs) were tolerated and even approved by their superiors, the company had a good-faith belief that they engaged in inappropriate conduct. *Balmat v. CertainTeed Corp.*, No. 04-2505, 2007 WL 4570928 (E.D. Pa. 12/28/07).

◆   Retired managers sued AT&T, claiming that it breached its fiduciary duties under ERISA by modifying its traditional defined benefit pension plan with a new cash balance plan and creating a "Special Update" plan for older employees that froze their benefits. They claimed that AT&T lured them into retirement with the "Special Update" as a means of reducing the work force prior to instituting a voluntary retirement plan for which they were no longer eligible. A New Jersey federal court and the Third Circuit ruled in favor of AT&T. **The retirees failed to show that the voluntary retirement plan was under serious consideration at the time they retired.** In order to be under "serious consideration," a change to an employee benefit plan must meet three requirements: 1) there must be a specific proposal; 2) it must be being discussed for the purpose of implementation; and 3) it must be discussed by senior management who have the authority to implement the change. Here, the earliest the company began seriously considering the plan was after all the retirees had retired. *Peterson v. American Telephone and Telegraph Co.*, 127 Fed.Appx. 67 (3d Cir. 2005).

◆   Employees of a company in South Carolina brought a lawsuit alleging that company officials used their healthcare contributions deducted from their paychecks for other business debts in violation of ERISA. A federal court granted pretrial judgment to the company, but the Fourth Circuit reversed. Funding the employees' health plan was a fiduciary function, not a business function, and there was a material question of fact as to whether the company deducted money from the employees' checks and then failed to pay it to the health plan's claims administrator. **Assets of ERISA-covered plans cannot inure to the benefit of employers.** A trial would determine whether the company had violated ERISA. *Phelps v. C.T. Enterprises*, 394 F.3d 213 (4th Cir. 2005).

◆   A technician on an offshore oil-drilling rig became eligible for retirement. He began to hear rumors that, in addition to regular retirement benefits, the company was going to be offering a lump-sum retirement incentive under a special ERISA welfare plan designed to induce employees to retire early. He asked several company officials about the incentive, and they told him truthfully that they knew nothing about it. A company attorney also told him that she could not confirm the rumors. Shortly thereafter, a vice president reviewed a proposal to provide an early retirement incentive, but no one told the technician. Two weeks after he retired, the company announced the incentive. He sued under ERISA, and a California federal court granted pretrial judgment to Exxon. The Ninth Circuit reversed and remanded, finding issues of fact that required a trial. If the incentive was under "serious consideration" when the technician tried to confirm the rumors, then the company had a fiduciary duty to provide him with complete and truthful information. **A plan is under serious consideration when it is specific and it is being discussed for purposes of implementation by senior management** who can implement it. However, if the plan was not under serious consideration at that time, then the company owed him no duty to follow up with information about the plan unless the officials promised to do so. *Bins v. Exxon Co.*, 220 F.3d 1042 (9th Cir. 2000).

◆   A division head for a Kentucky company told a manager that he wanted to reduce salaries and cut medical costs. He asked the manager to put together information on employee birth dates, hire dates, smoking habits and benefits. Another supervisory employee prepared a reduction in work force memorandum entitled "High Risk," which flagged employees by salary, age, disability, premature births of children, surgeries, and exemption status. Two older employees, ages 60 and 59, were among the workers who were laid off. They sued the company under the Age Discrimination in Employment Act (ADEA) and ERISA, asserting that the company fired them due to their age and to interfere with their pension rights. A jury ruled against them on their ADEA claim, but ruled in their favor on the ERISA claim, awarding one employee $135,000 and the other $348,000. The Sixth Circuit Court of Appeals affirmed. The evidence indicated that the reasons the company had given for terminating the employees were false. The employees' supervisors had testified that their work was either "above quality" or excellent. The jury had properly found that **the company had fired the employees to interfere with their retirement benefits**. *Pennington v. Western Atlas, Inc.*, 202 F.3d 902 (6th Cir. 2000).

♦   Following a heart attack, the interim plant manager at a Texas plant went on medical leave to undergo open heart surgery. He was fired the day after he returned to work. He claimed the company fired him so it wouldn't have to restore him to his previous position, in violation of the Family and Medical Leave Act (FMLA), and so it wouldn't have to pay his medical benefits, in violation of ERISA. The company argued that it had decided to terminate him for substandard performance the day before he suffered the heart attack. A federal jury found that **the termination decision did not take place until after the manager returned to work and was made to keep him from staying in his position and to avoid paying medical benefits**. It awarded him more than $41,000 in past lost wages and employee benefits; $11,000 for mental anguish; and $5,166 in out-of-pocket expenses. The district court entered judgment for more than $119,000, which included liquidated (double) damages. The Fifth Circuit Court of Appeals upheld the verdict, but reversed the award of out-of-pocket expenses and damages for mental anguish. Damages under the FMLA and ERISA do not include out-of-pocket expenses or damages for mental anguish. *Nero v. Industrial Molding Corp.*, 167 F.3d 921 (5th Cir. 1999).

4.   Other Retirement Benefits Issues

The following cases address other issues that can arise in the retirement benefits area.

♦   Three employees of a Texas company participated in their employer's wealth accumulation plan, which was funded by employee and employer contributions. After the employees became separated from employment, they alleged that the plan's forfeiture provisions violated ERISA. A district court ruled for the employer, but **a federal appeals court reversed**. It said the employer's wealth accumulation plan was an employee pension plan under ERISA, and it remanded the case for a determination of whether the plan was exempt from ERISA's rules because it was a "top hat" plan. *Tolbert v. RBC Capital Markets Corp.*, 758 F.3d 619 (5th Cir. 2014).

♦   An Indiana employee discovered that money being withheld from his paycheck wasn't being deposited into his retirement account as it should have been. He complained to his superiors, including the CEO. He later received checks to make up for the difference, plus interest. But when company officials believed he had prematurely taken money out of his retirement account, he was fired. He demonstrated that he was correct about the vesting date of his account, but the company refused to rehire him, so he sued under ERISA. The case reached the Seventh Circuit, which held that **if he was fired for questioning what happened to the withheld money, he had a cause of action under ERISA**. This was an "inquiry" under Section 510 of the law, and ERISA's anti-retaliation clause protected him. *George v. Junior Achievement of Cent. Indiana, Inc.*, 694 F.3d 812 (7th Cir. 2012).

♦   A Wisconsin paper company decided to fire a 14-year employee, who believed he had a viable age discrimination claim. In exchange for agreeing not to sue, he negotiated a severance agreement with the company's HR manager, who also was the administrator for the company's employee pension plan. When she figured out the reduced monthly pension payments to which he would be entitled under one of five different options, she miscalculated the amount he would receive, telling him he would get $1,156 per month rather than the correct amount of $706 per month. He accepted the severance package. The HR manager later discovered the error and notified him. **He sued under ERISA, claiming that the company's pension plan had to pay him the higher amount because he had relied on that figure when giving up his right to sue.** A federal court and the Seventh Circuit ruled against him, noting that there was no evidence the misrepresentation was intentional. *Pearson v. Voith Paper Rolls, Inc.*, 656 F.3d 504 (7th Cir. 2011).

◆   A Pennsylvania nurse claimed that she was entitled to greater contributions to her retirement plans than her employer made because she had to work during meal breaks and before her shifts started, and the employer didn't properly document the work. She sued under ERISA. A federal court granted pretrial judgment to the hospital, and the Third Circuit Court of Appeals affirmed. The court noted that **the plans at issue determined the amount of benefits due by the amount of compensation paid.** Since the hospital made contributions based on the compensation she received, it was not liable for more. However, if she could prove that she had been underpaid in her state court lawsuit, she would be entitled to greater retirement plan contributions. *Henderson v. Univ. of Pittsburgh Medical Center*, 640 F.3d 524 (3d Cir. 2011).

◆   ERISA's "anti-cutback" rule generally prohibits employers from making plan changes that reduce a participant's benefits. When a Massachusetts employee retired at age 58, he stated his intention to start receiving annuity benefits at age 62. His retirement annuity would be $187 per month (defined benefit plan), while his profit-sharing account balance was $370,388 (defined contribution plan). Upon his retirement, he could have transferred his profit-sharing money to his retirement account to receive an estimated payment of $4,163 per month, but he failed to do so. Shortly thereafter, the company eliminated the transfer option. When he tried to exercise that option at the age of 62, his request was denied. He sued under ERISA but lost. The First Circuit noted that **the "anti-cutback" rule provides an exception allowing retirement plans to eliminate transfer options between defined benefit and defined contribution plans.** *Tasker v. DHL Retirement Savings Plan*, 621 F.3d 34 (1st Cir. 2010).

◆   A company in Ohio had a "top hat" retirement plan for a select group of its highest-paid executives. The plan provided no benefits if an otherwise eligible employee quit or was fired for cause. After the company removed its president and excluded him from its facilities as well as from contacting other employees or customers, it retained him to assist with a failing business deal, believing he was the best person to create a marketing plan. He believed he was entitled to "top hat" benefits, but the company disputed that assertion. At least twice, he threatened to thwart the deal until the company met his severance demands. The company asked for his personal phone records to determine if he was making unauthorized calls, but rather than turn them over, he sued under ERISA, seeking $300,000. A federal court and the Sixth Circuit ruled that **the company reasonably believed he had acted in his best interest at the expense of the company's interest and therefore properly denied him the "top hat" benefits**. *Whitescarver v. Sabin Robbins Paper Co.*, 313 Fed.Appx. 781 (6th Cir. 2008).

◆   Three former Home Depot employees brought a lawsuit against the company under ERISA, asserting that it allowed a company-appointed investment committee to invest in corporate stock even though **corporate officials were backdating stock options and making fraudulent transactions that artificially inflated the stocks' value**. The employees claimed that Home Depot and the investment committee breached their fiduciary duty. A Georgia federal court dismissed the case, ruling that the employees were seeking "damages" rather than "benefits" because they were not seeking a "readily ascertainable amount that could directly affect a payment" to them. However, the Eleventh Circuit ruled that they were seeking benefits. Nevertheless, the lawsuit was premature. The employees first had to exhaust their administrative remedies. *Lanfear v. Home Depot, Inc.*, 536 F.3d 1217 (11th Cir. 2008).

◆   Two companies converted the pension plans they offered employees to cash balance plans. Under a cash balance (or hybrid) plan, a hypothetical account is established in each participant's name. Benefits are credited to that "account" over time, driven by two variables: 1) the employer's hypothetical "contributions," and 2) hypothetical earnings expressed as interest credits. Employer "contributions" are usually expressed as a percentage of salary, the rate of which may vary with employee tenure. Interest credits are usually tied to an extrinsic index, like Treasury bills. Each year an employee receives a statement of her "account" balance. These features are designed to mimic the simplicity of a defined contribution plan. However, under hybrid plans, employers bear the market risks. When participants challenged the two companies' plans, asserting that they violated ERISA's rule against age-based reductions in the rate of benefit accrual, federal courts in New York held that the plans did not violate ERISA. The Second Circuit affirmed, noting that the plans did not inherently result in an age-based reduction in the rate of benefit accrual even though **younger employees might achieve greater growth because of the longer time they had until retirement**. *Hirt v. Equitable Retirement Plan for Employees, Managers, and Agents*, 533 F.3d 102 (2d Cir. 2008).

◆   A New Jersey employee participated in his company's 401(k) plan and directed that his money be put into a stock fund composed entirely of company stock. In March 2004, the stock traded at a 52-week high of $7.42 per share. By October 4, the stock was trading at $1.70 per share, and the employee cashed out. The employee claimed the stock price plummeted because of a risky and failed merger. He sued the company for breaching its fiduciary duties to him and other plan participants by offering the stock as an investment option despite knowing it wasn't a prudent investment. He also asserted that plan administrators made misleading statements about the merger that caused him to invest in the plan. A federal court ruled that he was not a "participant" for purposes of ERISA because he had already cashed out of the plan. However, the Third Circuit reversed. It ruled that **he could sue the plan administrator for mismanaging the plan before he cashed out**, causing him to have less than he was entitled to. *Graden v. Conexant Systems, Inc.*, 496 F.3d 291 (3d Cir. 2007).

◆   A new manager at a window plant in Minnesota told the engineers that he had higher performance expectations than his predecessor. An engineer began to receive poor evaluations and was told that he was going to be put on a Performance Improvement Plan (PIP). If he failed to improve in defined areas within 30 days, he would be fired. He then learned that a co-worker had avoided getting placed on a PIP by announcing his retirement. The engineer did the same, then sued the company under ERISA, asserting that he had been constructively discharged because the PIP set goals that could not be achieved. A federal court and the Eighth Circuit ruled against him. Here, **he presented no evidence that the company forced him to retire to avoid paying health benefits**, nor could he prove that the PIP set impossible goals. In fact, he conceded that the plan conformed with what one would expect from an engineer. *Fischer v. Andersen Corp.*, 483 F.3d 553 (8th Cir. 2007).

B. Vesting Rights and Plan Amendment Issues

1. Vesting Rights

Where employees work the minimum number of years to vest their pension rights, they are entitled to benefits. Where there is a break in service (like where an employee is laid off and has to find another job), plans usually spell out the kind of employment that can be taken to stay on course for vesting.

◆   Two New York motion picture studio mechanics sued their pension plan and its administrator under ERISA, **claiming that they did not receive sufficient pension credit for years in which they worked less than full time**. Essentially, they argued that the plan improperly substituted a 200-day year for a 150-day year in its determination of a "full year of participation." Under ERISA Section 204(b)(4)(B), an employee who works at least 1,000 hours a year must be given pension credit for a partial year of service of at least "a ratable portion of the accrued benefit to which he would be entitled under the plan if his customary employment were full time." The case reached the Second Circuit, which ruled that the 200-day year was not arbitrary and capricious. Although the current plan did not define a "year of participation," at least three earlier versions of the plan used the 200-day year. *Kammerer v. Motion Picture Industry Pension Plan*, 487 Fed.Appx. 597 (2d Cir. 2012).

◆   A number of employees filed a class action lawsuit against their employer, asserting that its amended pension plan disproportionately harmed older employees and also violated anti-cutback and anti-backloading rules under

ERISA. Under the amendment, early retirement benefits were actuarially reduced to account for the fact that each participant's cash balance was being distributed over a longer period of time. To mitigate the effects on older employees, the plan created a frozen "special update" benefit, which provided a significant, one-time increase to each participant's benefits and was subject to the generous early retirement subsidies available under the old plan. One result was that for many older employees, cash balances would grow but early retirement benefits wouldn't. A New Jersey federal court granted pretrial judgment to the company, and the Third Circuit affirmed. **Because the employees' cash balances continued to grow, there was no anti-backloading violation.** Further, there was no anti-cutback rule violation because there was no reduction of accrued benefits or imposition of greater restrictions on the receipt of accrued benefits. *Engers v. AT & T, Inc.*, 466 Fed.Appx. 75 (3d Cir. 2011).

◆ A Nevada retiree sued after his former employer's pension plan determined that he was not a "participant" and thus was not eligible for benefits. A federal court found that **the plan abused its discretion by denying benefits** and granted pretrial judgment to the retiree. The plan appealed to the Ninth Circuit, which affirmed in part. It noted that the plan improperly determined that even though the retiree met all the requirements of participation in the plan, he did not qualify because he had not been in compensable service on or after May 1, 1978. However, the plan's own provisions allowed for participation for retirees who had ceased working for the company prior to that date. The appellate court also held that the lower court should have considered awarding reasonable attorneys' fees and prejudgment interest to the retiree. It remanded the case for further proceedings. *Weaver v. Retirement Plan for Employees of Hanson Building Materials America, Inc.*, 323 Fed.Appx. 564 (9th Cir. 2009).

◆ Participants in a New Jersey company's pension plan sued the company, alleging that it violated ERISA by 1) illegally ceasing benefit accrual by reason of age; 2) backloading pension accruals; and 3) providing a benefit at normal retirement age that was less than the early retirement amount. A federal court dismissed the lawsuit, finding that the participants failed to show any of the claims they asserted were true. Their calculations on the issue of ceasing benefit accrual failed to take into account one step. They also failed to prove that pension accruals were backloaded by the plan or that someone retiring at normal retirement age would receive less than someone who retired early. Without specific facts to back up their claims, their lawsuit could not proceed. *Haesler v. Novartis Consumer Health, Inc.*, 426 F.Supp.2d 227 (D.N.J. 2006).

◆ An employee of a steel company with 14 years, 11 months, and 11 days of service had his continuous service terminated for pension purposes because he had been absent from work for two years with a heart condition. He was 19 days short of eligibility for the company's 70/80 pension. He claimed that he did not learn of the service being broken until eight years later. The benefits plan administrator had determined that since his disability had not been incurred during the course of his employment, his continuous service stopped after two years away from the job. He sued under Section 502(a)(3) of ERISA, asserting that he was entitled to the 70/80 pension and that, at the very least, the plan administrator had breached a fiduciary duty to notify him of how it was interpreting his disability and that it was about to break his service. A Pennsylvania federal court granted pretrial judgment to the company. The Third Circuit vacated in part. **The administrator had breached its fiduciary duty to him by failing to notify him of the break in service.** Had he known his service was broken earlier, he could have taken certain steps to protect himself from a total loss of his pension. The court remanded the case for further proceedings. *Harte v. Bethlehem Steel Corp.*, 214 F.3d 446 (3d Cir. 2000).

♦   A Chicago steel plant supervisor requested a two-year leave of absence to accommodate her husband's health problems. The employer accepted her request but issued a written memorandum stating that she would be rehired only if she was needed and that a company reorganization was already planned. When she requested reinstatement less than two years later, the employer stated that no position was available in her former department and that she would be discharged at the expiration of her leave. Although she was entitled to a deferred vested pension, she sought a comprehensive pension supplement available to participants whose employment termination resulted from a permanent plant shutdown or job elimination. The company refused to award the supplement, stating that the separation had been caused by the leave of absence. The U.S. Court of Appeals, Seventh Circuit, found the administrator's interpretation of the plan reasonable. **The discharge had been due to the lack of an available position at the time she returned from her scheduled leave of absence.** Plan language could reasonably be read as requiring a direct cause and effect between job elimination and employment termination, a condition that was not satisfied where the employee initiated the separation. *Brehmer v. Inland Steel Industries Pension Plan*, 114 F.3d 656 (7th Cir. 1997).

♦   A California construction worker became permanently disabled at age 56. He was erroneously advised by union officials that he was two months short of the 15-year eligibility requirement for the normal retirement benefit from the Construction Laborers Pension Trust (CLPT) for Southern California. Thus, he did not apply for pension benefits when he turned 62, even though he had actually accrued 23 years of service. Plan trustees then lowered the eligibility requirement to 10 years. The laborer applied for pension benefits, but the plan awarded retroactive benefits covering only the time period after he had turned 65. He was denied benefits retroactive to the age of 62 because he had failed to apply for them. He sued, asserting violations of ERISA. The U.S. Court of Appeals, Ninth Circuit, stated that the CLPT plan had **only three requirements for eligibility**: the completion of the credited service requirement, the attainment of age 62, and the performance of a minimal requirement of covered service. Plan trustees had been arbitrary and capricious in adding further requirements for eligibility. The administrative requirement of applying for benefits was not a prerequisite to eligibility. *Canseco v. Construction Laborers Pension Trust for Southern California*, 93 F.3d 600 (9th Cir. 1996).

2. Plan Amendment Issues

Employers can generally adopt, modify or terminate pension plans just as they can welfare benefit plans. Where employers amend plans in their capacity as employers (and not as fiduciaries), they will not have liability under ERISA as long as they act consistently with ERISA, its regulations and the plans' requirements.

◆   An aircraft manufacturer doing business in Arizona and California established a "defined benefit" pension plan for its employees in 1951. By 1986, plan assets exceeded the value of accrued plan benefits by almost $1 billion. Even though the plan was funded by both employer and employee contributions, the employer ceased its contributions to the plan and used part of the surplus to fund a separate early retirement plan for current employees. A group of retired participants in the pension plan filed a California federal court action against the employer and plan, asserting violations of ERISA. The court dismissed the lawsuit, and the participants appealed. The U.S. Court of Appeals, Ninth Circuit, held that the employer's actions violated ERISA.

The case then came before the U.S. Supreme Court, which noted that **the retirees, as members of a *defined benefit plan*, had no interest in the plan's surplus**. This was so despite the fact that the plan surplus was partially attributable to the investment growth of the retirees' contributions. Defined benefit plan members have a non-forfeitable right to accrued benefits, and the employer is responsible for any shortages. By the same token, the employer is entitled to any windfall produced by the plan. Had this been a *defined contribution plan*, the retirees would have been entitled to whatever assets were dedicated to their accounts, and the employer could not have used the plan surplus to provide early retirement benefits to current employees. Because no fiduciary duty existed to prohibit the plan's amendment, the Court reversed the court of appeals' decision and held for the employer. *Hughes Aircraft Co. v. Jacobson*, 525 U.S. 432, 119 S.Ct. 755, 142 L.Ed.2d 881 (1999).

◆   An aircraft manufacturer rehired an employee who had left to work for a competitor earlier in his career. He was 61 years old at the time of reemployment and was excluded from participation in the employer's retirement plan because of his age. Congress amended ERISA to disallow age-based exclusions in 1979, and the manufacturer amended the plan. Employees previously excluded on the basis of age were allowed to participate, but without credit for service prior to plan enrollment. The manufacturer then offered two programs encouraging early retirement. Acceptance of early retirement benefits was expressly conditioned on the waiver of any employment-related claims. The employee retired without seeking such benefits. Instead, he sued the employer and plan in a California federal court, seeking a declaration that they violated their duty of care under ERISA and engaged in a prohibited transaction by funding the early retirement plan with surplus plan assets. The case reached the U.S. Supreme Court, which held that **the inducement of early retirement through waivers such as that used here did not violate ERISA**. Plan sponsors who amend plans in their capacity as employers are not fiduciaries under ERISA. Because the plan amendments were enacted in an employer capacity, the manufacturer was under no ERISA fiduciary duty. *Lockheed Corp. v. Spink*, 517 U.S. 882, 116 S.Ct. 1783, 135 L.Ed.2d 153 (1996).

On remand, the court of appeals observed that because the employer was not acting in a fiduciary capacity when amending the plan, the employee could not recover on his ERISA claims. However, he had alleged sufficient facts that he had relied upon the employer's promises of his entitlement to participate in the retirement plan as an inducement to return to work to support his claim for detrimental reliance. He was thus entitled to pursue his claim for benefits for the first four years of his reemployment, and the court reversed this portion of the judgment. *Spink v. Lockheed Corp.*, 125 F.3d 1257 (9th Cir. 1997).

◆   A 30-year flight attendant based in Georgia participated in Delta's retirement plan, which calculated years of service, earnings at Delta, and an offset for the amount of her Social Security benefit. The earliest retirement age under the plan was age 52. She sued after the plan amended its calculation of the Social Security offset, at which time she was not yet 52. She claimed that the amendment violated ERISA's anti-cutback rule, which forbids pension plan amendments that decrease a participant's accrued benefits. The case reached the Eleventh Circuit, which upheld the amendment under ERISA. **Since she had not yet become eligible as of the time of the amendment, her benefits had not accrued** under ERISA. Where the right to future benefit accruals are contingent on additional service, such future increases are not presently accrued benefits. Thus, a plan may freely amend how benefits are accrued in the future (or even end their accrual) so long as the amendment "goes to the terms of compensation for continued, future employment." *Cinotto v. Delta Air Lines Inc.*, 674 F.3d 1285 (11th Cir. 2012).

◆   Two unions in New Jersey merged, and their pension and welfare plans were combined. Before the merger, one union allowed its pension plan participants to choose between a lump-sum payout and periodic monthly payments. After the merger, that union's plan was amended so that retirees had to choose not to receive the lump-sum payout if they wished to receive healthcare benefits. A group of current and retired union members sued, claiming the amendment violated ERISA, and a federal court held that **the amendment violated the anti-cutback rule of ERISA (which prohibits any plan amendments that decrease a participant's accrued benefits)**. The Third Circuit affirmed, noting that because the amendment imposed a condition on the receipt of the pension plan's lump-sum payout, it decreased an accrued benefit. *Battoni v. IBEW*, 594 F.3d 230 (3d Cir. 2010).

◆   A California gas company changed its defined benefit pension plan to a cash balance plan. The amended plan included a "grandfather provision" that allowed eligible participants to continue to accrue benefits under the pre-conversion formula until June 30, 2003, at which time those benefits were frozen. If a participant did not begin receiving a payout on or before that date, the amount of accrued benefits would be determined by a "wear away" provision. Two older workers, whose benefits would be frozen because of the switch to the cash balance plan, sued under ERISA, alleging that the plan discriminated on the basis of age. They also asserted that the amended plan violated the anti-backloading provisions of ERISA. A federal court dismissed their claims, and the Ninth Circuit largely affirmed.

The court of appeals found that the cash balance plan did not violate ERISA's anti-age discrimination provision. It also did not violate the 133-1/3% anti-backloading provision – which stated that benefits accruing in any year could not exceed 133-1/3% of the benefit accrued in any prior year. **ERISA's anti-backloading provisions are designed to prevent companies from providing inordinately low rates of accrual in employees' early years of service**, when the employees are most likely to leave the job. However, the employees did adequately allege that the plan violated the notice requirement regarding plan amendments by failing to provide adequate notice so that they could adjust their retirement strategies. That part of the case was allowed to proceed. *Hurlic v. Southern California Gas Co.*, 539 F.3d 1024 (9th Cir. 2009).

◆   IBM amended its defined benefit pension plan by adopting a new way to calculate how benefits would accrue to the plan – the pension credit formula. Under the formula, an employee who began working for IBM at 35 and earned an annual salary of $60,000 until his employment ended at 50 would have an age-65 accrued benefit equal to $15,110 per year, while an employee who began working at age 50 (also making $60,000) would be left with an age 65 accrued benefit of $13,189 per year. Later, IBM amended the plan again, adopting a cash balance formula for determining benefits. Under this formula, a 49-year-old employee with 20 years' service would accrue an age-65 annuity of $8,093 in the year 2000. The following year, he would accrue an additional $622, and by 2010 his additional accrual would be $282. A court held that **the plan amendments violated ERISA because they provided lesser benefits for older employees**. *Cooper v. IBM Personal Pension Plan*, 274 F.Supp.2d 1010 (S.D. Ill. 2003).

◆   A pension committee made up of employer representatives and union representatives voted to increase union members' benefits after learning that the employer's contributions to the plan might result in a surplus. The employer contended that **the committee did not have the authority to increase union members' benefits**. A lawsuit resulted, and a Vermont federal court ruled for the employer. The Second Circuit Court of Appeals affirmed, noting that the collective bargaining agreement (CBA) did not give the committee power to increase benefits. Nor did employees have an automatic interest in a surplus that occurs when employer contributions turn out to be more than the amount needed to fund the plan at current levels. The CBA reserved to the company the right to amend the plan, including the right to increase benefits. *Bozetarnik v. Mahland*, 195 F.3d 77 (2d Cir. 1999).

◆   A corporation amended its pension plan to change the definition of "normal retirement age" from 65 to 67. Several retirees elected to take early retirement and received a lower benefit under the new plan. Whereas the old plan included a subsidy to raise the amount of early retirement benefits, the new plan eliminated their opportunity for further accrual of retirement subsidies. The retirees sued the corporation and plan in a Utah federal court, which ruled for the employer and plan. The retirees appealed, asserting that ERISA requires a plan to define normal retirement age only as age 65 or earlier. The Tenth Circuit Court of Appeals, however, stated that ERISA permits normal retirement to be defined as an age over 65 where an employee has participated in a plan for less than five years. ERISA does not require normal retirement age to be defined in a plan the same way it is defined in the statute. Although the amended plan established age 67 as the benchmark for determining plan benefits, 65 was maintained as the age for benefit accrual and vesting requirements as per the language of ERISA. As a result, employees retiring at age 65 received only 86.7% of the accrued benefit as calculated by the plans. Since these benefits were protected against elimination by plan amendment, **the plan complied with ERISA even though the early retirement subsidy eliminated the further accrual of early retirement benefits**. *Lindsay v. Thiokol Corp.*, 112 F.3d 1068 (10th Cir. 1997).

C. Coordination of Benefits

Coordination of benefits refers to a procedure whereby an employee receiving one type of benefit (like workers' compensation) is prevented from receiving another kind of benefit (like pension benefits) at the same time. These benefits are sometimes coordinated (offsetting one against the other) to prevent employees from receiving a windfall.

♦   A steelworker in Illinois suffered two on-the-job injuries and received workers' compensation settlement awards for permanent partial disabilities that totaled almost $84,000. He later took an early retirement rather than be laid off and he sought retirement benefits. However, the retirement plan committee determined that it had to offset the workers' compensation permanent partial disability awards against his pension such that he would not be entitled to receive benefits for approximately 10 years. **The retirement plan provided that the company would offset regular pension benefits against permanent disability payments.** He sued under ERISA and lost. A federal court and the Seventh Circuit ruled that the plan administrator did not make an arbitrary and capricious decision to deny benefits. Even though the plan could be interpreted to require an offset only where permanent total disability benefits (rather than permanent partial disability benefits) were paid, it could also be interpreted as it was here. *Frye v. Thompson Steel Co., Inc.*, 657 F.3d 488 (7th Cir. 2011).

♦   Three employees of Xerox received lump sum payments when they retired. They returned a few years later and did not repay any of the retirement money they had received. When they later retired again, Xerox reduced their final retirement benefits to account for the earlier distribution by calculating the amount they had received plus any increase the distribution would have earned had it remained in the plan. By doing so, it drastically reduced the monthly payments due the three employees (from $1,600 to $83, from $2,000 to $260, and from $2,800 to $550). The employees challenged the offset, and a California federal court ruled for Xerox. The Ninth Circuit reversed and remanded the case, noting that **the method of accounting Xerox used for calculating the prior accrued benefit distributions used to offset the final retirement amounts owed violated the actuarial equivalency requirements of ERISA**. *Miller v. Xerox Corp. Retirement Income Guarantee Plan*, 464 F.3d 871 (9th Cir. 2006).

◆   A New Jersey employee retired at the age of 69 and, as a highly compensated former employee, was a participant in three separate retirement plans. He ultimately sued the plan administrator, challenging the calculation of his benefits under one of the plans. A federal court and the Third Circuit ruled against him. The plan at issue was a "top hat" plan maintained for the purpose of providing deferred compensation to a select group of top managers. It contained a Social Security benefits offset. **The employee asserted that the offset ought to be only the amount he would receive if he retired at 65 rather than the greater amount he actually received for retiring at 69.** The courts instead noted that the plan administrator acted within its discretion in selecting the greater offset amount. Since there was no showing of bad faith, the plan administrator's decision was entitled to deference. *Ahearn v. Marsh & McLennan Companies, Inc.*, 124 Fed.Appx. 118 (3d Cir. 2005).

◆   Michigan brewery employees were laid off in a plant closing. Both were inactive due to work injuries at the time and were receiving workers' compensation. Before the closing, the employer's pension plan administrator presented plant employees with the option of receiving a lump sum of their pension benefits or transferring retirement funds into an insurance annuity trust. Both employees opted to take a lump sum. They applied for and were granted continuation workers' compensation benefits. The state Worker's Compensation Appeal Board held in one case that lump-sum pension distributions and workers' compensation benefits could not be coordinated. A contrary result was reached in the other case. The Supreme Court of Michigan decided **employees should be limited to the receipt of one wage loss benefit at a time**. The coordination of workers' compensation benefits with lump-sum pension distributions properly prevented duplicate wage loss benefits. *Drouillard v. Stroh Brewery Co.*, 449 Mich. 293, 536 N.W.2d 530 (Mich. 1995).

II.   WELFARE AND HEALTH BENEFIT PLANS

ERISA also covers employee welfare benefit plans. ERISA participation, vesting and funding requirements do not apply to welfare benefit plans, but such plans may create vested rights by an agreement of the parties. Employers generally can adopt, modify or terminate welfare benefit plans as long as they act consistently with ERISA, its regulations and the plans' requirements.

A.   ERISA Applicability and Compliance

ERISA, at 29 U.S.C. § 1002(1), defines an employee welfare benefit plan as any plan, fund, or program established or maintained by an employer or an employee organization, or both, for the purpose of providing for its participants or their beneficiaries, through the purchase of insurance or otherwise, (A) medical, surgical, or hospital care or benefits, or benefits in the event of sickness, accident, disability, death or unemployment, or vacation benefits, apprenticeship or other training programs, or day care centers, scholarship funds, or prepaid legal services, or (B) any benefit described in section 186(c) of this title (other than pensions on retirement or death, and insurance to provide such pensions).

ERISA applies to an employee benefits plan if it is established or maintained by an employer or an employee organization engaged in commerce or in any industry or activity affecting commerce [29 U.S.C. § 1003(a)]. This section applies to both pension benefit plans and welfare benefit plans.

However, group or group-type insurance programs are not employee welfare benefit plans for purposes of ERISA:
1) where they are offered by an insurer under which the employer does not contribute any funds,
2) where participation is voluntary,
3) where the employer does not endorse the program but merely collects premiums, and
4) where the employer receives no compensation in connection with the program.

See 29 C.F.R. § 2510.3-1(j).

1. Supreme Court Cases

♦   An employee in Texas went through a divorce, during which his wife agreed to divest herself of all rights to his employee benefit, retirement and pension plans. However, the divorce decree did not spell out a number of specific things necessary for it to be considered a "qualified domestic relations order." Nor did the employee change the beneficiary designation on his savings and investment plan (SIP). He did appoint his daughter as a new beneficiary for his pension and retirement plan. When he died, the SIP administrator paid $400,000 to the ex-wife. His estate sued under ERISA. The case reached the U.S. Supreme Court, which held that the administrator properly paid the benefits to the ex-wife. **The employee never changed the beneficiary designation on the SIP even though the plan provided an easy way for him to do so.** *Kennedy v. Plan Administrator for DuPont Savings and Investment Plan*, 555 U.S. 285, 129 S.Ct. 865, 172 L.Ed.2d 662 (2009).

♦   A Sears employee was diagnosed with a heart condition that prevented her from performing her job. She received disability benefits under the company's plan for 24 months, and applied for Social Security benefits as well. An administrative law judge found her eligible for benefits, which Sears' insurer took by right of offset. Sears' insurer then found her ineligible for long-term disability benefits on the ground that she could do sedentary work. She sued under ERISA.

An Ohio federal court ruled for the insurer, the Sixth Circuit reversed, and the U.S. Supreme Court affirmed the ruling for the employee. The Court noted **the conflict of interest where an insurer decides if an employee is eligible for benefits and is also responsible for paying the claim**. *Metropolitan Life Insurance Co. v. Glenn*, 554 U.S. 105, 128 S.Ct. 2343, 171 L.Ed.2d 299 (2008).

◆   After a Maryland employee and her husband were injured in an automobile accident, the employee's ERISA-covered health insurance plan paid the couple's medical expenses. They then sued several third parties for injuries they suffered as a result of the accident. The health plan administrator sent them a letter asserting a lien on any proceeds from the lawsuit. After the lawsuit settled for $750,000, the plan administrator sued to recover the medical expenses it had paid. A federal court ordered the couple to reimburse the plan administrator for the medical expenses, and the Fourth Circuit affirmed in part. The U.S. Supreme Court also affirmed, noting that **the plan properly provided for beneficiaries to reimburse the plan from any recovery from outside sources**. This was a claim for equitable relief that could be brought under ERISA. The couple had to reimburse the plan. *Sereboff v. Mid Atlantic Medical Services, Inc.*, 547 U.S. 356, 126 S.Ct. 1869, 164 L.Ed.2d 612 (2006).

◆   Two Texas employees sued their health plan administrators when their respective HMOs refused to cover their physicians' recommended medical treatment and they suffered medical setbacks as a result. Federal courts dismissed the cases as preempted by ERISA, but the Fifth Circuit reversed. On further appeal, the U.S. Supreme Court reversed the Fifth Circuit, noting that **ERISA preempted their state law claims for medical negligence**. The employees' claims fell squarely within the parameters of Section 502(a), which has extraordinary preemptive power and which allows plan participants to sue to enforce rights or recover benefits under their plans. Here, contrary to the employees' argument, the plan administrators were making eligibility decisions, not treatment decisions. Also, the failure of the plans to cover the requested treatment was the proximate cause of the employees' injuries, not the denial of coverage. *Aetna Health Care v. Davila*, 542 U.S. 200, 124 S.Ct. 2488, 159 L.Ed.2d 312 (2004).

◆   A Black & Decker employee alleged that a mild degenerative disc condition made him eligible for long-term disability benefits under ERISA. Although his personal physician backed up his claim, a separate neurologist recommended by Black & Decker concluded that he could perform "sedentary work" if aided by pain medication. Based on this opinion and the recommendation of its insurer, Black & Decker denied the employee's claim. He sued in a California federal court to overturn this determination. The judge ruled in favor of Black & Decker, but the Ninth Circuit reversed, holding that the company had not come up with adequate reasons for rejecting the opinion of the employee's treating physician. The Supreme Court, however, held that **plan administrators are not obliged to accord special deference to the opinions of treating physicians** when making benefit determinations. ERISA and its regulations "require 'full and fair' assessment of claims and clear communication to the claimant of the 'specific reasons' for benefit denials," the Court explained. "But these measures do not command plan administrators to credit the opinions of treating physicians over other evidence relevant to the claimant's medical condition." *Black & Decker Disability Plan v. Nord*, 538 U.S. 822, 123 S.Ct. 1965, 155 L.Ed.2d 1034 (2003).

◆   Employees of a railway subsidiary were entitled to railroad retirement benefits and pension, health and welfare benefits under collective bargaining agreements covered by ERISA. When the contract between the railway and the subsidiary was terminated, the railway hired another service to do the work. The new contractor retained some of the subsidiary's employees; however, it was not required to make railroad retirement contributions and its welfare plan was inferior to the subsidiary's plan. Employees who continued to work for the new contractor sued the railroad, the subsidiary and the new contractor in a California federal court, asserting that the manner of the discharge interfered with their pension and welfare benefits. The court dismissed the ERISA claims. The Ninth Circuit reinstated the claim for interference with pension benefits, but agreed that ERISA did not protect employees from elimination of welfare benefits that did not vest.

The U.S. Supreme Court found that Section 510 of ERISA prevents an employer from discharging a plan participant or beneficiary for the purpose of interfering with the attainment of any right to which the participant might be entitled. Section 510 draws no distinction between those rights that vest under ERISA and those that do not. Further, **although an employer has the right to unilaterally amend or eliminate a welfare benefit plan, Section 510 requires the employer to follow the plan's formal amendment process**. The Court vacated the judgment and remanded the case for further proceedings. *Inter-Modal Rail Employees Ass'n v. Atchison, Topeka and Santa Fe Railway Co.*, 520 U.S. 510, 117 S.Ct. 1513, 137 L.Ed.2d 763 (1997).

◆   A manufacturer transferred its money-losing divisions to a new subsidiary and told employees in these divisions that their benefits and salaries would remain the same if they transferred. Many employees transferred to the subsidiary, which went into receivership within two years. Employees and retirees who participated in the subsidiary's welfare benefit plan asserted that the manufacturer fraudulently induced them to accept the transfers. They sued in an Iowa federal court, which held that the manufacturer violated its obligation under ERISA to administer the plan in the employees' interest. The court awarded damages to the participants and ruled that they had a right to appropriate equitable relief including reinstatement into the manufacturer's plan. The U.S. Court of Appeals, Eighth Circuit, affirmed much of the district court decision but disallowed a $46 million damage award.

The manufacturer appealed to the U.S. Supreme Court, which found that the manufacturer had been **acting as both a plan fiduciary and an employer when it promised to preserve employee benefits and salaries after the transfer**. Accordingly, its actions were held to the standard of fiduciary care that subjected it to potential ERISA liability. The Court rejected the argument that ERISA did not allow individual equitable relief and affirmed the lower court decisions. *Varity Corp. v. Howe*, 516 U.S. 489, 116 S.Ct. 1065, 134 L.Ed.2d 130 (1996).

♦   A corporation maintained and administered a single-employer health plan for its employees. After closing a New Jersey facility, the corporation's executive vice president notified retirees of the facility by letter that their post-retirement health benefits were being terminated. The retirees sued the corporation, alleging that the company's summary plan description lacked a valid amendment procedure and that the action constituted a plan amendment. The court agreed with the retirees and ordered the corporation to pay them over $2.6 million in benefits. The Third Circuit affirmed.

The U.S. Supreme Court agreed with the corporation that the minimal language in its summary plan description satisfied the amendment procedure requirement of ERISA Section 402(b)(3). Under the plan description, the corporation "reserve[d] the right at any time to amend the plan. ..." ERISA creates no substantive entitlement to employer-provided welfare benefits and employers are allowed to freely modify, amend or terminate welfare plans under most circumstances. **A plan that simply identified the person or persons having authority to amend a plan necessarily indicated the amendment procedure.** The Court reversed and remanded the case. *Curtiss-Wright Corp. v. Schoonejongen*, 514 U.S. 73, 115 S.Ct. 1223, 131 L.Ed.2d 94 (1995).

♦   A corporation operated a self-funded healthcare plan under which plan members agreed to reimburse it for benefits paid if the member recovered on a claim in a liability action against a third party. The daughter of a plan member was seriously injured in an automobile accident, and the plan paid part of her medical expenses. A negligence action against the driver of the vehicle settled, and the plan member refused to reimburse the plan, asserting that Pennsylvania law precluded subrogation by the plan. A federal court held that the state statute prohibited the plan from enforcing the subrogation provision. The case reached the U.S. Supreme Court, which stated that ERISA preempted the application of the Pennsylvania law, and that the plan could seek subrogation. State laws that directly regulate insurance are "saved" from preemption, but this does not apply to **self-funded employee benefit plans** because they are not insurance for purposes of such laws. *FMC Corp. v. Holliday*, 498 U.S. 52, 111 S.Ct. 403, 112 L.Ed.2d 356 (1990).

♦   A District of Columbia workers' compensation statute required employers who provided health insurance for their employees to furnish equivalent health insurance coverage for injured employees eligible for workers' compensation benefits. An employer sued the district and its mayor, claiming that the act was preempted by ERISA. The U.S. Supreme Court held that **employer-sponsored health insurance programs are subject to ERISA regulation**, and any state law imposing requirements by reference to such covered programs is preempted by ERISA. ERISA superseded the workers' compensation act because the act related to a covered plan. The district could not require employers to provide equivalent health insurance coverage for injured employees eligible for workers' compensation. *District of Columbia v. Greater Washington Board of Trade*, 506 U.S. 125, 113 S.Ct. 580, 121 L.Ed.2d 513 (1992).

2. Preemption Cases

The same rationale for preemption used in retirement cases is applied here: namely, that it is better to have a single, federal law applied uniformly than different laws for each state. If a state law and ERISA both address employee benefit plans, courts will preempt the state law with ERISA to resolve any conflict.

◆   In 2006, San Francisco passed an ordinance requiring employers with more than 20 employees to either spend a certain amount on employee health care or pay the city a fee based on the number of employees and the hours they work. A restaurant association sued, claiming that ERISA preempted the ordinance. A federal court ruled in the association's favor, but the Ninth Circuit reversed. It held that the ordinance did not establish a "plan" within the meaning of ERISA. Nor did the ordinance have an impermissible "connection with" or "reference to" employee benefit plans that were subject to ERISA. It did not require employers to change the way they administered or managed an existing ERISA plan. **The plan allowed employers to structure their minimum payments in a variety of ways, not forcing them to provide a specific kind of healthcare benefit.** As a result, the ordinance was not preempted by ERISA. *Golden Gate Restaurant Ass'n v. City and County of San Francisco*, 546 F.3d 639 (9th Cir. 2008).

◆   Through payroll deductions, an Oregon employee obtained life insurance from a group plan. After she was diagnosed with terminal cancer and went on disability leave, her employer canceled the group plan and changed to a new plan for insurance. Under the new plan, the employee was not eligible for benefits because of her condition. The company offered employees the option of converting old policies to individual policies, but under the conversion provision, the employee would only have been eligible for $5,000 in coverage. When she died, her children sued the company, claiming that company officials had told the employee and her daughter that the employee was covered by a $150,000 insurance policy. They sought the benefits. A federal court dismissed the case, finding that ERISA preempted it. However, the Ninth Circuit reversed, holding that the children could pursue a breach of contract and negligence claim against the company. **ERISA did not preempt the lawsuit because the employee was not covered by an ERISA plan at the time of her death.** *Miller v. Rite Aid Corp.*, 504 F.3d 1102 (9th Cir. 2007).

◆   Maryland passed a law requiring employers with 10,000 or more employees that spend less than 8% of total wages on health insurance to pay the state the difference. A trade association filed a lawsuit to challenge the law, and the case reached the Fourth Circuit. The court of appeals held that the law was preempted by ERISA. A state law has an impermissible "connection with" an ERISA plan if it directly regulates or effectively mandates some element of the structure or administration of employers' ERISA plans. Here, **the law essentially mandated that employers provide a certain level of benefits, thus bringing it within the scope of ERISA**. The law was not enforceable. *Retail Industry Leaders Ass'n v. Fielder*, 475 F.3d 180 (4th Cir. 2007).

◆   A Georgia company allowed an insurer to publicize a disability plan to its employees. The company collected premiums through payroll deductions and remitted the payments to the insurer (satisfying the safe harbor exemption from ERISA). However, it also decided on the 90-day eligibility period, identified the plan as a benefit in its handbook and allowed the insurer to distribute booklets stating that the plan was covered by ERISA. When an employee with rectal cancer was denied benefits he thought he deserved under the plan, he sued the employer under state law. A federal court and the Eleventh Circuit ruled that the plan was governed by ERISA, which preempted the employee's state law claims. **Even though the company's involvement in the plan was minimal, it was enough that the plan did not qualify under the safe harbor exemption of ERISA.** The employee had to pursue his claim using ERISA's procedures. *Moorman v. UnumProvident Corp.*, 464 F.3d 1260 (11th Cir. 2006).

◆   A marketing specialist for a Massachusetts company was offered a position 100 miles from her home. After commuting for several weeks, she experienced increasing back pain and applied for relocation benefits. The company denied her request, and she went on disability leave. Later, the company decided that she was no longer disabled under its policy and required her to return to work. She worked intermittently for three days and was fired on the fourth day as part of a work force reduction. Instead of following the company's procedure for appealing a denial of short-term benefits or for requesting an application for long-term benefits, the employee sued the company for breach of contract, negligence, and violations of ERISA. The First Circuit held that **the company's short-term disability plan qualified as an ERISA plan**. ERISA preempted her state law claims because they were dependent on the ERISA plan. Further, because the employee failed to follow the company's appeals procedure, she was barred from bringing the ERISA claim. *McMahon v. Digital Equipment Corp.*, 162 F.3d 28 (1st Cir. 1998).

3.   Amending Welfare Benefit Plans

Employers can generally adopt, modify or terminate welfare benefit plans. Where employers amend plans in their capacity as employers (and not as fiduciaries), they will not have liability under ERISA as long as they act consistently with ERISA, its regulations and the plans' requirements.

With the astronomical increase in medical care costs, many companies have amended their healthcare plans to eliminate or reduce such benefits, particularly for retirees. Generally, unless the employer has contractually agreed not to amend the plan, this is permissible.

◆   An Illinois employee diagnosed with HIV began experiencing severe symptoms and filed a claim for total disability benefits under the company's long-term disability plan. The plan administrator then changed its standard for awarding total disability benefits, **now requiring him to show he could not work any job for which he was qualified, rather than just that he couldn't perform his last job**. Yet it continued to pay him benefits until it learned that he had traveled to London the previous year – a trip that was arguably at odds with his condition. Two doctors determined that his T-cell count had stabilized and that, at 200 pounds, he wasn't wasting away. A third doctor found that he suffered from moderately advanced AIDS, but that he might be able to perform sedentary work with frequent breaks. The plan administrator stopped paying benefits, and he sued under ERISA. A federal court ruled against him, and the Seventh Circuit affirmed. Medical evidence supported the plan's determination that he could work a sedentary job. *Jenkins v. Price Waterhouse Long Term Disability Plan*, 564 F.3d 856 (7th Cir. 2009).

♦   A real estate investment company offered an ERISA plan with a reservation of rights that allowed it to terminate the plan at any time. When two Iowa employees left the company, they each received a letter informing them that the company would continue to provide medical and life insurance benefits. After the company closed its U.S. operations, it terminated the ERISA plan. The two employees sued, claiming the letters they received constituted separate ERISA plans that offered lifetime benefits which could not be terminated by the company. A federal court and the Eighth Circuit disagreed. The letters merely stated that the employees would continue to receive benefits the same as their current coverage and instructed them to complete and return a "continuation of insurance upon retirement form" if they wanted the continued coverage. **Since the letters were not freestanding ERISA plans, the employees were not entitled to continuing coverage.** *Johnson v. Lend Lease Real Estate Investment*, 467 F.3d 1131 (8th Cir. 2006).

♦   From 1974 until a 1993 collective bargaining agreement (CBA) went into effect, a Pennsylvania manufacturer agreed to pay all of its hourly retirees' healthcare benefits. In 1991, industry-wide accounting guidelines for reporting employee benefits changed. As a result, the manufacturer reduced the benefits it provided active employees. After the terms of the 1993 CBA were agreed upon, the manufacturer retroactively eliminated or modified health and life insurance benefits for retirees, so employees who retired before the CBA became effective were no longer eligible for those benefits. The union sued, alleging violations of Section 301 of the Labor Management Relations Act and ERISA. The district court ruled for the manufacturer, and the Third Circuit affirmed. Because ERISA did not require automatic vesting of employee welfare benefit plans, an employer's commitment to vest such benefits had to be stated in clear and express language. Contract phrases stating that the company would continue to provide certain coverage **did not explicitly indicate that the benefits would continue indefinitely**, and a more reasonable interpretation was that the benefits would continue for the life of the CBA. *Int'l Union v. Skinner Engine Co.*, 188 F.3d 130 (3d Cir. 1999).

♦   A collective bargaining agreement (CBA) between a Michigan manufacturer and the machinists' union provided lifetime healthcare benefits to members who retired between 1985 and 1988. In the negotiations for the 1988-1991 contract, the parties made some significant changes to the insurance agreement, increasing, among other things, the amount of paid-up life insurance by $1,000. However, the later contract did not include language found in the 1985-88 agreement continuing retirees' benefits until death. When the company sold its assets, closed its Michigan plant and terminated its employees, it notified the employees who had retired after 1988 that they would no longer receive healthcare benefits to which they had been entitled under the CBAs. The union sued, and the case reached the Sixth Circuit, which rejected the company's argument that benefits had not vested because the parties agreed to time limits on them as a trade-off for increased benefits.

The court noted that whether benefits survive the termination of a CBA depends on the intent of the parties. Retiree benefits "are in a sense 'status' benefits which ... carry with them an inference ... that the parties intended those benefits to continue as long as the beneficiary remains a retiree." This conflicted with the Third Circuit's decision in *Int'l Union v. Skinner Engine Co.* above, where the Third Circuit held that retired workers' health benefits ended with the expiration of their contract. Since the language of the contract was unclear as to the intent of the parties, the court looked to affidavit testimony that supported the union's assertion that **time limits were not proposed as a trade-off for increased benefits during CBA negotiations**. *Int'l Union, UAAAIWA v. BVR Liquidating, Inc.*, 190 F.3d 768 (6th Cir. 1999).

◆ A series of collective bargaining agreements between an employer and several unions provided that the employer would pay full medical insurance premiums for company retirees. The employer amended the medical plan so that retirees would pay a portion of the premium if costs increased at a rate higher than the annual increase in the consumer price index. The unions and retirees sued in a New York federal court, asserting violations of the Labor Management Relations Act (LMRA) and ERISA, arguing that the bargaining agreements had promised lifetime medical benefits. The court ruled that the benefits were not vested under either plan documents or the bargaining agreements, which had by then expired. The Second Circuit affirmed. An employer can generally give notice to amend or terminate a welfare plan at any time. Under the LMRA, **an employer may modify or terminate employee medical benefits after the expiration of a bargaining agreement**. The bargaining agreements in this case specifically limited benefits to the term of each agreement and the benefits did not vest. The summary plan documents contained an express reservation of the employer's right to terminate the plan, which alerted retirees to that right. *American Federation of Grain Millers, AFL-CIO v. Int'l Multifoods Corp.*, 116 F.3d 976 (2d Cir. 1997).

4. Notice Issues

ERISA establishes notice requirements for denying benefit claims. According to regulation 29 C.F.R. § 2560.503-1(f), the initial notice must contain:

1) The specific reason or reasons for the denial,
2) Specific reference to pertinent plan provisions on which the denial is based,
3) A description of any additional material or information necessary, and

4) Appropriate information as to the steps to be taken if the participant or beneficiary wishes to submit his or her claim for review.

Employers also have a duty to provide notice with respect to plan terminations or modifications.

♦   An employee suffering from sleep apnea was referred to a specialist in her network. He couldn't treat her successfully, so he referred her to an out-of-network doctor who could, and he wrote to the insurer seeking a retroactive referral because he didn't know of any provider in the network who could provide the device necessary to treat her. After she was treated, she applied for benefits, which her plan denied because she failed to get pre-approval. She sued. A Texas federal court granted pretrial judgment to the healthcare plan, but the Fifth Circuit reversed. **The plan summary never made clear to the employee that she could lose coverage if she didn't get approval first.** Instead, the plan was confusing about when the requirement applied. *Koehler v. Aetna Health, Inc.*, 683 F.3d 182 (5th Cir. 2012).

♦   An Illinois employee selected a healthcare plan that cautioned her to check on whether healthcare providers were in the network so as to avoid paying out-of-pocket expenses. Later, a CT scan by her primary doctor revealed that she had lung cancer that had spread to her brain. She saw a neurologist without first checking to determine if he was in the network. Her husband called the insurer to inform it of her hospitalization for surgery, but neither he nor the insurer representative brought up the out-of-network issue. After the insurer determined that the doctors and hospital were out-of-network and denied coverage, the employee died. Her husband sued under ERISA, but a federal court and the Seventh Circuit held that **the insurer didn't violate the statute by denying coverage or failing to tell him that the wife's providers weren't in the network**. However, the insurer did violate ERISA by failing to provide a summary plan description (SPD). *Killian v. Concert Health Plan*, 680 F.3d 749 (7th Cir. 2012). Upon rehearing en banc, those conclusions were left undisturbed (*Killian v. Concert Health Plan*, 742 F.3d 651 (7th Cir. 2013)).

♦   A Wisconsin employee who had undergone stomach stapling got a new job and then began suffering severe acid reflux – a complication from her surgery. The new health plan didn't provide coverage for morbid obesity, but it paid for a procedure to help her. However, when the acid reflux returned, she sought to undergo another procedure. She called the customer service number listed in the health plan's summary plan description (SPD), and a representative told her she was covered except for a $300 deductible. The procedure cost $78,000, and the health plan refused to pay for it. When she sued under ERISA, a federal court granted pretrial judgment to the health plan, but the Seventh Circuit vacated the ruling. Here, **the health plan might be liable for failing to provide clarity as to what was covered and what wasn't**. Nothing in the SPD informed her that she couldn't rely on the customer service representative's interpretation of the plan. However, she would be limited to injunctive relief, like forcing the plan to properly train its employees, because her claimed loss was to herself only, not to the plan as a whole. *Kenseth v. Dean Health Plan, Inc.*, 610 F.3d 452 (7th Cir. 2010).

◆ An employee of a company in Michigan became disabled by depression and received short-term disability benefits. She applied for long-term disability benefits and was informed that payment of future benefits was dependent on her continuing disability, requiring her to visit her doctor once a month and attend therapy on the same day. After the company learned that she missed multiple sessions, it terminated her benefits because of her failure to comply with the terms of her treatment plan. She sued for ERISA violations, including failure to give notice that one of the reasons it was terminating benefits was because she was no longer disabled. A federal court and the Sixth Circuit ruled against her. Since she had missed her sessions, there was no continuing medical evidence that she was still disabled. **Even though the company failed to give proper notice of all its reasons for denying benefits, it still provided a reasonable basis for denying benefits** – her refusal to comply with her treatment plan. *McCartha v. National City Corp.*, 419 F.3d 437 (6th Cir. 2005).

◆ An Indiana clinical supervisor was diagnosed with chronic fatigue syndrome and fibromyalgia and received disability benefits under her employer's employee welfare benefit plan. The plan discontinued disability payments and sought further information (including an independent medical examination) concerning her application for long-term disability benefits when it learned that she had regularly been attending sales shows throughout the Midwest to sell jewelry she had made. The employee sued the plan administrator and provider under ERISA. The court ruled for the administrator and provider. The employee appealed, claiming that the plan had failed to provide her with adequate notice of its review process and that she was excused from exhausting the plan's internal appeal procedure. The Seventh Circuit Court of Appeals disagreed, observing that while ERISA establishes minimum notice and procedure requirements when a plan administrator denies a claim, **these safeguards do not apply until a claim is actually denied**. The plan had not denied the claim here, but had only discontinued payments while seeking further information about the employee's condition. The administrator and provider did not violate ERISA, and the district court had therefore properly ruled in their favor. *Robyns v. Reliance Standard Life Insurance Co.*, 130 F.3d 1231 (7th Cir. 1997).

5. Other Applicability and Compliance Cases

ERISA protects against actions taken by employers to either prevent the use of benefits or retaliate against employees for asserting rights under the act.

ERISA does not apply to independent contractors.

ERISA does not protect employee rights to job benefits that are provided solely at the discretion of the employer. Only where the employee has an entitlement to certain benefits can ERISA be used to protect those benefits.

♦   A Nebraska employee filed a claim for short-term disability benefits approximately a month after her employment was terminated. The claim was denied on the basis that she did not become disabled until after the employer terminated her coverage. The employee sued the employer. She claimed the employer knew she was going to file the claim and interfered with her ERISA rights by terminating her coverage and terminating her employment before she filed to keep her from getting insurance benefits. The court rejected her claims. **She did not show the employer stopped paying the premium for unlawful reasons,** and it provided legitimate reasons for terminating her employment, including tardiness and poor job performance. *Barnhardt v. Open Harvest*, 742 F.3d 365 (8th Cir. 2014).

♦   The administrator of a Michigan employer's health plan secretly added fees to employees' hospital costs and kept the fees for itself. The employer sued the administrator, and a trial court determined that the administrator breached its fiduciary duty to the employer by self-dealing. **It awarded the employer $5 million in damages.** A federal appeals court decided the administrator was an ERISA fiduciary that breached its fiduciary duty, and it upheld the trial court's decision. *Hi-Lex Controls, Inc. v. Blue Cross Blue Shield of Michigan*, 751 F.3d 740 (6th Cir. 2014).

♦   The Catholic owners of a company in Colorado **challenged the Affordable Care Act's requirement that the company provide coverage for contraception and abortion**. They asserted that the law violated the Religious Freedom Restoration Act (RFRA) as well as the First and Fifth Amendments. They asked for a preliminary injunction to prevent having to comply with the law until the case could be decided in court, and a federal court granted them the injunction. It noted that they were likely to win on their claim that the mandate violated the RFRA. *Newland v. Sebelius*, 881 F.Supp.2d 1287 (D. Colo. 2012).

♦   A conductor for a railway told his supervisor he needed a three-month absence for medical reasons. The supervisor forwarded his request to HR, which told the conductor he needed to provide more information to qualify for FMLA leave. He failed to provide the requested information and did not return to work when ordered to do so. After the railway fired him, he sought income replacement benefits from the union, but the plan administrator determined that he had been fired for insubordination and thus was not entitled to them. He sued under ERISA, but an Ohio federal court and the Sixth Circuit ruled against him. **It was clear that he had been fired for insubordination, for which the plan explicitly excluded coverage.** *Farhner v. United Transportation Union Discipline Income Protection Program*, 645 F.3d 338 (6th Cir. 2011).

♦   An Iowa employee was diagnosed with multiple sclerosis shortly after she began working for a convention center. She was fired five years later for poor performance. The general manager cited her failure to request menus in a timely fashion, selling more rooms than were available and not charging the correct amount for events. She later met with the company's CEO and **claimed that he**

told her he couldn't afford her health benefits. He disputed her version of events. When she sued under the ADA and ERISA, the Eighth Circuit rejected her claims. Here, her poor performance was well documented, and she could not show that the manager who fired her was simply being used as a conduit for the CEO's alleged bias. *Libel v. Adventure Lands of America*, 482 F.3d 1028 (8th Cir. 2007).

♦   A Kentucky plant manager was suspended for three days without pay because he took too long to respond to a malfunction in a conveyor belt. The year before, he was suspended for negligently operating a forklift. While he was on suspension, his doctor diagnosed him with a heart condition and determined he was unable to work. He was not allowed to return to the job and was fired for violating company policy regarding plant safety. When he sought short-term disability benefits, they were denied. He sued under ERISA, but the Sixth Circuit ruled against him, noting that **he was not actively at work when he notified his employer of his disability**. The plan defined "actively at work" as being actually at work on the day immediately preceding an excused leave of absence. The court rejected the manager's argument that a suspension was the same as an excused leave of absence. *Pollett v. Rinker Materials Corp.*, 477 F.3d 376 (6th Cir. 2007).

♦   The benefits administrator at a Philadelphia law firm was also a member of the HMO that provided health care to firm employees. The HMO sent her a letter advising her that she could request information about physician compensation. Instead, she sued, claiming that the HMO had a fiduciary duty to disclose detailed information about its physician incentive plan. A federal court ruled against her, and the Third Circuit affirmed. It ruled that **ERISA does not impose a duty on an HMO to disclose physician incentive information** unless the employee requests the information, the HMO has notice that the employee needs the information to prevent her from making a harmful decision about her health care, and the employee suffers some harm. Here, the employee never requested the information, and the employee suffered no harm because the law firm offered only the HMO plan to employees. It offered no alternatives. *Horvath v. Keystone Health Plan East, Inc.*, 333 F.3d 450 (3d Cir. 2003).

♦   A customer service representative was fired after 11 months on the job, allegedly for poor performance. However, she claimed that she was really fired in violation of ERISA because the company wanted to avoid the increased health insurance costs it would have incurred because of her son's hydrocephalus (water on the brain). An Ohio federal court granted pretrial judgment to the company, but the Sixth Circuit reversed. Here, **the employee did not have to show that the sole purpose in firing her was to interfere with her right to receive benefits under ERISA**; she only had to show that the interference was a motivating factor. She presented evidence that: 1) she was fired just two weeks after her supervisor learned of her son's condition, 2) all the customer complaints cited by the company for her poor performance dated from that two-week period, 3) a company official stated that families like hers were the cause of rising insurance costs and were a drain on the company, and

4) she received an 8% pay raise six weeks before she was fired. *Smith v. Hinkle Manufacturing, Inc.*, 36 Fed.Appx. 825 (6th Cir. 2002).

◆   The U.S. Court of Appeals, Seventh Circuit, held that **ERISA does not prevent the discharge of an employee for excessive absenteeism** unless the employee can demonstrate a specific intent by the employer to either prevent the use of benefits or retaliate against her. The case arose from the discharge of an Illinois inventory control analyst for violating her employer's no-fault attendance policy. Some of the absences were considered excused for the purposes of the company's short-term disability plan, but the company counted all absences, whether excused or unexcused, under the no-fault policy. The employer fired the employee, and she sued, asserting a violation of ERISA Section 510 (29 U.S.C. § 1140), which prohibits the discharge or discipline of plan participants and beneficiaries for exercising rights under the plan. The court ruled for the employer. The Seventh Circuit affirmed, holding that the employee presented no evidence of the employer's specific intent to interfere with her ERISA rights. Excessive absenteeism is a legitimate reason for termination, as long as there is no connection between the discharge and any entitlement to benefits. *Lindemann v. Mobil Oil Corp.*, 141 F.3d 290 (7th Cir. 1998).

B. Coverage Issues

Many of the ERISA cases that arise have to do with either the denial of benefits or the improper administration of plans (for example, failing to notify a departing employee of his or her COBRA continuation coverage rights). Where an employer, rather than an outside entity, acts as the plan administrator, its actions will be more closely scrutinized for self-dealing.

1. COBRA Cases

The Consolidated Omnibus Budget Reconciliation Act of 1985 (COBRA) was enacted as an amendment to ERISA (among other statutes) and requires employers who sponsor group health plans to give the plans' qualified beneficiaries the opportunity to elect <u>continuation coverage</u> under the plans when the beneficiaries might otherwise lose coverage upon the occurrence of certain qualifying events (like the termination or death of an employee).

When the qualifying event is termination or reduced hours (so as to make the employee no longer eligible under the company health plan), the maximum period of coverage is generally <u>18 months</u>. The benefits offered must be the same, but the employee is now the party responsible for paying for that coverage.

COBRA coverage can stop when the qualified beneficiary "first becomes, after the date of the election … covered under any other health plan … which does not contain any exclusion or limitation with respect to any preexisting condition of such beneficiary."

✦   COBRA amended ERISA by authorizing qualified beneficiaries of employer group health plans to obtain continuation coverage in specified circumstances, including employment termination. A Missouri medical corporation discharged an employee with cancer who was covered under its group health plan. It informed the employee that he had COBRA continuation coverage rights, and he participated in the plan for six months. At that time, the employer notified him that he was not entitled to COBRA benefits because he was already covered by a group health plan supplied by his wife's employer as of his election date. The former employee sued for wrongful denial of coverage. The case reached the U.S. Supreme Court.

The Court stated that the COBRA amendments to ERISA require group health plan sponsors, including employers, to provide continuation coverage when plan beneficiaries might otherwise lose coverage upon the occurrence of a qualifying event, such as termination or divorce. COBRA coverage may cease on the date on which the qualified beneficiary first becomes covered, after the date of election, under any other group health plan that does not limit or exclude a beneficiary's preexisting health conditions. The employer and plan argued that the former employee was "first" covered by his wife's plan after the time of the election. The Court disagreed, finding that **the former employee had been continuously covered by his wife's group health plan and did not "first become" covered under the wife's plan after the date of election**. The employer could not cut off the former employee's COBRA coverage. *Geissal v. Moore Medical Corp.*, 524 U.S. 74, 118 S.Ct. 1869, 141 L.Ed.2d 64 (1998).

✦   Along with his wife, a Nebraska employee who was severely injured when he fell from a railcar sued the Professional Employer Organization (PEO) that had entered into a staff servicing agreement to provide employment and HR services for another company. The couple claimed that the PEO violated ERISA by failing to give proper COBRA notice after firing the employee, and that it wrongfully denied health insurance benefits. They also asserted a claim for breach of fiduciary duty. The PEO claimed that he was never covered by insurance and thus was not entitled to COBRA coverage, but that it had sent a COBRA notice anyway. A federal court held that the PEO breached its fiduciary duty and that since **the PEO had wrongfully denied health insurance coverage while the employee was still working, it would have been futile for the couple to elect COBRA coverage upon his termination**. The ex-employee and his wife were entitled to the medical expenses they would have received had they elected COBRA coverage. However, the Eighth Circuit Court of Appeals limited the time period in which the couple could claim unreimbursed medical expenses and denied them statutory penalties of $110 per day. *Delcastillo v. Odyssey Resource Management, Inc.*, 292 Fed.Appx. 519 (8th Cir. 2008).

✦   A Michigan cemetery fired an employee and discontinued her health insurance coverage at that time. However, the employee did not learn of the discontinuation until two months later. She sued the cemetery for violating COBRA. The cemetery asserted that it did not have to comply with COBRA's requirements because it did not have at least 20 employees. A federal court and the Sixth Circuit agreed with the cemetery. Further, equitable estoppel (a legal doctrine barring a party from using its misrepresentation to another party for the purpose of gaining an advantage) did not apply here because the cemetery never misrepresented to the employee that she had any COBRA rights. *Thomas v. Miller*, 489 F.3d 293 (6th Cir. 2007).

✦ A South Dakota employee worked for an oil company until the retail location where she was assigned closed. She then developed health problems that required surgery. Three months after her job ended, she received a letter stating that she was no longer eligible for continuing COBRA benefits. She sued, claiming that the company had failed to appropriately notify her of her COBRA rights. A federal court ruled for the company, but the Eighth Circuit reversed. **It was not enough for the company to show that a notification letter had been generated and that it had a mailing process for letters.** The company also had to show that the notice was sent by means reasonably calculated to reach the employee. Among the ways it could do this were: photocopying a letter addressed to the employee or providing a report showing the date the notice was mailed. *Crotty v. Dakotacare Administrative Services, Inc.*, 455 F.3d 828 (8th Cir. 2006).

✦ The wife of an Oklahoma employee filed for divorce and obtained three protective orders requiring him to stay away from her. She sent a letter to the company asking that her "estranged husband" not be informed of any medical services she received. The company then determined that the couple had legally separated, which would be a qualifying event under COBRA, and notified the wife of her right to elect continuing health insurance coverage. She did not pay the premiums. When the divorce became final, she asked for COBRA coverage, and the company refused to reinstate the policy. She sued and won. The Tenth Circuit ruled that **the company violated COBRA by sending out the notice prematurely**. Divorce proceedings did not amount to a legal separation (qualifying event) under COBRA. *Simpson v. T.D. Williamson*, 414 F.3d 1203 (10th Cir. 2005).

✦ An employee who had enrolled himself, his wife and his children in his employer's group health insurance plan told his employer that he had divorced his wife and that he wanted to drop her from his medical coverage. Because a divorce is a qualifying event under COBRA, the employer gave the employee the necessary paperwork so he could give it to his wife. He apparently failed to give it to her. When she underwent medical treatment and discovered that she no longer had health insurance, she sued the employer to recover the money she had spent for her treatment. A New York federal court dismissed the case, ruling that because the employee's divorce had actually been invalid under state law, there was no "qualifying event" under COBRA. The Second Circuit reversed. **The employer should have notified the wife that she had been dropped from her husband's coverage**, rather than relying on him to notify her. Further, the act of telling the employer about the divorce (a qualifying event) triggered the employer's COBRA obligations, regardless of the validity of the divorce. *Phillips v. Saratoga Harness Racing, Inc.*, 240 F.3d 174 (2d Cir. 2001).

♦   A Wal-Mart employee resigned and sought continuing medical coverage under COBRA. She was rehired a month later. When she returned to work, she asked about the status of her COBRA premiums because she had become pregnant while she was not an employee. An in-store contact for the health plan administrator told her that she would be covered under the original plan and that she would not need COBRA coverage. As a result, she did not pay the COBRA premium for the month she was not employed. After the plan administrator refused to pay her pregnancy-related medical expenses, she sued. An Indiana federal court ruled in her favor, and the Seventh Circuit affirmed. Because of misleading statements and the unclear wording of Wal-Mart's health plan (particularly the Summary Plan Description), **she was entitled to coverage for her pregnancy-related medical expenses** as long as she paid the premium for the month she was not an employee. *Bowerman v. Wal-Mart Stores,* 226 F.3d 574 (7th Cir. 2000).

♦   Under COBRA, employers must notify plan administrators of a qualifying event, including termination, within 30 days, and the plan administrator is then responsible for notifying employees of their continuation rights within 14 days of receiving the employer's notice. An Illinois retail manager claimed that she was not provided with a COBRA notice upon her resignation. A federal court held that employers and plan administrators can prevail when they show that they have made good-faith attempts to comply with COBRA. **Notice by first class mail sent to a former employee's last known address is an acceptable method of COBRA notification.** Here, the employer and plan administrator presented unrefuted evidence that they had satisfied the good-faith standard for compliance with COBRA notice requirements. *Keegan v. Bloomingdale's, Inc.,* 992 F.Supp. 974 (N.D. Ill. 1998).

2. Denial of Benefits

Where an employer self-administers an employee welfare benefit plan, there is a conflict of interest between the employer's interest and the employees.' As a result, the denial of benefits is more likely to be construed as arbitrary and capricious in such cases.

♦   An Arkansas truck driver who lost his commercial license due to his diabetes filed a claim for disability benefits. Short-term benefits were granted, but long-term benefits were denied on the basis that the driver was not totally disabled under the plan. A federal appeals court rejected the driver's claim that the denial of benefits violated ERISA. Losing the license did not show total disability, and **the driver did not specifically show how his diabetes limited what he could do**. *Hampton v. Reliance Standard Life Insurance Co.,* 769 F.3d 597 (8th Cir. 2014).

♦   A Connecticut insurance adjuster with a back condition sought long-term disability benefits under her employer's insurance plan. The plan denied the claim **based on its conclusion that the employee could perform her job with accommodations**. She sued the plan and alleged a violation of ERISA.

The court rejected her claim, finding that the plan conducted a thorough review of the claim and amply supported its decision. *St. Onge v. Unum Life Insurance Co. of America*, 559 Fed.Appx. 28 (2d Cir. 2014) (Unpublished).

♦   An employee in Alabama participated in an employer-sponsored accidental injury/death insurance policy. He was found unresponsive in his truck after having worked outside in warm weather for approximately two hours. The cause of death was listed as cardiac arrest with heat as a possible contributing factor. His wife filed a claim for benefits under the policy, and the claim was denied on the basis that the employee did not die as a result of a covered accident. The wife sued under ERISA, but she lost. The plan defined covered accident as an injury caused "directly and exclusively" by a sudden, violent, unexpected external event, and **the employee's death did not meet the definition**. Cardiac arrest is not an external event, and the wife did not show the death was caused solely by a heat-related accident within the meaning of the policy. *Parsons v. Metropolitan Life Insurance Co.*, 571 Fed.Appx. 269 (5th Cir. 2014) (Unpublished).

♦   After receiving long-term disability benefits for 11 years, an Iowa software developer asked his insurance plan if he could work on a part-time basis without losing his benefits. The plan then determined that he was able to work and stopped providing the benefits because eligibility depended on total disability. **The employee sued under ERISA, but he lost.** The Eighth Circuit ruled that the insurer had discretionary authority to interpret the plan and did not abuse its discretion when it terminated the benefits. *Siegel v. Connecticut General Life Insurance Co.*, 702 F.3d 1044 (8th Cir. 2013).

♦   **A Minnesota employee married a transgender woman** who was born a male. He enrolled her in his health plan as an eligible family dependent. Some years later, his wife sought to replace a ruptured implant, and the plan denied her benefits under an exclusion for sex-transformation surgery. It terminated her eligibility because it considered her a man in an illegal marriage. She sued under ERISA, and the plan countersued to recover more than $80,000 in benefits it had already paid on her behalf. A federal court dismissed the counterclaim. The plan then amended its definition of eligible spouses to clarify that it would only recognize the individual's anatomical sex at birth. The court held that the plan had to provide coverage to the wife, noting that Minnesota law recognized her as a female in an opposite-sex marriage – not as a man in a same-sex marriage. *Radtke v. Miscellaneous Drivers & Helpers Union Local 638 Health, Welfare, Eye & Dental Fund*, 867 F.Supp.2d 1023 (D. Minn. 2012).

♦   A California employee, considered one of the best at his company, developed chronic fatigue syndrome after 15 years on the job. It took a year to diagnose his condition by conducting tests that ruled out other illnesses. When he applied for long-term disability benefits, the plan administrator denied them. He sued, and a federal court granted pretrial judgment to the plan. However, the Ninth Circuit reversed and ordered the lower court to award benefits. **The administrator demanded objective evidence of chronic**

fatigue syndrome even though the condition can't be diagnosed with objective tests. She also failed to consider that he received Social Security disability benefits, and she changed her reasons for denying benefits each time her reason for the denial was refuted by his doctors. She failed to engage in meaningful dialogue with the employee, and her decision was "illogical, implausible and without reasonable support." *Salomaa v. Honda Long Term Disability Plan*, 642 F.3d 666 (9th Cir. 2011).

◆   A Pennsylvania pilot suffered a psychotic episode on duty and began seeing a psychiatrist. His FAA certification was revoked, and he began receiving long-term disability benefits from the airline's benefits plan. Four years later, without receiving any new medical information, the plan stopped paying him benefits. He sued, and the Third Circuit ruled in his favor, noting that the plan arbitrarily stopped paying benefits. **The plan, operated by the airline, relied on the same medical evidence it had used to grant benefits to now deny benefits.** Also, the airline told him he had to reapply for FAA certification, but the plan had no such requirement. And because the airline ran and funded the plan, there was a conflict of interest that weighed in the pilot's favor. *Miller v. American Airlines, Inc.*, 632 F.3d 837 (3d Cir. 2011).

◆   A Yellow Book account representative in Minnesota obtained short-term disability benefits for his arthritis. However, when he applied for long-term disability benefits, the insurer (and plan administrator) denied them. The insurer referred to the Department of Labor's Dictionary of Titles, which stated that an account executive job required light physical demands, including frequent walking and/or standing; frequently having to carry, lift or pull up to 10 pounds; and occasionally having to carry, lift or pull 20 pounds. The account rep's doctors had stated that he was capable of performing those kinds of activities, but the account rep claimed his job actually required him to lift and carry around 35 pounds, which he was unable to do. He sued under ERISA and lost when the Eighth Circuit held that **the insurer could rely on the general description provided by the Department of Labor** rather than the specific requirements he claimed the job demanded. The appellate court noted that his doctors' opinions about his disability were mostly conclusory and that his actual job description closely tracked the Department of Labor's description. *Darvell v. Life Insurance Co. of North America*, 597 F.3d 929 (8th Cir. 2010).

◆   An Ohio accountant stopped working because of pain in her hands. She believed the pain was related to her rheumatoid arthritis, but her rheumatologist thought it might be related to work stress. He determined that her arthritis had stabilized enough that she could return to work with limitations. She saw a physical therapist who found that she could not return to work, and her rheumatologist agreed with that finding. When she applied for long-term disability benefits, the company's health plan administrator sent her to an independent physician, who found her arthritis was in remission. The administrator relied on the independent physician's opinion and paid her long-term disability benefits for 25 months but refused to continue paying them beyond that point. When she sued the administrator under ERISA, a federal district court and the Sixth Circuit ruled against her. **ERISA plan administrators do not have to give special deference to a treating physician's opinion.** *Balmert v. Reliance Standard Life Insurance Co.*, 601 F.3d 497 (6th Cir. 2010).

♦   A driver for a trucking company in Arkansas sustained injuries to her neck, back and knee. The company's employee welfare plan administrator initially awarded her long-term disability benefits, but after a year (when the plan used a different definition of "disabled"), it determined that she no longer qualified for long-term disability because, although she was unable to perform her job, she was not unable to perform "any gainful occupation." Her attorney sought documents supporting the administrator's position but did not receive them. When she sued under ERISA, a federal court dismissed her claim because she failed to exhaust her administrative remedies. However, the Eighth Circuit reversed in part. It ruled that because **the administrator failed to provide the employee with documents** that would give her a reasonable opportunity to review the denial of benefits, she had to be permitted to continue her challenge to the denial of benefits. *Brown v. J.B. Hunt Transport Services, Inc.*, 586 F.3d 1079 (8th Cir. 2009).

♦   A Michigan employee stopped working because of severe abdominal pain. Her doctor diagnosed mesenteric panniculitis and advised her not to return to work. She applied for long-term disability, but her doctor never responded to requests for documentation explaining how her condition prevented her from working. The company denied benefits. It later received surveillance video from an insurance company (with which the employee had a policy) showing the employee driving long distances, loading groceries into her car and carrying a rug. Two doctors reviewed the video and agreed that the employee ought to be able to do her job. When she sued under ERISA, a federal court and the Sixth Circuit ruled against her. Although the video wasn't necessarily inconsistent with her claim of intermittent disabling pain, **she never provided a doctor's documentation to back up her claim that she couldn't work.** *Kiel v. Life Insurance Co. of North America*, 345 Fed.Appx. 52 (6th Cir. 2009).

♦   The obese wife of an Oklahoma employee sought to have gastric bypass surgery. Her surgeon requested authorization for the procedure, but the company's health plan denied the request because the surgeon did not provide medical documentation that the procedure was necessary. Further, the wife had not participated in a clinically supervised weight reduction program for six months in the year prior, which was a prerequisite for gastric bypass surgery under the company's healthcare plan. She had the surgery anyway and then sued the company's health plan under ERISA. A federal court ruled in favor of the healthcare plan. Even though the wife's doctor had discussed dieting with her and had issued a prescription for a diet drug, which she filled one time, **she did not participate in a clinically supervised weight reduction program as required by the plan.** *Franke v. State Farm Group Medical PPO Plan for U.S. Employees*, No. CIV-07-1366-HE, 2008 WL 5429619 (W.D. Okla. 12/30/08).

✦   An Arkansas employee suffered from fibromyalgia and degenerative arthritis in her hand. She filed a claim for benefits under the company's short-term disability plan. The plan administrator denied her claim and subsequent appeals. She then sued the plan for violating her ERISA rights to a full and fair review. A federal court and the Eighth Circuit ruled for the plan. Although two physicians who examined her determined that she could not work full time, **the plan produced eight doctors who reviewed her medical reports and determined that she could continue to work at her sedentary job**. The plan acted reasonably in relying on those eight medical opinions. *Midgett v. Washington Group Int'l Long Term Disability Plan*, 561 F.3d 887 (8th Cir. 2009).

✦   On the way home from a company meeting that included a boat cruise, a Rhode Island employee drove his car into a tree and died. He had stopped off at a bar on the way home and had also consumed a few drinks on the cruise. His blood alcohol level was three times the legal limit. His widow sought to recover accidental death benefits from the company's insurer, but the insurer offered to pay only the basic life insurance policy proceeds. The widow then sued under ERISA, and a federal court ruled against her. The First Circuit affirmed, noting that the ERISA plan granted the insurer discretionary authority to make benefit determinations, and that the decision here was not arbitrary and capricious or an abuse of discretion. **Alcohol-related deaths and injuries are not "accidental" under insurance contracts governed by ERISA.** *Stamp v. Metropolitan Life Insurance Co.*, 531 F.3d 84 (1st Cir. 2008).

✦   A Wisconsin employee had health insurance through work. When his three-year-old son was diagnosed with brain cancer, the company's insurer paid for the surgery to remove the tumor. Following the surgery, the doctor recommended high-dose chemotherapy with stem cell rescue because it had a higher cure rate and was less risky for a young child. The insurer then terminated coverage, finding that the treatment was experimental. An independent doctor reviewed the case and agreed that the treatment was experimental. However, the doctor recommended approving the treatment because it was standard for a young child with brain cancer. Also, because there were no alternatives with superior or proven results, the doctor considered the treatment to be medically necessary. The insurer denied coverage, and the boy received the treatment anyway. His father then sued under ERISA. The Wisconsin Supreme Court ordered the insurer to resume coverage. It noted that **the insurer acted arbitrarily when it stopped coverage by failing to give specific reasons for its decision**, and by failing to refer to the specific plan provision that precluded coverage. *Summers v. Touchpoint Health Plan, Inc.*, 749 N.W.2d 182 (Wis. 2008).

✦   A Massachusetts employee became disabled as a result of a work-related hand injury. She received workers' compensation benefits. When those benefits ended, she applied for long-term disability benefits. She asserted that it was not the work-related hand injury that caused the disability but rather her worsening diabetes. The company's group disability plan allowed employees who were no longer active to receive benefits if the disability that led to the leave of absence was caused by a non-occupational injury or sickness. Her application for benefits was denied, and she sued the employer and its insurer. A federal court dismissed the lawsuit, and the First Circuit Court of Appeals affirmed. Here, the employee first became disabled as a result of her hand injury, not her non-occupational sickness. Thus, since she was not rendered disabled as a result of her diabetes, **she was not entitled to long-term disability benefits**. *Perry v. New England Business Service*, 347 F.3d 343 (1st Cir. 2003).

◆   A District of Columbia man lost his left eye in an explosion and required brain surgery. Over 30 years later, he was hired by a hospital. Before starting work, he was required to receive an MMR vaccination. Two days later, he began to have seizures that caused him to lose consciousness. Over the next six years, he had 39 seizures. The Department of Employment Services granted him temporary total disability benefits, and the hospital appealed. The D.C. Court of Appeals affirmed. Even though the vaccination occurred before the insured reported for work, he had been hired at the time of the inoculation, which was administered by and at the behest of the employer. Therefore, **there was an employer-employee relationship at the time of the vaccination**. The fact that the requirement of vaccination was imposed by law did not alter this conclusion. In receiving the vaccination, he furthered the employer's interests in avoiding liability and absenteeism. Also, he had suffered no seizures in the 32 years between his accident and the vaccination. *Washington Hospital Center v. D.C. Dep't of Employment Services*, 821 A.2d 898 (D.C. 2003).

3. Intentionally Harmful Conduct

Employers can be liable under ERISA where they engage in intentionally harmful conduct toward eligible employees. They may not retaliate against employees for availing themselves of their ERISA rights, nor may they interfere with the attainment of ERISA rights.

◆   A husband and wife who had worked for a utility company for many years were fired for falsifying their time sheets shortly after their son suffered a relapse of his brain cancer. The couple asserted that the real reason for the termination was the company's desire to avoid the insurance costs. They sued under the ADA and ERISA. A Wyoming federal court granted pretrial judgment to the company, but the Tenth Circuit reversed, finding issues of fact that required a trial. Besides the timing of the firings, the investigation itself was suspicious. **The company relied on logs that were known to be inaccurate, and also fired the employees while docking the pay of and using progressive discipline on other employees** who had been accused of falsifying time sheets in the past. The company may have illegally discriminated against the couple based on their association with a disabled person and also may have violated Section 510 of ERISA, which bars employers from discriminating against employees who exercise their rights under an employer-provided health plan. *Trujillo v. PacifiCorp.*, 524 F.3d 1149 (10th Cir. 2008).

◆   An Ohio refinery employee was allowed to retire in lieu of being fired after a number of incidents, including the contamination of two fuel tanks. The employee sued the refinery, claiming it did so to interfere with his ability to attain his full pension, and asserting that the incidents had not been his fault. A federal court ruled in favor of the refinery, noting that **the employee failed to prove a causal connection between his "forced" resignation and his entitlement to a full pension**. He still had 13 years to go until that event, and the refinery did not force him to retire. It would have been happy to fire him for potentially dangerous performance of duties. *Zbuka v. Marathon Ashland Petroleum, LLC*, 447 F.Supp.2d 845 (N.D. Ohio 2006).

◆   An Illinois sales employee had a bad relationship with his manager. His physician called the manager and stated that the employee suffered from severe job-related stress and should not return to work before seeing a psychiatrist. Although a psychiatric appointment was made for the following week, the manager fired the employee the day before the appointment, which was coincidentally the first day the employee would have been eligible to participate in the company's short-term disability benefits plan. The manager back-dated the action to the previous day. The action was justified as being pursuant to a longstanding, unwritten policy applicable to employees who failed to report to work for three consecutive days without calling the office. The employee sued, asserting that he had been discharged to deny his participation in the short-term disability plan in violation of ERISA. The court held for the employee, and the Seventh Circuit affirmed. **The manager's action of back-dating termination documents provided the necessary inference of intent to interfere with benefits.** The employer's assertion that it maintained a well-established employment abandonment policy was contradicted by the testimony of a former human resources administrator. *Salus v. GTE Directories Service Corp.*, 104 F.3d 131 (7th Cir. 1997).

◆   A health and welfare fund created under collective bargaining agreements between a local and international union and several employers was fully insured during the first 16 years of its existence. The plan administrator caused the cancellation of insurance due to late payments. The plan became self-insured but was later terminated due to inability to pay its claims. Plan trustees then transferred the plan's remaining assets to another plan which refused to assume liability for existing claims. The trustees offered to settle these claims for 25 cents on each dollar claimed. A participant in the plan underwent kidney dialysis, incurring over $66,000 in medical expenses that were not covered due to the plan's insolvency. When a medical provider sued him for unpaid bills, he sued the plan in federal court, seeking damages and restitution. The court refused to grant pretrial judgment to the plan on the claim for restitution because there was evidence that plan trustees had breached their fiduciary duties by causing the plan to default in its obligations. ERISA confers equitable powers upon courts to protect participants from fiduciary breaches by plan trustees and administrators. **There was also evidence that plan trustees and administrators had misrepresented the financial health of the plan.** Accordingly, the case had to proceed to trial. However, the employee was not entitled to a monetary damage award under ERISA. *Jackson v. Truck Drivers' Union Local 42 Health and Welfare Fund*, 933 F.Supp. 1124 (D. Mass. 1996).

◆   An Alabama marketing manager participated in his employer's medical, life, and disability insurance plans, for which he authorized payment by payroll deduction. The plan's underwriter claimed that the employee's premiums were delinquent. When the employee had a heart attack requiring hospitalization, the plan issued a letter retroactively canceling coverage due to nonpayment. The employee sued the underwriter and employer under ERISA. He also sought payment of his medical expenses and brought other state law claims. The court held that ERISA foreclosed any state law claims and did not authorize extra-contractual or punitive damages. The Supreme Court of Alabama ruled that the state law claims for fraud and breach of contract were barred by ERISA. However, ERISA allows state and federal courts **authority to develop remedies beyond those expressly stated in ERISA**. This included claims for extra-contractual and punitive damages if the facts of a case required such remedies. Because the employee had stated a valid ERISA complaint, the trial court had improperly foreclosed the possibility of a punitive damage award. The ERISA claims were reversed and remanded for reconsideration. *Weems v. Jefferson-Pilot Life Insurance Co., Inc.*, 663 So.2d 905 (Ala. 1995).

4. Other Coverage Issues

ERISA does not provide a statute of limitations. Thus, courts must borrow the most applicable state statute of limitations in cases brought under the act.

ERISA generally does not allow for money damages (except when the plan is suing a fiduciary for breach of duty). Only equitable remedies are available for individuals asserting violations of the act. This is because ERISA was enacted to protect whole employee benefit plans rather than the rights of individual employees.

◆   Three family businesses challenged Affordable Care Act provisions requiring employers to provide employee health coverage fo 20 contraceptive methods approved by the Food and Drug Administration. They specifically objected to paying for their employees' use of four methods of contraception. Their objection was based on religious grounds. The U.S. Supreme Court held that federal regulations enforcing the contraception mandate violated the Religious Freedom Restoration Act. **The mandate burdened the families' exercise of religion**, and it was not shown to be the least restrictive way to carry out the government's interest in ensuring cost-free access to contraception services. *Burwell v. Hobby Lobby Stores, Inc.*, 134 S.Ct. 2751 (U.S. 2014).

◆   After a car accident, a California woman became a quadriplegic. Her husband's employee benefit plan paid over $411,000 in medical expenses. The plan included a reimbursement provision that permitted the plan to recover from the beneficiary any third-party payments made to her, up to the amount of benefits paid out by the plan. When the woman sued various third parties to recover for her injuries, she reached a settlement of $650,000. A court ordered her to pay the plan $13,828 as her share of the medical costs, but the plan sought to be reimbursed for the full amount of benefits it had paid out. It sued the beneficiary under ERISA, and the case reached the U.S. Supreme Court. The Court held that the plan was not entitled to impose personal liability on the beneficiary for the contractual obligation. **Under Section 502(a)(3), only equitable relief is available, and the plan here was seeking a legal remedy** – the payment of money damages. The plan was not entitled to reimbursement of the $411,000 it had paid out. *Great-West Life & Annuity Insurance Co. v. Knudson*, 534 U.S. 204, 122 S.Ct. 708, 151 L.Ed.2d 635 (2002).

◆   A Michigan hospital employee was required to "occasionally" lift and carry 10 pounds, "frequently" stand and walk, and "occasionally" climb stairs. She suffered from numerous joint and spinal conditions that required more than 10 surgeries. Eventually, she stopped working and filed for long-term disability (LTD) benefits under a policy issued to the hospital under ERISA. The policy provided benefits if she was unable to perform all the material duties of her regular occupation. She also applied for Social Security benefits, which were awarded. The insurer then offset her LTD benefits against her Social Security benefits. It later conducted surveillance of her and determined that she could perform sedentary work. It decided that her prior job was sedentary and terminated her benefits. She sued under ERISA, and a federal court ruled for the insurer. However, the Sixth Circuit reversed, finding that the insurer's actions had been arbitrary and capricious. The policy clearly stated that she was due benefits if she couldn't perform <u>all</u> the material duties of her regular occupation. And **the insurer improperly reclassified her job as sedentary**. *Hunter v. Life Insurance Co. of North America*, 437 Fed.Appx. 372 (6th Cir. 2011).

◆   A new employee of a company in Michigan had a history of heart problems. Sometime during the three-month exclusionary period of the welfare benefits plan, he went to the doctor for an unrelated problem. The doctor found his blood pressure dangerously high and sought to admit him to a hospital, but he stated that he hadn't taken his blood pressure medicine that day and refused to go to the hospital. He later suffered a heart attack and collected short-term disability benefits. However, the company's welfare benefit plan denied him long-term disability benefits on the grounds that he had a preexisting condition. When he sued under ERISA, a federal court and the Sixth Circuit ruled against him. The court of appeals noted that **he was admittedly taking prescription medication for extreme hypertension during the three-month exclusionary period**, and that the heart attack had most likely been caused by the hypertension. *Estate of Blanco v. Prudential Insurance Co. of America*, 606 F.3d 399 (6th Cir. 2010).

◆   A wife and her husband were fired (two months apart) by their New Jersey employer after they told the owner that their supervisor was sexually harassing two subordinates. The wife underwent surgery the day before the husband was fired. Two months later, the husband learned that the employer had cancelled his health insurance after he was fired, backdating the cancellation to a few days before his termination. More than two years later, the husband and wife sued the employer for retaliation. The case reached the New Jersey Supreme Court, which held that they sued too late with respect to the retaliatory discharge claim.

However, **they could sue for retaliation with respect to the post-discharge cancellation of the insurance policy** because two years had not yet elapsed from that event. *Roa v. Roa*, 985 A.2d 1225 (N.J. 2010).

❖   A South Carolina employee began suffering from vertigo and stopped working. He made a claim for long-term disability benefits. Aetna, the plan's administrator and insurer, paid him monthly benefits after accepting the claim. He later filed for workers' compensation, claiming he developed asbestosis on the job. The company settled the claim, and he received over $39,000. Aetna then offset his workers' compensation benefits against his long-term disability benefits, paying him $665 less per month for the next 60 months. He sued Aetna under ERISA, asserting that it could not reduce his long-term disability benefits because **his workers' compensation award was for a separate and unrelated illness**. However, a federal court and the Fourth Circuit ruled against him, noting that the purpose of the employee benefits plan was to provide a steady stream of income, and that Aetna had discretion under the plan to make the offset. *Carden v. Aetna Life Insurance Co.*, 559 F.3d 256 (4th Cir. 2009).

❖   A co-worker caused an Arkansas employee to fall, aggravating a pre-existing back and shoulder injury. The employee tried to file an accident report, but was told that the accident would be taken care of "informally." A few days after he informed his supervisor that he needed time off for shoulder surgery, he was laid off due to a "lack of work." He obtained unemployment benefits, then alleged ERISA and ADEA violations, claiming he was really fired so the company could avoid paying his insurance benefits. When the EEOC sought information, **the company claimed it fired him for disciplinary reasons, despite the fact that it did not follow its own policies for a disciplinary termination**. In the lawsuit that resulted, the Eighth Circuit reversed pretrial judgment for the company on the ERISA claim, noting that questions of fact existed as to the real reason for the firing. *Fitzgerald v. Action, Inc.*, 521 F.3d 867 (8th Cir. 2008).

❖   A company in Illinois had a "Sickness and Accident Disability Benefit Plan" covered by ERISA, which provided disability benefits for accidents that arose out of and in the course of employment. Compensable injuries had to arise solely from an accident during and in direct connection with the performance of the employee's duties. When an employee slipped and fell in a restroom, suffering disabling injuries, she collected workers' compensation, then sought benefits under the plan. **The plan administrator granted sickness benefits (with a maximum 52 weeks of coverage)** but not potentially unlimited accident benefits. She sued, and the Seventh Circuit ruled against her. It refused to find the administrator's decision arbitrary and capricious. *Sisto v. Ameritech Sickness and Accident Disability Benefit Plan*, 429 F.3d 698 (7th Cir. 2005).

III. EMPLOYER LIABILITY AND RECOUPMENT

A plan may incur liability not only by failing to pay benefits that are due participants, but also by withdrawing from a multi-employer plan. Under the

Multi-employer Pension Plan Amendments Act, employers who withdraw from under-funded multi-employer pension plans must pay a <u>withdrawal liability</u>.

However, employers may also <u>recoup</u> excess funds from terminated defined benefit plans if the funds do not have to be paid out as accrued benefits (non-forfeitable benefits) or as other benefits under the plans.

A. Supreme Court Cases

◆   A paper company and its parent entity employed 2,600 people in seven paper mills. A union represented employees covered by 17 of the companies' defined benefit pension plans. When the companies filed for bankruptcy, they considered, as ERISA allows, terminating the plans through the purchase of annuities. The union proposed that the companies merge the plans with its multi-employer pension plan, conveying the plans' assets to the union's plan, which would then assume the liabilities of the companies' plans. However, the companies discovered that by purchasing annuities, they could satisfy their obligations to plan participants and retain a $5 million surplus. They rejected the union's proposal and purchased the annuities. A California bankruptcy court ruled that the companies breached a fiduciary duty to fully consider the union's proposal, and the Ninth Circuit agreed. The U.S. Supreme Court reversed. It noted that the Pension Benefit Guaranty Corporation (PBGC) – the entity administering the federal insurance program that protects plan benefits – took the position that **ERISA did not permit merger as a method of terminating a defined benefits plan because the statute provides for merger as an alternative to plan termination**. The PBGC's interpretation was reasonable. *Beck v. PACE Int'l Union*, 551 U.S. 96, 127 S.Ct. 2310, 168 L.Ed.2d 1 (2007).

◆   The Multi-employer Pension Plan Amendments Act of 1980 (MPPAA), 29 U.S.C. §§ 1381-1461, requires employers who withdraw from under-funded multi-employer pension plans to pay a withdrawal liability. Employers may contest an assessed liability but are required to make payments pending appeal. An employer made contributions to a multi-employer pension fund for laundry workers in the San Francisco Bay area for several years and then ceased making contributions. The fund's trustees demanded payment of a withdrawal liability and notified the employer of its payment options. The employer refused to make payments. However, the fund did not sue the employer until eight years after it withdrew from the fund and over six years after missing its first scheduled payment. A federal court dismissed the case as barred by the MPPAA's six-year statute of limitations, and the Ninth Circuit affirmed.

The fund appealed to the U.S. Supreme Court, which rejected the employer's claim that its withdrawal commenced the statute of limitations, because the MPPAA does not require a withdrawing employer to pay anything until the plan demands payment. **The cause of action did not accrue until the employer was assessed a liability, notified of the amount and means of payment, and failed to make a required payment.** Although over six years had passed from the employer's failure to pay the first installment, the fund was entitled to recover all but the first of the installment payments. The Court reversed and remanded the lower court decisions. *Bay Area Laundry and Dry*

Cleaning Pension Trust Fund v. Ferbar Corp. of California, Inc., 522 U.S. 192, 118 S.Ct. 542, 139 L.Ed.2d 553 (1997).

◆ The MPPAA requires employers who withdraw from under-funded multi-employer pension plans to pay a fair share of the plan's unfunded liabilities. It gives withdrawing employers the option to pay their withdrawal liability in a lump sum, or to amortize the amount in level annual payments "calculated as if the first payment were made on the first day of the plan year following the plan year in which the withdrawal occurs and as if each subsequent payment were made on the first day of each subsequent plan year." A Wisconsin brewing company withdrew from an under-funded plan with a withdrawal charge of $23.3 million. Although the plan and the brewery agreed on the amount of withdrawal liability, the parties disagreed on the amount of interest that had accrued during the withdrawal year. The case reached the U.S. Supreme Court, which stated that **nothing in the MPPAA required withdrawing employers to pay an actuarially perfect fair share of withdrawal liability**. The MPPAA provision describing withdrawing employer liability did not cause interest to start accruing during the withdrawal year itself. Rather, it called for calculation as if the first payment were made on the first day of the plan year following the plan year in which withdrawal occurs. Because a withdrawing employer owed nothing to a plan until the plan demanded payment as set forth by the MPPAA, the employer was unable to determine its liability until sometime after the beginning of the withdrawal year. The Court affirmed the decision for the brewery. *Milwaukee Brewery Workers' Pension Plan v. Jos. Schlitz Brewing Co.*, 513 U.S. 414, 115 S.Ct. 981, 130 L.Ed.2d 932 (1995).

◆ A former employee of a closely held corporation claimed that the corporation and a corporate officer/shareholder violated ERISA by failing to properly administer the corporation's employee pension plan. The former employee sued the corporation and the officer/shareholder, obtaining a judgment of $187,000 against the corporation. The former employee was unable to collect on his judgment, even though the shareholder/officer continued to take cash out of the corporation as a favored creditor. The former employee then sued the corporate officer for engaging in a civil conspiracy to siphon assets from the corporation to prevent satisfaction of the ERISA judgment. The court allowed the employee to collect his judgment from the officer. The Fourth Circuit, affirmed, but the Supreme Court reversed. **ERISA contains no authority for imposing liability for an existing ERISA judgment against a third party.** There were no independent grounds for a federal court to exercise jurisdiction in this case under a corporate veil-piercing argument. There was also no merit to the former employee's argument that a federal court could exercise jurisdiction over the matter as factually interdependent with and related to the prior lawsuit. Because the case was based on theories of relief that did not exist, the district court lacked jurisdiction to hear it. *Peacock v. Thomas*, 516 U.S. 349, 116 S.Ct. 862, 133 L.Ed.2d 817 (1996).

◆ The U.S. Supreme Court held that the **Coal Industry Retiree Health Benefit Act of 1992 unconstitutionally deprived a Massachusetts employer**

of property by requiring it to fund healthcare benefits for retired coal miners and their dependents, which created a severe, disproportionate and retroactive burden on the employer. The Act imposed severe retroactive liability on a class of employers that could not have anticipated it, and the liability was substantially disproportionate to the parties' experience. The employer's liability under the act was estimated at $50 to $100 million, even though it had employed no miners since before 1965, when the retirement and healthcare benefits offered were far less extensive. The act retroactively divested the employer of property long after it believed its liabilities were settled. *Eastern Enterprises v. Apfel*, 524 U.S. 498, 118 S.Ct. 2131, 141 L.Ed.2d 451 (1998).

◆   A corporation sold a subsidiary and terminated the ERISA retirement plan it funded. As a single-employer plan, all accrued benefits automatically vested. The corporation paid out the benefits that had vested, including non-reduced early retirement benefits to those employees who met both the age (62) and years of service (30) requirements. A group of employees who did not meet both requirements sued the corporation because it recouped nearly $11 million. They maintained that it was first required to distribute contingent early retirement benefits, even if unaccrued, before recouping plan assets. A Virginia federal court ruled for the corporation, and the Fourth Circuit reversed. The case reached the U.S. Supreme Court, which held that **the section of ERISA under which this lawsuit was brought did not create benefit entitlements** but merely provided for the orderly distribution of plan assets. However, since there were two alternative sections of ERISA, which could potentially lead to a recovery by the employees, the Court remanded the case. *Mead Corp. v. Tilley*, 490 U.S. 714, 109 S.Ct. 2156, 104 L.Ed.2d 796 (1989).

◆   A New York corporation filed for Chapter 11 bankruptcy (reorganization). At that time, it was the sponsor of three defined benefit pension plans covered by Title IV of ERISA that were chronically under-funded. At the corporation's request, the Pension Benefit Guaranty Corporation (PBGC) terminated the plans. The corporation and its employees then **negotiated new pension arrangements that provided substantially the same benefits as before**. The PBGC then issued a notice of restoration to undo the termination because the new "follow-on" plans were abusive of the insurance program. When the corporation refused to comply with the restoration, a lawsuit followed. The U.S. Supreme Court found that the PBGC's restoration decision was not arbitrary or capricious. As such, the corporation had to restore the plans that had been terminated. *Pension Benefit Guaranty Corp. v. LTV Corp.*, 496 U.S. 633, 110 S.Ct. 2668, 110 L.Ed.2d 579 (1990).

B. Other Employer Liability Cases

As more employers move toward 401(k) plans and away from defined benefit plans, the number of employer liability cases should decrease. However, employers can still be liable for improper conduct of supervisory employees who serve as plan administrators.

* An Arkansas employee was insured under her employer's life and accidental death plan. After she died of a drug overdose, the plan denied her son's claim for accidental death benefits on the basis that the manner of death could not be determined. The son filed a lawsuit claiming an ERISA violation. The court ruled in his favor, saying **there was insufficient evidence of suicide** and the death fell squarely within the meaning of "accident." *Nichols v. Unicare Life and Health Insurance Co.*, 739 F.3d 1176 (8th Cir. 2014).

* The owner of an Illinois company was also the 401(k) plan and the profit-sharing plan trustee for his 100 employees. After the profit-sharing plan lost $400,000 and the 401(k) plan lost $700,000 from 2000 to 2002, an employee sued the company and its owner for breach of fiduciary duty under ERISA. A federal court granted pretrial judgment to the defendants, but the U.S. Court of Appeals, Seventh Circuit, reversed in part. Although the owner did not owe employees a fiduciary duty under the 401(k) plan to investigate each participant's investments, **he might have improperly delegated his responsibilities to manage the profit-sharing plan**. *Jenkins v. Yager*, 444 F.3d 916 (7th Cir. 2006).

* A couple with a construction company in Oklahoma made payments to a multi-employer fund for employee benefits under a collective bargaining agreement. When their business worsened, they stopped making contributions to the fund. After they filed for Chapter 7 bankruptcy protection, an audit determined that they owed more than $121,000 to the fund. The fund's trustees sought the unpaid contributions and the case reached the Tenth Circuit. The court of appeals held that the couple's decision to pay other business expenses rather than make contributions was a business decision and not a breach of fiduciary duty. Accordingly, **they were entitled to discharge the pension fund debt in bankruptcy** and were not personally liable for the unpaid amount. *In re Luna*, 406 F.3d 1192 (10th Cir. 2005).

* Two family-owned Massachusetts construction companies operated from the same building, shared employees, worked on the same projects and were managed by the same persons. One of the companies entered into a collective bargaining agreement with its employees and signed a statewide agreement with a carpenters' union requiring it to make pension contributions for each hour of work performed by its employees. However, it did not make all required contributions, and the union collection agency sued both businesses for failing to make required contributions under ERISA. It sought unpaid contributions from the non-signatory business under the theory that it was the alter ego of the signatory business. The court ruled for the collection agency, awarding damages and penalties in excess of $121,000. The First Circuit affirmed. The alter ego theory of entity liability may apply to ERISA cases. It may also apply to parallel companies, such as those involved here. Courts must consider factors including continuity of ownership, similarity of business purposes, management relations, operations, equipment, customers, supervisors, and anti-union sentiment. Although there was no finding of anti-union sentiment here, enough other factors demonstrated that **the non-signatory entity was the alter ego of the**

signatory business and both were liable. *Massachusetts Carpenters Cent. Collection Agency v. Belmont Concrete Corp.*, 139 F.3d 304 (1st Cir. 1998).

◆ A Connecticut employer maintained an ERISA-qualified employee benefits plan. The employer contracted with a private company to provide administrative case management services. An employee who received inpatient treatment at a psychiatric hospital sought benefits for her hospitalization costs from the plan. When they were denied, she sued the employer. A federal court held that the employer had control over the plan's administration and could therefore be sued and held liable for benefits. However, the Second Circuit rejected the employee's assertion that an **employer acting as a co-administrator of an ERISA plan** is always jointly liable with the named plan administrator. The employer was entitled to dismissal of the claims against it because it was neither the designated plan administrator nor a plan trustee. *Crocco v. Xerox Corp.*, 137 F.3d 105 (2d Cir. 1998).

◆ A corporation with three subsidiaries in California sponsored an ERISA-qualified retirement plan. Two subsidiaries closed and the corporation made contributions to the plan through the third subsidiary. It later sold the third subsidiary and discontinued making contributions for all three subsidiaries. The retirement fund assessed a withdrawal liability against the corporation for withdrawing from the two closed subsidiaries, but not for the sold subsidiary, as its purchaser continued making contributions. The selling corporation argued that it could not be liable for withdrawing from the retirement plan because the cessation of contributions came as a result of a changed corporate structure as defined by the Multi-employer Pension Plan Amendments Act of 1980 (MPPAA). A California federal court held for the fund, and the Ninth Circuit Court of Appeals affirmed. **The corporation's withdrawal liability for the two closed subsidiaries had been shielded from assessment because the third subsidiary had continued making contributions to the plan.** However, upon the sale of the third subsidiary, the corporation was no longer shielded from liability under the MPPAA, and the district court had properly awarded judgment to the pension fund. *Penn Cent. Corp. v. Western Conference of Teamsters Pension Trust Fund*, 75 F.3d 529 (9th Cir. 1996).

IV. SEVERANCE BENEFITS

Employee severance pay or retirement incentive plans may be qualified under ERISA, if they are part of a written employee benefit plan that creates a reasonable expectation for the payment of benefits. One-time-only lump sum payments that are not subject to an ongoing administrative program are typically not covered by ERISA.

◆ A packaging and processing company discontinued operations at a plant, laying off almost all its employees. Some of the former employees then filed suit against the company, seeking severance pay under Maine law. The company asserted that ERISA preempted the plant-closing statute (which required the company to provide severance pay). The Supreme Judicial Court of Maine held that the company was liable for severance pay because ERISA only preempted state laws that relate to benefit plans created by employers or employee organizations. The U.S. Supreme Court held that the Maine statute was not subject to ERISA preemption. **The state law merely required a one-time lump-sum payment triggered by a single event** (the plant closing). There was no ongoing administrative program the employer had to meet. Thus, there was no potential problem of multiple regulation by state and federal statutes. Also, the Maine statute was not preempted by the National Labor Relations Act because it did not impermissibly intrude upon the collective bargaining process. *Fort Halifax Packing Co. v. Coyne*, 482 U.S. 1, 107 S.Ct. 2211, 96 L.Ed.2d 1 (1987).

◆   Two employees of a Wisconsin paper mill that was about to shut down left for other jobs before the shutdown occurred. They were denied severance benefits that were made available to employees who were involuntarily terminated. They sued under ERISA, claiming they should have received the severance benefits. The Seventh Circuit rejected their claim, finding that **the denial of benefits was not arbitrary and capricious**. Nor was the denial a breach of fiduciary duty or a breach of contract. *Reddinger v. SENA Severance Pay Plan*, 707 F.3d 702 (7th Cir. 2013).

◆   Johns Manville fired a senior vice president and paid him his annual salary of $312,000 plus $212,000 – a prorated portion of its annual incentive plan. He claimed that under the company's 1997 separation pay plan he was also entitled to a post-termination payment under both the company's annual incentive plan and its long-term incentive plan. The company rejected his demand, asserting that its 2006 separation pay plan ruled. He sued and lost. A Colorado federal court and the Tenth Circuit held that **the later separation pay plan clearly superseded the earlier plan**. The 2006 plan stated that employees who were eligible for severance pay under an employment agreement – as the vice president was – were not entitled to annual or long-term incentive pay under the plan. *Rosenzweig v. Manville*, 422 Fed.Appx. 709 (10th Cir. 2011).

◆   The CEO of a company in North Carolina signed an employment agreement that allowed him to collect severance benefits if he was terminated for other than cause or if the company sold substantially all its assets. When the company began proceedings to sell 90% of its business, the CEO became the lead negotiator until problems arose and the chairman of the board replaced him, locking him out of the office. When he sought severance benefits, the company first claimed that he had quit but then learned that he had gotten reimbursed for business travel despite using frequent flyer miles for certain flights (about $22,000 worth). It claimed it would have fired him had it known about the reimbursements earlier, but a federal court and the Fourth Circuit ruled against the company, noting that the CFO had known about the CEO's reimbursements and yet the company didn't fire him. **The CEO was entitled to severance benefits of around $1 million.** *Rinaldi v. CCX, Inc.*, 388 Fed.Appx. 290 (4th Cir. 2010).

✦   A director at a Missouri company told his supervisor he intended to leave the company to pursue other opportunities. He offered to stay on to train his replacement. However, he criticized the replacement and the company at a staff meeting and was then fired for insubordination. The company offered him only eight weeks of severance pay, which he refused. Instead, he sued under ERISA, asserting that he was entitled to more, and that he was fired so he would be forced to sell back his company stock. A federal court and the Eighth Circuit ruled against him, noting that **even if he had not been fired for cause, he did not meet the company's severance package criteria** because he was neither disabled nor eligible under the Rule of 75 (age plus years of service equals 75). It did not matter that the company had paid other ineligible employees a better severance package than he was offered. *Pendleton v. QuikTrip Corp.*, 567 F.3d 988 (8th Cir. 2009).

✦   An insurance company in Illinois, anticipating the sale of a business unit, decided to revoke severance benefits for employees who sold life and long-term healthcare insurance. The company posted the change on its intranet but did not highlight, underline or otherwise draw attention to the newly added language. Over six months later, and four days before it terminated its life and long-term healthcare insurance sales people, it sent them written copies of the change. The employees sued under ERISA, claiming they were not given "reasonable" notice as required by the severance plan's summary plan description. The company sought pretrial judgment, but a federal court refused to grant it. A trial was required because **the intranet posting did not amount to an "alert" to the sales people that the severance plan had changed**. Department of Labor guidelines clearly stated that the mere placement of material in a location frequented by participants was insufficient for electronic notice. *Rosenberg v. CNA Financial Corp.*, No. 04 C 8219, 2007 WL 2126085 (N.D. Ill. 7/23/07).

✦   A bank developed a severance plan that disallowed benefits for covered employees who were fired "for cause." The plan defined "cause" as "gross and willful misconduct," including acts or omissions that violated the bank's policies. A Minnesota employee working as a financial analyst accessed a personnel salary file and allegedly told two subordinates that he had information about personnel changes in two divisions. **After he was fired for violating company policy on confidentiality, he sought severance benefits, which were denied.** He then sued under ERISA and lost. Even though he claimed he had accessed the file for business reasons, he did not state what those reasons were. Benefits were properly denied. *Anderson v. U.S. Bancorp*, 484 F.3d 1027 (8th Cir. 2007).

✦   As part of a company-wide layoff, a vice president was told that he would be offered a severance package. At that time, the company's severance plan provided up to 26 weeks of salary, conditioned on the employee signing a release of claims. However, the next day, the company offered the vice president a new severance plan calling for 32 weeks of pay if the vice president would sign a non-compete clause. A week later, the company formally adopted this amendment to the severance plan. The vice president's last day of work came the following week. Without signing the non-compete agreement, the vice president sought severance benefits. The company denied them, and a lawsuit resulted. A Texas federal court and the Fifth Circuit ruled that the vice president's lawsuit under ERISA could not succeed. **The company had the right to amend its severance plan, and the vice president was not entitled to benefits because he didn't sign the non-compete agreement.** *Chacko v. Sabre, Inc.*, 473 F.3d 604 (5th Cir. 2006).

◆   In accepting a job with a Michigan company, a vice president signed a contract that provided a financial penalty if he quit within the first year, and also offered to pay him a separation allowance (representing the difference between his first year's compensation and the payments he'd already received) if he was fired other than for cause. This second clause did not specifically state that it applied only to the first year of employment, but it immediately followed the preceding clause, which did. Six years later he was laid off and offered a severance package of nine months' pay plus continued health insurance coverage. He refused to sign the release offered by the company and sued, claiming he was owed his compensation for the six years he'd worked for the company, minus his first year's compensation. A federal court and the Sixth Circuit ruled for the company. Here, the two clauses in the contract had to be read together. They offered reciprocal obligations and were only meant to apply to the first year of the contract. *Reardon v. Kelly Services, Inc.*, 210 Fed.Appx. 456 (6th Cir. 2006).

◆   After rumors circulated that a division of a company was going to be sold, a company official read a letter to employees indicating that if there were a change of control or sale of a business unit resulting in job loss, employees would receive a severance package. Eventually the company folded the division and paid employees severance benefits and cooperation bonuses as it had for earlier internal consolidations. However, that amount was less than it would have been if the division had been sold to an outside party. A number of terminated employees sued under ERISA, claiming that the letter served as a summary plan description (SPD) and that the company owed them the larger benefits promised therein. An Iowa federal court held that the letter was a faulty SPD that conflicted with the severance plan. It awarded the employees an additional $1.6 million in benefits. The Eighth Circuit reversed. Here, **although the letter was confusing and deceiving, it was not an SPD because it did not contain the information required by ERISA regulations**. Thus, the employees could not use the letter to obtain extra benefits. *Antolik v. Saks, Inc.*, 463 F.3d 796 (8th Cir. 2006).

◆   An Illinois company hired an employee under a written contract that required it to pay her one year's base salary as severance if she was terminated "for reasons other than cause." Later, the company fired the employee for failing to meet a $380,000 billing quota. It claimed this was a "for cause" reason under the contract and refused to pay severance. The employee sued, and a federal court granted pretrial judgment to the company. The Seventh Circuit reversed and remanded the case, noting that **there can be a difference between cause for discharge and cause for the denial of severance benefits**. Here, the employee's performance was deemed unsatisfactory based on criteria selected after she began working, and was not specified in the contract. Thus, a factual issue existed as to whether there was cause to deny severance benefits. *Joy v. Hay Group, Inc.*, 403 F.3d 875 (7th Cir. 2005).

◆   An insurance company in Maryland hired an employee under a written contract that required it to pay him one year's base salary as severance if he was terminated "without cause." Subsequently, the company sold his division to another insurer and arranged for his transfer to the new company. He sought severance benefits after the sale, claiming that he had been "terminated" without cause even though he continued to perform the same job for a new employer. The case reached the Fourth Circuit, which held that he was entitled to severance pay. Most courts agree that **when a company sells a business unit, that unit's employees are terminated, even if they continue working for the buyer**. Such terminations are not "for cause." *Gresham v. Lumbermen's Mutual Casualty Co.*, 404 F.3d 253 (4th Cir. 2005).

◆   An employee of a risk management and insurance company in Massachusetts forwarded seven internal emails containing confidential information to a former co-worker who had become a senior official with a direct competitor. When the company learned of the emails, it fired him. He asked for severance benefits, which the company denied, noting that **severance pay was barred for employees who were fired for just cause**. Rather than make a written claim for benefits or appeal internally, he sued, claiming ERISA violations. The First Circuit ruled against him, holding that he had to exhaust his administrative remedies before filing suit. He could not just assume that an internal appeal would be futile. Further, the company's decision to fire him was reasonable. *Madera v. Marsh USA, Inc.*, 426 F.3d 56 (1st Cir. 2005).

◆   A company in Minnesota laid off an employee while it had a severance plan in place. By the time it actually terminated him, however, it had replaced its severance plan with a new one that paid less benefits. When the employee attempted to collect his benefits from the human resources department, he was informed that he was only entitled to benefits under the new plan, and that he had to sign a waiver of any rights under the old plan to get any benefits at all. He instead sued the company. A federal court held that ERISA governed the situation and that the company had to pay the employee his severance benefits under the new plan even though he did not sign the waiver. The Eighth Circuit reversed, holding that the employee could be required to sign a waiver as a condition of receiving benefits under the new plan. Since **the company had no legal obligation to pay any severance benefits**, there was no ERISA violation in requiring a waiver. The employee was not entitled to severance pay. *Petersen v. E.F. Johnson*, 366 F.3d 676 (8th Cir. 2004).

◆   The head of security for a pharmaceutical company in Missouri learned that his job was going to be cut as a result of corporate restructuring. Rather than relocate to New Jersey, he decided to participate in the company's ERISA-qualified severance plan. He began to pursue a real estate career and charged more than 3,000 minutes on his company cell phone in violation of company policy. He also misused a confidential employee list by mailing real estate notices to the employees. When the company fired him for misconduct, he became ineligible for severance pay. He objected to the disqualification, asserting that other employees committed misconduct without being similarly punished. A federal court ruled in favor of the company, and the Eighth Circuit affirmed. It did not matter if the company inconsistently disciplined its employees as long as **it did not intentionally interfere with his severance benefits**. Since he could not prove that the termination was designed to interfere with his ERISA-protected rights, he was not entitled to severance pay. *Koons v. Aventis Pharmaceuticals*, 367 F.3d 768 (8th Cir. 2004).

♦   A chef in Rhode Island received an employee handbook that described the company's severance policy, which was based on tenure and salary. The handbook also contained a disclaimer stating that it was not intended to be a contract, and that the company reserved the right to revise any or all policies contained therein, even without notice. The company then abandoned the severance policy and told the chef about the company's new completely subjective, or arbitrary, severance approach. A month later, **the chef was fired without severance for planning to open a competing restaurant nearby**. He sued for severance benefits, but the Supreme Court of Rhode Island ruled against him. The only document he produced to support his claim of entitlement to severance pay was the employee handbook, which clearly stated that it was not a contract and that it could be modified at any time. *D'Oliveira v. Rare Hospitality Int'l, Inc.*, 840 A.2d 538 (R.I. 2004).

♦   Sixteen utility company employees in Washington, D.C., asked company officials whether the company was considering a retirement incentive program. After being informed that no such plan was being considered, they retired between January and June. In fact, the company implemented such a program at the end of June, **offering employees in their classification a one-time opportunity to receive specified severance benefits if they would retire early**. They sued the utility under ERISA, asserting that it had breached its fiduciary obligations by failing to inform them of the program. A federal court dismissed the lawsuit, and the D.C. Circuit Court of Appeals affirmed. It noted that the retirement incentive program was not covered by ERISA because it could be implemented with a straightforward factual determination of whether an employee qualified for it. The program was based on a one-time triggering event. Since this was not the kind of administrative decision that required the protection of ERISA, the federal court had no jurisdiction to hear the retirees' claims. *Young v. Washington Gas Light Co.*, 206 F.3d 1200 (D.C. Cir. 2000).

♦   An Indiana woman worked for a General Motors (GM) facility for 19 years, at which time the facility was sold to another company. She continued working there. Less than three years later, the facility was sold again, this time to a GM subsidiary. She was offered a job but refused it, instead seeking severance benefits under GM's employee welfare plan, which was covered by ERISA. The U.S. Court of Appeals, Seventh Circuit, held that the woman had quit her job voluntarily when she chose not to continue her employment after the sale of the facility. Because the employee handbook clearly explained that **refusing a suitable offer of employment amounted to quitting** the job, the woman was not entitled to severance benefits. *James v. General Motors Corp.*, 230 F.3d 315 (7th Cir. 2000).

✦   A Wisconsin paper manufacturer established a severance package for certain employees prior to a hostile takeover. The plan called for the payment of a lump sum to employees who suffered a material reduction in compensation or authority. The successor's health plan offered less favorable benefits than the manufacturer's plan, prompting many employees to select the severance package. Several employees retired and claimed that because the new employer's health package was less favorable, they were entitled to severance benefits. The plan administrator denied the claims, and the retirees sued the plan, administrator, and both employers under ERISA. The court ruled against the retirees on all claims, and the Seventh Circuit Court of Appeals affirmed. Here, **the anticipated reduction in benefits did not trigger the severance package eligibility clause** because the employees had retired instead of switching to the new plan. The court of appeals rejected the retirees' argument that the plan and employers had a fiduciary duty to fully advise them that selecting early retirement would make them ineligible for the severance package since ERISA does not require a plan administrator to prepare an advisory opinion for each plan participant. *Chojnacki v. Georgia-Pacific Corp.*, 108 F.3d 810 (7th Cir. 1997).

V.   VACATION AND SICK LEAVE BENEFITS

Vacation and sick benefits are generally a matter of contract interpretation and require an examination of the employment contract. No federal or state law requires an employer to offer paid sick leave or vacation leave.

In recent years, many employers have lumped vacation and sick leave benefits into one unified bank of hours, generally called personal leave. For example, an employee with 18 days (or 144 hours) of personal leave could use any portion of that time for sickness or vacation.

The U.S. Supreme Court has held that a policy of paying discharged employees a lump sum out of corporate general assets does not constitute an employee welfare benefit plan under ERISA.

A.   Vacation Benefits

✦   A Massachusetts bank discharged two vice presidents and allegedly failed to compensate them for vacation time they had accrued but not used. The state charged the bank president with criminal violation of a state law that prohibited this. The bank president moved to dismiss the case against him on the ground that ERISA preempted all state laws relating to an "employee welfare benefit plan." The question of whether payments for unused vacation time constitutes an employee welfare benefit plan came before the U.S. Supreme Court. The Court noted that **the creation of a separate fund to pay employees vacation benefits would bring the plan under ERISA coverage**. However, the employer here had a policy of paying vacation benefits out of its general assets. Because ERISA had been enacted to prevent mismanagement of accumulated plan funds and to prevent failure to pay benefits from such funds, it did not apply to the situation involved here. The vacation pay owed in this case was fixed, payable from general assets, and not dependent on contingencies outside the employee's control. Accordingly, the criminal action against the bank president was not preempted by ERISA. *Massachusetts v. Morash*, 490 U.S. 107, 109 S.Ct. 1668, 104 L.Ed.2d 98 (1989).

◆   A collection agency obtained money judgments against 25 people who were participants in an employee welfare benefit plan covered by ERISA. The covered workers drew their vacation benefits from the plan annually. The collection agency sought to garnish the debtors' plan benefits to collect the money judgments. A state court allowed the garnishment, but the court of appeals reversed, holding that a Georgia statute barred the garnishment of funds of an employee benefit plan subject to ERISA. The Georgia Supreme Court reversed, deciding that ERISA preempted the Georgia statute. The case reached the U.S. Supreme Court, which first noted that ERISA preempted the state law because it related to a pension plan described under ERISA. It then stated that Congress did not intend to preempt state-law garnishment of ERISA welfare benefit plans even where the purpose was to collect judgments against plan participants. ERISA only placed a ban on alienation or assignment of *pension* benefits. Here, **the vacation benefits could be garnished because they were not part of a pension plan**. The Court affirmed the decision in favor of the collection agency. *Mackey v. Lanier Collections Agency & Service*, 486 U.S. 825, 108 S.Ct. 2182, 100 L.Ed.2d 836 (1988).

◆   A Louisiana employer had a policy that permitted employees to accrue paid days off. Employees received paid days off in lieu of vacation and holidays. A licensed practical nurse resigned and demanded to be paid for her unused vacation time. A state appeals court reversed a decision for the employer, **rejecting its argument that the vacation time was a gratuitous benefit**. Under state law, unused vacation time was a wage due an employee if the employer let employees earn or accrue the time. *Davis v. St. Francisville Country Manor, LLC*, No. 136 So.3d 20 (La. Ct. App. 2013).

◆   A company hired a salesman's son and by letter agreed that the son could take over the father's accounts when the father retired. Before the father retired, the company transferred many of his accounts to other employees. The son took over the remaining accounts after his father retired, but he was later fired and sued for breach of contract, citing the letter agreement referencing taking over his father's accounts. He also **claimed that the employee handbook created an implied contractual obligation to pay him for unused vacation time**. The New York Supreme Court, Appellate Division, held that the company did not have to maintain the father's accounts as they were at the time of the agreement and that the handbook did not create an implied contract to pay unused vacation time because of its disclaimer language stating that it did not create a binding contract. *Martin v. Southern Container Corp.*, 92 A.D.3d 647, 938 N.Y.S.2d 335 (N.Y. App. Div. 2012).

◆   A California employee sued his former employer, claiming that he was owed for an eight-week sabbatical that he had earned but not taken at the time he resigned. Under the sabbatical policy, salaried employees with seven years of service were eligible for an eight-week fully paid sabbatical. The leave was forfeited if the employee did not use it before employment terminated. **The employee claimed that the sabbatical was just extra vacation time for long-term employees and that the company couldn't make him forfeit vested vacation pay.** A state court granted pretrial judgment to the company. However, the Court of Appeal reversed, finding issues of fact that required a trial. The Department of Labor Standards and Enforcement rule regarding sabbaticals noted that sabbaticals should: 1) be granted infrequently, 2) be long enough to achieve the employer's purpose, 3) be granted in addition to regular vacation, and 4) incorporate some feature demonstrating that the employee will return to work after the sabbatical is over. The court remanded the case for further proceedings. *Paton v. Advanced Micro Devices, Inc.*, 129 Cal.Rptr.3d 784 (Cal. Ct. App. 2011).

◆   A dental hygienist in West Virginia left her job and sought to be paid for unused, accrued vacation time. She filed a Request for Assistance form with the Wage and Hour Section of the Division of Labor. Indicating that the dentist had no written paid leave policy, she alleged that he failed to pay her $1,472 for unused paid leave (representing the 64 hours shown on her final pay stub multiplied by her regular rate of pay of $23 per hour). A compliance officer determined that she was owed 40 hours of vacation pay. The dentist asserted that she was owed only 4.2 hours but eventually issued a check for $920 to close the matter. However, the hygienist claimed that he still owed her liquidated damages for failing to comply with the law. The case reached the Supreme Court of Appeals of West Virginia, which ruled that she was entitled to only 4.2 hours of unused, accrued vacation pay. However, **the dentist had violated the wage and hour act by failing to provide accurate information regarding how much vacation time she was due.** The court ordered the dentist to pay the settlement amount in order to dismiss the action. *Isaacs v. Bonner*, 225 W.Va. 460, 694 S.E.2d 302 (W.Va. 2010).

◆   A Minnesota clinic employed a dialysis patient care technician and issued her a copy of the employee handbook, which explained the Paid Time Off (PTO) policy. The handbook also provided that an employee who resigned would be paid for earned but unused paid time off if she gave proper notice, but specified that an employee who resigned without giving proper notice or who was terminated for misconduct would not be eligible for payment of earned but unused PTO. The clinic fired the technician for a "pattern of behavior" that resulted in "performance and patient safety issues." She sued the clinic to recover her unused vacation time, alleging that she had 181 hours of PTO worth over $3,000. The case reached the Minnesota Supreme Court, which noted that the handbook constituted a valid contract between the clinic and the technician. **The clinic could set conditions that the technician would have to meet to become eligible for paid vacation** because nothing in state law mandated the terms on which PTO must be offered, or that it be offered at all. The clinic's decision not to offer the benefit of payment in lieu of paid time off to employees terminated for misconduct did not violate state law. *Lee v. Fresenius Medical Care, Inc.*, 741 N.W.2d 117 (Minn. 2007).

◆   Two Indiana employers published handbooks that contained policies regarding the payment of vacation time upon termination of employment. The handbooks did not constitute a contract. Two employees were involuntarily terminated by the employers. Both employees had accrued vacation time prior to termination, and both employers refused to pay the employees for the unused vacation time. The question that arose before the Court of Appeals of Indiana was whether, as a matter of law, the non-contractual published policies in the employee handbooks relieved the employers of any obligation to pay the employees for the accrued, but unused, vacation time. The court held that **the handbooks properly relieved the employers of the obligation to pay the unused vacation time**. The problem for the employees was that they were claiming they were entitled to accrued vacation pay granted by the handbooks while at the same time repudiating the terms of the handbooks that took away their right to the pay. *Mitchell v. Universal Solutions of North Carolina, Inc.*, 853 N.E.2d 953 (Ind. Ct. App. 2006).

◆   A Louisiana long-term acute care hospital maintained a written employment policy calling for the forfeiture of all accrued benefits when an employee abandoned a position. A licensed practical nurse employed by the hospital twice threatened to leave work but was reminded by the hospital's director of nursing that quitting without notice violated company policy. She later walked off the job without notice, and her employment was deemed terminated by the hospital. It confiscated her accrued vacation pay in compliance with hospital policy. She sued, asserting violations of state wage law. The case reached the Supreme Court of Louisiana, which noted that **the employee's accrued vacation pay constituted "wages" under state law**. Quitting a job abruptly without notice to the employer does not justify the withholding of earned wages. The court also stated that the employer's reliance on an unlawful company policy did not provide it with a good-faith defense to the imposition of penalty wages. *Beard v. Summit Institute of Pulmonary Medicine and Rehabilitation*, 707 So.2d 1233 (La. 1998).

◆   To reduce its work force size, a Missouri employer offered a severance package to employees who accepted voluntary retirement or separation. Acceptance of the severance benefits required separation on the last day of the current fiscal year – the date when earned vacation benefits ordinarily became available for use during the following year. Employees accepting severance benefits were required to waive all claims against the employer. A number of employees who accepted benefits claimed that they were entitled to the vacation benefits that had vested on the day they accepted the severance packages. After they sued the employer to recover vacation benefits, a federal court ruled for the employer. The Eighth Circuit affirmed. **The severance waiver barred the claims against the employer**, since the waiver encompassed any claim related to employment. *Mange v. Petrolite Corp.*, 135 F.3d 570 (8th Cir. 1998).

B. Sick Leave Benefits

Many of the issues that arise with respect to sick leave are issues that also arise under the *Family and Medical Leave Act* (FMLA). Although leave under the FMLA is unpaid, employees can request (and employers can require) that paid leave run concurrently with FMLA leave. For cases involving the FMLA, please see Chapter Six, Section V.

◆   An Indiana not-for-profit penal facility hired a corrections officer as an at-will employee making $9.25 an hour. Its handbook provided that after 90 days, she would be eligible for benefits, including sick time. It also stated that the company did not pay employees for unused sick time upon termination. Moreover, the handbook described the vacation time policy and stated that employees would not be paid for unused vacation time if they were fired or gave less than two weeks' notice. The officer was fired 45 days later and was paid only minimum wage for her final pay period. She sued under the state's Wage Claims Statute, asserting that she was entitled to 7.4 hours of accrued sick pay, 14.76 hours of vacation pay and the difference between $9.25 per hour and $5.15 per hour for her final pay period. The case reached the Court of Appeals of Indiana, which held that she was entitled to the difference between her agreed-upon salary and minimum wage, but that she was not entitled to her accrued but unused sick pay or vacation. She never met the requirements for vacation pay because she did not work at least 90 days. **As for the sick pay, the handbook clearly limited its use and did not allow it to be converted or otherwise made available to the employee.** Further, even if the sick pay were analogous to vacation pay, she was still not eligible for it because she did not meet the handbook's requirements for eligibility. *Williams v. Riverside Community Corrections Corp.*, 846 N.E.2d 738 (Ind. Ct. App. 2006).

◆   An accountant in Nebraska gave his employer 90 days' notice as required by his contract, stating that he intended to open a competing accounting firm. The company fired him on the spot, not letting him work out the remainder of the 90 days. It also sued him for breach of the non-compete agreement. A trial court ruled that the non-compete agreement was more restrictive than was reasonably necessary to protect the company's rights and was therefore unenforceable. However, the company properly fired the accountant for malfeasance after he gave his 90-day notice. The court also held that the accountant was entitled to 32 hours of unused vacation pay and 72 hours of unused sick leave under the employment handbook. The Nebraska Supreme Court affirmed. The non-compete clause was overly restrictive. And although the accountant was entitled to his earned but unused vacation and sick leave pay as of the day he gave notice, **he was not entitled to the vacation and sick leave he would have accrued during the 90-day notice period**. *Professional Business Services Co. v. Rosno*, 680 N.W.2d 176 (Neb. 2004).

◆   An airline paid employees for sick leave during their own illnesses, but it did not permit the use of sick leave for parental leave. Employees received sick pay at the same time they received their regular pay during the period when leave was taken. The airline denied use of paid sick leave to two Oregon-based employees for parental leave. The employees contended that Oregon's parental leave law required the airline to allow the use of accrued sick leave for this purpose and filed complaints against the airline with the state Bureau of Labor and Industries. The bureau issued cease and desist orders against the airline, and it brought a federal court action against the bureau, seeking declaratory and injunctive relief from the orders. The court granted pretrial judgment to the bureau, and the airline appealed to the U.S. Court of Appeals, Ninth Circuit.

The airline argued that the state law claims were preempted by ERISA, but the court noted that **ERISA regulations exempt certain payments as payroll practices** where the compensation is normal, paid out of an employer's general assets and payable on account of time during which the employee is physically or mentally unable to perform job duties. The sick leave payments in this case satisfied these elements. The compensation system utilized by the employer had the characteristics of an unfunded payment, rather than an ERISA trust fund payment. The sick pay plan was not subject to ERISA preemption, and the court affirmed the district court judgment. *Alaska Airlines, Inc. v. Oregon Bureau of Labor*, 122 F.3d 812 (9th Cir. 1997).

◆   A Utah bank required employees to sign an agreement that called for them to submit written requests for sick leave. One department manager announced a no-leave policy during the bank's acquisition of another bank and conversion to a new computer system. The manager repeatedly denied an employee's request for a full day off to have a lump removed from her lip. After four months, she was allowed a day off. She was diagnosed with an aggressive malignant melanoma. She sued for breach of contract and breach of an implied covenant of good faith and fair dealing. The court granted the bank's motion for pretrial judgment, finding no employment contract between the parties. The Court of Appeals of Utah observed that even though the employment relationship was at will, there was still an employment contract. And the at-will relationship did not negate the sick leave contract between the parties. The court remanded the case for a determination of **whether the bank had breached the contract by denying permission to use sick leave** and whether it had acted unreasonably and in violation of its obligation of good faith and fair dealing. *Cook v. Zions First National Bank*, 919 P.2d 56 (Utah App. 1996).

◆   An Illinois hospital employee with 20 years of experience was fired for taking a $25 gift certificate a few weeks before they were scheduled to be given out to employees. Because the employee was qualified to participate in the hospital pension plan, she requested her pension benefits on the same day she was fired. However, the hospital denied her request for payment of accumulated unused sick days, stating that she had been fired and had not retired. The employee filed a lawsuit against the hospital in an Illinois circuit court, which granted the hospital's pretrial judgment motion. On appeal, the Appellate Court of Illinois observed that the hospital's employee handbook stated that employees who retired became immediately eligible to receive payment for their unused sick time. **The handbook was sufficiently definite to create a binding contract to pay for sick time** and failed to distinguish between voluntary retirement and retirement caused by firing. The employee was over 55 years of age and had five years of service, which were the only requirements for payment of accrued sick time. The employee was entitled to an award of over $9,000 plus interest. *Dow v. Columbus-Cabrini Medical Center*, 655 N.E.2d 1 (Ill. App. Ct. 1995).

CHAPTER FIVE

Labor Relations

I. WAGE AND HOUR LAWS

The Fair Labor Standards Act of 1938 (FLSA), 29 U.S.C. § 201 *et seq.*, is a comprehensive federal statute that mandates the payment of <u>minimum wage</u> and <u>overtime</u> compensation to covered employees.

States have laws that are similar to the FLSA. Most employees are covered under these laws, but there are some exceptions (such as disabled workers, full-time students and tipped employees, among others).

The FLSA prohibits employment of any covered employee in excess of 40 hours per week unless the employee is paid at least time-and-a-half. The FLSA also requires employers to pay at least the minimum wage ($7.25 per hour as of July 24, 2009).

State laws generally provide similar requirements, though the minimum wage may be slightly higher or lower. If your state's minimum wage requirement is higher than that of the FLSA, you will have to comply with the higher state minimum wage requirement.

A. The Fair Labor Standards Act (FLSA)

The FLSA applies where there is an employer/employee relationship (it does not apply to independent contractors). Although the FLSA sets minimum wage and overtime requirements, it does not require employers to provide sick leave, vacation time, holiday pay or severance pay.

The FLSA is enforced by the Wage and Hour Division of the federal Department of Labor, which conducts investigations, usually in response to complaints by employees or former employees. It is a violation of the FLSA to <u>retaliate</u> against an employee for making a complaint or participating in an investigation (or other legal proceeding) under the FLSA.

If an employer is found to have violated the minimum wage or overtime provisions of the FLSA:

1) the Wage and Hour Division may supervise the payment of back wages
2) the Secretary of Labor may sue for back wages and an equal amount as liquidated damages
3) the employee may sue for back pay, liquidated damages, attorneys' fees and costs, or
4) the Secretary of Labor may obtain an injunction against the employer.

1. Supreme Court Cases

♦ A Nevada employer subjected hourly warehouse workers to security checks at the end of their workdays. Two of the employees sued, claiming they were entitled to be paid for the time it took to go through the checks, which lasted up to 25 minutes. The U.S. Supreme Court held that **the time the employees spent waiting to undergo and undergoing the checks was not compensable under the FLSA**. The screenings were not the principal activities the employees were hired to perform, and the screenings were not integral and indispensable to those activities. *Integrity Staffing Solutions v. Busk*, 135 S.Ct. 513 (U.S. 2014).

♦ A group of Indiana steelworkers claimed their employer violated the FLSA by failing to pay them for the time they spent donning and doffing protective gear. The steelworkers' union contract excluded time spent "changing clothes" from their paid time, but they claimed the protective gear was not clothing. The U.S. Supreme Court rejected their claim. It said that **for steelworkers, "clothes" under the FLSA includes protective gear**. *Sandifer v. United States Steel Corp.*, 134 S.Ct. 870 (U.S. 2014).

♦ A registered nurse claimed that her former employer violated the FLSA by deducting time for meal breaks even when employees worked during them. She sought damages for herself and other similarly situated individuals. Before any similarly situated workers joined the suit, the employer offered to settle by paying her an amount that was equal to the total value of her individual claim. She did not respond to the offer. The employer then filed a dismissal motion, arguing that the case was moot. A federal appeals court said the worker's collective action was not moot, but the Supreme Court reversed. **The collective action claims were not a matter in controversy**, the Court decided. *Genesis Health Care Corp. v. Symczyk*, 133 S.Ct. 1523 (U.S. 2013).

♦ Two pharmaceutical sales reps sued their employer for overtime, claiming that they didn't meet the FLSA's "outside sales" exemption because they were primarily engaged in promoting the company's products and did not finalize any sales. An Arizona federal court rejected their argument, and the Ninth Circuit affirmed. The U.S. Supreme Court also affirmed. It rejected the Department of Labor's position that the pharmaceutical sales reps didn't fall under the FLSA's outside salesmen exemption. **The sales reps here didn't technically sell the drugs** because the law prohibits them from doing so. However, they earned high salaries and worked with minimal supervision, setting them apart from hourly workers. They were not entitled to overtime. *Christopher v. SmithKline Beecham Corp.*, 132 S.Ct. 2156, 183 L.Ed.2d 153 (U.S. 2012).

♦ An employee in Wisconsin complained verbally but not in writing that the placement of time clocks in the worksite violated the FLSA because it prevented employees from being paid for donning and doffing protective gear. After he was fired, he sued the company for retaliation in violation of the FLSA. The case reached the Supreme Court, which ruled that **the anti-retaliation**

provision of the FLSA protects oral as well as written complaints under the act. The Secretary of Labor has consistently held the view that "complaints" include both oral and written ones, and the Secretary's views are entitled to deference. *Kasten v. Saint-Gobain Performance Plastics Corp.*, 131 S.Ct. 1325, 179 L.Ed.2d 379 (U.S. 2011).

♦   The FLSA was amended in 1974 to exempt from minimum wage and maximum hours rules persons "employed in domestic service employment to provide companionship services for individuals ... unable to care for themselves." A Department of Labor regulation includes in the exemption companionship workers employed by an agency other than the family or household using the services. A domestic worker in New York who provided companionship services sued her former employer (a third-party agency) for minimum and overtime wages. The case reached the U.S. Supreme Court, which held that the third-party regulation was valid and binding, meaning **the worker was not entitled to minimum or overtime wages**. *Long Island Care at Home, Ltd. v. Coke*, 551 U.S. 158, 127 S.Ct. 2339, 168 L.Ed.2d 54 (2007).

♦   Employees of meat and poultry processing plants in Washington and Maine brought class action lawsuits against the plants' owner, alleging FLSA violations. They asserted that the company owed them for the time they spent waiting to change into and out of required specialized clothing and safety gear, and that it owed them for the time it took to walk between the locker room and the production floor. The case reached the U.S. Supreme Court, which determined that **the time spent walking between the locker room and the production floor was compensable**. The Portal-to-Portal Act does not exclude such time from the FLSA's coverage. Further, the time spent waiting to doff the protective gear was covered by the FLSA. However, the time spent waiting to don the protective gear before the start of each shift was not compensable. Donning and doffing gear that is integral and indispensable to employees' work is a "principal activity" under the Portal-to-Portal Act, but waiting to don the first piece of gear is two steps removed from the productive activity on the assembly line. *IBP, Inc. v. Alvarez*, 546 U.S. 21, 126 S.Ct. 514, 163 L.Ed.2d 288 (2005).

♦   A nonprofit religious organization derived most of its income from the operation of commercial businesses staffed by its "associates." These people, former drug addicts and criminals, received no cash salaries, but were provided with food, clothing, shelter and other benefits. The Secretary of Labor sued the organization and its officers for violating the FLSA. An Arkansas federal court held that the organization was an "enterprise" within the meaning of the FLSA, and that the associates were employees protected by the FLSA. The case reached the U.S. Supreme Court, which affirmed, noting that the FLSA contained no express or implied exception for commercial activities conducted by religious or other nonprofit organizations. Further, even though the associates claimed that they were not employees, they did expect compensation of a sort; thus, **the economic reality was that they were employees under the FLSA**. Finally, the Court held that application of the FLSA did not violate the Free Exercise Clause or the Establishment Clause of the First Amendment. The

FLSA did not require the payment of cash wages, so the employees could still be paid in the form of benefits. Also, they could return any payments made to them if they so wished, and provided it was voluntary, this would not violate the FLSA. Nor did the FLSA's recordkeeping requirements inhibit religious activities undertaken with a business purpose. The FLSA applied to the organization. *Tony & Susan Alamo Foundation v. Secretary of Labor,* 471 U.S. 290, 105 S.Ct. 1953, 85 L.Ed.2d 278 (1985).

2. Exempt Employees

In addition to the students and disabled workers discussed above, there are other exceptions to covered employment. These include executives, bona fide administrative employees and professional employees paid on a salaried basis.

◆   Audit associates for a New York accounting firm sued for overtime under the FLSA. Their jobs involved counting, recording and checking client inventory; reviewing client financial reporting requirements with clients; and itemizing and preparing audit documents. **They claimed they were entitled to overtime** because they did not exercise specialized knowledge or professional discretion. The court disagreed. It found the employees work required advanced knowledge and specialized academic training. The employees were not entitled to overtime. *Pippins v. KPMG LLP*, 759 F.3d 235 (2d Cir. 2014).

◆   Three former employees of a lumberyard in Arkansas claimed that they were improperly classified as exempt from overtime. A lower court ruled for the employees, but a federal appeals court partially reversed. It said **two of the employees did not have hiring and firing authority** and so were not exempt from overtime. However, a third employee did have hiring and firing authority. Therefore, the third employee was exempt. *Madden v. Lumber One Home Center, Inc.*, 745 F.3d 899 (8th Cir. 2014).

◆   A personnel supervisor at a tire manufacturing plant in Virginia sued for overtime after he quit his job. He conceded that he met the salary test for exempt employees and that they customarily and regularly directed two or more other employees. However, he claimed he was entitled to overtime because he was not directly engaged in management. The court disagreed. The employee was accountable for his shift's production. He provided production reports every two hours, and he ran monthly safety drills. In addition, **upper management gave sufficient weight to his input**. The employee was exempt from overtime. *Martin v. Yokohama Tire Corp.*, No. 7:22-CV-00244, 2013 WL 6002344 (W.D. Va. 11/12/13).

◆   An Ohio insurance company classified its special investigators as administrative employees who were not entitled to overtime pay. The special investigators sued to recover overtime pay, claiming they were not exempt from overtime because they did not exercise independent judgment and discretion over significant matter related to their job. The Sixth Circuit appeals court affirmed a ruling against them. Though the special investigators were subject to quality control standards, **they nonetheless exercised independent judgment and discretion** when resolving fraud claims. *Foster v. Nationwide Mutual Insurance Co.*, 710 F.3d 640 (6th Cir. 2013).

♦ A pharmacist was paid a guaranteed salary of more than $1,250 per week based on a 44-hour week. The pharmacist worked 16 to 36 hours beyond 44 hours per week, but the employer classified him as a salaried employee who was exempt from overtime. It compensated him for the extra hours by using a formula that added "premium pay" for the extra hours. The pharmacist earned more than $100,000 annually. When he sued for overtime, he lost. Though he argued that he was entitled to overtime because his guaranteed salary was not reasonably related to his actual earnings, **the reasonable relationship requirement did not apply** because he always made more than $100,000 annually. *Anani v. CVS RX Services, Inc.*, 730 F.3d 146 (2d Cir. 2013).

♦ A staffing firm placed a computer employee with an employer. The firm paid the employee under a plan in which he was not paid for more than eight hours in a day unless he worked more than 11 hours. When he sued for overtime, **the employer argued he was an exempt computer employee because he was always paid an hourly wage well above $27.63**. However, because he was not paid anything for this ninth and tenth hours he did not meet the salary requirement and was not exempt from overtime. *Jones v. Judge Technical Services, Inc.*, No. 11-6910, 2013 WL 5777159 (E.D. Pa. 10/25/13).

♦ Team leaders for a New York food distributor oversaw a team of employees who retrieved products from a warehouse and loaded them onto delivery trucks. The team leaders arrived 30 minutes early to set up, and they stayed after each shift to write up a production report. **When a group of eight team leaders sued for overtime under the FLSA, the company asserted that they were executive employees exempt from overtime.** A federal court and the Second Circuit agreed. The team leaders made $700 a week (more than the $455 required by law), their primary duty involved directing the work of two or more employees, and management gave "particular weight" to their recommendations and suggestions for promoting and firing team members. *Ramos v. Baldor Specialty Foods, Inc.*, 687 F.3d 554 (2d Cir. 2012).

♦ A Dollar Store manager in South Carolina regularly worked more than 40 hours a week. He sued for overtime, **claiming that he was not an exempt "executive" employee because he spent between 75% and 90% of his time doing nonexempt work**. However, a federal court ruled against him, noting that he was responsible at all times for the store's operations, including directing employees and apportioning tasks, deciding how to display merchandise and taking care of inventory. If he failed to perform his managerial duties, the store would not function at all because no one else could perform them. *Gooden v. Dolgencorp., Inc.*, No. 3:10-cv-1059, 2012 WL 1110085 (D.S.C. 4/3/12).

♦ A store manager for Family Dollar Stores in North Carolina brought a lawsuit on behalf of herself and other store managers under the FLSA. She asserted that she was improperly classified as exempt from overtime because she spent 99% of her time doing manual, non-managerial tasks like running the register, stocking shelves and unloading freight. A federal court ruled for the company, and the Fourth Circuit affirmed. It noted that at the same time the manager was performing those routine tasks, she also had to perform the managerial tasks that kept the store operating – checking for theft and thinking about future tasks she needed to perform. **Department of Labor regulations explicitly recognize this multi-tasking as a duty of management.** *In re: Family Dollar FLSA Litigation*, 637 F.3d 508 (4th Cir. 2011).

◆   A New York magazine paid a regional director of sales a salary plus commission. She was responsible for generating sales in the northeastern U.S. and Canada for the magazine's travel and finance sections. After her employment ended, she sued the magazine for overtime, but a federal court ruled that she was an exempt administrative employee and granted pretrial judgment to the magazine. The Second Circuit vacated that ruling, finding that she was not an exempt employee because **her job did not relate directly to management policies or business operations**. Instead, she was a salesperson, making specific sales to individual customers and not developing promotions or policies aimed at increasing sales generally. *Reiseck v. Universal Communications of Miami, Inc.*, 591 F.3d 101 (2d Cir. 2010).

◆   A recruiter (who later became a recruiter manager) for a staffing company in Maryland brought a lawsuit against the company for unpaid overtime. The case became a class action lawsuit, and the company defended itself by asserting that she and all recruiters fit under the administrative exemption of the FLSA because they **performed work directly related to company management or general business operations**, and they also exercised discretion and independent judgment. A federal court agreed with the company and ruled that the class was not entitled to overtime. The recruiters interviewed clients and negotiated pay for the candidates, and also determined which candidates would be the best fit, making decisions about whom to recommend for various jobs. *Andrade v. Aerotek, Inc.*, 700 F.Supp.2d 738 (D. Md. 2010).

◆   A company that made hydraulic power units hired a New York man who had 20 years of mechanical engineering experience – but no college degree – as a product design specialist. It classified the position as exempt from overtime under the "professional" employee exemption of the FLSA and paid him $62,000 a year. After the employee was laid off, he sued for overtime, claiming the company had misclassified him. The Second Circuit agreed that he should have been paid overtime. **A company can't use the "professional exemption" for a position that doesn't meet the FLSA's educational requirements.** The company had to pay overtime going back three years for its willful violation of the FLSA. *Young v. Cooper Cameron Corp.*, 586 F.3d 201 (2d Cir. 2009).

◆   An underwriter at a New York bank evaluated whether individual loans should be approved based on the bank's detailed guidelines. He had some ability to make an exception to the guidelines by applying specific factors. The bank classified him as "administrative" exempt from overtime. When he later sued under the FLSA, asserting that he had been misclassified, a federal court granted pretrial judgment to the bank. However, the Second Circuit reversed. **The underwriter performed day-to-day sales activities that weren't exempt.** He was not performing work directly related to management policies or general business operations. Nor was he exercising discretion and independent judgment. *Davis v. J.P. Morgan Chase & Co.*, 587 F.3d 529 (2d Cir. 2009).

♦   A Florida marketing executive for a title insurance company received a 50% commission on all orders for title insurance from clients. After leaving the company, the executive sued for overtime under the FLSA, **claiming she was not an exempt "outside sales" employee because she didn't close the sales**, but rather referred business to the company, which closed the deals. A federal court and the Eleventh Circuit ruled for the company, noting that her primary duty was to obtain commitments to buy title insurance, she was credited with the sale when the deal closed, and she received income as a result of the orders. It did not matter that the company technically closed and processed the deal separately. *Gregory v. First Title of America*, 555 F.3d 1300 (11th Cir. 2009).

♦   A gaming company in West Virginia employed three racing officials as required by state law. The officials helped secretaries with clerical duties when there wasn't a race. Otherwise, they made sure horses were wearing the proper equipment, ensured that grooms were properly preparing horses, checked the horses' papers and watched races, using a computer system to determine the final outcome, when necessary. After they were fired for posting the wrong finish order, they sued for overtime. The company claimed they were exempt administrative employees because their jobs were required by state law. A federal court ruled for the company, but the Fourth Circuit reversed. Although the officials made at least $455 a week, **their duties were not directly related to the company's general business operations merely because the state required and regulated the racing official position.** *Desmond v. PNGI Charles Town Gaming, LLC*, 564 F.3d 688 (4th Cir. 2009).

♦   An Ohio gas and convenience store manager, who was expected to work 50 hours a week, received a salary of $522 per week, with a bonus of up to 5% of the store's gross profit margin on the sale of certain products, up to $2,500 per month. She spent 60% of her time performing nonmanagerial tasks like stocking shelves, cleaning restrooms and operating the cash register. She also hired employees, trained them, set schedules, wrote formal evaluations and frequently recommended terminations to her district manager. After she was fired, she sued for overtime under the FLSA, claiming she was not exempt as a bona fide executive employee. A federal court and the Sixth Circuit ruled against her. **Even though she spent 60% of her time performing nonexempt tasks, she exercised discretion every day**; her district manager adopted a largely hands-off approach; and her "primary" duties were those inherent to the management of the business. *Thomas v. Speedway SuperAmerica*, 506 F.3d 496 (6th Cir. 2007).

◆   After a merger, a company in Maine assigned a salesman accounts with chronic service problems. Although those accounts would not generate new sales opportunities, the salesman was still required to handle their service requests. As a result, he spent 70% of his time in the office receiving customer calls instead of out in the field generating new sales. When the company quintupled his sales quota, then fired him, he sued for unpaid overtime under the FLSA and the Maine Prompt Pay Act. A federal court and the First Circuit ruled against him. **Even though the Prompt Pay Act allows commissioned salespeople to earn overtime where their employer exerts substantial control over hours and work location, the company here did not do so.** It merely required the salesman to answer customers' service calls without detailing how that should be done. *Palmieri v. Nynex Long Distance Co., d/b/a Verizon Enterprise Solutions*, 437 F.3d 111 (1st Cir. 2006).

3. Commuting, Breaks and Other 'Time' Issues

On-call time is considered to be working time if the employee is sufficiently restricted in the ability to pursue nonwork activities. In other words, if the employee is called often and required to give repeated assistance, she is probably going to have to be paid for such on-call time.

Break time is not compensable under the FLSA if the employee has no job responsibilities during the break. If the employee is expected to help out during a break (for example, where a store or restaurant is extremely busy), then the break time is compensable under the FLSA.

◆   A foreman for a plumbing subcontractor in Connecticut sued under state law to be paid for the time he spent commuting to work in a company pick-up truck and for other time. A trial court awarded him $641.44 for time spent stopping at the company warehouse after work to pick up tools for the next day. It also said he was not owed time for cleaning the truck, even though he said he had to stay after work to do so, because the employer gave him time during the day to clean the truck. It further decided that **the claim relating to commuting time was preempted** by the FLSA and he was not entitled to pay for the time. On appeal, the trial court's ruling was affirmed. *Sarrazin v. Coastal, Inc.*, 89 A.3d 841 (Conn. 2014).

◆   Three Pennsylvania employees claimed they were entitled to time spent before and after their shifts donning and doffing gear and providing shift relief. During their shifts, the employees were paid for one to three 30-minute meal breaks. The court said **the employer could use the paid meal breaks to offset unpaid pre- and post-shift work**. The breaks did not need to be considered hours worked because there was no evidence they benefited the employer. *Smiley v. E.I. du Pont de Nemours and Co.*, No. 12-cv-2380, 2014 WL 5762954 (M.D. Pa. 11/5/14).

◆   Florida delivery drivers sued to be paid for on-call time. The employer argued that the drivers weren't entitled to FLSA protection because the business did not make enough money and was not involved in interstate commerce. The court held that **the drivers were covered because they regularly and directly participated in the movement of persons or things in interstate commerce**. The case could proceed. *Gregory v. Quality Removal, Inc.*, No. 14-21480, 2014 WL 549448 (S.D. Fla. 10/30/14).

◆   A technician who was paid for commutes to customer homes only if the commute exceeded 35 minutes claimed that a supervisor instructed him to underreport commute times so the employer could pay him less. **In one instance, he reported taking 15 minutes to drive 100 miles.** When he sued for overtime, the court decided that although the 35-minute rule was permissible, a question was present as to whether the supervisor in fact pressured the employee to underreport his commute times. The court denied the employer's motion for pretrial judgment. *Arnett v. Sears, Roebuck and Co.*, No. SA-12-CA-488, 2013 WL 3324070 (W.D. Tex. 7/1/13).

◆   A Black & Decker (B&D) employee in New York had to visit Home Depot stores to check stock of B&D products. He also had to do in-home paperwork, such as reviewing sales reports and checking emails before and after visiting stores. He was paid for the work he did at home, which added up to 30 or more minutes a day, and he also received payment for any part of his commute that exceeded 60 miles each way. When he sought to be paid for all his commuting time, a federal court and the Second Circuit ruled against him. **The FLSA's "continuous workday" rule didn't apply to his at-home work** because he didn't have to do the work immediately before and after his store duties. The rule requires an employer to pay for all time between the first task that's "integral and indispensable" to the employee's principal activity and the last task that's "integral and indispensable" to that activity. The at-home work here didn't fall into that category. *Kuebel v. Black & Decker, Inc.*, 643 F.3d 352 (2d Cir. 2011).

◆   An employee at a Tennessee food plant sued to get paid for the time she and her fellow workers spent donning and doffing uniforms and equipment. However, the Sixth Circuit ruled against her, noting that before it became unionized, the plant had a policy of not paying employees for that activity. Also, when the union negotiated a bargaining agreement, that issue never came up, so the contract was silent on the matter. Thus, under Section 203(o) of the FLSA, the plant didn't have to pay for the changing of clothes. But the court said that **the plant might have to pay for the time employees spent walking to and from the time clock to change in and out of their work clothes**. The court remanded the case for a determination of whether that time was negligible. *Franklin v. Kellogg Co.*, 619 F.3d 604 (6th Cir. 2010).

◆   A technician for Lojack – a company that installs tracking devices on vehicles so police can locate them if stolen – used a company car to commute from his house to customers' locations. He could not use the car for personal errands. He also was not paid for his commute. When he sued the company for lost overtime under the FLSA and the Employee Commuting Flexibility Act, a California federal court and the Ninth Circuit U.S. Court of Appeals ruled against him, noting that **his commute was not compensable even though he was required to drive a company car**. However, he might be able to make a claim for the time he spent at the end of every day transmitting information about the work he performed from a portable data terminal to the company. This task took him about 15 minutes every day (more than an hour a week) and was for the benefit of the company. *Rutti v. Lojack Corp.*, 596 F.3d 1046 (9th Cir. 2010).

◆   Maintenance workers for a Wisconsin paper mill regularly showered after each shift and sought to be paid for that activity under the FLSA. The mill asserted that it had a policy in place by which it paid employees to immediately shower and change clothes if they became exposed to a hazardous chemical while working, and that it shouldn't have to pay for showers at the end of the day for workers not exposed to the hazardous chemical. The case reached the Seventh Circuit, which ruled that **the mill did not have to pay for the daily showers by the workers** because they failed to show that the showers were an integral and indispensable part of their job. Workers who discovered they'd been exposed to the chemical after their shifts could seek compensation under the mill's policy for extra time spent showering and changing. *Musch v. Domtar Industries, Inc.*, 587 F.3d 857 (7th Cir. 2009).

◆   A Maryland nonprofit corporation operated community living facilities for disabled residents and employed community living assistants (CLAs) to check on the residents every two hours around the clock. A Department of Labor (DOL) investigator determined that the weekend CLAs, who worked 48 hours straight over the weekend, but were only paid for 40 hours, were entitled to be paid for their full shifts (as well as overtime). **The unpaid four-hour break periods the CLAs received each day amounted to work because the CLAs could not leave the premises during the breaks, and their breaks were frequently interrupted.** A federal court and the Fourth Circuit agreed with the DOL that the CLAs were entitled to be paid for the break time as well as for overtime. However, since the violation of the FLSA was not willful, the company's liability reached back only two years instead of three. Damages were assessed at $527,900. *Chao v. Self Pride, Inc.*, 232 Fed.Appx. 280 (4th Cir. 2007).

◆   A company that drilled and serviced oil and gas wells in New Mexico distributed a travel policy informing employees that it did not require them to travel to the drilling rigs with their crew supervisors. However, as a practical matter, employees met their foremen at a convenience store near company headquarters, then drove together to the drilling rigs. Bad roads, limited parking, permits and gate keys, as well as pressure on foremen to arrive with a full crew drove the decision to commute together. **When a group of employees brought a collective action under the FLSA to be paid for their travel time, the Tenth Circuit ruled against them.** The Portal-to-Portal Act (which states that the FLSA does not require employers to compensate an employee for time spent traveling to or from work) barred the employees' claims. *Smith v. Aztec Well Servicing Co.*, 462 F.3d 1274 (10th Cir. 2006).

✦   A Michigan company paid all its employees, whether salaried or hourly, under a single payroll system. Because some salaried employees worked 36 hours one week and 48 hours the next, the company told them to report 40 hours in the weeks they worked 36. This would ensure that they received 1/26th of their annual salary biweekly. When some exempt employees accidentally underreported their hours, they were underpaid. They sued under the FLSA, claiming they had been misclassified as exempt. A federal court and the Sixth Circuit disagreed. **The company allowed them to report hours in excess of what they worked to generate their full pay for each biweekly period.** Even though the company paid the employees on an hourly basis, they were still salaried employees. *Acs v. Detroit Edison Co.*, 444 F.3d 763 (6th Cir. 2006).

4. Retaliation

Retaliation is illegal under the FLSA. Several circuit courts have held that even informal complaints under the FLSA are protected. However, mere disagreements about whether a job is exempt do not amount to protected activity under the statute.

✦   A Virginia employee told the company's chief operating officer (COO) that she believed her supervisor was violating the FLSA because he deliberately changed time sheets to remove any overtime employees worked. The COO told her he would look into her complaint. Six days later, she was fired for having too many conflicts with her supervisor. She sued the company for violating the FLSA. A federal court dismissed her lawsuit, but the Fourth Circuit reversed and allowed the case to proceed. **Her internal complaint was sufficiently clear and detailed for the company to understand it**, and she was asserting her rights under the FLSA and asking for protection. As a result, a trial would have to determine whether she was fired for improper reasons. *Minor v. Bostwick Laboratory, Inc.*, 669 F.3d 428 (4th Cir. 2012).

✦   A Virginia employee sued her former employer for overtime under the FLSA. Around that same time, she applied for a job with another company. The second company offered her a job contingent on passing a drug test and verifying and transferring her security clearance. However, the company later withdrew the offer. She believed it did so because of her lawsuit against her prior employer for overtime, and she sued the second company for retaliation under the FLSA. A federal court dismissed the case, and the Fourth Circuit affirmed. The court of appeals held that **the FLSA doesn't prohibit prospective employers from refusing to hire someone because she sued a former employer under the act**. The FLSA only authorizes "employees" to sue for retaliation. *Dellinger v. Science Applications Int'l Corp.*, 649 F.3d 226 (4th Cir. 2011).

✦   A Florida employee complained on Facebook about her employer's payment practices – in particular, overtime wages. The company fired her and she sued it under the FLSA. A federal court held that **her Facebook posting was not the same thing as a complaint to the employer**. Therefore, even if she was fired in retaliation for her posting, that action didn't violate the FLSA.

She couldn't prevail in her lawsuit. *Morse v. JP Morgan Chase & Co.*, No. 8:11-CV-779 (M.D. Fla. 6/23/11).

◆   A Missouri CEO asked an employee to perform work that two other employees had performed in the past. He also asked her not to record overtime. She claimed she needed to work overtime to get the work done. When she recorded the overtime, she was paid for it. But he again asked her not to record overtime, and she did it again. After paying overtime again, the CEO fired her. She sued for retaliation under the FLSA, but she lost when the Eighth Circuit noted that she had not filed a "complaint" under the law. **Her informal complaint to the CEO wasn't protected activity.** Moreover, her recording of overtime could be deemed insubordination. *Ritchie v. St. Louis Jewish Light*, 630 F.3d 713 (8th Cir. 2011).

◆   A satellite dish company in Texas decided to change its technicians' schedules to eliminate overlapping time. It went from two four-day shifts of 10 hours to a four-day shift and a three-day shift of 12 hours. Under the old schedule, technicians earned a considerable amount of overtime pay. A manager believed that under the new schedule, technicians would earn less overtime even though he was assured that that was not the case. He was told to assure subordinates about the positive features of the change. Instead, he told them it would likely lead to less overtime and that they should find out from an HR manager. When he was then fired for poor performance and insubordination, he sued under the FLSA, asserting retaliation for protected activity. A federal court and the Fifth Circuit ruled against him, noting that **his personal objections to the new schedule did not amount to protected activity**. And asking the HR manager to answer his subordinates' questions about the schedule did not amount to protected activity either. *Hagan v. Echostar Satellite, L.L.C.*, 529 F.3d 617 (5th Cir. 2008).

5. Recordkeeping

In addition to minimum wage and overtime requirements, the FLSA has certain basic recordkeeping requirements. The basic information that must be kept is:

1) Employee's full name and Social Security number
2) Address, including zip code
3) Birth date, if younger than 19
4) Sex and occupation
5) Time and day of week when employee's workweek begins
6) Hours worked each day
7) Total hours worked each workweek
8) Basis on which employee's wages are paid (hourly, weekly, piecework)
9) Regular hourly pay rate
10) Total daily or weekly straight-time earnings
11) Total overtime earnings for the workweek
12) All additions to or deductions from the employee's wages

    13) Total wages paid each pay period

    14) Date of payment and the pay period covered by the payment

◆   A housekeeper who had worked for a small hotel in South Dakota claimed that she was entitled to overtime for a three-month period. Near the end of her employment, during that three-month period, her time cards went missing. She filed a claim under the FLSA. Later, **time cards were found and they appeared to indicate that her hours worked were greater than what she was paid for**. However, they were not stamped by the time clock or initialed by a manager as all the other time cards were. In the lawsuit that followed, a federal court held that a jury would have to decide whether the time cards were accurate and whether the employee had actually worked the hours she indicated she had. The company could present the pay stubs from that three-month period to indicate the true hours worked, and a jury would determine the truth. *Mendoza v. Addar, Inc.*, No. 10-4077-KES, 2012 WL 1665425 (D.S.D. 5/11/12).

◆   After being demoted from a supervisor to a security guard, a security company employee sued for overtime under the FLSA. Eventually the case came down to overtime wages for a single day. **A company representative admitted that the company didn't pay overtime to the employee on that day**, but company records showed that he wasn't scheduled to work that day. An Alabama federal court held that the company violated the FLSA, and a jury awarded the employee $1,100 in overtime, which the court doubled to $2,200. However, the Eleventh Circuit reversed, noting that there was an issue of fact that should have been decided by a jury – namely, whether the employee had actually worked on that day. *Jarmon v. Vinson Guard Services, Inc.*, 488 Fed.Appx. 454 (11th Cir. 2012).

◆   A cashier at an Indiana store was promoted to assistant manager. After the store manager was fired, she took on some of the manager's responsibilities while remaining an hourly employee. She was promoted to manager, after which she requested a transfer. The following month she was fired. She then sued for overtime under the FLSA. A federal court noted that she couldn't specifically identify the hours or even days she worked overtime without pay. The court granted pretrial judgment to the store. However, the Seventh Circuit reversed, noting that **when an employer fails to keep proper records required by the FLSA, an employee can still proceed with her claim**. Here, although employees submitted accurate time sheets, the company could and apparently did use a computer to alter the hours employees said they worked. The store even showed the manager clocking out before closing time on several occasions even though she was the only employee who could lock up. *Brown v. Family Dollar Stores of Indiana, LP*, 534 F.3d 593 (7th Cir. 2008).

◆   After a Texas husband and wife were fired, they sued their former employer under the FLSA, asserting that they were entitled to unpaid wages. They put together records documenting their hours worked. The employer submitted her own records, which were not fully complete. Nevertheless, the court used the employer's records because **the employees' records were a reconstruction**

after the fact and were insufficient to allow a "just and reasonable inference" of hours worked. Also, witness testimony supported the employer's version. The Fifth Circuit U.S. Court of Appeals ruled that the employer's records had properly been used to determine hours worked. *Rosales v. Lore*, 149 Fed.Appx. 245 (5th Cir. 2005).

◆   A husband and wife took a job with a Virginia storage facility. They lived on the premises and agreed to be paid for 40 hours a week each as a reasonable estimate of the time they would have to work. If unusual circumstances caused them to exceed a 40-hour week, they were supposed to notify the owner within 24 hours. They submitted only one such notification and were paid accordingly. Four years later they were fired. They sued under the FLSA, seeking overtime for many other weeks, but a federal court and the Fourth Circuit ruled against them. The agreement they had signed was reasonable under 29 CFR § 785.23 – a regulation applying to situations where employees reside on the owner's premises – and they chose not to adhere to it. *Garofolo v. Donald B. Heslep Associates, Inc.*, 405 F.3d 194 (4th Cir. 2005).

6.   Other FLSA Issues

◆   Part-time sales assistants for a Texas homebuilder sued the employer for unpaid wages and overtime under the FLSA. The court said the employees could take their overtime claims to trial **even though they never told the employer they were working unreported overtime** because there was a question about whether the employer knew they were working the time. *Carman v. Meritage Homes Corp.*, No. 4:11-CV-1824, 2014 WL 808257 (S.D. Tex. 2/28/14).

◆   When she was hired, a clerk agreed in writing to arbitrate any future disputes between her and the employer. She later filed a class action against the employer, claiming she was wrongfully classified as exempt from overtime. The court decided that the FLSA does not bar the waiver of class action claims, and it concluded that the agreement to arbitrate was valid. **The potentially prohibitive cost of pursuing a claim individually was not a good reason to invalidate the arbitration agreement.** *Sutherland v. Ernst & Young LLP*, 726 F.3d 290 (2d Cir. 2013).

◆   Cable technicians filed a collective action against their employer, asserting violations of FLSA requirements relating to overtime and minimum wages. The employer argued that the technicians' claims failed because they were independent contractors, but the Eleventh Circuit decided that **there were factual issues present as to the question of whether the technicians were employees** under the FLSA. There was evidence that the employer exercised significant control over the technicians; that the technicians' opportunity for loss and profit was limited; and that the services performed by the technicians were integral to the employer's business. *Scantland v. Jeffry Knight, Inc.*, 721 F.3d 1308 (11th Cir. 2013).

◆   Supermarket employees filed a collective action against their employing entity and its owner, asserting FLSA violations relating to overtime. A court awarded damages, after which the entity defaulted. When **the employees then asked the court to hold the owner personally liable**, the Second Circuit determined the owner could be held liable because he exercised functional control over the company's daily operations. *Irizarry v. Catsimatidis*, 722 F.3d. 99 (2d Cir. 2013).

◆   Two employees of a Florida installer of shutters sued their employer for unpaid overtime. They also sued the company CEO and two directors in their individual capacities. A jury found in favor of the employees, and damages were awarded. The two directors appealed, but the Eleventh Circuit ruled against them. First, it decided that **even if one of the workers was in the country illegally, he was still due overtime** because undocumented workers are "employees" under the FLSA. It further held that the directors could be personally liable under the FLSA based on their ownership interest in the company and the degree to which they controlled its day-to-day operations. *Lamonica v. Safe Hurricane Shutters, Inc.*, 711 F.3d 1299 (11th Cir. 2013).

◆   A helper at a New York bakery typically worked more than 60 hours over a six-day workweek. When she was terminated, she sued for minimum wages and overtime under the FLSA. The bakery offered its tax returns to support its argument that it did not gross enough ($500,000) annually to be covered by the statute. However, **the helper offered a sworn statement indicating that the bakery grossed at least $2,000 daily and was open every day**. Thus, a jury could conclude that the earnings threshold was met. *Lin v. Yeh's Bakery, Inc.*, No. 12-cv-2146, 2013 WL 867436 (E.D.N.Y. 3/7/13).

◆   DHL, a national shipping company, contracted with an Alabama staffing firm to provide it with drivers. One of the drivers sued DHL for overtime on behalf of himself and 49 others. **DHL asserted that it couldn't be liable under the FLSA because it wasn't the drivers' employer** for purposes of the act. The case reached the Eleventh Circuit Court of Appeals, which noted that DHL didn't involve itself with the specifics of how its contracted-for goals were met. Further, it bore no financial responsibility for the drivers. The staffing firm handled all the details and paid the drivers, who could deliver packages for companies other than DHL. Accordingly, DHL was not liable for overtime. *Layton v. DHL Express (USA), Inc.*, 686 F.3d 1172 (11th Cir. 2012).

◆   Wal-Mart locked its doors when crews stayed after hours to clean its stores. It contracted with outside companies for cleaning services. Some companies brought in illegal workers, who eventually sued under RICO and the FLSA, **claiming they were falsely imprisoned by the lock-ins** and that Wal-Mart knew they were illegal aliens because of its policy of cleaning stores "on the cheap." The case reached the Third Circuit, which ruled against the workers. They showed up for work knowing the stores would be locked, so they couldn't claim they were falsely imprisoned under the FLSA. Also, the stores had functioning emergency exits that they chose not to use out of fear of being fired or an alarm going off. Finally, there was no evidence that Wal-Mart helped them enter or remain in the country illegally, so the RICO claim couldn't succeed. *Zavala v. Wal-Mart Stores, Inc.*, 691 F.3d 527 (3d Cir. 2012).

♦   An Indiana manager routinely showed up for work before the start of her shift and performed small tasks to prepare for the day, but she never informed the company's two owners that she did so. After she quit, she sued for overtime under the FLSA. The company argued that she wasn't entitled to overtime, and the Seventh Circuit agreed. Although she spent between 10 and 40 minutes preparing the workplace for her employees, the company's owners had no reason to know that she was voluntarily doing this in violation of their business policy, which **required prior approval before working overtime**. *Kellar v. Summit Seating, Inc.*, 664 F.3d 169 (7th Cir. 2011).

♦   A real estate appraiser in Illinois worked for a firm that classified her as administrative exempt so it would not have to pay her overtime. After it fired her, she sued under the FLSA, alleging that she had been improperly classified as exempt and seeking overtime for almost 1,500 hours. A federal court agreed that she had been misclassified and that the firm had acted in bad faith. However, it allowed the firm to calculate her overtime using the fluctuating work week method. Under that method, her hourly pay varied each week even though her salary remained the same. And as a result, she received only $12,000 in overtime (which was doubled to $24,000 for the firm's bad faith) instead of $56,000 (doubled to $112,000) under the standard method of determining overtime. When she appealed, **the Seventh Circuit upheld the fluctuating work week methodology as a legitimate means of determining how much overtime she was due**. *Urnikis-Negro v. American Family Property Services*, 616 F.3d 665 (7th Cir. 2010).

♦   A payroll manager for a company operating in Wyoming consulted an attorney about wage and hour laws because of concerns about overtime. Employees worked 12-hour shifts, seven days a week. The company didn't keep track of overtime but instead paid them a set "day rate" for the first eight hours and a set overtime rate for the remaining four hours. The attorney informed her that the company had to pay overtime for each hour in excess of 40 per week, but the company ignored the advice and continued to pay employees the old way. In the lawsuit that later ensued, the U.S. Court of Appeals, Tenth Circuit, said that **the company couldn't use the fact that it had consulted an attorney to prove that it had acted in good faith** under the FLSA. The company disregarded the attorney's advice to pay overtime. Therefore, the lower court properly awarded liquidated damages for the company's willful violation of the FLSA. *Mumby v. Pure Energy Services (USA), Inc.*, 636 F.3d 1266 (10th Cir. 2011).

♦   Landscapers, security technicians and construction workers for six companies claimed they weren't paid minimum wage or overtime as required by the FLSA and sued. The companies asserted that they weren't covered by the FLSA, which applies to employers with at least $500,000 in gross sales and who have employees handling, selling or otherwise working on goods or materials that are moved in or produced for interstate commerce. A Florida federal court found that the employees didn't handle materials produced for interstate commerce because the companies purchased the materials in Florida regardless of where they came from. The Eleventh Circuit reversed. **What mattered was where the materials were produced and if they were moved interstate**, not where they were ultimately purchased. Materials also must have a significant connection to the business to be counted for purposes of the FLSA. The court remanded the case for further action. *Polycarpe v. E&S Landscaping Service, Inc.*, 616 F.3d 1217 (11th Cir. 2010).

◆   Nurses at a California hospital asked to work 12-hour shifts (instead of eight) so they could have more days off. The hospital agreed to the change, but lowered the hourly wages of those nurses who chose to work 12-hour shifts so that they would still earn the same amount per pay period. The hourly wage change was necessary because nurses received overtime pay for work in excess of eight hours a day. A nurse sued the hospital under the FLSA, alleging that the lowering of nurses' wages was an "artifice" designed to avoid the FLSA's overtime requirements. A federal court ruled for the hospital, and the Ninth Circuit affirmed. The 12-hour nurses made more than the minimum wage and made the same amount per pay period as those who continued to work eight-hour days. **The hospital did not have to pay them the same hourly rate as it paid the eight-hour nurses.** *Parth v. Pomona Valley Hospital Medical Center*, 630 F.3d 794 (9th Cir. 2010).

◆   A life insurance company used a pyramid system of sales agents, each of whom agreed to work as independent contractors. The company promoted some of the agents to "sales leader" management positions while still keeping them as independent contractors. The company retained the authority to hire and fire agents under their supervision, and it determined sales territories while preventing sales leaders from selling competing products. When 14 former sales leaders sued for overtime under the FLSA, a Texas federal court and the Fifth Circuit ruled in their favor, finding that **they were actually employees and not independent contractors**. Because of all the restrictions on the sales leaders, they lacked real control over their jobs and were thus entitled to overtime. *Hopkins v. Cornerstone America*, 545 F.3d 338 (5th Cir. 2008).

B. State Laws

State wage and hour laws are similar to the FLSA. They may apply to more employers than the FLSA, and they may cover more employees. They may also have a higher minimum wage. If a state's minimum wage is less than the FLSA, and if the FLSA applies to the employer, then the employer must pay the higher federal rate.

1. Federal Preemption

Preemption occurs when a state and federal law address the same subject matter. In such cases, the federal law takes precedence over the state law by virtue of the Supremacy Clause (U.S. Constitution, Article VI, clause 2).

✦   California's prevailing wage law is based on the federal Davis-Bacon Act. It requires contractors working on public works projects to pay their employees at least the general prevailing wage rate for similar work being performed in the locality. Both laws allow public works contractors to pay apprentices less than the prevailing journeyman wage where they participate in approved programs complying with the National Apprenticeship Act. The California Apprenticeship Council charged a subcontractor working on a county construction project with improperly paying apprentices in a nonapproved program the apprentice wage rather than the appropriate journeyman wage. It ordered the county to withhold payments to the contractor for the violation. The contractor sued, claiming that the prevailing wage act was preempted by ERISA. The court agreed with the contractor that the apprenticeship training system under which the apprentices worked was an employee welfare benefit plan under ERISA and that the prevailing wage statute related to it. However, it held that the state wage act was not preempted. The U.S. Supreme Court affirmed, noting that **the California prevailing wage act was not preempted because it referred to approved apprenticeship programs that did not necessarily have to be ERISA plans**. Here, the prevailing wage statute merely offered economic incentives to apprenticeship programs to comport with the state's requirements. *California Division of Labor Standards Enforcement v. Dillingham Construction*, 519 U.S. 316, 117 S.Ct 832, 136 L.Ed.2d 791 (1997).

✦   Undocumented aliens who worked for a contractor on construction projects with the New York City School Construction Authority and the New York City Housing Authority filed a lawsuit claiming that the contractor failed to pay them the prevailing wage as required by law. The contractor asserted that the Immigration Reform and Control Act (IRCA) preempted the lawsuit and sought to have the case dismissed. A New York trial court refused to dismiss the lawsuit. It noted that **IRCA did not preempt New York law with respect to paying prevailing wages**. The court also held that the undocumented workers could seek wages for work they had already performed even if they allegedly offered fraudulent documents to obtain employment. *Pineda v. Kel-Tech Construction, Inc.*, 832 N.Y.S.2d 386 (N.Y. Sup. Ct. 2007).

✦   A Massachusetts pavement contractor received an administrative ruling by the state Commissioner of Labor and Industries that it was required to comply with a state prevailing wage law that covered the construction of public works. The contractor argued that the law was inapplicable to its activities because its work was limited to maintenance and repair work and was not "construction." It also asserted that the act was preempted by ERISA, since the contractor was bound by collective bargaining agreements to make contributions to ERISA plans and the statute credited amounts placed in the plans for each hour an employee worked against the employee's hourly wage as determined by the commissioner. The Supreme Judicial Court of Massachusetts found that **the prevailing wage law was applicable to the contractor's employees despite the claim that its work was limited to repairs**. The commissioner's interpretation of the act concerning road work was permissible. ERISA does not preempt state wage laws that have a minimal effect on an ERISA plan, and the state prevailing wage law did not "relate to any [ERISA] plan" by listing ERISA benefits as an example to be factored into the prevailing wage. The prevailing wage law applied to the contractor. *Marino Co., Inc. v. Commissioner of Labor and Industries*, 426 Mass. 458, 689 N.E.2d 495 (Mass. 1998).

2. Applicability

The following cases address the applicability of state wage and hour laws to various situations.

♦   Pizza delivery drivers worked for a Minnesota employer that charged customers a delivery fee. The drivers claimed that customers were confused about the fee and that it should be paid to the drivers as a tip. When they sued to recoup the money, a district court certified a class of about 1,600 drivers. However, the Eighth Circuit ruled that class certification was improper because **the circumstances of each transaction varied** from driver to driver and customer to customer. The case could not proceed as a class action. *Luiken v. Domino's Pizza, LLP*, 705 F.3d 370 (8th Cir. 2013).

♦   A Nebraska employer had a paid time off (PTO) plan that allowed employees to use PTO for any absence. It did not provide separate vacation leave and sick leave benefits, and its handbook said employees would not be paid for unused PTO when they became separated from employment. Two employees sued to recover PTO after they stopped working for the employer. The state's highest court upheld a ruling for the employees, finding that under state law **unused PTO was considered to be the same as unused vacation time** – which is an earned benefit that is treated as unpaid wages. And since unpaid wages were to be paid upon separation, the employees were entitled to the money. *Fisher v. PayFlex Systems USA, Inc.*, 829 N.W.2d 703 (Neb. 2013).

♦   Costco converted some managers from salaried employees who were exempt from overtime to salaried employees who were eligible for overtime. Before and after the change, it expected them to work 45 hours a week. To make the change, it reduced their base salaries so that with the addition of five hours of overtime a week, they would make exactly what they made before the change. However, managers who worked fewer than 45 hours a week would receive less pay. A group of managers sued, claiming the reclassification violated state wage laws. The California Court of Appeal disagreed. **Costco was free to reclassify the at-will managers as non-exempt and reduce their base salaries** as long as the company complied with minimum wage laws and gave sufficient notice, which it did. And the managers impliedly consented to the reclassification by continuing to work there after the change. *Head v. Costco Wholesale Corp.*, No. B222841, 2011 WL 452970 (Cal. Ct. App. 2011).

♦   Three Oracle employees who were non-residents of California performed some of their work in the state. They sued Oracle under state law, seeking overtime for full days and weeks they worked in California. The company sought pretrial judgment, which a court granted, but the Supreme Court of California then granted review and noted that California's labor statutes applied to non-residents who work in the state. However, the labor laws did not require Oracle to pay overtime to non-residents who performed work outside the state, assuming the wages were not paid in the state. **For those full days and weeks worked in California, the non-resident employees were entitled to any overtime due under state law.** *Sullivan v. Oracle Corp.*, 51 Cal.4th 1191 (Cal. 2011).

◆   A Pennsylvania borough maintained that a street resurfacing project was "maintenance" and not "construction, reconstruction, demolition, alteration and/or repair work." The state Department of Labor and Industry determined that the resurfacing was not maintenance and that the borough had to pay prevailing wages for the project. The borough appealed, and the case reached the Pennsylvania Supreme Court, which ruled that **the resurfacing was principally a reconstruction project and not mere maintenance**. Accordingly, the borough had to pay prevailing wages. *Borough of Youngwood v. Pennsylvania Prevailing Wage Appeals Board*, 947 A.2d 724 (Pa. 2008).

◆   A company in New Mexico paid an employee under an agreement that provided a fluctuating rate of pay. She received a basic salary each week that didn't change regardless of the number of hours worked. However, if she worked more than 40 hours in a week, her overtime was calculated by taking her weekly pay and dividing the number of hours worked to reach her regular hourly rate. This meant that **the more hours she worked, the smaller her regular hourly rate became, giving her diminishing overtime wages**. She filed a wage claim under the state's minimum wage law. The case reached a state appeals court, which ruled that the agreement violated the law because in extreme cases, overtime wages would be less than minimum wage. *New Mexico Dep't of Labor v. Echostar Communications Corp.*, 134 P.3d 780 (N.M. Ct. App. 2006).

II. THE NATIONAL LABOR RELATIONS ACT

The National Labor Relations Act (NLRA) guarantees employees "the right to self-organization, to form, join, or assist labor organizations, to bargain collectively through representatives of their own choosing, and to engage in other concerted activities for the purpose of collective bargaining or other mutual aid or protection." [29 U.S.C. § 157] The National Labor Relations Board has taken a relatively expansive view relating to the scope of "concerted activities" within the meaning of this section, construing it to include activities such as employee use of social media.

Employees also have "the right to refrain from any or all of such activities except to the extent that such right may be affected by an agreement requiring membership in a labor organization as a condition of employment." [29 U.S.C. § 157]

The NLRA makes it an <u>unfair labor practice</u> for an employer "to interfere with, restrain, or coerce employees" in the exercise of their Section 157 rights

[29 U.S.C. § 158(a)(1)]. The NLRA also prohibits employers from refusing to bargain collectively with the employees' representatives.

Employers covered by the NLRA must post a notice of employee rights under the Act, including the right to act together to improve wages and working conditions, the right to form, join and assist a union, and the right to refrain from any of those activities.

A. Applicability

Not all employees of a company qualify as "employees" under the NLRA. For example, any individual employed as a "supervisor" is not considered an employee for purposes of the NLRA.

A supervisor is an employee who has the authority to use independent judgment to "hire, transfer, suspend, lay off, recall, promote, discharge, assign, reward, or discipline other employees, or responsibly to direct them, or to adjust their grievances, or effectively to recommend such action," and the employee holds that authority "in the interest of the employer."

◆   The U.S. Chamber of Commerce sued the state of California to challenge a law that barred private employers who received more than $10,000 in state funds in a year from using those funds "to assist, promote, or deter union organizing." It claimed that the law illegally **required employers to take a neutral position with regard to unions**, that it was preempted by the NLRA and that it violated the First Amendment. A federal court agreed, but the Ninth Circuit reversed. On further appeal, the U.S. Supreme Court reversed, holding that the NLRA preempted the state statutes. Here, the statutes attempted to regulate within a zone protected and reserved for market freedom. *Chamber of Commerce of U.S. v. Brown*, 554 U.S. 60, 128 S.Ct. 2408, 171 L.Ed.2d 264 (2008).

◆   The U.S. Supreme Court overturned a decision by the National Labor Relations Board (NLRB) awarding back pay to an undocumented alien worker who was laid off in retaliation for his role in union organization activities. The Court held that the award exceeded NLRB powers, trivialized immigration laws and encouraged future violations. Here, the employer laid off a worker who supported a union organization campaign and distributed authorization cards to co-workers. The NLRB imposed sanctions and ordered the employer to offer to reinstate the laid-off worker. However, the worker admitted that he used fraudulent documents to get the job. An administrative law judge found that an award of back pay would be contrary to Supreme Court precedent and the Immigration Reform and Control Act of 1986 (IRCA), but the NLRB held that the worker was entitled to almost $67,000 in back pay and interest. The case reached the Supreme Court, which held that **the NLRB had no power or authority to award back pay to the illegal alien**, since to do so was contrary to policies underlying the IRCA. The employer was still subject to other sanctions imposed by the NLRB. *Hoffman Plastic Compounds, Inc. v. NLRB*, 535 U.S. 137, 122 S.Ct. 1275, 152 L.Ed.2d 271 (2002).

✦   A Minnesota electrical contractor refused to grant employment interviews to 10 job applicants who were union members. The only union applicant accepted for employment was fired after a few days on the job. The union members filed a complaint against the contractor with the NLRB, asserting that the contractor had failed to hire or retain them because of their union affiliation in violation of the NLRA. An administrative law judge held for the union members, and a panel of the NLRB affirmed. The U.S. Court of Appeals, Eighth Circuit, reversed the NLRB's decision, finding that the job applicants were not "employees" for the purposes of the NLRA because they were being paid by the union to organize the company. They were, therefore, not protected from anti-union discrimination. The U.S. Supreme Court stated that the NLRB's broad, literal interpretation of the statutory term "employee" was consistent with NLRA purposes, one of which was to protect the right of workers to organize for mutual aid without employer interference. The contractor argued that common law agency principles prohibited this interpretation, and that the applicants were paid union organizers who could only serve the union's interest. The Court noted that common law agency principles did not prohibit workers from accepting employment from more than one employer. **Union organizing was equivalent to performing work for another employer during non-work hours, which no employer had a legal right to prevent.** The Court held that the NLRB's interpretation of the term "employee" was correct. *NLRB v. Town & Country Electric, Inc.*, 516 U.S. 85, 116 S.Ct. 450, 133 L.Ed.2d 371 (1995).

On remand, the Eighth Circuit found that substantial evidence supported the NLRB's ruling that the firing of the union electrician had been retaliatory and motivated by the contractor's anti-union sentiment. It enforced the NLRB order. *Town & Country Electric, Inc. v. NLRB*, 106 F.3d 816 (8th Cir. 1997).

✦   A poultry processing corporation purchased a company that operated a production plant in North Carolina. The plant employed crews of workers who collected live chickens for slaughter from independent contractor farmers. Before the sale was completed, a labor organization filed a petition to represent crew workers who worked out of the plant. The NLRB approved the crew workers as a bargaining unit that was protected by the NLRA and determined that **they were not excluded from coverage as agricultural laborers**. It ordered the corporation to recognize the union and bargain with it. The U.S. Supreme Court upheld the NLRB's ruling. The NLRB had properly focused on the status of the corporate employer, which was not a farmer, and noted that despite doing their work at farm locations, the employees began and ended each workday at the production plant. *Holly Farms Corp. v. NLRB*, 517 U.S. 392, 116 S.Ct. 1396, 134 L.Ed.2d 593 (1996).

✦   "Supervisors" are not covered under the NLRA if they have the authority to use independent judgment to "hire, transfer, suspend, lay off, recall, promote, discharge, assign, reward, or discipline other employees, or responsibly to direct them, or to adjust their grievances, or effectively to recommend such action," and they hold that authority "in the interest of the employer." The NLRB issued a complaint against the owner and operator of an Ohio nursing home, alleging that unfair labor practices had been committed in the disciplining of four licensed practical nurses. It determined that the nurses were not supervisors. The U.S. Supreme Court held that the NLRB's test for determining whether nurses were supervisors was inconsistent with the NLRA. Here, **the NLRB had erroneously concluded that the nurses were not supervisors because their focus was on the well-being of the nursing home residents**, not on the interests of the employer. The Court noted that because patient care is a nursing home's business, attending to residents' needs is in the employer's interests. Thus, the nurses were supervisors outside the coverage of the NLRA. *NLRB v. Health Care & Retirement Corp.*, 511 U.S. 571, 114 S.Ct. 1778, 128 L.Ed.2d 586 (1994).

◆   A Massachusetts corporation that operated a textile dyeing and finishing plant laid off all its employees and went out of business. One of its officers then teamed up with a former customer, acquired the plant, and began to operate a similar business. The new company hired many ex-employees of the old corporation. The union that had represented those employees asked the new company to recognize it as the collective bargaining agent for the new company's employees. The company refused. The union then filed an unfair labor practice charge with the NLRB. An administrative law judge found that the new company was a "successor" to the old corporation and that its refusal to bargain was an unfair labor practice. The U.S. Supreme Court agreed, holding that **there was "substantial continuity" between the two enterprises since the employees' jobs remained essentially unaltered**. Further, at the time one full shift of workers had been hired, a majority were ex-employees of the old corporation. Accordingly, even though the union's demand for bargaining had been premature, the new company was under an obligation to bargain once it had a "substantial and representative complement" of its work force in place. *Fall River Dyeing & Finishing Corp. v. NLRB*, 482 U.S. 27, 107 S.Ct. 2225, 96 L.Ed.2d 22 (1987).

◆   After employees of two small Illinois leather processing firms elected a union as their collective bargaining representative, the firms challenged the election on the ground that six of the seven eligible voters were illegal aliens. When the NLRB denied the challenge, the firms sent a letter to the Immigration and Naturalization Service (INS), asking it to check into the status of a number of employees. The NLRB determined that the firms had committed an unfair labor practice by reporting the employees to the INS in retaliation for their union activities, and ordered reinstatement with back pay. The U.S. Court of Appeals, Seventh Circuit, modified the NLRB's order, keeping the reinstatement offers open for four years and requiring the offers to be written in Spanish. It also held that even though the employees were not entitled to back pay when they were not legally entitled to be present in the United States, an award of six months' back pay would be appropriate.

On further appeal, the U.S. Supreme Court held that **the NLRA applied to undocumented aliens with respect to unfair labor practices committed against them**. Accordingly, the firms had committed an unfair labor practice against the illegal aliens by constructively discharging them (by reporting them to the INS). However, back pay can only reimburse for actual, not speculative, consequences of an unfair labor practice. The court of appeals exceeded its authority by keeping the offers open for four years and by requiring them to be written in Spanish. The Court remanded the case to the NLRB so appropriate relief could be determined. *Sure-Tan, Inc. v. NLRB,* 467 U.S. 883, 104 S.Ct. 2803, 81 L.Ed.2d 732 (1984).

◆   A union that represented certified nursing aides at a Florida nursing home wanted to represent the facility's licensed practical nurses (LPNs). The NLRB certified the union as the LPNs' bargaining representative, but the facility refused to recognize the union based on its belief that the LPNs were supervisors who could not be unionized. The NLRB determined that the facility thus violated the NLRA, but the Eleventh Circuit reversed. The evidence showed that **LPNs had the authority to discipline, suspend or discharge other employees**. *Lakeland Healthcare Associates, LLC v. NLRB,* 696 F.3d 1332 (11th Cir. 2012).

◆   An Arizona company created workplace rules that: 1) prohibited employees from talking about work-related "legal matters" on social networking sites without permission from the company's legal department; 2) prohibiting employees, through a confidentiality policy, from discussing discipline with co-workers; and 3) prohibiting "unnecessary conversations" at work. The question of whether these rules violated the NLRA came before an administrative law judge, who determined that they did violate the law because **they tended to chill employees' right to engage in conduct protected by the NLRA**. *G4S Secure Solutions (USA) Inc. and Int'l Union, Security, Police and Fire Professionals of America,* No. 28-CA-23380 (NLRB, San Francisco, 3/29/12).

◆   An employee of a New York services agency sent co-workers text messages criticizing their work and told one of them she was going to raise her concerns with the agency's executive director. One of the co-workers posted a message on Facebook on her day off, stating that the employee didn't believe the agency's workers helped their clients enough. She asked other workers to respond. Four employees did. The employee then complained to the executive director, who fired the five co-workers. The fired workers filed an unfair labor practices charge with the NLRB, which ruled in their favor and ordered their reinstatement. It didn't matter that the agency was non-union or that the co-workers weren't trying to change the work environment, or even that they never raised their concerns with the executive director. **Their Facebook comments were still protected concerted activity under the NLRA.** *Hispanics United of Buffalo, Inc. and Ortiz,* No. 3-CA-27872 (NLRB, Div. of Judges, 9/2/11).

◆   A condominium association in Florida provided maintenance and security services to individual condo owners. A union sought to bargain for the maintenance employees after they voted for representation, but the association refused to bargain, claiming that the employees were domestic employees who were excluded by the NLRA. The National Labor Relations Board ruled that the employees were not domestic employees and ordered the association to bargain with the union. The Eleventh Circuit enforced the board's order. **The** maintenance employees were not employed by the individual homeowners but rather by the condominium association. They were thus not exempt domestic employees. *Shore Club Condominium Ass'n, Inc. v. NLRB*, 400 F.3d 1336 (11th Cir. 2005).

B. Handbilling and Picketing

As a general rule, employers do not have to allow non-employee <u>organizers</u> on their property for the purpose of distributing union literature. However, where the employees are beyond the reach of reasonable union efforts to communicate with them, employers may have to allow handbilling on company property. However, the burden is on the union to show that no other reasonable means of communicating its organizational message to the employees exists. Off site, employers do not have the right to prevent the distribution of <u>union literature</u>.

Employees have the right to peacefully picket an employer during a strike. As long as the employees can lawfully assemble in a place (usually a sidewalk area), employers cannot prevent them from doing so.

1. Handbilling

Handbilling is the distribution of union literature for the purpose of unionizing a workplace. Sometimes such information is distributed to employees; however, it is often targeted to customers.

◆   A food and commercial workers union attempted to organize employees at a Connecticut retail store. When the employer refused to allow the union on store property to distribute handbills, the union filed a complaint with the NLRB, which ordered the employer to cease and desist barring the union from the parking lot. The Fifth Circuit affirmed the NLRB's decision, but the U.S. Supreme Court reversed, noting that "the right to distribute [handbills] is not absolute, but must be accommodated to the circumstances." If it is unreasonable for a union to distribute literature to employees entirely off the employer's premises, distribution in parking lots or other common areas may be warranted. The Court concluded that there were no "unique obstacles" hindering the union from reaching the employees because it had access to the list of names and addresses. Therefore, **the employer did not violate the NLRA by preventing union organizers from distributing handbills in the parking lot**. *Lechmere, Inc. v. NLRB*, 502 U.S. 527, 112 S.Ct. 841, 117 L.Ed.2d 79 (1992).

◆   A contractor was hired to build a department store in a Florida mall. A union believed the contractor was paying substandard wages and fringe benefits. It thus engaged in **peaceful handbilling of the businesses in the mall**, asking customers not to shop there until the mall's owner publicly promised that all construction at the mall would be done using contractors who paid fair wages. The mall owner, after failing to convince the union to alter the handbills to state that the dispute was not with the owner, filed a complaint with the NLRB, charging the union with engaging in unfair labor practices under Section

8(b)(4) of the NLRA. The NLRB dismissed the complaint, concluding that the handbilling was protected by Section 8(b)(4)'s proviso exempting non-picketing publicity intended to truthfully advise the public that products are produced by an employer with whom the union is involved in a labor dispute. The Eleventh Circuit affirmed, but the U.S. Supreme Court reversed on the ground that the mall owner and its other tenants did not distribute the contractor's products. *Edward J. DeBartolo Corp. v. NLRB,* 463 U.S. 147, 103 S.Ct. 2926, 77 L.Ed.2d 535 (1983).

On remand, the NLRB ordered the union to stop distributing the handbills because the handbilling was an attempt to inflict economic harm on secondary employers. This constituted economic retaliation and was therefore a form of coercion prohibited by Section 8(b)(4)(ii)(B). The Eleventh Circuit refused to enforce the NLRB's order, holding that there was no clear congressional intent to proscribe such handbilling in the NLRA. The U.S. Supreme Court then held that **Section 8(b)(4) did not contain any clear expression of congressional intent to prohibit this kind of handbilling**. Further, since there were serious constitutional problems, including First Amendment free speech concerns, with the NLRB's construction, a clear expression that that was Congress' purpose would be required before such an interpretation would be adopted. The Court affirmed the decision denying enforcement of the NLRB's order. *Edward J. DeBartolo Corp. v. Florida Gulf Coast Building & Construction Trades Council,* 485 U.S. 568, 108 S.Ct. 1392, 99 L.Ed.2d 645 (1988).

◆ A Nevada casino leased space to a restaurant company to provide food service facilities inside its hotel and casino complex. When employees of the restaurant company sought to unionize, they distributed handbills on casino property to customers of the casino and restaurants. The handbills asked the customers to urge management of the restaurants to sign a union contract. Casino security told the employees they could not distribute literature on casino property, but the employees refused to leave. The police were called, and most of the handbilling employees were cited for trespassing. The union then filed unfair labor practice charges against the casino, asserting that the restaurant employees could handbill in non-work areas during non-work times. **The casino asserted that the restaurant employees were not casino employees and thus had no Section 7 organizing rights** under the NLRA. The NLRB ruled in favor of the employees, but the U.S. Court of Appeals, D.C. Circuit, refused to enforce the NLRB's order. Instead, it remanded the case for a determination of whether the restaurant employees enjoyed the same Section 7 rights as casino employees. On remand, the NLRB again determined that in general, a property owner cannot bar employees of an onsite contractor from distributing union-related handbills on the property. It also found that the handbilling did not pose any safety issues. As a result, the NLRB reaffirmed its earlier finding that the casino committed an unfair labor practice. The casino filed another appeal, and the NLRB cross-appealed to have its order enforced. The casino argued that an onsite contractor's employees should be treated as non-employees rather than employees for purposes of determining whether they have a right to distribute union-related handbills on an owner's property. But the U.S. Court of Appeals, D.C. Circuit determined that the NLRB had discretion to decide how to treat employees of onsite contractors for such purposes, and it found that the NLRB permissibly exercised its discretion when it determined that the casino committed an unfair labor practice. As a result, the order of the NLRB was enforced. *New York-New York, LLC v. NLRB*, 676 F.3d 193 (D.C. Cir. 2012).

◆   A grocery store manager in California called the police when union organizers handed out flyers to customers in the parking lot and refused to leave. The store had a no-solicitation policy prohibiting solicitors from operating on store premises. The NLRB determined that the store violated Section 8(a)(1) of the NLRA by calling the police, but the U.S. Court of Appeals, District of Columbia Circuit, held that the store did not commit an unfair labor practice. The NLRB had relied on a California Supreme Court case that had a labor-picketing exception to the trespass laws, but that had since been discredited. Here, **the store's policy clearly prohibited all picketers, regardless of the content of their speech**, and this did not violate the First Amendment or the NLRA. *Waremart Foods v. NLRB*, 354 F.3d 870 (D.C. Cir. 2004).

2. Secondary Picketing

Secondary picketing is picketing targeted at entities that are not the employees' direct employer – for example, a union may picket the largest customer of a nonunionized employer to pressure the employer to unionize.

A union cannot <u>threaten, coerce, or restrain</u> an entity that is not a party to a labor dispute "where … an object thereof is … forcing or requiring [the entity] to cease using, selling, handling, transporting, or otherwise dealing in the products of any other producer … or to cease doing business with any other person …" [29 U.S.C. § 158(b)(4)(ii)(B)]

Not all peaceful picketing at secondary sites is prohibited. Where such picketing is designed only to persuade the picketed entity's customers not to buy the struck product, it is allowed.

◆   After contract negotiations between a title insurance company and its employees' union reached an impasse, the employees went on strike. They also picketed five local title companies who derived over 90% of their gross incomes from the sale of the insurer's policies. The U.S. Supreme Court held that **the secondary picketing amounted to coercion of neutral parties** with the object of forcing them to cease dealing in the primary party's product. Successful secondary picketing would force the local title companies to choose between survival and cutting their ties with the insurer. Section 8(b)(4)(ii)(B) of the NLRA barred such coercive activity, and its application to the picketing involved here did not violate the First Amendment. The NLRB's order to stop the picketing had to be enforced, held the Court. *NLRB v. Retail Store Employees Union, Local 1001*, 447 U.S. 607, 100 S.Ct. 2372, 65 L.Ed.2d 377 (1980).

◆   A union had a dispute with a railroad over the renewal of a collective bargaining agreement. The union struck the railroad and then extended its picketing to other railroads that interchanged traffic with the struck railroad. These railroads sued to enjoin the picketing, and an Illinois federal court issued an injunction against the picketing. The court found that the case did not "grow out of a labor dispute" as defined by the Norris-LaGuardia Act, and that none of the picketed railroads were "substantially aligned" with the struck railroad. The court of appeals reversed, and the U.S. Supreme Court affirmed that decision. It held that **the district court did not have jurisdiction to enjoin the secondary picketing in the railway labor dispute**. The Norris-LaGuardia Act was enacted to preclude courts from enjoining secondary as well as primary activity. Railroads were to be treated no differently than other industries in this regard. Because the definition of "labor dispute" is broad, the adoption of the "substantial alignment" test (which would narrow that definition) would defeat Congress' intent by requiring courts to second-guess which activities are truly in the union's interest. Further, there was nothing in the Railway Labor Act to indicate that Congress intended to permit federal courts to enjoin secondary activity as a means of settling strikes and avoiding interruptions to commerce. *Burlington Northern Railroad Co. v. Brotherhood of Maintenance of Way Employees,* 481 U.S. 429, 107 S.Ct. 1841, 95 L.Ed.2d 381 (1987).

◆   Members of a local union in Georgia began picketing a resort to protest a construction company the resort had hired. The union members believed the construction company was violating its collective bargaining agreement by hiring employees represented by another union to work on the project. The picketers gathered adjacent to a highway that was a major artery for traffic in the county. The resort became concerned about a potential safety hazard and called the police, who informed the picketers they needed to obtain an assembly permit. The picketers left peaceably. When they later decided not to wait a week for the permit and resumed picketing, the police again asked them to leave. However, the city attorney, after conferring with the police, allowed them to stay. They then filed an unfair labor practice charge with the NLRB, which determined that the resort had violated the NLRA by calling the police. The case reached the Fourth Circuit, which disagreed. **The resort did not interfere with the union members' Section 8(a)(1) rights under the NLRA by calling the police because of the potential safety hazard** created by the picketers. *CSX Hotels, Inc. v. NLRB,* 377 F.3d 394 (4th Cir. 2004).

◆   A national railway carrier with a major hub in Seattle terminated its contract with a subcontractor that provided loading and unloading services to the carrier. The union representing the subcontractor's employees threatened to picket after the carrier entered into an agreement with another company to provide those same services. The carrier sued and a Washington federal court granted it an injunction to prevent the picketing. The Ninth Circuit reversed, finding the dispute covered by the Norris-LaGuardia Act because it centered on who would perform work at the hub, which union would represent employees of the carrier's subcontractors, and the terms of the workers' employment. Even though there was no employer-employee relationship between the carrier and the union, the "matrix" of the dispute was the employer-employee relationship. Thus, **the Norris-LaGuardia Act applied** to prevent the court from stopping the picketing. *Burlington Northern & Santa Fe Railway v. Int'l Brotherhood of Teamsters Local 174*, 203 F.3d 703 (9th Cir. 2000).

◆   An unincorporated association of affiliated labor organizations representing Pennsylvania workers engaged in a course of illegal secondary boycotts and picketed work sites to exert pressure on nonunion employers. The NLRB entered into a consent judgment with the association and its business agent prohibiting further secondary boycotts, but the association continued the practice. Over the next 15 years, the NLRB entered four contempt adjudications against the association for repeated violations of the consent decrees. By 1989, the NLRB had increased the fine against the association to $250,000 for past noncompliance and increased prospective fines to $100,000 per violation as well as $10,000 per day. For six years the association discontinued its picketing and then filed a motion to vacate the prior contempt adjudication. The Third Circuit held that **the passage of time did not constitute a change in circumstances that justified lifting the injunction.** Compliance with prior orders was also insufficient, especially given the association's history of noncompliance. Because the association failed to identify a significant hardship caused by the decrees, the court refused to dissolve the consent judgments or the contempt adjudications. *Building & Construction Trades Council of Philadelphia v. NLRB*, 64 F.3d 880 (3d Cir. 1995).

C. Strikes and Strike Replacement Workers

Where a strike is determined to be an <u>unfair labor practices strike</u> (a strike caused in whole or in part by an employer's unfair labor practices), employers cannot permanently replace the striking workers.

In an unfair labor practices strike, employers cannot refuse to reinstate striking workers upon their <u>unconditional offer</u> to return to work (unless they can show "legitimate and substantial business justifications" for their refusal).

Where a strike is an <u>economic strike</u>, employers can hire permanent replacement workers and refuse to immediately reinstate strikers who offer to return to work. The employer only has to reinstate strikers as vacancies arise (unless the union can force the employer to discharge the replacement workers as a condition for ending the strike).

◆   Some time after Wisconsin employees went on strike to protest an unfair labor practice, their union made an unconditional offer to return to work, thereby ending the strike. **The company delayed the return of many employees and refused to reinstate others.** After the NLRB found that the company's actions violated the NLRA, it ordered the company to pay back pay to 42 former strikers and asked the Seventh Circuit to enforce the order. The company challenged the order as to 11 employees, arguing that it shouldn't have to pay five employees who accessed their 401(k) accounts because they had permanently resigned. And three employees allegedly took too long to find other jobs, while another three quit their interim jobs without good reason.

However, the court of appeals ruled that all 11 employees were entitled to back pay. A manager told employees the only way they could access 401(k) funds was to resign. As for the three employees who didn't look for work right away, they didn't have to start looking for work immediately if the company gave them optimism about the prospect of reinstatement. Finally, the other three who quit their interim jobs all did so for good reasons. *NLRB v. KSM Industries, Inc.*, 682 F.3d 537 (7th Cir. 2012).

◆   A union brought multiple unfair labor practice charges against the owner of a senior living facility in California after negotiations on a new bargaining agreement fell apart and a strike authorization vote was conducted. While the vote was taking place, management asked a number of off-duty union members assisting in that process to leave the premises. A strike was called, and the facility hired temporary workers, later offering them permanent employment. It continued to offer permanent employment to temporary workers even after the strikers submitted an unconditional offer to return to work. The NLRB sought an injunction to force the facility to reinstate the strikers. A federal court granted the injunction, finding that the union was likely to succeed in showing that **the facility violated the NLRA by denying off-duty employees access to workplace premises during the vote and by refusing to reinstate the strikers**. *Baudler v. American Baptist Homes of the West*, 798 F.Supp.2d 1099 (N.D. Cal. 2011).

◆   Employees of a garbage company in Texas voted to join a union, which then attempted to bargain with the company, starting with the maintenance unit and then the drivers. The parties reached an impasse, and the maintenance workers voted to strike. A number of drivers joined the strike. The company hired replacement workers and notified employees that it deemed the strike to be economic rather than an unfair labor practice strike. Subsequently, the union made an unconditional offer to return to work, which the company rejected. The new workers disavowed the union, and the company then informed the union it would no longer bargain with it. An administrative law judge determined that the company violated the NLRA by bargaining in bad faith, so that the strike was an unfair labor practice strike. A federal court agreed with the NLRB and **ordered the company to temporarily reinstate the striking workers**. On further appeal, the Fifth Circuit largely affirmed, finding a causal link between the employer's bad faith bargaining and the strike. Thus, the lower court properly ordered the reinstatement of the strikers so that any changes to the terms or conditions of employment could be bargained over. *Overstreet v. El Paso Disposal, L.P.*, 625 F.3d 844 (5th Cir. 2010).

◆   After collective bargaining between a union and a company in Tennessee broke down, 53 of the 75 employees in the bargaining unit went on strike. The company hired "permanent" replacement workers, though it stated that it reserved the right to terminate the replacement workers when the strike ended. Several months later, the union, on behalf of the striking employees, made an unconditional offer to return to work. The company refused to immediately reinstate the striking workers, but offered to put them on a preferential recall list. About a month later, the company offered reinstatement to 47 strikers, and 18 accepted. The union then filed charges against the company over its refusal to reinstate the strikers. It **argued that the replacement workers were in fact temporary and not permanent.** The NLRB disagreed, and the union appealed to the Seventh Circuit, which upheld the NLRB's decision. The company offered legitimate and substantial business justifications for retaining the permanent replacement workers following the unconditional offer to return to work. *United Steel, Paper and Forestry, Rubber, Manufacturing, Energy, Allied Industrial and Service Workers Int'l Union v. NLRB*, 544 F.3d 841 (7th Cir. 2008).

♦   A healthcare provider in Kentucky operated a rehabilitation center that employed therapists and rehabilitation technicians. It announced a wage cut for its rehabilitation employees, who discussed what actions to take to reverse that decision. Five of them wrote a grievance letter and decided to stop seeing patients until upper management met with them to discuss issues. They instead would perform necessary paperwork. Their manager, after speaking with upper management, sent them home. They chose not to picket, instead demanding a meeting. The company fired them for insubordination, and they filed an unfair labor practice charge. The case reached the Sixth Circuit, which ruled that **the employees' actions were not protected because they amounted to a partial strike.** To be protected, they would have had to completely stop work. They could not simultaneously walk off the job and retain the benefits of working. *Vencare Ancillary Services, Inc. v. NLRB*, 352 F.3d 318 (6th Cir. 2003).

♦   During negotiations for a new collective bargaining agreement, a newspaper publisher in Pennsylvania hired stringers to perform night/weekend photography assignments without first notifying the union or giving it the chance to bargain over the issue. The union filed an unfair labor practice complaint with the NLRB. Shortly thereafter, the union and publisher failed to come to terms on the bargaining agreement, and the publisher's employees voted to strike. The publisher hired temporary replacement workers and later informed the union that it considered the strike to be an economic strike such that it could permanently replace the strikers. **The strikers then made an unconditional offer to return to work, but the publisher refused to let them.** The NLRB ruled that the publisher had engaged in an unfair labor practice, and the Third Circuit upheld the NLRB's order. The unilateral subcontracting of the night/weekend work during negotiations was an unfair labor practice; the strike was not an economic one; and even if it was, the publisher's efforts to prevent the strikers from making the unconditional offer to return to work (by sending the union a letter stating that the replacement workers were permanent) violated the NLRA. *Citizens Publishing and Printing Co. v. NLRB*, 263 F.3d 224 (3d Cir. 2001).

♦   A food processor and the union representing its employees reached a collective bargaining impasse. The union organized a strike that lasted over two years and resulted in the loss of two recertification elections. The employer used replacement workers, and the strike was characterized by violence. A group of strikers sought reemployment prior to the second election, and **the employer rehired them in positions that were less desirable and lower paying** than those they had formerly held. The employer feared that reemployment in their former positions created the possibility of industrial sabotage and more violence that could affect plant security. After losing the second reelection, the union filed an unfair labor practices complaint against the employer with the NLRB, which agreed that the employer had discriminated against the returning strikers. The U.S. Court of Appeals, D.C. Circuit, held that the NLRB could not have reasonably found a risk of industrial sabotage with regard to one returning striker who operated a forklift. However, there were valid safety concerns with respect to an employee in a quality control position. *Diamond Walnut Growers, Inc. v. NLRB*, 113 F.3d 1259 (D.C. Cir. 1997).

◆   A union successfully organized many electrical workers employed by an Indiana industrial contractor. The contractor then transferred almost all union supporters to a single job site and employed an "expediter" with no electrical work experience to enforce company rules. Five union members at the site commenced a weeklong unfair labor practice strike to protest this tactic. They then approached a supervisor and indicated their willingness to return to work but were advised that the contractor considered them to have quit. Although the union provided the contractor three written notices of their willingness to return to work, the contractor refused to reinstate the employees, and the union filed an unfair labor practice complaint with the NLRB. The NLRB ordered the contractor to reinstate the employees. The U.S. Court of Appeals, Seventh Circuit, enforced the board's order, holding that **unfair labor practice strikers are entitled to reinstatement upon making an unconditional offer to return to work** and that an employer violates the NLRA by failing to offer immediate reinstatement. The resumption or continuance of picketing is not inconsistent with an offer to return to work. *Dilling Mechanical Contractors, Inc. v. NLRB*, 107 F.3d 521 (7th Cir. 1997).

◆   A labor organization filed numerous unfair labor practice charges against a Michigan employer for coercing, intimidating and discriminating against union supporters and refusing to bargain with the union in good faith. The charges included retaliation against returning strikers who protested unfair labor practices. The employer claimed that the strikers had not been engaged in an unfair labor practice strike and asserted that replacement workers had been hired in their place. The NLRB ruled that the employer had violated the NLRA by failing to reinstate some of the strikers but had properly refused to reinstate one striker for failing to communicate his unconditional offer to return to work. The Sixth Circuit found substantial evidence that the employees had engaged in protected conduct. **A strike caused in whole or in part by unfair labor practices is an unfair labor practice strike**, and the employer must reinstate striking employees unless there is a legitimate and substantial business justification for refusing to do so. The court enforced the NLRB order. *Allied Mechanical Services, Inc. v. NLRB*, 113 F.3d 623 (6th Cir. 1997).

◆   In a Texas case, employees called an economic strike after a collective bargaining agreement expired. The employer hired permanent replacement employees. When the union attempted to accept the employer's previous offer, the employer informed it that the offer was no longer available. It then withdrew recognition from the union, refusing to further bargain with it. The employer felt that the union was no longer supported by a majority of the employees in the unit. The union then filed an unfair labor practice charge with the NLRB, asserting that the employer had violated the NLRA. The NLRB found that the employer's evidence of its replacements' union sentiments was not sufficient to rebut the presumption of the union's majority support. The Fifth Circuit held that the NLRB had to presume that strike replacements opposed the union. But the U.S. Supreme Court held that **the NLRB did not have to presume opposition to the union by the replacements**. A replacement who otherwise supports the union may be forced by economic concerns to work for a struck employer. The Court reversed and remanded the case. *NLRB v. Curtin Matheson Scientific, Inc.*, 494 U.S. 775, 110 S.Ct. 1542, 108 L.Ed.2d 801 (1990).

◆   Some local labor unions engaged in a number of unauthorized, "wildcat" strikes at several West Virginia coal mines in violation of the collective bargaining agreements in place between the employer and the international union. The regional subdivision of the international was unsuccessful in attempting to persuade the miners not to strike and to return to work. The employer then sued the international, the regional subdivision, and the local unions under Section 301 of the LMRA. The U.S. Supreme Court held that **neither the international nor the regional subdivision could be held liable for the unauthorized strikes**. There was no obligation implied in law on their part to use all reasonable means to prevent and end unauthorized strikes. If the strike had been authorized (and in violation of the collective bargaining agreements), then the international would have been liable under Section 301, but such was not the case here. *Carbon Fuel Co. v. United Mine Workers of America*, 444 U.S. 212, 100 S.Ct. 410, 62 L.Ed.2d 394 (1979).

◆   A Massachusetts linen supply company was a member of an association formed to negotiate collective bargaining agreements with a truck drivers' union as a multi-employer unit. During negotiations for a proposed agreement, an impasse was reached, and the union began a selective strike against the company. The company hired permanent replacements and notified both the union and the association that it was withdrawing from the association. When a collective bargaining agreement was later executed, the company refused to sign it. The U.S. Supreme Court held that **the bargaining impasse did not justify the company's withdrawal from the multi-employer bargaining unit**. Here, there was no unusual circumstance to justify the unilateral withdrawal. To permit withdrawal at an impasse would undermine the utility of multi-employer bargaining as a practical matter. The Court required the company to implement the new agreement. *Charles D. Bonanno Linen Service v. NLRB*, 454 U.S. 404, 102 S.Ct. 720, 70 L.Ed.2d 656 (1982).

D. Unfair Labor Practices

The NLRA makes it an unfair labor practice for an employer "to interfere with, restrain, or coerce employees" in the exercise of their organizational rights under Section 157 [29 U.S.C. § 158(a)(1)]. The NLRA also prohibits employers from refusing to bargain collectively with the employees' representatives.

Because of the greater protections available for unfair labor practice strikers, workers will generally seek to find some element of an unfair labor practice so that a strike will not be deemed an economic strike.

1. Terms and Conditions of Employment

It is an unfair labor practice to refuse to bargain over terms and conditions of employment. A plant closure or partial closure (or consolidation) is not a term or condition of employment; nor is a relocation. Although such a decision can affect employees' tenure, it does not affect their terms and conditions of employment.

If an employer bargains to impasse over terms and conditions of employment, it may effect a unilateral change in such terms or conditions without committing an unfair labor practice.

◆   An Arizona company that sold pharmaceuticals from a mail order facility had a program that gave employees "WOW" awards for exceptional performance. The company believed that customers would view the program as evidence of its commitment to service. When clients and potential clients toured the facility, they were shown slides about the award program and were taken to a cafeteria to view a "Wall of WOW." On a day when a client was scheduled to take a tour, **an employee wore a shirt with a union logo on the front and "I don't need a WOW to do my job" on the back**. The general manager had the employee remove the shirt, and the employee's union filed an unfair labor charge. An ALJ ruled against the employer, but the D.C. Circuit reversed. It ruled that the shirt could be banned because its "gibe at management" threatened to harm the company's relationship with its customers. *Medco Health Solutions of Las Vegas, Inc. v. NLRB*, 701 F.3d 710 (D.C. Cir. 2012).

◆   To protect its bidding process, a temporary staffing firm in Rhode Island required employees to sign a confidentiality agreement prohibiting them from discussing their salaries and terms of employment with other parties. While in a placement with an energy company, an employee of the firm complained to a company official that he was not being paid in a timely manner. He wondered if he could continue to work for the company through a different staffing agency. His request was denied. He also complained to the firm when the computer reimbursement amount he received for using his own computer was dropped from $15 per day to $12 per day, and he informed the company about that as well. He was fired for violating the confidentiality agreement. However, the NLRB ruled that the agreement violated Section 7 of the NLRA, and the

First Circuit affirmed that decision. It didn't matter that this wasn't a union situation. What mattered was that **the agreement chilled the employee's right to discuss working conditions**. *NLRB v. Northeastern Land Services, LTD*, 645 F.3d 475 (1st Cir. 2011).

◆   A nurse with a pharmaceutical research company in Maryland spoke with a co-worker who had left the company and returned, asking him if he received a raise when he came back. He lied and said he did. He also said his wife was going to return to the company with a raise – another lie. The nurse then spoke with a supervisor about having the entire unit quit and come back with raises. Her supervisor reported the comments to the operations manager, who met with the nurse. The nurse recounted what she'd learned and said, and then she indicated that she'd only spoken with her supervisor about the issue. The manager fired her a week later. When she claimed a violation of the NLRA, a three-member panel of the NLRB ruled that **the company violated the nurse's Section 7 rights by firing her to prevent her from engaging in future concerted activity** – talking to other employees about perceived wage favoritism. *Parexel Int'l, LLC v. Neuschafer*, No. 5-CA-033245 (NLRB 1/28/11).

◆   A company purchased a circuit board manufacturing facility in New York and laid off 200 employees. The union contacted an employee about speaking to a newspaper, which the employee did, stating that the layoffs would hurt the company over the long term, and that there were gaping holes in the business. A vice president of IBM then called one of the owners to determine if the company was still viable. The owner later met with the employee and threatened to fire him if he disparaged the company again. The employee then posted a message on a newspaper's website stating that the business was being "tanked" by a group of people who did not have the ability to manage it. He was then fired. The NLRB found that the threat and the firing violated Section 8(a)(1) of the NLRA, but the U.S. Court of Appeals, D.C. Circuit, held that **the employee's disloyal, disparaging and injurious attacks on the company deprived him of the protection of Section 8(a)(1)**. The company did not commit an unfair labor practice by firing the employee. *Endicott Interconnect Technologies, Inc. v. NLRB*, 453 F.3d 532 (D.C. Cir. 2006).

◆   Lead care aides at an assisted living facility in Ohio circulated a petition criticizing work conditions and planning a daylong strike. Managers interviewed all the aides to determine who had spearheaded the effort, then fired one lead care aide and demoted another. The strike never happened. After an unfair labor practices charge was filed, the NLRB ruled in favor of the employees, ordering reinstatement and full back pay. The Fourth Circuit enforced the order, finding that **the drafting of the petition was protected as a concerted activity under the NLRA**. Also, the managers committed an unfair labor practice by coercively interviewing the aides about the strike and the petition without assuring the aides that there would be no reprisals. *Sunrise Senior Living, Inc. v. NLRB*, 183 Fed.Appx. 326 (4th Cir. 2006).

◆   A newspaper employee in North Carolina was also the president of his union's local bargaining unit. He called his supervisor a racist and stated that the newspaper was a racist place to work. His supervisor told him such behavior was unacceptable and threatened to suspend him if it did not stop. He nevertheless again called the supervisor and newspaper racist and also cursed at the supervisor. After an investigation, he was fired. He filed a complaint with the NLRB, claiming that he was fired in retaliation for engaging in protected union activity under Section 7 of the NLRA. The case reached the Fourth Circuit Court of Appeals, which held that **his behavior could not be deemed to be protected activity**, and that his discharge for insubordination was lawful. *Media General Operations, Inc. v. NLRB*, 394 F.3d 207 (4th Cir. 2005).

◆   A company in New York had a decades-old tradition of giving employees paid time off to donate blood. Twice a year during blood drives, employees could receive up to four hours of paid time to travel to the site, give blood, recover, and return to their jobs. In 2001, the company decided to stop paying employees for time off to give blood because of the disruption it caused in the workplace. The union filed a grievance, and the NLRB found that the company violated Section 8(a)(5) of the NLRA by failing to give the union a chance to bargain over the change to employees' wages and hours as established by longstanding company policy. The U.S. Court of Appeals affirmed. Even if the company established the policy for charitable reasons, it had an effect on employees' hours and wages the same as if the company had given them four hours' paid time off twice a year. As a result, the company had to bargain before changing the policy. *Verizon New York v. NLRB*, 360 F.3d 206 (D.C. Cir. 2004).

◆   An Illinois steel plant used more than 100 "plain view" video cameras to monitor areas of the plant, and it also used hidden cameras at various times over the years to investigate specific cases of theft, vandalism and other kinds of wrongdoing. Using a hidden camera, the plant ascertained that an employee was using a manager's office to make unauthorized long-distance phone calls. It fired him. During the grievance process that followed, the local union president learned that the NLRB had concluded in another case that the use of hidden surveillance cameras was a mandatory subject of collective bargaining. The union asked the company for information about the hidden cameras, and the company refused to provide it. The union filed unfair labor practice charges, and **the NLRB determined that the company had to bargain over the use of the hidden cameras**. The Seventh Circuit Court of Appeals enforced the NLRB's order. It noted that the use of hidden cameras was analogous to physical exams, drug testing and polygraphs. The NLRB's order did not strip the company of the right to use the cameras; it attempted to preserve the confidentiality necessary for the company to effectively use the hidden cameras. *National Steel Corp. v. NLRB*, 324 F.3d 928 (7th Cir. 2003).

◆   A production operator at a New York brewery allegedly obstructed an independent contractor doing work at the brewery. The following morning, two senior managers approached the operator and began questioning him. He promptly requested the assistance of a shop steward in his department, who was aware of the facts underlying the incident. The managers denied the request because the shop steward was at lunch. They called for another steward, who arrived 15 minutes later. The employee refused to talk and was sent home for the day. The next day, he again requested the shop steward be there for the investigation, and the request was again denied. He was disciplined for the incident. The union then filed an unfair labor practices complaint, and the administrative law judge found that **he should have been allowed the representative of his choice**. The NLRB agreed and so did the Fourth Circuit Court of Appeals. This "Representation Rule" furthers workers' ability to seek mutual aid and protection under the NLRA. *Anheuser-Busch v. NLRB*, 338 F.3d 267 (4th Cir. 2003).

◆   Two nonunion employees were asked to attend a disciplinary meeting after criticizing their boss in a memo to his supervisor. One of the employees refused to attend the meeting without the other and was fired. The other employee agreed to meet, received a warning about gross insubordination, and was fired three months later for refusing to sign performance objectives. The employees filed an unfair labor practices complaint with the NLRB, and an administrative law judge found no NLRA violation. The NLRB reversed, extending the *Weingarten* rule to nonunion workers. (In *NLRB v. Weingarten*, 420 U.S. 251 (1975), the Supreme Court held that employees in a unionized workplace may request the presence of a union representative at an investigatory interview that the employee reasonably believes might result in disciplinary action.)

The case reached the U.S. Court of Appeals, D.C. Circuit, which upheld the NLRB's decision. Section 7 of the NLRA (29 U.S.C. § 157) gives employees the right "to engage in other concerted activities for the purpose of collective bargaining or other mutual aid or protection." Here, **even though the workers did not belong to a union, they had the right to have a co-worker present at the investigatory interview**. *Epilepsy Foundation of Northeast Ohio v. NLRB*, 268 F.3d 1095 (D.C. Cir. 2001).

On June 9, 2004, the NLRB reversed itself and ruled that nonunion employees do not have the right to demand that a co-worker be present during investigatory interviews.

◆   A manufacturer of trailers in Pennsylvania began to negotiate with its employees' union over a new collective bargaining agreement. Negotiations became heated, and the company instituted a new attendance policy, reducing the number of unexcused absences allowed before an employee could be fired. After the employees went on strike, the company decided to purchase a new plant in Georgia. The employees then unconditionally offered to return to work. However, the company rehired only some of them. A few months later, it closed the Pennsylvania plant and fired all the employees. The NLRB charged the company with violating Sections 8(a)(1), 8(a)(3) and 8(a)(5) of the NLRA. The company was found to have violated Section 8(a)(1) (unfair labor practice to interfere with employee rights to organize and bargain collectively), **Section 8(a)(3) (unfair labor practice to discriminate with respect to hiring, or length or term of employment to discourage union membership),** and Section 8(a)(5) (unfair labor practice to refuse to bargain collectively with the employees' representatives) as well as Section 8(d) (unfair labor practice to refuse to bargain over terms and conditions of employment).

The company appealed the NLRB's ruling to the Fourth Circuit Court of Appeals, which affirmed in part and reversed in part. Here, the company violated Sections 8(a)(1) and 8(a)(5) by unilaterally instituting the new attendance policy. It also violated Sections 8(a)(1) and 8(a)(3) by refusing to reinstate some of the employees after the unconditional offer to return to work. However, it did not violate Section 8(a)(3) by closing the plant. Nor did it violate Section 8(a)(5) by refusing to bargain to impasse over the plant's relocation. Because economic reasons largely drove the decision to relocate, that decision was not a term or condition of employment over which the company had to bargain. *Dorsey Trailers, Inc. v. NLRB*, 233 F.3d 831 (4th Cir. 2000).

◆   Two unions negotiating over contracts with an Illinois utility company failed to reach an agreement nine months after the previous contracts expired. Rather than strike, they decided to initiate an "inside game" strategy wherein their members would refuse to work voluntary overtime and generally "work to rule," strictly adhering to all company safety and other rules, doing exactly and only what they were told, reporting to work precisely on time, and parking work trucks at company facilities at the end of the day, which would prevent the company from responding to after-hours emergencies. Union members also agreed to present all grievances as a group and to advise non-employees to report unsafe conditions. Two months later, the company instituted a lockout that lasted for three months. The unions eventually reached an agreement with the company. However, they filed unfair labor practice charges with the NLRB. The U.S. Court of Appeals, D.C. Circuit, noted that lockouts are not inherently anti-union. **The lockout here was not an unfair labor practice.** It was supported by a legitimate business interest in stopping the "inside game" and in getting the unions to place the company's offer before their memberships. *Local 702, IBEW v. NLRB*, 215 F.3d 11 (D.C. Cir. 2000).

◆   A California manufacturer purchased the assets of a bankrupt company and notified employees that they were being discharged because of the sale. However, the employees were also told that some of them would be hired back immediately and that others would be hired as needed. All of the initial employees hired to run the new business had worked for the bankrupt company. The manufacturer set the terms of employment without bargaining with the employees' former union. It also stated that there would be no union in its workplace. A lawsuit resulted. The case reached the Ninth Circuit Court of Appeals, which held that **a successor employer has a duty to bargain with an incumbent union** before imposing terms when it hires an essentially intact bargaining unit from its predecessor. However, it has no obligation to accept the predecessor's labor agreement. Therefore, if it bargained to impasse, it could then set the initial terms of employment. Here, because the employees all came from the predecessor, it was clear that the union represented a majority of the employees hired by the manufacturer. The manufacturer had violated its duty to bargain with the union, and a court would have to determine whether the manufacturer would have bargained to impasse, thus giving it the right to impose terms like pay rate. *NLRB v. Advanced Stretchforming Int'l*, 233 F.3d 1176 (9th Cir. 2000).

♦ A manufacturer assigned salaried, nonunion employees to work the third shift at an Ohio plant. A union representing nonsalaried plant employees filed a grievance claiming that the collective bargaining agreement required the assignment of union employees to perform the work. Union representatives met with a company HR manager, who asserted that the grievance could lead to the elimination of the entire shift. The employer later eliminated the shift for economic reasons. The union filed a complaint with the NLRB, and an administrative law judge (ALJ) agreed that the employer had violated the NLRA by failing to provide prior notice and an opportunity to bargain before eliminating the shift. The Sixth Circuit noted that the decision to lay off employees is a mandatory subject of bargaining but disagreed with the administrative rulings that the decision to abolish the third shift had to be negotiated. **The bargaining agreement reserved scheduling, assignment, hiring and layoff decisions to the employer**, which satisfied the NLRB's notice requirement. Also, since there were legitimate business reasons for the layoffs, this portion of the decision was remanded for further consideration. *Uforma/Shelby Business Forms, Inc. v. NLRB*, 111 F.3d 1284 (6th Cir. 1997).

♦ A New Mexico trucking company employed a casual dock worker under a contract that required him to be available prior to a shift in case he was needed. The company fired the employee in a dispute over the contract provision, but he was reinstated after filing a grievance and an unfair labor practice charge. He was fired a second time for allegedly failing to respond to a call and was again reinstated after a successful grievance. The company then instituted a new policy calling for discharge of employees who were late for work twice without good cause. The employee was late for work twice within six days, and on the second occasion called to explain that his car had broken down. The company determined that he had been lying and fired him again. He filed a second unfair labor practice charge against the company and repeated his false story at a hearing. An administrative law judge determined that the third discharge had been based upon good cause. The NLRB reversed the ruling. Even though the employee had lied about his reason for being late, the company had not actually discharged him for lying. The company had instituted a retroactive policy and had used it as a pretext to discharge him. Accordingly, the discharge was unlawful and the board reinstated the employee with back pay. The Tenth Circuit affirmed, and the U.S. Supreme Court also affirmed. **Because the NLRB's authority to order reinstatement was not restricted, it was not required to adopt a strict rule barring reinstatement with back pay for an employee who falsely testified.** *ABF Freight System, Inc. v. NLRB*, 510 U.S. 317, 114 S.Ct. 835, 127 L.Ed.2d 152 (1994).

2. Organization Issues

It is an unfair labor practice for an employer to interfere with employees' rights to organize and bargain collectively. Thus, if employees engage in organizing activity, they cannot be threatened, disciplined, transferred or fired.

Employers can explain the predicted negative effects that will result from unionization. However, such statements are often deemed to be threats, so any such statement should be cleared with an attorney before being made to ensure that it will not be found unlawful.

If an employee would have been otherwise disciplined for legitimate reasons, the employee may still be disciplined. However, any action taken is likely to be heavily scrutinized. Thus, it is important to be consistent with any action taken. Don't just discipline the union organizer for being late if you don't discipline others for tardiness.

Where employees seek to de-certify their union, only ministerial aid can be offered.

◆ When the Communication Workers of America tried to organize an Arizona hospital's housekeeping staff, the hospital president met with workers. He told them he didn't think a union was necessary and said he would not be able to have the same kind of direct conversation with them if a union was formed. A federal appeals court decided that the president's conduct did not amount to a threat and did not violate the NLRA. **Employers may "explain the advantages and disadvantages of collective bargaining"** to convince employees they would be better off without a union. *Flagstaff Medical Center, Inc. v. National Labor Relations Board*, 715 F.3d 928 (D.C. Cir. 2013).

◆ After an Iowa welder contacted a union to learn about union representation, the company CEO called a meeting to explain why he opposed the union. When the welder asked the CEO if the welder could talk to workers about forming a union, **the CEO told him to "shut up and sit down."** Three weeks later, the welder was fired. Another worker who supported the union was terminated, and a third was terminated after he accused the employer of overcharging workers for the cost of cleaning employee uniforms. Still another worker was fired after he directly contacted the uniform cleaning service. Two more workers were fired after they supported other fired workers, while still another two were let go after they called a co-worker to investigate a rumor that he had been fired. The court decided all of the firings violated the NLRA because they punished employees for engaging in protected activity. *National Labor Relations Board v. RELCO Locomotives, Inc.*, 734 F.3d 764 (8th Cir. 2013).

◆ Starbucks issues employees multiple pins and buttons to reward them for their performance and to promote its products. But it limited employees to wearing only one pro-union button. When employees and a union in New York challenged the policy, the NLRB ruled that it violated the NLRA and ordered Starbucks to allow employees to wear more than one pro-union button. However, the Second Circuit refused to enforce the order. It held that **Starbucks could implement a dress code policy prohibiting multiple pro-union buttons or pins** to prevent distractions from the messages it wished to send to its customers. *NLRB v. Starbucks Corp.*, 679 F.3d 70 (2d Cir. 2012).

◆   Off-duty employees joined union members outside a California grocery store in handing out pro-union flyers. After customers complained, the store required on-duty employees to hand out flyers explaining that the store was a great place to work. However, the flyers contained two misleading statements. The first was that the people handing out the store's flyers weren't employees, and the second was that the grocer's employees didn't support a union. Yet a majority of employees had asked the store to recognize a union without an election. After unfair labor practice charges were filed, **the NLRB held that the grocer violated the NLRA by forcing employees to take an anti-union stand**. *Tesco PLC and United Food and Commercial Workers Int'l Union*, Nos. 31-029913, 31-030021, and 31-030088 (NLRB 6/25/12).

◆   An Ohio supervisor **claimed that his boss asked him to build a case against employees who were trying to unionize and to then fire them**. He refused to do so. The following year, he was transferred to the least desirable part of the plant, and two years after that, he was fired for "badging" an employee (clocking in a worker under a different employee's time badge). He filed a complaint with the NLRB, but it informed him that it had found no evidence he was fired for refusing to commit an unfair labor practice. Rather than appeal that ruling, he withdrew the charge and sued. A federal court and the Sixth Circuit ruled against him, noting that his lawsuit was preempted by the NLRA and that he waived his right to appeal the adverse ruling by withdrawing the complaint. *Lewis v. Whirlpool Corp.*, 630 F.3d 484 (6th Cir. 2011).

◆   A nonunion janitorial company took over a Florida university's cleaning contract from a unionized business and hired a number of employees from the unionized business. It refused to recognize the union, however, and a low-level supervisor told an employee that three other employees hadn't been hired because of their strong support for the union. He also told the employee he could be fired too if he voiced support for the union. The union filed unfair labor practice charges, and the National Labor Relations Board ruled that **the company had violated the NLRA by refusing to hire the union supporters** and by threatening the other employee. *TCB Systems, Inc.*, Case 12-CA-25299, Slip Opinion #355-162 (NLRB 8/27/10).

◆   An Oregon newspaper publisher had a computer policy that prohibited employees from using email to solicit or proselytize for commercial, religious, political or other non-job-related reasons. After it issued an employee two disciplinary warnings for soliciting union business in violation of its email policy, the employee's union filed unfair labor practice charges against it, claiming a violation of the employee's Section 8(a)(1) and 8(a)(3) rights. It claimed interference with the employee's right to organize and discrimination because of union membership. The case reached the U.S. Court of Appeals, D.C. Circuit, which held that **the publisher violated the NLRA by selectively enforcing its email communications policy**. The publisher let employees send non-job-related messages, such as offers to sell sports tickets and party invitations, so it could not discipline the employee for discussing union matters in his email. *Guard Publishing Co. v. NLRB*, 571 F.3d 53 (D.C. Cir. 2009).

◆   A uniform supply business had a dress code that required employees to wear navy blue pants and a light blue shirt provided by the company. The company allowed employees at a North Carolina facility to wear decorative and holiday pins but refused to let employees wear pro-union stickers on their shirts. A supervisor also removed pro-union flyers from the break room and made an employee take down one from her work area, claiming that they violated the company's no-solicitation policy. When the union alleged unfair labor practices, the National Labor Relations Board and the Eighth Circuit agreed. **The selective enforcement of the dress code combined with the removal of the flyers amounted to a violation of the NLRA.** *Cintas Corp. v. NLRB*, 589 F.3d 905 (8th Cir. 2009).

◆   Two employees of a Las Vegas casino also served as union organizers. They approached some co-workers during lunch to ask if the co-workers wanted to sign union cards. After watching this for a moment, a vice president of HR walked over to their table and said she wanted to make sure they had all the facts before they signed the cards. She pointed out that signing the cards was "legal and binding," and also stated that the cards authorized the union to start taking dues out of the employees' paychecks. She further told the employees that union dues were $32.50 a month. This interruption lasted about eight minutes. The vice president then walked away. When the union filed unfair labor practice charges with the NLRB, the case reached the Ninth Circuit. The court of appeals held that **the vice president did not violate the NLRA because her statements to the employees were not coercive or threatening**. Thus, she did not interfere with the employees' right to organize. *Local Joint Executive Board of Las Vegas v. NLRB*, 515 F.3d 942 (9th Cir. 2008).

◆   A company operated several hospitals and related facilities in Ohio. When a union began organizing efforts at several of those facilities, the company hired consultants to provide labor relations training to managers and supervisors. A few months later, the union filed unfair labor practice charges with the NLRB, asserting that **the company selectively enforced its "no solicitation/no distribution" policy**, disciplined employees based on their union activities, created the impression of surveillance among its employees, and unlawfully threatened its employees. The NLRB ordered the company to take various remedial measures, which it refused to do. The Sixth Circuit held that the "coachings" (warnings) given to employees involved in organizing activities amounted to disciplinary action in violation of the NLRA. Also, the company selectively enforced its no-solicitation policy only against union organizing material. Further, it improperly gave the impression that employees' union activities were under surveillance. Finally, a warning to an employee not to talk to other employees about the union while on the job amounted to an implied coercive threat. The court ordered enforcement of the NLRB's order in part. *NLRB v. Promedica Health Systems, Inc.*, 206 Fed.Appx. 405 (6th Cir. 2006).

◆   A nonunion company in Nebraska advertised for electricians. Eight union employees who applied for the job were not hired. A ninth union employee was hired, but he went on strike because he was not being paid union wages. The company's president told him that he viewed the action as a "voluntary quit." He then told employees that the electrician's recruiting efforts could cost them their jobs, and denigrated the union and its members. The union filed an unfair labor practice charge, and the NLRB found that **the company violated the NLRA by threatening employees with plant closure and job loss**. It ordered various remedies. The U.S. Court of Appeals, D.C. Circuit, granted the NLRB's petition for enforcement, ruling that the president's comments violated the NLRA. *Progressive Electric, Inc. v. NLRB*, 453 F.3d 538 (D.C. Cir. 2006).

◆   A driver for a trucking company in Florida had three separate incidents in less than a month in which a client's merchandise was damaged. On the day of the third incident, he faxed a letter to his supervisors stating that he intended to form a union. He was fired three days later. He then filed unfair labor charges with the NLRB. An administrative law judge and the NLRB ordered his reinstatement, but the Fourth Circuit reversed. Here, the driver was fired because of his pattern of negligence, which cost the company over $2,000. **Even though he engaged in protected activity, he was not shielded from termination for his poor performance.** *TNT Logistics of North America, Inc. v. NLRB*, 413 F.3d 402 (4th Cir. 2005).

◆   A Wal-Mart employee in Oklahoma wore a pro-union T-shirt into the store during off-duty time but did not discuss union matters with fellow employees. Store managers nonetheless escorted him out. The next day, he invited several co-workers to a union meeting and told one co-worker he wanted her to sign a union authorization card. He was then subjected to a written "coaching session" – the first step in Wal-Mart's progressive disciplinary process. The union filed an unfair labor practice charge with the NLRB, which held that Wal-Mart violated Section 8(a)(1) and (3) of the NLRA. The Eighth Circuit upheld that decision in part. **Wal-Mart should not have escorted the employee out of the store, and disciplining him for inviting others to a union meeting was improper.** However, Wal-Mart could, in keeping with its anti-solicitation policy, discipline him for asking the co-worker to sign the union authorization card. *Wal-Mart Stores v. NLRB*, 400 F.3d 1093 (8th Cir. 2005).

◆   A maintenance mechanic for an Arizona company had a perfect attendance record and no disciplinary problems. He became a vocal supporter of a union that had begun a union-organizing campaign. When he was temporarily assigned to work the night shift, he left work early on two consecutive days after day shift maintenance mechanics arrived and told him the floor was covered. The company treated his actions as job abandonment under the code of conduct rather than an attendance problem. It fired him, and the union filed an unfair labor practice charge with the NLRB. The NLRB ruled against the company, citing four incidents demonstrating anti-union animus: making the employee remove a union button because of a ban on jewelry, but not requiring anyone else to remove their jewelry; barring talk about the union because of a so-called ban on non-work conversations that never existed; forcing the employee to cover up his union T-shirt while walking through the shop to collect his personal belongings after being fired; and commenting to the employee about his bad attitude. The Seventh Circuit upheld the NLRB's order, finding that **the company's inconsistency in enforcing its policies justified the ruling against it**. *SCA Tissue North America LLC v. NLRB*, 371 F.3d 983 (7th Cir. 2004).

◆   Bowling Transportation had a single client: AK Steel. AK Steel awarded safety bonuses to Bowling of up to $1 for each employee-hour of injury-free work. It encouraged Bowling to pass the entire bonus on to its employees, but Bowling kept half the money for a Christmas party and some safety equipment. When two Bowling employees complained to an AK Steel manager about not receiving the entire bonus, AK Steel instructed Bowling to remove the employees from its premises. Bowling fired the employees, who then filed a complaint with the NLRB. An administrative law judge determined that the employees had engaged in "protected concerted activity" under the NLRA, and that Bowling had violated their rights when it fired them. The Sixth Circuit agreed with that assessment. Even though the employees' complaints about the safety bonuses had nothing to do with union activity, **their actions qualified as protected concerted activity**. Despite the difficult position Bowling was in, it could have sued AK Steel for breach of contract or sued under federal labor laws if AK Steel had thrown it off site for noncompliance. *Bowling Transportation, Inc. v. NLRB*, 352 F.3d 274 (6th Cir. 2003).

◆   An HR manager at a Tennessee plant overheard two stockroom employees talking about paying union dues. The HR manager talked with a stockroom team leader, who promised to reprimand employees for punching in early even though the company had tolerated punching in early in the past. The stockroom team leader then told an employee that the HR manager was on the warpath and that the "union stuff" had management "stirred." A few days before union elections, the division president held a series of meetings at which he warned employees that the plant might have to shut down if they voted for the union. When the union lost the election, it filed charges with the NLRB. An administrative law judge found that **the stockroom team leader was properly considered part of management** for NLRA purposes when he threatened to impose more stringent working conditions on employees because of their union activity, and also determined that the division president had improperly threatened to close the plant. However, the company did not violate the NLRA when it removed union flyers from the bulletin board because it had a consistently enforced policy of allowing only personal postings. The Seventh Circuit upheld that ruling. *Fleming Companies, Inc. v. NLRB*, 349 F.3d 968 (7th Cir. 2003).

◆   A Louisiana man and his wife owned all the shares of an electrical company that provided residential and commercial contracting services. The man agreed to recognize a union as the collective bargaining agent of the company's employees and paid union wages to employees working on commercial jobs. The company, with the knowledge of the union's business manager, followed a longstanding industry practice of using nonunion labor at nonunion wages for residential projects. When a new business manager later complained about that practice, a payment was made to the union's apprentice fund to resolve the matter. However, the man then resigned as president of the company and opened another business with his wife, providing the same services and using the old company's employees, building and three of its five trucks. The stock of the old company was transferred to the man's father without compensation. The new business did not pay union wages. When the union complained, the NLRB concluded that **the man had violated the NLRA by forming a new company that was the alter ego of the first company** in order to avoid his collective bargaining obligations. The Fifth Circuit U.S. Court of Appeals upheld the board's order in favor of the union. *Vallery Electric, Inc. v. NLRB*, 337 F.3d 446 (5th Cir. 2003).

◆   A nonunion company "lent" several thousand temporary construction workers a year to contractors on the West Coast. The company implemented a 30% rule with respect to wages (refusing to hire applicants whose recent wages were 30% higher or lower than its starting wages), and it also began a better screening process in an effort to retain more employees. When a union targeted the company as part of a "salting" campaign, two union employees obtained jobs with the company. When their projects were completed, they were let go and were not offered any further positions because the company knew that they were pro-union. An unfair labor practices charge was filed, and the NLRB determined that the 30% rule was discriminatory under the NLRA. It also found that the two employees should be reinstated with make-whole damages. The U.S. Court of Appeals, D.C. Circuit, enforced the NLRB's order only in part. It noted that **the 30% rule was not discriminatory against union employees** because the rule was motivated by legitimate business objectives. *Contractors' Labor Pool, Inc. v. NLRB*, 323 F.3d 1051 (D.C. Cir. 2003).

◆   A Massachusetts employer recognized a union as the collective bargaining representative of its employees and negotiated a series of agreements with it over an 11-year period. Contract negotiations for a new agreement were unsuccessful, and employees struck for over a month. The employer then made an acceptable contract offer. The union accepted by telegraph. The following day, the employer disavowed the agreement and denied any duty to continue bargaining, claiming that 13 of the 23 bargaining unit employees had resigned from the union and that nine had crossed the picket line during the strike. The union filed a complaint with the NLRB, which determined that the employer's action violated the NLRA. It ordered the employer to reduce the agreement to writing. The First Circuit enforced the NLRB order, and the U.S. Supreme Court affirmed. **Unions were entitled to a presumption of majority status for one year following certification and for up to three years during the term of any bargaining agreement.** The employer could not raise the issue of majority support after the acceptance of a collective bargaining agreement because to do so would give the employer an unfair advantage in contract negotiations. The Court required the employer to bargain. *Auciello Iron Works, Inc. v. NLRB*, 517 U.S. 781, 116 S.Ct. 1754, 135 L.Ed.2d 64 (1996).

E. Union Elections

The NLRB has wide discretion in establishing procedures to ensure the fair and free choice of bargaining representatives by employees. However, it cannot act arbitrarily and capriciously in doing so. Employers can withdraw recognition from a union, or conduct an internal poll of employee support for a union, only where they have a good-faith reasonable doubt about the union's majority support. They may also request a formal, NLRB-supervised election where they doubt a union enjoys majority support.

♦   The managers of a Pennsylvania truck parts and service factory branch purchased the branch and began operating it. They hired 32 of the 45 branch employees and learned that eight of them had expressed doubt about support for their existing union. The new employer rejected the union's request for recognition as the employees' bargaining representative and then conducted a poll that resulted in a 19-13 loss by the union. The NLRB determined that the employer had inherited the branch's bargaining obligation under the presumption of continuing majority support. The poll was unlawful because the employer had no objective reasonable doubt about continuing majority support for the union. It ordered the employer to recognize and bargain with the union. The U.S. Court of Appeals enforced the order.

The U.S. Supreme Court upheld the NLRB's standard for reviewing employer polling, even though it resembled the high standard required for evaluating an employer's withdrawal of recognition. However, the NLRB's decision in this case was contrary to the standard since at least 20% of the employees had expressed doubt about continuing support for the union. The NLRB had disregarded important statements by two employees who had stated that the union would not win an election, supporting the inference of reasonable uncertainty by the employer. Because **the employer had a reasonable, good-faith ground to doubt the union's majority support**, the Court reversed the judgment and remanded the case with instructions to deny enforcement of the NLRB's order. *Allentown Mack Sales and Service, Inc. v. NLRB*, 522 U.S. 359, 118 S.Ct. 818, 139 L.Ed.2d 797 (1998).

♦   The NLRB certified a local union in Washington as the collective bargaining representative of a bank's employees. Eight years later, in an election in which only union members were allowed to vote, the local voted to affiliate with an international labor organization. It then petitioned the NLRB to amend its certification to reflect this change. The NLRB initially granted the petition, finding that the bank had committed an unfair labor practice by refusing to bargain with the new entity. Eventually it decided that, because nonunion employees had not been allowed to vote in the affiliation election, the election did not meet minimal due process standards. It found the affiliation invalid. The U.S. Court of Appeals, Ninth Circuit, remanded the case because it deemed the NLRB's requirement that nonunion employees be allowed to vote on affiliation questions inconsistent with the NLRA.

The U.S. Supreme Court affirmed the Ninth Circuit's decision, holding that **the NLRB had exceeded its authority in requiring that nonunion employees be allowed to vote for affiliation** before it would order the employer to bargain with the affiliated union. Here, the NLRB effectively circumvented the NLRA's decertification procedures and allowed for outside interference in union decisionmaking. *NLRB v. Financial Institution Employees of America Local 1182*, 475 U.S. 192, 106 S.Ct. 1007, 89 L.Ed.2d 151 (1986).

◆   An employee asked a union to help him get his employer's safety and maintenance workers unionized. A union representative prepared union authorization cards with his name and phone number on them and solicited them to the corporation's workers. The employee helped hand out authorization cards. However, he also became aggressive, telling six co-workers they would be fired if they didn't vote for the union. The six co-workers reported the threats to management, which assured them that no jobs would be lost either way. After the union was elected, the corporation refused to bargain with it because of the threats and harassment. However, the NLRB and the D.C. Circuit ruled that the election was still valid. **The union wasn't responsible for the employee's actions, which were outside the scope of what the union authorized him to do**, and the corporation had assured employees that they wouldn't be fired. *NLRB v. Downtown BID Services Corp.*, 682 F.3d 109 (D.C. Cir. 2012).

◆   After 57 of 91 union-eligible employees of a California company signed union authorization cards, the company disciplined and fired two employees because of their support for the union. It also disciplined a third employee and threatened a fourth. When the election was held, only 37 of 79 votes cast were in favor of representation by the union. The union filed an unfair labor practice charge with the NLRB, and an administrative law judge (ALJ) found that the company had violated the NLRA. The ALJ recommended a number of remedies, including reinstatement of the fired workers and a *Gissel* order requiring the company to recognize and bargain with the union. The NLRB affirmed the ALJ's recommendations except for the *Gissel* order. Instead, the NLRB determined that the other remedies would enable the union to get a fair rerun election, and satisfactorily protect and restore employees' section 7 rights. The case reached the Ninth Circuit, which held that **the NLRB did not abuse its discretion in refusing to impose the extreme remedy of a *Gissel* order on the company**. *United Steel Workers of America AFL-CIO-CLC v. NLRB*, 482 F.3d 1112 (9th Cir. 2007).

◆   Shortly before a union election at a Virginia plant, a union circulated a "vote yes" petition, after a voluntary meeting where a union representative told employees that everyone should sign the petition. After several employees complained that they felt intimidated by the union's actions, the company sent out a memo in which it characterized the "vote yes" petition as a straw vote, and emphasized that regardless of whether employees felt pressured to sign the petition, they should not feel pressured to vote for the union. The memo told employees they had an "absolute right to vote NO" in the election. When employees voted for union representation, the company refused to bargain with the local, and the international union filed an unfair labor practices charge. The NLRB found in favor of the union, and the Fourth Circuit Court of Appeals granted its request for an enforcement order. Although employers cannot poll employees prior to a union election, unions can – provided their actions are not coercive. Here, a reasonable employee would not have felt "intimidated, threatened or coerced" because **the company sent out a memo countering the union's allegedly coercive actions**. *NLRB v. Media General Operations*, 360 F.3d 434 (4th Cir. 2004).

* Prior to a union election, an organizer for the Communications Workers of America invited the employees of a Michigan cable company to Chicago for a two-hour meeting on cable industry issues. The meeting was to take place on the weekend after the election, and the union promised to pick up all the expenses for the weekend (about $50 per person). After the employees voted 31 to 17 in favor of the union, the company refused to bargain. The union filed an unfair labor practice charge with the NLRB, which ruled in its favor. The Sixth Circuit Court of Appeals reversed the ruling and invalidated the election. It found that **the offer of a free weekend in Chicago had the potential to influence employees' votes**. Earlier cases had invalidated elections where unions had given away benefits that were far less substantial. *Comcast Cablevision-Taylor v. NLRB*, 232 F.3d 490 (6th Cir. 2000).

* After a California concrete manufacturer's contract with a local teamsters bargaining unit expired, the unit went on strike. The manufacturer hired replacement workers who signed a de-certification petition. The company then withdrew its recognition of the union. The union filed unfair labor charges with the NLRB, asserting that the company's requirement that replacement employees list their union affiliation on the job application form illegally coerced them into signing the union de-certification petition. An administrative law judge (ALJ) held that the inquiry into union membership of replacement applicants and a manager's later interrogation of a replacement driver each violated Section 8(a)(1) of the NLRA. The ALJ concluded, however, that neither violation tainted the signatures supporting de-certification. The Board reversed, and the company appealed to the D.C. Circuit Court of Appeals. Finding **no causal connection between the application form and the de-certification petition**, the court held for the company. Nothing about the way the request for union information in the form was presented would draw attention to it or suggest that it would leave a memorable impression. *Mathews Readymix, Inc. v. NLRB*, 165 F.3d 74 (D.C. Cir. 1999).

* A union local won an election at an Atlanta transportation service center by a wide margin. However, the employer refused to bargain, accusing the union of unlawfully conducting video and photographic surveillance of employees in the election area. It argued that the union intimidated and coerced employees by conducting a raucous rally within the hearing of a polling station and within sight of employees waiting to vote. The union stated that it had only conducted a cookout that was not characterized by electioneering. The NLRB found that the employer unlawfully refused to bargain and certified the union as the exclusive bargaining representative for the employees. The employer appealed to the D.C. Circuit, arguing that the video and photo surveillance had interfered with the election and required setting it aside. The union stated that the activity was not attributable to it but rather to certain union-supporting employees and that a lower standard for third-party conduct applied, requiring enforcement of its order. The court stated that **misconduct attributable to third parties may result in the setting aside of a union election only where it is so aggravated as to create a general atmosphere of fear and reprisal**. The alleged misconduct did not create an atmosphere of fear and reprisal so as to require

setting aside the election. The court enforced the NLRB's order. *Overnite Transportation Co. v. NLRB*, 140 F.3d 259 (D.C. Cir. 1998).

✦   A Pennsylvania employer complained of **pro-union songs blaring from a truck loudspeaker parked at a plant on the day of a union election**. It refused to negotiate with the union after the election. An administrative law judge found that the employer did not commit an unfair labor practice by doing so. The NLRB disagreed, finding that the campaign songs did not constitute campaign speech because the songs were void of specific campaign promises. The U.S. Court of Appeals, Third Circuit, reversed the decision of the NLRB, holding that it was inconsistent with earlier NLRB determinations. The court observed that music might appeal to the visceral emotions of workers and have a potentially larger impact upon them than an actual speech. The court refused to enforce the NLRB's order requiring the employer to bargain with the union. *Bro-Tech Corp. v. NLRB*, 105 F.3d 890 (3d Cir. 1997).

✦   A management employee of a New England pharmaceutical distributor gave speeches discouraging unionization and referred to possible closure of the warehouse, loss of jobs and loss of benefits should the union win an election. The union won the election by three votes; however, the vote of regular employees was evenly split. The distributor contested votes cast by temporary employees, asserting they had no community of interest with regular employees sufficient to allow them to vote in the election. When the distributor refused to bargain, the NLRB issued a bargaining order to recognize the union. The Second Circuit stated that a bargaining order is a rare administrative remedy that is to be used only when other remedies cannot eliminate an employer's unfair labor practices. Here, the management employee had a right to tell employees his opinion of the economic consequences of unionization. The only unfair labor practice of the employer was a threat of discharge that had later been retracted. Because of this mitigating factor, the NLRB had inappropriately issued a bargaining order. There was a genuine fact issue concerning **whether some of the temporary employees had a community of interest sufficient to allow them to vote**. The NLRB was required to either order a new election or reconsider the validity of the temporary employees' ballots. *Kinney Drugs, Inc. v. NLRB*, 74 F.3d 1419 (2d Cir. 1996).

✦   A paper manufacturer and two unions representing employees of a Maine paper mill were unable to renegotiate their collective bargaining agreement, and union members engaged in an economic strike. The company hired replacement workers and laid off 151 striking union employees. Some of the union employees petitioned the NLRB to hold an election to de-certify the union. Prior to the election, the unions ended the strike with an unconditional offer to return to work. The parties entered into an agreement to recall former strikers when positions occupied by replacement workers became available. The union members then voted for de-certification. The manufacturer advised the unions and some of the laid off employees that they no longer had recall rights. The unions sued, arguing that the recall agreement had survived the de-certification election and remained binding. The court held for the manufacturer, and the

First Circuit affirmed. It found **no evidence that the parties had contemplated the survival of the recall agreement in the event of de-certification**. *United Paperworkers Int'l, Local 14 v. Int'l Paper Co.*, 64 F.3d 28 (1st Cir. 1995).

F. Arbitration

This section addresses arbitration in the context of labor relations. For cases involving arbitration with respect to other employment issues, see Chapter Six, Section VI.

The Supreme Court has found a presumption of arbitrability with respect to collective bargaining agreements (CBAs) in Section 301 of the Labor Management Relations Act (LMRA), noting that arbitrators are in a better position than courts to interpret the terms of a CBA.

However, where the question is not one of interpreting a CBA but rather a federal statute, the presumption in favor of arbitrability fails.

◆　The U.S. Supreme Court held that **a collective bargaining agreement's general arbitration clause did not require a covered employee to use arbitration to redress alleged violations of the Americans with Disabilities Act (ADA)**. The Court left open the question of whether such a clause would be enforceable if it provided a clear and unmistakable waiver to redress those rights in federal court. The case involved a longshoreman who brought suit under the ADA. A South Carolina federal court dismissed the case because the longshoreman had failed to pursue his administrative remedies. However, the Supreme Court held that the general arbitration clause was not specific enough to require arbitration. The Court also refused to reconcile two earlier Supreme Court cases on arbitration: *Alexander v. Gardner-Denver Co.*, 415 U.S. 36 (1974), where the Court held that an individual subject to a collective bargaining agreement's arbitration clause does not forfeit his or her right to sue in court for discriminatory discharge under Title VII, and *Gilmer v. Interstate/Johnson Lane Corp.*, 500 U.S. 20 (1991), where the Court held that a security broker's federal age discrimination claim could be subject to compulsory arbitration under a clause in the security registration form that the broker had to sign in order to work. *Wright v. Universal Maritime Service Corp.*, 525 U.S. 70, 119 S.Ct. 391, 142 L.Ed.2d 361 (1998).

◆　The collective bargaining agreement between an airline and a union included an agency shop clause, under which nonunion pilots had to pay a monthly agency fee of 81% of union dues. The fee was based only on expenditures attributable to collective bargaining. A number of nonunion pilots sued the union, asserting that the agency fee overstated collective bargaining expenses. Union policies and procedures provided for the arbitration of fee calculations, but the bargaining agreement did not specify arbitration. The union treated objections to the fee calculation as requests for arbitration and referred them to an arbitrator, who consolidated the cases and recalculated the agency fee. The union then moved for pretrial judgment, asserting that the pilots were required to exhaust their arbitral remedies before filing suit. The court agreed, finding that 62 pilots who had not joined the arbitration were bound by the decision. The U.S. Court of Appeals, D.C. Circuit, reversed. The U.S. Supreme Court noted that *Chicago Teachers Union v. Hudson*, 475 U.S. 292 (1986), required public employee unions to provide objecting employees a reasonably prompt opportunity to challenge the amount of an agency fee by appeal to an impartial decision maker. This rule did not require a party to accept arbitration where no arbitration agreement existed, since arbitration is a matter of contract. The requirement of an impartial decision maker did not bar the dissenting pilots' immediate resort to federal court. **The Court rejected the union's assertion that arbitration was necessary to assure a prompt decision by an impartial decisionmaker.** The Court affirmed the court of appeals. *Air Line Pilots Ass'n v. Miller*, 523 U.S. 866, 118 S.Ct. 1761, 140 L.Ed.2d 1070 (1998).

◆   A Michigan company discharged two employees for "just cause," and the employees disputed this. They believed there had been no just cause as required by the collective bargaining agreement. They invoked the agreement's grievance procedures without success and then filed suit against the company under Section 301 of the Labor Management Relations Act. A federal court granted pretrial judgment to the company, and the Sixth Circuit Court of Appeals affirmed, holding that a strike or other job action is the proper remedy for failure to successfully resolve a grievance where arbitration is not required. The U.S. Supreme Court reversed the appellate court's ruling. It noted that Section 301 provides a federal remedy for breach of a labor agreement and that there was **a strong presumption that the federal courts would provide access for the peaceful resolution of labor disputes**. Here, since the parties had not agreed to arbitration, a neutral forum would be provided. Even though the collective bargaining agreement allowed strikes or lockouts upon exhaustion of the grievance process, this did not mean that the employees had to resort to such economic weapons as strikes. The Court remanded the case for further proceedings. *Groves v. Ring Screw Works*, 498 U.S. 168, 111 S.Ct. 498, 112 L.Ed.2d 508 (1990).

◆   A carman, employed by a railroad, brought a lawsuit against the railroad under the Federal Employers' Liability Act (FELA). He claimed that fellow employees had harassed, threatened and intimidated him, causing him emotional injury, and that the railroad had condoned these acts. The railroad asserted that the employee's sole remedy was through the National Railroad Adjustment Board, according to the Railway Labor Act (RLA). The U.S. Supreme Court held that **although the injury at issue might have been subject to arbitration under the RLA** (a dispute arising out of workplace conditions which was similar to a "minor" labor dispute), it was also possibly the type of injury that the FELA was enacted to address. The Court remanded the case for a determination of whether emotional injury was cognizable under the FELA. *Atchison, Topeka and Santa Fe Railway Co. v. Buell*, 480 U.S. 557, 107 S.Ct. 1410, 94 L.Ed.2d 563 (1987).

◆   A California grocery clerk worked under a collective bargaining agreement that called for binding arbitration to resolve disputes arising from termination or suspension. After the employer fired the clerk, it refused to comply with her demand for the immediate payment of wages owed. Full payment was made by mail three days later. When the clerk filed a claim for a penalty, the California Division of Labor Standards Enforcement (DLSE) refused to take action to enforce the claim, advising her by letter that it did not resolve disputes arising from bargaining agreements that contained arbitration clauses. The clerk sued under 42 U.S.C. § 1983, claiming that the DLSE's policy violated her rights under the NLRA. The U.S. Supreme Court held that **the issue of whether the employer had willfully failed to pay the clerk's wages was independent of the bargaining agreement** and was a matter of state law. It was unnecessary to look to the bargaining agreement except to compute damages. Therefore, there was no federal preemption of the state law claim. The employee was entitled to relief under Section 1983 for violation of her rights under the NLRA. *Livadas v. Bradshaw*, 512 U.S. 107, 114 S.Ct. 2068, 129 L.Ed.2d 93 (1994).

◆ A corporation operated a check-printing plant in California. After the collective bargaining agreement expired, 10 of the plant's employees were laid off. The union filed grievances, claiming a violation of the agreement. The corporation refused to process the grievances or submit to arbitration. The NLRB determined that the corporation had violated the NLRA and ordered it to process the grievances and to bargain with the union over the layoffs, but it refused to order arbitration. The Ninth Circuit enforced the NLRB's order except that it found the layoff grievance arbitrable. The corporation appealed to the U.S. Supreme Court, which held that the layoff dispute was not arbitrable. It refused to impose a statutory duty on the corporation to arbitrate a post-expiration dispute. **Arbitration will not be imposed if to do so would go beyond the scope of the parties' consent.** Further, since the layoff dispute did not arise under the collective bargaining agreement, its arbitration provisions could not be used to force arbitration. *Litton Financial Printing v. NLRB*, 501 U.S. 190, 111 S.Ct. 2215, 115 L.Ed.2d 177 (1991).

◆ Managers at a Florida clothing store sued under the FLSA, claiming their employer improperly classified them as exempt from overtime. The employer then instituted **a new alternative dispute resolution program** and told managers who potentially could opt in to the lawsuit that they had to sign an arbitration agreement as a condition of their employment. The court refused to compel the managers to arbitrate and said they could opt in to the suit. *Billingsley v. Citi Trends, Inc.*, 560 Fed.Appx. 914 (11th Cir. 2014) (Unpublished).

◆ A union entered into an agreement with a healthcare company setting forth rules governing the parties' conduct during a union organizational drive. One of the promises the company made was that it would not imply that employees would lose benefits, wages or be subject to less favorable working conditions by unionizing. After the union lost the election, it sent a letter to the company, charging it with engaging in 18 incidents that violated the pre-election agreement, including granting more favorable working conditions to employees on the hospital's "Vote No" committee. When it sought to arbitrate the dispute, the company denied the request. The union sued to compel arbitration, and a

California federal court dismissed the case. The Ninth Circuit Court of Appeals reversed, noting that **arbitration should have been ordered because the heart of the case was contractual** and not representational. Under Section 301 of the LMRA, federal courts have jurisdiction over cases involving the violation of private labor agreements. Since the agreement called for arbitration, the district court should have compelled arbitration. *Service Employees Int'l Union v. St. Vincent Medical Center*, 344 F.3d 977 (9th Cir. 2003).

◆   A manufacturer employed a unionized work force at an Illinois engine plant. A plant employee who was fired filed a grievance under the collective bargaining agreement. He then requested an arbitration hearing to challenge the action. A plant manager testified at the arbitration hearing that the employee slept on the job and falsified employment records. When the employee sued the manager and former employer for defamation, the court dismissed the case, ruling that the manager and former employer were protected by absolute immunity for their statements in the arbitration proceeding. The employee appealed to the Appellate Court of Illinois, which followed the majority of jurisdictions and held that **absolute immunity protects witnesses testifying before grievance and arbitration hearings**. The prospect of criminal prosecution for perjury acted as a check against false statements before an arbitrator. The court affirmed the dismissal of the case. *Bushell v. Caterpillar, Inc.*, 683 N.E.2d 1286 (Ill. App. Ct. 1997).

◆   The union representing steelworkers at a Missouri plant negotiated a collective bargaining agreement containing a "contracting out" prohibition. Under the agreement, the employer was forbidden from contracting out work that was normally performed by employees where there was appropriate equipment and time, and enough qualified employees to perform the work. The employer nonetheless transferred work from the Missouri plant to a nonunion Illinois facility that it operated, resulting in layoffs and other adverse effects for 60 employees. The union sought arbitration, and the arbitrator agreed that intra-corporate transfers of work violated the contracting out prohibition. The U.S. Court of Appeals, Eighth Circuit, observed **that an arbitrator's interpretation of a collective bargaining agreement is entitled to extreme judicial deference** so long as it is not unlawful and draws its essence from the bargaining agreement. Because the arbitrator's decision drew its essence from the bargaining agreement, the court upheld it. *American National Can Co. v. United Steelworkers of America*, 120 F.3d 886 (8th Cir. 1997).

◆   The U.S. Court of Appeals, Second Circuit, held that a federal court had improperly refused to enforce an arbitration order requiring the conditional reinstatement of a New York nuclear power employee who adulterated a urine sample and then tested positive for cocaine use. The conditional reinstatement did not violate public policy, as the lower court had held. **The public policy exception to the finality of arbitration awards is limited**, the Supreme Court has held, to cases where a labor contract or arbitration award actually violates laws or legal precedent. This was not such a case, since federal nuclear regulations do not require the discharge of employees who adulterate a drug test or submit a single positive test. The regulations specify a two-week suspension, encouraging employee retention and rehabilitation. The employer had never discharged an employee for a single positive drug test, and the award did not conflict with nuclear safety goals. *Int'l Brotherhood of Electrical Workers v. Niagara Mohawk Power Corp.*, 143 F.3d 704 (2d Cir. 1998).

III. LABOR ASSOCIATIONS AND COLLECTIVE BARGAINING AGREEMENTS

Labor associations may be liable to their members for unfair labor practices under the NLRA and may also be liable for violating the Labor Management Relations Act (LMRA), which requires labor associations (unions) to act on behalf of their members in good faith and to fairly represent them.

A labor association that engages in conduct that is <u>arbitrary, discriminatory, or in bad faith</u> may be liable for breach of the duty of good faith and fair representation of its membership. Unions also have a duty, when collecting fees from nonmembers, to use those fees only for collective bargaining.

A. Agency Fees and Union Security Agreements

The NLRA permits parties to a collective bargaining agreement to include <u>union shop clauses</u> under which the employer agrees to condition employment in a bargaining unit upon union membership. However, the U.S. Supreme Court has held that employers may not compel employees to support a union's political activities through their union dues.

Dissenting employees may avoid union membership by paying an <u>agency fee</u>, which is the portion of union dues representing only union expenditures for collective bargaining activities.

♦   The U.S. Supreme Court held that **a union does not breach its duty of fair representation by negotiating as part of its collective bargaining agreement a union security clause that tracks the language of Section 8(a)(3) of the NLRA**. A union cannot be said to be acting arbitrarily or in bad faith by failing to explain in the clause that membership is required only insofar as the "member" is required to pay fees used to support the union's collective bargaining activities. The case involved a part-time actress who obtained a one-line role in a television series. After she accepted the part, the Screen Actors Guild required her to pay the $500 union fees before she could start working. When she failed to pay, she was replaced. She sued the Screen Actors Guild for violating its duty of fair representation. The Supreme Court held that her claim could not succeed. By tracking the statutory language, the clause incorporated all of the judicial fine-tuning that has been associated with it in cases like *Beck*, below. *Marquez v. Screen Actors Guild*, 525 U.S. 33, 119 S.Ct. 292, 142 L.Ed.2d 242 (1998).

◆   Employees of a Maryland company, who chose not to become union members, were required to pay the union agency fees under the applicable collective bargaining agreement. A group of these employees sued the union, challenging its use of agency fees for purposes other than collective bargaining. A federal court found that such expenditures violated the First Amendment rights of nonmembers and enjoined the collection of fees for purposes other than collective bargaining. The U.S. Court of Appeals, Fourth Circuit, agreed that the **agency fees could not be used for nonrepresentational purposes**, but based its ruling on Section 8(a)(3) of the NLRA. The U.S. Supreme Court affirmed, finding that Section 8(a)(3) did not permit a union to expend funds collected from nonmember employees, over objection, on activities unrelated to collective bargaining. *Communications Workers of America v. Beck*, 487 U.S. 735, 108 S.Ct. 2641, 101 L.Ed.2d 634 (1988).

◆   A union and airline entered into an accretion agreement for non-unionized customer service agents to add them into the union for other service employees. Although they hadn't voted on a contract, the agents were required to pay union dues. They did receive some benefits as a result of the agreement. When the existing bargaining agreement expired and became open for negotiation, Northwest was on the verge of bankruptcy. **During Chapter 11, wages were cut. A number of agents then sought to become dues-objectors** by signing a petition letter. However, Northwest policy required dues-objectors to provide individual letters with names and addresses. Eventually the objecting agents sued the union for breaching the duty of fair representation with respect to how it handled their dues-objector status requests. A Michigan federal court and the Sixth Circuit ruled for the union and awarded Rule 11 sanctions against the agents for bringing a frivolous lawsuit. The union didn't breach a duty to process the procedurally defective requests. *Merritt v. Int'l Ass'n of Machinists & Aerospace Workers*, 613 F.3d 609 (6th Cir. 2010).

◆   A mechanic for TWA was subject to the collective bargaining agreement's union security clause, meaning he had to either join the union or pay an agency service fee (under which he would not be paying for any political activities of the union). After initially joining the union and having his union dues deducted from his paycheck, the mechanic requested that he be placed on agency fee payer status. The union complied, and TWA stopped deducting his union dues from his paycheck. However, he then stated that he would only pay the agency fees if they were deducted from his paycheck; he would not write a separate check to the union to cover his agency fees. He was fired for violating the bargaining agreement and sued under the Railway Labor Act (RLA) and the First Amendment. A Missouri federal court ruled against him, and the Eighth Circuit affirmed. Here, the RLA allowed TWA and the union to negotiate a check-off procedure that best suited their interests, and **nothing in the bargaining agreement required TWA to deduct agency fees**. Also, there was no First Amendment violation because the refusal to offer payroll deduction did not infringe on the mechanic's speech or association rights. *Conrad v. Int'l Ass'n of Machinists*, 338 F.3d 908 (8th Cir. 2003).

♦   A clerical worker in Virginia was employed by a company that withheld union dues and initiation fees from his paycheck without his authorization. The collective bargaining agreement required employees to become and remain union members in good standing under a security clause that required full union membership. When the worker requested a breakdown of how his union dues were being spent, he was not told that he could object to the withholding of fees for nonrepresentational activities and could only be compelled to pay the amount spent on representational activities. He was instead threatened with employment termination if he failed to become a union member. He filed an unfair labor practices charge against the employer and union with the NLRB. The employer and union settled the matter with the NLRB, and the U.S. Court of Appeals, Eighth Circuit, held that the settlement was proper. **A security clause can track the language of Section 8(a)(3) of the NLRA, using terms of art that employees may not understand without further explanation.** *Bloom v. NLRB*, 209 F.3d 1060 (8th Cir. 2000).

♦   A number of nonunion machinists whose bargaining units were represented by a union filed a complaint with the National Labor Relations Board (NLRB), challenging the union's assessment of dues. They claimed that the union should not be allowed to pool expenditures among all workers in the union, arguing that the agency fee should be limited to expenses from their own bargaining unit. They also claimed that audits should be performed by certified public accountants rather than union employees, and that the union had failed to properly notify them of their right to avoid union membership. The NLRB issued an order specifying procedures by which the union had to protect the dissenting employees' rights but upholding the union's pooling of expenditures, audit method and notification of rights through a union newsletter. It agreed with the dissenting machinists that the union could not require the payment of full union dues for the rest of the year for union members who quit after the "window" period. The U.S. Court of Appeals, Seventh Circuit, found a reasonable basis for the NLRB's decision as to each issue. **It was appropriate to allow the pooling of expenditures given the interdependence of each bargaining unit in the union,** and the notice to employees was reasonably calculated to notify employees of their rights. The court enforced the order. *Int'l Ass'n of Machinists and Aerospace Workers v. NLRB*, 133 F.3d 1012 (7th Cir. 1998).

♦   An employee of a New York aircraft manufacturer decided to resign from the union after more than 20 years of membership. Because union membership was a condition of continued employment under the union security clause, he had to pay almost 80% of normal union dues as "membership" dues despite resigning from the union. The dues deduction authorization he originally signed provided for a 10-day window each year during which he could revoke it. He attempted to revoke the payroll deduction authorization despite the passage of the revocation window period for that year. The company honored his demand to revoke the payroll deduction, and the union filed a grievance against the company. The employee filed a complaint with the NLRB, asserting that the union had committed an unfair labor practice in violation of the NLRA, which prohibits unions from causing an employer to discriminate against an employee.

The NLRB determined that the union action did not constitute an unfair labor practice, and the U.S. Court of Appeals, Second Circuit, agreed that **the employee's fee should be deducted from his wages by the employer until he made a timely revocation**. *Williams v. NLRB*, 105 F.3d 787 (2d Cir. 1997).

B. Union Representational Duties

The Supreme Court has held that Section 301(a) of the Labor Management Relations Act (LMRA), 29 U.S.C. § 185, authorizes lawsuits by and against individual employees as well as between unions and employers, including actions against employers for wrongful discharge.

Unions have a <u>duty of fair representation</u>, which is inferred from their exclusive authority under the NLRA to represent all employees in a bargaining unit. This duty requires unions "to serve the interests of all members without hostility or discrimination toward any [individual member], to exercise [their] discretion with complete good faith and honesty, and to avoid arbitrary conduct." *Vaca v. Sipes*, 386 U.S. 171, 87 S.Ct. 903, 17 L.Ed.2d 842 (1967).

Hybrid lawsuits brought under Section 301 of the LMRA assert breach of contract against the employer and breach of the duty of fair representation against the union. In such actions, employees need to show not only that the employer breached the collective bargaining agreement, but also that the union breached its duty of fair representation to the employee.

1. Unfair Labor Practices

It is an unfair labor practice for a union to restrain or coerce an employer in the selection of its representatives for the purposes of collective bargaining or the adjustment of grievances. A union also cannot restrict the right of employees to resign from the union.

◆ A union representing employees at a Pennsylvania manufacturing plant claimed that their employer fraudulently induced them to enter into a bargaining agreement that prohibited strikes for any reason. According to the union, absent the employer's fraud, it would not have entered into either the bargaining agreement or a separate memorandum agreement requiring the employer to give the union a seven-day notice prior to subcontracting out work. The union made the assertion after the employer announced its intention to contract out work, which would cause many union members to lose their jobs. A federal court dismissed the complaint as not arising under the LMRA since it alleged no violation of a labor contract. The U.S. Supreme Court agreed, noting that **the LMRA limits federal court jurisdiction to lawsuits for violations of labor contracts, not claims asserting that a contract is invalid**. This case had no purpose or object of demonstrating a violation of any contract, as the union argued. The bargaining agreement had already expired. *Textron Lycoming, AVCO Corp. v. United Automobile, Aerospace and AI Workers of America*, 523 U.S. 653, 118 S.Ct. 1626, 140 L.Ed.2d 863 (1998).

◆   A labor union fined two of its members who worked as supervisors for violating its constitution by working for employers who did not have collective bargaining agreements with the union. The employers then filed unfair labor practice charges with the NLRB, alleging that the union had violated Section 8(b)(1)(B) of the NLRA by restraining or coercing an employer in the selection of its representatives for the purposes of collective bargaining or the adjustment of grievances. An administrative law judge agreed with the employers, and the board entered an order against the union. However, the U.S. Court of Appeals reversed the board's order. The U.S. Supreme Court held that **discipline of a supervisor union member is prohibited under Section 8(b)(1)(B) only when that member is engaged in Section 8(b)(1)(B) activities**, like collective bargaining and grievance adjustment, or some other closely related activity. Since neither supervisor had such responsibilities, the union discipline was not an unfair labor practice. Further, the absence of a bargaining relationship between the union and the employers made the possibility of employer coercion too attenuated to form the basis of an unfair labor practice charge. Finally, the employers were not coerced by reason of the supervisors being fined by the union. The Court affirmed the ruling for the union. *NLRB v. Int'l Brotherhood of Electrical Workers, Local 340*, 481 U.S. 573, 107 S.Ct. 2002, 95 L.Ed.2d 557 (1987).

◆   A national union amended its constitution to provide that resignations or withdrawals from the national or its locals would not be permitted during a strike or lockout, or at a time when either appeared imminent. Ten Illinois union members violated this provision by resigning during a strike and returning to work. After the strike ended and a new bargaining agreement was signed, the union fined the 10 employees. The employers' representative then filed charges with the NLRB against the union, claiming that the imposition of fines was an unfair labor practice. The board agreed that it was unfair – in violation of Section 8(b)(1)(A) of the NLRA – and the U.S. Supreme Court upheld that decision. The levying of fines against the employees here violated their Section 7 rights because it coerced or restrained them from choosing not to engage in "concerted activities." Further, the board had justifiably concluded that **by restricting the right of employees to resign from the union, the provision in question impaired the policy of voluntary unionism implicit in Section 8(a)(3) of the NLRA**. Finally, Congress' intent to preserve for unions the control over their own "internal affairs" did not suggest an intent to authorize restrictions on the right to resign. *Pattern Makers' League of North America v. NLRB*, 473 U.S. 95, 105 S.Ct. 3064, 87 L.Ed.2d 68 (1985).

◆   A union representing laborers in Minnesota, North Dakota and Wisconsin had a labor dispute with a nonunion Wisconsin company. It refused to sign a collective bargaining agreement with a newly formed subcontractor because the subcontractor intended to do business with the company. The subcontractor filed unfair labor practice charges against the union, and the NLRB ordered the union to stop threatening or coercing the subcontractor in violation of Section 8(b)(4) of the NLRA – which prohibits using a secondary employer to coerce a primary employer to do what the union wants. The Eighth Circuit upheld the NLRB's order, finding that **the union had improperly pressured**

subcontractors not to do business with the company. *Laborers Dist. Council of Minnesota and North Dakota v. NLRB*, 688 F.3d 374 (8th Cir. 2012).

♦   An employee of a home health services company in New York was fired after she refused to enter a patient's apartment and cancelled several meetings to discuss the incident. She filed a grievance, and the union pursued the matter through various procedures. However, it ultimately declined to arbitrate the termination because it determined that it was well founded and arbitration would be futile. She then sued the company and the union under Section 301 of the LMRA. A federal court and the Second Circuit ruled against her, noting that **she failed to prove a breach of the bargaining agreement by the company or a breach of the duty of fair representation by the union.** *Pinkney v. Progressive Home Health Services*, 367 Fed.Appx. 210 (2d Cir. 2010).

♦   An Ohio company fired an employee because of her excessive absenteeism and prior disciplinary history. The union filed a grievance for her, but chose not to take the grievance to arbitration and notified her that it would take no further action on her behalf. She brought a hybrid suit under Section 301 of the LMRA, claiming that the employer violated the collective bargaining agreement by firing her and that the union breached its duty of fair representation. A federal court held that her lawsuit was untimely, but that even if she had filed it in time, she could not prove that the firing had been in violation of the bargaining agreement. **The company had taken numerous disciplinary actions against her prior to her termination.** Further, she failed to provide the company or the union with medical documentation to support her absences. Also, the union's decision not to arbitrate her grievance was not arbitrary or discriminatory. The hybrid lawsuit failed. *Burrell v. Henderson*, 504 F.Supp.2d 330 (S.D. Ohio 2007).

♦   A trailer manufacturer experienced a backlog of work orders at a Pennsylvania plant due to increasing customer demand. Without notifying the employees' collective bargaining representative, the manufacturer entered into a subcontracting agreement under which it shipped materials to the subcontractor for assembly. The union filed an unfair labor practices complaint against the employer for unilaterally implementing new job duties and wages and for subcontracting bargaining unit work. The NLRB ordered the employer to rescind the agreement. The Third Circuit held that a decision to subcontract bargaining unit work must be evaluated to determine the underlying management reasons for the agreement. Here, **the employer entered into the agreement for economic reasons.** There was substantial evidence that it was unable to meet customer demand at its Pennsylvania plant and would lose business if it did not subcontract the work. Also, the employer's motivation for the changes in wages and job duties was based on a desire to fill orders and not to eliminate overtime at the plant. The court denied enforcement of the NLRB's order. *Dorsey Trailers, Inc. v. NLRB*, 134 F.3d 125 (3d Cir. 1998).

♦   A California publishing company proposed a new wage system to its employees when the collective bargaining agreement of the parties expired. The parties deadlocked over wage terms, and, following an impasse, the employer awarded wage increases to employees based upon merit without consulting the union. The union filed an unfair labor practice complaint with the NLRB. The NLRB held that the employer was obligated to bargain with the union prior to changing any employee's pay and that the unilateral merit increases constituted an unfair labor practice. The union had not waived its right to be consulted about wage changes as contained in the bargaining agreement. The NLRB then determined that while **an employer generally satisfies its statutory duty by bargaining to impasse over a discretionary pay proposal**, the facts of this case presented an exception due to the lack of a waiver by the union as to its right to be consulted about wage changes. The U.S. Court of Appeals, D.C. Circuit, found that the NLRB could permissibly create an exception to the bargaining to impasse rule, since the employer's wage action was inherently destructive of fundamental principles of collective bargaining and allowed it to circumvent its statutory bargaining obligation. The court affirmed the NLRB's decision concerning implementation of the merit increase. *McClatchy Newspapers, Inc. v. NLRB*, 131 F.3d 1026 (D.C. Cir. 1997).

2. Breach of Duty

A union breaches its duty of fair representation if it acts in an irrational, arbitrary fashion that fails to provide its members with fair and adequate representation.

The arbitrary, discriminatory or bad faith standard applies to all union activity – not just contract negotiation – and the behavior must be so far outside a "wide range of reasonableness" as to be irrational.

◆   Non-union employees from different companies represented by different unions filed unfair labor practice charges to challenge policies that required them to annually opt out of paying for union political activity. The NLRB determined that **the renewal policies violated the unions' duty of fair representation** and struck them down. Although it denied a request for refunds because the unions were not on notice that the policies were unlawful, the Seventh Circuit preserved the NLRB's determination with respect to the legality of the policies. *Richards v. National Labor Relations Board*, 702 F.3d 1010 (7th Cir. 2012).

◆   A group of machine repairmen working for Chrysler in Ohio became dissatisfied with the way their jobs were classified by a new collective bargaining agreement. They felt that the union and Chrysler had reassigned significant portions of their work to millwrights and electricians, favoring those two groups more than the repairmen. They filed a lawsuit against the union for breach of the duty of fair representation. A federal court ruled for the union, and the Sixth Circuit affirmed. **The union was not acting as a "hiring hall" when it made decisions regarding work assignments, so it could not be held to a higher duty of representation.** Further, the new work assignments were not irrational. Therefore, the union didn't breach its duty of fair representation. *Bowerman v. Int'l Union, UAW, Local No. 12*, 646 F.3d 360 (6th Cir. 2011).

◆   An Arizona union employee was suspended and warned after a former lover alleged that she used profanity in the parking lot before work. She asked the union to file a grievance on her behalf and a field representative promised to do so but never did. She was fired after another incident of alleged profanity during an argument over a pay error. The union filed a grievance over the termination but refused to arbitrate it. **The employee then sued the union for sex discrimination and breach of the duty to represent her.** A federal court ruled in her favor, and the Ninth Circuit affirmed. Here, the employee presented evidence that the union aggressively represented two male employees who had been involved in tussles with co-workers, including one who threatened a fellow employee with a knife. She also presented evidence that the union did not aggressively represent another female employee who allegedly extended the expiration date on some meat, even though two male employees who allegedly engaged in the same behavior were not fired. The employee was entitled to her award of $16,304 in lost wages, $125,000 in compensatory damages and $50,000 in punitive damages. *Beck v. United Food and Commercial Workers Union, Local 99*, 506 F.3d 874 (9th Cir. 2007).

◆   United Parcel Service (UPS) fired two Kansas and Missouri employees for job abandonment. Their union filed grievances on their behalf and represented them. UPS nevertheless upheld the terminations. The two employees then filed hybrid suits against UPS and the union under Section 301 of the LMRA, claiming UPS breached the collective bargaining agreement, and that the union breached its duty of fair representation. They also asserted a claim under the Labor Management Reporting and Disclosure Act (LMRDA), arguing that the new union leadership retaliated against them for supporting the opposition slate of candidates. The case reached the Eighth Circuit, which ruled that **the union did not breach its duty of representation to the employees**. Thus, it did not even have to decide whether UPS breached the collective bargaining agreement because both claims had to be proved to prevail in a hybrid lawsuit. The union represented both employees adequately. For the same reason, the LMRDA claim failed. *Jones v. United Parcel Service*, 461 F.3d 982 (8th Cir. 2006).

◆   The union representing passenger service employees of US Airways negotiated a collective bargaining agreement that changed the system for business-necessitated layoffs. Under the agreement, the most senior employee would displace the most junior employee, the second most senior would displace the second most junior, etc. Under the older system, the most senior employee bumped a less senior employee, who in turn bumped a less senior employee, etc. After the September 11 attacks, the airline had to close operations at 1small locations, and it attempted to reduce its work force under the old system. Instead, the union forced it to use the displacement system in the bargaining agreement, which resulted in certain senior employees being left without jobs or in less desirable assignments, but reduced by more than 100 the number of displacements system-wide. A number of senior employees adversely affected by the bargaining agreement sued the union for breaching its duty of fair representation. A Virginia federal court ruled for the union, and the Fourth Circuit affirmed. **The union's conduct in forcing the airline to adopt** the bargaining agreement was not arbitrary, discriminatory or in bad faith, and did not breach its duty to the employees. *Jeffreys v. Communications Workers of America, AFL-CIO*, 354 F.3d 270 (4th Cir. 2003).

◆   An employee of a Massachusetts sporting goods company was accused of spreading false rumors that a female co-worker and a male co-worker were having an affair. Not only did the employee tell the female co-worker's husband, but he also told his supervisor and another employee. He was fired for violating the company's sexual harassment policy. The union initially filed a grievance on his behalf, but when the company refused to resolve the complaint, the union accepted the company's response and failed to pursue the matter. The employee sued the company and the union under Section 301 of the LMRA, alleging that the company fired him without proper cause (as required by the collective bargaining agreement) and that the union breached its duty of fair representation by failing to pursue the grievance. A federal court ruled for the defendants, and the First Circuit Court of Appeals affirmed. Since there was substantial evidence to support the discharge decision, the company had proper cause to fire the employee. He could not have thought he was reasonably justified in discussing the alleged affair with third parties who had no legitimate interest in the subject matter. **Because the firing was proper, the union did not breach its duty of fair representation, and the Section 301 claim failed.** *Mulvihill v. The Top Flite Golf Co.*, 335 F.3d 15 (1st Cir. 2003).

◆   An Ohio truck driver was fired for intentionally destroying the brake pedal of a tractor he was instructed to drive. He was suspected of deliberately damaging the vehicle, which he had earlier referred to as a "piece of junk." However, another driver corroborated the driver's statement that the brakes had failed at an intersection. The union filed a grievance against the employer, but an arbitration panel upheld the discharge. The driver sued the employer and union under Section 301 of the LMRA. The jury returned an $850,000 verdict for the driver, which the court apportioned between the employer and union. The Sixth Circuit affirmed. **Evidence indicated that the union had failed in its duty to fairly represent the driver**, since it did not call an expert witness who might have contradicted the testimony of the employer's expert. There was strong circumstantial evidence in the driver's favor suggesting that the employer had "set him up." In Section 301 cases, the focus is on whether the employer has breached the contract and the union has contributed to the erroneous outcome of contractual proceedings. Here, the union's conduct had tainted the arbitration, and the employee was entitled to judgment. *Schoonover v. Consolidated Freightways Corp. of Delaware*, 147 F.3d 492 (6th Cir. 1998).

◆   Continental Airlines filed a petition for reorganization under Chapter 11 of the Bankruptcy Code. It then repudiated its collective bargaining agreement with the pilots' union and cut pilots' salaries and benefits by more than half. This resulted in a strike that lasted for more than two years. During the strike, Continental set up a system of bidding for vacancies and assigned all the positions to working pilots, effectively ending the strike. The union then entered into an agreement with Continental to allow striking pilots to participate in the bidding allocation. Thereafter, a group of pilots sued their union, alleging that it had breached its duty of fair representation by negotiating an agreement that arbitrarily discriminated against striking pilots. A Texas federal court ruled for the union, but the Fifth Circuit reversed. The U.S. Supreme Court held that the rule announced in *Vaca v. Sipes*, 386 U.S. 171, 87 S.Ct. 903, 17 L.Ed.2d 842 (1967) – that a union breaches its duty of fair representation if its actions are either "arbitrary, discriminatory, or in bad faith" – applies to *all* union activity, including contract negotiation. The Court then stated that a union's actions would be arbitrary only if the union's behavior was so far outside a "wide range of reasonableness" as to be irrational. This issue had to be considered in light of the factual and legal landscape at the time of the union's actions. Here, **even if the union made a bad settlement, its actions at the time of the settlement were not irrational**. Thus, it did not breach its duty to the pilots. The Court reversed the court of appeals' decision. *Air Line Pilots Ass'n Int'l v. O'Neill*, 499 U.S. 65, 111 S.Ct. 1127, 113 L.Ed.2d 51 (1991).

3. Federal Law Preemption

When a state law claim is based on an analysis of the terms of a collective bargaining agreement (CBA), the state law claim will be preempted by Section 301 of the Labor Management Relations Act (LMRA). However, where the state law claim can be resolved without reference to the CBA (or independently of the CBA), the LMRA will not preempt the state law claim.

◆   After an underground fire at an Idaho mine, the survivors of four miners filed a state-law wrongful death action against the miners' union, alleging that, based on a collective bargaining agreement, it had negligently conducted safety inspections. The Idaho Supreme Court eventually determined that the survivors had stated a valid claim under state law that was not preempted by Section 301 of the LMRA. The U.S. Supreme Court reversed, holding that the survivors' claims (that the union had been negligent in its safety inspections) were not independent of the collective bargaining agreement. Here, the union's representatives were participating in the inspection process according to the provisions of the agreement. Thus, **any duty owed the miners arose out of the agreement, and the state-law tort claim was preempted by Section 301**. Also, the Section 301 claim could not succeed against the union because the complaint had alleged only negligence. More than mere negligence was needed for liability under Section 301. *United Steelworkers of America v. Rawson*, 495 U.S. 362, 110 S.Ct. 1904, 109 L.Ed.2d 362 (1990).

◆   An electrical apprentice, who was a member of a union, worked for a Florida power company. She was assigned to a job in an electrical substation and was injured when she came into contact with some highly energized components. Two years later, she sued her union, alleging that it had a duty to ensure that she was provided safety in her workplace and that she not be required to take undue risks while performing her duties – risks that were beyond her training and experience. She claimed that the tasks she had been performing at the time of her injury were beyond the scope of her training and experience. The union removed the case to a federal court, which dismissed the suit as untimely, but the U.S. Court of Appeals reversed. The U.S. Supreme Court noted that **the LMRA preempted any state-law action she might have had because interpretation of the collective bargaining agreement would be necessary**. Under federal law, the court of appeals would be required to determine whether the apprentice's claim was time-barred by the six-month limitations period of the National Labor Relations Act, or whether some other period should be used. The Court vacated the court of appeals' decision and remanded the case. *Int'l Brotherhood of Electrical Workers, AFL-CIO v. Hechler,* 481 U.S. 851, 107 S.Ct. 2161, 95 L.Ed.2d 791 (1987).

♦   Three gas company employees in Atlanta were bumped out of their positions by employees with more seniority during a statewide reduction in force. They refused offers to transfer to other locations and were laid off. The company denied their grievances and the union chose not to take the matter to arbitration. They then sued the company for breach of contract and emotional distress, and also raised other claims.

A Georgia federal court granted pretrial judgment to the company, and the Eleventh Circuit largely affirmed. Here, the breach of contract claims were preempted by the LMRA because they were substantially dependent on analyzing the terms of the collective bargaining agreement between the company and the union. Also, the emotional distress claims were preempted because they revolved around the alleged failure to provide proper notice of termination or the meaningful opportunity to consider transfers. As such, those claims also required analysis of the bargaining agreement. Finally, the court noted that the employees could not proceed under the LMRA because their claims were properly considered hybrid Section 301 claims, and they waited more than the allowed six months to file suit. *Bartholomew v. AGL Resources, Inc.,* 361 F.3d 1333 (11th Cir. 2004).

♦   A California employer installed video cameras and listening devices behind two-way mirrors in its employee restrooms, ostensibly to detect drug use by employees. After the equipment was discovered, employees filed two class action lawsuits against the company for invasion of privacy and infliction of emotional distress. They sought injunctive relief to end the use of the surveillance devices. The company asserted that the lawsuits were preempted by Section 301 of the LMRA because the claims required interpretation of the collective bargaining agreement (CBA) to determine the employees' reasonable expectations of privacy. A federal court dismissed one of the lawsuits and found the other one preempted by Section 301. The Ninth Circuit Court of Appeals reversed, holding that **a state law claim is not preempted by Section 301 unless it requires a court to interpret part of a CBA that is relevant to the resolution of the dispute**. Here, the invasion of privacy claims were based on California constitutional and statutory rights of privacy guaranteed to all persons, whether or not they happen to work subject to a CBA. And even if the CBA allowed the use of two-way mirrors to detect drug use, that provision would be illegal under California law and thus unenforceable. Also, the emotional distress claims were not preempted by Section 301 because the conduct alleged violated California penal law and therefore was per se outrageous. *Cramer v. Consolidated Freightways, Inc.*, 255 F.3d 683 (9th Cir. 2001), *cert. denied*, 534 U.S. 1078 (2002).

◆   A mechanic at a New Mexico facility also served as a union steward. His supervisor confronted him about leaving his post to conduct union business, and he asserted that he had the right to do so under the collective bargaining agreement. Management then conducted surveillance on him, allegedly to catch him misusing his time card. Based on this surveillance, the company terminated him. An arbitrator ordered reinstatement. The mechanic claimed that the company then stripped him of a security clearance needed for career advancement. He sued the company, but the case was dismissed on the ground that Section 301 of the LMRA preempted his lawsuit. The Tenth Circuit reversed, finding that he could pursue his retaliation claim against the company. **His lawsuit was not about interpreting a collective bargaining agreement**, but rather about the motivation behind the company's actions. *Garley v. Sandia Corp.*, 236 F.3d 1200 (10th Cir. 2001).

◆   A California tire plant hired strike replacement workers. When the strikers returned, 207 replacement workers were laid off, but not those replacement workers who were promised they would not be. The company and the union then entered into a new collective bargaining agreement (CBA), and the retained replacement workers became members of the union. Subsequently, diminished sales forced the layoff of 175 more employees, including the replacement workers who had been promised no layoffs when the strikers returned. The laid-off workers sued the company for fraud and breach of contract under state law, but a federal court ruled in favor of the company. The Ninth Circuit affirmed, holding that **Section 301 of the LMRA preempted the lawsuit because the workers had become part of the bargaining unit** covered by the CBA, and because the CBA dictated how seniority-driven layoffs would take place. The lawsuit could not be resolved without interpreting the CBA's layoff and seniority provisions. *Aguilera v. Pirelli Armstrong Tire Corp.*, 223 F.3d 1010 (9th Cir. 2000).

◆   Meter readers for a gas company in California were paid according to a collective bargaining agreement that set forth a complex arrangement. The meter readers were paid a flat sum that was calculated by multiplying a standard rate ($16.56 per hour) by the amount of time the company expected them to complete their routes. Meter readers who worked more than eight hours in a day received an adjustment to the flat sum. They sued the company under state law, asserting that under the formula in place, they were actually being paid less than $16.56 per hour for overtime. The Ninth Circuit held that **their lawsuit was preempted by Section 301 of the LMRA** because resolution of their claim depended on an interpretation of the bargaining agreement. *Firestone v. Southern California Gas Co.*, 219 F.3d 1063 (9th Cir. 2000).

◆   After a female longshore worker sued the local union and an association of employers, asserting that she had been denied entry into a higher classification of workers because of her gender, the parties entered into a settlement agreement whereby the association agreed not to deny the worker entry into the higher classification the next time classifications were organized. However, when the association refused to register any workers into the higher classification, a number of workers sued under the LMRA. A Washington federal court dismissed the suit because it was filed after the six-month statute of limitations had passed. When the workers then sued under state law, the case was again dismissed. The Ninth Circuit Court of Appeals affirmed, finding that **the LMRA preempted the state law action** because resolving whether the settlement agreement had been breached required interpreting the bargaining agreement. As a result, Section 301 of the LMRA was the appropriate mechanism to be used. And since the statute of limitations had passed on their LMRA cause of action, the workers' lawsuit had to be dismissed. *Audette v. Int'l Longshoremen's and Warehousemen's Union*, 195 F.3d 1107 (9th Cir. 1999).

◆   A claims processor for a service center worked under a collective bargaining agreement that contained a nondiscrimination clause prohibiting discrimination on the basis of sexual orientation. The employee's supervisor allegedly began to harass him after learning of his homosexuality, and the employee was later laid off. His union filed grievances against the employer on his behalf. While the grievances were pending, the employee sued the employer and supervisor for breach of contract and intentional infliction of emotional distress. A federal court dismissed the action as preempted by LMRA Section 301, finding that resolution of the claims depended upon analysis of the collective bargaining agreement. The Eighth Circuit affirmed, observing that the contract alleged to have been breached in this action was the bargaining agreement. Because **the claims alleged by the employee were inextricably intertwined with the consideration of the bargaining agreement**, they were preempted by the LMRA. This was also true of the emotional distress claim, which was also grounded in the bargaining agreement. *Oberkramer v. IBEW-NECA Service Center, Inc.*, 151 F.3d 752 (8th Cir. 1998).

◆   A South Carolina electric company foreman was a union member for 38 years. The union constitution prohibited members from "working for any company declared in difficulty" with the union. When the union and company were unable to renegotiate a collective bargaining agreement, the union called a strike. The foreman resigned from his union executive board post and stopped paying membership dues. The union terminated his membership for failure to pay dues and filed internal charges against him for continuing to work for the employer after the union declared a strike. The union also declared him ineligible for his union pension. The foreman sued the union for violating the state Right-to-Work Act, which prohibits employer-labor agreements that make union membership a condition of employment. The court awarded the foreman over $100,000 in damages. The Court of Appeals of South Carolina held that **the LMRA preempted the Right-to-Work Act because reference to the union constitution was necessary to determine whether the foreman had a property interest in his union pension**. The state supreme court affirmed. *Lewis v. Local 382, IBEW*, 518 S.E.2d 583 (S.C. 1999).

C. The Labor-Management Reporting and Disclosure Act (LMRDA)

The LMRDA was enacted to guarantee union members equal voting rights, rights of free speech and assembly, and the right to sue to protect those rights. It aims to ensure that unions are democratically governed and responsive to the will of their memberships.

The LMRDA makes it unlawful for a union to "fine, suspend, expel or otherwise discipline" any of its members for exercising rights secured by the LMRDA. Thus, for example, it is unlawful for a union to refuse to refer union members for jobs in retaliation for those members' opposition to union policies.

◆   An auto company employee worked full time in an elected union position. When he learned that local union leaders had agreed silently to end a production process that would have resulted in the loss of several hundred jobs, he refused to sign a settlement agreement and told the media that the union had sold out its membership. Problems erupted between the employee and the union's leaders. They urged acceptance of the agreement and allegedly disparaged him in doing so, while he urged the agreement's defeat. After the agreement passed, he claimed that the union cancelled a meeting to discuss his charges against union leadership and ignored his charges against union leaders. He retired early, then sued under the LMRDA. A Michigan federal court ruled against him, and the U.S. Court of Appeals for the Sixth Circuit affirmed. Here, **the employee failed to show that he was "disciplined" for exercising his legal rights**. He also failed to show that union leaders defamed him or intentionally caused him emotional distress. *Webster v. United Auto Workers, Local 51*, 394 F.3d 436 (6th Cir. 2005).

◆   Two union members in New York violated their union constitution by being disruptive at union meetings. After hearings, both were suspended and fined by the union. They sued under the LMRDA, asserting that the union violated their speech rights under the law. A federal court held for the union, and the Second Circuit affirmed. Here, **the employees had been suspended for their disruptive and abusive actions, not their words**. Further, even though the union constitution did not specifically allow for suspensions, it did allow for discretionary discipline as well as greater punishments than they received. The suspensions did not violate the LMRDA. *Hughes v. Bricklayers and Allied Craftworkers Local #45*, 386 F.3d 101 (2d Cir. 2004).

◆   An international labor organization imposed a trusteeship on a local union representing Tennessee office workers because of a paralyzing division in the local's executive board. The division resulted from the activities of a business agent who questioned the local's election processes, selection of delegates, membership dues increases and failure to process grievances. The union trustee reprimanded the business agent for his continuing criticism of the union and then fired him and revoked his union membership without notice or a hearing. Union reform candidates who supported the business agent eventually won election to the local board, and the trusteeship was lifted. The new board reinstated the agent, and he sued the international. The court denied relief based upon claims that the trusteeship had been improperly imposed, but awarded compensatory and punitive damages to the business agent for the international's violation of the LMRDA. The Sixth Circuit considered the international's argument that the business agent was not entitled to protection under the LMRDA because he was a union employee and was not required to be a union member. The LMRDA was enacted to ensure that unions were democratically governed and responsive to their memberships. **Because the agent was a voluntary union member who was subjected to retaliatory action and deprived of his union membership, he was entitled to LMRDA protection.** The jury properly considered the appropriateness of the trusteeship as it had a direct bearing on the claim for damages. There was also substantial evidence supporting the award of damages. *Thompson v. Office and Professional Employees Int'l Union, AFL-CIO*, 74 F.3d 1492 (6th Cir. 1996).

◆   A member of a local electrical union sued the union and its officers in an Ohio federal court. He asserted that, because of his opposition to proposed union actions, they had discriminated against him with respect to certain job referrals in violation of the LMRDA. He also alleged that their conduct breached Section 301 of the LMRDA by violating the union's constitution and bylaws. The district court dismissed all the claims, and the Sixth Circuit Court of Appeals affirmed in part, reversing the dismissal of the LMRDA claim. The U.S. Supreme Court then held that **the union member was entitled to a jury trial on the LMRDA claim**. Even though he sought injunctive relief as well as damages, the court compared an LMRDA action to a personal injury action for which a jury trial right existed. Further, federal courts have jurisdiction to hear suits brought against unions by individual members under the LMRA. Here, even though the union member's suit under the LMRA was a third-party suit seeking to enforce a contract between the local and international union, Section 301 of the LMRA did not limit itself to suits by the contracting parties. His suit was governed by federal law. The Court remanded the case. *Wooddell v. Int'l Brotherhood of Electrical Workers, Local 71*, 502 U.S. 93, 112 S.Ct. 494, 116 L.Ed.2d 419 (1991).

◆   A local union in the midst of a financial crisis asked its international union for help. A trustee was sent to put the local back on sound economic ground. At a special meeting set up to vote on a dues increase, one of the local's officials voiced opposition to the increase because the trustee would not commit to lowering expenditures. After the vote for a dues increase failed, the trustee removed the elected official because of his outspoken opposition to the increase in union dues. In a California federal court, the official challenged his removal as violative of his free speech rights under the LMRDA. The court ruled for the international, but the court of appeals reversed. On further appeal, the U.S. Supreme Court held that **the removal of the elected union official, in retaliation for the statements he made at the dues meeting, violated the LMRDA**. It not only interfered with his Title I rights – which protected him if he spoke out against the union leadership – but it also denied the members who voted for him the representative of their choice, chilling their Title I free speech rights as well. The Court affirmed the court of appeals' decision, holding that the official's statements were entitled to protection. His removal was invalid even though it was carried out during a trusteeship that was lawfully imposed. *Sheet Metal Workers' Int'l Ass'n v. Lynn,* 488 U.S. 347, 109 S.Ct. 639, 102 L.Ed.2d 700 (1989).

◆   A local union operated a hiring hall through which it referred members and nonmembers for construction work. A member brought sued the union for violating its duty of fair representation by passing him over in making job referrals and in refusing to honor employer requests for his services – all because he supported a rival business manager candidate. He also alleged that the union's actions violated the LMRDA. An Ohio federal court dismissed the suit as outside its jurisdiction, and the Sixth Circuit affirmed. The U.S. Supreme Court granted review and held that the union member stated a valid claim for breach of the duty of fair representation. However, the failure of the business manager and business agent to refer him for employment could not be attributed to the union for the purpose of maintaining a claim under Sections 101(a)(5) and 609 of the LMRDA. Here, **the union was not attempting to discipline the member for his political convictions; it was only individual officers who allegedly did so**. Also, the fair representation claim did not require a concomitant claim against an employer for breach of contract; whatever an employer's liability, the union member would still have a legal claim against the union. The Court reversed in part and remanded the case. *Breininger v. Sheet Metal Workers Int'l Ass'n Local Union No. 6,* 493 U.S. 67, 110 S.Ct. 424, 107 L.Ed.2d 388 (1989).

IV. OSHA AND OTHER SAFETY REGULATIONS

The Occupational Safety and Health Act of 1970, 29 U.S.C. § 651 *et seq.,* (OSH Act), requires employers to provide a place of employment that is "free from recognized hazards that are causing or are likely to cause death or serious physical harm."

Employers' duties are of two kinds:

—first is the general duty to provide a safe work environment, and
—second is the specific duty to conform to particular health and safety standards that are promulgated by the Secretary of Labor and the Occupational Safety and Health Administration (OSHA).

It is important for employers to know which OSHA standards apply to their workplaces. The standards are published and are organized by industry. Also, a great deal of information about OSHA standards and procedures is available from the OSHA website at *www.osha.gov/.*

◆   A pilot for NetJets Aviation, which operates chartered business jets, made repeated safety reports. He claimed two superiors criticized him for doing so. Later, he applied for a promotion that he had previously sought on 25 occasions without success. When he didn't get the promotion again, he filed a charge with OSHA, **asserting that he hadn't gotten the promotion because of the safety reports**. An administrative judge in Washington, D.C., rejected his complaint, and the Sixth Circuit affirmed that decision. It found clear and convincing evidence that he would not have been promoted even if he hadn't engaged in protected activity. All 30 candidates were evaluated using the same three-point system, and he placed 27th out of 30. Nineteen candidates who ranked higher than him didn't receive promotions either. *Hoffman v. Solis*, 636 F.3d 262 (6th Cir. 2011).

A. Regulatory Interpretations

OSHA can set safety standards on its own initiative or as a result of petitions from other parties, including the Secretary of Health and Human Services. Problems arise when those standards exceed the requirements of the Occupational Safety and Health (OSH) Act.

◆   A Colorado steel corporation equipped 28 of its employees with respirators that failed an "atmospheric test" designed to ascertain whether such respirators would protect the wearers from carcinogenic emissions. As a result, some employees were exposed to coke-oven emissions exceeding the regulatory limit. A compliance officer, under the direction of the U.S. Secretary of Labor (Secretary), issued a citation to the steel company for violating an OSH Act regulation. The company contested the citation, and the Occupational Safety and Health Review Commission (Commission) vacated the citation because the officer had cited the wrong regulation. The Secretary appealed to the U.S. Court of Appeals, Tenth Circuit, which affirmed the Commission's order. The U.S. Supreme Court then examined to whom a reviewing court should defer when **the Secretary and the Commission have reasonable but conflicting interpretations** of an ambiguous Department of Labor regulation. The Court decided that it would defer to the Secretary, who is more likely to develop the expertise relevant to assessing the effect of a particular regulatory interpretation. The Court thus reversed the court of appeals' decision and remanded the case for a determination of whether the Secretary's interpretation was reasonable. *Martin v. OSHRC*, 499 U.S. 144, 111 S.Ct. 1171, 113 L.Ed.2d 117 (1991).

◆   Two employees of an Ohio corporation refused to perform their usual maintenance duties on a suspended wire-mesh screen that hung about 20 feet above the plant floor. They believed the screen was unsafe (and in fact, one fatality had already resulted from an employee's fall through an old part of the screen). The corporation suspended the employees and placed written reprimands in their files. The U.S. Secretary of Labor then sued the corporation for discriminating against its employees in violation of the OSH Act. A federal court held for the corporation, but the Sixth Circuit Court of Appeals reversed. The U.S. Supreme Court affirmed, holding that the regulation, which allowed an employee to choose not to perform an assigned task because of a reasonable apprehension of death or serious injury (coupled with a reasonable belief that no less drastic alternative was available), was valid. **Here, the employees had exercised their rights under the OSH Act, and the corporation had taken adverse actions against them.** The regulation helped effectuate the general duty clause of the act, which requires employers to provide a place of employment free from recognized hazards that are likely to cause serious injury or death. The corporation had to pay the employees for the period of time they were suspended and remove the reprimands from their files. *Whirlpool Corp. v. Marshall*, 445 U.S. 1, 100 S.Ct. 883, 63 L.Ed.2d 154 (1980).

✦　The OSH Act gives the U.S. Secretary of Labor (Secretary) broad authority to establish standards to ensure safe and healthy working conditions. With respect to carcinogens, the Secretary stated that no safe exposure level could be determined, and that the OSH Act required the exposure limit to be set at the lowest technologically feasible level that would not impair the viability of the industries regulated. The Secretary then lowered the benzene exposure limit to one part per million, prompting Texas benzene producers to challenge the standard. The Fifth Circuit held the standard invalid, and the U.S. Supreme Court affirmed.

The Secretary of Labor had not made a finding that the workplace was "unsafe" before creating the standard. The Court noted that "safe" is not the equivalent of "risk-free." There must be a significant risk of harm before a workplace can be termed "unsafe." Even though certain assumptions indicated that the number of leukemia cases might be reduced by lowering the exposure level, there had never been a finding that leukemia was caused by exposure to low levels of benzene. **The Secretary had exceeded his power in setting the new standard.** *Industrial Union Dep't v. American Petroleum Institute,* 448 U.S. 607, 100 S.Ct. 2844, 65 L.Ed.2d 1010 (1980).

✦　A foreman violated an OSHA regulation by digging himself into an 11-foot wall of dirt while looking for a utility cable. The DOL argued that the foreman knew he was violating an OSHA regulation and that his actions should be imputed to the employer. An ALJ agreed, but the Eleventh Circuit reversed. It found that **the DOL did not prove the employer knew about the violation**, and it determined that the employee's knowledge of his wrongdoing could not be imputed to his employer. *ComTran Group, Inc. v. U.S. Dep't of Labor*, 722 F.3d 1304 (11th Cir. 2013).

✦　The DOL discovered a safety violation at a New York nursing home. It categorized the nursing home as a repeat offender based on violations that had occurred at two other facilities that were under the same corporate umbrella. The Occupational Safety and Health Review Commission determined that the facility was not a repeat offender because **the three facilities were not a single employer**. The Second Circuit upheld that decision. The three facilities were located in different cities and separately handled matters related to safety. *Solis v. Loretto-Oswego Residential Health Care Facility*, 692 F.3d 65 (2d Cir. 2013).

✦　The Occupational Safety and Health Act requires companies to record work-related injuries and illnesses, and it allows them seven days to prepare an incident report and injury log. They also have to prepare a year-end summary of all recordable injuries within the calendar year that is certified by a company executive. If they fail to comply, they can be cited and fined. When OSHA learned that a construction company had not been diligent in completing its logs, forms and summaries between 2002 and 2006, it issued 171 citations, which the company sought to have dismissed because OSHA only had six months within which to issue citations and all of these were untimely. OSHA asserted that the citations were timely under the continuing violation doctrine because the most recent violation occurred two days less than six months before it began its inspections. However, the D.C. Circuit Court of Appeals disagreed with OSHA and held that **the citations were untimely. Each violation was a discrete act.** *AKM LLC, d/b/a Volks Constructors v. Dep't of Labor*, 675 F.3d 752 (D.C. Cir. 2012).

✦ A final OSHA stated that **each failure to provide a respirator or workplace training to an employee working with asbestos could constitute a separate violation** of the regulation. Certain trade associations petitioned for judicial review, asserting that the Secretary of Labor exceeded the authority granted by Congress in creating the rule. The case reached the U.S. Court of Appeals, District of Columbia Circuit, which ruled in favor of OSHA. By giving the Secretary the power to define what constitutes a violation, the OSH Act necessarily gave the Secretary the authority to define the unit of prosecution, meaning that the rule could make each individual failure a separate violation. *National Ass'n of Home Builders v. OSHA*, 602 F.3d 464 (D.C. Cir. 2010).

✦ UPS contracted with a consultant to conduct a study of its aircraft facilities throughout the country to determine what hazards were present in those work environments and the personal protective equipment necessary to protect workers from those hazards. The consultant determined that UPS could satisfy its obligations under OSHA by conducting a single representative assessment at its central hub in Louisville. Targeting two Michigan facilities, a union complained to the state's occupational safety and health administration, which found no safety violations but issued citations after determining that UPS's safety assessment was inadequate. UPS appealed, and the Michigan Court of Appeals held that **the state's OSHA rule did not require employers with multiple similar workplaces to perform a separate hazard assessment at each workplace.** Rather, it allows for representative assessment. The citations were vacated. *UPS v. Bureau of Safety and Regulation*, 745 N.W.2d 125 (Mich. Ct. App. 2007).

✦ Under the OSH Act, parties adversely affected by an occupational safety or health standard may file a petition for review "at any time prior to the sixtieth day after such standard is promulgated." In 1983, OSHA promulgated the Hazard Communication Standard (HCS), which imposed obligations on manufacturers based on the "latest edition" of a list of dangerous chemicals published by a private group of industrial hygienists. When the hygienists added several chemicals to the list in 2006, industry groups filed a petition for review, alleging that publication of the privately created list effectively amended the standard without notice and comment. The U.S. Court of Appeals, D.C. Circuit, disagreed. The HCS provisions referencing the list were promulgated in 1983. Thus, the groups were about two decades too late in filing their challenge. The conditions required of the regulated parties did not change at all in 2006. **Both before and after publication of the new list, regulated parties were required to treat as hazardous any chemical listed in the then-current version of the**

list. Since the new additions to the list did not modify the HCS, the challenge to the HCS was untimely. *National Ass'n of Manufacturers v. OSHA*, 485 F.3d 1201 (D.C. Cir. 2007).

✦ The owner of a stucco company contested a citation issued by a Department of Labor inspector for violating the OSH Act. He claimed that he was not involved in a business affecting interstate commerce and that he had no employees. The case reached the Tenth Circuit Court of Appeals, which ruled in favor of OSHA. First, the stucco company, as part of the construction business, was in a "class of activity that affects interstate commerce" even if it did not have a specific impact on interstate commerce. Second, the owner was paying a helper $8 an hour to assist in the project. He controlled the scope of the helper's work and provided all the materials. Accordingly, **he was an employer for purposes of the OSH Act.** *Slingluff v. Occupational Safety & Health Review Comm'n*, 425 F.3d 861 (10th Cir. 2005).

✦ A water and sewer company in Wisconsin was excavating along a public street when an OSHA compliance officer drove by. He noticed the excavation, stopped his car and walked up to the trench. He saw an employee in the trench while a supervisor worked up above. This was a violation of OSHA regulations. He began videotaping the scene and identified himself to the project superintendent. The superintendent let him continue his inspection. Based on soil samples and measurements of the trench, as well as the video, OSHA issued the company three citations. The company claimed that the citations should not be enforced because the OSHA officer violated its Fourth Amendment right to be free of unreasonable searches and seizures. The Seventh Circuit disagreed. Here, **the excavation occurred along a public street, and the superintendent did not object to the inspection or demand a warrant** before letting the officer proceed. Thus, the evidence collected against the company was admissible. *Lakeland Enterprises of Rhineland, Inc. v. Chao*, 402 F.3d 739 (7th Cir. 2005).

✦ A company purchased a gas grill with a 20-pound propane tank for an outdoor barbecue at its bread-baking plant in Denver. A plant official determined that the 20-pound tank was not big enough to handle the barbecue and ordered a 40-pound tank. The 40-pound tank came with a warning that it was not to be used with a grill equipped for a 20-pound tank. The plant superintendent ignored the warning and directed a plant engineer to install the 40-pound tank. When the flow of gas was insufficient to cook the meat, the superintendent asked the engineer to reposition the tank. A fire erupted when some fuel escaped, and the engineer was burned. An OSHA investigator issued the company a citation, charging it with violating the OSH Act's general duty clause. The Tenth Circuit upheld that decision. Here, **the hazard was obvious and recognizable; it was likely to cause death or serious injury; and it could have been avoided**. The court of appeals also rejected the company's assertion that the improper installation of the 40-pound tank was not a "condition with respect to work." Even though this was a barbecue, the engineer was "working" when he was instructed to improve the flow of fuel to the grill. *Safeway, Inc. v. OSHRC*, 382 F.3d 1189 (10th Cir. 2004).

◆   A compliance officer for OSHA videotaped construction activities at a Florida work site from a rooftop adjacent to the site. He taped two employees who were working about 80 feet above the ground without adequate safety cables. OSHA held an evidentiary hearing to determine whether a violation of its regulations had occurred. An administrative law judge determined that one of the employees was a foreman and imputed his knowledge of safety violations to the employer based on his supervisory authority. The employer appealed the imposition of a $7,000 fine to the Fourth Circuit.

The court of appeals rejected the employer's privacy claim. The employer had no reasonable expectation of privacy in the work site since it was a public place, and the surveillance did not create an unreasonable intrusion into it. **The surveillance did not violate the OSH Act, which allows reasonable entry by OSHA officials to inspect and investigate work sites** during an employer's regular work hours, provided that the OSHA inspector presents his credentials before any inspection. The long distance observation by the inspector did not constitute an entry onto the work site. However, the foreman's knowledge of the violation could not be imputed to the employer. *L.R. Willson and Sons, Inc. v. OSHRC*, 134 F.3d 1235 (4th Cir. 1998).

B. Willful Violations

—Repeat and willful violations of OSHA standards may have penalties as high as $70,000.
—Serious violations may have penalties of up to $7,000.
—Where a violation is deemed "other than serious," there will often be no monetary penalties, though such penalties can be imposed up to $7,000.

◆   A husband, wife and son held close control over two New Jersey construction companies. During a construction project, OSHA officials inspected the site and found numerous problems with the fall protection equipment, such that employees were at risk of falling 79 feet. It issued citations for willful violations to the husband and son, as well as to both companies. The husband, son and companies challenged the citations, asserting that the companies should not be treated as a single entity, that the danger existed for only three weeks, and that no one got hurt. An OSHA review board imposed a penalty of $336,000 ($56,000 for each violation), and the Third Circuit upheld those fines. It found that **the two companies were correctly treated as a single employer**. Both husband and son could fire employees and enforce safety regulations at both companies. *Altor, Inc. v. Secretary of Labor*, 498 Fed.Appx. 145 (3d Cir. 2012).

◆   An administrative law judge (ALJ) with the Occupational Safety and Health (OSH) Review Commission found that two related companies in Texas committed 59 willful violations of the recordkeeping regulation by intentionally and knowingly failing to record certain work-related accidents or illnesses. The Secretary of Labor sought a penalty of $9,000 per violation for one company and $8,000 per violation for the other. The ALJ instead treated the companies as if they had each committed only one willful violation and assessed a penalty of $70,000 each. The case came before the Fifth Circuit, which held that although the OSH Review Commission had the authority to assess all civil penalties, and could assess a penalty anywhere between $5,000 and $70,000 for each willful violation, the commission could not group separately charged and proven willful offenses for the purposes of assessing a penalty. On remand, the ALJ would have to assess penalties based on the number of proven willful violations. *Chao v. Occupational Safety and Health Review Comm'n*, 480 F.3d 320 (5th Cir. 2007).

♦   A Pennsylvania foundry doing work on a furnace believed that any asbestos had been removed. It also believed that any new insulation added would be asbestos-free. Therefore, it did not conduct tests to determine if asbestos was present. However, an employee noticed that some insulation in a dumpster appeared to contain asbestos. Testing revealed that it contained 5% asbestos, and **OSHA issued a citation for failure to determine the presence, location and quantity of asbestos** at the work site and for failing to notify employers whose employees might be working there that they could be exposed to asbestos. OSHA characterized these violations as "serious." The OSH Review Commission upheld the two violations but reclassified them as "non-serious." The Secretary of Labor contended that the commission erred in reclassifying the violations, and the Third Circuit agreed. Under the OSH Act, when the violation of a regulation makes the occurrence of an accident with a substantial probability of death or serious physical harm possible, the employer has committed a serious violation. The substantial probability part of the act refers not to the probability that an accident will occur but to the probability that, an accident having occurred, death or serious injury could result. *Secretary of Labor v. Trinity Industries, Inc.*, 504 F.3d 397 (3d Cir. 2007).

♦   A Nevada company was cited for willfully violating the federal fall protection regulations of the state Occupational Safety and Health Review Board after a worker fell 90 feet to his death. The company was fined $56,000 for failing to ensure that a proper fall protection system was in place and utilized by employees. The company asserted that its violations, if any, were only "serious" and not "willful." The case reached the Supreme Court of Nevada, which noted that state law essentially mirrored federal law on willful violations. Thus, **the court relied on federal case law standards to define a willful violation**. Under those standards, there was substantial evidence to support the willful violation. In addition to the employee who was killed, two other employees were observed working without fall protection one day and one week after the fatal fall. *Century Steel, Inc. v. State, Division of Industrial Relations*, 137 P.3d 1155 (Nev. 2006).

♦   An OSHA compliance officer visited a Wal-Mart store in Alabama to investigate a complaint about dangerous conditions in the store's stockroom. She found that **an emergency exit was blocked by a knee-high rail conveyor system and a stack of boxes**. The Department of Labor issued a citation, characterized it as a repeat violation (because of an incident in Georgia where shopping carts blocked an exit) and recommended a $25,000 fine. An administrative law judge assessed a penalty of $5,000, which the U.S. Court of Appeals, D.C. Circuit, upheld. Even though the conveyor system could be taken apart easily and the boxes could be moved, the regulation requires emergency exits to be "continuously maintained free of obstructions." *Wal-Mart Stores v. Secretary of Labor*, 406 F.3d 731 (D.C. Cir. 2005).

◆   OSHA cited a manufacturing plant in Illinois for violating safety regulations. One of the manufacturer's machines (a "track press") had an exposed hole that could impede the machine's operations if debris fell into it. A worker who failed to stop the machine before removing the debris could get his or her fingers crushed. The manufacturer had placed a cover over the hole, but when it became damaged it was removed. The investigation revealed that workers had disabled an electric eye on the press. The "eye" automatically stopped the press when someone put his or her hand near the hole. Two years earlier, the manufacturer had been cited for failing to provide another press with a barrier guard for its hole.

The OSH Review Commission (Commission) fined the manufacturer $10,000 for engaging in a "willful" violation of the OSH Act and $12,000 for a "repeat" violation of the act. The U.S. Court of Appeals, Seventh Circuit, sustained the order. With respect to a willful violation, there was substantial evidence for the Commission to find that the manufacturer knew the cover had come off the press machine and failed to fix the problem in conscious disregard of the regulations. With respect to a repeat violation, the Seventh Circuit rejected the notion that the term implies more than two violations but not necessarily of a similar character. Instead, it examined **whether the first violation was "substantially similar" to the second one so as to alert the employer to the condition that brought about the later violation**. Here, even though the first problem was mechanical and the second was electrical, they both involved "interchangeable methods of protecting the operator's hands from moving machinery" and were substantially similar. *Caterpillar, Inc. v. Herman*, 154 F.3d 400 (7th Cir. 1998).

◆   OSHA conducted an investigation into a workplace accident at a South Dakota car dealership that resulted in an employee's death. The employee habitually used the facility's freight elevator instead of its stairs because he had bad knees. The elevator was three-sided; there was no door, gate, or interlock safety device on the open side. Controls were located on each floor outside the elevator and could be reached from inside once the elevator stopped, but when the elevator was moving, there were no controls inside it to stop it or reverse its movement. The employee was killed when his head was caught in a shear as the elevator ceiling lowered past the floor of the second floor. The Eighth Circuit Court of Appeals found substantial evidence to support a ruling that **the dealership knew the elevator's unprotected shear points posed a safety hazard**. The configuration of the elevator and its lack of safety features made the risk plainly obvious. The court also affirmed a finding that the safety violation was "willful." The fact that the dealership had no meaningful safety program, that another employee had been injured in a similar accident, and that the dealership continued to let employees ride the elevator demonstrated that the dealership was "plainly indifferent" to the hazard. *McKie Ford v. Secretary of Labor*, 191 F.3d 853 (8th Cir. 1999).

◆ Three employees of a Milwaukee contractor were killed by a methane gas explosion in a sewage tunnel. OSHA performed an investigation and cited the contractor for 68 willful violations of OSHA standards. The case was referred to the U.S. Department of Justice for criminal prosecution while OSHA proceedings were stayed. The prosecution resulted in criminal fines of $750,000 for 49 OSHA violations. The Department of Labor then resumed administrative hearings on the civil OSHA claims. The parties settled claims arising from the 19 violations not prosecuted in the criminal proceeding, and the contractor asserted that further review of the previously adjudicated 49 violations would violate the Double Jeopardy Clause of the Fifth Amendment. An administrative law judge imposed additional fines in excess of $300,000. The Seventh Circuit enforced the OSHA order, noting that under a recent Supreme Court decision, **the Double Jeopardy Clause does not forbid OSHA sanctions following criminal punishment for the same conduct**. *S.A. Healy Co. v. Occupational Safety and Health Review Comm'n*, 138 F.3d 686 (7th Cir. 1998).

◆ A heavy equipment manufacturer utilized a forging press to make track links for earth-moving equipment. Regular maintenance procedures for the press involved removing the hub of the press by placing great pressure on it. During these maintenance operations, metal fragments were sometimes thrown for long distances, and in some cases came close to hitting employees. In one maintenance procedure, pressure propelled a nine-pound metal fragment 121 feet, causing serious injury when it struck an employee. The manufacturer had placed warning markers 90 to 100 feet from the press but had not employed recommended safety precautions. The OSH Review Commission affirmed a citation against the manufacturer for willful violation of the general duty clause of the OSH Act. In doing so, it increased the penalty from $30,000 to $49,000. The manufacturer appealed to the Seventh Circuit, where it argued that it had taken appropriate precautions for the foreseeable hazards of the operation. The court observed that a violation of the OSH Act is established where a hazard is likely to cause death or serious physical harm, and the employer, aware of the hazard, fails to implement known feasible abatements. In this case, the manufacturer **had a heightened awareness of the risk of flying metal fragments and failed to employ recommended safety precautions**. This evidenced a plain indifference to employee safety. The penalty was appropriate, and the court affirmed the Commission's order. *Caterpillar, Inc. v. Occupational Safety and Health Review Comm'n*, 122 F.3d 437 (7th Cir. 1997).

◆ A North Carolina employer was cited for several serious violations of the OSH Act, including failure to provide machine guards on an assembly line. The employer obtained a time extension for abatement of the violations. Before the extension ended, an employee was severely injured when emergency cutoff switches malfunctioned on the equipment. The employee sued the employer and two supervisors for negligence. The Court of Appeals of North Carolina held that where an employer intentionally engages in misconduct substantially certain to cause serious injury or death and an employee is injured or killed by the misconduct, workers' compensation exclusivity does not bar a negligence action. Here, although the employer had been aware of the OSH Act violation, **it did not operate the equipment with substantial certainty of causing serious injury or death**. The employer had received permission to continue operations without abating the hazard, and there was no evidence that the supervisors had engaged in reckless or willful conduct. *Regan v. Amerimark Building Products, Inc.*, 489 S.E.2d 421 (N.C. Ct. App. 1997).

◆   Employees working at a Maryland steel plant placed a toaster oven in the employee break room. The toaster was placed on a floor-mounted air conditioner for several years and became dilapidated. An employee was then killed during his break when he placed his arm on the toaster and was electrocuted. The Maryland Occupational Safety and Health Administration cited the employer for violating state and federal employment safety laws and fined it for violating a federal regulation requiring employers to maintain electrical equipment in a condition that is free from recognized hazards likely to cause death or serious physical harm. The penalty was based on willful or repeated violations of safety laws. The Court of Appeals of Maryland reviewed the federal regulation and found that the employer could be held responsible for electrical hazards caused by equipment brought to a work site by employees. The regulation obligated employers to abate electrical hazards and maintain worker safety without regard to the source of the risk. The court also upheld administrative findings that **the outer condition of the oven, which was in an obvious state of deterioration, put the employer on notice of the risk of electrocution**. The court remanded the case for further consideration of whether the employer was guilty of repeated violations. *Commissioner of Labor and Industry v. Bethlehem Steel Corp.*, 344 Md. 17, 684 A.2d 845 (Md. 1996).

◆   An OSHA regulation prohibits workers from riding on a load suspended from a crane except where the use of a conventional personnel platform or scaffold would be more hazardous. A contractor demolished a bridge in West Virginia using a backhoe suspended by a crane. An OSHA compliance officer determined that the backhoe was a load, not a personnel platform, and that the arrangement violated the regulation. The employer disregarded the officer's instruction to discontinue the operation, and the work was completed without incident. OSHA cited the employer for a willful violation. An administrative law judge found that the backhoe arrangement was a personnel platform, not a load, and did not violate the regulation. The OSH Review Commission (Commission) reversed the administrative ruling, and the employer appealed, arguing that under the OSH Act, the backhoe was a nonconforming personnel platform, and that a nonconforming platform did not warrant a citation. The D.C. Circuit Court of Appeals agreed with the employer. **The regulation did not prohibit the conversion of equipment designed for one function to other purposes.** The court vacated and set aside the Commission's order. *S.G. Loewendick & Sons, Inc. v. Reich*, 70 F.3d 1291 (D.C. Cir. 1995).

C. Federal Law Preemption

Generally, the OSH Act preempts state safety laws that address the same area.

◆   While working on a boat in Louisiana, a contractor's employee fell down a manhole as he descended into the rudder room. Although he had safely negotiated the angle iron steps several times previously, this time he slipped and fell as a result of some anti-corrosive material. He sued the boat owner for negligence, seeking to recover for his injuries. The boat owner sought pretrial judgment, asserting that it did not violate its duties under the LHWCA, and also maintaining that **Coast Guard regulations preempted OSHA regulations as they related to inspected vessels**. The court agreed with the boat owner, noting that it was not liable for failing to warn the contractor's employee of the hazard, and that the presence of the anti-corrosive material was open and obvious. On appeal, the Fifth Circuit affirmed in part, agreeing that the boat owner had no duty to warn of the open and obvious hazard. However, there were questions of fact as to whether the boat owner had active control of the vessel and the welder's work area, making it possible for him to prove negligence in a trial. *Romero v. Cajun Stabilizing Boats, Inc.*, 307 Fed.Appx. 849 (5th Cir. 2009).

◆   A mechanic who worked for a Kansas paper manufacturer was disciplined for arguing with his supervisor about the safety of a piece of machinery. He filed a complaint about the machinery's safety with OSHA, which conducted a surprise investigation and found that some of the mechanic's complaints were valid. The mechanic was fired a month later, and he sued, claiming wrongful discharge under Kansas common law and retaliatory discharge pursuant to Section 11(c) of the OSH Act. He withdrew the OSH Act claim after an OSHA employee told him that the claim was no longer valid because the machinery had been fixed. The Kansas Supreme Court determined that **the remedy provided by the OSH Act for retaliatory discharge was not sufficiently adequate to prevent fired employees from suing for wrongful discharge** under state law. Using the "adequate remedy" standard, the court found that the mechanic could pursue his state law claim because the remedies provided by the OSH Act limited his rights of redress to filing a complaint with the Secretary of Labor (Secretary). Under the OSH Act, the mechanic could not file a lawsuit himself, and he was afforded no right of appeal if the Secretary declined to do so. *Flenker v. Willamette Industries*, 967 P.2d 295 (Kan. 1998).

◆   A Houston pipe and tubing company vice president was killed while unloading a truck after regular working hours when no appropriate help was available. The Workers' Health and Safety Division of the state Workers' Compensation Commission identified the company as an extra-hazardous employer under its regulatory guidelines. The company was able to escape the designation after six months of compliance with the accident prevention plan developed for it. However, it challenged the designation in state court, asserting that the regulatory basis for the designation was preempted by the OSH Act. The case reached the Court of Appeals of Texas, which held that the OSH Act generally preempts state workplace safety regulations unless they fall within the act's savings clause. This includes federally approved state regulatory regimes under which the state agrees to enforce the act. Another area of state authority that is not preempted is a state workers' compensation system. Here, although the state extra-hazardous designation arose under a program closely related to the state workers' compensation system, it did not affect any award or amount of compensation and focused on accident prevention and safety. Because **this was the exact area of OSHA application, and the state program was not a federally approved OSHA enforcement regime**, the state program was preempted by OSHA. *Ben Robinson Co. v. Texas Workers' Compensation Comm'n*, 934 S.W.2d 149 (Tex. Ct. App. 1996).

◆   A building subcontractor's employee was injured when he fell from the second floor of a building that was under construction. He filed a lawsuit against another subcontractor at the work site, claiming that it was liable for his injuries because it had control of the unfinished staircase from which he had fallen. He also alleged that state and federal OSHA standards imposed a duty of care upon the subcontractor and added claims based on alternate theories. A Delaware trial court determined that **state Occupational Safety and Health standards were inapplicable because they were preempted by the federal OSH Act** as concerning identical areas of workplace safety regulation. Federal OSHA standards did not create a private cause of action for injured workers by establishing a duty of care on the part of subcontractors. Even though the employee was deprived of this cause of action, OSHA workplace regulations served as a guide for a standard of conduct that bound the subcontractor. The negligence action against the subcontractor could not be dismissed. *Figgs v. Bellevue Holding Co.*, 652 A.2d 1084 (Del. Super. Ct. 1994).

◆   A laboratory technician at a nuclear fuels production facility complained to management and to the Nuclear Regulatory Commission about perceived violations of nuclear safety standards. When the company did not adequately address her concerns, she deliberately failed to clean some contamination left by a previous work shift. She outlined the contaminated areas with red tape and then pointed them out to her supervisor a few days later (when they still had not been cleaned). Her employer discharged her for her knowing failure to clean up radioactive contamination. After unsuccessfully pursuing an administrative remedy, the technician sued the employer in a North Carolina federal court for intentional infliction of emotional distress. The court dismissed her claim as conflicting with Section 210 of the Energy Reorganization Act. The Fourth Circuit affirmed. The U.S. Supreme Court held that **the technician's claim was not preempted by Section 210**. This section was primarily intended to protect employees even though it did bear some relation to the field of nuclear safety. Accordingly, not all state law claims arising from the section were included in the field (nuclear safety) that Congress intended to preempt. The Court reversed and remanded the case for a trial on the merits. *English v. General Electric Co.*, 496 U.S. 72, 110 S.Ct. 2270, 110 L.Ed.2d 65 (1990).

V. OTHER LABOR REGULATIONS

There are many federal and state statutes and regulations that affect labor relations and employment. The FLSA, the NLRA and the OSH Act are among the most litigated. The cases below involve some of the other labor statutes and regulations with which employers must contend.

A. The Railway Labor Act

The Railway Labor Act (RLA) governs labor relations in the railroad and airline industries by imposing a comprehensive scheme for dispute resolution. The federal goal of keeping labor disputes in these areas out of lengthy court proceedings is reflected in the relegation of "minor disputes" to compulsory arbitration, and the requirement of bargaining and mediation for "major disputes," with arbitration of a major dispute if mediation fails.

Minor disputes are defined as those arising out of the interpretation of collective bargaining agreements concerning rates of pay, rules, or working conditions.

Major disputes relate to the formation of collective bargaining agreements or efforts to secure them, and concern rates of pay, rules or working conditions.

◆   A Hawaii aircraft mechanic recommended replacement of a part during an inspection of an aircraft. His supervisor refused to replace the part. At the end of the shift, the mechanic refused to sign a maintenance record approving the plane for flight. The supervisor suspended the mechanic pending a termination hearing, and the mechanic reported the incident to the Federal Aviation Administration. The mechanic filed a grievance under the collective bargaining agreement, which prohibited discharge without just cause and prohibited discipline for refusing to perform work in violation of safety laws. The hearing officer recommended termination for insubordination, and the employee sued for violation of the Hawaii Whistleblower Protection Act, among other claims. His claims were dismissed as preempted by the RLA. The Supreme Court of Hawaii held that the state tort actions were not preempted by the RLA.

The U.S. Supreme Court affirmed. The RLA and other federal labor statutes promoted stability in labor-management relations by offering comprehensive frameworks for resolving labor disputes. **Although the RLA preempted minor disputes under collective bargaining agreements, it did not preempt substantive protections under state laws.** Here, the mechanic alleged that the airline had a state law obligation not to fire him in violation of public policy or in retaliation for whistleblowing. The RLA and other similar federal labor statutes did not preempt such claims. *Hawaiian Airlines, Inc. v. Norris*, 512 U.S. 246, 114 S.Ct. 2239, 129 L.Ed.2d 203 (1994).

◆   A railroad with operations in Pennsylvania agreed to sell its assets to a newly formed subsidiary of another railroad (buyer). The buyer did not intend to assume the seller's collective bargaining contracts, needing only 250 of the 750 employees then working for the seller. The Railway Labor Executives' Association sued to determine the seller's obligations under the RLA and to enjoin the sale until those obligations could be met. The unions representing the seller's employees filed RLA Section 156 notices proposing extensive changes in existing agreements and went on strike. The buyer obtained an exemption from the ICC, which essentially amounted to an approval of the sale, and a federal court enjoined the work stoppage. The court also issued an injunction against the sale, and the Third Circuit affirmed in part but set aside the injunction against the strike. The U.S. Supreme Court held that the RLA did not require or authorize an injunction against the sale of the seller's assets to the buyer. Also, the Section 156 notices did not obligate the seller to postpone the sale beyond the approval date set by the ICC. However, the seller did have a limited duty to bargain regarding the effects of the sale. This obligation ceased on the date for closing the sale. The Court remanded the case for a determination as to **whether the RLA created a duty not to strike while its dispute resolution mechanisms were under way**. *Pittsburgh & Lake Erie Railroad Co. v. RLEA,* 491 U.S. 490, 109 S.Ct. 2584, 105 L.Ed.2d 415 (1989).

◆   A union representing flight attendants declared a strike after reaching a collective bargaining impasse over wages and working conditions, and after pursuing the required dispute resolution mechanisms of the RLA. The airline hired permanent replacements to help those who had not gone out on strike or who had abandoned the strike. After the strike ended, an agreement was entered into whereby strikers who returned to work would be reinstated with their seniority rights intact. The union then sued, contending that even if the strike was economic, the full-term strikers were entitled to displace junior crossover attendants. A Missouri federal court denied relief to the union, but the Eighth Circuit held that the less senior crossovers could be displaced. Further appeal was taken to the U.S. Supreme Court, which held that **the RLA did not require the airline to lay off the junior crossovers**. Since new hires could not be displaced after an economic strike, it would be unfair to differentiate between them and junior crossovers. The airline had lawfully exercised its economic power during the strike. *Trans World Airlines v. Independent Federation of Flight Attendants,* 489 U.S. 426, 109 S.Ct. 1225, 103 L.Ed.2d 456 (1989).

◆   While Northwest Airlines was in Chapter 11, a bankruptcy court gave it the right to reject its collective bargaining agreement with the union representing its flight attendants. The union characterized this as unilateral action allowing it to strike. Northwest petitioned the bankruptcy court to enjoin the flight attendants from striking, but the court denied the motion for injunctive relief. Northwest then asked a New York federal court to issue a preliminary injunction to prevent the strike. The court issued the injunction, finding that **the rejection of the bargaining agreement did not automatically terminate the dispute resolution process under the Railway Labor Act**. Here, the rejection of the bargaining agreement did not constitute an act of bad faith, or an arbitrary or unilateral change in the status quo so as to give the union the right to strike. The union was required to exert every reasonable effort to resolve the dispute before striking so as not to disrupt commerce. The flight attendants were not allowed to strike. *In re Northwest Airlines Corp.*, 349 B.R. 338 (S.D.N.Y. 2006).

◆   An airline required its pilot trainees to agree to compulsory arbitration of statutory claims as a condition of employment. The pilots' union, which did not represent the trainees, sued the airline under the RLA, asserting that the arbitration clause was a mandatory subject of bargaining that could not be enforced because the airline had not bargained over it. The U.S. Court of Appeals, D.C. Circuit, ruled in favor of the airline, noting that unions cannot use an individual's statutory right to a judicial forum in the collective bargaining process. In other words, a union cannot lawfully agree to binding arbitration. As a necessary consequence of this ruling, **the arbitration clause could not be a mandatory subject of bargaining**, and the airline could require its pilots to agree to arbitration without bargaining over the issue. *Airline Pilots Ass'n Int'l v. Northwest Airlines, Inc.*, 199 F.3d 477 (D.C. Cir. 1999).

◆   A New York commuter railroad dispatcher was accused of drug use by her supervisor in the presence of two other supervisors. She requested a grievance hearing under the applicable collective bargaining agreement and also commenced a defamation lawsuit against the supervisor in state court. A jury awarded her $1.2 million. The court refused to set aside the verdict on the grounds of preemption by the RLA. The New York Court of Appeals held that **state law actions for retaliatory discharge do not involve minor disputes and are not preempted by the RLA** because they do not involve the interpretation of a bargaining agreement. Although the state law claim involved some factual consideration of the bargaining agreement, it required no construction of contractual terms so as to be preempted by the RLA. *Harris v. Hirsh*, 86 N.Y.2d 207, 654 N.E.2d 975 (N.Y. 1995).

◆   An association was certified as the representative of the flight attendants of an airline with operations in Oregon. However, over a year and a half later, negotiations between the union and the airline were still unproductive, despite the intervention of the National Mediation Board. The union sued the airline under the RLA, asserting that it had violated its statutory duty to "exert every reasonable effort" to reach an agreement. A federal court held that the airline had violated the RLA. The U.S. Court of Appeals, Ninth Circuit, noted that it is proper for federal courts to consult NLRA cases for assistance in construing the RLA. The U.S. Supreme Court has held that **"the duty to exert every reasonable effort imposed by the RLA requires at least the avoidance of bad faith** as defined under the NLRA, that is, going through the motions with a desire not to reach an agreement." Here, the district court had relied on the NLRA cases solely to impose on the airline the duty which the Supreme Court had held to be common to both statutes. Since the district court had merely ordered the airline to perform its existing duty under the RLA (without imposing upon it any duties derived from the NLRA) the court of appeals affirmed the district court's decision. *Ass'n of Flight Attendants v. Horizon Air Industries, Inc.*, 976 F.2d 541 (9th Cir. 1992).

B. The Worker Adjustment and Retraining Notification Act

The Worker Adjustment and Retraining Notification (WARN) Act, 29 U.S.C. § 2101 *et seq.*, requires large companies to serve written notice upon employees or their representatives 60 days in advance of a plant closing or mass layoff where a third of the work force at a single site and 50 or more employees lose their jobs during a 30-day period, or where 500 or more employees lose their jobs.

Where an employer violates the notice requirement, it becomes liable for back pay for each day of the violation, as well as lost benefits, civil penalties and attorneys' fees. The statute does not contain a limitation on actions.

1. Notice Requirements

Although the WARN Act generally requires a 60-day advance notice in cases of mass layoffs and plant closings, it contains an exception for:

—unforeseeable business circumstances (sudden, dramatic and unexpected actions outside the employer's control), and

—situations where the employer is pursuing a reasonable possibility of future business that would avoid the plant closing or mass layoff, and the giving of notice would jeopardize the possibility of acquiring that business.

◆   An Oklahoma wholesale grocery distributor announced that it would be laying off 200 employees three business days after its largest customer said it was going to get its supplies from another distributor, and shortly after its bank declined to loan it $15 million. The laid-off employees sued for benefits under the WARN Act on the grounds that the distributor failed to give the required 60 days' notice. A federal court and the Tenth Circuit ruled for the distributor, holding that **the "unforeseen business circumstances" clause permitted the distributor to lay off the employees with less than 60 days' notice**. Even though the customer had warned the distributor that it might have to start placing more orders with other suppliers because of low inventories, its sudden decision to terminate the relationship was not reasonably foreseeable. *Gross v. Hale-Halsell Co.*, 554 F.3d 870 (10th Cir. 2009).

◆   When a New York mortgage company could not fund its continued operations, it retained money owed to a creditor by falsifying certain data. Eventually, the creditor discovered the misappropriations. It refused to do business with the individuals responsible for the fraud. Those people resigned, and a new manager was brought in. The creditor worked with the business, but eventually the business failed and the creditor issued a default notice. Two days later the business closed. **Employees who were let go filed a WARN Act suit against the creditor, alleging that it was the employer for WARN Act purposes** and failed to give proper notice before closing it down. A federal court and the Second Circuit ruled for the creditor, finding that it was not liable as an employer under the WARN Act because it was not operating the business as a going concern at the time it closed. Instead, it acted to shore up the business in the short term to facilitate the sale of the business and recover the $5.6 million in loans that had been misappropriated. It did not exercise control over the business beyond that which was necessary to recoup some or all of what was owed it, and it took no long-term control over the business. *Coppola v. Bear Stearns & Co., Inc.*, 499 F.3d 144 (2d Cir. 2007).

◆   A Texas-based company provided personnel management, payroll and other administrative services for a manufacturer of men's clothing, essentially acting as an off-site human resource department. When the manufacturer closed its plant without providing 60 days' advance notice as required by the WARN Act, the union representing the manufacturer's employees demanded that the human resources (HR) company compensate each member of the bargaining unit for 60 days' pay plus benefits. The HR company refused to pay, and a Texas federal court ruled in its favor. The Fifth Circuit affirmed, noting that the HR company played no role in the closing of the plant, and did not even know of the closing until after the fact. Further, even though it was a co-employer for purposes of providing group medical benefits and workers' compensation, it did not employ the workers in the normal business sense. **The HR company could not be held liable as a joint employer under the WARN Act.** *Administaff Companies, Inc. v. New York Joint Board*, 337 F.3d 454 (5th Cir. 2003).

◆   A school bus transportation company notified its seasonal and year-round employees in July 1995 that it would be closing its local terminal because it had not been assigned any transportation routes for the upcoming school year. In the same notice, the employees were advised that they would not be rehired in September. The union and eight nonunion employees sued, alleging that the employer violated the WARN Act by failing to provide its seasonal and non-seasonal employees with 60 days' notice of an impending plant closing. A Missouri federal court found that the seasonal workers received adequate notice but that the nonseasonal employees did not. Both sides appealed. The Eighth Circuit Court of Appeals affirmed, holding that although the seasonal employees on temporary layoff were "employees" under the act, **they did not suffer an "employment loss"** so as to be entitled to damages. Despite evidence that the employer knew it would probably close the terminal sometime before September 1995, the seasonal employees would have been laid off in June of that year anyway. At most, they lost the immediate expectation of being rehired, and a loss of an expectation is not an "employment loss" under the act. *Teamsters Local 838 v. Laidlaw Transit*, 156 F.3d 854 (8th Cir. 1998).

◆   The WARN Act allocates the notice responsibility in the case of a sale of an employer's assets to the party actually making the decision that creates an employment loss. A business seller is responsible for giving the notice up to and including the effective date of sale. After the effective date of sale, the purchaser is responsible for any required notice. A Nebraska optical company negotiated with another business to sell the company. The parties contemplated the continuing operation of the seller's plant until several days before the sale, when the purchaser suddenly determined that it would only buy the seller's equipment, tools, supplies and inventory. Two days after the parties signed a purchase agreement, the seller announced the plant closing to employees. The purchaser hired some of the seller's former employees, and several of the others sued the buyer and seller, asserting WARN Act violations. The case reached the U.S. Court of Appeals, Eighth Circuit, which found that **the responsibility for giving notice had never passed to the purchaser** and that the seller became obligated to provide notice two days prior to the plant closing, when it learned of the sale of assets. The seller was liable for damages resulting from the violation. *Burnsides v. MJ Optical, Inc.*, 128 F.3d 700 (8th Cir. 1997).

◆ An Ohio barge company purchased the assets of a Kentucky barge and towing company and offered to rehire the seller's employees. It circulated job applications to most of the seller's employees and eventually hired 49 of 160 affected workers. Some former employees of the seller filed a lawsuit against both companies in a Kentucky federal court for WARN Act violations. The court granted pretrial judgment to the employers, but the Sixth Circuit found that the district court had improperly held that each of the barges utilized by the seller constituted a single site of employment for WARN Act purposes. Because the employees all reported to a single site in Kentucky, the boats were based there and all work assignments originated there, it constituted a single site for WARN Act purposes. However, there was **no employment loss under the WARN Act because all but 24 of the 160 affected employees had received an opportunity to continue employment** with the purchaser. *Wiltz v. M/G Transport Services, Inc.*, 128 F.3d 957 (6th Cir. 1997).

◆ A mining company sold the entire annual coal output from a particular Virginia mine to a Canadian steelmaker under annual contracts that were renegotiated each year. After 30 years, the parties were unable to reach an agreement, and the coal company closed the mine, giving employees only a one-day notice. The employees' union sued under the WARN Act. A federal court ruled for the employer, and the Fourth Circuit affirmed. One of the exceptions to the general WARN Act requirement for a 60-day advance notice of a plant closing or mass layoff is a closing caused by business circumstances that are not reasonably foreseeable as of the time that notice would have normally been required. In those situations, an employer must give as much notice as is practicable and explain the reason for reducing the notification period. Here, **the loss of the contract was not reasonably foreseeable in view of the previous 30 years of successful contract negotiations**. The employer had made an economic decision that could not have been made at a prior time. *Local Union 7107, UAW v. Clinchfield Coal Co.*, 124 F.3d 639 (4th Cir. 1997).

◆ A manufacturing company advised the labor union representing employees working at a Missouri plant that a permanent layoff of 277 employees would occur 60 days later. The union charged that the manufacturer had already begun the layoff in violation of the WARN Act. An employer violating the notice requirement of the act must pay each employee wages for each day of the violation, and unions are specifically authorized to file suit on behalf of injured employees. The union sued, but the court dismissed the lawsuit, finding that the union could not recover monetary damages on behalf of individual union members without their participation in the lawsuit. The Eighth Circuit affirmed, but the U.S. Supreme Court reversed. **The WARN Act explicitly allows unions to recover damages on behalf of individual union members.** The Constitution did not prohibit Congress from conferring legal standing upon labor organizations to sue for damages on behalf of their individual members. Earlier decisions of the Court restricting monetary damage claims by representative organizations prohibited such claims as a matter of judicial convenience, and not as a constitutional prohibition. *United Food and Commercial Workers Union Local 751 v. Brown Group, Inc.*, 517 U.S. 544, 116 S.Ct. 1529, 134 L.Ed.2d 758 (1996).

✦   In a case involving the statute of limitations under the WARN Act, the U.S. Supreme Court observed that where Congress fails to specify a limitations period in a federal law, the appropriate **statute of limitations** is drawn from the state in which the case is venued. Since 1830, state laws have supplied the appropriate limitations period for such claims under federal law, except where to do so would frustrate an important Congressional purpose. In this case, it was entirely appropriate to apply Pennsylvania law as the limitations period for WARN Act actions. The employers had set forth no reason to deviate from the general rule, and the court of appeals' decision was affirmed. *North Star Steel Co. v. Thomas,* 515 U.S. 29, 115 S.Ct. 1927, 132 L.Ed.2d 27 (1995).

2. Number of Employees

A <u>mass layoff</u> includes any employment loss at a single site of employment that involves one-third of the employees at that site and at least 50 employees, or alternatively, at least 500 employees.

✦   An Arkansas employer laid off 62 employees, most of whom then sued the company for violating the WARN Act by failing to give proper notice. They sought 60 days of back pay and lost benefits. A federal court ruled that there was no WARN Act violation because the company had 202 qualified employees at the time of the layoff, not the 191 claimed by the plaintiffs. The 11 employees at issue had been hired more than six months prior to the layoffs and were thus not part-time employees for WARN Act purposes. Also, four employees resigned prior to the layoffs because they knew a layoff was inevitable. So instead of 66 employees being laid off, only 62 were. And **the four employees who resigned did not count for purposes of the WARN Act**. Since 33% (or 66) employees had to be laid off to reach the mass layoff trigger requirements, the 62 who were laid off had no claim. *Guinn v. Timco Aviation Services, Inc.*, 317 F.Supp.2d 888 (W.D. Ark. 2004).

✦   An Ohio plant superintendent announced the permanent closing of the facility, providing employees with only 10 days written notice. Employees were offered tentative positions with a facility located in another city, but only 17 of over 100 employees accepted employment there. Fifty-one separated employees sued the company under the WARN Act. The court held for the employees, finding that the factory was subject to WARN Act coverage since it employed over 100 workers at the relevant time, and that the employer had failed to make them a reasonable transfer offer. It awarded damages to the employees for 60 calendar days of pay and attorneys' fees. The U.S. Court of Appeals, Sixth Circuit, found that the employer had over 100 employees at the plant during the relevant time period, despite employment fluctuations due to leave, vacation and temporary layoffs. It agreed with the employer, however, that the district court had improperly awarded damages based on calendar days, rather than work days. **WARN Act damages should be equal to wages that would have been received** had employees remained on the job during the violation period. The district court had also erroneously failed to credit from the damage award the 10 days of actual notice given by the employer. The court affirmed the finding of liability and vacated and remanded the damage award for reconsideration. *Saxion v. Titan-C-Manufacturing, Inc.*, 86 F.3d 553 (6th Cir. 1996).

♦   A Louisiana grocery retailer operated three stores in a metropolitan area. Although about 30% of its employees had been permanently or temporary transferred between stores on at least one occasion, the stores maintained separate payroll records, and no employee was paid at his or her base store when working at another. The retailer announced that it was closing the three stores due to decreased sales, and those employees who did not accept transfers to other stores were discharged. A number of former employees sued, arguing that the three area stores constituted a "single site of employment" under the WARN Act. The court held that because none of the individual stores employed the statutory minimum 50 full-time employees, the WARN Act was inapplicable. The Fifth Circuit Court of Appeals affirmed. WARN Act regulations state that **noncontiguous sites in the same geographic area that do not share the same staff should not be considered a single site**. The retailer had taken steps to ensure that transferred employees were paid by their temporary store rather than their base store and stores did not routinely share employees and equipment. Because occasional transfers of employees did not establish the necessary connection for a single site, the WARN Act claims failed. *Viator v. Delchamps, Inc.*, 109 F.3d 1124 (5th Cir. 1997).

♦   A California videotape business was acquired by a holding company, with only a few days notice to employees. Most of the company's employees accepted employment with the new entity, but many suffered a pay cut and loss of fringe benefits under collectively bargained-for union health and pension plans. The new employer refused to recognize the union's representation of approximately one-third of the transferred employees, and the union sued the selling company for damages under the WARN Act. A federal court held that there had been no employment loss under the WARN Act because fewer than 50 employees lost their jobs. The union appealed to the Ninth Circuit.

The union argued that the definition of "employment loss" under the WARN Act should encompass a reduction in pay and benefits resulting from a business sale. It also claimed that the sale had been a sham and that the new entity was the alter ego of the former employer. The court found no WARN Act violation, accepting the U.S. Department of Labor's interpretation that a business seller is liable for violations of the act only up to the date of sale. The buyer is responsible thereafter. Also, the WARN Act applied only to employees who actually experienced a covered employment loss and not a technical termination through sale. The WARN Act did not apply to modifications of the terms of employment, such as compensation and benefits. **The sale in this case was not an event that triggered the coverage of WARN**, and the district court had properly held for the former employer. *Int'l Alliance v. Compact Video Services, Inc.*, 50 F.3d 1464 (9th Cir. 1995).

◆   An industrial products manufacturer closed a department and laid off 41 employees there. It also laid off 15 employees who worked in the same division in departments related to the one that had been dissolved. The employees sued under the WARN Act. A federal magistrate judge found that the corporation did not order a "mass layoff" under the statute but that it had ordered a "plant closing" without providing the required 60-day notice. A Rhode Island federal court agreed, finding that the department was an "operating unit" for purposes of the WARN Act. The corporation considered the department to be a separate organizational unit, and it planned and executed a shutdown of that unit. Even though some of the department's work was picked up by other departments, **the department was a distinct organizational and production entity that was closed by the corporation**. Also, more than 50 employees lost their jobs within a 30-day period. Even though the general downturn in the economy was the reason the additional 15 employees were not reassigned to other groups, the employment loss was caused by the closure of the department. *Pavao v. Brown & Sharpe Manufacturing Co.*, 844 F.Supp. 890 (D.R.I. 1994).

C. Other Statutes

The following cases address the Hours of Service Act and the Immigration Reform and Control Act.

◆   Arizona passed a law requiring employers to use E-Verify to determine if potential employees are eligible to work. The law also allowed the state to suspend and revoke business licenses for employing unauthorized aliens. A number of groups challenged the law, and the case reached the U.S. Supreme Court, which held that the law was valid. The law was not preempted by federal law, including the Immigration Reform and Control Act (IRCA). **The IRCA specifically allows states to impose sanctions for employing illegal aliens through licensing and similar laws.** *Chamber of Commerce v. Whiting*, 131 S.Ct. 1968, 179 L.Ed.2d 1031 (U.S. 2011).

◆   The federal Hours of Service Act (HSA) states that railroad employees can work shifts of up to 12 consecutive hours. The employer must then allow the employee at least 10 consecutive hours off or face considerable penalties. The HSA states that time spent in transportation to a duty assignment is on-duty time, but time spent in transportation from a duty assignment at the end of a shift is neither time on duty nor off duty. Because many railroad workers spend considerable time periods being transported from work sites, the HSA recognizes a category, known as limbo time, which applies to employees who are not working but are being transported from a work site. This time is not assessed against the 12-hour limitation. The Federal Railroad Administration (FRA) then declared time spent waiting to travel to be on-duty time that counted against the 12-hour prohibition. Nine major railroads filed a lawsuit in the U.S. Court of Appeals, Seventh Circuit, for review of the FRA's changed interpretation. The court agreed with the railroads and held that time spent waiting for transportation is limbo time.

The U.S. Supreme Court stated that the HSA treats time spent in transit to a work site as on-duty time because this time contributes to worker fatigue. However, the HSA does not treat time spent traveling from a work site at the end of a shift as on-duty time because there is no similar safety concern in transporting an employee to an eventual point of release from work. For the same reason, **time spent waiting to be transported to a work site should be regarded as on-duty time** (to be assessed against the 12-hour limitation) while time spent waiting for transportation at the end of a shift should be treated as limbo time, which did not count against the 12-hour limit. Because this interpretation supported HSA safety goals and granted the railroads a necessary measure of flexibility, the Court affirmed the Seventh Circuit decision. *Brotherhood of Locomotive Engineers v. Atchison, Topeka & Santa Fe Railroad Co.*, 516 U.S. 152, 116 S.Ct. 595, 133 L.Ed.2d 535 (1996).

◆   An Illinois contracting firm challenged **the state's Employee Classification Act**, alleging that it violated due process. The contractor had been cited for violating the act by misclassifying six workers as independent contractors on two construction projects over a three-month period. It claimed that it should have received notice and an opportunity to respond before being penalized and fined. It sought a preliminary injunction to prevent the department of labor from enforcing the act while it sued. A court granted the injunction, but the Appellate Court of Illinois vacated and remanded the case. Since the department did not adjudicate whether the contractor had violated the act but only investigated and determined whether to bring actions in court, there was no due process violation. *World Painting Co., LLC v. Costigan*, 967 N.E.2d 485 (Ill. App. Ct. 2012).

◆   An illegal immigrant purchased a New Jersey woman's name and Social Security number for $800 from an unidentified person in New York and used the documents to get a job as a maid at a hotel. When the identity theft victim applied for unemployment benefits, they were denied on the grounds that she had a job as a maid at the hotel. The identity theft victim called the police, and the immigrant was deported. The identity theft victim then sued the hotel under the Immigration Reform and Control Act (IRCA). A state court found that the hotel conducted a reasonable inspection of the documents. The appellate division court ruled that **the identity theft victim could not bring a private cause of action under the IRCA.** Further, she could not sue the hotel for negligence because there was no relationship between the identity theft victim and the hotel. *Piscitelli v. Classic Residence by Hyatt*, 973 A.2d 948 (N.J. Super. Ct. App. Div. 2009).

◆   A group of businesses and civil rights organizations brought a lawsuit challenging the Legal Arizona Workers Act (LAWA), asserting that it was preempted by the Immigration Reform and Control Act of 1986 (IRCA) and by the Illegal Immigration Reform and Immigrant Responsibility Act of 1996. The LAWA allows the state to revoke businesses' licenses if they don't fire all unauthorized workers, and it requires businesses to use the E-Verify system to check the work-authorization status of employees. A federal court held that the state law was not preempted, and the Ninth Circuit affirmed. The court of appeals noted that IRCA allows for state licensing laws, and that LAWA is such a law. Further, **even though the E-Verify system was enacted as a voluntary system, that did not mean Congress intended to prevent states from making participation mandatory**. *Chicanos Por La Causa, Inc. v. Napolitano*, 558 F.3d 856 (9th Cir. 2009).

◆   A company in California was notified by the Social Security Administration (SSA) that information the company reported about 48 employees did not match what the SSA had on file. In response to the "no-match" letter, the company gave the employees three days to provide proof that they had applied for new Social Security cards. It then fired 33 employees who didn't provide the proof after seven days. The employees' union filed a grievance. The case reached the Ninth Circuit, which held that **a "no-match" letter, by itself, does not put a company on constructive notice that the employees named in the letter are undocumented**. Further, the short turnaround time the company gave the employees to provide documentation did not allow the company to draw the inference that the employees were undocumented. Since the arbitrator who heard the union's grievance found no convincing evidence that any of the employees were undocumented, the employees were entitled to be reinstated with back pay. *Aramark Facility Services v. Service Employees Int'l Union*, 530 F.3d 817 (9th Cir. 2008).

◆   A Kansas restaurant manager agreed to pay an illegal immigrant $6 an hour for work as a cook. The cook worked 50 to 60 hours a week but was paid $50 or $60 per week on top of his rent for six months ($100/month). He sought to be paid the agreed-upon amount, and a hearing officer determined that the restaurant owed him $3,720 in wages, $217 in interest, and $3,720 in penalties for the willful withholding of his wages. A federal court then held that the cook could only receive the minimum wage because he was an undocumented worker. However, the Kansas Supreme Court disagreed and reinstated the award for the cook. Here, **the Immigration Reform and Control Act (IRCA) did not bar his recovery because he did not obtain the work by fraudulent means or fake documents**. The court held that enforcing state wage laws actually furthers IRCA's goals by creating disincentives for employers to hire illegal immigrants and pay them low or no wages. *Coma Corp. d/b/a Burrito Express v. Kansas Dep't of Labor*, 154 P.3d 1080 (Kan. 2007).

CHAPTER SIX

Employment Practices

I. HIRING PRACTICES

Employers use various pre-employment measures to ensure that applicants will be suited for the positions available. Among the options most frequently used are physical and mental tests, psychological examinations, and of course the interview process, during which the applicant's intelligence and personality are gauged (even through such clues as dress and mannerisms).

Generally, the problem isn't choosing between a qualified and a non-qualified candidate. More often, the problem is in choosing between two or more seemingly equal candidates. Here are several potential solutions:

1) having each qualified candidate work a week or a pay period for an amount not less than minimum wage to see who is most qualified – any candidate refusing to participate can be eliminated,

2) obtaining more information through the use of additional tests or reference and background checks – some candidates may withdraw during this process, making your job easier, and

3) adding an additional interview stage with the employees the candidate will be working with to see which one is most compatible with the group.

Part of what employers do in the hiring process is discriminate against applicants who are perceived to be less qualified or less easy to work with. This is not against the law.

However, employers must be careful not to discriminate or otherwise refuse to hire applicants for reasons that violate public policy. For discrimination cases involving race, sex, religion, national origin, age and disability, please see Chapter One.

Employers also have to be careful not to let information about prior workers' compensation claims, union activity, National Guard duty, lawsuits against former employers, marital status, children and (in some states) sexual orientation color their decision-making process.

Employers should also try to keep as much objectivity in the hiring process as possible to avoid charges of unfairness.

A. Negligent Misrepresentation

Occasionally, lawsuits will arise when employees or applicants claim that certain representations were made to them that never materialized. These cases tend to be for negligent, as opposed to intentional, misrepresentation. Often, they arise because of <u>casual or careless statements</u> by company managers, or because a company official asserted an opinion that was taken as more than an opinion.

♦   After a salesman at an Oregon car dealership had a heart attack, his doctor told him to find a less stressful job. The salesman received an offer to work at a local newspaper. He claimed that when he told the dealership manager he was planning to accept the offer, the manager promised him a less stressful corporate job at the dealership. Based on this promise, the salesman turned down the job at the newspaper. The dealership did not give the manager the corporate position, and the salesman sued it for promissory estoppel and fraudulent misrepresentation. Oregon's highest court reversed a ruling for the dealership, finding that **the salesman's status as an at-will employee did not bar his claims**. It is not unreasonable for a prospective employee to rely on the promise of a job just because the job is at will. *Cocchiara v. Lithia Motors, Inc.*, 297 P.3d 1277 (Or. 2013).

♦   A South Carolina employee sued his former employer, alleging that the non-compete clause he'd signed was not enforceable. He also claimed that his former employer had negligently misrepresented that he was not a candidate for termination prior to his signing of a revised shareholders' agreement, which contained the non-compete clause at issue. A federal court and the Fourth Circuit held that **the former employer did not make negligent misrepresentations about the employee's subsequent termination**. A supervisor's statement that he should keep his head down and keep doing good work was merely an expression of opinion. However, the court of appeals did determine that the non-compete clause was void because it lacked any geographic limitation and was not reasonably limited to protect the employer's interests. *Lampman v. DeWolff Boberg & Associates, Inc.*, 319 Fed.Appx. 293 (4th Cir. 2009).

♦   A New Mexico physician's assistant resigned from a hospital and sued for constructive discharge, alleging that mismanagement in the ER compromised patient care, forcing him to resign. He was then provisionally hired by another hospital, pending receipt of information from his former employers. He signed several releases of liability during the application process, discharging third parties from liability for providing answers to the new hospital's questions about his prior employment. After the old hospital provided responses, some of which were negative, the physician's assistant was not hired at the new hospital. He sued the old hospital for intentional interference with contractual relations and intentional infliction of emotional distress. The Court of Appeals of New Mexico ruled for the old hospital. Here, it had a duty of care to **third parties who could be physically injured by the physician's assistant if the**

information provided in its reference was a negligent misrepresentation of the employee's work history. The physician's assistant failed to prove that the old hospital abused its conditional privilege to provide information about him to his new employer. *DiMarco v. Presbyterian Healthcare Services, Inc.*, 141 N.M. 735, 160 P.3d 916 (N.M. Ct. App. 2007).

◆   An executive at a venture capital firm that invested in Internet start-up companies offered a high-level job to a prospective employee, indicating that the firm was close to raising a $40 million venture capital fund. The prospective employee accepted the job, turning down an offer from another Internet company. When the funding fell through, the firm exercised its option to fire the employee. He sued the firm and the executive for negligent representation. A New York federal court ruled in favor of the defendants, noting that they made efforts toward raising the money. **They did not lure the employee into a job while never intending to raise the capital needed**; they merely were unable to obtain it. Thus, there was no negligent misrepresentation. *Elliot v. Nelson*, 301 F.Supp.2d 284 (S.D.N.Y. 2004).

◆   An Illinois employer solicited applications for a marketing manager position. It hired an applicant who later asserted that the company's vice president told him during his employment interview that the company's size was going to double over the next few years and that it had impressive sales figures. Shortly after he started, he learned that the company was in a deteriorating financial condition and he was soon fired as part of a restructuring. He sued for negligent misrepresentation, breach of fiduciary duty and breach of contract. The Supreme Court of Illinois held for the employer, stating that there is no duty to avoid misrepresentations that cause only emotional harm. In order **to state a claim for negligent misrepresentation, there must be a communication of false information that results in physical injury or harm to property**. While other states have recognized a duty to avoid negligent misrepresentations in employment cases, the court refused to expand the scope of employer liability for negligent misrepresentation in Illinois. *Brogan v. Mitchell Int'l, Inc.*, 181 Ill.2d 178, 692 N.E.2d 276 (Ill. 1998).

B.   Mental and Physical Tests

As mentioned above, employers often require prospective employees to undergo psychological and/or physical examinations prior to employment. As long as such requirements apply to all prospective employees (and not just those who seem disabled, for example), the testing requirements will be upheld.

For pre-employment drug screening tests, please see Section II.

◆   An Oregon mill employee took a medical leave for knee surgery. After her doctor authorized her return to work with certain restrictions, the mill required her to undergo a physical capacity evaluation. After conducting the exam, the mill determined that her permanent lifting restrictions prevented her from returning to work in either her last job or the job she could next bid on under the collective bargaining agreement. Her doctor removed the lifting restrictions, but the mill still refused to rehire her. She sued under the ADA, and a federal court granted pretrial judgment to the mill. However, the Ninth Circuit vacated and remanded the case. It found that **the physical capacity evaluation was, in fact, a medical exam under the ADA**, and also stated that the mill could not require a medical exam that wasn't consistent with business necessity. There were factual questions about whether the exam was necessary given that the employee's doctor had removed the lifting restrictions. *Indergard v. Georgia-Pacific Corp.*, 582 F.3d 1049 (9th Cir. 2009).

♦   An applicant for a bank position in Illinois received a job offer that was conditioned on her successful completion of a drug test. She told the bank she'd recently received a cervical epidural shot that might result in additional medication showing up on the test. And indeed her test results showed phenobarbital in her system. The bank rescinded the offer of employment, and she sued under the ADA. When the bank sought to dismiss her lawsuit, a federal court refused to do so. **The applicant stated a claim that the bank used the drug test to discriminate even against applicants who took legally prescribed medications**, without regard to whether the medication might impair their ability to perform the essential functions of the job. The case required a trial. *Connolly v. First Personal Bank*, 623 F.Supp.2d 928 (N.D. Ill. 2008).

♦   An Indiana manufacturer of mineral wool insulation hired an applicant on the condition that he pass a physical examination. The applicant suffered from type I diabetes and was insulin dependent. A doctor examined the applicant, administering a urine glucose test and interviewing him. The doctor determined that his diabetes was not under control and that he was not capable of performing the physical requirements of the job. When the manufacturer withdrew its employment offer, he sued it under the ADA. He claimed that the manufacturer unreasonably relied on the doctor's opinion because the doctor did not perform an adequate, individualized assessment of his ability to do the job. A federal court and the Seventh Circuit ruled for the employer. Here, **the manufacturer reasonably relied on the doctor's opinion** because the applicant admitted to the doctor that he had a history of poor compliance and failure to seek medical attention. He even became angry when the doctor suggested he could do better at controlling his blood sugar levels. Thus, the doctor did not need to do more testing. The evidence also suggested that the applicant posed a direct threat to the safety of the workplace because of the environment where he would be working. *Darnell v. Thermafiber, Inc.*, 417 F.3d 657 (7th Cir. 2005).

♦   An employee began work at a company in Minnesota but was told that he would have to pass a pre-employment examination that took place a week later. **Although he had had an MRI of his back, he did not mention that to the doctor.** He passed the exam, then injured his back and went on short-term disability leave. After 26 weeks, when the leave expired, he got a note from his doctor stating that he could return to work. However, the company believed he could not perform the essential functions of the job and fired him. He sued for discrimination, claiming the real reason was his race, but a federal court ruled against him. Here, the company legitimately believed he could not do the job, based in part on statements he had made while on leave. *Lavela v. S.B. Foot Tanning Co.*, No. Civ 034115 (JRT/JSM), 2005 WL 1430302 (D. Minn. 3/7/05).

C. Employment Agencies

Employment agencies provide employers with prospective employees for a fee. Lawsuits arise when employers hire employees without paying the employment agency fee or otherwise violate the agency agreement.

◆   **A Minnesota nursing home contracted with a recruiting service to bring in foreign registered nurses.** The nursing home retained final discretion on whether to accept an individual nurse as an employee, and was not required to accept a specific number of nurses under the contract. The contract also allowed either party to terminate it on 30 days' notice, and stated that all applications already submitted to the Immigration and Naturalization Service would be considered valid and carried in accordance with the terms of the agreement. When the nursing home terminated the contract and wrote to the Justice Department, withdrawing the I-140 (Immigrant Petition for Alien Worker) petitions pending for 34 foreign nurses recruited by the service, the service sued it for the fees on those 34 nurses. It claimed that the nursing home had to pay those fees under the "Duration of Agreement" clause. A federal court and the Eighth Circuit ruled for the nursing home. The "Duration of Agreement" clause was subordinate to the "Final Discretion" clause, which stated that the nursing home was not required to hire a specific number of nurses. *Team Nursing Services, Inc. v. Evangelical Lutheran Good Samaritan Society*, 433 F.3d 637 (8th Cir. 2006).

◆   An Illinois company contacted several employment recruiters, seeking a new controller. A recruiter found a candidate for the company, but he lived in Iowa and made more than the company wanted to pay. The company informed the recruiter that it would not consider the candidate. Two weeks later, another recruiter gave the company the same candidate's name, location and salary information. The company now needed to hire someone quickly, and its CFO did not remember seeing the candidate's name earlier. After discussions among the second recruiter, the candidate and the company, the candidate accepted the job. The company paid the second recruiter, and the first recruiter sued for its fee as well. The Appellate Court of Illinois held that **although the first recruiter did discuss the candidate with the company, it did not follow up after the company rejected the candidate**. The second recruiter did the work in putting the two sides together. The first recruiter was not entitled to its fee. *Vinzenz v. Hintzsche Fertilizer, Inc.*, 783 N.E.2d 1087 (Ill. App. Ct. 2003).

D. Bankruptcy

It is not unlawful for private sector employers to refuse to hire applicants who have declared bankruptcy. However, employers cannot discriminate against current employees who file for bankruptcy, nor can those employees be fired for exercising their rights under the bankruptcy code.

♦   A Texas company withdrew its job offer to an applicant after a background check revealed that she had filed for bankruptcy. She sued for unlawful discrimination on the basis of her bankruptcy status, but a federal court and the Fifth Circuit ruled against her, noting that **the Bankruptcy Code did not bar a private employer from denying employment to a prospective employee because of a bankruptcy filing**. The code instead applied only to public employers. *In re Burnett*, 635 F.3d 169 (5th Cir. 2011).

♦   A Pennsylvania man filed for bankruptcy. Six years later, he interviewed for a job with an investment firm, but it refused to hire him because of his earlier bankruptcy. He sued it for violating Section 525(b) of the Bankruptcy Act, which **prohibits private sector employers from terminating or discriminating against someone who is or has been in bankruptcy because of said bankruptcy**. He claimed that denying him a job was discrimination because of his bankruptcy, but the Third Circuit Court of Appeals disagreed. It held that the act's prohibition on denying a job because of bankruptcy applied only to public employers, not to the private sector. *Rea v. Federated Investors*, 627 F.3d 937 (3d Cir. 2010).

II. DRUG TESTING

Challenges to drug testing in the private sector are less likely to succeed than their counterparts in the public sector. For instance, the Fourth Amendment only prohibits unreasonable searches and seizures by the government. It does not prohibit unreasonable searches by private employers.

However, discriminatory drug testing is illegal, so any drug testing plan must target all employees and not just a select few. Further, privacy issues may arise, so any drug testing plan should provide for confidentiality of information obtained.

For cases involving drug testing and unemployment benefits, please see Chapter Eight.

A. Pre-Employment Testing

Employers often present job applicants with conditional offers of employment, contingent upon the successful completion of a drug screening test. This is perfectly legal as long as it is not done as a pretext to discriminate against certain applicants.

♦   A Massachusetts job applicant was given a conditional job offer and required to pass a drug screen, which included a test for nicotine. As part of its wellness plan, the company had a policy of not hiring smokers. The applicant submitted a urine sample and began working for the company pending the test results. When his urine tested positive for nicotine, he was told he would not be permanently hired. He sued, asserting that he had been "fired" in violation of his ERISA rights. A federal court ruled against him, noting that he was not an employee who "may become eligible to receive a benefit from an employee benefit plan." **His "regular" employment was clearly contingent on passing the background check and urinalysis screening.** He also could not claim a violation of his privacy rights because he smoked in public and received a warning after his supervisor noticed his cigarettes on his dashboard. *Rodrigues v. EG Systems d/b/a Scotts Lawnservice*, 639 F.Supp.2d 131 (D. Mass. 2009).

♦   A North Carolina applicant with depression, bipolar disorder and ADHD received a conditional offer of employment, contingent on passing a drug test. He did not mention that he was taking medication for his condition and then tested positive for amphetamines. When the job offer was withdrawn, he did not contact the company's medical review officer to provide proof that he was taking legal medication. Instead, he sued under the ADA. A North Carolina federal court ruled for the company, noting that **its drug-free workplace policy did not improperly prohibit employees' use of prescription drugs**. In fact, several other applicants had contacted the medical review officer after testing positive for amphetamines, and provided documentation that they were taking prescription medication. They were subsequently hired. Thus, the company did not discriminate against the applicant in violation of the ADA. *Meyer v. Qualex, Inc.*, 388 F.Supp.2d 630 (E.D.N.C. 2005).

♦   After Wal-Mart offered a West Virginia applicant a job, it required her to give a urine sample. The test came back negative for drugs, and the employee began working. She later quit and sued the company for invasion of privacy. The case reached the Supreme Court of Appeals of West Virginia, which noted that an employer may not require an employee to submit to drug testing unless it has a reasonable good-faith suspicion of drug use, or the employee's job responsibilities involve public safety or the safety of others. However, **in the pre-employment context, the individual has a lower expectation of privacy**. Background checks, references and medical examinations all contribute to that lower expectation. The urine sample requirement did not violate the employee's privacy rights. *Baughman v. Wal-Mart Stores*, 592 S.E.2d 824 (W.Va. 2003).

♦   A manager accepted a conditional offer of employment that required him to pass a drug test prior to beginning the job. He succeeded in delaying the test until four days after his eventual date of hire and then submitted a test indicating marijuana use. The employer withdrew its offer of employment, and the manager sued, claiming that he could not be tested for drugs without individualized suspicion of drug use. The Court of Appeal of California noted that the state **approved of drug testing without individualized suspicion for job applicants**. Suspicionless testing is appropriate in such cases, because prospective employers have not had the opportunity to observe them and may have a need to evaluate their drug usage. In contrast, an employer generally should not have to resort to suspicionless testing of current employees. In this case, the manager had not performed any work for the new employer and was properly viewed as a job applicant. An applicant could not avoid drug testing by delaying a test beyond the date of hire. *Pilkington Barnes Hind v. Superior Court (Visbal)*, 77 Cal.Rptr.2d 596 (Cal. Ct. App. 1998).

◆   An electrical contractor hired employees for construction projects in North and South Carolina. A labor organization charged that the contractor violated federal labor law at the North Carolina site by refusing to hire, threatening and interrogating union-affiliated applicants, and for devising and enforcing a drug testing policy to discourage union activities. The union also claimed that the contractor failed to offer work to 16 union-affiliated employees at the South Carolina site based on their union activities or sympathies. The National Labor Relations Board (NLRB) affirmed the findings of an administrative law judge (ALJ) in favor of the union and ordered the contractor to reinstate two union-affiliated employees who had been fired for refusing to take a drug test. The contractor appealed. The Fourth Circuit rejected the contractor's claim that the ALJ was biased and held that the contractor had committed unfair labor practices. However, the drug testing policy had been **legitimately enacted in response to information that employees of other contractors at the two work sites were using drugs**. The drug testing policy had been uniformly applied to all new employees. The court reversed the NLRB's decision concerning the drug testing policy. *Eldeco, Inc. v. NLRB*, 132 F.3d 1007 (4th Cir. 1997).

B. Employee Testing

Employees may also remain subject to drug testing throughout their employment. Some employer policies rely on <u>random testing</u> (usually for "safety-sensitive" positions), while other policies require <u>reasonable cause</u> or suspicion before testing an employee.

Where an employee has a history of drug use or alcohol abuse but is currently clean and sober, that past history generally cannot be used against the employee.

Absent a <u>last chance agreement</u> (an agreement wherein an employee who has tested positive agrees to be tested in the future in order to save his or her job, with any further positive result allowing the employer to fire him or her), testing targeted to employees with only a past history of drug or alcohol use can be a violation of the Americans with Disabilities Act.

◆   When a railway engineer reported for work in Indiana, he was informed that he had been selected for random drug testing. He was unable to provide a sample and was given a second opportunity some time later. On the second try, he provided an insufficient sample. According to then-existing Federal Railroad Administration regulations, he was to be afforded two hours to produce an adequate sample. Failure to produce would result in dismissal, unless the failure was medically excusable. When he again **failed to produce a sample**, he was removed from service. A doctor's exam found no medical explanation for his failure to provide a sample. An arbitration panel upheld his dismissal, finding that the railway's actions were not "unjust." A federal court and the Seventh Circuit affirmed. A court's role is not to judge whether the arbitrator's contract interpretation is right or wrong but solely to review whether the arbitrator interpreted the contract at all. If so, that interpretation is conclusive. *Lyons v. Norfolk & Western Railway Co.*, 163 F.3d 466 (7th Cir. 1999).

1. Privacy Claims

It is not uncommon for invasion of privacy and defamation claims to arise as a result of drug testing policies. Although such claims usually fail, they can succeed where the employer goes out of its way to publicize the results of a test, or where it breaches its own policy of confidentiality.

◆ A temporary employee of a nonprofit agency in New Jersey was taking six different medications for degenerative disc disease. When he applied for a permanent job with the agency, he was required to provide a urine sample, which came back positive for morphine. After the agency fired him, he sued for invasion of privacy, negligence and wrongful discharge. The case reached the Superior Court of New Jersey, Appellate Division, which ruled in favor of the agency. **The employee had no reasonable expectation of privacy with regard to the drug testing**, and the actions taken by the agency and its laboratory did not amount to negligence even though it used an older opiate cutoff level that might pick up on innocent activity, like eating a poppy seed muffin. Here, the employee's level was above what might be expected from such an occurrence. Also, it was not unlawful for the agency to perceive that the employee was taking illegal drugs. *Vargo v. National Exchange Carriers Ass'n, Inc.*, 870 A.2d 679 (N.J. Super. Ct. App. Div. 2005).

◆ A Texas employer periodically tested its employees for use of illegal controlled substances and randomly tested an employee who yielded a positive result for a cocaine metabolite. He told his supervisor that the result was due to his consumption of herbal teas and offered to have the teas tested by an independent laboratory. A doctor hired by the employer stated that tea could not have caused a positive drug test, and the employee was fired. He sued the employer and physician for discrimination, false light invasion of privacy, negligence, and intentional infliction of emotional distress. The court stated that **Texas does not recognize claims for false light invasion of privacy** because of concerns that doing so would duplicate other claims, including defamation. It dismissed the negligence claims since the employee had sought to impose upon the employer a duty of good faith and fair dealing, which was nonexistent in Texas. In the absence of any evidence of outrageous conduct by the employer, there was also no basis for the intentional infliction of emotional distress claim, and the court granted a partial dismissal of the case. Only the discrimination claims remained. *Quintanilla v. K-Bin, Inc.*, 993 F.Supp. 560 (S.D. Tex. 1998).

◆ A hotel employee signed a consent form required by her employer under which she agreed to participate in a random drug and alcohol testing program.

She tested positive for illegal drug use and requested another test from a different laboratory. The employer declined the request but offered to retest the original sample, which the employee refused. The employer then discharged her, and she sued it for wrongful discharge and invasion of privacy. A state court dismissed her lawsuit, and the court of appeals affirmed. The employee appealed to the Supreme Court of Tennessee, arguing that Tennessee public policy protected her against wrongful discharge because the employer had violated a clear mandate of public policy. The court **rejected her claim that the state constitutional guarantee of privacy restricted the right of a private employer to fire an at-will employee who tested positive for drug use**. Privacy standards applicable to public employers were inapplicable in private employment cases and to the extent that public policy existed concerning drug screening, it favored drug-free workplaces. The court affirmed the ruling for the employer. *Stein v. Davidson Hotel Co.*, 945 S.W.2d 714 (Tenn. 1997).

◆ A Texas employer required its employees to participate in random drug testing. The testing laboratory informed the employer's vice president that one employee tested positive for drug use, and the vice president told the employee's supervisors not to assign him hazardous work. The confirming test result was negative, and the supervisors apologized to the employee for telling him he had failed the drug test. The employee was fired the next year for an unrelated matter, and he sued the employer for negligent and intentional infliction of emotional distress, breach of contract, defamation and invasion of privacy. The court ruled for the employer, and the Court of Appeals of Texas affirmed. Although it agreed with the employee that the employer had breached its own policy of confidentiality in reporting lab results, its report was not false. **Truth was a complete defense to the slander cause of action.** The employee's breach of contract claim also failed, because the employment relationship was at will. The employee was unable to show that the employer's conduct had been intentional, reckless, extreme or outrageous. Accordingly, it did not support a claim for emotional distress. *Washington v. Naylor Industrial Services, Inc.*, 893 S.W.2d 309 (Tex. Ct. App. 1995).

◆ A Massachusetts tool grinder was never under any reasonable suspicion that she ingested illegal drugs. However, one of the company's owners became concerned about drug use by employees and decided to initiate a drug testing policy. When the tool grinder refused to take the test because she found the testing procedure degrading, the company fired her. She sued, alleging a violation of her statutory right to privacy and wrongful termination in violation of public policy. The Supreme Judicial Court of Massachusetts ruled for the employer. Although submission to urinalysis involves a significant invasion of privacy, especially when employees are required to submit to a visual inspection to ensure that they are not concealing vials of urine, the company had a legitimate business interest in protecting its employees and customers, and the owner had a strong basis for suspecting that employees were using drugs. Further, the owner had promised that anyone who tested positive would not be fired, but would be retested in 30 days and given an opportunity to undergo counseling at company expense. Thus, **the drug testing policy was reasonable**

and did not violate the tool grinder's right to privacy. *Folmsbee v. Tech Tool Grinding & Supply, Inc.*, 630 N.E.2d 586 (Mass. 1994).

2. Consent

Employees can be required to consent to drug testing as a condition of employment.

♦   A full-time warehouse employee for a Minnesota company also served as a part-time driver. When he was selected for random drug testing, he refused to take the test. After he was suspended and fired, he sued under state and federal drug testing laws. A federal court ruled for the company, and the Eighth Circuit Court of Appeals affirmed. **Even though the employee was only a part-time driver, he was still subject to random testing under the federal law**, and the refusal to take that test could be treated as a positive test justifying his discharge. Also, state law did not prevent the company from firing him for refusing to take a federally mandated test. *Belde v. Ferguson Enterprises, Inc.*, 460 F.3d 976 (8th Cir. 2006).

♦   An employee attempted to steal a surge protector and made several misrepresentations to different employees in his effort to conceal the theft. His behavior prompted the employer to conduct a fitness-for-duty evaluation, which included a drug test. He tested positive and was offered enrollment in an employee assistance plan. However, he was fired after submitting another positive result in a random drug test. He sued for violations of the state workplace drug testing law. The court found that the employer lacked probable cause to suspect the employee of drug use. It also refused to include testimony suggesting that the employer could have fired the employee solely on the basis of the theft incident. The employer appealed. The Supreme Court of Connecticut held that **private sector employees could waive their statutory rights by giving their consent to be tested**. Waiver rights ensured that employees maintained the option of entering employee assistance programs and keeping their jobs. The trial court had improperly excluded testimony concerning the employee's state of mind at the time of the waiver, and a new trial was required at which evidence concerning the theft incident would be considered. *Poulos v. Pfizer, Inc.*, 244 Conn. 598, 711 A.2d 688 (Conn. 1998).

♦   A California employer maintained a drug testing policy under which employees could be tested where reasonable cause or suspicion of drug or alcohol use was present. **Employees consented in writing to testing as a condition of employment.** The policy stated that disciplinary action, including discharge, could be imposed for refusing to consent to a test. The employer hired an executive secretary, then discharged her eight months later when she refused to take a drug test after two co-workers observed her slumping over her desk. She sued the employer for wrongful discharge, intentional infliction of emotional distress and violation of the California Constitution, which has been interpreted by state courts as creating a right of action against private employers for invasion of privacy. The Court of Appeal of California stated that employee drug testing claims under the state constitution required balancing the employee's reasonable privacy expectations against the employer's legitimate business interests. The employee had presented evidence that the employer had no reasonable cause to suspect her of drug abuse, and had offered an alternative explanation for the discharge (retaliation against her for refusing to work uncompensated overtime). A trial was required on the wrongful discharge and invasion of privacy claims. However, the trial court had properly dismissed the claim for intentional infliction of emotional distress. *Kraslawsky v. Upper Deck Co.*, 65 Cal.Rptr.2d 297 (Cal. Ct. App. 1997).

3. Adequacy of Testing

The employer should put in place procedures that ensure the testing will be accurate so that any challenge to the procedures will be unsuccessful. The lab used to test the samples should comply with the guidelines of the U.S. Department of Health and Human Services.

◆   An Oklahoma UPS driver was subject to the federal Omnibus Transportation Employee Testing Act, which requires drug and alcohol testing of employees in "safety sensitive" jobs in various transportation industries. After he swerved onto the shoulder of a highway, overturning the two trailers he was pulling, he was ordered to submit to a drug test. When his tests came back positive, he was fired. He sued under Oklahoma's drug testing law, **claiming he did not receive proper notice of the first test as required by federal DOT regulations**. He sought reinstatement, back pay and lost benefits – remedies not available under the federal law. The Tenth Circuit ruled against him, noting that he was not entitled to his job back or any monetary compensation. Here, the driver was required to be tested by federal law; therefore, the Oklahoma statute exempted him from its protections. *Williams v. United Parcel Service, Inc.*, 527 F.3d 1135 (10th Cir. 2008).

◆   A Kentucky truck driver was fired after testing positive for drugs. However, **the testing was not conducted in a manner required by federal regulations,** and the results were inaccurate due to the improper handling of the sample and the driver's use of legal over-the-counter medications. He submitted to a later, more accurate test, which demonstrated that the earlier test had indicated a false positive. After he had trouble finding another job due to disclosures by his former employer that he had tested positive for drugs, he sued for wrongful termination and defamation. A trial court dismissed the lawsuit, and the Kentucky Court of Appeals agreed that his wrongful discharge claim could not stand because he was an at-will employee and there was no public policy against firing someone based on a violation of federal regulations. However, he did state a claim for defamation based on the release of the drug test information. That part of the lawsuit required a trial. *Shrout v. The TFE Group*, 161 S.W.3d 351 (Ky. Ct. App. 2005).

◆   A Texas truck driver was required to submit to random drug testing pursuant to Department of Transportation (DOT) regulations. He tested positive for THC (marijuana) in two different urine samples and was fired after the second test. He sued the company for violating five of the DOT collection protocols. A jury found that the company was negligent in collecting his urine sample and awarded him more than $800,000 in damages, as well as exemplary damages of $100,000 after finding that the company acted with malice. The court of appeals affirmed, but the Supreme Court of Texas reversed. It found no basis for holding an employer liable for firing an at-will employee for a positive drug test. Under the at-will employment doctrine, an employer does not have to determine if a termination was based on correct information. **The court refused to adopt a new theory of negligent drug testing.** *Mission Petroleum Carriers, Inc. v. Solomon*, 106 S.W.3d 705 (Tex. 2003).

◆   A North Carolina employer asked an employee to submit to random drug screening. The employee tested positive for drug use and was fired. He filed a wrongful discharge action against the employer, asserting that the laboratory used for the testing was not approved by the state as required by law. The court granted pretrial judgment to the employer, but the court of appeals reversed, holding that state law established procedures required of employers to conduct drug screening on employees to protect them from unreliable or inadequate testing. It agreed with the employee that the law was an express policy declaration by the state and that any discharge inconsistent with the law violated a public policy exception to the presumption of employment at will. The employer here had violated public policy by utilizing an unapproved laboratory. On further appeal, the North Carolina Supreme Court reversed, holding that **the employer's failure to use an approved laboratory for the drug testing did not give rise to a claim for wrongful discharge**. There must be more than a statutory violation; there must also be an unlawful reason or purpose that violates public policy. Here, there was no evidence of such a purpose. *Garner v. Rentenbach Constructors, Inc.*, 515 S.E.2d 438 (N.C. 1999).

4. Collective Bargaining Agreements

In unionized workplaces, collective bargaining agreements generally define the nature of drug testing policies and limits. They also generally provide a disciplinary procedure and a grievance process for employees who wish to challenge positive test results.

◆   A West Virginia truck driver, who was subject to Department of Transportation regulations requiring random drug testing for workers engaged in "safety-sensitive" tasks, tested positive for marijuana on two occasions. Both times, his employer sought to discharge him, but the union went to arbitration on both occasions and obtained awards that ordered his reinstatement. The employer then sued to nullify the arbitrator's award. A federal court enforced the award, and the Fourth Circuit affirmed. The U.S. Supreme Court also affirmed. It held that **public policy did not require the courts to prevent the driver's reinstatement despite the positive drug tests**. Federal law encourages rehabilitation where possible. Here, the arbitration award did not condone the driver's conduct or ignore the risk to public safety that drug use by truck drivers may pose, but punished the driver by placing conditions on his reinstatement. He had to pay both parties' arbitration costs, undergo further substance abuse treatment and testing, and provide a signed letter of resignation in the event he failed any more drug tests. *Eastern Associated Coal Corp. v. UMW of America*, 531 U.S. 57, 121 S.Ct. 462, 148 L.Ed.2d 354 (2000).

◆   An employee of an aircraft manufacturing corporation was fired after his second positive drug test. He sued the company and the union under Section 301 of the LMRA, alleging wrongful discharge by the company and breach of the duty of fair representation by the union. A Connecticut federal court and the Second Circuit ruled against him. **Firing the employee for the second positive drug test did not violate the collective bargaining agreement.** Further, the union's decision not to arbitrate the employee's claim was not irrational or arbitrary so as to constitute a breach of the duty of fair representation. *Verrilli v. Sikorsky Aircraft Corp.*, 221 Fed.Appx. 8 (2d Cir. 2007).

◆   A New Jersey brewery worker submitted a hair for drug testing and was fired when a positive result came back. He and his wife sued the brewery, alleging that although the drug test reading was below the "minimum detection level," and thus was not reliable, the brewery nonetheless discharged him. They asserted breach of contract and intentional infliction of emotional distress, among other claims. A federal court ruled against them, noting that the breach of contract action was preempted by Section 301 of the LMRA because a collective bargaining agreement was in place at the time of the firing and any resolution of the claim would demand the interpretation of the agreement. Further, the emotional distress claim could not survive because the brewery's action in firing the worker was not so extreme and outrageous that it went beyond all possible bounds of decency. *Brandt v. Anheuser-Busch, Inc.*, No. 06-5424 (WJM), 2007 WL 1175751 (D.N.J. 2007).

◆   An electrical contractor in Illinois agreed to abide by the collective bargaining agreement between a contractors association and the International Brotherhood of Electrical Workers. **The bargaining agreement contained a drug testing provision for all employees of each participating firm.** When the contractor refused to implement the drug testing rule for employees other than electricians represented by the union, an arbitration board ordered the electricians' union not to refer any of its members to the contractor for employment. The contractor sued, and a federal court held the board's order invalid, but the Seventh Circuit Court of Appeals reversed. It held that the contractor had agreed to be bound by the bargaining agreement, and that federal labor law allowed bargaining agreements to reach beyond the certified unit of workers. Thus, the contractor could not test only the electricians. However, if the separate bargaining agreement between the contractor and the operating engineers' union had its own drug testing rules, the contractor would have to abide by those rules for those employees. *Lid Electric, Inc. v. IBEW, Local 134*, 362 F.3d 940 (7th Cir. 2004).

◆   A bus driver for the New York City Transit Authority was randomly called to the office for a drug test. She was unable to provide an adequate sample of at least 45 ml of urine and was required to drink 40 ounces of liquid within a three-hour period. She still could not provide an adequate sample and was referred to a doctor, who could find no medical reason for the failure. This was deemed a "refusal" to provide a sample and resulted in the employee's suspension. The transit authority also told her it intended to fire her. Doctors later found that she had slow urine flow and urgency incontinence, but that she should have been able to provide a sample within the three-hour period. Her union filed a grievance, and an arbitration panel determined that she should not be disciplined. The Supreme Court, Appellate Division, held that **Department of Transportation regulations specified removal from a safety-sensitive position (like driving a bus) where an employee "refuses" to provide a sample**. However, the Court of Appeals reversed, ruling that the appellate division improperly substituted its factual finding for that of a majority of the arbitration panel. *Dowleyne v. NYCTA*, 816 N.E.2d 191 (N.Y. 2004).

◆   A collective bargaining agreement provided that where a company had reasonable cause to believe that an employee was working while under the influence of drugs, the employee would be required to submit to a blood or urine test or be fired. After the company received anonymous phone calls accusing an employee of drug trafficking, it used a machine to sweep the employee's car and work area for drug residue. Cocaine was detected in both places. The company asked the employee to take a drug test. But he refused to take the test and was thereafter fired.

The union took the case to arbitration, where the arbitrator determined that the company **could require the drug test only if there was reasonable cause to believe the employee was on drugs at the time** he was asked to submit to the test. Since the company did not believe the employee was on drugs at the moment it asked him to take the drug test, it could not fire him for refusing to submit. The Seventh Circuit Court of Appeals affirmed the arbitrator's order that the employee be reinstated. Although it would not have read the bargaining agreement so literally, it refused to overturn the ruling because the ruling was not arbitrary and capricious. *Int'l Truck and Engine Corp. v. United Steel Workers of America, Local 3740*, 294 F.3d 860 (7th Cir. 2002).

III. NON-COMPETITION AGREEMENTS AND TRADE SECRETS

Employers, particularly in specialized areas (like broadcasting), often require employees to enter into non-compete agreements that prohibit employees from leaving their employment and competing against their former employer.

Non-compete agreements are generally valid if supported by consideration. In other words, if both sides give something of value, they will be upheld. This means they should be signed prior to employment (as a condition of employment) wherever possible.

However, non-compete agreements must also be <u>reasonable in scope, geographic area and duration</u>. A non-compete agreement that lasts for three years will likely be struck down as too harsh, as will one that includes too great a geographical area.

Agreements that prevent an employee from soliciting all potential customers, even those who are not currently customers of the employer, may also be struck down as too broad in scope.

Although non-compete agreements are not appropriate for many employees, trade secret and <u>confidentiality agreements</u> should be used more frequently – first, to protect confidential information, and second, to establish that the employer considers certain information confidential.

A. Non-Compete Agreements

The key to restrictive covenants and covenants not to compete is that they must be reasonable or courts will not uphold them. There is no automatically reasonable agreement; each agreement will be examined in light of the individual facts pertinent to it.

Courts look to the scope, duration and geographic limitations of "no compete" clauses to test their validity.

◆   The COO of a company in Rhode Island signed a contract that **barred him from competing with the company in the New England area for two years if he was fired for "cause."** When he violated a direct order not to deliver granite to a customer until the customer paid for the order, the president of the company fired him on the spot. He acquired a competing business, and his former employer sued to enjoin him from competing. In his defense, he asserted that the company should have given him due process (notice and a hearing) before firing him for cause. The Rhode Island Supreme Court disagreed. The COO admittedly defied the president's directive, giving the president a good-faith basis to fire him for cause. As a result, by the terms of the non-compete clause, he was barred from opening the competing business. *New England Stone, LLC v. Conte*, 962 A.2d 30 (R.I. 2009).

◆   The manager of a trucking company in St. Louis made plans to leave the company and join a competitor. She let the renewal deadline for the company's lease of its premises pass without informing company officials, then **gave confidential information about the company to the competitor**. When the company sued her for breach of the duty of loyalty (and sued the competitor for conspiracy), she claimed that as an at-will employee who had never signed a non-compete agreement, she could not be held liable. A jury and the Missouri Supreme Court disagreed. However, the verdict ($54,000 against the manager and $254,000 against the competitor) could not stand because it included preparations the manager made. Instead, the jury could only consider actions taken beyond the preparation stage. The case had to be re-tried. *Scanwell Freight Express STL, Inc. v. Chan*, 162 S.W.3d 477 (Mo. 2005).

1. Enforceability of Agreements

Where a non-compete agreement is not supported by valid consideration (usually, where all the burden is on the employee and there is no cost or burden on the employer), it is not enforceable. Thus, where possible, an employer should condition employment on the signing of the agreement. If an employer wishes to ask a current employee to sign such an agreement, it should probably provide extra benefits (independent consideration) to support the contract.

Continued employment is often not sufficient consideration to support such a contract, though each state has different laws. Such benefits should only be given to employees who sign the agreement.

If the benefits are provided to other employees who do not sign (or who are not asked to sign), the contract will not be enforced.

◆   A chemist in Georgia signed an employment agreement that included a non-competition clause. A week later, he signed another agreement that did not have such a clause. He did not deliver the first agreement to the employer until after he had signed the second agreement. When he began working for another company, the employer sued him for violating the agreement with the non-competition clause. The court ruled for the employee. **The agreement signed second superseded the agreement that was signed first.** *Mapei v. Prosser*, 761 S.E.2d 500 (Ga. Ct. App. 2014).

◆   An assistant showroom manager for an Indiana appliance sales and service company signed a non-compete agreement that restricted him from providing "any service" that would compete with the services offered by the employer for two years after he left. The agreement barred the employee from providing the services to anyone who was a customer of the employee during the 14 years the employee worked for the employer. The employee went to work for a competitor, and the employer sued to enforce the agreement. **The court held the agreement could not be enforced because it was too broad.** The employer could not restrict the employee from servicing customers he never had contact with or from providing competing services in any county where the employer had any customers. *Clark's Sales and Service, Inc. v. Smith*, 4 N.E.3d 772 (Ind. Ct. App. 2014).

◆   After he had been employed there for some time, an employee of a fitness club in Washington state signed an agreement that barred him from working for a competing business for three years after his employment ended. The employee was later fired, and he sought a court order to stop the employer from enforcing the agreement. A state appeals court held that **the agreement could not be enforced under state law** because the employee received no additional consideration in exchange for his promise to be bound by its terms. *McKasson v. Johnson*, 315 P.3d 1138 (Wash. Ct. App. 2013).

◆   A recruiter for an Indiana information technology staffing (IT) firm signed a non-compete agreement that barred him from working for a competitor or a competitor of a current or potential customer in the event of employment separation. It also barred him from recruiting for any job in the IT industry or working as an HR employee in a non-IT company. **In addition, it banned him from recruiting anywhere in the country.** When the recruiter stopped working for the firm and began placing ads for jobs in the IT field, the firm sued for breach of the agreement. A trial court ruled in its favor, but a state appeals court reversed. It found that the agreement too severely restricted the recruiter's ability to utilize the experience he acquired with the firm. *Buffkin v. Glacier Group*, 997 N.E. 2d 1 (Ind. Ct. App. 2013).

◆   A software developer signed a non-competition agreement that barred him from performing services for any competing business for a year after he left employment with his company. **He left the company and developed a product he believed did not compete with the company's products.** The company disagreed and sued him for violating the agreement. A state appeals court said a fact-finder would have to decide if the new product directly competed with the company's products. While the new product was similar to one sold by the company, there was a question as to whether the developer marketed it to the same audience that the company targeted. *Strange v. HRsmart, Inc.*, 400 S.W.3d 125 (Tex. Ct. App. 2013).

◆   When an Illinois employee began working for an employer, he signed a non-compete that said if he left, he would not compete with the employer for two years. He left after three months and began working for a competitor. He sued to have the non-compete declared invalid, and he won. **Under state law, such agreements were not valid unless the employee worked for the employer for at least two years.** *Fifield v. Premier Dealer Services, Inc.*, 993 N.E.2d 938 (Ill. App. Ct. 2013).

◆   A Missouri employer had one of its salesmen sign a non-compete agreement and then reduced his salary. The salesman quit and began working for a competitor, and the employer sued to enforce the agreement. A state appeals court held that **a jury was to decide whether it was the employer who breached the agreement** by cutting the salesman's salary. *Jumbo Sack Corp. v. Buyck*, 407 S.W.3d 51 (Mo. Ct. App. 2013).

◆   A New Jersey food distributor sued a former employee for tortious interference with a prospective economic advantage or contractual relationship after the former employee, while still employed there, placed customer orders with a competing business. It also sued the competing business, making an additional claim for misappropriation of confidential information. Finally, it asserted breach of contract claims. However, a federal court dismissed the breach of contract claims because the handbook clearly stated that it was not a contract even though it contained a non-compete agreement. Also, **the competing business couldn't be sued for misappropriation of confidential information because all the improper activity was conducted by the former employee**. On the other hand, the tortious interference claim could proceed to a trial. *Metropolitan Foods, Inc. v. Kelsch*, No. 11-3306 (JLL), 2012 WL 956178 (D.N.J. 2/4/12).

◆   A Virginia pest control company required a new employee to sign a non-compete agreement that barred him from having any contact with another pest control company in any capacity after leaving the job, even as a stockholder of a conglomerate with a pest control subsidiary. After he resigned and went to work for a competing pest control company, his former employer sued. The Supreme Court of Virginia ruled that the non-compete agreement was invalid because it was overbroad. **The agreement could only legally prohibit activity that was of the same type the employee engaged in.** *Home Paramount Pest Control Companies, Inc.*, 718 S.E.2d 762 (Va. 2011).

◆   An insurance company developed a stock option plan to give select employees an incentive to become part owners of the company. In exchange, the company required selected employees to sign a non-solicitation/non-compete agreement and submit payment for the stock at a discounted price. A managing director exercised his option on 3,000 shares and signed the three-year non-compete agreement. Less than three years later, he resigned and immediately began working for a competitor. The company sued for breach of contract. The case reached the Texas Supreme Court, which held that **the stock options could be valid consideration to support the agreement**. *Marsh USA, Inc. v. Cook*, 354 S.W.3d 764 (Tex. 2011).

◆   Several employees of a service company in Georgia signed an employment agreement with a non-compete clause that restricted their ability to compete for two years, even in counties in which they had conducted no business. When the employees grew dissatisfied and went to work for competitors, the company sued. A trial court and the Georgia Court of Appeals ruled against the company, finding that **the non-compete clause was overbroad and unreasonable with respect to its geographic restrictions**. The company included counties where it expected the employees to make cold calls on potential customers even though the employees had conducted no business there. This attempt to limit the potential customer base for competing ex-employees went too far. *Gordon Document Products, Inc. v. Service Technologies, Inc.*, 308 Ga. App. 445 (Ga. Ct. App. 2011).

◆   A Pennsylvania company fired an insurance salesman because of the high commissions he was making. He had signed a non-compete agreement that prevented him from soliciting current or prospective clients for two years after his employment ended. He had also signed an agreement putting his formerly exempt clients on the non-solicitation list and had received $300,000 in exchange for that sale. When he sought to compete with the company, a lawsuit resulted. He claimed that the non-solicitation clause was invalid, and a trial court agreed. However, the Superior Court of Pennsylvania held that **the**

agreement could still be valid even though he'd been fired for making too much money. Other factors had to be considered, including whether the clause unreasonably limited his ability to earn a living. *Missett v. Hub Int'l Pennsylvania, LLC*, 6 A.3d 530 (Pa. Super. Ct. 2010).

◆ The owner of a company in Georgia sold the company to new owners and agreed to stay on as a vice president. As part of the deal, he signed a non-compete clause, **agreeing not to compete within 100 miles for a year** if he left the company. When he later resigned and began to compete, the new owners sued. The Georgia Court of Appeals ruled that he was bound by the non-compete clause. The agreement was not overbroad because it came as part of the sale of the company and not as part of a contract under which his continuing employment was conditioned on signing the non-compete clause. He was barred from competing for one year. *American Control Systems, Inc. v. Boyce*, 694 S.E.2d 141 (Ga. Ct. App. 2010).

◆ A staffing firm in Maryland hired a recruiter, who signed a non-compete covenant in which he agreed not to engage in the recruiting of technical, industrial, administrative and support staff personnel for a period of 18 months within a 50-mile radius of the office after he stopped working for the firm. He quickly rose to the position of director of strategic accounts, but then went to work for a competitor, causing the firm to sue to enforce the non-compete covenant. A federal court found the covenant enforceable because it was reasonable as to time, geography and scope of activity. And **the recruiter failed to show that the restrictions presented an undue hardship** because he never tried to find employment outside the restricted region. *TEKsystems, Inc. v. Bolton*, No. RDB-08-3099, 2010 WL 447782 (D. Md. 2/4/10).

◆ An at-will sales rep for a company worked out of his Ohio home. He was told that his job would be in jeopardy if he didn't sign a non-compete contract, so he signed the contract, which also changed his salary and commission structure. He later resigned after his largest client determined that it would only deal with the company through its corporate headquarters in Tennessee, and he chose not to move there. Instead, he began working for a competitor. The company sued him for violating the non-compete clause, and the Court of Appeals of Tennessee ruled in its favor, noting that **the agreement was supported by adequate consideration – the sales rep's continued employment** if he signed it. *Cummings, Inc. v. Dorgan*, 320 S.W.3d 316 (Tenn. Ct. App. 2009).

◆ A Pennsylvania salesman working in a three-state area signed a non-compete agreement that prevented him from working for a competitor for 12 months following his departure. **The agreement covered a 10-state area as well as any area in which the company's products were sold, and it listed nine competitors by name as prohibited employers** during that time. When the employee went to work for one of the competitors in the 10-state area (but outside the three-state area where he had worked), he and his new employer sued for a declaration that the non-compete agreement was invalid.

A federal court dismissed the case on the pleadings, finding the agreement unenforceable. However, the Third Circuit vacated and remanded the case, finding that the district court should have considered the fact that the agreement only restricted the salesman from working for nine named competitors. It also should have considered that the 10-state limitation might be reasonable. The case should not have been dismissed on the pleadings. *Victaulic Co. v. Tieman*, 499 F.3d 227 (3d Cir. 2007).

2. Terms and Conditions

The terms and conditions of non-compete agreements must be <u>reasonable</u> to be enforced. Where parts of the agreement are not reasonable, some courts will strike down the entire agreement. Other courts will strike down only those elements that are unreasonable. Still other courts will strike down the unreasonable elements and substitute their judgment of what is reasonable.

◆   A manager at a Massachusetts recruiting company signed a non-compete agreement. The agreement provided that if the manager left the company, she would wait a year before placing employees in professions that the employer serviced. It also banned her from soliciting, recruiting or hiring employees away from the company. Within a year of her departure, the manager began working for a competitor and recommended a former colleague at the company to a potential employer. She also told a friend who worked for one of the company's clients about her new job, pointing out that part of her new job involved servicing clients that her former employer did not. **The company sued, claiming both actions violated the non-compete agreement.** The court disagreed. The manager did not solicit, recruit or hire when she gave the potential employer the former colleague's name, and her simple mention to her friend was permissible because it involved a field of clients that the former employer did not solicit. *KNF&T Staffing Resources v. Muller*, No. 13-3676 (Mass. Commw. Ct. 10/24/13).

◆   The director of a mental health counseling company in Washington signed a non-compete agreement that barred her from soliciting clients for three years if she left the company. After the company gave her notice of termination and instructed her not to do any more work for it, the director treated clients who approached her. The company then terminated her and refused to pay her for her final 60 days. When she sued for wrongful termination, the company filed a counterclaim alleging breach of the non-compete agreement. A state appeals court decided that **the manager did not violate the agreement** because she did not solicit clients. Instead, they approached her. *Burton v. Becker*, 175 Wash.App. 1073 (Wash. Ct. App. 2013).

◆   A seasonal tax preparer for H&R Block signed a non-compete/non-solicitation agreement that prohibited her from soliciting business or preparing and filing returns for people with whom she worked at the company. The restriction lasted two years and covered a 25-mile radius of the office. After the company audited some of her tax returns and refused to rehire her for the following season, she started her own company about 13 miles away. H&R Block sued her for violating the agreement. A Georgia federal court found the agreement unenforceable because it prevented her from accepting unsolicited business from former clients, but the Eleventh Circuit reversed. It held that the restriction was narrow in scope, **limiting her only with respect to soliciting clients from the past year**, and its geographic limitation was reasonable, even including a map to clarify the restricted area. *H&R Block Eastern Enterprises, Inc. v. Morris*, 606 F.3d 1285 (11th Cir. 2010).

◆   A company with its headquarters in Ohio required a sales rep to sign a non-compete clause when it promoted him to account manager for its Illinois and Indiana regions. While working for the company, the manager was contacted by a competitor's HR director. He submitted his résumé to the competitor and eventually accepted an offer to become a vice president of sales. After resigning and going to work for the competitor, he was sued by the company for breaching the agreement. A federal court held that although he had violated the agreement, **the agreement was overbroad because it did not contain a geographic limitation**. The court refused to rewrite the non-compete clause to make it enforceable, and the Seventh Circuit upheld that decision. Under Ohio law, the court had the discretion to decide whether to modify the agreement. *Cintas Corp. v. Perry*, 517 F.3d 459 (7th Cir. 2008).

◆   A company in Michigan asked an employee to sign a non-compete agreement that prohibited him from "directly or indirectly" engaging in the operation of a competing business, except for a county in which the employee already owned a competing business. After the employee signed the agreement, he allegedly carried out some sales and deliveries in the prohibited area. The company sued him for violating the non-compete agreement, and a federal court ruled in favor of the employee. The U.S. Court of Appeals, Sixth Circuit, affirmed the decision, reading the non-compete agreement narrowly. It stated that **the transactions the employee engaged in did not amount to management or oversight of the competing business**. It was the mere soliciting of customers or selling of products, which was technically not the same thing as "operating a business." *United Rentals (North America), Inc. v. Keizer*, 355 F.3d 399 (6th Cir. 2004).

◆   An insurance agent signed an employment contract in which he agreed not to disclose proprietary information or to compete with the company within a 25-mile radius for five years. The restrictive covenants contained no information concerning assignability. Later, the company sold its insurance business assets, and the buyer told the agent it was going to eliminate his position. The agent sought employment with a competitor and also sought to obtain the business of one of the buyer's largest clients. The buyer and seller objected, and the competitor refused to hire the agent. When the agent sued, a state court held that the non-compete agreement was assignable to the buyer but modified its terms because it was not reasonable as to time and distance. The Supreme Court of Pennsylvania reversed, holding that **the non-compete agreement was not assignable without the employee's consent**. Further, the non-compete agreement could not be enforced by the seller because the seller did not have a legitimate interest that needed protecting. The seller was no longer in the insurance business. *Hess v. Gebhard & Co.*, 808 A.2d 912 (Pa. 2002).

◆   A New York title insurance company's highest paid salesman, represented by his lawyer, agreed to a non-compete provision that prohibited him from selling title insurance in New York for six months after he left the company. A direct competitor subsequently offered him a job and agreed to pay him a salary during that six-month period. Before he resigned, the salesman spoke to 20 of the company's customers, informing them of his interest in joining a competitor and expressly asking one to follow him. The company applied for an injunction to have the agreement enforced, and a federal court ordered him to abide by the terms of the agreement. The Second Circuit Court of Appeals upheld the order. First, **the agreement was reasonable in time (six months) and in its geographic scope (the state of New York)**. Second, the salesperson's services were unique, making the agreement valid, for three reasons: 1) the title insurance business relies heavily on personal relationships; 2) because potential clients are limited, maintaining current clients from this group is crucial; and 3) the salesman negotiated the agreement with the assistance of counsel. *Ticor Title Insurance Co. v. Cohen*, 173 F.3d 63 (2d Cir. 1999).

B. Trade Secrets

Most states have enacted the Uniform Trade Secrets Act, which states that trade secrets must be subject to efforts that are reasonable to maintain their secrecy. If information is readily available, or if the employer does not take reasonable steps to protect it, it will not be given trade secret protection.

Following are a few ways to demonstrate that an employer is making reasonable efforts to keep information secret:

1) Require every employee to sign trade secret or confidentiality agreements,
2) Restrict visitor access to sensitive areas of the workplace,
3) Separate sensitive departments or processes from the main workplace,
4) Keep secret documents in locked file cabinets or safes, and
5) Distribute confidential information on a strictly need-to-know basis.

Note that customer lists can be trade secrets if they are properly protected, and if they cannot be obtained by other (legal) methods.

1. Defining "Trade Secrets"

Generally, a trade secret is "information" that derives independent economic value (actual or potential) from not being generally known and not being generally ascertainable (by legal means) by competitors.

◆ An Internet company in California hired a writer to post video blogs and tweet about the company. He was given use of and maintained a Twitter account. He quit his job and **changed his Twitter name while keeping his 17,000 followers**. Eventually he went to work for a competitor and sued the company for unpaid wages. The company then sued him for interference with prospective business and misappropriation of trade secrets, as well as conversion. It sought $340,000 in damages ($2.50 per follower). He sought to dismiss the case, but a federal court allowed the trade secret and conversion issues to proceed. The company would have to prove that the account password and the account's followers were trade secrets. *PhoneDog v. Kravitz*, No. C 11-03474 MEJ, 2011 WL 5415612 (N.D. Cal. 11/8/11).

◆ An employee of a company that produced and sold a vinyl-silane treated talc known as 604AV left the company and started his own consulting business. He contracted with another company to develop and market a vinyl-silane talc called Genera. His former employer sued him for misappropriating a trade secret, but he claimed that the knowledge for how to make the formula was in the public domain. A Colorado federal court granted pretrial judgment to the former employee, but the Tenth Circuit reversed. It stated that a jury had to decide whether the making of 604AV was a trade secret. **A trade secret can exist in a combination of characteristics and components, each of which by itself is in the public domain.** A jury might decide that the exact amount of silane content necessary to make 604AV could not be determined from public sources. The jury would also have to decide if the company took reasonable steps to guard the secrecy and whether the customer list was a trade secret. *Hertz v. The Luzenac Group*, 576 F.3d 1103 (10th Cir. 2009).

◆ An Illinois manufacturer of tubes used in filtration devices hired an employee and required him to sign two non-compete agreements during his tenure with the company. He later left, formed his own business and began to compete with his old company. The company sued him for misappropriating trade secrets and violating the non-compete agreements. An Illinois court determined that the company's customer information was protected as a trade secret. The Appellate Court of Illinois disagreed. The company **failed to take reasonable steps to protect the customer information as a trade secret**. All it did was require its employees to sign a confidentiality agreement. Thus, the customer information was not protected. Further, the non-compete agreements were invalid because they were blanket prohibitions on competition. *Arcor, Inc. v. Haas*, 842 N.E.2d 265 (Ill. App. Ct. 2005).

◆ A Texas company performed high performance upgrades on motor vehicles. An employee who gained substantial knowledge of the business began competing with the company after resigning without notice. A state court granted temporary injunctive relief to the employer, forbidding the new venture from performing a variety of acts including disclosing information and servicing motor vehicles of the type that the company upgraded. The former employee appealed to the Court of Appeals of Texas, asserting that the relief granted was excessive. The court held that **the employer's information was**

protectable as a trade secret. The employee had a duty arising from the employment relationship not to use confidential or proprietary information in a manner adverse to the employer. The court modified the scope of the trial court order. Here, the employer had argued that its sales might drop $2 million in the absence of such protection, and injunctive relief was appropriate. The parties settled after an appeal to the state supreme court. *T-N-T Motorsports, Inc. v. Hennessey Motorsports, Inc.*, 965 S.W.2d 18 (Tex. Ct. App. 1998).

✦   A Georgia computer software developer hired two employees under written agreements to develop programs for tracking assets. The employees breached a restrictive covenant in their employment agreements by forming a competing venture and offering to sell similar software to the employer's customers. The employer sued them for breach of contract, seeking an injunction against violation of the covenants. The court found that the former employees had misappropriated the employer's trade secrets and were currently using them in violation of the covenants. However, it found that the former employees had not been unjustly enriched and should not pay any damages. Instead, it imposed a 7% royalty upon them for four months for use of the trade secrets and enjoined them from soliciting the former employer's customers according to the terms of the covenants, which were to expire in three days.

The Supreme Court of Georgia found that **computer software constituted trade secrets** that were a proper subject of the covenants. The evidence sufficiently detailed the existence of trade secrets, and the trial court had permissibly imposed a royalty payment for their improper use. The trial court had also properly enjoined the former employees from soliciting customers for the duration of the covenants, even though they were set to expire only three days beyond its order. The court refused to extend the duration of the covenants by excluding the time of the litigation from the two-year period contained in them, noting that the parties could have included a tolling provision. *Electronic Data Systems Corp. v. Heinemann*, 493 S.E.2d 132 (Ga. 1997).

2. Employer Protections

Generally, employers wish to protect themselves by obtaining <u>injunctive relief</u> (usually in the form of a court order prohibiting a competitor from using trade secrets to its advantage) in addition to money damages and attachment of future royalties. However, courts will generally not issue an injunction unless there is more than a suspicion of injury.

✦   A Massachusetts recycler of nonfunctioning electronics (e-waste) sued an independent contractor, accusing him of misappropriating trade secrets such as customer lists, pricing information, amounts sold and purchased, billing procedures and other information. The court rejected the claim on the basis that **the recycler did not show it took adequate measures to keep the information from being disclosed** to outsiders. *C.R.T.R., Inc. v. Lao*, 31 Mass.L.Rptr. 635 (Mass. Super. Ct. 2014).

◆   An Ohio tool company sued three former employees for misappropriating trade secrets relating to a tool line. It claimed the employees stole its trade secrets so they could make "knock-off" products. The employees argued that the allegations were speculative, but the court disagreed and refused to dismiss the case. The tool company **sufficiently alleged that the employees had access to information about trade secrets** and used the information in an unauthorized way. *Apex Tool Group, LLC v. DMTCO, LLC*, No. 13-cv-00372, 2014 WL 580 3021 (S.D. Ohio 11/7/14).

◆   A branch manager for an Illinois company that inspected petroleum products and chemicals signed a confidentiality and non-solicitation agreement. He supplied company information to a competitor. **He then resigned and went to work for the competitor, which was set to open a new office.** The company filed a trade secrets claim, and the court concluded it was likely to succeed on that claim. It enjoined the competitor from opening the new office for two months. *Intertek USA Inc. v. AmSpec LLC*, No. 14-CV-6160, 2014 WL 4477933 (N.D. Ill. 9/11/14).

◆   A Mississippi plant worker sued his employer, accusing it of violating the ADA by denying his requests for breaks. The employee wore a prosthetic leg below the knee. When the company claimed he was not physically able to operate his machine, the employee sought to submit video evidence of the machine to show he could operate it. **The company refused to let him do so, citing issues relating to trade secrets.** The employee filed a motion to compel the employer to allow him to gather the video evidence. The court decided the worker could gather the evidence. But it also restricted who could view it and ordered that it be returned to the company or destroyed when the case ended. *Morton v. Cooper Tire & Rubber Co.*, 288 F.R.D. 126 (N.D. Miss. 2012).

◆   A manufacturer of industrial plastic bags hired a sales rep and required her to sign a confidentiality agreement. When the company determined that she was bad-mouthing it and selling products for competitors during its bankruptcy proceedings, it fired her. **She went to work for a competitor and told it that she wasn't bound by a non-compete agreement or a confidentiality agreement** and that she had a list of customers she had developed over the years. She gave the list to the competitor, who earned millions off of it. When the manufacturer sued the competitor for misappropriating confidential information, the New Jersey Supreme Court held that there were issues about whether the competitor knew the list was the manufacturer's proprietary information. A trial was required. *Fox v. Millman*, 45 A.3d 332 (N.J. 2012).

◆   A company that offered training programs to professional managers fired an instructor in Georgia after his credential lapsed and he used a company credit card without authorization. He had signed a confidentiality agreement and assured the company that he had returned all teaching materials. However, he then formed his own company and began teaching managers using company materials. The company sued him under the Uniform Deceptive Trade Practices Act and won. The jury had sufficient evidence that **he had used company**

materials and engaged in misleading advertising. The Georgia Court of Appeals upheld the award of $147,750 to the company. *Trotman v. Velociteach Project Management, LLC*, 715 S.E.2d 449 (Ga. Ct. App. 2011).

♦ A former vice president for a bakery in Pennsylvania sought to work for another bakery despite the existence of a confidentiality agreement. He claimed that he could block the old bakery's trade secrets from his mind. The old bakery sought an injunction preventing him from working for the new bakery until after a trial, and the Third Circuit granted that request. It noted that the vice president had accessed confidential information at the old bakery after accepting the similar job at the new bakery but before telling anyone at the old bakery about it. And he copied trade secret information from his work laptop onto external storage devices. Accordingly, **the court found it substantially likely that he would disclose trade secrets at his new job**. Thus, it upheld the injunction preventing the vice president from starting at the new bakery until a trial could be held. *Bimbo Bakeries USA v. Botticella*, 613 F.3d 102 (3d Cir. 2010).

♦ Two managers of a Dallas consulting firm's claims office were approached by a competitor about selling off the claims practice. The managers prepared a detailed proposal without informing their employer of the competitor's interest in buying the practice. When the deal fell through, they continued to try to sell the claims practice to other competitors, hoping to route the transaction through a company they owned. They eventually left to work for one of the competitors, and the firm sued them for breach of contract, breach of fiduciary duty and misappropriation of trade secrets. A jury awarded the firm over $2 million in damages, including punitive damages, and the Fifth Circuit upheld the award. The jury had properly determined that **the managers breached their fiduciary duty, breached the contract, and misappropriated trade secrets** by disclosing confidential information to the firm's competitors. *Navigant Consulting, Inc. v. Wilkinson*, 508 F.3d 277 (5th Cir. 2007).

♦ A chiropractor, while working for a clinic, began looking for another job and agreed to work for a nearby clinic that would pay her $3,800 per month plus a $100 bonus for every new client. The chiropractor appropriated the confidential client list from the first clinic over the next few months, then urged clients to switch to the nearby clinic. The chiropractor who owned the first clinic **sued the former employee as well as the owner of the nearby clinic for violating the Uniform Trade Secrets Act (UTSA)**. A jury awarded $89,000 against the defendants, and the trial judge doubled the damages award on the grounds that the former employee acted willfully. The Washington Court of Appeals held that the nearby clinic could be vicariously liable for the UTSA violation. However, it did not clearly establish at trial that the former employee had been acting as the nearby clinic's agent when she stole the confidential list. The nearby clinic claimed to be unaware of the theft until the lawsuit. Thus, the case had to be retried. *Thola v. Henschell*, 164 P.3d 524 (Wash. Ct. App. 2007).

• Two salesmen for a Missouri medical devices company signed confidentiality agreements, pledging not to disclose or use any confidential information acquired during their employment. While with the company, the salesmen decided to create a competing product. They hired the engineer who had built the company's device to create a similar product. He did so using spare parts from the company and with the assistance of a company employee. The salesmen then used sales information acquired while with the company to compete with it. When the company sued, a jury awarded it over $2 million in damages. The Eighth Circuit upheld the award. Here, **the employees violated the confidentiality agreement and misappropriated the company's trade secrets**. *Synergetics, Inc. v. Hurst*, 477 F.3d 949 (8th Cir. 2007).

• A Minnesota insurance agency hired a salesman from a competitor after checking the non-compete agreement that the salesman had signed. The agreement stated that the salesman could solicit business from his close family and friends even if they were on the competitor's list of policyholders. The agency gave the salesman stationery and other supplies, and he proceeded to solicit approximately 250 people from the competitor's list, which was about 200 more than he was entitled to solicit. A lawsuit arose under the Minnesota Trade Secrets Act, and a trial court found that the salesman had violated the act but that the agency was not liable because the salesman had been acting outside the scope of his employment when he violated the non-compete agreement. The court of appeals held that the agency was liable because it should have supervised the salesman, but the Minnesota Supreme Court held that the agency was not vicariously liable. Here, although vicarious liability was possible under the act, **the competitor failed to show it was foreseeable that the salesman would misappropriate trade secrets**. *Hagen v. Burmeister & Associates, Inc.*, 633 N.W.2d 497 (Minn. 2001).

IV. COMPENSATION DISPUTES

There is no federal law that sets guidelines regarding wage disputes (like deducting an amount for damage to company property). Each state has its own laws and regulations regarding what is permissible.

The following cases deal with wage disputes, including the payment of commissions and bonuses. For wage deductions generally (like for union dues, charitable contributions, stock purchases and loans made by the employer), employers usually need the written permission of employees.

Each state has its own laws concerning whether and how an employer can make a wage deduction for faulty workmanship, loss, theft or damage to employer property. As a general rule, employers should assume that they cannot make deductions from wages or commissions without the written permission of employees unless a court rules that the employees are liable for the loss or indebtedness.

State laws also allow for the garnishment of wages for certain debts (especially delinquent child support). Title III of the federal *Consumer Credit Protection Act* (CCPA) prohibits employers from discharging employees whose earnings have been subject to garnishment for any one debt. However, it does not prohibit discharging employees who have been subject to garnishment for more than one debt.

Title III of the CCPA also sets limits for how much money can be garnished (usually the lesser of 25% of disposable earnings or the amount by which disposable earnings are greater than $217.50 per week – 30 times $7.25). Where garnishment is made for child support or alimony, Title III allows for more money to be withheld (usually 50 or 60% of disposable earnings).

If state laws allow garnishments that are more restrictive than federal law (in other words, if the employer cannot deduct as much under state law), the state law applies over the federal law. Also, if state law prohibits discharging an employee with two or more debts that are subject to garnishment, then state law applies there as well.

For cases involving minimum wage and overtime compensation under the Fair Labor Standards Act, please see Chapter Five, Section I.

A. Wage Disputes

Wage disputes usually arise as a result of unpaid wages or reductions in wages by the employer. As a general rule, when there is a wage dispute, the wise course of action is to pay the employee and then seek any amounts improperly received through the legal system (like small claims court).

Obviously, this is not completely satisfactory, but the alternative may be even less so. Where an employee makes a wage complaint to the state department of labor, a hearing will usually be required, costing time and money. Often the amount in dispute is not great enough to warrant the inconvenience such a hearing brings.

◆   A Massachusetts company provided janitorial services to business customers through "janitorial franchise agreements" it had with individual janitors. Under the agreements, the individual janitors had to wear approved uniforms and ID badges and had to complete a training program. The company agreed to perform all billing and collection services and pay the individual janitors after taking out certain fees. A group of janitors sued the company for **misclassifying them as independent contractors**. After they won, certain aspects of the case reached the Supreme Judicial Court of Massachusetts, which held that the company couldn't withhold wages until customers paid for the services rendered. Further, the company couldn't enter into an agreement to have the janitors pay their own workers' compensation insurance premiums. Nor could the company and the janitors agree that the janitors would pay for bond and liability insurance. All these practices violated the state's wage act. *Awuah v. Coverall North America, Inc.*, 952 N.E.2d 890 (Mass. 2011).

◆   A Rhode Island medical practice contracted with a payroll company to directly deposit employees' wages in their accounts. The contract specified that the payroll company should act according to the instructions it received from the practice's designated contact, who happened to be its office manager. After the office manager told the payroll company to pay her over $200,000 more than she was owed, it did so. The medical practice then sued it for breach of contract, asserting that it had an obligation to verify that the amounts it deposited matched each salary. However, the First Circuit disagreed. Nothing in the contract stated that the payroll company was supposed to do so. Rather, **the contract required the payroll company to act as the office manager specified**. The practice could not recoup the money overpaid to the office manager from the payroll company. *Ophthalmic Surgeons, Ltd. v. Paychex, Inc.*, 632 F.3d 31 (1st Cir. 2011).

◆   A Florida employee claimed he was owed $1,500 in overtime wages. When he sued for $3,000 ($1,500 in wages and $1,500 in liquidated damages), the company offered to settle for $637 and sought to dismiss the case. A court refused to do so because of the difference between what he was claiming and what the company asserted was its liability. The company then offered him $3,000, which he accepted. At that point, the court dismissed his case and rejected his request for attorneys' fees because he had not won a court judgment so as to make him a prevailing party. *Dionne v. Floormasters Enterprises, Inc.*, 667 F.3d 1199 (11th Cir. 2012).

◆   A group of baristas sued Starbucks for violating California labor law by requiring them to share their tips with their shift supervisors. A trial court awarded them $86 million, finding that the shift supervisors were agents of Starbucks because they handled scheduling and could tell baristas to leave early if business was slow. However, the California Court of Appeal reversed the award, holding that **the shift supervisors were entitled to share the tips**. They performed virtually the same services (waiting on customers, making drinks and serving food), and customers left tips in a box for both the baristas and shift supervisors. *Chau v. Starbucks Corp.*, 94 Cal.Rptr.3d 593 (Cal. Ct. App. 2009).

◆   Verizon signed a collective bargaining agreement that required it to notify the union before creating a new job title or classification (or restructuring an existing job) so that the union could bargain over the starting wage. The agreement also limited retroactive back pay awards to 150 days. **Verizon later assigned additional duties to its voice mail clerks, which the union claimed was a restructuring or reclassification** of the job to a more skilled position, and that they were entitled to a higher wage rate. The union filed a grievance, and an arbitrator ruled that Verizon should have negotiated this change. A second arbitrator awarded increased pay to the voice mail clerks retroactively, going back over five years. The D.C. Circuit held that the arbitrator's decision drew its essence from the bargaining agreement. Even though the retroactive award exceeded the limit of 150 days set by the agreement, the employer's failure to give notice of the change in classification justified the retroactive increase. *Verizon Washington, D.C. Inc. v. Communications Workers of America, AFL-CIO*, 571 F.3d 1296 (D.C. Cir. 2009).

♦ An Indiana company fired two employees and paid them their accrued vacation/sick leave/personal time 14 days after it paid them their wages earned for their last pay period. They filed a class action lawsuit against the company, claiming it violated the state's Wage Claims Statute. The company claimed it could pay them after the date specified by the statute because of its employee manual. A court granted pretrial judgment to the company, but the Court of Appeals of Indiana reversed. Although the company could have completely denied payment of accrued vacation/sick leave/personal time according to the terms of its employee manual, having chosen to pay the employees, it was bound by the Wage Claims Statute. **The vacation/sick leave/personal time became "wages" under the statute and had to be paid within the time frame specified by law.** *Reel v. Clarian Health Partners, Inc.*, 873 N.E.2d 75 (Ind. Ct. App. 2007).

♦ A mechanic for a company in Wyoming was given a check for $2,500 and told that the company could no longer afford to employ him. He filed a claim with the state Department of Employment for the remainder of his unpaid wages. The company agreed that it owed him an additional $944 but disputed the remainder of his claim. A hearing officer ruled that the company owed him $8,700 in wages but that it could award a maximum of two months' wages by statute – in this case, $6,400 – because the mechanic did not file a civil suit. She also denied his request for interest, attorneys' fees and costs on the grounds that the department did not have the authority to make such an award. The Supreme Court of Wyoming upheld the hearing officer's decision. **The company was not entitled to offset the mechanic's wages for gas and parts for his pickup or for a lost toolbox.** Further, the department did not exceed its authority by requiring an employee's written authorization before certain sums could be deducted from wages. Finally, the department had the power to award interest, attorneys' fees and costs. The court remanded the case. *Diamond B Services, Inc. v. Rohde*, 120 P.3d 1031 (Wyo. 2005).

B. Commissions

In some positions (usually sales positions), employees receive commissions as a part of their compensation packages. Generally, commissions are paid against a draw – that is, the employee earns the higher commission wage after reaching a certain preset goal.

If the employee fails to reach the goal, he or she is paid only the draw amount. An employee who fails to reach the goal (or sales quota) for a certain number of pay periods generally becomes subject to termination.

1. Commission Arrangements

The commission arrangements outline the payment terms of the commission, such as what percentage amount of the sale comprises the commission. Withholding commission payments may subject the employer to substantial damage awards, including punitive damages.

◆ An account executive for a maker of corrugated cardboard boxes was hired pursuant to an offer letter that paid him a base salary and said he would receive commissions for two years on sales to customers he procured. It also provided that he would stop getting commissions after the two years. The employer later terminated the employee and stopped paying him commissions. **The employee sued, claiming he was owed commissions on sales made after his termination.** The court said he was entitled to the commissions because he was hired to procure customers. His right to earn commissions did not end when his employment was terminated, the court said. *Dietrich v. Bell, Inc.*, 554 Fed.Appx. 418 (6th Cir. 2014) (Unpublished).

◆ A company in Colorado provided a salesman with a letter that outlined its commission structure but also stated that it was not a contract and that the company reserved the right to change or cancel the commission structure at any time until payments had been earned. Later, the company notified the salesman that he wouldn't receive a commission for the following month. He quit and sued for the unpaid commission, but the Tenth Circuit ruled against him. **The company had changed the commission structure before the salesman had earned the commission, which was allowed** by the letter. Further, the letter explicitly stated that it wasn't a contract. *Geras v. Int'l Business Machines Corp.*, 638 F.3d 1311 (10th Cir. 2011).

◆ Outside sales reps for a company in California used their cars to perform their duties. They brought a lawsuit under Labor Code § 2802 seeking expenses incurred in using their own vehicles. The company asserted that it could meet its obligations under state law by paying the outside sales reps more than the inside sales reps. Eventually the case reached the Supreme Court of California, which held that the company could use a "lump-sum" method to reimburse the sales reps for work-required automobile expenses, provided that the amount paid was sufficient to provide full reimbursement for actual expenses necessarily incurred. Of course, the sales reps had to be permitted to challenge the lump-sum payments as being insufficient. The court also held that **the company could combine wages and business expense reimbursements in a single enhanced employee compensation payment of salary and commissions**, so long as the company established some means to identify the portion of the compensation that was intended as expense reimbursement, and provided that the amounts paid were sufficient to cover actual expenses incurred. *Gattuso v. Harte-Hanks Shoppers, Inc.*, 169 P.3d 889 (Cal. 2007).

◆ An account manager for a Kansas company sold training seminars by telephone. She was paid an hourly wage as well as commissions. The company changed its compensation policy from one of paying commissions upon a signed contract to one of paying commissions upon the buyer paying for the seminar. When the account manager quit, the company offset her hourly wages against what it claimed were prepaid, unearned commissions. She filed a claim for withheld wages with the Department of Labor, and the case reached the Court of Appeals of Kansas, which held that the offset was impermissible. **The employment agreement did not permit the offsetting of unearned**

commissions against accrued and earned hourly wages. The company had to pay the account manager the $822.25 it withheld, plus interest. *Graceland College Center for Professional Development and Life-Long Learning, Inc. v. Kansas Dep't of Labor*, 131 P.3d 1281 (Kan. Ct. App. 2006).

◆   A South Carolina harbor pilot was paid commissions by a towing company for guiding ships into port. After several years, he made plans to form a competing business. While he continued working for the towing company, he made loan applications, filed registration and insurance forms and solicited most of the towing company's existing customers for the new venture. The towing company fired the pilot when it learned of the competing venture and refused to pay him $4,200 in accrued commissions. The pilot sued the towing company under the South Carolina Wage Payment Act, asserting breach of contract and other claims. The towing company counterclaimed on the basis of employee disloyalty. A jury awarded the pilot his claimed commissions. The court then trebled the damage award pursuant to the wage payment act and awarded him attorneys' fees. The court of appeals reversed, stating that an employee's duty of loyalty continues throughout the term of employment. Although employees may make pre-termination plans to compete with an employer, an employee is disloyal if there is a direct solicitation of the employer's customers. The court determined that the common law duty of employee loyalty could properly be applied to deny a claim for unpaid commissions under the wage payment act. Here, the pilot had been disloyal by soliciting customers prior to employment termination. The South Carolina Supreme Court reversed, finding that **when an employee is disloyal, he forfeits compensation for only that period of time**. Here, the pilot should have been paid his claimed commissions for the period in which he was loyal to the company. *Futch v. McAllister Towing of Georgetown, Inc.*, 518 S.E.2d 591 (S.C. 1999).

◆   A Pennsylvania company hired independent sales reps under written contracts calling for compensation on the basis of a percentage of their gross sales. Sales reps were paid a monthly draw against expected commissions and were required to repay any excess draws within 90 days of contract termination. A sales rep who worked for almost two years had more than $34,000 in draws over and above commissions earned at the time of his termination. The employer filed a breach of contract action against him for repayment of the amount with interest. The court held for the employer but denied an award of interest, and the rep appealed. The Superior Court of Pennsylvania held that the state wage act was inapplicable to the dispute because it involved only the right to enforce payment of wages, and the rep conceded that he was paid all the commissions due him. Instead, the action involved the interpretation of the contract, which apparently failed to anticipate earnings remaining below the amount of advance draws. **Because the contract did not provide for the situation here, its repayment requirement was enforceable by its terms, and the rep had to repay the draw.** The court acknowledged that 22 other states, including New York, California and Illinois, refuse to impose personal liability on salespersons to repay draws against commissions. *Banks Engineering Co., Inc. v. Polons*, 697 A.2d 1020 (Pa. Super. Ct. 1997).

2. Damage Awards

State law defines the damages that are due where an employer improperly withholds payment of wages or commissions. Often, the employer has to pay, in addition to the withheld wages, interest, a <u>liquidated damages</u> penalty (usually an amount equal to the improperly withheld wages) and any attorneys' fees and costs the employee incurred.

♦   An Alabama employment agency salesperson was promoted to an account executive position. Despite imposing a higher quota upon her sales production, the agency did not increase her salary or commission rate. When her commissions were cut from an average of $23,000 to about $4,000 in one quarter, she learned that the agency's management had arbitrarily changed her commission calculations and retroactively imposed the higher sales quota requirements. It also failed to credit her for certain new accounts. The salesperson sued the agency, claiming that it owed her $186,000 in underpaid commissions for three quarters of employment. A jury awarded her $300,000 in compensatory damages for fraud and $3 million in punitive damages. The court reduced the punitive damage award to $2 million. Before the Supreme Court of Alabama, the agency argued that the verdict had been inconsistent since it did not award any damages for breach of contract and the fraud claim was based on breaching the contract. The court found no error since the $300,000 awarded for compensatory damages did not have to be specified as breach of contract damages. **The agency committed affirmative misconduct by concealing and falsifying the commission figures.** The Supreme Court requires state courts to review punitive damage awards for excessiveness by comparing them with the civil or criminal penalties that could be imposed for comparable misconduct. The court reduced the punitive damage award to $1.5 million and conditionally affirmed the trial court judgment. *Talent Tree Personnel Services, Inc. v. Fleenor*, 703 So.2d 917 (Ala. 1997).

♦   An independent sales rep sold an apparel line for a clothing company in Alabama, Georgia and Florida on a commission basis, receiving 5% of gross sales. Sales increased dramatically over eight consecutive years. After attempting to reduce the commission rate, the company decided to eliminate independent reps altogether. It offered the representative and his two associates a salary plus a commission of one-half percent of sales. The representative and his associates decided to quit rather than become salaried under these terms but continued to book orders until the effective date of their resignations. They **accused the company of tampering with their orders by crediting other salespersons**, improperly crediting returns against their accounts, canceling orders and other misconduct, which deprived them of almost $1 million in commissions. The reps sued the company in an Alabama court, which awarded them $15 million, including punitive damages for fraud and mental anguish. The Supreme Court of Alabama substantially affirmed, but imposed a $3.5 million reduction in the damages for mental anguish. *Duck Head Apparel Co., Inc. v. Hoots*, 659 So.2d 897 (Ala. 1995).

♦   A South Carolina radio advertising salesman was employed under a contract that called for the payment of sales commissions for separating employees only when the advertisements were actually broadcast. When his employment was terminated, the employer refused to pay commissions on seven contracts under which no advertisements had been broadcast. A South Carolina trial court directed a verdict in favor of the employer for three contracts, but allowed a jury to consider the remaining contract claims, which related to the employee's work for a division of the employer. This resulted in an award of damages for the employee plus attorneys' fees. Both parties appealed to the Supreme Court of South Carolina. The employee argued that he was entitled to treble damages under the state wage act, but the court held that **treble damages are not payable where a good-faith wage dispute exists between employer and employee.** The trial court had properly withheld an award of treble damages and allowed the question of the four contracts to appear before the jury. It had also made an appropriate partial award of attorneys' fees. The trial court's judgment was affirmed. *Rice v. Multimedia, Inc.*, 456 S.E.2d 381 (S.C. 1995).

3. Salary Deduction Policies

Because there is no federal law in this area, employers need to know the laws and regulations of the states in which they have workers. Any questions that arise as to whether a deduction is allowable can be addressed to the state department of labor or an employment attorney in that state.

However, when in doubt, employers should pay wages first (certainly any undisputed portion of the wages or commissions) and seek reimbursement later.

♦   A Massachusetts recycling company instituted a policy whereby employees who were in preventable accidents with company vehicles could either be disciplined or pay for the damage. The company determined whether the accident was preventable, and those findings could not be appealed. When the state attorney general's office audited the company, it determined that the practice of taking deductions violated the state's wage law. The case reached the Supreme Judicial Court of Massachusetts, which upheld that determination. The policy amounted to a "special contract" allowing wage deductions even though state law only allowed wage deductions against an "established" debt or stolen property. **Because the company was the sole arbiter of whether the accidents were preventable, the debt could not be said to be "established."** *Camara v. Attorney General*, 458 Mass. 756, 941 N.E.2d 1118 (Mass. 2011).

♦   A company in New York gave its temporary employees the option of receiving a paycheck or cash. Those who chose the cash option were given a voucher that could only be redeemed at a cash dispensing machine owned by a subsidiary of the company. Each transaction cost a dollar plus the number of cents in the employee's wages – up to $1.99. A lawsuit resulted from the practice, and the Court of Appeals of New York – the state's highest court – ruled that **the company's voucher policy amounted to an unlawful**

deduction from the wages of the temporary workers. The vouchers were not negotiable instruments that could be exchanged for cash. Also, the receipt of the voucher and subsequent receipt of cash could not be viewed as two separate transactions voluntarily made by the employees. *Angello v. Labor Ready, Inc.*, 7 N.Y.3d 579, 825 N.Y.S.2d 674 (N.Y. 2006).

♦   A California department store imposed a wage deduction on its sales personnel that represented a prorated share of commissions on returned items for which the salesperson could not be identified. The store justified the policy as a response to employee abuse for failing to follow procedures that would allow the identification of the affected salesperson. A sales employee sued the store, claiming that it had violated a California law prohibiting employers from recapturing wages already paid. The court granted pretrial judgment to the store, and the employee appealed. The California Court of Appeal observed that the state had a strong public policy against deductions from employee wages for cash shortages, breakages, and other business losses resulting from simple negligence by employees. Employers were not allowed to make their employees insurers against business losses. **The store's policy penalized conscientious employees who accurately reported their returns by charging a portion of the returns of dishonest employees against their wages.** The store had other options to prevent employee fraud that did not violate California law. The court reversed the trial court decision. *Hudgins v. Neiman Marcus Group, Inc.*, 41 Cal.Rptr.2d 46 (Cal. Ct. App. 1995).

♦   A Wisconsin convenience store manager was paid a fixed salary and also received a commission based on a percentage of store sales. Company policy was to hold store managers responsible for cash and merchandise shortages, returned checks, bad credit card charges and damaged or unreturned videos. For five years, the manager claimed that he lost over $26,000 due to the company policy. He sued in a Wisconsin trial court seeking twice the amount of the deductions under a state wage statute. The court determined that the store manager's commissions were not wages and dismissed the lawsuit. The court of appeals affirmed, and the manager appealed. The Supreme Court of Wisconsin reversed. The statute did not operate as a minimum wage law or fairness guarantee as the court of appeals had ruled. Rather, it was intended to protect employees from arbitrary salary reductions attributable to performance. The court ruled that **commissions were included in the statutory definition of wages.** *Erdman v. Jovoco, Inc.*, 512 N.W.2d 487 (Wis. 1994).

C. Bonuses and Other Cash Incentives

Bonuses represent another form of compensation provided by many employers. Bonus rights generally must arise at the beginning of the employment relationship and be for an exact amount or based upon a formula or method of determining the exact amount of the bonus.

In other words, if any bonus due is payable at the discretion of the employer, and is not ascertainable through the use of a formula or from a written promise, it likely will not be enforceable through a court action.

◆   A physical therapist in Kansas, who was employed on an at-will basis, said she was told when she was hired that she would receive a bonus of $10,000 every year. The employer's business manager said she told the physical therapist that the bonus was promised for the first year only. The employer then implemented a bonus plan that calculated bonuses based on a percentage of business receipts, and after her first year the therapist received annual bonuses that were less than $10,000. **She sued for breach of contract, but she lost.** Because she was employed on an at-will basis, the employer was free to change the bonus terms. *Smith v. Kansas Orthopedic Center P.A.*, 316 P.3d 790 (Kan. Ct. App. 2013).

◆   A Massachusetts sales director was fired four months before he was due to be paid a $60,000 bonus. The employer said it fired the director because he failed to manage his district properly. The director sued, claiming he was fired without cause. He also claimed the employer breached a contract with him when it failed to pay the bonus. The First Circuit rejected his claim related to the bonus, finding that **the employer permissibly concluded the director was not entitled to the bonus** because he was fired for good cause. *Weiss v. DHL Express, Inc.*, 718 F.3d 39 (1st Cir. 2013).

◆   Before she was laid off, a marketing executive for a Missouri greeting card and gift company signed a separation agreement in which she agreed not to disclose or retain confidential information and not to work in the industry for 18 months following her separation from employment. **In exchange, she was paid $735,000.** After she left, she disclosed confidential information to a competitor. The company sued the executive to recover the $735,000, and it won. The agreement clearly stated that its purpose was to preserve confidential information, and the executive did not do so. *Hallmark Cards, Inc. v. Murley*, 703 F.3d 456 (8th Cir. 2013).

◆   The managing director of a New York start-up investment firm lured a broker from another firm by promising him a salary of $175,000 and a bonus of $175,000. The start-up took longer than anticipated, and the director asked if he could delay the bonus for a year. The broker agreed. However, after the following year, the director paid him only a $20,000 bonus. He rejected it, after which he was fired for insubordination and for making derogatory comments. When he sued, a jury rejected the director's claim that he had never promised the broker the money. It awarded the broker the bonus. The New York Court of Appeals upheld the award. **It didn't matter that the bonus promise was never reduced to writing.** *Ryan v. Kellogg Partners Institutional Services*, 19 N.Y.3d 1 (N.Y. 2012).

◆   After a sales manager for an Ohio consulting business was fired, he claimed he was due money under a bonus plan in his employment agreement. He sued. The company claimed there was no breach of contract because it had discarded the bonus plan formula as it was entitled to do under at-will principles. A court granted pretrial judgment to the company, but the Ohio Court of Appeals reversed. There were questions over whether the president of the company modified the bonus plan and notified the sales manager. **Even though the** company had the right to modify the plan, it had to inform the manager of the new employment terms to make him bound by them. *Pate v. Quick Solutions, Inc.*, No. 10AP-767, 2011 WL 3449619 (Ohio Ct. App. 8/9/11).

◆   A pharmacist at a New York CVS store was paid a base salary of $100,031 based on a 44-hour work week. CVS classified him as a professional employee exempt from overtime, but it paid him a premium for working extra shifts. To calculate the premium, it divided his weekly salary by 44 to get his compensation rate, then paid him his compensation rate plus $6 per hour. He often worked between 60 and 80 hours a week. When he quit, he sued for overtime, alleging he was not an exempt employee. However, a federal court disagreed, noting that CVS didn't deduct from his pay if he worked less than his usual number of hours. **The bonus payments did not convert him from exempt to non-exempt.** *Anani v. CVS RX Services, Inc.*, 788 F.Supp.2d 55 (E.D.N.Y. 2011).

◆   A New Jersey Macy's employee worked in the "gold bay" of the store's jewelry department. She claimed that the store refused to let her fill in for absent "diamond bay" associates, depriving her of the opportunity to earn bonuses on sales of more expensive products. When she sued under Title VII for race discrimination, most of her claims were dismissed. However, a federal court held that her "bonus" claim could proceed. Further, under the Lily Ledbetter Fair Pay Act, she could potentially recover back pay going back two years before she filed her claim with the EEOC. *Gilmore v. Macy's Retail Holdings*, No. 06-3020 (JBS), 2009 WL 305045 (D.N.J. 2009).

◆   An Indiana surgeon was paid $250,000 a year, plus a bonus based on collections for services rendered. After the surgeon resigned, the institute he had worked for continued to receive collections for services he rendered prior to his resignation. However, it maintained he was not entitled to further compensation. The surgeon sued for his bonus, and the case reached the Supreme Court of Indiana, which held that **the post-termination bonus was to be calculated the same way as earlier bonuses**. Under the parties' contract, there was no indication that the surgeon was to be denied his bonus after his resignation. Thus, the surgeon was entitled to his bonus. However, it was not a "wage" governed by the state's Wage Payment Statute, so he was not entitled to double the bonus amount. *Highhouse v. Midwest Orthopedic Institute, P.C.*, 807 N.E.2d 737 (Ind. 2004).

◆   A financial analyst elected to receive an annual salary of $40,000 so that he would be eligible for participation in the company's bonus/profit-sharing pool, which required the company to meet certain financial goals. According to two memos, the shared distributions would be paid in quarterly installments at the sole discretion of the chief executive officer (CEO), and they were contingent on the recipient's continued employment. After the CEO allocated $160,000 to the analyst and paid him the first $40,000, the analyst resigned. He then sued to recover the remaining $120,000, claiming that the money was either "wages" to which he was entitled, or that his right to the bonus was vested. The New York

Court of Appeals held that the bonus money could not be construed as "wages." The money was not sufficiently linked to the analyst's labor or services to the company. It was instead tied to the company's financial success. Further, his right to the bonus was not vested because **the plan clearly required him to continue working for the company to be eligible for future payments**. *Truelove v. Northeast Capital & Advisory, Inc.*, 715 N.Y.S.2d 366 (N.Y. 2000).

◆   A Pennsylvania chemist notified his employer that a competitor held a patent for a manufacturing process that was similar to a patent owned by the employer. The employer initiated a patent infringement action against the competitor. The competitor refused to permit any of the employer's current employees to review pretrial documents from the case, and the chemist agreed to retire from active employment to serve as a consultant in the patent litigation. The employer agreed to retain him on a per-diem basis for consulting work and agreed to pay him a bonus equaling 1% of the award should the employer prevail. The case was settled when the competitor agreed to undertake some shipping for the employer but involved no cash payment. The employer refused to pay the former employee a bonus, and he sued for breach of contract. He asserted that the employer was bound by a duty of good faith to reach a reasonable result in the patent litigation since he had voluntarily accepted early retirement to facilitate the case. The court observed that **the employer's duty required only the reasonable exercise of discretion to conduct the litigation and determine whether the former employee was entitled to a bonus**. The employer's independent self-interest was congruent with its duty of good faith, and there was no violation of the duty of good faith in settling the case. *Fremont v. E.I. DuPont DeNemours & Co.*, 988 F.Supp. 870 (E.D. Pa. 1997).

◆   A Maine employer instituted an employee suggestion program that awarded cash incentives for ideas that produced savings or increased profits. The maximum award for employee suggestions was $50,000, and the program also offered initial awards of $5,000 based on estimated savings. An employee with over 30 years of experience submitted a cost-saving idea that he expected would qualify for the maximum award. Although the employer paid him the maximum initial award of $5,000, further awards were not paid pending determination of first-year savings for the company. The employee retired, incorporating the expected maximum award into his retirement plans. The company later advised him that he would receive only $17,500 for his idea. He rejected the award and sued the employer. The case reached the First Circuit, which rejected his argument that the company had reserved excessive discretion over the program, making it void and legally unenforceable. **The terms of the program gave the employer appropriate discretion while giving employees incentives to participate.** However, there was evidence that the employer had failed to live up to its obligations by withdrawing the offer. The court remanded this part of the case for further proceedings. *Hodgkins v. New England Telephone Co.*, 82 F.3d 1226 (1st Cir. 1996).

V. THE FAMILY AND MEDICAL LEAVE ACT

The Family and Medical Leave Act of 1993 (FMLA), 29 U.S.C. §§ 2601-2654, grants eligible employees the right to take up to 12 weeks of unpaid leave per year under specified circumstances related to family healthcare and childbirth, and (with the passage of amendments in 2008) for military caregiver leave or in exigent circumstances relating to the National Guard or Reserves. Employees become eligible by working:

1) for an employer with at least 50 employees,
2) for the employer for at least 12 months, and
3) at least 1,250 hours in the previous year.

Eligible employees are expressly authorized by the act to take leave upon the birth of a child by the employee or the employee's spouse, or by the placement of a child for adoption or foster care with the employee.

The act also applies when the employee is needed to care for a child, spouse or parent who has a serious health condition, and when the employee is unable to perform employment duties because of her own serious health condition.

♦   An Arkansas employee was diagnosed with cancer and requested medical leave. Her employer granted her request and allowed her to take seven months of leave. However, the company did not inform her of her eligibility under the FMLA, nor did it inform her of her right to have the leave designated as FMLA leave. When she exhausted the seven months of company-provided leave, she was fired. Her request for additional FMLA leave was denied. She sued, and a federal court ruled for the employer. The Eighth Circuit affirmed, holding that the employer's failure to designate any part of the leave as FMLA leave did not prevent the FMLA leave from expiring. The court struck down the Department of Labor regulation that required the employer to provide more than 12 weeks of leave because of its failure to designate the leave as FMLA leave. The court refused to penalize the employer because its leave program was more generous than the FMLA. The U.S. Supreme Court also affirmed, noting that **employers who provide more than 12 weeks of family and medical leave cannot be penalized for failing to give proper FMLA notice**. *Ragsdale v. Wolverine World Wide, Inc.*, 535 U.S. 81, 122 S.Ct. 1155, 152 L.Ed.2d 167 (2002).

A. "Serious Health Condition"

Under the FMLA regulations, a serious health condition is one requiring an overnight stay in a hospital, hospice or residential medical care facility or a period of incapacity requiring more than three calendar days' absence and two visits to a healthcare provider.

Under the new regulations, the first healthcare provider visit must occur within seven days of the first day of incapacity, and the second visit must occur within 30 days. For chronic health conditions, the employee must make at least two visits to a healthcare provider per year.

A serious health condition can also involve a period of incapacity due to pregnancy, a chronic serious health condition (like asthma, diabetes or epilepsy) or a permanent or long-term condition like Alzheimer's, a severe stroke or the terminal stages of a disease.

◆   A Home Depot employee in Illinois admitted she had an alcohol problem and sought help through the company's employee assistance program (EAP). She later got a DUI, and her EAP caseworker told her she had to be evaluated at a treatment facility. She scheduled the evaluation but showed up to work under the influence prior to that time. After Home Depot fired her, she checked herself into a hospital and sued under the FMLA, claiming retaliation. However, the Seventh Circuit ruled against her, noting that **her alcoholism was not a serious health condition under the FMLA**. She didn't check herself into the hospital until after she was fired. And she was properly fired for violating the company's substance abuse policy. *Ames v. Home Depot*, 629 F.3d 665 (7th Cir. 2011).

◆   A Pennsylvania medical receptionist was diagnosed with a urinary tract infection and low back pain. She got a prescription for antibiotics from her doctor, who also provided a note stating that it was likely she'd be able to return to work within a day or two, though it was possible she wouldn't be able to return to work after three days. She stayed out for a week and was fired for performance reasons. When she sued under the FMLA, she presented her doctor's note and her testimony that she was incapacitated. A federal court ruled that she failed to prove she had a "serious health condition" under the act. However, the Third Circuit held that her testimony, combined with the doctor's note, was sufficient to prove she had a serious health condition. The court remanded the case for a determination of whether she provided sufficient notice of her need for leave and whether she was improperly fired. *Schaar v. Lehigh Valley Health Services, Inc.*, 598 F.3d 156 (3d Cir. 2010).

◆   While riding his bike, a UPS employee in Michigan was hit by a car. He refused medical treatment at the scene, but went to the emergency room that night. Doctors noted contusions on his back and legs and prescribed pain medication, but he didn't fill the prescription. He returned to the ER the next night with back pain, but again refused to fill the prescription for pain medication. He called his supervisor to report that he'd been struck by a car and submitted vague doctors' reports that contained no details. After UPS fired him for unexcused absenteeism, he sued under the FMLA. The Sixth Circuit ruled against him, finding that **his contusions and sore back did not amount to a serious health condition**. *Stimpson v. UPS*, 351 Fed.Appx. 42 (6th Cir. 2009).

◆   A janitor for a property management company in Illinois notified his employer that he was having medical problems, including a weak bladder. He also told his supervisor he was having a biopsy to determine whether he had prostate cancer. After the biopsy, he returned to work with a temporary restriction on heavy lifting and a treatment plan, which his supervisor allegedly ignored. He said he was going home because he felt sick. The next day he was fired. After being diagnosed with prostate cancer, he sued under the FMLA and ADA. His FMLA suit was allowed to move forward. **Even though he didn't know of his diagnosis until after he was fired, he was entitled to FMLA protection.** However, he could not show that he was disabled under the ADA. *Burnett v. LFW Inc.*, 472 F.3d 471 (7th Cir. 2006).

◆ When a company refused to allow an employee time off to care for his 13-year-old son who had severe attention deficit disorder, the employee sued under the FMLA. A Michigan federal court ruled in favor of the company, and the Sixth Circuit Court of Appeals affirmed. Here, the son did not qualify as having a serious health condition because even though he saw his doctor every six months to monitor his medication, he was not incapacitated during the requested leave time. He was able to attend school and do the same activities most children do; he simply had to be watched all the time. *Perry v. Jaguar of Troy*, 353 F.3d 510 (6th Cir. 2003).

◆ A clerical worker at a Florida hospital was disciplined three times for unscheduled absences and was given a final written warning. Later, she slipped and fell at work, fracturing an elbow and ankle. She returned to work on her doctor's recommendation after he put her arm in a sling. She left work early on several days and took two days off the following week without informing her supervisor. The following Monday she was fired. She sued the hospital under the FMLA, and a federal court ruled against her. The Eleventh Circuit affirmed. Here, the employee did not have a "serious health condition" under the FMLA because **her injury did not require her to miss three consecutive full calendar days of work**. Even though the several partial days and two non-consecutive days she took off added up to more than three days away from work during a 10-day period, she was not protected by the FMLA. The regulations clearly require some fraction more than three consecutive calendar days to constitute the period of incapacity. The termination was justified. *Russell v. North Broward Hospital*, 346 F.3d 1335 (11th Cir. 2003).

◆ A California truck driver's sister was murdered by her ex-husband. The truck driver moved to Reno temporarily to be with his father, who had fallen into a depression. He drove his father to counseling sessions and did household chores. While on leave, he agreed with the company's HR manager that he would resign from his job and would be rehired if he returned to work within six months. When he sought reinstatement, the company cited union-related restrictions and refused to reinstate him with seniority. It did, however, give him a position as a probationary truck driver. He sued under the FMLA, and a federal court granted pretrial judgment to the company. The Ninth Circuit reversed, finding an issue of fact as to whether the leave of absence qualified as FMLA leave. Here, if the father had a "serious health condition" and if the truck driver cared for him within the meaning of the FMLA, then he should have been reinstated to his position with seniority. *Scamihorn v. General Truck Drivers*, 282 F.3d 1078 (9th Cir. 2002).

◆   A West Virginia employee was warned about poor attendance. She then came down with the flu and missed a week of work. She saw her doctor twice during the week and requested FMLA leave when she returned to work. Her employer denied her request and fired her for excessive absenteeism. The Fourth Circuit affirmed a ruling in her favor, holding that **an employee with the flu could be suffering from a "serious health condition"** where the employee cannot work for at least three consecutive days and receives continuing treatment from her doctor. "Treatment" includes examinations and evaluations of the seriousness of the illness. Here, even though the employee's second visit to the doctor was to evaluate her condition, this constituted continuing treatment for a serious health condition. *Miller v. AT&T Corp.*, 250 F.3d 820 (4th Cir. 2001).

B. Notice

The FMLA requires employees to give employers sufficient notice, usually 30 days, to prevent unduly disrupting employer operations. However, lesser notice may be sufficient when a 30-day notice is impossible.

Under the regulations, employees have to follow the employer's usual and customary call-in procedures for reporting an absence unless unusual circumstances exist to excuse that lack.

The FMLA also requires employers to give notice to employees who request leave. Under the regulations, the notice has to be given within five business days and must contain the following:

1)   a statement that the leave will be counted against the employee's annual FMLA entitlement,
2)   any requirements for the employee to furnish medical certification of a serious health condition,
3)   a statement of the employee's right to substitute paid leave and whether the employer will require the substitution of paid leave,
4)   any requirement for the employee to make any premium payments to maintain health benefits,
5)   any requirement for the employee to present a fitness-for-duty certificate to be restored to employment,
6)   if the employee is a "key employee," a statement explaining that status and the potential consequence that restoration may be denied following the leave,
7)   a statement of the employee's right to restoration to the same or an equivalent job upon return from leave, and
8)   a statement of the employee's potential liability for payment of health insurance premiums paid by the employer during the leave if the employee fails to return to work after the leave.

◆   An employee of a Florida-based security company sent his supervisor an email titled "Vacation Schedule" and listed dates he wanted to take as vacation time for the next two years. The supervisor denied the request, and the employee answered that his "medical/health professionals" told him he could not wait to use his vacation time. The employee said he also called the supervisor to say he needed the leave for medical reasons, but the supervisor denied that happened. The employee was then fired for insubordination and poor job performance. He sued, claiming the employer violated the FMLA by denying him leave and firing him because he requested it. The court ruled against him. It found that **his request did not qualify for protection under the FMLA** because he did not request the leave to address an actual incapacity. *Hurley v. Kent of Naples*, 746 F.3d 1161 (11th Cir. 2014).

♦   An Iowa employee missed work on a number of occasions because of depression. Her employer transferred her to a position where daily attendance wasn't so crucial. She then missed a month of work around the time of her father's death, and the company fired her. When she sued under the FMLA, a federal court awarded her $296,112 – $80,793 in back pay, $80,793 in statutory liquidated damages, and $134,526 in front pay. It said she qualified for FMLA leave with a serious health condition and notified the employer of her need for it. Yet **the company never informed her of her FMLA rights** and fired her rather than reinstating her when she was able to return to work. On appeal, the court took away the award of front pay, finding it was based on speculation. *Dollar v. Smithway Motor Express, Inc.*, 710 F.3d 798 (8th Cir. 2013).

♦   A research clerk at a Minnesota bank failed to show up for work on the date he was scheduled to return from military leave. Three days later, he called his manager and said he felt ill. He went to a doctor, but a test for pneumonia came back negative. Still, the clinic faxed a note saying that he was ill. For a few days, he called in each day and left a voice mail for his manager. The bank's policy required employees to report all absences directly to their supervisor (no voice mails, emails or notification to co-workers). A few days after he stopped calling in, the bank determined that he had abandoned his job and terminated him. When he sued under the FMLA, he lost. A federal court held that **the employer could expect him to follow its call-in procedures**. *To v. U.S. Bancorp*, No. 08-5979 (JRT-JJK), 2010 WL 3546823 (D. Minn. 9/7/10).

♦   An assembly line worker at a Ford plant in Indiana requested leave for stress. Her doctor faxed a form to the plant's clinic stating that she needed until August 28, then referred her to a psychiatrist, who could not see her until August 29. She asked her doctor to let the plant clinic know she needed more time off, but she did not notify the clinic herself. When the clinic didn't hear from her, it sent her a "quit notice" via certified mail, which she waited a few days to pick up. After her termination, she sued under the FMLA but lost. A federal court and the Seventh Circuit ruled that she could be fired for violating the FMLA's "two-day" rule, which required her to give notice of unforeseeable need for leave within two days. Although that rule has since been replaced by **a rule requiring employees to comply with the employer's usual and customary policy on notice of need for leave**, the two-day rule applied here. And the employee failed to show that extraordinary circumstances prevented her from complying. *Brown v. Automotive Components Holdings, LLC*, 622 F.3d 685 (7th Cir. 2010).

◆   A Texas medical center employee with a seizure disorder had a history of FMLA-approved absences and unexcused absences. One day, her mother found her hallucinating at home and contacted her supervisor. She was told to take the employee to the emergency room. The employee was later transferred to a behavior center, where she was diagnosed with bipolar disorder. When she sought to obtain additional FMLA leave, she learned that she had been fired for failing to contact the medical center's third-party administrator within two days of her release from the hospital. She sued. A federal court granted pretrial judgment to the medical center, but the Fifth Circuit reversed, finding issues of fact over **whether the center's strict notice policy should be set aside** because her mother tried to comply with it by speaking with her supervisor. *Saenz v. Harlingen Medical Center, LP*, 613 F.3d 576 (5th Cir. 2010).

◆   An Arkansas steel mill employee with two unexcused absences sought a day off for his ex-father-in-law's funeral on the following Wednesday. He was told to swap with another employee on Sunday, but instead he called up on Sunday, intoxicated and emotional, and said he was "through" with the company. He then called his supervisor on Monday and claimed he'd had a nervous breakdown. But because he had previously been dishonest, his supervisor thought he was making an excuse not to come to work. He stayed away all week. The next week he called an HR manager and claimed an alcohol problem and depression. The manager referred him to the Employee Assistance Program, and he underwent treatment, after which he was demoted because of his unexcused absences. When he sued under the FMLA, he lost. A federal court and the Eighth Circuit ruled that **his shifting explanations for why he couldn't work did not provide sufficient notice of his need for FMLA leave**. *Scobey v. Nucor Steel-Arkansas*, 580 F.3d 781 (8th Cir. 2009).

◆   A service manager for a New Jersey company had a chronic heart condition, which his employer knew about. About two weeks after he returned from quintuple bypass surgery, he received a written warning about his job performance. He later told a supervisor that his doctor had found more blockages, that he was going to have to undergo medical monitoring, and that he might need more surgery. A week later he was fired for performance-related reasons. When he sued under the FMLA, a federal court granted pretrial judgment to the company. However, the Third Circuit reversed, finding issues of fact that required a trial. Here, **the employee's statement to his supervisor was sufficient to provide notice of his need for FMLA leave**. *Sarnowski v. Air Brooke Limousine, Inc.*, 510 F.3d 398 (3d Cir. 2007).

◆   An Illinois employee with a previously unblemished record got dizzy and felt her neck muscles tighten when a stray dog entered the facility where she worked. She began yelling to her supervisor that "f——— animals shouldn't be in the workplace." Two hours later she went home ill. She called in sick the next day, but the following day, she charged into the company president's office and began screaming and cursing at him for allowing a dog to enter the facility. She then missed three more days, and when she returned to work, she found the contents of her desk moved to another room to accommodate her fear of animals. She called the police, believing she was being harassed, then went home early. She went to a doctor but did not provide written or oral notice of her need for FMLA leave. After she was fired, she sued. A federal court granted pretrial judgment to the employer, but the Seventh Circuit reversed, finding issues of fact that required a trial. **Her unusual behavior may have provided the employer with constructive notice of her need for FMLA leave.** *Stevenson v. Hyre Electric*, 505 F.3d 720 (7th Cir. 2007).

◆   A Maryland employee missed two-and-a-half days of work because of illness. She saw a doctor and returned to work with medical reports diagnosing her with a possible peptic ulcer. She worked four days. On the fifth day she told her supervisor she was sick and had to leave early for a doctor's appointment. She was absent for the next eight days, but failed to inform her superiors that she would be gone, instead telling three co-workers to inform her supervisor that she was sick. She was fired, then provided documentation of her absence, and was offered a lower-paying position. She turned it down, then sued under the FMLA. A federal court ruled against her, noting that **her minimal notice to the employer did not satisfy the requirements of the FMLA**. *Rodriguez v. Smithfield Packing Co.*, 545 F.Supp.2d 508 (D. Md. 2008).

◆   A Louisiana employee called her supervisor on a Monday to tell him she was sick. She also told him she was pregnant, but did not say that the sickness was related to pregnancy complications. When she called back on Tuesday, she was told to get a medical release. She told her supervisor she had a doctor's appointment on Wednesday, meaning more than a week later. However, her supervisor thought she meant the next day. She had no further contact with her employer for 10 days. When she was fired for violating the "no call/no show" policy, she sued under the FMLA. A federal court and the Fifth Circuit ruled against her. **She failed to give her supervisor enough information to put the employer on notice that she had a "serious health condition."** *Willis v. Coca-Cola Enterprises*, 445 F.3d 413 (5th Cir. 2006).

◆   An attendance-challenged Wisconsin employee in danger of being fired left work early because she was sick. She submitted a form from the company's health center stating that she should be off work for three days. Several months later, after more absences, she was fired. She was diagnosed with a head tumor and sued under the FMLA, claiming the three-day absence should not have been counted against her. The Seventh Circuit ruled against her. **The note from the health center did not inform the company that she had a serious health condition**, and she did not tell the company she was taking prescribed antibiotics. *Phillips v. Quebecor World RAI, Inc.*, 450 F.3d 308 (7th Cir. 2006).

C. Employer-Paid Leaves and State Statutes

Sometimes employer-paid leaves and state statutes provide different types of coverage for employees requiring leaves. Employer policies and state statutes may provide more protection than the minimum requirements of the FMLA. However, they may not provide less protection.

◆   After 10 months on the job, a Minnesota employee asked for leave to treat depression and chronic migraines. Since he didn't yet qualify for FMLA leave, the company granted him short-term disability leave. During his leave, the company informed him it was removing him from his position but that he would remain an employee and retain his benefits while on leave. Shortly after his 12-month anniversary, he was cleared to return to work, but the company had no job openings and discharged him. He sued under the FMLA, **asserting that he became eligible for FMLA leave during his disability leave**. A federal court disagreed. The determination of FMLA eligibility must be made as of the date leave commences. This was unlike a situation where an employee uses vacation time to get to the 12-month eligibility requirement. *Adly v. SuperValu, Inc.*, No. 06-CV-5108 (PJS/RCE), 2007 WL 2226040 (D. Minn. 8/3/07).

◆   An Alabama manager took a 15-week pregnancy leave, during which she received 13 weeks of pay under the employer's disability plan. Upon her return to work, she was demoted to assistant manager based on the expiration of the FMLA's maximum 12-week leave period. The employee resigned and sued, claiming that she had been constructively discharged in violation of the FMLA. The court considered FMLA language describing the relationship between the FMLA's maximum 12-week leave period and employer-provided paid leaves of absence. It noted a conflict between the statutory language and federal regulations published by the Department of Labor. **The FMLA does not require employers to provide 12 weeks of unpaid leave in addition to any paid leave provided by an employer plan.** Because the employee in this case had taken more than 12 weeks of leave, she had received all that she was entitled to receive under the FMLA. The court granted the employer pretrial judgment. *Cox v. AutoZone, Inc.*, 990 F.Supp. 1369 (M.D. Ala. 1998).

◆   A flight attendant, who normally worked less than 1,000 hours per year, missed substantial amounts of work due to illnesses she claimed were severe enough to qualify for coverage under the FMLA. The airline disputed the seriousness of the illnesses and fired her. She sued it in a Georgia federal court. The airline claimed that the injuries were not covered by the FMLA and that she did not work enough hours to qualify for coverage. The employee argued that the airline's policy provided substantial benefits to flight attendants working at least 540 hours per calendar year. Because **an FMLA regulation required employers to observe any benefit programs providing greater family or medical leave rights than the FMLA minimum**, she claimed coverage under the airline's internal policy. The court disagreed, stating that the regulation simply preserved contractual rights and did not alter FMLA jurisdictional requirements. Since she worked less than 1,250 hours per year, the act did not apply. *Rich v. Delta Air Lines, Inc.*, 921 F.Supp. 767 (N.D. Ga. 1996).

◆   New Jersey's Family Leave Act requires employers to grant employees leave for reasons including childbirth or the illness of a family member. "Employer" is defined by the act as a person, corporation or other business entity employing 50 or more employees. Unlike the federal FMLA, the state act does not specify that the minimum number of employees be located in a particular geographic location, and the act does not state whether they must work within the state. An employee filed a complaint with a state agency against her employer, claiming that it had violated the state act. The employer responded that while it employed 164 persons in six states, it had fewer than 12 New Jersey employees and that the act did not apply to it. The agency found probable cause of a violation of the act, and the New Jersey Superior Court, Appellate Division, affirmed. The absence of a geographic limitation in the statute indicated that **the legislature intended all employers doing business in the state having a total of 50 employees to come within the scope of the act**. Not all employers having less than 50 employees in the state were small; they could have hundreds or thousands of employees in other states. *Essex Crane Rental Corp. v. Director, Division on Civil Rights*, 294 N.J.Super. 101, 682 A.2d 750 (N.J. Super. Ct. App. Div. 1996).

D. Certification

Employers can require employees to provide medical certification issued by a healthcare provider to ensure that the employees have a serious health condition, but must allow 15 days for the certification to be provided.

Under the regulations, employers can request recertification of an ongoing medical condition every six months in conjunction with an absence.

The regulations also place strict limitations on who is allowed to contact the employee's healthcare provider, and prohibit the employee's direct supervisor from doing so.

◆   In an attempt to curb what it perceived as FMLA abuse, an Oregon employer instituted a policy requiring all employees approved for intermittent FMLA leave to submit a note from their medical provider each time they missed work for an FMLA-related reason. The employer then filed lawsuits seeking a declaration that the policy was valid. A federal district court consolidated the lawsuits and decided that the policy was not valid because **it directly conflicted with an FMLA regulation** that allows employers to seek recertification no more than once every 30 days. The policy impermissibly required employees to reestablish their FMLA eligibility every time they were absent. *Oak Harbor Freight Lines, Inc. v. Antti*, 998 F.Supp.2d 968 (D. Ore. 2014).

◆   A Texas employee's daughter was flown to Miami for emergency surgery during a vacation. He received permission to use FMLA leave, but when he filled out the forms, they were incomplete. He returned to Texas from Miami a few weeks before his leave was scheduled to end, while his wife stayed in Miami to look after their daughter. When he finally returned to work, the company asked him to complete the paperwork. Instead, he walked out. The company fired him, and he sued for retaliation under the FMLA. However, he lost because **he failed to show that he was needed to provide actual care** "in close and continuing proximity" to his daughter during the weeks he was back in Texas. *Baham v. McLane Foodservice, Inc.*, 431 Fed.Appx. 345 (5th Cir. 2011).

+   After being injured on two occasions by developmentally disabled students, an employee of a school in Illinois went to work in the kitchen, where students were not allowed. When a student later came into the kitchen, the employee complained to the HR department about the unsafe environment. She asked for an FMLA certification form and went to a doctor, who filled out the form, certifying her condition as severe recurrent headaches and pain in her upper body from the student attacks. The employee added the words "plus previous depression" to the form and turned it in late. The school denied her FMLA request and fired her for excessive absenteeism. When she sued, she lost. The Seventh Circuit held that **she was not entitled to FMLA leave after altering the certification form**, even though she would have qualified for such leave had she not done so. *Smith v. Hope School*, 560 F.3d 694 (7th Cir. 2009).

+   An Illinois employee with Graves' disease took three weeks of FMLA leave to have her thyroid removed. She returned to work, but the replacement hormones made her feel fatigued. She began leaving work an hour early, taking work home in the evenings and on weekends. Her supervisor later told her she had to resume an eight-hour day and issued her a corrective action report (CAR) when she failed to do so. Her supervisor also told her she would have to provide FMLA certification. When she failed to turn it in on time, she was given two more CARs. The company then suspended and fired her. She sued under the FMLA and lost. A federal court and the Seventh Circuit held that she failed to comply with the time restrictions imposed by the FMLA, so even though the company made some mistakes – it failed to let her know she might qualify for FMLA leave when it issued the first CAR, and it referred to the leave as "intermittent" rather than "reduced schedule" leave – **it properly fired her for failing to return the paperwork in a timely fashion**. *Ridings v. Riverside Medical Center*, 537 F.3d 755 (7th Cir. 2008).

+   An Ohio employee with attendance problems missed two weeks of work for back pain, her 18-year-old daughter's post-partum depression, and her grandson's illness. This put her over the minimum number of points for unexcused absences under her employer's attendance policy. She sought FMLA leave to stave off her termination but failed to submit proper certification from her doctor for her back pain. She offered a form that her doctor had signed. However, her doctor had not examined her so did not provide information about the date the medical condition began or its likely duration. After she was fired, she sued under the FMLA and lost. The Sixth Circuit noted that her daughter was not a minor child and that **the company did not have to seek a second opinion before denying her leave. Nor was it barred from challenging her certification simply because it didn't obtain a second opinion.** *Novak v. MetroHealth Medical Center*, 503 F.3d 572 (6th Cir. 2007).

+   A Tennessee welder requested FMLA leave for surgery. Her doctor scheduled a follow-up for her the day after she was to return to work. Six days before she was due back, she asked for an extension and was told to get a statement from her doctor. Believing she had 15 days to do so, she did not immediately get the statement. The company fired her the day she was scheduled to return to work even though her doctor faxed a statement to the company that day. She sued under the FMLA and obtained an award of $55,000. The Sixth Circuit upheld the award, noting that **federal regulations require employers to allow 15 days for certification submissions**. *Killian v. Yorozu Automotive Tennessee, Inc.*, 454 F.3d 549 (6th Cir. 2006).

* An emergency medical technician in Michigan suffered from migraine headaches and was allowed to take intermittent leave under the FMLA. However, her employer **spotted what it believed was an inconsistency in her medical certification** and asked her to correct it. She refused to do so, believing that if she did so, the employer would force her to work part time. After submitting to a fitness-for-duty exam, she told her supervisor to "quit f—— with [her]." She repeated the profanity the next day and was fired a few weeks later. When she sued for retaliation under the FMLA, a federal court and the Sixth Circuit ruled against her. She was legitimately fired for insubordination. *Hoffman v. Professional Med Team*, 394 F.3d 414 (6th Cir. 2005).

* A mechanic suffered a work-related injury that resulted in episodes of neck pain and numbness in his hands. He went on short-term disability leave, during which he received a letter from the employer, informing him that his leave qualified as FMLA leave, and that he had to produce a doctor's certificate to return to work. The day after his 12-week FMLA leave expired, he called the company to inquire about reinstatement, but was told that he was fired for not returning to the job within the 12-week period (the employer claimed that the 12-week period ran from before it sent the mechanic the FMLA notice letter). A week later, the mechanic received a letter confirming that he was fired. He sued the employer under the FMLA and the Arkansas Civil Rights Act, and a jury awarded him damages of $305,000. The Eighth Circuit affirmed the award, holding that **the jury had properly found that he had attempted to return to work**, that he had obtained a doctor's certificate releasing him to work, and that he was able to perform the essential functions of the job. *Duty v. Norton-Alcoa Proppants*, 293 F.3d 481 (8th Cir. 2002).

E. Post-Leave Issues

The FMLA requires covered employers to restore employees to their former positions or an equivalent position but does not confer a right, benefit or position to which the employee was not entitled in the absence of a leave.

* A Wal-Mart employee took FMLA leave. When she sought to extend the leave under the employer's personal leave policy, the employer sent her paperwork and told her to return it within 15 days. She missed the 15-day deadline, and her employment was terminated. **She sued the employer, accusing it of retaliating against her by denying her extended leave under the personal leave policy.** The court allowed the claim to proceed, noting that while the employer was awaiting return of the additional paperwork it already had her FMLA certification file. *Scorsone v. Wal-Mart Stores, Inc.*, No. 13-cv-14418, 2014 WL 2207002 (E.D. Mich. 5/28/14).

◆   A home healthcare nurse in Pennsylvania allegedly showed a patient and his wife lewd cell phone photos of her boyfriend. She took FMLA leave shortly thereafter for surgery, during which time the company learned of the allegation. When she returned to work two months later, the company confronted and then fired her. She sued but lost. The Third Circuit held that **there was nothing sinister about the company waiting until her leave expired to confront and fire her**. *Adams v. Fayette Home Care and Hospice*, 452 Fed.Appx. 137 (3d Cir. 2011).

◆   A Pennsylvania warehouse manager with a history of performance problems took a series of FMLA leaves. He claimed that for the next six months, his co-workers and the regional manager were antagonistic toward him. At that point, he was fired for asking an employee not to report the actual time a customer picked up an item, which violated company policy. He sued for retaliation but lost. A federal court found **no evidence linking the leaves with the firing**. *Ellison v. Oaks 422 LLC*, No. 11-2943, 2012 WL 876723 (E.D. Pa. 3/15/12).

◆   A Maryland employee who had never fully met all expectations in any performance review began to suffer from insomnia and saw a doctor. She took four sick days and was granted FMLA leave for three weeks. All her lab tests were normal, but her doctor wrote a note restricting her to an eight-hour day. The company asked her to submit a plan describing how she would perform the necessary functions of her job. In her plan, she committed to working only from 11:00 a.m. to 4:00 p.m. When the company found the plan inadequate and fired her, she sued under the FMLA and ADA. She lost. A federal court found that **she failed to show she suffered from a serious medical condition or from a disability**. *Anderson v. Discovery Communications*, 814 F.Supp.2d 562 (S.D. Md. 2011).

◆   A drug company vice president in Georgia was placed on a performance improvement plan because of complaints about her confrontational and inflexible management style. While on the plan, she took FMLA leave for a pregnancy. Her subordinates informed the HR department that her region functioned significantly better under her replacement. Her replacement also learned that she had ignored scores of expense reports and had failed to pay several outside creditors. When the vice president sought to return to work, the company offered her a demotion. She accepted the demotion but later sued under the FMLA. However, she lost when the Eleventh Circuit noted that the company had a valid reason for demoting her. **It didn't discover the full extent of the problem with her management until she was on leave.** *Schaaf v. SmithKline Beecham Corp.*, 602 F.3d 1236 (11th Cir. 2010).

◆   A Michigan mechanical engineer with epilepsy worked for a contractor at a joint venture project for the city of Detroit. Despite medication, he continued to have seizures. His doctor recommended surgery as a way to alleviate the seizures. He scheduled the surgery and informed the contractor that he wanted to take FMLA leave. The contractor granted the leave, but when the engineer tried to return to work 12 weeks later, it refused to take him back. When he sued under the FMLA, the contractor claimed it was not required to comply with the law because it did not have 50 employees within a 75-mile radius of his work site. It also asserted that the job had been eliminated from the project. A federal court ruled for the contractor, and the Sixth Circuit affirmed. **The engineer couldn't show that he relied on a misrepresentation by the contractor because he had already scheduled the surgery when he asked for the leave.** *Dobrowski v. Jay Dee Contractors, Inc.*, 571 F.3d 551 (6th Cir. 2009).

✦   A staffing agency employee working in the IT division of an automotive industry company had to be hospitalized for asthma. While she was on FMLA leave, the company eliminated her position. It used another contractor from the staffing agency to perform her duties and later hired him directly. When she sued the agency and the company under the FMLA, a Michigan federal court granted pretrial judgment to the defendants. However, the Sixth Circuit found issues of fact requiring a trial. It noted that the defendants could be liable as joint employers for interfering with her reinstatement rights. Also, the employee presented **evidence that the restructuring was done to get around the requirements of the FMLA**. *Grace v. USCAR and Bartech Technological Services, LLC*, 521 F.3d 655 (6th Cir. 2008).

✦   An IT employee in Virginia took FMLA leave to have hip surgery. While he was gone, his position was eliminated, and he was offered another project to work on with the same salary, title, bonus eligibility, and health and retirement benefits. However, he no longer oversaw the IT department budget and no longer had purchasing authority. Four months later, his job was eliminated because of a merger, and by the end of the year, all IT functions had been transferred to Toronto. He sued under the FMLA and the ADA. A federal court and the Fourth Circuit ruled against him. **There was no FMLA violation in the assignment to the equivalent position**, and he could not prove he was disabled under the ADA. *Csicsmann v. Sallada*, 211 Fed.Appx. 163 (4th Cir. 2006).

✦   After receiving complaints about the HR department and one of its employees, a Louisiana company developed a plan to improve the department and reassigned the employee. Her supervisor later met with her to discuss areas where she needed improvement. She took FMLA leave for anxiety and stress. While on leave, she was granted a merit increase in salary, but the vice president of HR remained concerned about her performance. When she returned from leave, she was told that she would be fired if her performance did not improve. The plant manager micro-managed her work, and she was ridiculed at a meeting. She resigned, then sued under the FMLA. A federal court and the Fifth Circuit ruled against her. **She was not demoted when she returned from leave**, and the ridicule at the meeting was not enough to prove constructive discharge. *Haley v. Alliance Compressor, LLC*, 391 F.3d 644 (5th Cir. 2004).

F.   Other FMLA Issues

The FMLA sometimes creates special issues under the Americans with Disabilities Act and state workers' compensation law. Each statute has its own requirements. As the following cases show, the FMLA can also present a variety of other issues as well.

◆   A Pennsylvania clerical worker broke the bone connecting her right wrist to her pinky finger. The employer told her she could not work full duty with the injury, and it supplied her with FMLA certification forms. The employee gave the employer a doctor's note that said she could return to work without restrictions on a specified date. She returned with a splint, **and the employer told her to get a doctor's excuse from work until she could use all her fingers to type**. The employer replaced her, and she sued under the FMLA. The court held that the employee raised trial questions as to whether the employer interfered with the employee's right to be restored to her position. A jury could find the employer improperly disregarded the doctor's conclusion that the employee could return to work without restrictions. *Budhun v. Reading Hospital and Medical Center*, 765 F.3d 245 (3d Cir. 2014).

◆   An options trader at a Kentucky brokerage firm took FMLA leave to have knee replacement surgery. She was approved for FMLA leave until October 11, **but the employer's short-term disability carrier calculated a return-to-work date of September 22**. The carrier extended coverage through October 1, but when the employee did not return until October 6, she was issued a "final" warning. Nine days later, her employment was terminated. She sued the employer for interfering with her right to take FMLA leave and retaliating against her because she took it. The court said a jury could find that the employer's decision to terminate the employee was motivated by her use of FMLA leave. *Wallner v. Hilliard*, No. 13-6548, 2014 WL 5488172 (6th Cir. 10/31/14) (Unpublished).

◆   An employee of an Illinois residential nursing facility took FMLA leave to care for her daughter, who was being treated for thyroid cancer, and her daughter's children. Assuming she would not return to work before her leave expired, the employer replaced her before her leave ran out. She sued under the FMLA, and she won. **The employee was not required to tell the employer exactly how much leave she needed** because she did not know, and the FMLA covers employees who provide a combination of care to an adult child and grandchildren. *Gienapp v. Harbor Crest*, 756 F.3d 527 (7th Cir. 2014).

◆   An analyst for a Florida insurance company submitted a request for FMLA leave. She then received a negative performance review. The employer told her she could accept severance benefits or agree to a performance improvement plan. It also told her that if she chose the severance benefits, **she would need to waive any claims she might have under the FMLA**. The employee signed the agreement, but she later sued under the FMLA. She claimed the employer interfered with her FMLA rights and retaliated against her for seeking FMLA leave. The court rejected her claim, holding the waiver validly blocked claims based on past employer conduct. *Paylor v. Hartford Fire Insurance Co.*, 748 F.3d 1117 (11th Cir. 2014).

◆   An assistant store manager at a Wal-Mart in Wisconsin was placed on a performance improvement plan. She was then granted FMLA leave to undergo surgery. When she returned to work, her job performance did not rise to an acceptable level and she was terminated. She sued, claiming she was fired because she took FMLA leave. She said the employer set her up to fail by placing her on the night shift and giving her bad reviews. The court rejected her claim. **Neither the shift assignment nor the negative reviews were adverse actions**, and she did not show she was fired because she took FMLA leave. *Langenbach v. Wal-Mart Stores, Inc.*, 988 F.Supp.2d 1004 (E.D. Wis. 2013).

◆   A banquet steward at an Illinois hotel took FMLA after he suffered an eye injury. He was provided 12 weeks of FMLA leave and took additional leave that was provided by his union's contract with the employer. While he was on leave, he provided conflicting doctors' notes regarding his ability to return to work. One said he could return with restrictions, while others said he couldn't work at all. He finally returned to work in the same position after about a year, and he then sued the hotel for violating the FMLA by not returning him to work right after one doctor released him for light duty. The Seventh Circuit rejected his claim. **The release did not release him to perform all essential job functions**; the steward submitted other notes that contradicted the release; and the steward failed to respond to the employer's requests that he clarify his medical condition. *James v. Hyatt Regency Chicago*, 707 F.3d 775 (7th Cir. 2013).

◆   A telecommunications technician in Ohio began taking intermittent FMLA leave due to a back condition. Even though his doctor said the flare-ups requiring leave were not predictable, he often took Thursdays and Fridays as leave days when he had the weekend off. **The employer investigated and observed him working in his yard and garage while he was supposedly experiencing a flare-up.** It fired him, and he sued under the FMLA. The Sixth Circuit rejected his claim because the employer acted based on its honest belief that he was abusing FMLA leave and thus violating its code of conduct. *Tillman v. Ohio Bell Telephone Co.*, 545 Fed.Appx. 340 (6th Cir. 2013).

◆   An Ohio employer approved a customer service representative's request for intermittent FMLA leave after a therapist said the leave was needed due to the employee's anxiety. **The employee was an aspiring writer, and she told a newspaper that a person has to "take off work to make [her] dreams come true."** In addition, she began taking every Monday off and then misled supervisors into thinking she needed to attend the funeral of her biological granddaughter. In fact, the funeral was for her step-granddaughter, and she was evasive when pressed for details. The employer fired the employee, and she sued for retaliation under the FMLA. The Sixth Circuit rejected her claim because the employer showed it investigated the employee's actions in good faith and made a reasonably "informed and considered" decision to fire her. *Hall v. Ohio Bell Telephone Co.*, 529 Fed.Appx. 434 (6th Cir. 2013).

◆   A sales employee in Texas took her entire 12 weeks of FMLA leave in one three-month block to care for her sick daughter. After she returned, her job performance slipped and she continued to miss time from work. She was eventually terminated, and she sued under the FMLA. The Fifth Circuit affirmed a federal district court's ruling that she failed to show the employer retaliated against her for taking FMLA leave. The evidence showed the employee was fired for poor job performance and not because she took FMLA leave. *Lorentz v. Alcon Laboratories, Inc.*, 535 Fed.Appx. 319 (5th Cir. 2013).

◆   A New Jersey nurse took extensive leave under the FMLA. She missed deadlines for submitting paperwork related to the leave, and she handed in forms that were incomplete or inaccurate. Her employer alerted her when her paperwork was insufficient, sent her forms when she missed deadlines, and applied FMLA leave retroactively when she failed to make a timely request for it. She was fired after her FMLA leave ran out, and she failed to submit required forms in support of a request for additional personal leave. **She claimed the employer illegally retaliated against her for taking FMLA leave by repeatedly rejecting her paperwork**, but a federal district court rejected the claim. Requiring an employee to clarify information on FMLA certification forms is not an adverse action. *Ehling v. Monmouth-Ocean Hospital Service Corp.*, 961 F.Supp.2d 659 (D.N.J. 2013).

◆   An Iowa claims supervisor with a history of unexcused absences also took intermittent FMLA leave for a bad back. After several years of continuing unexcused absenteeism, the company fired her following two days of no call/no show absenteeism. She sued under the FMLA, claiming that the company failed to include 18 hours of FMLA time from the previous year in its calculation of unexcused absenteeism. A federal court and the Eighth Circuit ruled against her. **She failed to show that the mistake about the 18 hours caused or influenced the decision to issue her an excessive absenteeism warning** and then fire her. *Lovland v. Employers Mutual Casualty Co.*, 674 F.3d 806 (8th Cir. 2012).

◆   The American Medical Association (AMA) decided to lay off more than 100 employees. One of the employees selected for layoff was a director who was planning to take FMLA leave for a knee replacement. He sued. An Illinois federal court granted pretrial judgment to the AMA, but the Seventh Circuit found issues of fact that required a trial. **The AMA had provided inconsistent explanations for the director's layoff as well as backdated notes of a meeting about the layoff** and an email by the director's boss apologizing for his "11th hour change of heart" about recommending the director for termination instead of another candidate he initially recommended. *Shaffer v. American Medical Ass'n*, 662 F.3d 439 (7th Cir. 2011).

◆   An Indiana machine operator with bouts of leg pain and anxiety saw a physician every two or three months and took medication for his conditions. He missed a lot of work. One day, he missed an entire shift to go to his doctor's office and get a prescription for a refill, as well as to go to an appointment at a clinic 25 miles away. There was some question as to whether he asked for just the afternoon off or his entire shift. The company fired him for having too many absences in a four-month period, and he sued under the FMLA. A federal court and the Seventh Circuit ruled for the company, noting that **missing work to get a prescription filled wasn't covered by the FMLA**. This was not treatment. *Jones v. C&D Technologies, Inc.*, 684 F.3d 673 (7th Cir. 2012).

◆   A Kansas employee with a history of job-related problems, including tardiness, applied for two months of FMLA leave to have surgery on a bunion in February. Her doctor submitted a note stating that the surgery was serious and that she would need two months to recuperate. Eventually, an HR assistant informed the employee that FMLA leave would be approved. The company later sent her a letter notifying her that her leave was approved and would extend to April 1. She claimed she never got this letter and did not call in her absences from work on April 2, 3 and 4. The company fired her for violating its call-in policy. When she sued under the FMLA, she lost. A federal court and the Tenth Circuit held that **she was properly fired for violating the call-in policy**. *Twigg v. Hawker Beechcraft Corp.*, 659 F.3d 987 (10th Cir. 2011).

◆   An Illinois employee took 12 weeks of leave under the FMLA for his gastric reflux disease. When he returned to work, he was assigned to a different position because his job had been eliminated during his leave. He claimed that his supervisor harassed him for taking the leave, which resulted in him having to take another five-month leave for surgery, then a third leave for another surgery. After he was fired, he sued under the FMLA, claiming that the supervisor's harassment exacerbated his condition and made the surgery necessary. However, the Seventh Circuit ruled against him, noting that **the FMLA doesn't concern itself with the cause of an injury**. He exhausted his available leave under the statute and thus was not entitled to recover any damages. *Breneisen v. Motorola, Inc.*, 656 F.3d 701 (7th Cir. 2011).

◆   An Arkansas employee got in a car accident and suffered injuries that left him in considerable pain. A month later, he took leave and sought treatment. The company mistakenly told him he was eligible for FMLA leave even though he wasn't yet eligible. After a couple of surgeries, he still wasn't able to return to work. Several months later, the company fired him for job abandonment and he sued. The case reached the Eighth Circuit, which ruled against him. **It didn't matter which eligibility date was used for FMLA purposes because he wasn't able to work after the expiration of either period.** *Hearst v. Progressive Foam Technologies, Inc.*, 641 F.3d 276 (8th Cir. 2011).

◆   A housekeeper for a hospital in Arkansas submitted a request for FMLA leave because she needed back surgery. The hospital's HR director allegedly discouraged her from taking the leave by telling her not to talk to anyone about the fact that she had been informed of her rights under the FMLA. Also, **her immediate supervisor called her weekly while she was out to find out when she was coming back to work**. After she returned to work, the hospital fired her for allegedly attempting to steal money from a co-worker. When she sued under the FMLA, a federal court held that she presented enough evidence of interference with her FMLA rights to warrant a trial. However, the hospital's decision to fire her, even though made without proof, was not retaliatory because it sincerely believed she had tried to steal the money. *Terwilliger v. Howard Memorial Hospital*, 770 F.Supp.2d 980 (W.D. Ark. 2011).

♦   A Michigan Kmart employee took FMLA leave for surgery. While she was gone, the company instituted a reduction in force (RIF). Her store manager rated her poorly and noted that she was on leave. As a result, Kmart laid her off. She sued under the FMLA, claiming that her earlier evaluations rated her as meeting or exceeding expectations, and noting that if she had been rated consistently with the earlier evaluations, she wouldn't have been selected for the RIF. A federal court granted pretrial judgment to Kmart, but the Sixth Circuit reversed, finding issues of fact that required a trial. **A jury could consider Kmart's claim that her manager rated her higher in earlier evaluations to avoid confrontation.** *Cutcher v. Kmart Corp.*, 364 Fed.Appx. 183 (6th Cir. 2010).

♦   For years, an insurance company employee in Pennsylvania worked extra hours outside the office. For a time, her supervisor allowed her to accrue "comp" time for them. At one point, she began working part time to care for a daughter with Down syndrome. Three weeks after she asked for FMLA leave to prepare her daughter for school, she was fired. When she sued under the FMLA, the insurer asserted that she had been fired for using profanity to describe the company on a phone call and that she'd worked only 1,222 hours in the prior year. It claimed she'd been told not to work any extra hours. A federal court granted pretrial judgment to the insurer, but the Third Circuit reversed. It noted that the 77 extra hours the employee worked at home should not necessarily have been discounted. She had sent a new supervisor an email seeking clarification on whether she could continue to work extra hours and never received a reply. Thus, **she might be able to show that the insurer did not clearly ban her from working the extra hours, in which case she would meet the 1,250-hour threshold**. *Erdman v. Nationwide Insurance Co.*, 582 F.3d 500 (3d Cir. 2009).

♦   A vice president of information technology at a nonprofit in Indiana was disciplined for sending abusive emails to several employees. He was also told that due to pressing business, he could not take a monthlong vacation he had planned. He immediately left work, saw his doctor and returned with a request for FMLA leave, which the nonprofit granted. While he was out, the nonprofit discovered multiple problems with its computer system and fired him. He sued under the FMLA and lost. A federal court and the Seventh Circuit ruled that **the nonprofit would have fired him had he not taken leave** and that it could do so despite his taking the leave. *Daugherty v. Wabash Center, Inc.*, 577 F.3d 747 (7th Cir. 2009).

♦   A New Jersey employee fell outside her doctor's office and developed pregnancy complications. She missed work from July to December and resumed working in January. At the end of April, she injured her back at work and was absent until she was terminated in October for violating the company's no-fault leave policy. She sued, claiming the company violated the FMLA, but a federal court and the Third Circuit ruled against her. First of all, **her FMLA leave expired after 12 weeks**, so only about half of her first leave had been protected. And her second leave didn't fall under the FMLA because she hadn't yet worked the necessary 1,250 hours to qualify. *Smith v. Medpointe Healthcare, Inc.*, 338 Fed.Appx. 230 (3d Cir. 2009).

♦ A Utah company promoted an employee and gave her a $10,000 raise after a competitor offered her a job. She also received many emails praising her performance. But when she told her supervisor she needed six weeks off after a hysterectomy, she was fired the next day. The company claimed she was fired because her subordinates had complained about her, but there were no emails supporting that position. Also, company policy dictated giving employees written warnings before terminating them. When she sued under the FMLA, the Tenth Circuit ruled that she was entitled to a trial. It also noted that the company handbook never mentioned the FMLA, and the supervisor admitted he knew nothing about it until the employee notified him of it. *DeFreitas v. Horizon Investment Management Corp.*, 577 F.3d 1151 (10th Cir. 2009).

♦ A manager for a freight company terminal in Illinois went out on FMLA leave, and the company hired several replacement employees to perform his job duties while he was absent. The replacement employees found several problems with the terminal's management while he was gone. The company's head of operations then investigated and discovered even more problems. On the day the manager returned from FMLA, leave, he was fired. He sued and lost. The Seventh Circuit held that **the FMLA permits an employer to fire an employee based on performance problems it discovers while the employee is on leave**. *Cracco v. Vitran Express, Inc.*, 559 F.3d 625 (7th Cir. 2009).

♦ A North Carolina drug company employee informed his superiors that he needed to make two trips to Russia to complete the adoption process for a baby girl. He took along some drug samples to give to the orphanage, allegedly with the knowledge of his superiors. However, when he returned from his second trip, the company fired him for giving the drug samples to the orphanage. He sued under the FMLA, asserting that the company required him to work one day while he was on leave and **retaliated against him for taking the leave**. A jury ruled in his favor, and a judge awarded him over $700,000 in damages. The Fourth Circuit Court of Appeals upheld the award, noting that the jury had permissibly determined that the drug company had violated the FMLA and that the employee's superiors had known he was donating the samples to the orphanage but never stopped him. *Dotson v. Pfizer, Inc.*, 558 F.3d 284 (4th Cir. 2009).

♦ A Missouri assembly line worker began seeing a chiropractor, who diagnosed him with arthritis, a bulging disc and a lesion on his spine. The worker had attendance problems and received a warning for accumulating absences. He submitted his chiropractor's certification to HR and **continued to miss work even though the certification stated that he was not incapacitated**. The company informed him that any work time he took off before his FMLA request was officially approved would not be protected if his request was ultimately denied. After he was fired for accumulating too many absenteeism points, he sued. A federal court and the Eighth Circuit ruled against him, noting that he should have known his absences weren't covered. *Reed v. Lear Corp.*, 556 F.3d 674 (8th Cir. 2009).

♦   A company in Indiana used a point system to track and discipline employees for absenteeism. A recovering alcoholic employee who had worked there for 15 years was nine points (three absences) short of termination. He had a relapse on a Friday evening, and his wife called the hospital the next day to see if she could bring him in for treatment. He reached his doctor on Wednesday and, after obtaining insurance approval, was admitted to the hospital on Friday. However, he missed three scheduled days of work prior to his admittance. He sought FMLA protection. The company fired him, and he sued. A federal court and the Seventh Circuit ruled against him, noting that **the three days he missed prior to his hospitalization (but after he and his wife contacted his doctor) did not count as "treatment" under the FMLA.** *Darst v. Interstate Brands Corp.*, 512 F.3d 903 (7th Cir. 2008).

VI. ARBITRATION

Arbitration has become a popular method for resolving employment disputes, mainly because of the lower cost as compared to litigation. For cases involving arbitration with respect to labor relations, please see Chapter Five, Section II.F.

To be enforceable, an arbitration agreement has to be fair.

—It cannot place undue costs or obstacles on employees.
—It cannot require a forum that is convenient for the employer without considering the ability of employees to reach that forum.
—It cannot force employees to arbitrate but not make the same requirement of employers.
—It cannot change the law. In other words, it cannot provide less in the way of remedies than employees would be entitled to under federal and state law.

♦   An employer secured a confidentiality and non-competition agreement from two employees. The agreement also included a provision requiring any dispute between the parties to be settled by arbitration. When the employees left for a competitor, the employer sought arbitration. The employees sued in state court, seeking a declaration that the non-competition agreements were invalid. Oklahoma's highest court decided that the agreement was not enforceable. The U.S. Supreme Court vacated and remanded, finding that **attacks on the validity of the agreement were to be resolved by an arbitrator.** *Nitro-Lift Technologies v. Howard*, 133 S.Ct. 500 (2012).

♦   An employee of a rental center in Nevada signed an arbitration agreement as a condition of employment but later sued the center for race discrimination and retaliation under 42 U.S.C. § 1981. The center sought to enforce the agreement under the Federal Arbitration Act while the employee claimed that it was not enforceable because it was unconscionable under state law. The case reached the U.S. Supreme Court, which held that **because the agreement** included a clause allowing the arbitrator to determine the enforceability of the agreement, an arbitrator would have to make that determination. Had the employee challenged the provision granting the arbitrator that authority, a court would have been able to rule on that issue. *Rent-A-Center, West, Inc. v. Jackson*, 561 U.S. 63, 130 S.Ct. 2772, 177 L.Ed.2d 403 (2010).

• As a condition of employment, a South Carolina man signed an arbitration agreement (agreeing to arbitrate employment-related disputes). He then began work as a grill operator for a restaurant. Sixteen days later, he suffered a seizure at work and was discharged shortly thereafter. He did not initiate arbitration proceedings, but instead filed a disability discrimination charge with the Equal Employment Opportunity Commission (EEOC), alleging that his firing violated the Americans with Disabilities Act (ADA). The EEOC filed an action against the restaurant seeking injunctive relief to eradicate past and present unlawful employment practices, and also seeking specific relief to make the employee whole. The employee was not a party to the case. A federal court refused to compel arbitration under the Federal Arbitration Act. The Fourth Circuit held that the arbitration agreement did not prevent the EEOC from bringing the action, but that it could not seek relief for the employee. The U.S. Supreme Court then determined that the EEOC could seek relief on behalf of the employee despite the existence of the arbitration agreement. **The EEOC's statutory right to compel enforcement of Title VII and the ADA is not altered by an arbitration agreement** between employer and employee. *EEOC v. Waffle House, Inc.*, 534 U.S. 279, 122 S.Ct. 754, 151 L.Ed.2d 755 (2002).

• A gay employee of Circuit City claimed that he was subjected to harassment because of his sexual orientation. He quit and sued the company under California law. A federal court ordered him to arbitrate his claim because when he signed the application for the job, he agreed to arbitrate any disputes arising out of or relating to his employment. The Ninth Circuit reversed the order to arbitrate, finding that the Federal Arbitration Act excluded all employment-related agreements from its reach because of language exempting "seamen, railroad employees or any other class of workers engaged in foreign or interstate commerce." The case reached the U.S. Supreme Court, which held that employers could enforce arbitration agreements under the Federal Arbitration Act, even where employees wanted to sue for employment discrimination. **Only transportation employees engaged in interstate or foreign commerce are exempt from the application of the Federal Arbitration Act.** *Circuit City Stores, Inc. v. Adams*, 532 U.S. 105, 121 S.Ct. 1302, 149 L.Ed.2d 234 (2001).

On remand, the Ninth Circuit ruled that the arbitration agreement was not enforceable because it was both procedurally and substantively unconscionable. The agreement was a standard form contract that put the employee in a "take it or leave it" position by conditioning employment on signing the contract. Further, the agreement required employees to arbitrate while not requiring the employer to do so, and made them pay half the arbitrator's fees. *Circuit City Stores, Inc. v. Adams*, 279 F.3d 889 (9th Cir. 2002).

✦   A store manager in New Jersey signed an arbitration agreement. The form she signed in connection with the agreement indicated in bold type that the agreement was "an important legal document." After she was fired, the employee sued the company, alleging race discrimination and other claims. **She said she was not bound by the arbitration agreement because she did not sign it knowingly or voluntarily.** She said the employer did not explain what rights she was giving up. The court rejected her claim that the arbitration agreement was unenforceable. Its terms were clear and conspicuous, and she accepted them. *Fave v. Neiman Marcus Group*, No. A-0, 2014 WL 1884337 (N.J. Super. Ct. App. Div. 5/13/14) (Unpublished).

✦   A homebuilder began requiring employees to sign arbitration agreements that banned class action arbitrations. An employee challenged the ban, and the NLRB agreed that it violated the NLRA. However, **a federal appeals court refused to enforce the NLRB's ruling**. It found that the agency's order was contrary to the Federal Arbitration Act, which requires that arbitration agreements be enforced unless a conflicting statute says otherwise. Nothing suggested that the NLRA should override the Federal Arbitration Act in this case, the court said. *D.R. Horton, Inc. v. National Labor Relations Board*, 737 F.3d 344 (5th Cir. 2013).

✦   A Washington Macy's employee injured herself at work. She filed a workers' compensation form, then claimed that Macy's retaliated against her and eventually fired her. When she sued, Macy's asserted that she had to submit to arbitration because she had not opted out of it when she completed most of the new-hire paperwork electronically. **It provided her e-signature as evidence that she had filled out the paperwork without opting out of arbitration.** However, the Washington Court of Appeals found that the electronic signature wasn't sufficient to prove that she hadn't opted out. Macy's couldn't prove that only she had access to the information (Social Security number, birth date, zip code) that comprised the e-signature. Her claim that a Macy's employee could have back-dated the documents required a trial. *Neuson v. Macy's Dep't Stores, Inc.*, 249 P.3d 1054 (Wash. Ct. App. 2011).

✦   An eBay manager in Utah signed **an arbitration agreement requiring both parties to arbitrate any dispute arising from their relationship, including those under Title VII and the ADEA**. After eBay fired the manager, he sued it for violating Title VII and the ADEA. A federal court compelled arbitration, and the Tenth Circuit Court of Appeals affirmed that decision. Even though the agreement permitted the arbitrator to award costs to the prevailing party, which meant that it violated public policy, that provision could be severed from the agreement as a whole. As a result, the remainder of the agreement was enforceable, and the manager had to arbitrate his claims. *Kepas v. eBay*, 412 Fed.Appx. 40 (10th Cir. 2010).

✦   A Michigan husband and wife applied for paramedic positions with a nonprofit organization and filled out applications, which included a section stating that all employment-related disputes would be exclusively reviewed by a grievance review board. Nearly a month after they were hired, they attended an orientation at which they received information about arbitration procedures. When the husband was later fired, he and his wife sued. The employer asserted that they had to arbitrate their claims, but the Sixth Circuit disagreed. It held that the husband and wife **did not knowingly, intelligently and voluntarily sign the waivers included in their employment applications** because they were not given any information about the grievance review board procedures. Thus, their lawsuit could proceed. *Alonso v. Huron Valley Ambulance, Inc.*, 375 Fed.Appx. 487 (6th Cir. 2010).

♦ A Texas employee hit his head on a pipe and sustained spine injuries. He filed a workers' compensation claim and received physical therapy. A month later he told his supervisor his neck was still bothering him. He was fired the next day and sued for retaliatory discharge under the state's workers' compensation statute. The company asserted that he had to arbitrate his claims. The case eventually reached the Supreme Court of Texas, which noted that **even though there was an invalid provision in the arbitration agreement, that provision could be severed and the employee could be required to arbitrate his claim**. The invalid provision prohibited the employee from receiving punitive damages or reinstatement, both of which were available remedies under the law, and the company could not force the employee to waive those substantive rights. The court remanded the case for arbitration. *In re Poly-America*, 262 S.W.3d 337 (Tex. 2008).

♦ Jack-in-the-Box representatives met with some Missouri employees to discuss a dispute resolution agreement that required arbitration of any claims made against the company. One employee allegedly refused to sign the agreement, but his misspelled signature appeared on one form along with his Social Security number, which was off by two numbers. He continued to work for the company until he was fired, at which time he sued for age and gender discrimination. The company sought to force him to arbitrate his claims, but the Missouri Court of Appeals held that **his continued work for the company did not necessarily mean he agreed to be bound by the arbitration clause**. It could also have been a counteroffer to continue working under the old conditions, which the company accepted by not firing him. A trial was required. *Kunzie v. Jack-in-the-Box, Inc.*, 330 S.W.3d 476 (Mo. Ct. App. 2010).

♦ A Michigan car dealership created a binding arbitration agreement for its employees, **requiring them to deposit $500 or five days' pay with the general manager within 10 days after the third stage of the arbitration process**. The agreement allowed employees to seek a waiver of part or all their financial obligation so long as the request was made within that same 10-day period. After an employee who earned $10 an hour was fired, he sued the dealership, which asserted that he was required to arbitrate his claims. A federal court found the $500 deposit prohibitively expensive, but the Sixth Circuit Court of Appeals disagreed. Even though the dealership had the sole authority to grant waivers, its attorney indicated that the dealership would likely waive or reduce the deposit, making the cost-splitting arrangement valid. *Mazera v. Varsity Ford Services LLC*, 565 F.3d 997 (6th Cir. 2009).

◆   A company in Virginia entered into an agreement with an executive, in which the parties agreed that all disputes would be resolved by arbitration and that any arbitration award would be considered "final" for purposes of a judicial proceeding to enforce the award. However, the agreement did not state that a court could enter judgment on an arbitrator's award. An arbitrator awarded the company $300,000 after finding that the executive was developing his own business while working for the company. The executive then argued that a court could not enter judgment on the award because of the missing clause. The Fourth Circuit disagreed. **The parties agreed to abide by the Judicial Arbitration and Mediation Services' rules**, which authorized judicial enforcement. So despite the missing clause, the award was enforceable by a court. *Qorvis Communications, LLC v. Wilson*, 549 F.3d 303 (4th Cir. 2008).

◆   A Nebraska insurance company employee signed an agreement to arbitrate any employment-related claims against the company. She later filed charges with the EEOC, claiming sexual harassment by male subordinates. The EEOC brought a Title VII enforcement action and she sought to intervene in the case. The Eighth Circuit held that she could not do so. Although she had filed for Chapter 7 bankruptcy and could no longer afford her half of the arbitration fee, her employer had agreed to pay both halves and, even if it hadn't, **she could still be compelled to arbitrate her Title VII claims**. *EEOC v. Woodmen of the World Life Insurance Society*, 479 F.3d 561 (8th Cir. 2007).

◆   An Oklahoma pawnshop and check-cashing store introduced a mandatory dispute resolution program requiring employees to resolve their employment disputes through arbitration. The company made clear that **any employee who remained with the company after March 1, 2003 would be deemed to have accepted the arbitration program**. A manager who explicitly rejected the arbitration language nonetheless continued to work for the company. After she was fired, she tried to sue for sex discrimination, but the Tenth Circuit Court of Appeals held that because she had continued to work for the company, she was required to arbitrate her claim. *Hardin v. First Cash Financial Services, Inc.*, 465 F.3d 470 (10th Cir. 2006).

◆   A new employee of a staffing firm in Washington, D.C., signed **an arbitration agreement that prohibited the awarding of punitive damages** in any proceeding required by the agreement. It also contained a severability clause, stating that if any part of the agreement were ruled to be invalid, that part would be severed from the rest of the agreement, which would continue to remain in effect. When the employee later sued for race discrimination, seeking punitive damages, the firm sought to compel arbitration. The U.S. Court of Appeals, D.C. Circuit, severed the invalid punitive damages waiver and ordered arbitration. *Booker v. Robert Half Int'l*, 413 F.3d 77 (D.C. Cir. 2005).

◆   A company in Massachusetts created a new dispute resolution policy and sent out a mass email, referring employees to two links at the bottom of the message. The message informed employees they were covered by the new policy if they continued working after the policy's effective date, and warning that the company would seek to dismiss any employment-related lawsuit they might file. When an employee with sleep apnea was fired for too many absences, he sued under the ADA, and the company sought to compel arbitration. A federal court and the First Circuit refused to do so. Here, **the mass email did not mention the mandatory arbitration procedure in the body of the message**. Nor did it require employees to respond with an acknowledgement that they had read and understood the policy's terms. It also did not mention that the new policy would become automatically binding on any employee who showed up for work the next day. *Campbell v. General Dynamics Government Systems Corp.*, 407 F.3d 546 (1st Cir. 2005).

* Employees of a restaurant chain in Tennessee brought a lawsuit to collect overtime they believed they were owed under the Fair Labor Standards Act. The restaurant asserted that the employees were bound by the arbitration agreements they had signed and thus could not sue. The case reached the Sixth Circuit, which ruled that **the arbitration agreements were not enforceable**. Here, the restaurant did not allow enough time for job applicants to review the arbitration agreements; they were not allowed to take the agreements home to review them; and the agreements failed to explicitly state that applicants were giving up their right to a jury trial by signing the agreements. This was not a knowing and voluntary waiver. Also, although applicants were required to arbitrate their claims against the company, the restaurant was not required to arbitrate its claims against employees. *Walker v. Ryan's Family Steak Houses, Inc.*, 400 F.3d 370 (6th Cir. 2005).

VII. OTHER EMPLOYMENT PRACTICES CASES

Any employment practice can lead to litigation. Thus, employers should try to implement practices and policies that will minimize the chances of being sued. Start with:

—written job descriptions,
—flexible disciplinary procedures,
—consistent application of company rules,
—a good handbook that contains anti-harassment policies, and
—an awareness of what the law allows and prohibits.

* A New Jersey county enacted **a living wage ordinance** affecting businesses that contracted with the county to provide home healthcare, food and janitorial services. Under the ordinance, the contractors had to provide their employees with health benefits and pay them 150% of the federal minimum wage. A lawsuit ensued, and the Superior Court, Appellate Division, held that the ordinance did not violate the contractors' constitutional right to equal protection by arbitrarily imposing requirements on some businesses but not others. The county had a legitimate interest in increasing the standard of living for low-wage workers while decreasing the tax burden of caring for the uninsured. *Visiting Homemaker Service of Hudson County v. Board of Chosen Freeholders*, 883 A.2d 1074 (N.J. Super. Ct. App. Div. 2005).

◆   An engineer worked at Intel for nine years until he was fired. He then joined with several other former and current Intel employees in forming an organization that was critical of Intel's employment policies. He became the organization's spokesperson and, in a 21-month period, sent out six mass emails on behalf of the organization to employee addresses on Intel's email system. Besides criticizing Intel policies, the emails also suggested moving to other companies and joining the organization. Intel demanded that he stop sending the messages through its computer system. He refused, and it sued him for trespass. The case reached the Supreme Court of California, which ruled that **Intel could not succeed in its trespass lawsuit because the unwanted emails caused no property damage** to the company's computer system. Here, the harm Intel claimed to have suffered (lost productivity from employees reading and reacting to the emails) was not an injury to the company's interest in its computers. *Intel Corp. v. Hamidi*, 71 P.3d 296 (Cal. 2003).

◆   A Wal-Mart employee was fired after the company's loss prevention district supervisor determined that she had removed store property without authorization. The investigating supervisor obtained statements from several witnesses and also interviewed the employee, who wrote a two-page statement. After losing her job, the employee wrote to the store manager explaining her version of the events. She requested a copy of her personnel file and the documents relating to the investigation. Wal-Mart gave her copies of the documents in her personnel file, but did not give her any of the documents relating to the supervisor's investigation. The supervisor kept those documents in his home office. The employee sued under a Maine law requiring disclosure of "formal or informal employee evaluations and reports relating to the employee's character, credit, work habits, compensation and benefits."

A court determined that the investigation records were components of her personnel file pursuant to the statute and that Wal-Mart should have produced them. It ordered the documents to be disclosed and fined the company $500. The Supreme Judicial Court of Maine upheld the ruling in favor of the employee. It noted that **the statute did not limit disclosure to those documents actually placed in the employee's personnel file**, but rather included all employee records in the employer's possession. Even though Wal-Mart had sought to maintain witness confidentiality and protect itself from releasing possibly defamatory statements, it was required by law to disclose the documents. *Harding v. Wal-Mart Stores*, 765 A.2d 73 (Me. 2001).

◆   An engineer working in the Denver office of an international petroleum company requested and was given a five-month unpaid educational leave so that he could attend a semester of classes on a full-time basis. He signed a memorandum stating that there was no guarantee a position would be available when he returned, and that he would be considered for open positions, but that the company was under no obligation to hire him for them. However, his supervisor allegedly told him that he could return to his old job any time. During his leave, the company reduced part of its work force and informed the engineer that his position had been eliminated. He turned down a temporary job and an offer to relocate to Houston, and the company fired him. A federal court ruled for the company, and the U.S. Court of Appeals, Tenth Circuit, affirmed. The general rule in Colorado is that **there can be no implied promise where an express contract covers the same subject**. Here, because the written memo expressly outlined the terms of unpaid leave, there could be no implied promise from the engineer's supervisor that he could return to his old job any time. *Flint v. Amoco Corp.*, 173 F.3d 863 (10th Cir. 1999) (Unpublished).

A. Discrimination and Nepotism

The following cases address discrimination issues other than those presented in Chapter One. For example, some states' civil rights laws protect against marital status or sexual orientation discrimination.

Appearance and dress code policies are generally permissible as long as they are not used in a discriminatory manner. For example, it may not be appropriate to ban cornrows because such a policy might be construed to have a discriminatory impact on African-Americans.

Nepotism (hiring family, friends and insiders) can be illegal where it leads to discrimination against protected minorities.

Anti-nepotism policies are generally legal. Only where they are used as a means of discriminating against protected minorities are they likely to be struck down.

♦   A longtime employee of a company in Florida married one of the company's three operating partners and was then fired. She sued, alleging she had been fired because of her marital status in violation of the state's Civil Rights Act, which bars marital status discrimination. However, the Florida District Court of Appeal ruled against her, noting that **the reason for her termination was not her marital status, but rather the specific identity of her spouse** – one of three hands-on partners who operated the business. The court noted that she was replaced in her job by another married woman, undermining her marital status claim. *Industrial Affiliates, Ltd. v. Fish*, 25 So.3d 629 (Fla. Dist. Ct. App. 2009).

♦   A Minnesota company fired a husband and wife who worked as managers. The wife claimed that the CEO told her he was eliminating her position because he expected her to relocate with her husband. She **sued for marital status discrimination**, and a trial court dismissed the lawsuit. However, the Minnesota Court of Appeals reversed, allowing the case to go to trial. State law prohibits discrimination based on the "identity and situation" of the employee's spouse. As a result, the wife was entitled to proceed with her lawsuit. *Taylor v. LSI Corp. of America*, 781 N.W.2d 912 (Minn. Ct. App. 2010).

♦   A native Alaskan, who was a member of the Kenaitze tribe, wore his hair long. He worked for a supermarket that had a dress code/grooming policy requiring men to wear their hair no longer than collar length. However, he was told that if he kept his hair tied back, he would not have to cut it. After he'd been on the job for more than two years, the store was sold, then closed. He was offered a transfer to another location, but only if he cut his hair. He refused to do so and was fired. When he sued, his constitutional claims failed because there was no state action. He also alleged a breach of the covenant of good faith and fair dealing, but lost that claim too. The company had a legitimate reason for its grooming policy, and **the employee never claimed, prior to his discharge, that he had religious reasons for wearing his hair long**. Further, his constitutionally protected liberty and privacy interest in wearing his hair long was outweighed by the company's legitimate interest in its grooming policy. *Miller v. Safeway, Inc.*, 170 P.3d 655 (Alaska 2007).

♦   A country club in Michigan refused to renew the contract of its golf professional after he moved out of his marital home and began having an adulterous affair with a married woman. He sued for marital status discrimination, claiming that the nonrenewal of his contract violated the state's Civil Rights Act. The case reached the Supreme Court of Michigan, which noted that **an employee who is fired solely because of conduct such as adultery is not protected by the Civil Rights Act**. However, because there was some evidence that the country club may have considered the golf pro's marital status in addition to the adultery when it made the decision not to renew the contract, the case was remanded for further consideration. *Veenstra v. Washtenaw Country Club*, 645 N.W.2d 643 (Mich. 2002).

♦   An employer belonging to the National Association of Securities Dealers (NASD) sold securities registered with the SEC. NASD requires all employees who participate in securities sales to be individually registered, and in order to obtain registration, agents must have no statutory disqualification. A felony conviction within 10 years of an application is a statutory disqualification unless an employer is willing to undertake certain obligations, such as paying substantial fees and making daily reviews of the applicant's securities work. An employer rejected an applicant based on his three-year-old conviction for helping deliver a controlled substance. He filed a complaint with the state Department of Industry, Labor and Human Relations. A hearing officer found no discrimination because, based on his NASD disqualification, he was not qualified for the position. She held that an employer need not accommodate an applicant's conviction record. The applicant appealed. The Court of Appeals of Wisconsin agreed with the administrative finding that **an employment applicant must be qualified for a position in order to trigger statutory protections against unlawful discrimination**. The employer gave a legitimate, nondiscriminatory reason for refusing to hire felons based on its previous problems with NASD compliance prior to instituting its policy. Its refusal to voluntarily take steps which might have made him employable did not transform him into a qualified applicant, and nothing in Wisconsin law mandated such action. The court affirmed the ruling for the employer. *Knight v. Labor and Industry Review Comm'n*, 582 N.W.2d 448 (Wis. Ct. App. 1998).

◆   Washington's Law Against Discrimination prohibits employment discrimination based on marital status. A title company employee began to experience conflicts with her co-workers as a result of her husband's conduct. Her husband was an independent contractor who provided the company with janitorial services. A co-worker obtained a restraining order against him, and the company manager warned the employee, co-worker and husband that they would all be fired if they could not work together. The co-worker later complained of an obscene phone call by the husband, and the manager fired the employee and co-worker, and terminated the janitorial contract. The employee sued for discrimination based on marital status. The case reached the Supreme Court of Washington, where the employee argued that **marital status discrimination under state law included actions based on a spouse's misconduct**. The court agreed with the employee, stating that the law against discrimination was to be broadly construed to prohibit discrimination on the status of being married or single. This included the conduct of an employee's spouse. Because the question of discrimination should have been resolved by a jury, the trial court had improperly granted pretrial judgment to the company. *Magula v. Benton Franklin Title Co., Inc.*, 930 P.2d 307 (Wash. 1997).

B. Privacy Rights

Many states recognize a right of privacy. At times, employment policies will come into conflict with this right. For example, where a company official tells a prospective employer about a former company employee, there might be a defamation claim or an invasion of privacy claim brought.

Invasion of privacy lawsuits are difficult for employees to win, but the cost of defending them can be high. Thus, the dissemination of personal information about employees should be strictly forbidden.

◆   A New York employee fell off her chair at work and sued both her employer and the maker of the chair for her injuries, claiming that she was bed-ridden and confined to her home. However, her public Facebook and MySpace pages showed her engaging in an active lifestyle, including trips to Pennsylvania and Florida during the time of her supposed confinement. A state court **ordered her to give Facebook and MySpace written permission to allow her employer to review her private pages** on the social media sites to determine if they contained information contradicting her claims. *Romano v. Steelcase, Inc.*, 907 N.Y.S.2d 650 (N.Y. Sup. Ct. 2010).

◆   An Ohio claims adjuster joined a class action lawsuit against her employer under the Equal Pay Act. Her supervisor then allegedly began retaliating against her. Her attorneys asked her to provide any documentation that related in any way to the litigation. She gave confidential insurance files to the attorneys, even though the files had nothing to do with her case, because she thought the files might help "jog" her memory. When the company discovered the wrongdoing, it fired her. She sued for retaliation and lost. A federal court and the Sixth Circuit ruled that **the company properly fired her for violating**

its privacy policy. *Niswander v. The Cincinnati Insurance Co.*, 529 F.3d 714 (6th Cir. 2008).

1. Invasion of Privacy

There are basically four types of invasion of privacy:

1) appropriation of an employee's name or picture for commercial advantage,
2) intrusion by an employer upon an employee's private affairs or seclusion,
3) publication by an employer of facts placing an employee in a false light, and
4) public disclosure of private facts about an employee.

The most common types of invasion of privacy claims employers face are false light claims (putting the employee in a false light) and lawsuits alleging public disclosure of private facts.

♦   NASA's jet propulsion laboratory (a federal contractor) in California required its employees to complete a new background check asking whether they had used or been treated for using illegal drugs, and also asking their references whether they had any reason to question the employees' honesty, trustworthiness, financial integrity and mental or emotional stability. A group of 28 employees sued, claiming that NASA's new requirement violated their privacy rights. The U.S. Supreme Court ruled that **the questions about drug use did not violate any constitutional right to privacy**. And the open-ended questions to the employees' references did not violate any constitutional privacy right either. *National Aeronautics and Space Administration v. Nelson*, 131 S.Ct. 746, 178 L.Ed.2d 667 (U.S. 2011).

♦   During a team-building retreat, **two vice presidents of a company took photos of an employee in his underwear** in the hotel room he was sharing with one of the vice presidents – passed out after drinking too much. The vice presidents also invited male and female employees into the room to have a look at him. He awoke with no memory of what happened, but learned of the pictures later. He quit and sued the company and the vice presidents – one of whom had been fired and the other reprimanded – for invasion of privacy. A court granted pretrial judgment to the defendants, but the Arkansas Court of Appeals reversed, finding issues of fact that required a trial. The vice presidents may have been acting within the scope of their employment when they took the photos, and the company could be liable if that was the case. *Coombs v. J.B. Hunt Transport, Inc.*, 388 S.W.3d 456 (Ark. Ct. App. 2012).

♦   The CEO of a Georgia printing company read a manager's emails from the manager's personal laptop while investigating rumors that the manager had violated the company's non-compete policy. The manager used the laptop at work to conduct company business. After the emails confirmed that the manager was working for a competing business on the side, he was fired. He sued for invasion of privacy and computer theft under state law but lost. The Georgia Court of Appeals held that **the CEO had the authority to inspect the laptop pursuant to the company's computer usage policy**, which the manager had agreed to when he started the job. Further, the CEO did not unreasonably intrude on the manager's privacy. Also, there was no violation of the computer theft statute. *Sitton v. Print Direction, Inc.*, 718 S.E.2d 532 (Ga. Ct. App. 2011).

♦   A Muslim at a Pennsylvania company broke his hand and sought workers' compensation benefits. His employer's insurer hired an investigator to conduct surveillance on him, and the investigator filmed him praying at an Islamic center, which had windows to the outside, through which the employee was clearly visible to the investigator in the parking lot. The employee became upset about the surveillance and sued the investigator and his employer for invasion of privacy. The Superior Court of Pennsylvania ruled against him, noting that **he did not have a reasonable expectation of privacy while praying in public**. It also noted that he had a reduced expectation of privacy because he'd filed a workers' compensation claim. *Tagouma v. Investigative Consultant Services, Inc.*, 4 A.3d 170 (Pa. Super. 2010).

♦   A computer specialist for a children's center in California determined that numerous pornographic websites had been viewed late at night from a computer lab and a clerical employee's computer. Because the computer lab was too busy to be monitored properly, the center's director installed a surveillance camera behind the clerk's computer to catch the perpetrator. The director didn't suspect the clerk and never activated the camera while she was working. When she and her office mate found the camera, the director removed it, explaining why the camera had been placed there in the first place. The clerk and her office mate sued for invasion of privacy, but the Supreme Court of California ruled against them. It noted that **the surveillance was narrowly tailored** to address legitimate business concerns, and it was limited in place, time and scope. *Hernandez v. Hillsides, Inc.*, 211 P.3d 1063 (Cal. 2009).

♦   A New Jersey employee used a company computer to access her private email account and send messages to her attorney about her intent to sue the company. After she resigned and brought the lawsuit, the company extracted and created a forensic image of the hard drive from her computer. Its attorney discovered and read a number of emails between the employee and her attorney. When the employee and her attorney learned of that fact, they asked the company to return the originals and all copies of the communications. The company refused, and a trial court ruled for the company. However, an appellate court reversed, holding that **the company's broad monitoring policy had to give way to the attorney-client privilege**. *Stengart v. Loving Care Agency, Inc.*, 973 A.2d 390 (N.J. Super. Ct. App. Div. 2009).

♦   An employee of an Ohio company had her ribs broken by her live-in boyfriend, who also worked for the company. The police were called, and the boyfriend was convicted of domestic violence. While on probation, he was arrested again. The company learned of the domestic violence conviction and, pursuant to its anti-violence policy, questioned the employee on several occasions about whether the boyfriend was a threat. She was uncooperative. It fired the boyfriend and asked the employee to notify it if he made threats against it or its employees. She refused to do so and was fired. When she sued it for violating her privacy rights, she lost. **She failed to show that the questions intruded into her private life or that her answers were substantially certain to become public knowledge outside the company.** *Rowe v. Guardian Automotive Products, Inc.,* No. 3:04CV7145, 2005 WL 3299766 (N.D. Ohio 12/6/05).

2. Wiretapping and Stored Communications

Wiretapping is generally illegal under the federal Omnibus Crime Control and Safe Streets Act. However, the act creates an exception for conversations that are recorded by the user of communication services in the ordinary course of business.

The act also creates an exception for a person who "is a party to the communication or where one of the parties to the communication has given prior consent to such interception."

♦   The food service director for an elder care company quit after she reported harassment by her supervisor, and the company's investigation revealed no wrongdoing. Though she used only the company's Comcast account for work emails, her replacement searched 36 of her personal emails from her AOL account – which she kept on her work computer – to make sure no vendor orders slipped through the cracks. Her replacement also printed emails she sent from her AOL account after leaving the job (that had nothing to do with work) and shared them with a superior, who shared them with a board member and the company's attorneys. She sued the company for violating the Stored Communications Act. A state court granted pretrial judgment to the company, but the Appellate Court of Illinois held that **the company may have gone too far in its search of her private emails** and thus violated the federal electronic privacy law. *Borchers v. Franciscan Tertiary Province of the Sacred Heart, Inc.,* 962 N.E.2d 29 (Ill. App. Ct. 2011).

♦   An employee at an executive search firm in California left to start a competing business. He convinced some former colleagues, who were still working there, to assist him. They used their passwords to download information from a confidential database and transferred the information to him. The government later prosecuted him for trade secret theft, mail fraud, conspiracy and violating the Computer Fraud and Abuse Act (CFAA). A federal court dismissed the charges under the CFAA, and the Ninth Circuit affirmed. It disagreed with holdings by the Fifth, Seventh and Eleventh Circuits and found **the CFAA was meant to outlaw hackers and thus couldn't be used to prosecute the former employee in this case.** *U.S. v. Nosal,* 676 F.3d 854 (9th Cir. 2012).

• While dictating a report, two department heads at an Illinois hospital turned off the recorder and began criticizing the hospital's planned reorganization. The employee in charge of transcription then entered the office and allegedly turned the recorder back on while picking up some papers. She denied doing so. After the recording of their later conversation was transcribed, they were disciplined. They sued under the Wiretap Act, which prohibits intentionally intercepting oral conversation and intentionally disclosing the conversation while knowing it was unlawfully intercepted. A federal court granted pretrial judgment to the hospital, but the Seventh Circuit reversed, finding issues of fact that required a trial over **whether the employee activated the recorder so as to intentionally eavesdrop**. It was significant that the recording did not record the whole of their conversation but rather picked up their voices in mid-conversation. *McCann v. Iroquois Memorial Hospital*, 622 F.3d 745 (7th Cir. 2010).

• A New Jersey restaurant employee showed a supervisor (who was also a friend) a website created by a co-worker to vent against management. The website contained ethnic slurs, derogatory sexual comments and information confidential to management. Later, another supervisor asked her to provide her password so the site could be accessed. The employee provided it, and the co-worker who set up the site was fired. He sued the restaurant for violating the Stored Communications Act, which prohibits intentionally accessing electronically stored information without authorization to do so. A jury awarded him $12,500 in compensatory and punitive damages. The restaurant moved for a new trial, but the court refused to grant the motion. **The jury believed that the employee had been coerced by the second supervisor to provide her password**, making the access of the site unauthorized and intentional. *Pietrylo v. Hillstone Restaurant Group*, No. 06-5754 (FSH), 2009 WL 3128420 (D.N.J. 9/25/09).

• The president of a company in Rhode Island surreptitiously monitored certain employees' phone calls and fired a vice president who used "salty language" to describe him to a colleague. The vice president then sued the company for violating the federal wiretap statute, 18 U.S.C. § 2510(5)(a), and a corresponding state law. A jury awarded him $50,000 for the violation of federal law and another $25,000 for invasion of privacy. The case reached the Supreme Court of Rhode Island, which held that the monitoring without consent was not within the company's ordinary course of business. Generally, monitoring must be done as part of the ordinary course of business, and the employer must notify the parties or obtain their consent. Thus, **the company violated the wiretap statute and invaded the vice president's privacy**. *Cady v. IMC Mortgage Co.*, 862 A.2d 202 (R.I. 2004).

• A Pennsylvania agent agreed to sell insurance policies as an independent contractor on an exclusive basis for an insurer. The contract was terminable at will. After the agent filed a complaint about the insurer with the state attorney general's office, the insurer performed a search of its main file server for any emails written by or to the agent that might indicate whether he had been revealing company secrets to competitors or violating the exclusivity agreement. It opened emails whose headers contained relevant information, and the attorney testified that the emails confirmed the agent's disloyalty. When it fired the agent, he sued under Title II of the Electronic Communications Privacy Act of 1986 (ECPA). A federal court ruled against him, and the Third Circuit affirmed. Title II of ECPA does not provide privacy protection for emails authorized "by the person or entity providing a wire or electronic communications service." Since the emails were stored on the insurer's own computer system, it could search those emails under the Title II exception. *Fraser v. Nationwide Mutual Insurance Co.*, 352 F.3d 107 (3d Cir. 2003).

◆   A consultant for an annuity association in New York City fielded calls from association clients and was told that his calls would be monitored as a way of evaluating the quality of service the consultants were providing. He was also allegedly told that his personal calls would not be monitored. During a party to celebrate a co-worker's promotion, a team leader exposed himself to the consultant and attempted to kiss him. He told the consultant that **another team leader had monitored one of the consultant's personal phone calls** and learned that he was gay, drank excessively and had problems in his personal life. The consultant complained about the incident and claimed that he was then subjected to retaliation in the form of discipline for tardiness, which had not been the cause of discipline before. He sued the association under federal, state and city law, and most of his claims were dismissed. However, a federal court refused to dismiss his claim against the association for violating the federal Wiretap Act (by intercepting and monitoring a personal call without his consent). A jury would have to decide that issue. *Devlin v. Teachers' Insurance & Annuity Ass'n of America*, No. 02 Civ. 3228 (JSR), 2003 WL 1738969 (S.D.N.Y. 2003).

◆   A New York alarm services company conducted 24-hour recording of incoming and outgoing telephone calls through a machine hooked up to its telephone system. Two employees sued under the federal wiretapping statute (Title III of the Omnibus Crime Control and Safe Streets Act) asserting the illegal interception of their private phone calls without their consent. They claimed that even if the recording was supported by a legitimate business purpose, the company failed to provide notice. The Second Circuit ruled in favor of the company. Although Title III generally prohibits the intentional interception of private phone conversations, it makes an **exception for conversations that are recorded by the user of communication services in the ordinary course of business**. Here, continual recording was standard practice within the central alarm industry because it ensured accurate reporting of emergencies and safeguarded sensitive information. Further, the company's underwriter recommended continual recording and some regulatory authorities even required it. Finally, the company did not violate the law by failing to notify employees that their private conversations were being recorded. *Arias v. Mutual Cent. Alarm Service, Inc.*, 202 F.3d 553 (2d Cir. 2000).

C. Polygraphs

Lie detector tests are generally illegal under the federal Employee Polygraph Protection Act, which forbids an employer from directly or indirectly requiring, requesting, suggesting or causing any employee or prospective employee to take or submit to any lie detector test. Employers also cannot fire or otherwise discipline employees for refusing to take a lie detector test.

There are exceptions for public employers, security providers, power and water facilities, employers dealing with hazardous waste, and employers who are authorized to make, distribute or dispense controlled substances.

♦   After a branch manager for a bank in Georgia was transferred to a new location, his replacement conducted an audit and discovered that $58,000 was missing from the two cash dispenser machines. Fraud investigators looked into the matter and found that surveillance footage showed the former manager had repeatedly violated bank policy by failing to have two employees present when cash was handled or when certain secure areas were accessed. They asked the former manager to take a polygraph, and he refused. The bank then fired him for violating the dual control policy. **He sued under the Employee Polygraph and Protection Act**, but a federal court and the Eleventh Circuit ruled against him. The bank met the four conditions required by the act: 1) it determined that he had access to the property being investigated; 2) it gave him a signed statement detailing his alleged misconduct; 3) it made the request in connection with an ongoing investigation into economic loss; and 4) it had a reasonable suspicion that he was involved. *Cummings v. Washington Mutual*, 650 F.3d 1386 (11th Cir. 2011).

♦   A mail room supervisor for a defense contractor in Florida discovered 14 opened and undelivered Christmas cards in a wastebasket. She told her superior and notified him that a subordinate had been assigned to the front desk that day. He arranged for the subordinate to undergo a polygraph test, which indicated deception when he denied opening the mail. Later, **the company asked all the mail room employees to submit to a polygraph**. The mail room supervisor refused and was fired a week later for allegedly permitting package deliveries through the back door in violation of security procedures. She sued under the Employee Polygraph Protection Act (EPPA). The wrongful discharge claim settled, and the Eleventh Circuit held that the company also had liability under the EPPA for requesting the polygraph. Here, the company failed to show that it had a reasonable suspicion that the supervisor was involved with the wrongdoing. Instead, it sought the polygraph to absolve it of any potential liability for the opened and undelivered Christmas cards. *Polkey v. Transtecs Corp.*, 404 F.3d 1264 (11th Cir. 2005).

♦   The owner of a Florida bar suspected that employees were violating certain employment policies and hired a company to investigate their conduct. An agent for the company observed one employee taking multiple drink orders from different customers without recording them, ringing up no sales on the cash register when cash was taken from customers, and placing money in a tip jar when no sales were registered. Based on the report, the employer asked the employee to take a polygraph examination. She took the examination, then voluntarily resigned and sued the employer for violating the federal EPPA. The court observed that **there had been no improper disclosure of polygraph information by the employer**. Although the owner told other employees that the employee had failed a polygraph test, the comment had come after the filing of the lawsuit. The court rejected the employee's assertion that the employer had no reasonable suspicion giving rise to an investigation since there was evidence of business losses that could be attributable to employees. Although the EPPA forbids an employer from discharging or disciplining an employee for refusal to take a lie detector test, this issue was moot since the employee had voluntarily resigned. The court ruled in favor of the employer. *Long v. Mango's Tropical Cafe, Inc.*, 972 F.Supp. 655 (S.D. Fla. 1997).

◆   An Iowa grocery store employee was suspected of stealing money from a cash register. The store manager called the police. An officer stated that the police would need the store's agreement to examine the suspected employee by polygraph. The employee agreed to take a polygraph test to clear his name. His test results showed emotional distress or deception, and he did not pass the exam. Although no criminal charges were brought against the employee, the store manager and owner decided to take away his cash handling responsibilities and return him to stock work. The employee resigned and sued the store in federal court, alleging violations of the EPPA and state law.

The court noted that **the EPPA prohibits an employer from using, accepting, or inquiring about the results of any lie detector test**, and makes it an unlawful practice to fire, discipline, or discriminate against an employee on the basis of a polygraph test result. Here, while the employer had not required the employee to take the test, it had clearly violated the EPPA by using the test results to discipline him. Conditions at the store became intolerable for the employee, and he was constructively discharged when he was demoted. He was entitled to lost wages plus interest in excess of $22,000. He was also entitled to a $15,000 damage award for emotional distress and attorneys' fees. *Mennen v. Easter Stores*, 951 F.Supp. 838 (N.D. Iowa 1997).

D. Investigations

Employer investigations into employee wrongdoing should be conducted carefully. Employers should include in their handbooks a statement that employees have no right of privacy in their desks, work areas, lockers, etc.

If the employer suspects wrongdoing and has established that employees have no reasonable expectation of privacy, it may conduct a search without prior permission from the employee.

◆   A group of California truck drivers became dissatisfied with their working conditions and began bringing their concerns to their supervisors. They also openly discussed supporting a union. The company then fired four of the most vocal drivers. The regional director of the National Labor Relations Board then petitioned for a temporary injunction ordering that the four employees be offered full interim reinstatement to their prior positions. The company asserted that it had legitimate reasons for firing the four drivers. One left work early without permission, one repeatedly refused to work more than eight hours a day, one submitted a false application that omitted criminal convictions, and the fourth **refused to cooperate into an investigation of vandalism** and was insubordinate. As a result, the federal court refused to grant the temporary injunction. *Small v. Swift Transportation Co., Inc.*, No. CV 09-4751 PSG (FMOX), 2009 WL 3052637 (C.D. Cal. 9/18/09).

◆   The security manager for a medical center was accused of leaving an obscene message on the voice mail of a nurse. When several co-workers identified the speaker as the manager, the medical center began an investigation and submitted the obscene call for voice print analysis. The security manager refused to provide a voice exemplar for testing and was fired. He sued for wrongful discharge, claiming that such testing was prohibited by an Iowa law barring employers from conditioning employment on submission to a polygraph exam. A trial court ruled against the manager, and the Supreme Court of Iowa affirmed. First, **the manager was an at-will employee who could be fired for failing to cooperate in the investigation**. Second, the purpose of the voice print analysis was identification, not verification of truthfulness or deception. Finally, the medical center was not liable for defamation for stating the reason for his discharge and for having a security officer escort him from the building. *Theisen v. Covenant Medical Center, Inc.*, 636 N.W.2d 74 (Iowa 2001).

◆   A 16-year-old Maryland retail store employee was interrogated by store security employees for over four hours. When he sued for false imprisonment, a trial court awarded him $110,000 in compensatory damages and $9 million in punitive damages. The court of appeals noted that the U.S. Supreme Court has held that a punitive damage award cannot be grossly excessive in relation to deterrence and punishment interests. The amount of such an award must not be disproportionate to the harm done or the party's ability to pay the award. Another appropriate consideration is to compare the award with awards in other cases in the jurisdiction in somewhat comparable cases. The court had never upheld a punitive damage award of over $700,000, and the largest possible penalty for any state criminal law violation was $1 million. Most punitive damage awards were for less than $100,000. **Although the interrogation by the security guards was heinous, it was not life threatening**, and the employee had suffered no permanent injuries. The award could not stand. A remand was necessary to determine a proper punitive damages amount. *Bowden v. Caldor, Inc.*, 350 Md. 4, 710 A.2d 267 (Md. 1998).

E. Dress Codes and Personal Appearance

Employers can implement personal appearance and dress code policies so long as they do not more harshly impact one group than another. In other words, the policy can't target women more than men or favor one religion over another.

♦ A Nevada casino instituted a "Personal Best" program under which female bartenders and beverage servers had to wear makeup and nail polish, while male bartenders and beverage servers had to keep their hair short and have clean, trimmed fingernails. A female bartender refused to comply with the makeup policy and never applied for a position that did not require makeup. She was fired, and sued the casino under Title VII, alleging sex bias. A federal court and the Ninth Circuit ruled against her. The policy did not burden female servers more than males. **Different grooming standards are discriminatory only when they impose a greater burden on one sex than the other.** Accordingly, the casino could legally enforce its personal appearance policy. *Jespersen v. Harrah's Operating Co.*, 392 F.3d 1076 (9th Cir. 2004).

♦ A cashier in Massachusetts with multiple body piercings and tattoos claimed that she was **required by her religion – the Church of Body Modification – to display her body piercings** to the public. Her employer had a dress code policy that forbade the wearing of any facial jewelry except earrings. It rejected her suggested accommodation that she cover her eyebrow piercings with a flesh-colored Band-Aid and fired her for unexcused absences as well as failure to comply with the dress code. During Equal Employment Opportunity Commission mediation, the employer offered to let her return to work with her jewelry covered, but she then took the position that she should be exempted from the dress code for religious reasons. When she sued under Title VII, a federal court ruled against her, and the First Circuit Court of Appeals affirmed the ruling. Granting such an exemption would be an undue hardship to the employer because it would adversely affect the employer's public image. *Cloutier v. Costco Wholesale Corp.*, 390 F.3d 126 (1st Cir. 2004).

♦ The District of Columbia Code prohibits employment discrimination on the basis of personal appearance, including grooming, hairstyles and beards. An exception exists where an employer has a reasonable business purpose for restricting the style of dress or grooming. A maintenance contractor doing business in the District had a written personal appearance policy requiring employees to maintain good hygiene, a neat hairstyle and a clean shaven face. One maintenance employee began wearing his hair in a ponytail and refused to cut it when his supervisor told him to get a haircut or wear a hat. He sued the employer for violation of the D.C. human rights act. The D.C. Court of Appeals ruled against him. The evidence indicated that the employer communicated a general rule that employees must conform to traditional grooming styles and that the supervisor's interpretation of the rule as forbidding ponytails was not unreasonable. There was a reasonable business purpose for the rule as there was evidence that customers were concerned about employee appearances. **Application of the grooming rule did not violate the human rights act.** *Turcios v. U.S. Services Industries*, 680 A.2d 1023 (D.C. 1996).

CHAPTER SEVEN

Workers' Compensation

I. EXCLUSIVE REMEDY

Workers' compensation is a system designed to protect both employer and employee. Generally, an employee gives up the right to sue his employer in exchange for the security of obtaining workers' compensation benefits for accidental injuries that <u>arise out of</u> and <u>occur in the course of</u> employment.

Where an accidental injury or illness arises out of and in the course of employment, workers' compensation is generally the exclusive remedy available to the employee. Thus, even where the employer is not at fault, it becomes liable for benefits under workers' compensation when an employee is injured.

The trade-off is that the <u>employee cannot sue</u> the employer in tort (e.g., for negligence) to recover for her injuries. She is limited to the statutory recovery provided by the workers' compensation system. Thus, even where the employer is at fault, the employee's recovery is limited to the statutory schedule of benefits for the type of injury suffered.

However, where the injury is not sufficiently work related, or where the injury is caused by an intentional tort, employer liability may result. For other cases involving employer liability, please see Chapter Two, Section I.

A. Exclusive Remedy Applied

Employees injured at work occasionally seek to avoid the application of workers' compensation in order to sue for negligence or another tort. By doing so, they hope to obtain a larger damage award than they could achieve with workers' compensation (including, potentially, punitive damages). In the following cases, courts applied the exclusive remedy doctrine to bar lawsuits against the employers.

◆   A manager for a Georgia Wal-Mart was abducted from the store parking lot while walking toward the store to begin her shift. The manager was driven to a wooded area and raped for approximately 90 minutes. The manager later sued Wal-Mart for negligence, claiming the attack lasted longer because Wal-Mart did not provide police with store surveillance video in a timely manner. A state appeals court rejected the claim, finding that **workers' compensation was the manager's exclusive remedy because the attack arose out of her job**. *Dawson v. Wal-Mart Stores*, 751 S.E.2d 426 (Ga. Ct. App. 2013).

◆   While pursuing a shoplifting suspect, a loss prevention employee at a North Carolina Wal-Mart collided with a door greeter. The door greeter later died from injuries sustained as a result of the collision. The door greeter's estate filed a wrongful death claim against Wal-Mart, asserting it should not be limited to workers' compensation benefits because the employee's misconduct caused the death. **The court rejected the claim that misconduct caused the death.** Though Wal-Mart allegedly required loss prevention employees to catch at least eight shoplifters each month, it also had a "no-chase" policy that was motivated by safety concerns. As a result, workers' compensation was the exclusive remedy. *Pender v. Lambert*, 737 S.E.2d 778 (N.C. Ct. App. 2013).

◆   Two Wyoming employees drove to a work site to repair a truck bed. They left at 5:00 a.m. and worked on the truck bed until about midnight. On the way back to the company shop, the employee driving the vehicle fell asleep and the car went into the ditch, causing back injuries to the other worker. He sued his co-worker for intentionally causing his injuries. He maintained that the workers' compensation exclusive remedy provisions didn't apply because the driver engaged in willful and wanton misconduct by driving when he was too tired to do so. The case reached the Supreme Court of Wyoming, which ruled that the co-worker was bound by the exclusive remedy of workers' compensation. **The driver didn't intentionally act to cause harm to the co-worker, and his actions were not highly likely to cause harm.** *Formisano v. Gaston*, 246 P.3d 286 (Wyo. 2011).

❖   A 17-year-old North Carolina employee was killed while working at a pallet shredder. No one witnessed the accident, but the state Occupational Safety and Health Administration conducted an investigation and issued two citations listing 11 safety violations. The employee's estate sued the company for wrongful death, and the company asserted that workers' compensation was the estate's exclusive remedy. The estate argued that the company had removed safety guards to increase productivity, assigned an underage person to work on heavy equipment and failed to ensure that trained personnel were present when the shredder was operating. A court granted pretrial judgment to the company, and the court of appeals affirmed. **The estate failed to prove that the company knew its actions were substantially certain to cause serious injury** or death. Workers' compensation was the estate's only remedy. *Valenzuela v. Pallet Express, Inc.*, 700 S.E.2d 76 (N.C. Ct. App. 2010).

❖   A Vermont employee was ordered by his supervisor to drive an ATV up a steep incline. The ATV flipped over, causing severe injuries to the employee. He sued his supervisor for negligence, and his supervisor sought to have the case dismissed on the grounds that workers' compensation was his exclusive remedy. The employee asserted that the supervisor was a person other than his employer, such that he did not have to abide by the exclusivity provisions of workers' compensation. The case reached the Supreme Court of Vermont, which ruled that the employee was barred by the exclusivity provisions of workers' compensation. **The supervisor was exercising a non-delegable duty of the company (to provide a safe workplace) when he ordered the employee to drive up the steep incline.** As a result, workers' compensation was the employee's exclusive remedy, and he could not sue the supervisor for negligence. *Garger v. Desroches*, 974 A.2d 597 (Vt. 2009).

❖   A CVS employee in Massachusetts attempted to apprehend a suspected shoplifter, who responded violently, stabbing him in the neck with a knife. The employee died at the scene shortly thereafter. At the time of his death, he was an 18-year-old high school student who lived at his mother's home. He was financially dependent on both parents and had no dependents himself. As a result, no workers' compensation benefits were paid. His parents sued CVS for wrongful death, and CVS sought to have the case dismissed, arguing that even though no workers' compensation benefits were paid, the employee would have been eligible had he survived or had dependents. Thus, his parents could not sue for wrongful death because of the exclusive remedy of workers' compensation. The Supreme Judicial Court of Massachusetts agreed with CVS that the employee's injury was technically compensable under the workers' compensation statute. So **even though no workers' compensation benefits were actually paid, the exclusive remedy prevented the parents' wrongful death lawsuit.** *Saab v. Massachusetts CVS Pharmacy, LLC*, 896 N.E.2d 615 (Mass. 2008).

❖   For economic reasons, a Florida bank decided to eliminate the security guard position. It did so despite an earlier robbery in which a teller was pistol-whipped. Afterward, two armed men entered the bank, robbed it, then shot the branch manager in the face. She sued the bank for negligence and for intentionally creating an unsafe environment. A federal court and the Eleventh Circuit ruled against her. The negligence claim failed because **injuries sustained during robberies in the workplace are deemed to "arise out of" employment**. Thus, workers' compensation provided immunity. And the exception for intentional torts failed because she could not show that the decision not to have a guard on duty amounted to conduct that was "substantially certain" to result in her injury or death. Accordingly, she was limited to workers' compensation benefits for her injuries. *Locke v. SunTrust Bank*, 484 F.3d 1343 (11th Cir. 2007).

♦   An Illinois worker suffered a heart attack and stroke, and was left lying on a loading dock for eight hours until help arrived. He filed for workers' compensation benefits and, when the company challenged the claim, sued the company for negligence before the workers' compensation commission ruled on the matter. The company then asserted that workers' compensation was his exclusive remedy. A federal court and the Seventh Circuit agreed with the company. However, the court of appeals noted that **the company, by insisting the worker had to rely on workers' compensation, was in essence conceding that some of the worker's injuries were compensable under that law**. *Dunlap v. Nestle USA, Inc.*, 431 F.3d 1015 (7th Cir. 2005).

♦   An employee at a company in Minnesota received a "birthday spanking" from five co-workers with a two-by-four that had been fashioned into a paddle. He suffered injuries to his buttocks, wrists and elbow, then sued the company and his co-workers for assault and battery, among other claims. The case reached the Supreme Court of Minnesota, which held that the state's workers' compensation act was the employee's exclusive remedy against the company. Even though the company knew about the tradition of "birthday spankings" employees visited on each other, it did not intend to harm the employee. **Its inaction with respect to stopping the spanking was not sufficient to satisfy the intentional injury exception to workers' compensation.** However, there was a question of fact regarding the co-workers' intent or gross negligence. The court remanded the case for a determination of that question. *Meintsma v. Loram Maintenance of Way, Inc.*, 684 N.W.2d 434 (Minn. 2004).

♦   A suspended police officer went to work for Sears as a security guard at its Hackensack, New Jersey, store. Two armed assailants killed him while he was trying to transport money from the warehouse to the main building after the store closed for the evening. Even though Sears had a regional directive requiring money to be transported in the morning and in the presence of two security guards, the Hackensack store had not implemented the directive. The guard's family obtained workers' compensation benefits. It then sued Sears for wrongful death, asserting that it had actual knowledge of the parking lot dangers and engaged in intentionally wrongful conduct by disregarding the corporate policy. A court ruled for Sears, and the Superior Court of New Jersey, Appellate Division, affirmed. The family's lawsuit was barred by the exclusive remedy provision of the state's workers' compensation law. They **failed to show that**

Sears committed an intentional wrong – that it knew harm was "substantially certain" to result from its failure to follow corporate policy. Also, Sears did not violate OSHA or other governmental regulations. *Fisher v. Sears, Roebuck & Co.*, 833 A.2d 650 (N.J. Super. Ct. App. Div. 2003).

◆   A security guard for a car rental agency at the Cleveland airport backed out of the parking lot at the end of his noon-to-6 p.m. shift and hit a co-worker who was verifying a customer's paperwork. The co-worker received workers' compensation benefits for his injury and then sued the guard for negligence. The case reached the Ohio Supreme Court, which noted that employees who are injured in their employers' parking lots on their way home from work have been injured "in the course of and arising out of" their employment. Therefore, an employee who **injures a co-worker in the parking lot while on his way home** has also injured the co-worker "in the course of and arising out of" employment. As a result, the workers' compensation statute was the co-worker's exclusive remedy, and the guard was immune to a lawsuit for negligence. *Donnelly v. Herron*, 88 Ohio St.3d 425, 727 N.E.2d 882 (Ohio 2000).

◆   A utility worker for a Virginia power company participated in a company-sponsored lunch time aerobics class and developed a severe headache. The company's health services coordinator took her to the "quiet room" for employees who become ill at work but did not call any medical or emergency personnel. Two hours later, the coordinator returned to check on the worker and found her in a coma-like state. The worker was then taken to the hospital, where she was diagnosed with a cerebral aneurysm and hemorrhaging. She sustained partial paralysis and brain damage, and she sued the company for negligence. After her lawsuit was dismissed, the Virginia Court of Appeals affirmed that decision, finding her injuries covered by workers' compensation. The worker suffered an "injury by accident" because **the injury she sustained was the delay in treatment caused by the company's negligence**, not the aneurysm itself. Also, the injury arose out of and in the course of her employment. As a result, her exclusive remedy was workers' compensation. *Combs v. Virginia Electric and Power Co.*, 525 S.E.2d 278 (Va. Ct. App. 2000).

◆   The Court of Appeals of Georgia affirmed a ruling in favor of a convenience store sued by an employee who asserted a job-related emotional injury after being robbed at gunpoint. She filed a state court negligence action against the employer, claiming that it rejected her request for a transfer to the day shift without a cut in pay. The court dismissed the action under the exclusivity provision of the state workers' compensation act. On appeal, the court of appeals stated that even if an employer's **willful failure to afford employees a safe workplace** results in injury to an employee, the only recourse for the injury is under the workers' compensation act. *Boulware v. Quiktrip Corp.*, 486 S.E.2d 662 (Ga. Ct. App. 1997).

◆   A Vermont employee was placed at a factory by a temporary employment agency. Under the agreement between the temp agency and the manufacturer, the agency paid the temporary workers and provided their workers' compensation insurance. When the employee was injured at the factory, she obtained workers' compensation benefits from the temp agency and sued the manufacturer and one of its supervisors in state court. The court ruled for the manufacturer and supervisor under the borrowed servant doctrine. The Supreme Court of Vermont affirmed, finding that the manufacturer was the employee's statutory employer under the state workers' compensation act. **The act allowed an employee to have two contemporaneous employers**, and because the manufacturer qualified as an employer under the law, it was entitled to immunity. The employee could not collect workers' compensation benefits from the agency and bring a personal injury lawsuit against the manufacturer. *Candido v. Polymers, Inc.*, 687 A.2d 476 (Vt. 1996).

B. Exceptions

Workers' compensation will not be the exclusive remedy in certain situations – most notably, where the employer is accused of intentional wrongdoing against the employee.

If the employer commits an intentional tort (e.g., assault, battery, false imprisonment, intentional infliction of emotional distress), an employee injured as a result will be able to sue to recover for that injury.

Also, where an employer acts with deliberate indifference to its employees' welfare, and where harm is substantially certain to result, courts will assume that the employer intended to harm the employees, and they will be able to sue to recover for injuries sustained as a result.

For example, where an employer removes a safety device from a piece of machinery to speed up production, the employer will be deemed to have intended harm to employees using the machine. Any injury that results will allow for a tort lawsuit that could yield punitive damages.

Employers can also be sued for discrimination or where the injury does not arise out of and in the course of the employment relationship.

♦   A UPS supervisor in Texas had a congenital heart condition and worked in an office without air conditioning. He collapsed at work and died from a heart attack. His fiancée, on behalf of his son, filed a claim for workers' compensation, which was denied because of his preexisting condition. The fiancée then sued for wrongful death, claiming gross negligence, and UPS sought to have the case dismissed. A trial court did so, but the Court of Appeals of Texas reversed, noting that the issues weren't the same in this case as they had been in the workers' compensation proceeding. Here, the question was not whether the employee's work was a substantial contributing factor to the heart attack, but rather whether the employer's conduct involved an extreme degree of risk and whether the employer was aware of and indifferent to that risk. **A jury could decide that the failure to install air conditioning was gross negligence.** *Barnes v. United Parcel Service, Inc.*, No. 01-09-00648-cv, 2012 WL 112252 (Tex. Ct. App. 1/12/12).

♦   The manager and a number of employees of a Florida bank became sick as a result of exposure to concrete dust, glue and paint fumes, and fiberglass particles – all of which came from a renovation project. The bank, hoping to stay open during the renovation, built a temporary wall between the new construction and the old bank, but it didn't build the wall all the way to the ceiling. Bank officials refused to relocate the employees even after they became sick. When the manager sued for the injuries she sustained, the bank argued that workers' compensation was her exclusive remedy. A court granted the bank pretrial judgment, but the court of appeal reversed, finding issues of fact that required a trial. **Requiring an employee to work in an area containing harmful fumes, without providing masks,** satisfies the substantial certainty standard needed for the exception to workers' compensation exclusivity. *Barnett v. Bank of America Corp.*, 45 So.3d 948 (Fla. Dist. Ct. App. 2010).

♦   A Delaware grocery store employee socialized with the night manager in the parking lot after the store closed. Somehow he climbed up on the hood of the manager's car and rode there while the manager drove around the lot. He fell off, sustaining serious injuries, and sued the store for negligent supervision and retention of the manager. A trial court ruled for the store, and the Supreme Court of Delaware affirmed. The employee's injuries were not a reasonably foreseeable consequence of the manager's inappropriate social behavior so as to establish a duty to the employee on the part of the store. Further, **the employee's parking lot injuries after the store closed occurred outside the scope of his employment, so workers' compensation exclusivity did not apply**. *Matthews v. Food Lion, L.L.C.*, 970 A.2d 257 (Del. 2009).

♦   An employee at a Florida store complained to his manager about an old wooden ladder that was wobbly and undersized. The manager in turn complained about it to her supervisor. Subsequently, the employee, while trying to retrieve merchandise from a high shelf, fell from the ladder. He sued for an intentional tort, claiming his injury was substantially certain to occur such that workers' compensation was not the sole remedy at his disposal. A jury awarded him $118,000 after making a reduction for comparative fault, and the store appealed. The district court of appeal reversed, finding no liability under the intentional tort exception to workers' compensation because the store did not conceal the dangerous nature of the ladder. On further appeal, the Florida Supreme Court held that **the store did not have to conceal the danger in order to be liable under the exception to workers' compensation**. The supreme court reversed the lower court decision and remanded the case. *Bakerman v. The Bombay Co., Inc.*, 961 So.2d 259 (Fla. 2007).

♦   A 12-year employee of a missile systems company was diagnosed with testicular cancer. He sued the company for fraudulently concealing the fact that he was exposed to carcinogenic chemicals in the workplace (an exception to the exclusive remedy provisions of workers' compensation law). A court dismissed his action, finding that he had to seek a remedy under the state's workers' compensation law. The California Court of Appeal reversed and remanded the case. It noted that an employee can avoid workers' compensation and recover in an action for damages where the employer knew he had suffered a work-related injury, the employer concealed that knowledge from the employee, and the injury was aggravated as a result of the concealment. Here, as a result of chronic overexposure to carcinogenic chemicals for many years, the employee suffered an injury. He also alleged that the company concealed the knowledge of his overexposure and that if he had known, he could have sought treatment earlier. As a result, **he was not bound by the exclusivity provisions of workers' compensation law**. He could sue for damages. *Palestini v. General Dynamics Corp.*, 120 Cal.Rptr.2d 741 (Cal. Ct. App. 2002).

✦ A lube technician for a trucking company contracted pneumonia and then bronchitis, partly as a result of acid mist and fumes from a chemical mixture used for cleaning the exteriors of trucks. He filed a workers' compensation claim for his lung condition, but benefits were denied because he failed to prove that his work exposure was the major contributing cause of his lung disorder. He then sued the company to recover for his bronchitis. The case eventually reached the Supreme Court of Oregon, which held that **he could proceed with his common law action despite the exclusive remedy provisions of workers' compensation law**. The court remanded the case for further proceedings. *Smothers v. Gresham Transfer, Inc.*, 332 Or. 83, 23 P.3d 333 (Or. 2001).

✦ A California employee claimed that her unborn child was exposed to toxic levels of carbon monoxide at her workplace. The allegation arose from the employer's use of a propane-powered machine in an inadequately ventilated location at which she was working. The employee and several others fainted from carbon monoxide fumes, and the employee alleged that her daughter was born with cerebral palsy and other disabilities as a result. She sued the employer for negligence on behalf of her child. The court held that the complaint was barred by the exclusivity provision of the state workers' compensation act. The court of appeal reversed, and the Supreme Court of California affirmed. Here, both the mother and child had been exposed to toxic levels of carbon monoxide. **The child had asserted a viable claim for injury to herself and was not claiming any damages for injury to her mother.** Because the child's claim for damages did not legally depend on injuries suffered by the mother, the workers' compensation act did not bar the claim. The court noted that many other state courts, including appellate courts in Colorado, Louisiana, Illinois, Indiana, Alabama, Pennsylvania and Georgia, have found prenatal injuries to be separate and distinct from injury to the mother. *Snyder v. Michael's Stores, Inc.*, 16 Cal.4th 991, 68 Cal.Rptr.2d 476, 945 P.2d 781 (Cal. 1997).

✦ An Arkansas employee sustained bilateral carpal tunnel syndrome from repetitive motion in her workplace. She filed a workers' compensation claim that was not challenged by her employer, and she resumed work while receiving treatment. Her physicians released her from treatment and rehabilitation with a permanent restriction from repetitive motion and a 5% permanent physical impairment in her arms. However, upon returning to work, the employer discharged her. She sued the employer for discrimination on the basis of disability in violation of the state civil rights act. The court dismissed the case on the grounds that the employee's sole remedy was workers' compensation, but the Supreme Court of Arkansas reversed. The workers' compensation act did not afford any remedy for the employee here because she had alleged discharge on the basis of a disability. Because **the employee had alleged discrimination, and not refusal by the employer to allow her to return to work**, the complaint had been erroneously dismissed. The court remanded the case. *Davis v. Dillmeier Enterprises, Inc.*, 956 S.W.2d 155 (Ark. 1997).

◆   A West Virginia truck driver suffered a spinal injury and filed a claim for workers' compensation benefits. His employer contested the claim and asserted that no job-related injury had occurred. The claim was denied, but on appeal, benefits were awarded including a retroactive sum of over $95,000. The employee then sued the employer for fraud and for wrongfully opposing his workers' compensation complaint. The West Virginia Supreme Court of Appeals observed that **the workers' compensation act pertained to employee injuries suffered as the result of workplace negligence** and that the fraud claim concerned alleged intentional acts by the employer. Because this was outside the scope of the compensation act, a separate action could survive if the injury giving rise to the claim was not suffered in the course of employment, if the employer fraudulently misrepresented facts, and if the misrepresentation was an attempt to deprive the employee of benefits covered by workers' compensation. *Persinger v. Peabody Coal Co.*, 474 S.E.2d 887 (W.Va. 1996).

◆   A Montana mining safety employee believed that his employer negligently disregarded his safety recommendations, leading to avoidable employee deaths and injuries. He reported depression and physical symptoms including chronic fatigue, insomnia, nausea and headaches, and he filed for workers' compensation benefits. The claim was denied, and the employee sued the employer for negligence. The court dismissed the lawsuit, determining that the state workers' compensation act barred the action – the act prohibited workers' compensation recovery for injuries that were purely mental or emotional. The Supreme Court of Montana determined that the employee had properly been denied a workers' compensation recovery because **his physical and mental injuries were expressly excluded by the statute**. As a result, personal injury remedies were available, and the district court had erroneously dismissed the case. *Kleinhesselink v. Chevron, USA*, 920 P.2d 108 (Mont. 1996).

◆   An employee worked for over 30 years for a Kentucky food distributor. He received positive employment evaluations until coming into conflict with a new marketing manager, who ordered him to obtain competitor price lists in violation of the company's ethics policy and employment manual. A manager then evaluated his job performance as poor, and he was presented with a resignation letter and severance package. The company also misleadingly offered him a position at a South Carolina bakery. After learning that no position was available as promised, the former employee suffered an emotional breakdown and attempted suicide. He sued the employer in a Kentucky court, which awarded him over $180,000 for wrongful discharge, $70,000 for intentional infliction of emotional distress and $500,000 in punitive damages. The court of appeals and the Supreme Court of Kentucky affirmed. The workers' compensation act did not bar the damage award, as the claim for **intentional infliction of emotional distress arose after the employment relationship had terminated**. There was evidence that the employer had induced the employee to resign with a nonexistent job offer and other intentional acts of fraud, deceit, slander and interference with his rights. *Kroger Co. v. Willgruber*, 920 S.W.2d 61 (Ky. 1996).

❖   A resident of the District of Columbia (D.C.) was hired there by a company, but he also worked for the company in the state of Virginia. He sustained a back injury while working in Virginia and received benefits under Virginia's workers' compensation law. Subsequently, he received a supplemental award under D.C.'s workers' compensation law. His employer and its carrier challenged this second award because Virginia law excluded any other recovery "at common law or otherwise." Thus, D.C. should have given the first award "full faith and credit." An administrative order upholding the second award was reversed by the U.S. Court of Appeals. The U.S. Supreme Court then held that **the Constitution's Full Faith and Credit Clause did not preclude successive workers' compensation awards** where the second state would have had the power to apply its workers' compensation law in the first place. Here, since the employee could have sought a compensation award from D.C. in the first place, the employer and its insurer would have had to measure their liability exposure by the more generous workers' compensation scheme anyway. Accordingly, Virginia's interest was not enough to prevent D.C. from making the supplemental award. The Court reversed the case. *Thomas v. Washington Gas Light Co.,* 448 U.S. 261, 100 S.Ct. 2647, 65 L.Ed.2d 757 (1980).

II. CONNECTION WITH EMPLOYMENT

Workers' compensation will not be paid merely because an injured person happens to be employed. The injury must be <u>connected</u> with the employment for benefits to become payable. The injury must either arise out of and in the course of the employment, or it must be an occupational disease.

A. Arising from Employment

For an injury to be compensable under workers' compensation, it must "arise out of and in the course of" employment. An injury that <u>arises out of employment</u> has a causal connection to the employment. In other words, there must generally be:

1) some proximity between the scene of the accident and the place of employment,
2) some degree of control exercised by the employer over the scene of the accident, and
3) some benefit the employer received from the injured employee's presence at the scene of the accident.

An injury that occurs <u>in the course of employment</u> generally occurs:

1) during working hours,
2) at the place of employment, and
3) while the employee is fulfilling his working duties.

Not every element listed above must be present in every case for employees to qualify for workers' compensation. However, the more elements present, the greater the likelihood that an injury will qualify for workers' compensation, and that the employer will not be liable in a lawsuit for negligence.

◆   A Missouri employee slipped and fell after work in an icy parking lot next to his office. The employer fought his claim for workers' compensation benefits, arguing that he was going home when he got hurt and the hazard that caused the injury was not specifically related to his job. The court rejected the argument and decided **the employee could collect workers' compensation benefits under the state's "extended premises" doctrine**, which allows employees to receive workers' compensation benefits for injuries sustained as a result of accidents on property they customarily use to get to and from work if the property is owned or controlled by the employer. *Scholastic, Inc. v. Viley*, No. WD 77546, 2014 WL 5462306 (Mo. Ct. App. 10/28/14).

◆   When she moved to newly remodeled offices, an attorney in Washington state noticed a strange odor and reported a metallic taste in her mouth. She then started getting nosebleeds, and she felt disoriented and fatigued. She began working from home and got sick again when she tried to return. A medical specialist diagnosed her as having multiple chemical sensitivity and filed a workers' compensation claim on her behalf. However, **there was no concrete evidence tying her symptoms to the exposure**, and a hygienist who evaluated the office found nothing remarkable. A state appeals court decided the attorney was not entitled to workers' compensation benefits because she did not show her disorder was caused by the work environment. *Potter v. Dep't of Labor and Industries*, 289 P.3d 727 (Wash. Ct. App. 2012).

◆   A Virginia nurse lost control of her car when she glanced over at her flashing cell phone. Her tires slid on some gravel, and she skidded to the other side of the road, then crashed, sustaining injuries. She used the phone for work because the pager supplied by the hospital was unreliable. At the time of the accident, she was driving home from a mandatory training session and was on call. Although the hospital didn't call her, there was no evidence as to who had done so or even if there was a call at all. She applied for workers' compensation benefits, and the Virginia Court of Appeals held that she was entitled to them. **The hospital required her to monitor her cell phone at all times when she was on call, so her injuries arose out of her employment.** *Wythe County Community Hospital v. Turpin*, No. 0208-11-3, 2011 WL 4552277 (Va. Ct. App. 10/4/11).

◆   A billing clerk in a Missouri hospital office fractured her pelvis when she fell in the office kitchen after making a pot of coffee. Apparently she tripped over her sandal as she was turning around. She was taken to the emergency room and later applied for workers' compensation benefits. An administrative law judge denied benefits, but the state industrial and labor commission reversed, finding she was entitled to them under the "personal comfort" doctrine, which allows recovery when an employee is injured while tending to a basic personal need. The Missouri Supreme Court reversed the commission, finding that the personal comfort doctrine was no longer applicable. **The then-current law required an employee's injury to be caused by a risk or hazard she would not be exposed to in her "normal nonemployment life."** Her accident didn't arise out of and in the course of her employment. *Johme v. St. John's Mercy Healthcare*, 366 S.W.3d 504 (Mo. 2012).

◆   With the owner's permission, a Tennessee employee went to work early after dropping his wife off at her job. When the owner arrived, he found the employee shot dead near a shop door. The police never found a motive for the shooting, but the business was located along a highway corridor in a high crime area. When the widow sought workers' compensation death benefits, the Supreme Court of Tennessee held that she was not entitled to them. The trial court had found that **the shooting was a "neutral assault" with no tie to the job** and that the "street risk" doctrine didn't apply because the business wasn't the sort of enterprise that attracted outside burglaries. Since the widow failed to show a job-related connection, no benefits were due. *Padilla v. Twin City Fire Insurance Co.*, 324 S.W.3d 507 (Tenn. 2010).

◆   A Maine paper mill employee injured his neck, back and arm at work. Ten years later, he injured his back again and was placed in a light-duty position. But his back continued to worsen, and he eventually filed a workers' compensation claim following a third injury. While driving to a mediation conference regarding all his work injuries, he was involved in a car accident and injured his shoulder. He filed a claim for that injury as well. A hearing officer awarded him benefits for the three work injuries but denied benefits for the car accident. The case reached the Supreme Judicial Court of Maine, which held that **the injury he sustained while traveling to a workers' compensation mediation did not arise out of and in the course of his employment**. *Feiereisen v. Newpage Corp.*, 5 A.3d 669 (Me. 2010).

◆   A nursing assistant for a rehab clinic in Arkansas attended a mandatory training seminar, after which she was to receive her paycheck and fill out paperwork for a flu shot. She was not allowed to clock out until she received her paycheck. After the seminar, while approximately 200 employees waited in line to get their paychecks and fill out their paperwork, she decided to grab a quick smoke because of the long line. She went to the smoking area, had a cigarette and while walking back, fell and broke her arm. **The center challenged her workers' compensation claim on the grounds that picking up a paycheck was a personal activity not in its interest.** But the Supreme Court of Arkansas disagreed. She was still on the employer's premises and required to be clocked in at the time of her injury. *Jonesboro Care & Rehab Center v. Woods*, 2010 Ark. 482 (Ark. 2010).

♦   A custom decorator with J.C. Penney worked out of her home or met with customers in their homes. She kept fabric samples in her garage. One day, while going to the garage to get some fabric samples, she tripped over her dog and fell, breaking her wrist. She filed for workers' compensation benefits, but the workers' compensation board denied them on the grounds that her injury didn't "arise from her employment." When she appealed, the Oregon Court of Appeals reversed, noting that **her injury arose out of her job because it occurred as a result of a risk of her work environment**. The court remanded the case to the board for a determination of whether the injury "occurred in the course of" her employment, which the employee could prove by showing it occurred at a place she was reasonably expected to be while reasonably fulfilling her job duties. *Sandberg v. J.C. Penney Co., Inc.*, 243 Or. App. 342 (Or. Ct. App. 2011).

♦   A migrant worker with a company in South Carolina lived in employer-supplied housing. He slipped on a wet sidewalk caused by overflow from an outdoor sink being used by a fellow worker and broke his ankle. After the company fired him, he filed for workers' compensation benefits. The case reached the Supreme Court of South Carolina, which ruled that he was entitled to them. **He was essentially required, by the nature of his work, to live in employer-supplied housing.** Living on premises benefited both the employee and the employer. Thus, his injury arose out of and in the course of his employment. He would not have been injured had he not lived there, and the injury was caused by the overflowing sink, which apparently did not have proper drainage. The injury was compensable. *Pierre v. Seaside Farms, Inc.*, 689 S.E.2d 615 (S.C. 2010).

♦   For 10 years, an employee in Connecticut walked around the company's grounds during her half-hour unpaid lunch break. One day, while walking along a service road, she stepped aside for an oncoming car and fell on some gravel, injuring her right shoulder. She received physical therapy and applied for workers' compensation benefits. A judge awarded benefits, finding that her walk was incidental to her employment and that it benefited both her and the company. An appeals board and the Connecticut Court of Appeals reversed. The court stated that **although her injury arose out of and in the course of her employment, she was engaged in a voluntary recreational activity at the time**. Thus, there was no coverage. *Brown v. United Technologies Corp.*, 963 A.2d 1027 (Conn. App. Ct. 2009).

♦   A valet driver for a company in Pennsylvania got into a breakroom fight with a co-worker after the two taunted each other at lunch. He suffered broken ribs and sought workers' compensation benefits, which were denied. The two men had been verbally jousting for a year, and the fight was precipitated when the co-worker implied that he had slept with the valet driver's wife. As a result, **the injury resulted from personal animosity over issues unrelated to the job**. *Waszewski v. Workers' Compensation Appeal Board*, No. 486 C.D. 2008, 2008 WL 9405111 (Pa. Commw. Ct. 10/27/08) (Unpublished).

◆   A Kmart employee in Oklahoma took an evening assignment guarding merchandise left outside overnight for a sale. Because the store was locked, he was told to go to the nearest convenience store if he had "issues with anything." Around 3:15 a.m., he went to use the bathroom at the nearest convenience store, but the place was closed. He then went to the nearest McDonald's, but only the drive-through was open there. He decided to get a hamburger and was shot while he was in his car. When he sought workers' compensation benefits, the Supreme Court of Oklahoma ruled that he was entitled to them. Here, his injuries occurred in the course of his employment and also arose out of his employment because **he had to leave the store to minister to his personal needs, and his shift put him at higher risk than the general population**. *Kmart v. Herring*, 188 P.3d 140 (Okla. 2008).

◆   Over a two-month period, a Chinese stir-fry cook at a restaurant in Arizona endured teasing at the hands of his supervisor and co-workers, who mimicked his accent and poor English. They thought it was just good fun, but he felt it was harassment and demeaning. After his supervisor mocked him for taking a bone home to make soup, he told off his supervisor. The supervisor pushed him away, and he fell, injuring his shoulder and pelvis. He sought and was awarded workers' compensation benefits. The Arizona Court of Appeals held that under **the "friction and strain" rule**, his injuries arose out of his employment. The "friction and strain rule" provides that, even if the subject of the altercation in which the employee is injured is unrelated to the work, the injuries are compensable if work brought the participants together and created the relations and conditions which resulted in the altercation. *PF Chang's v. Industrial Comm'n of Arizona*, 166 P.3d 135 (Ariz. Ct. App. 2007).

◆   While making lunch in her kitchen, a telecommuter in Tennessee was assaulted by her neighbor without provocation or explanation. He knocked on her door, and she let him in. He left after a few minutes but returned a moment later, saying he had forgotten his keys. When she turned away from him, he beat her until she lost consciousness. She sought workers' compensation benefits for her injuries, asserting that her work arrangement placed her in a position that facilitated the assault. However, the Tennessee Supreme Court ruled against her. **Although her injuries occurred in the course of her employment, they did not arise out of her employment** so as to be covered by workers' compensation. There was no evidence that she was singled out because of her work duties or business relationships. *Wait v. Travelers Indemnity Co. of Illinois*, 240 S.W.3d 220 (Tenn. 2007).

◆   A 50-year-old mechanic with a history of back problems reinjured his back when he jerked loose a card stuck in a knitting machine. He tried to return to work on light duty, but was told that there were no light-duty positions available. **He was fired a week later and committed suicide two weeks after that. His widow sought workers' compensation death benefits**, asserting that his injury caused him to become clinically depressed and that the termination exacerbated his depression to the point of suicide. The case reached the Massachusetts Court of Appeals, which upheld the award of death benefits. The court rejected the "independent, intervening factor" test – used in tort cases to break the chain of causation – noting that workers' compensation principles don't award or deny benefits based on fault. *In re Dube's Case*, 872 N.E.2d 1171 (Mass. App. Ct. 2007).

• An Ohio cook apparently had a tense relationship outside of work with a co-worker. One day he accidentally or carelessly spilled hot water from a wok on the co-worker. After the cook turned away, the co-worker hit him in the back of the head with a large cooking utensil, knocking him unconscious. He suffered permanent paralysis to his left side and filed a claim for workers' compensation benefits. The industrial commission awarded benefits, a trial court reversed, and the Ohio Court of Appeals reinstated them. Here, **it did not matter that the injury was intentional** or that the two men allegedly had a poor relationship outside of work. What mattered was that the cook sustained his injury during the course of and arising out of his employment. As a result, he was entitled to workers' compensation benefits. *Luo v. Gao*, No. 23310, 2007 WL 675635 (Ohio Ct. App. 3/7/07).

• A 70-year-old cashier at a store in South Dakota completed her shift at 7:00 p.m. and punched out at 7:04. She bought a few items at 7:07 and, on her way out the door, tripped over a rug near the exit. She fell and sustained injuries to her head and leg, aggravating an ulcer in her ankle. Eventually she was forced to quit. She sought workers' compensation benefits, and an administrative hearing officer found that she was permanently disabled. The case reached the Supreme Court of South Dakota, which noted that **the cashier's activities were "reasonably incidental" to her work**. The store allowed employees to shop during breaks, and even though the cashier waited until the end of her shift, her deviation from her usual route before leaving was less than 10 minutes. She was entitled to benefits. *Fair v. Nash Finch Co.*, 728 N.W.2d 623 (S.D. 2007).

• A temporary employee in Tennessee was assigned to a hotel construction project in another town and returned at the end of the day to collect his paycheck. He waited for his paycheck outside the office along with other employees. A truck then pulled up, and a woman passenger asked to use the bathroom. The manager denied the request pursuant to company policy, and an altercation ensued during which the driver shot and killed the employee. His children filed for workers' compensation benefits. The Tennessee Supreme Court ruled that the children were entitled to them because **the shooting outside the office arose out of the employment**. *Hurst v. Labor Ready*, 197 S.W.3d 756 (Tenn. 2006).

• On his way back to work after a bathroom break, a forklift operator for a company in Arkansas tried to cross a board that had been set on concrete and placed over a muddy ditch. While he was on the board, it slipped off the concrete and he fell, twisting his knee. He filed for workers' compensation benefits, which were denied on the grounds that he was not performing employment-related services at the time of his injury. The Arkansas Supreme Court disagreed with that finding. **A bathroom break is a necessary function,**

and it directly or indirectly advances the interests of the employer. Here, the worker was still on the clock and unable to leave the worksite. Also, he would have had to cut his break short if his supervisors needed him. *Wallace v. West Fraser South, Inc.*, 225 S.W.3d 361 (Ark. 2006).

◆ An Indiana DaimlerChrysler employee parked in a lot owned by a shopping mall across the street from the plant where he worked even though he wasn't supposed to. As he crossed the street on his way to work, he was struck by a car and killed. His widow applied for death benefits, which were denied. Here, the employee had not been acting in the course of his employment at the time of his death. Further, DaimlerChrysler provided plenty of parking for its plant that, even though it was farther away, did not require crossing a busy street. Benefits were properly denied the widow. *Mueller v. DaimlerChrysler Motors Corp.*, 842 N.E.2d 845 (Ind. Ct. App. 2006).

◆ An Arkansas employee was told to plan and coordinate a mandatory company retreat at an Ozarks resort. She rented a boat and wave runners, and obtained a map of the places where employees could jump off cliffs. When she attempted to follow some co-workers off a cliff, she fell and hit the rocks below. She filed for workers' compensation benefits, which a compensation judge denied. An appeals commission affirmed, but the Arkansas Court of Appeals reversed. Here, **the employee was acting within the course and scope of her employment when she fell off the cliff**. It did not matter that her employer did not expressly order her to jump off the cliff. She was entitled to benefits. *Engle v. Thompson Murray, Inc.*, 96 Ark.App. 200 (Ark. Ct. App. 2006).

◆ A New Jersey construction worker rode into New York City with his supervisor on September 11, 2001 to work at a job site there. After the terrorist attacks, the bridges and tunnels connecting New York and New Jersey closed, and the supervisor suggested they get an early dinner and return to the job to work until the bridges reopened. On the way back to the job site, they were in a car crash, and the employee suffered injuries. He sought workers' compensation benefits, and the New Jersey Supreme Court held that he was entitled to them. Even though he was hurt off the job site, **he was directed or "compelled" to participate in the activity by his supervisor.** *Sager v. O.A. Peterson Construction Co.*, 862 A.2d 1119 (N.J. 2004).

◆ An employee of an Illinois industrial cleaning service was assigned to help carry 500 45-pound bags of asbestos down several flights of stairs to a dumpster. The temperature was 5 degrees Fahrenheit. He suffered chest pains, went to the hospital and had an angioplasty to open up a blocked artery. He filed for workers' compensation benefits, and an arbitrator awarded them. The court of appeals reversed the award, but the Supreme Court of Illinois reinstated it. There was sufficient evidence for the arbitrator to find a connection between the employee's work and his heart attack. Even though the employee's blocked artery was a preexisting condition, **his symptoms began while he was performing heavy labor under extreme conditions**, and the conditions contributed to the risk of heart attack in persons with blocked arteries. *Twice Over Clean, Inc. v. The Industrial Comm'n*, 827 N.E.2d 409 (Ill. 2005).

◆   A contract laborer who worked for a contractor in New Jersey did not have a driver's license and relied on his boss to drive him to job sites. After work at a customer's house one day, the contractor and the customer drove go-carts around a track on the property. The contractor then told the laborer to drive the go-cart. The laborer refused, saying he did not know how to drive, but the contractor persisted, insisting it was easy. When the laborer then crashed and broke his ankle, he sued for workers' compensation benefits. The case reached the Supreme Court of New Jersey, which ruled that **if an employee reasonably feels compelled to participate in a recreational activity, that activity becomes work related**, and workers' compensation benefits are available. The court remanded the case for a determination of whether the laborer had an objectively reasonable basis for believing he had to ride the go-cart. *Lozano v. Frank De Luca Construction*, 842 A.2d 156 (N.J. 2004).

◆   When a female worker brought a sexual harassment lawsuit against a Colorado company, a 25-year employee agreed to testify on her behalf. He claimed he was then ostracized and harassed in retaliation for his testimony. He brought a union grievance against a male co-worker for remarks made during a confrontation, but he refused to testify at the grievance hearing (allegedly because of pressure from the union president), and the grievance was dismissed. After being diagnosed with bipolar disorder, he sought workers' compensation benefits, which were awarded. The Colorado Court of Appeals affirmed, noting that even though the employee suffered from preexisting emotional problems, **his stress-related disability resulted primarily from his employment**. Also, it did not arise from noncompensable harassment, but from the work-related retaliation after his testimony in the harassment suit. *Public Service of Colorado v. Industrial Claim Appeals Office*, 68 P.3d 583 (Colo. Ct. App. 2003).

◆   An employee of a steel manufacturer accidentally killed a co-worker who stepped in front of a tow motor the employee was operating. After the accident, the employee sought treatment for severe depression and filed a workers' compensation claim that was denied. The case reached the Ohio Supreme Court, which held that the state's workers' compensation law allowed an employee to recover for psychiatric injuries that arose from "an injury or occupational disease." **The law did not specify that the person suffering the psychiatric injury had to be the same person who suffered the compensable injury.** Since the law had to be construed liberally in favor of employees, the court ruled that the employee was entitled to benefits. *Bailey v. Republic Engineered Steels, Inc.*, 741 N.E.2d 121 (Ohio 2001).

B. Occupational Diseases

Just like injuries, occupational diseases have to be causally connected to employment in order to be compensable under workers' compensation. Generally, the disease must occur as a result of <u>unusual, extraordinary or abnormal working conditions</u>. In other words, there must be something about these working conditions that is different than normal working conditions.

Most jobs, for example, are somewhat stressful. A heart condition that occurs as a result of stress is usually not going to be compensable under workers' compensation. But the stress in certain jobs is so high that a heart condition is not an unlikely scenario (e.g., police officers and firefighters often have a statutory presumption that heart conditions are caused by occupational stress).

Occupational disease cases are harder to prove than occupational injury cases because there is seldom one defining incident that occurs to pinpoint causation.

◆   A retired coal mine employee in Illinois filed a claim for workers' compensation to recover for his chronic obstructive pulmonary disorder (COPD). He had done a number of jobs for the mine, including working as an electrician, and had worked in areas that contained a lot of dust. The mine fought his claim, asserting that he suffered from COPD because he had been a smoker for 40 years. His medical expert testified that it was impossible to determine the relative contribution of each to his COPD. The mine's medical expert testified that the COPD came from his smoking and not from his exposure to coal dust, though he acknowledged that the coal mine dust could have exacerbated the employee's COPD. An arbitrator and a court denied benefits under the Occupational Diseases Act, but the Appellate Court of Illinois reversed and remanded the case. **The finding that the employee's COPD was caused only by smoking was against the manifest weight of the evidence** given that he had been exposed to both cigarette smoke and coal dust for about 40 years. *Gross v. Illinois Workers' Compensation Comm'n*, 960 N.E.2d 587 (Ill. App. Ct. 2011).

◆   An Idaho employee claimed that he suffered from non-acute lumbar spine occupational disease caused by repetitive heavy lifting, twisting and bending. He sought workers' compensation benefits, which were denied at the administrative level. When he sued, the Supreme Court of Idaho ultimately ruled against him, noting that **he failed to prove his lower back disease was caused by a work injury**. The doctor who conducted the independent medical examination testified that there was no specific injury and that he had multilevel degenerative disc disease that developed over years. And the employee never claimed to have suffered an acute injury that started the back pain. As a result, his back disease was not compensable. *Watson v. Joslin Millwork, Inc.*, 243 P.3d 666 (Idaho 2010).

◆   A Louisiana assembly worker filed a claim for workers' compensation because of herniated discs in her back. Her doctor opined that her degenerative disc disease was caused by changes in posture that resulted from her carpal tunnel syndrome. The company asserted that the worker's degenerative disc disease was not an occupational disease and that it should not have to provide workers' compensation benefits. The Office of Workers' Compensation dismissed her claim, but the Court of Appeal of Louisiana held that **there was sufficient evidence to establish that her herniated discs were due to her**

work-related carpal tunnel syndrome. No medical testimony contradicted her doctor's opinion as to causation. The worker was entitled to benefits. *Dorion v. Gulf States Asphalt Co., L.P.*, 14 So.3d 44 (La. Ct. App. 2009).

◆   A tool cutter and grinder in Florida was exposed to beryllium dust over a period of 17 years until he was laid off. The Department of Labor offered to test his blood for potential work-related disorders, and he tested positive for beryllium sensitivity. He then received two medical directives. First, he could no longer work in an occupation with risk of beryllium exposure. Second, he should undergo regular medical testing or monitoring to determine whether the beryllium sensitivity had advanced to a state of chronic beryllium disease. When he sought workers' compensation benefits, his former employers asserted that he did not yet have chronic beryllium disease, so he should not be entitled to workers' compensation benefits. However, the Florida District Court of Appeal held that **his beryllium sensitivity caused an objective and verifiable change in his body that required medical treatment**. Thus, he suffered an injury for purposes of workers' compensation. *Huff v. Loral American Beryllium Co.*, 967 So.2d 244 (Fla. Dist. Ct. App. 2007).

◆   A Delaware retiree died from lung cancer caused by his occupational exposure to asbestos. He had worked for his employer for 40 years, never filing a workers' compensation claim and receiving a pension after he voluntarily retired. When his widow filed a claim for death benefits, the employer asserted that she had no independent right to recover them. The case reached the Supreme Court of Delaware, which ruled that a surviving spouse can recover death benefits independently and irrespective of whether the deceased employee received wages or disability benefits arising from the occupational injury or disease that caused his death. **Since death benefits were not limited to wage replacement benefits, the widow was entitled to recover them.** *Hirneisen v. Champlain Cable Corp.*, 892 A.2d 1056 (Del. 2006).

◆   An employee of a meat company in Kansas whose job required him to put his gloved hands into dirty water to handle intestines full of fecal matter developed weak, painful, swollen, discolored hands. He was diagnosed with bilateral dermatitis and was transferred to another position. When he sought workers' compensation benefits, an administrative law judge found that he had a 10% impairment to the body as a whole. However, he had not suffered any wage loss as a result because he was making more now than he had been when the disease first affected his hands. The Workers' Compensation Board determined that he was nevertheless entitled to 41.5 weeks of permanent partial disability compensation at the rate of $278.25 per week, resulting in an award of $11,547.38. The employer appealed. The Kansas Court of Appeals held that **even though the employee was earning more than before, he was not precluded from receiving benefits for his disease**. It affirmed the award. *Garcia v. Tyson Fresh Meats, Inc.*, 125 P.3d 580 (Kan. Ct. App. 2006).

◆   For approximately 40 years, an employee had a job retreading truck tires. The process required the use of various chemicals and produced a fine dust that covered him on a daily basis. He developed lung cancer and died. He never smoked, and the two houses he had lived in tested negative for significant radon exposure. After his widow was awarded workers' compensation death benefits, the company and its insurer appealed. The Missouri Court of Appeals affirmed the award. It held that the workers' compensation commission appropriately found that the employee's experts were more credible. **Missouri law did not require the employee to prove which specific chemical caused the occupational disease in order to recover benefits.** *Kent v. Goodyear Tire and Rubber Co.*, 147 S.W.3d 865 (Mo. Ct. App. 2004).

◆   A Delaware tire shop repairman had to buff the insides of rubber tires to prepare them for patching. The process produced airborne particles of dirt and dust (including latex particles), which the repairman inhaled. After several months on the job, he was found to have an allergy to latex. He filed a claim for total disability workers' compensation benefits as well as his medical expenses. At his hearing, his expert witnesses testified that he was susceptible to allergies, noting that after he began working at the repair shop, he developed a number of allergies. The Delaware Industrial Accident Board denied him benefits, and the Superior Court of Delaware affirmed. It noted that although the repairman's allergy had been triggered by his exposure to latex particles at work, he was not entitled to benefits because there was an insufficient causal connection between the allergy and some distinctive feature of his job. He had **a predisposition to allergies that was triggered by his employment**. *Smith v. Service Tire Truck Center*, No. 98A-03-013-WCC, 2000 WL 145817 (Del. Super. Ct. 2000).

◆   A Nebraska bar and grill contracted with an exterminator to spray the premises each month for cockroaches. The exterminator sprayed the bar, and the following day an employee washed up the surfaces with towels and buckets of water, immersing her hands and arms in the water for over two hours. She experienced headaches, pain, seizures, blurred vision and memory loss. A physician diagnosed her as having organic brain damage due to toxic encephalopathy caused by poison. The employee submitted a claim for workers' compensation benefits. The workers' compensation court ruled that the employee was permanently totally disabled and entitled to benefits. The Court of Appeals of Nebraska affirmed that decision, stating that unless the nature and effect of an industrial injury is readily apparent, expert testimony is required to establish a causal relationship between the incident and the disability. The compensation court was entitled to consider evidence that would assist it in understanding the claimant's condition. **A claimant is not required to prove that a medical diagnosis is universally recognized** in the medical community to prevail. *Sheridan v. Catering Management, Inc.*, 5 Neb. App. 305, 558 N.W.2d 319 (Neb. App. 1997).

◆   A Pennsylvania district manager was promoted to manage a large territory that had been merged from two districts. Her workload increased from 55 to 70 hours weekly, and she began to suffer from severe depression. She successfully petitioned for workers' compensation benefits for suffering a psychic injury as a result of abnormal working conditions. The case reached the Supreme Court of

Pennsylvania, which held that the manager had failed to establish that the merger of the districts and her promotion to a new job with greater responsibilities established abnormal working conditions. An **increase in workload and responsibilities caused by promotion or job change does not establish an abnormal working condition** under state workers' compensation law. Such a finding could be determined only by reference to the job into which she was promoted, not by comparison to her former responsibilities. *Hershey Chocolate Co. v. Comwlth. of Pennsylvania, WCAB*, 682 A.2d 1257 (Pa. 1996).

◆   A 70-year-old South Dakota retiree worked part time at a grocery store. He unloaded a delivery truck for almost two hours one morning. That evening, he was taken to a hospital emergency room, where he was diagnosed as having a heart attack and massive gastrointestinal bleeding. He later died. His estate filed a claim for workers' compensation benefits that was denied by the state department of labor. The Supreme Court of South Dakota upheld that determination, observing that the employee had been a lifelong smoker who suffered from cardiovascular disease and chronic obstructive pulmonary disease for which he received medication. In workers' compensation cases resulting from heart attacks, claimants were required to establish a causal relationship between employment and the heart attack. Here, the department of labor was entitled to rely on testimony that **the employee was suffering angina while he was at work, rather than a heart attack**. *Helms v. Lynn's, Inc.*, 542 N.W.2d 764 (S.D. 1996).

◆   A Nebraska employee whose job was to change paint filters and maintain paint guns came into contact with a variety of solvents. He developed a rash and became dizzy when working around painting equipment and suffered seizures on three occasions. His employment was terminated, and he consulted two physicians who were unable to confirm that his seizures were caused by exposure to solvent toxicity. After a third physician attributed the seizures to repetitive solvent toxicity, the employee filed a claim for workers' compensation benefits. The employer contested the application and sought review by the state workers' compensation court, which awarded benefits. The court of appeals reversed the award. The employee appealed to the Supreme Court of Nebraska, which held that the compensation court was entitled to make a credibility determination among the physicians and agree with the third physician's opinion that **exposure to solvents caused the seizures**. The court reinstated the workers' compensation judgment. *Berggren v. Grand Island Accessories, Inc.*, 249 Neb. 789, 545 N.W.2d 727 (Neb. 1996).

C. Preexisting Conditions

Although an injury may occur on the job or appear to be work related, it may be the result of a preexisting condition or an aggravation of a preexisting condition. However, a preexisting condition does not necessarily bar a claim for benefits. It may simply limit the amount of benefits an employer has to pay.

There may be a <u>second injury fund</u> or some sort of special fund set up by a state to compensate workers with preexisting conditions. Also, there are almost always questions in these cases, such as:

—how much of an employee's disability is attributable to the preexisting condition?
—how much can be attributed to the workplace incident?
—was the employer aware of the preexisting condition? and
—what was the employee's level of impairment before the second injury?

Generally, the employer is only responsible for the amount of disability attributable to the workplace incident.

These are complicated issues, the resolution of which demands specialized knowledge of a particular state's workers' compensation laws. The following cases examine some of the issues that arise in cases involving preexisting conditions.

◆   A bus driver in Louisiana injured her back when she fell down some stairs while coming out of a hotel. Although in pain, she managed to drive the bus back to New Orleans. She reported the injury to her supervisor and sought treatment. She had never previously been treated for any injury to her back or neck. Since she could not go back to lifting luggage weighing up to 60 pounds, the company offered her a sedentary position. She declined it because no one knew what was wrong with her. When she filed for workers' compensation benefits, the company fought the request. The office of workers' compensation determined that her injuries were caused by a degenerative condition and that she was not entitled to further compensation. However, the Court of Appeal disagreed. It held that **her work-related accident caused an aggravation of a pre-existing condition in her back that required surgery**. She had performed her job, which demanded a certain amount of heavy lifting, without any problems before the accident. *Merrill v. Greyhound Lines, Inc.*, 70 So.3d 991 (La. Ct. App. 2011).

◆   A Mississippi nurse who had a history of injuries to her left leg, including injuries sustained in two serious car crashes, nevertheless passed the physical exam required by her nursing home employer every year. One day, while dispensing medication, she pivoted on her left leg to get a glass of water for a patient. The twisting motion caused her to break her leg, and she sought workers' compensation benefits. The commission denied benefits, but a court reversed that decision, and the Mississippi Court of Appeals affirmed. The injury came about as a result of doing the job, and **the employer takes the worker as the worker is found**. Accordingly, the nurse was entitled to benefits for her injury because her employment acted upon her preexisting condition to produce a disability. *Beverly Healthcare v. Hare*, 51 So.3d 223 (Miss. Ct. App. 2010).

◆   An obese Georgia custodian bent to pick up a diuretic pill she had dropped, heard something pop in her knee, and collapsed. She sustained an anterior dislocation of her knee, for which she had undergone two prior surgeries. An administrative law judge held that because she was on duty and her job required her to pick things up off the floor, she was covered by workers' compensation. A trial court reversed, finding that her obesity caused her injury and that it could have occurred on or off the job. The Georgia Court of Appeals reversed. Bending over to pick up her medication was an employment function even if the pill was hers, and **her predisposition to dislocate her knee did not necessarily render her injury noncompensable**. Further, taking required medication did not amount to more than a slight deviation from the course of her employment. She was entitled to benefits. *Harris v. Peach County Board of Commissioners*, 674 S.E.2d 36 (Ga. Ct. App. 2009).

♦   An electrician also worked as a minister for a church. He injured his knee while performing electrical work. The Montana State Fund, as the company's workers' compensation insurer, accepted workers' compensation liability for his injury. Eventually he had surgery, and for a while his knee performed well. The following year he took a buyout offer from the company and worked only for the church However, his knee deteriorated until he could no longer work as a minister either. He sought temporary total disability benefits, and the workers' compensation court determined that the state fund had to pay them. The Montana Supreme Court affirmed that decision, holding that **the temporary aggravation of his preexisting knee injury while working as a minister did not constitute the last injurious exposure**. Thus, the state fund (and not the church) was liable for the increased benefits. *Lanes v. Montana State Fund*, 192 P.3d 1145 (Mont. 2008).

♦   A Vietnam veteran working for a mining company in Pennsylvania filed a claim for workers' compensation benefits after experiencing harassing comments of a homosexual nature from the mine foreman. He claimed that he had been traumatized by numerous acts of homosexuality he observed in the military and that the foreman's comments about wanting to have sex with him aggravated his posttraumatic stress disorder. The company asserted that the psychological injury suffered was a preexisting condition for which it should not be held liable. The Supreme Court of Pennsylvania held that **the harassing behavior, which violated the union contract and which resulted in discipline for the foreman, constituted abnormal working conditions, thus entitling the employee to benefits**. The foreman's statements were more than mere joking, crude behavior. Also, it did not matter that the employee suffered from a preexisting condition. *RAG (Cyprus) Emerald Resources, L.P. v. WCAB*, 912 A.2d 1278 (Pa. 2007).

♦   An Arkansas Wal-Mart employee claimed that she fell off a ladder and hurt her back. No one saw the fall. Later in the day she had a friend drive her to the ER. After three days off work, she agreed to see the company doctor, but became argumentative and walked out. Eventually she saw the company doctor and another physician, neither of whom found bruising, swelling or muscle spasms consistent with the pain she claimed she was having. She also failed to tell them she had suffered a back injury 13 years earlier (and that she had filed a workers' compensation claim at that time) or that she had been hospitalized for back pain three years prior to the fall. When she sought workers' compensation benefits, the Arkansas Court of Appeals agreed with the workers' compensation commission that **she failed to prove the accident caused her back pain** rather than a preexisting condition. She was not entitled to benefits. *English v. Wal-Mart Associates, Inc.*, No. CA 06-220, 2006 WL 2848659 (Ark. Ct. App. 10/4/06).

♦   An employee at a shipyard in Maine suffered from an inherited neurological condition that caused involuntary shaking of his head and arms. The shaking became worse when he experienced stress. When his co-workers called him derogatory names and subjected him to practical jokes because of his symptoms, he worried that he could no longer safely perform his job. Eventually, his doctor advised him to stop working, and his symptoms improved. He filed for workers' compensation benefits, which the company fought. An administrative law judge found that the employee was subjected to dehumanizing remarks and pranks that aggravated his disorder, and that working conditions prevented him from returning to the shipyard. The First Circuit upheld the decision to award him total disability benefits. **The fact that his medical condition was preexisting did not prevent him from obtaining benefits.** *Bath Iron Works Corp. v. Preston*, 380 F.3d 597 (1st Cir. 2004).

♦   An Arizona cabinet manufacturer hired a service worker who indicated in his application that he had been "wounded in combat NAM." He initially denied having mental or physical disabilities. In a subsequent employment interview, he revealed that he had posttraumatic stress disorder that required him to work outside a plant, away from people. Although he indicated that he had been wounded in a helicopter crash and had a bad back, he stated that he could lift over 50 pounds. He later suffered a back injury and filed a workers' compensation claim. The employer's insurer assigned him a permanent impairment and applied for reimbursement from the state special fund for the employee's preexisting posttraumatic stress disorder. An administrative judge awarded reimbursement, finding that the employee had properly advised the employer of the existence of his mental impairment under the written records requirement of state law, even though the written application had been supplemented with oral testimony. The court of appeals reversed.

The Supreme Court of Arizona stated that the purpose of the second injury fund was to provide incentives to employers to hire disabled workers by relieving them of the risk of increased liability from preexisting impairments and industrial injuries. The written records requirement should not be interpreted in a manner that defeated this legislative purpose. **Credible oral testimony offered in conjunction with written documents was sufficient to establish employer knowledge of a preexisting injury.** Here, the employer had been advised of the employee's general disability by the written record and supplementing oral evidence. It was entitled to reimbursement from the special fund, and the court reinstated the award. *Special Fund Division v. Industrial Comm'n of Arizona*, 953 P.2d 541 (Ariz. 1998).

◆   An Arkansas employee suffered a work-related injury that resulted in some degree of permanent physical impairment but did not result in any reduction in his wage-earning capacity. Eight years later, he suffered another compensable injury. The impairment resulting from this injury was allegedly greater than that which would have occurred but for his previous injury. The Workers' Compensation Commission determined that the second injury fund was not liable because the employee's previous injury was work related and did not result in a loss of earning capacity. The Arkansas Court of Appeals utilized a three-part test to determine whether the fund was liable. First, it agreed that the employee's earlier injury was a compensable injury. Second, the injury resulted in a permanent impairment. The court held that **the prior impairment need not result in a loss of earning capacity** and may be caused by either a work-related or a non-work-related injury. A contrary holding would impermissibly distinguish between types of handicapped persons. The court did not address the third part of the test, which required that the compensable injury combine with the recent injury to produce the current disability status. The court affirmed the finding that the employee was permanently and totally disabled, reversed the finding as to the liability of the second injury fund and remanded the case. *White Consolidated v. Rooney*, 866 S.W.2d 838 (Ark. Ct. App. 1993).

◆   A New Hampshire employee with a history of back problems allegedly injured his back while shoveling gravel for his employer. He filed a claim for a permanent partial disability award with the department of labor. The hearing officer deemed medical evidence insufficient to support a finding that the injury was a result of the shoveling at work. The employee appealed, claiming that the hearing officer failed to apply the amended statute allowing permanent partial disability awards for spinal column or spinal cord injuries. Further, the employee claimed the hearing officer erred in determining that any permanent impairment that existed, existed before the alleged injury. On appeal, the Supreme Court of New Hampshire affirmed the hearing officer's finding and dismissed the employee's claims. The court agreed that **benefits should not be awarded because the employee did not prove his condition arose from his employment**. Moreover, the medical evidence showed no evidence of a definite new injury. *Petition of Hyde*, 605 A.2d 228 (N.H. 1992).

◆   A Nebraska nursing attendant suffered a back injury as a result of transferring a patient from a wheelchair to a bed. The employer gave her some time off and workers' compensation benefits for temporary disability. After returning to work, her back pains continued. She consulted a doctor who found that she suffered from a naturally progressing back problem that could have been a congenital condition. The employee and employer presented conflicting evidence regarding whether the initial back injury exacerbated her naturally progressing condition. The state Workers' Compensation Court denied her claim for benefits. The Supreme Court of Nebraska affirmed. It recognized the compensation court's authority to weigh the conflicting evidence and testimony. Additionally, the expert testimony supported the finding that **the employee's condition resulted from the natural progression of her back condition**. *Liberty v. Colonial Acres Nursing Home*, 481 N.W.2d 189 (Neb. 1992).

D. The Coming and Going Rule

Generally, employers are not liable under workers' compensation for injuries sustained by employees while in transit to and from work.

However, under the coming and going rule, an employer can be liable for workers' compensation where an employee is injured on the way to or from work while on a special mission for the employer – for example, a car accident on the way to the bank to make a deposit before going home for the night.

Employers can also be liable where employees are required to be away from home for their jobs. Thus, an accident that occurs on the way to the work site from a hotel would likely be covered under workers' compensation.

◆   A hotel employee in Maryland got into an argument with a co-worker over a supply cart. The co-worker called a friend, who followed the employee as he drove another co-worker home. When he stopped his car to let the co-worker out, the friend emerged from his vehicle and shot the employee, rendering him a paraplegic. When he sought workers' compensation benefits, the hotel argued that he was not entitled to them. The case reached the Court of Special Appeals of Maryland, which agreed with the hotel that he was not entitled to benefits. His injuries did not arise out of his employment, they were not directed at him in the course of his employment, and the "coming and going rule" barred recovery for injuries occurring on the way to or from work. *Doe v. Buccini Pollin Group, Inc.*, 29 A.3d 999 (Md. Ct. Spec. App. 2011).

◆   A Rhode Island employee worked out of a company-owned cargo van, traveling to customers' locations to perform routine and emergency maintenance. He kept the van at his apartment because he was on-call all the time. While on his way to a central location to await a maintenance call one snowy morning, he encountered a stranded motorist blocking his exit. He pushed her free but injured his back in the process. When he filed for workers' compensation benefits, the Supreme Court of Rhode Island awarded them. He was on his way to a central location, and he was engaged in removing an obstacle that would allow him to conduct his employer's work. Thus, the injury was compensable under an exception to the coming and going rule. *McGloin v. Trammellcrow Services, Inc.*, 987 A.2d 881 (R.I. 2010).

◆   On his day off, a Nevada construction company employee was asked to deliver equipment from the construction yard to a job site. He did so using a company truck he was authorized to keep at his home. After dropping off the equipment, he headed for a location where he was doing a personal job. He got in an accident and was seriously injured two miles from the job site. When he sought workers' compensation benefits, the Nevada Supreme Court held that under the "special errand" exception to the coming and going rule, he would be entitled to benefits if the accident occurred while he was on a part of the road he would only have been on because of the errand he was asked to perform. The case was remanded for that determination. *Bob Allyn Masonry v. Murphy*, 183 P.3d 126 (Nev. 2008).

◆   A bank in Kansas leased 94% of a building and 737 of 757 spaces in the adjoining parking lot. While crossing the lot after leaving work, a bank employee slipped on a patch of sand that had been put down to prevent people from slipping on ice. She injured her hip, shoulder and elbow on the pavement, then filed a claim for workers' compensation. The case reached the Supreme Court of Kansas, which ruled that she was entitled to benefits. Here, **the bank had enough control over the parking lot for it to be considered part of the bank's premises**. Thus, since the employee was still on bank property, the "coming and going" rule did not apply to bar benefits. *Rinke v. Bank of America*, 148 P.3d 553 (Kan. 2006).

◆   An office equipment technician in Pennsylvania agreed to work for a company if he was given a company car. He signed a one-year contract that was not updated in following years. After becoming a supervisor and spending most of his time at the office rather than at clients' businesses, he was killed while driving to the office to repair a client's fax machines. His widow filed a claim for workers' compensation benefits. A workers' compensation judge denied benefits on the grounds that the technician was not killed in the course and scope of his employment. The case reached the Supreme Court of Pennsylvania, which disagreed. **Because the technician's employment contract included transportation to and from work, the "coming and going rule" did not apply to bar coverage.** *Wachs v. Workers' Compensation Appeals Board*, 884 A.2d 858 (Pa. 2005).

◆   An employee at a Pennsylvania car dealership wore the "wrong" casual clothes to work – his shirt did not carry the dealership's logo. He was given the option of buying a shirt with the logo on it or returning home for a proper shirt. He elected to go home. On his way back to the dealership, he was involved in a serious car accident that left him in a persistent vegetative state. His wife applied for workers' compensation benefits on his behalf, and the Workers' Compensation Appeals Board upheld the decision to award benefits. The dealership appealed, but the Pennsylvania Commonwealth Court upheld the award. Here, **the employee had been on a "special mission" for the dealership at the time of the accident**. Therefore, he had been acting in the course and scope of his employment so as to entitle him to benefits. He did not eat lunch or do anything else that would put him on his "own" time; instead, he immediately headed back to the dealership after changing his shirt. *Sloane Nissan v. WCAB*, 820 A.2d 925 (Pa. Commw. Ct. 2003).

◆   When a sales rep was placed on full commission, he negotiated for the right to work out of the office in his home. He only had to drive to the company office once a week. On one occasion, he drove to work and then stopped at his mailbox to pick up his personal and company mail on the way home. The mailbox was two blocks from his home but was not out of the way. As he was retrieving the mail, he slipped on the ice and fell, injuring himself. The employer's insurer refused to pay reasonable medical and workers' compensation benefits, arguing that the employee was injured while commuting. The Workers' Compensation Court ruled that the employee's injury was work related, since it occurred in the course and scope of his employment and was therefore compensable. It held the insurer liable for the employee's costs. The Montana Supreme Court affirmed. Here, the employee was traveling between two job sites: his company office and his home office. This was more than just going to and coming from work. **Since the injury occurred in the course of required travel, it was compensable.** *Bentz v. Liberty Northwest*, 57 P.3d 832 (Mont. 2002).

◆ A North Carolina yarn-service packer left work for the night. Exiting the plant, he found the gate at the back parking lot's chain-link fence locked. When he could not squeeze through the opening, he tried to climb the fence, fell and broke his leg. He filed a claim for workers' compensation benefits. The commission awarded him benefits, finding that even though he could have waited for someone to unlock the gate or walked around to the front door, his injury arose from his employment because he was not disobeying an order or thrill-seeking when he climbed the gate and was injured. The court of appeals affirmed. It noted that the coming and going rule did not act to bar the employee's claim because the employee was injured in the parking lot adjacent to the company's premises. The employee's negligence was not a bar to benefits because he was not intoxicated and did not willfully intend to injure himself or another. The Supreme Court of North Carolina reversed, noting that **the company provided a known safe and secure exit, which the employee elected not to use**. Also, climbing the fence was not an incidental activity of employment. *Arp v. Parkdale Mills, Inc.*, 576 S.E.2d 326 (N.C. 2003).

◆ A Kentucky employer furnished a truck to an employee to allow him to report directly to job sites without first reporting to an office. He was not compensated for travel time to and from home, but was paid for travel time between the office and job sites and was issued a credit card for fuel purchases. After performing work at an Indiana job site and the employer's office, he was killed in a traffic accident while going home. His survivors sought workers' compensation survivor's benefits, which the employer resisted. The Supreme Court of Kentucky awarded benefits. The employee's use of the vehicle had benefited the employer by allowing him to begin his work duties earlier in the day and work longer in the evening by avoiding a stop at the office. Since the employee had performed a service to the employer at the time of his death, **the work-related exception to the going and coming rule applied**. *Receveur Construction Co./Realm, Inc. v. Rogers*, 958 S.W.2d 18 (Ky. 1997).

◆ A Louisiana employer furnished van transportation to employees to a heliport for further transportation to job sites. A roustabout who chose instead to drive himself to the heliport was injured in a traffic accident and filed for workers' compensation benefits. The state workers' compensation office dismissed his claim, and the Court of Appeal of Louisiana affirmed. While an employee who is **required to check in at a certain place** and is injured en route to a work site is considered to be within the course of employment, this rule does not apply between home and the check-in place. The court rejected the roustabout's claim that the employer had expressly agreed to provide employee transportation, since a written employer policy only promised to provide transportation from its facility to a job site and not from an employee's home. *Bergeron v. Mar-Con, Inc.*, 705 So.2d 232 (La. Ct. App. 1997).

♦   A Utah insurance company employee made deliveries for her employer when its normal courier service experienced delays. She **picked up documents on her way home from work on a route that created a five-mile detour** from her normal way home. The employer did not pay her for her extra time, mileage or other expenses. After dropping off documents on her way to pick up her children at day care, the employee was involved in an accident. When her insurer denied coverage, she applied for workers' compensation benefits. An administrative law judge held that her injuries arose out of and in the course of employment. The commission reversed, finding that the employee was not on a special errand for the employer because the deliveries were part of her routine and were outside the course of her employment. The Supreme Court of Utah agreed that the delivery was part of her normal job duties and not a special errand. The relative regularity, lack of onerous circumstances on the employee and lack of suddenness in the work assignment were all factors supporting the employer's view. The accident had not occurred as the result of a deviation from the employee's normal route home and was not substantial enough to make it any different from the normal risks presented to all commuters. *Drake v. Industrial Comm'n of Utah*, 939 P.2d 177 (Utah 1997).

♦   A maintenance supervisor at an Iowa plant responded to an emergency weekend call involving malfunctioning equipment. He made the repairs and left for home by an indirect route. He was severely injured in an accident and became quadriplegic. His wife received special training in caring for him, and their home was modified to accommodate his wheelchair use. The family also purchased a modified van and other adaptive equipment. He returned to work in a supervisory position at the same salary with the use of adaptive equipment. He filed for workers' compensation benefits since many of his expenses were not covered under his group health and accident insurance plan. The state industrial commissioner's office assigned an 80% industrial disability based on the severity of his injury and his compromised ability to compete for jobs. He was also awarded as reasonable medical expenses the cost of van conversion, home modification, appliances and home nursing services provided by his wife. An Iowa court and the Supreme Court of Iowa affirmed. **An employee responding to a weekend call apart from usual employment is acting for the benefit of the employer**, and the coming and going time of such a special errand is within the course of employment. Even though the employee had deviated from his normal return route, he had not abandoned his special errand. The injury was compensable. *Quaker Oats Co. v. Ciha*, 552 N.W.2d 143 (Iowa 1996).

♦   A New York security guard was required to wear a uniform provided by his employer, and he was subject to discipline if he failed to keep it clean. He used a dry-cleaning establishment at which the employer maintained an account for the purpose of encouraging guards to have their uniforms dry cleaned. After dropping off some uniforms on his way home from work, he had a car accident and sustained serious injuries. The state's Workers' Compensation Board ruled that he sustained an accidental injury arising out of and in the course of his employment. The Supreme Court, Appellate Division, reversed, finding that the guard was not on a special errand for the employer because he was not required to have his uniform dry cleaned. The New York Court of Appeals reinstated the holding of the Workers' Compensation Board. Here, the guard was engaged in a special errand at the time of his injury. **The employer encouraged its employees to have their uniforms dry cleaned** by paying for those services, and it received a benefit in the form of its employees' appearance being neat and clean. *Neacosia v. New York Power Authority*, 649 N.E.2d 1188 (N.Y. 1995).

III. MODIFICATION AND TERMINATION OF BENEFITS

Benefits can be increased where the injured employee's situation worsens, and they can be decreased where the employee's situation improves. They can be terminated completely if the employee recovers or is able to return to work. They can also be terminated or offset for other reasons.

A. Modification of Benefits

There are four basic kinds of workers' compensation benefit awards: permanent total disability, temporary total disability, permanent partial disability, and temporary partial disability.

— Total disability occurs where the employee cannot regularly engage in an ordinary occupation, given the employee's physical impairment, level of education, training, experience and age.
— Partial disability is a lesser degree of impairment and is assigned a numerical value (a percentage of disability).
— Permanent disability means there is no reasonable expectation of improvement.
— Temporary disability means that the employee is in the process of healing and has not reached the stage of maximum medical improvement.

These awards can be modified up or down as the employee's changing condition merits. Thus, an employee whose condition deteriorates can seek increased payments, just as an employer can seek to pay less where an employee's condition improves.

♦ An employee of an insulation company in North Carolina retired. Years later, he was diagnosed with mesothelioma, which is caused by asbestos. He filed a claim for workers' compensation benefits but died the next day. His widow then filed an amended claim for death benefits. The commission awarded 400 weeks of death benefits at $308 per week – the maximum compensation rate for 1987, which was his last year of employment. The widow appealed, and the Court of Appeals of North Carolina held that **the correct year**

for determining the maximum compensation rate was 2006 – the year the employee was diagnosed with mesothelioma. Using that latter year, the widow was entitled to receive $538 per week for 400 weeks. *Johnson v. Covil Corp.*, 711 S.E.2d 500 (N.C. Ct. App. 2011).

◆   A Pennsylvania baggage handler injured his back and began collecting workers' compensation benefits. Eight years later, **he filed an amended claim seeking benefits for treatment of depression and anxiety**, which he said he developed as a result of being in constant pain from the injury. A workers' compensation judge held the company liable for 50% of the employee's psychiatric treatment because the injury was not the sole cause of the depression. An appeals board reversed, but the Commonwealth Court reversed the board and ordered 100% reimbursement for psychiatric treatment. Here, the employee had no preexisting psychiatric problems, and apportionment was not available because there was only one injury, from which the depression stemmed. *Huddy v. Workers' Compensation Appeal Board*, 905 A.2d 589 (Pa. Commw. Ct. 2006).

◆   An employee at a Nissan plant in Tennessee claimed that he suffered a loss of hearing as a result of noise from the assembly line. He filed for workers' compensation benefits. A trial court found that his ability to hear was not paramount to his job performance and awarded him a 9% vocational impairment of 150 weeks. The court of appeals raised the award to 45%, noting as it did so his loss of enjoyment of everyday activities. On further appeal, the Tennessee Supreme Court affirmed in part, noting that the 9% figure was too low. However, **Tennessee law does not allow for hedonic damages** (loss of enjoyment of life). The court remanded the case for a determination of whether the court of appeals took that into account when it issued the 45% award. *Lang v. Nissan North America, Inc.*, 170 S.W.3d 564 (Tenn. 2005).

◆   An ironworker slipped on a beam and fell, injuring his back. He filed for workers' compensation benefits. An MRI revealed degenerative disc disease and conflicting testimony was offered at his hearing. An administrative law judge awarded him 25% permanent partial disability. On review, the Labor and Industrial Relations Commission (LIRC) modified the award, finding total and permanent disability. The employer appealed. The Missouri Supreme Court affirmed, noting that a reviewing court was not required to view the evidence and all reasonable inferences drawn therefrom in the light most favorable to the LIRC award. As a result, it needed only to determine whether there was sufficient evidence to support the award. Here, **despite the conflicting evidence about the severity of the injury, there was sufficient evidence to support the award of benefits**. *Hampton v. Big Boy Steel Erection*, 121 S.W.3d 220 (Mo. 2003).

◆   The West Virginia legislature responded to the threatened integrity of the state workers' compensation fund by amending state law to limit permanent partial disability awards. Such awards were limited to claimants having suffered a whole body medical impairment of at least 50% without regard to the economic effect of the injury. A workers' compensation claimant with a 32% whole body disability rating brought a lawsuit asserting that the act violated his rights under the state constitution. The Supreme Court of Appeals of West Virginia observed that while **the amendment created a high threshold for receiving a permanent partial disability award**, the amendment did not modify the act's traditional reliance on the nature of an industrial injury as opposed to the claimant's economic circumstances. Because the government had a legitimate purpose in preserving the financial integrity of the state workers' compensation fund and the legislation appeared to meet this purpose, the court refused to declare the amendment unconstitutional on equal protection grounds. However, the legislature had violated the claimant's due process rights by waiving the 90-day waiting period that normally affects new state legislation. This had a retroactive effect on the claimant's case, and he was entitled to consideration of his claim. *State of West Virginia ex rel. Blankenship v. Richardson*, 474 S.E.2d 906 (W.Va. 1996).

♦   The New Mexico workers' compensation act used current American Medical Association (AMA) guides to evaluate medical impairment for determining the appropriate level of permanent or partial disability benefits for workers' compensation claims. Two employees who were injured in the scope of their employment filed claims for workers' compensation benefits and were rated through use of the AMA Guide. They contested the ratings and appealed. Before the Supreme Court of New Mexico, **they asserted that use of the AMA Guide was an unconstitutional delegation of legislative power**. They also asserted that they had been denied their equal protection rights to determine the existence or extent of an industrial disability. The court observed that many states have delegated highly technical issues, such as industrial impairment, to an independent authority in order to take advantage of its expertise. Here, there was no delegation of legislative power to an outside entity. Workers' compensation judges retained the authority to decide cases and use their discretion. The act did not violate the state constitution, and the court affirmed the rulings on the appropriate level of benefits. *Madrid v. St. Joseph Hospital*, 928 P.2d 250 (N.M. 1996).

♦   A housekeeper employed by the Catholic Archdiocese of Seattle complained of sexual harassment by her supervisor. She later injured her hand at work and required a three-month medical leave. She obtained workers' compensation benefits. Her supervisor repeated the harassment when she returned to work. When her hand required further surgery, she was absent from work for eight months under assurances that her position would be kept open. However, the archdiocese failed to preserve the job and refused to hire her for other vacancies. The housekeeper sued the archdiocese for discrimination, among other claims. A trial court awarded $150,000 in damages plus $47,000 in attorneys' fees. The court of appeals held that the trial court had erroneously refused to offset the damage award by the amount of lost wages under the workers' compensation system. The Supreme Court of Washington held that **the employee was not required to mitigate her damages under the collateral source rule**. The compensation had been made for two different injuries:

discrimination and the hand injury. The trial court had not committed error by refusing to set off the damage award by the employee's workers' compensation benefits. The court reversed and remanded the case. *Wheeler v. Catholic Archdiocese of Seattle*, 880 P.2d 29 (Wash. 1994).

◆   A supermarket clerk slipped and fell on a wet floor, sustaining injuries that required medical treatment and vocational rehabilitation. She was paid temporary disability indemnity benefits and received a permanent disability indemnity of 61%. She sought a 50% increase in her award under Section 4553 of the California Labor Code, alleging serious and willful misconduct by the employer. At an administrative hearing, it was determined that there were no safety mats on the floor and that employees were advised to walk carefully because safety mats would be a nuisance. The workers' compensation judge found that the employee's injury occurred as a result of serious and willful misconduct and ordered a 50% increase in her total compensation benefits. The Workers' Compensation Appeals Board affirmed the finding of serious and willful misconduct. However, it held that the 50% increase in compensation applied only to compensation indemnity and not to non-indemnity benefits. The California Court of Appeal held that **the 50% increase recoverable under Section 4553 should include non-indemnity benefits, such as medical treatment payments, medical legal fees, and vocational rehabilitation costs**. It noted that the state labor code defined compensation to include every benefit or payment conferred upon an injured employee, including vocational rehabilitation. The 50% increase did not constitute punitive damages and was not constitutionally excessive so long as the total benefits payable were not more than was necessary to fully compensate the clerk for her damages. The court annulled the board's decision and remanded the case for further proceedings. *Ferguson v. WCAB*, 39 Cal.Rptr.2d 806 (Cal. Ct. App. 1995).

◆   An Iowa employee's arm was amputated after she caught her hand in a meat grinder. She received partial disability benefits for the impairment to her right arm (a scheduled injury to a specific part of the body). However, the industrial commissioner denied her benefits for an alleged injury to her central nervous system as a result of pain at the "limb's former situs" (an unscheduled injury – based on injury to the body as a whole). The employee challenged the denial of benefits, alleging that Iowa statute Section 8534(u) entitled her to further compensation for the phantom limb pain. The court held that, pursuant to paragraph (m), the employee was entitled only to compensation for scheduled injuries. The Iowa Court of Appeals determined that psychological conditions resulting from work-related physical trauma are compensable as unscheduled injuries. Although no Iowa decision addressed compensation for phantom limb pain, New Mexico and Pennsylvania have held phantom limb pain to be a disabling impairment. Here, the court of appeals determined that **the phantom pain experienced by the employee at the limb's former situs was analogous to a psychological condition**. Consequently, it was a compensable unscheduled injury under paragraph (u). The case was reversed and remanded for a determination of the functional loss to the employee's body. *Dowell v. Wagler*, 509 N.W.2d 134 (Iowa Ct. App. 1993).

♦   A Rhode Island painter sustained severe injuries to his right leg when he fell between a roof and scaffolding. He filed for benefits with the Workers' Compensation Commission, which awarded him 125 weeks of disfigurement compensation. However, due to complications, the employee's right lower leg was amputated. He then filed with the Workers' Compensation Court seeking additional disfigurement compensation. The trial judge ordered the employer to pay **15 weeks of additional disfigurement compensation**. The Appellate Division affirmed. Before the Supreme Court of Rhode Island, the employee contended that the disfigurement award of 140 total weeks of compensation was highly inadequate. The court noted that the original disfigurement was 125 weeks for what the physician termed as a crushed leg. However, the assessed compensation for the disfigurement caused by the amputation was for 15 weeks (approximately eight times less than the value of the initial award). Accordingly, the court determined that the award was inadequate and remanded the case for further proceedings to determine the proper assessment. *Johnson v. State*, 634 A.2d 863 (R.I. 1993).

♦   A Pennsylvania welder became disabled as a result of exposure to zinc fumes. He received workers' compensation benefits based upon an average weekly wage that included a prorated $2,750 annual bonus. One year later, the welder filed a petition to review the compensation award, claiming that the entire bonus should be included in the quarter in which it was actually paid and that the same quarter should be used in calculating his average weekly wage. The Supreme Court of Pennsylvania determined that where the employee was paid a wage that was determined annually, **the average weekly wage was to be calculated by dividing the annual wage by 52**. Because the bonus had been paid as an annual performance bonus, the welder's wage was an annual wage that required prorating the bonus over 52 weeks. *Lane Enterprises, Inc. v. WCAB*, 644 A.2d 726 (Pa. 1994).

♦   The Michigan legislature enacted a statute allowing "benefit coordination" to enable employers to decrease benefits to those disabled employees who were eligible to receive wage-loss compensation from other employer-funded sources. Certain employers attempted to apply the law retroactively. The legislature then enacted a law disapproving this practice and requiring reimbursement. The employers sought judicial relief, and the controversy eventually reached the U.S. Supreme Court. The employers argued that the reimbursement provision violated the Contract Clause and the Due Process Clause of the U.S. Constitution. The Court disagreed.

    With respect to the Contract Clause, there was no contractual relationship here that had been impaired by the new statute. Although employment contracts existed prior to the new law's enactment, they did not address the specific workers' compensation terms at issue. Further, there was no due process violation because **the reimbursement provision was a rational means of meeting a legitimate objective** – preserving injured workers' rights to their full benefits. The Court thus held that the Michigan statute did not violate the Constitution. *General Motors Corp. v. Romein*, 503 U.S. 181, 112 S.Ct. 1105, 117 L.Ed.2d 328 (1992).

B. Termination of Benefits

Where an injured employee is able to return to work without restrictions, or is able to take another job that is less physically demanding, but which pays the same or better, and the employee either takes the job or refuses the offer, workers' compensation benefits can often be terminated. Benefits can also be terminated where an employee acts fraudulently or unreasonably.

♦ A manual laborer in Pennsylvania injured his back when he pulled a heavy piece of equipment from a ditch. This aggravated his degenerative disc disease. He obtained workers' compensation and later went to work for another company as a driver. After injuring his back while sneezing, he obtained total temporary disability benefits for one month. He went to work for a third employer as a driver and injured his back again, this time while bending over to tie his shoe. He again sought total disability benefits, presenting evidence that he was in great pain and couldn't get around without a cane. However, surveillance video showed him going to a salvage yard with a friend, using a jack to get auto equipment, and jumping into the back of his pickup, all without a cane or a limp. The Commonwealth Court of Pennsylvania ruled against him, holding that **he failed to meet his burden of proof that his pain had persisted through the proceedings**. *Soja v. W.C.A.B.*, 33 A.3d 702 (Pa. Commw. Ct. 2011).

♦ A North Carolina employee suffered a knee injury and was told by her doctor that she could not kneel, squat or lift more than 40 pounds. Her employer offered her temporary light-duty work, but only during the daytime and at a rate of $6.50 per hour instead of her old rate of $10.50 per hour. She had previously worked the 3:00 – 11:00 shift for childcare reasons. She told her employer she couldn't work the day shift and was fired. Within two weeks, she found another job doing data entry part-time and earning $8.50 per hour. Her old company then sent her a formal offer of light-duty work and asserted that she wasn't entitled to medical and disability benefits because she had constructively refused suitable employment. The case reached the Court of Appeals of North Carolina, which held that **the company's offer of light-duty work was not an offer of suitable employment so as to permit the suspension or termination of benefits**. And the company failed to show that she could have found other work that paid as much as she had earned prior to her injury. *Wynn v. United Health Services/Two Rivers Health-Trent Campus*, 716 S.E.2d 373 (N.C. Ct. App. 2011).

♦ An Illinois carpenter suffered heatstroke on the job and was dropped on his head while being transported to the ambulance. He suffered head and neck injuries. A doctor recommended spinal fusion surgery, which he elected to delay until he could determine whether medication and physical therapy would work. He received temporary total disability (TTD) benefits and did light-duty work until he was fired for scrawling religious graffiti in a storage room. He sought to continue receiving workers' compensation because he had not reached maximum medical improvement, while the company sought to terminate his benefits because of his firing. The Illinois Supreme Court held that **his entitlement to TTD benefits was completely separate from the issue of whether he was properly fired**. Thus, he was entitled to benefits post-termination until his injury stabilized. *Interstate Scaffolding, Inc. v. Illinois Workers' Compensation Comm'n*, 923 N.E.2d 266 (Ill. 2010).

◆   A Missouri truck driver, who was also a Jehovah's Witness, suffered a severe injury at work and was taken to the hospital, where he refused a blood transfusion because he considered that a sin. Seven days later he died, and the company began paying death benefits to his widow. Two years after the accident, the company stopped paying the death benefits on the grounds that he had unreasonably refused medical treatment. The widow sued and won. The Missouri Court of Appeals noted that the state workers' compensation act allowed an employee to receive treatment "by prayer or spiritual means." Because the statute was meant to liberally accommodate an employee's religious beliefs, **the employee could not be deemed to have acted unreasonably in refusing the transfusion**. *Wilcut v. Innovative Warehousing*, 247 S.W.3d 1 (Mo. Ct. App. 2008).

◆   A Louisiana forklift operator suffered a back injury when her forklift hit a hole. She became unable to work, eventually being diagnosed with fibromyalgia and osteoarthritis, allegedly caused by the accident. Her employer paid her $267 a week for 535 weeks for total temporary disability (TTD). After her doctor sent the employer a letter stating that she had "significant permanent restrictions as far as work activities," but that she could resume some form of work, the employer terminated her benefits. She appealed, and the case reached the Supreme Court of Louisiana. The court held that she was entitled to supplemental earnings benefits, and the employer was not entitled to a credit for the TTD benefits it had already paid. However, **she was not entitled to permanent total disability benefits because she failed to prove by clear and convincing evidence that she was physically unable to engage in any employment at all**. *Frith v. Riverwood, Inc.*, 892 So.2d 7 (La. 2005).

◆   An Ohio man applied for a truck driver position and was required to list the most current five previous employers. He failed to include an employer he worked for during an eight-month period and under whom he made a workers' compensation claim. However, he did list another employer under whom he made such a claim. While working in the new job, he suffered a neck injury and was certified with a temporary total disability. The employer discovered the unlisted employer and fired the driver for falsifying his application. It also sought to stop paying workers' compensation. The Ohio Court of Appeals refused to find that the driver had voluntarily abandoned his employment by failing to list the prior employer. **The driver did not intend to deceive the employer when he failed to include the prior job; he merely forgot.** As a result, he was entitled to continuing benefits. *State ex rel. Strimbu, Inc. v. Industrial Comm'n of Ohio*, No. 03AP-71, 2004 WL 1277770 (Ohio Ct. App. 2004).

* An employee injured his back on the job while working for a manufacturer. He took a few weeks off work, then returned to a light-duty assignment. After a few months, he quit, but refused to sign a "quit slip." In response, the manufacturer terminated his employment when he failed to show up for work for several days. Nearly two years later, he applied for workers' compensation benefits, and almost two years after that, he offered to return to work. The case reached the Supreme Court of Michigan, which held that the employee was **not entitled to benefits because he had refused the manufacturer's offer of reasonable employment**. Although he would have been able to obtain benefits for the period of time following his offer to return to work, a workers' compensation judge had found that his disability ended 10 months before that time. *Perez v. Keeler Brass Co.*, 608 N.W.2d 45 (Mich. 2000).

* A Maryland worker qualified for temporary total disability benefits due to a work-related injury. Two years later, he was incarcerated. His employer quit paying his temporary total disability benefits for several months during the sentence and withheld benefits for one month after his release from prison. The state workers' compensation commission denied the employee's demand for benefits during the period of incarceration but reinstated his benefits for the month following his release. The Court of Appeals of Maryland held that **incarceration did not affect the employee's entitlement to benefits**. The state workers' compensation act did not expressly allow the suspension or termination of temporary total disability benefits to otherwise qualified workers during periods of incarceration. The only statutory exception allowing termination of benefits was where a claimant unreasonably refused to submit to a medical examination. The employee was entitled to continue receiving benefits so long as the disability persisted and continued to impair his wage-earning capacity. The court followed the majority of jurisdictions in reaching this conclusion, citing decisions of the Nevada and Wyoming Supreme Courts. *Bowen v. Smith*, 342 Md. 449, 677 A.2d 81 (Md. 1996).

* The Pennsylvania legislature amended the state workers' compensation act to authorize employers to stop paying total disability benefits to incarcerated claimants during their incarceration. A worker who received total disability benefits was jailed on the same day the amendment took effect. The employer quit paying benefits and filed a petition to suspend benefits. The employee sought reinstatement of benefits plus a statutory penalty. The workers' compensation appeals board held that the employer had violated the act but refused to award a penalty. The Commonwealth Court of Pennsylvania stated that **in general, suspension of benefits is appropriate when a claimant's earning power is no longer affected by a work-related injury**. The event that caused the suspension of the employee's benefits here was his incarceration, which occurred after the effective date of the amendment. The court affirmed the order denying the petition to suspend benefits. However, the employee was not entitled to a penalty because the amendment did not provide clear guidance or procedures for employers seeking to cut off benefits. *Banic v. WCAB*, 664 A.2d 1081 (Pa. Commw. Ct. 1995).

IV. EMPLOYEE MISCONDUCT

Where an employee commits misconduct in the workplace by, for example, violating known safety rules, the employer can raise this as a defense in an action for benefits. Further, disregard of a doctor's advice may be enough to allow for the cessation of benefits.

◆ A Tennessee truck driver claimed that he was told he had to make a delivery to California by a certain time four days later. While driving through New Mexico on a straight road, he lost control of his truck and overturned. He admitted that he might have fallen asleep at the wheel. When he applied for workers' compensation, the company fought the claim, asserting that **he failed to take a rest break after 10 hours, in violation of company policy**. Instead, his GPS system showed that he drove for 36 straight hours before the accident. The Tennessee Supreme Court upheld the denial of benefits, finding the company more credible than the driver. The driver lied on his application about taking methadone for a foot condition, which would have barred him from driving a truck in interstate commerce under DOT regulations. And the company had previously fired 36 drivers for violating the rest-break rule. *Keith v. Western Express, Inc.*, No. M2011-00653 WC R3 WC (Tenn. 2/16/12).

◆ A nurse aide in Nebraska applied for a job at a hospital. She disclosed that she had suffered a back injury while lifting a patient at a nursing home, but she failed to disclose another back injury she suffered while lifting a patient at another hospital. She injured her back a third time while lifting a patient. She sought workers' compensation benefits, which the hospital fought. It asserted that her misrepresentation barred her from recovering benefits. However, the Nebraska Supreme Court disagreed. It noted that **her misrepresentation occurred when she was an applicant, not an employee**. Accordingly, her misrepresentation could not be used to deny benefits. *Bassinger v. Nebraska Heart Hospital*, 806 N.W.2d 395 (Neb. 2011).

◆ A Florida welder sustained a compensable back injury and underwent surgery. He returned to work in a modified position but had trouble with even the reduced strain on his back. He resigned, writing to the company that he was taking a better offer with another company. However, he did not mention the difficulties he had experienced after his surgery. He stayed in the new job, which was much easier on his back (but which paid less than his earlier job) for a year until his back became worse and he had to quit that position as well. When he sought workers' compensation benefits from the first employer and its carrier, they asserted that his resignation letter amounted to misconduct. They claimed that he made intentional misrepresentations for the purpose of gaining benefits. A workers' compensation judge and the Florida appellate court disagreed. The judge believed his testimony that **the false assertion in his resignation letter was made to protect his future employment opportunities, not to further his chances of obtaining benefits**. *Steel Dynamics, Inc. – New Millenium v. Markham*, 46 So.3d 641 (Fla. Dist. Ct. App. 2010).

✦   A South Carolina construction worker sustained a back injury while moving lumber and removing a fence. He underwent lumbar fusion surgery and sought workers' compensation benefits. The employer asserted that he had misrepresented his back condition on his application and that he was not entitled to benefits because he was not really an employee (by virtue of the fraudulent medical statements on his application). In fact, the employee had previously injured his back while with the Navy and while working for a different construction company. The Workers' Compensation Commission awarded the employee benefits, but the Supreme Court of South Carolina reversed. **The employee's fraudulent responses on his application vitiated the employment relationship and barred his recovery of workers' compensation benefits.** *Brayboy v. Workforce*, 681 S.E.2d 567 (S.C. 2009).

✦   A Michigan employee of a company that promoted Martin Luther King's mission of racial equality and reconciliation refused to attend an annual staff development event in Dearborn because she had had bad experiences there as an African-American child. Her supervisor told her she would be docked a day's pay for refusing to attend. The CEO then docked her two days' pay and took away some of her responsibilities. The CEO also shook her finger at the employee and told her she didn't deserve a paycheck. As a result, the employee became deeply depressed and unable to work. She sought workers' compensation benefits. The Michigan Supreme Court held that she was not entitled to them. Here, **her illness arose out of her "intentional and willful" violation of a workplace rule** – that she attend the mandatory event. *Brackett v. Focus Hope, Inc.*, 753 N.W.2d 207 (Mich. 2008).

✦   A teenage employee of a restaurant in Ohio was told never to boil water in a pressure cooker to clean it. A supervisor saw him doing this and warned him against it, explaining that he could be severely injured if he did so. Later, an experienced co-worker saw him adding water again and told him to stop. Shortly thereafter, despite a warning from yet another co-worker not to open the lid, the employee did so and was severely burned by the boiling water that escaped under extreme pressure. Two others were also severely burned. He later obtained temporary total disability (TTD) benefits under workers' compensation, then was fired after an investigation. The company sought to discontinue paying benefits, but the Supreme Court of Ohio ruled that it had to keep paying them. **The employee's termination was causally related to his injury. Thus, his misconduct was not a voluntary job abandonment and did not preclude him from receiving TTD benefits.** *Gross v. Industrial Comm'n of Ohio*, 874 N.E.2d 1162 (Ohio 2007).

✦   While under the influence of methamphetamine, a construction worker in Arizona fell off his drywall stilts and injured himself. He applied for workers' compensation. An administrative law judge denied benefits. The case reached the Arizona Supreme Court, which consolidated it with another case involving an employee who had used alcohol the night before he had a workplace accident and tested positive for alcohol impairment. The court stated that the statute prohibiting recovery of benefits for alcohol or drug-impaired employees (unless they could prove that the impairment was not a contributing cause of the accident) was unconstitutional as applied here. **The statute eliminated claims for injuries partially caused by necessary risks or dangers** of employment, thereby conflicting with the state constitution. *Grammatico v. Industrial Comm'n of Arizona*, 117 P.3d 786 (Ariz. 2005).

✦   A New Jersey employee worked at a retail store where arm-wrestling matches were commonplace. He broke his arm during a match with his supervisor and submitted a claim for workers' compensation. The employer opposed the claim, asserting that the injury had involved a recreational activity and thus was not compensable under workers' compensation. It appealed a final administrative ruling in the employee's favor to the Superior Court of New Jersey, Appellate Division, which observed that state law allows for compensation where an employee is injured as the result of horseplay so long as the horseplay is not instigated by the employee. However, **compensation is disallowed unless the horseplay is a regular incident of employment** and produces a benefit to the employer that goes beyond improvement in employee health and morale. Because the employee could not show that the arm-wrestling conferred any such benefit upon the employer, the court reversed the award of benefits. *Quinones v. P.C. Richard & Son*, 310 N.J.Super. 63, 707 A.2d 1372 (N.J. Super. Ct. App. Div. 1998).

✦   However, in a Nebraska case, a roofing laborer challenged a co-worker to an arm-wrestling match in response to his taunting for carrying less paint than other employees. Both men fell from the roof, and the taunted employee broke his ankle. He filed a claim for workers' compensation benefits, which was allowed. The Supreme Court of Nebraska ruled that an **insubstantial deviation that does not measurably detract from work** does not take an employee's case out of the workers' compensation regime. Here, the injury had arisen from work-related banter and was the result of an accidental slip during the course of momentary horseplay. The court affirmed the ruling for the employee. *Varela v. Fisher Roofing Co., Inc.*, 253 Neb. 667, 572 N.W.2d 780 (Neb. 1998).

✦   A Virginia construction company hired an employee who responded negatively to a job application question asking whether he had been charged or convicted of any crime. He was soon fired for absenteeism but was rehired the following year. On his second job application, he left the criminal record question blank. When the employee submitted a workers' compensation claim, the employer learned that he had been convicted of breaking and entering. A company human resources representative testified at a workers' compensation hearing that the employee would not have been rehired had the company known of his criminal record. The state Workers' Compensation Commission held that the employer had not relied upon the employee's misrepresentation in rehiring him. The Supreme Court of Virginia affirmed. In order to defeat the application, the employer had to prove that it relied upon the false representation in the application, that the **employer's reliance on the misrepresentation resulted in injury** and that there was a causal relationship between the injury and the misrepresentation. The employer had made no attempt to verify the employee's application and had not relied upon his misrepresentation. *Falls Church Construction Co. v. Laidler*, 493 S.E.2d 521 (Va. 1997).

◆   A Virginia employer hired an applicant and requested evidence of U.S. citizenship, including a social security card and other identification, as required by the Immigration and Naturalization Service. The employer hired the applicant because it thought the forged documents he provided were valid. When the employee broke his ankle, the workers' compensation commission denied his claim for benefits because he had misrepresented his eligibility to work legally in the U.S. The employee appealed to the court of appeals, claiming that despite the misrepresentation, an employer-employee relationship existed and that the employer had failed to prove any causal connection between the misrepresentation and the injury. The court held that there was a causal connection between the claimant's inability to work legally and the injury received that defeated the claim for workers' compensation. The Supreme Court of Virginia disagreed with the reasoning of the court of appeals, but upheld the result. **As an illegal alien, the claimant was not an "employee"** for purposes of the workers' compensation act and thus was not entitled to benefits. *Granados v. Windson Development Corp.*, 509 S.E.2d 290 (Va. 1999).

◆   Georgia workers' compensation law disallows claims where a workplace injury or death is caused by intoxication by alcohol, marijuana, or a controlled substance. An employee who unjustifiably refuses to submit to drug testing must overcome **a rebuttable presumption that the accident or injury was caused by alcohol, marijuana or a controlled substance**. An employee of a self-insured employer was injured when he drove his forklift into a wall shortly after he had been observed smoking marijuana by a supervisory employee. He refused to take drug tests on three occasions during his week of hospitalization, asserting that he had been given narcotic pain medications in the ambulance. The employer contested his claim for workers' compensation benefits, and an administrative law judge agreed that he had unjustifiably refused the test and was subject to the rebuttable presumption that the injury was caused by marijuana. The Supreme Court of Georgia upheld that determination, finding that the employer did not have to give prior notice that refusing to submit to the test could result in the denial of benefits. *Georgia Self-Insurers Guaranty Trust Fund v. Thomas*, 501 S.E.2d 818 (Ga. 1998).

V. LONGSHORE AND HARBOR WORKERS' COMPENSATION ACT

The Longshore and Harbor Workers' Compensation Act (LHWCA) provides compensation for the death or disability of persons engaged in "maritime employment." For the LHWCA to apply,

—the injured person must have been injured in the course of employment,
—the injury must have occurred upon navigable waters (including adjoining areas like piers and wharfs),

—the employer must have employees engaged in maritime employment, and

—the employee must have been engaged in maritime employment.

The LHWCA was intended to supplement state workers' compensation laws and to provide a minimum federal remedy. Where state workers' compensation laws are more generous than the LHWCA, employees can avoid the LHWCA in favor of the state's system.

◆   The LHWCA allows awards to be modified upon a change in conditions or a mistake in a factual determination. A longshore worker injured his back and leg while working and received compensation under the LHWCA. He was retrained as a crane operator and was reemployed full time with additional work as a heavy truck operator. His earnings were about three times more than before his injury, and the employer moved to modify the disability award. An administrative law judge ordered disability payments discontinued even though the employee's physical condition had not improved. A benefits review board affirmed the modification order, but the U.S. Court of Appeals, Ninth Circuit, reversed, finding no authorization to modify the award absent changed physical conditions. The U.S. Supreme Court reversed and remanded, finding that modification of an LHWCA award is permissible where wage-earning capacity has been reduced, restored or improved.

The Ninth Circuit reversed the order to discontinue compensation payments, and the Supreme Court again accepted review. It observed that the uncertain nature of an employee injury and the need for swift resolution of compensation issues prohibited the complete foreclosure of an LHWCA remedy even where an employee's wage-earning capacity was not currently diminished. The employee was entitled to nominal compensation, which would hold open **the possibility of future modification should his earnings later fall below his pre-injury level**. An injured employee's disability is not necessarily reflected in actual wages earned after an injury, and an LHWCA fact-finder must make a determination that takes the future effect of a disability into account. The Court vacated the Ninth Circuit's judgment. *Metropolitan Stevedore Co. v. Rambo*, 521 U.S. 121, 117 S.Ct. 1953, 138 L.Ed.2d 327 (1997).

◆   A Mississippi shipbuilding company employee was exposed to asbestos at work. He was later diagnosed as suffering from asbestosis, chronic bronchitis and possible malignancy in his lungs. He filed a claim for disability benefits under the LHWCA, and his employer admitted liability. He then sued 23 manufacturers and suppliers of asbestos and entered into settlement agreements with eight of them. His wife joined in the settlements and released any cause of action she might have for wrongful death. None of these settlements were approved by the employer. After the employee died, the wife filed a claim for death benefits under the LHWCA, which was granted. The employer contested the claim on the ground that the wife had been a "person entitled to compensation" under the LHWCA who was required to obtain the employer's approval before entering into the settlements. Thus, because she had failed to do so, she forfeited her eligibility for death benefits. The U.S. Court of Appeals,

Fifth Circuit, affirmed the grant of death benefits to the wife. The U.S. Supreme Court held that **before the injured worker's death, his wife had not been a "person entitled to compensation" for death benefits**. Thus, she did not have to obtain the employer's approval of the settlements and did not forfeit her right to collect death benefits under the LHWCA. *Ingalls Shipbuilding, Inc. v. Director, OWCP*, 519 U.S. 248, 117 S.Ct. 796, 136 L.Ed.2d 736 (1997).

♦   Five employees were injured while involved in shipbuilding or ship repair activities. Although the LHWCA applied to the injuries sustained, they applied for benefits under Pennsylvania's workers' compensation law. The employer asserted that the LHWCA was the exclusive remedy, but the state administrative agency ruled that the LHWCA did not preempt state workers' compensation laws. The U.S. Supreme Court noted that **the LHWCA supplemented, rather than supplanted, state workers' compensation law**. It was intended to provide complete coverage to maritime laborers so that they would not have to guess which jurisdiction they were supposed to be in before filing a claim. Here, by filing under state law, the workers may have gotten better benefits than under an exclusively federal system, but the LHWCA was enacted to raise awards to a federal minimum because state compensation laws were generally less generous. Thus, the workers were entitled to state benefits. The Court affirmed the state court decisions. *Sun Ship, Inc. v. Pennsylvania*, 447 U.S. 715, 100 S.Ct. 2432, 65 L.Ed.2d 458 (1980).

♦   The U.S. Supreme Court held that an employee who worked as a **welder on a fixed platform oil rig in Louisiana territorial waters was not entitled to LHWCA benefits** because his employment was not "maritime." Not everyone involved in every task that is part and parcel of offshore drilling can be considered a maritime employee. Congress' purpose under the LHWCA was to cover those workers on a covered situs who are involved in the essential elements of the loading, unloading or construction of vessels. The welding work here was far from the traditional work covered by the LHWCA. Further, even though the employee would have been eligible for LHWCA benefits if he had been injured on the continental shelf, such was not the case here. Accordingly, the employee was only entitled to recover state workers' compensation benefits for his injuries. *Herb's Welding, Inc. v. Gray*, 470 U.S. 414, 105 S.Ct. 1421, 84 L.Ed.2d 406 (1985).

♦   A man worked for an iron works corporation for many years. After he retired, he learned that he suffered from a work-related hearing loss. An administrative law judge awarded him disability benefits under a combination of compensation systems set forth by the LHWCA. The Benefits Review Board affirmed, but the U.S. Court of Appeals reversed, finding that the worker should have been compensated under the LHWCA's scheduled injury plan. The U.S. Supreme Court held that **claims for hearing loss filed by either current workers or retirees were claims for scheduled injuries** that had to be compensated under the system of scheduled injury compensation, rather than under the system providing compensation for retirees who suffered from occupational diseases that did not become disabling until after retirement. As a scheduled injury type of loss, the worker is presumptively disabled simultaneously with the injury. It did not matter that the worker did not notice the hearing loss until after he retired. *Bath Iron Works Corp. v. Director OWCP*, 506 U.S. 153, 113 S.Ct. 692, 121 L.Ed.2d 619 (1993).

✦   The U.S. Department of Labor applied the "true doubt" rule to resolve claims under the Black Lung Benefits Act and the LHWCA. The rule shifted the burden of persuasion to a party opposing a claim for benefits so that in cases in which the evidence was evenly balanced, the claimant prevailed. In two separate cases arising under these federal acts, the U.S. Supreme Court determined that the department's analysis was incorrect. Under the true doubt rule, where evidence was evenly balanced, the claimant always won. However, because **the Administrative Procedure Act (APA) required a claimant to lose in the case of evenly balanced evidence**, the true doubt rule violated the APA. *Director, OWC Programs v. Greenwich Collieries*, 512 U.S. 267, 114 S.Ct. 2251, 129 L.Ed.2d 221 (1994).

✦   Three railroad employees worked at their employers' Virginia terminals, where coal was being loaded from railway cars to ships. Two of the employees were injured while they were cleaning spilled coal from loading equipment to prevent the machinery from fouling. The other employee was injured while repairing a mechanical device necessary for the loading of ships. All three employees brought suit in state court under the Federal Employers' Liability Act (FELA) (which provides a negligence cause of action for railroad employees), but the trial courts dismissed on the grounds that the LHWCA provided the exclusive remedy. The U.S. Supreme Court agreed, holding that the LHWCA provided the exclusive remedy. **Maritime employment includes not only those who physically handle cargo, but also land-based activity, which is an integral or essential part of loading or unloading a vessel.** Here, the employees were maintaining or repairing equipment which was essential to the loading process. Even though the work being performed might be considered traditional railroad work, it was being done at a relevant situs and involved integral elements of the loading process. *Chesapeake and Ohio Railway Co. v. Schwalb*, 493 U.S. 40, 110 S.Ct. 381, 107 L.Ed.2d 278 (1989).

VI. OTHER WORKERS' COMPENSATION CASES

Several other issues, representing a wide range of topics, can also arise in workers' compensation litigation. Some topics include discriminatory or unconstitutional statutes; classification of employees, employers, or dependents; and entitlement to benefits.

A. Discrimination

Employers should not inquire into whether applicants have filed workers' compensation claims. It is permissible to inquire as to whether an applicant can perform the essential functions of the position, and as to any accommodations that may be necessary for the applicant to do the job, but an inquiry into any past workers' compensation filing may violate state civil rights laws.

◆   The wife of a Missouri man died in a work-related accident in her employer's parking lot. Her husband filed a claim for death benefits under Missouri's workers' compensation law. However, the law provided that a widower could not receive death benefits unless he was either mentally or physically incapacitated from wage earning, or unless he could show actual dependency on his wife's earnings. His claim was denied because he did not fit into the statutory parameters. The case reached the U.S. Supreme Court, which held that the law indisputably mandated gender-based discrimination. Further, the discriminatory means employed were not substantially related to the achievement of the important governmental objective of providing for needy spouses. **Either all widows and widowers could be paid or only dependent surviving spouses could be paid.** The discriminatory law, then, simply did not stand up under the intermediate level of scrutiny applied by the Court in gender discrimination cases. The claim that it was administratively more convenient to have the law structured in this way was not sufficient to justify the different treatment for men. *Wengler v. Druggist Mutual Insurance Co.,* 446 U.S. 142, 100 S.Ct. 1540, 64 L.Ed.2d 107 (1980).

◆   A group of workers' compensation claimants in Montana filed a petition challenging the constitutionality of terminating their total permanent disability benefits at age 65, claiming age discrimination and a violation of their equal protection and due process rights. The case reached the Supreme Court of Montana, which ruled that the statute terminating the claimants' benefits was rationally related to the legitimate governmental interest in controlling costs and in assisting workers at a reasonable cost to their employers. Accordingly, the statute was not unconstitutional and **the claimants were not entitled to continue receiving workers' compensation benefits upon retirement at age 65.** *Satterlee v. Lumbermen's Mutual Casualty Co.,* 353 Mont. 265 (Mont. 2009).

◆   A workers' compensation claimant in Utah challenged the constitutionality of a statute providing that permanently disabled workers would receive disability compensation unaffected by the simultaneous award of any other benefit for six years, but after six years, disability payments would be reduced by half of the dollar amount of Social Security benefits received. The case reached the Utah Supreme Court, which held that the statute was unconstitutional. **It drew a distinction between those claimants eligible for Social Security and those who were not, without a rational basis for doing so.** Even if the purpose of the law was to account for additional income received by the claimant, it relied solely on income from Social Security rather than all other forms of income a claimant might receive. *Merrill v. Utah Labor Comm'n,* 223 P.3d 1089 (Utah 2009).

◆   A widow received workers' compensation death benefits under a 1989 amendment to the workers' compensation statute. She received benefits for 13 years until the Georgia Insurers Insolvency Pool began handling her claim. It then suspended her benefits, asserting that she had received more than the required 400 weeks of benefits required. The amendment stated that death benefits would terminate at age 65 or after 400 weeks of payments, "whichever occur[red] first." Prior to the amendment, the law required payment until age 65 or 400 weeks, whichever was the greater amount. And in 1990, the law was amended again to provide the greater of amount of benefits between age 65 and 400 weeks. The case reached the Georgia Supreme Court, which found that the 1989 amendment was unconstitutional because it was ostensibly enacted to correct grammatical errors and modernize language, but in fact it substantively changed the amount of time a surviving spouse was eligible to receive death benefits. *Sherman Concrete Pipe Co. v. Chinn*, 660 S.E.2d 368 (Ga. 2008).

◆   The Colorado legislature amended its workers' compensation law to disallow permanent total disability benefits to injured workers ages 65 and older. Two 64-year-old workers injured in the course of their employment turned 65 during administrative proceedings concerning their claims for permanent total disability benefits. In both cases, the state industrial claim appeals office affirmed denial of the claims based upon the amendment. The cases reached the Colorado Supreme Court, which held that the legislation **unconstitutionally denied workers' compensation benefits to individuals 65 and older who were permanently and totally disabled**, while allowing partially disabled workers over age 65 and other classes of younger disabled individuals to continue receiving benefits. This unequal treatment for Social Security recipients was not justified. Unlike workers' compensation benefits, Social Security retirement benefits were pension payments and were not intended to compensate workers for loss of income from work-related injury. *Industrial Claim Appeals Office v. Romero*, 912 P.2d 62 (Colo. 1996).

B. Retaliation

Employers should not <u>retaliate</u> against employees for filing workers' compensation claims. In many states, the workers' compensation act prohibits this; in some states, such action is a violation of public policy. For cases involving termination as a result of a workers' compensation filing, please see Chapter Three, Section IV.C.

◆   A property manager in Texas injured his back at work, and an office manager helped him file a workers' compensation claim. The employee took a medical leave of absence. He was later discharged after a leave of two months, and he said the owner told him he was let go because the owner didn't know how long he would be on workers' compensation. The property manager sued for retaliation, but he lost. **There was no evidence that the employer had any animosity toward the employee because he filed a workers' compensation claim.** *McClendon v. Deep East Texas Property Management LLC*, No. 12012-00331-CV, 2014 WL 13088618 (Tex. Ct. App. 3/31/14).

◆   A staffing service employee in Kentucky injured his chest on the job at a car manufacturing plant. He was taken to the emergency room, then placed on work restrictions for five days. He was released to work early, but was not dressed properly at that time. He claimed that his supervisor did not insist he return to work that day. She claimed that she told him to change his clothes and return to work. When he didn't return to work that day, he was fired for excessive absenteeism. He sued the staffing service, alleging retaliation for filing a workers' compensation claim. A state court granted pretrial judgment to the staffing service, but the Kentucky Court of Appeals reversed. It found **issues of fact as to whether the service fired him for filing the workers' compensation claim**. It also stated that he was not entitled to pursue punitive damages arising from his claim. *Bishop v. Manpower, Inc. of Cent. Kentucky*, 211 S.W.3d 71 (Ky. Ct. App. 2006).

◆   An Alabama employee injured his knee on the job and received medical expenses from his employer. He settled his workers' compensation claim against the employer. After returning to the job, he re-injured the knee a few years later and again settled a workers' compensation claim with the employer. However, he continued to have problems with the knee, then injured his back because his knee wouldn't bend properly. He was then fired for attendance problems. When he sued for retaliation under the state's workers' compensation law, **a jury awarded him $400,000 in compensatory damages and $200,000 in punitive damages**. The Supreme Court of Alabama upheld the jury's verdict, finding sufficient evidence that the reason for the discharge was pretextual and that the true reason was the employee's workers' compensation claims. *Flint Construction Co. v. Hall*, 904 So.2d 236 (Ala. 2004).

◆   A Kansas grocery store manager took time off work for surgery on his arm and filed a workers' compensation claim. He was demoted to another position with a reduction in pay upon returning to work. He sued the employer for demoting him in retaliation for filing the workers' compensation claim, and the court granted pretrial judgment to the employer. The court of appeals affirmed, and the employee appealed to the Supreme Court of Kansas. The court observed that state supreme courts in Illinois and California have recognized legal causes of action based upon retaliatory demotion, despite arguments that recognition of the cause of action would involve judicial micro-management of the workplace and lead to trivial lawsuits based on minor employment matters. The court held that **a cause of action for retaliatory demotion was necessary to supplement the existing cause of action for retaliatory discharge** in order to prevent an employer from demoting, rather than discharging, an employee in retaliation for filing a workers' compensation claim. The court reversed the lower court judgments and remanded the case. *Brigham v. Dillon Companies, Inc.*, 935 P.2d 1054 (Kan. 1997).

◆   An Alabama manufacturing employee missed approximately five months of work due to an injury for which he received workers' compensation benefits. On his first day back on the job he injured his back while repairing machinery and was absent for another five months. Upon his return to work, the employer fired him for allegedly falsifying his original job application regarding his prior compensation claims history. The employee sued for retaliatory discharge and won. The Court of Civil Appeals of Alabama affirmed, finding sufficient evidence that **the employer had retaliated against the employee for filing workers' compensation claims**. The employee had successfully rebutted the alleged falsification of the employment application with evidence that he had been instructed by a human resources employee to indicate "no" in response to an ambiguous question concerning whether he had previously filed a claim. Evidence indicated that the employee reasonably believed that he was honestly indicating only that he had never filed a lawsuit to obtain benefits. *Beaulieu of America, Inc. v. Kilgore*, 680 So.2d 288 (Ala. Civ. App. 1996).

◆ The Court of Appeals of Texas affirmed a trial court ruling for the employer of an injured driver who was fired while off work under doctor's orders following a job-related injury. Although the employer had created a new position to accommodate the driver's back injury, he never responded to the employer's request for a return-to-work date. The court found sufficient evidence that **the discharge action had been a legitimate response to changed business conditions** and that the employer did not fire the driver for discriminatory reasons in violation of the state workers' compensation act. *Hogue v. Blue Bell Creameries, L.P.*, 922 S.W.2d 566 (Tex. Ct. App. 1996).

C. Employment Relationship Issues

Independent contractors are generally not entitled to workers' compensation benefits, though they can sue the "employers" if their injuries resulted from employer negligence. Illegal immigrants may be entitled to workers' compensation despite their status.

◆ A Virginia carpenter went to work for a company as an independent contractor. When he fell from the second story of a home on which he was working, he filed for workers' compensation, which the company denied. However, the state's workers' compensation commission and the Virginia Court of Appeals ruled that the carpenter was an employee and thus entitled to workers' compensation. **The company retained control over his job performance and treated him like its hourly employees.** It paid him an hourly wage, and he performed the same duties as the hourly employees, working close to eight hours a day for the company. *Dillon Construction and Accident Fund Insurance Co. of America v. Carter*, 686 S.E.2d 542 (Va. Ct. App. 2009).

◆ An illegal alien used fraudulent documents to obtain a janitorial position with a company in Georgia. After she was injured on the job, she filed a claim for workers' compensation benefits. She obtained an administrative ruling in her favor, and the company appealed to the Georgia Court of Appeals, which affirmed the award of benefits. Even though federal law prohibited the employment of illegal aliens, the Immigration Reform and Control Act did not preempt state workers' compensation law so as to make the employment contract void. Further, since **there was no causal connection between the**

janitor's fraud and the injury she suffered, her fraud could not be used to deny her benefits. *Continental PET Technologies, Inc. v. Palacias*, 604 S.E.2d 627 (Ga. Ct. App. 2004).

◆   An illegal immigrant injured his back while working as a maintenance worker for a Pennsylvania company. A workers' compensation judge determined that **even though he did not have proper Immigration and Naturalization Service documentation to work in the United States, he was entitled to benefits** under Pennsylvania's workers' compensation act. The case reached the Commonwealth Court of Pennsylvania, which agreed that the worker was entitled to benefits. It joined courts in New Jersey, Florida, Louisiana and Oklahoma in finding illegal immigrants eligible for workers' compensation. To disallow benefits would be to potentially subvert the public policy against illegal immigration because employers might seek out illegal aliens who would not have to be paid workers' compensation. The court also held that the company could not suspend benefits on the ground that the immigrant would be unavailable for suitable alternative employment.

The Pennsylvania Supreme Court upheld the ruling that the illegal alien was entitled to workers' compensation benefits. It then held that the commonwealth court should not have required the employer to present evidence for purposes of the suspension of benefits that jobs were referred to or available to the immigrant. When an employer seeks to suspend workers' compensation benefits that have been granted to an illegal alien, a showing of job availability by the employer is not required. However, since the workers' compensation judge did not address the company's contention that benefits had to be suspended, the court remanded the case for a determination on that issue. *Reinforced Earth Co. v. WCAB*, 810 A.2d 99 (Pa. 2002).

◆   An undocumented alien lost a finger in an assembly line accident and later experienced psychological injuries including posttraumatic stress disorder and severe depression. The employer accepted responsibility for medical and temporary disability benefits but contested his claim for continuing medical benefits and psychiatric treatment. A workers' compensation judge denied the claim. The case reached the Superior Court of New Jersey, Appellate Division, which noted that **the workers' compensation system is fundamentally different than the unemployment compensation system (which disqualifies illegal aliens)**. The system was based on a contractual remedy that replaced the common law right of an employee to seek damages for personal injuries against employers. The compensation judge had improperly attempted to transport unemployment compensation principles to this claim. The court reversed and remanded the case. *Mendoza v. Monmouth Recycling Corp.*, 288 N.J. Super. 240, 672 A.2d 221 (N.J. Super. Ct. App. Div. 1996).

◆   A Colorado man worked for a ski resort as a part-time ski instructor in exchange for a pass that allowed him to ski free at any time. Subsequently, the resort notified its ski instructors that it needed persons with CPR qualifications and first aid training to work on ski patrol. The instructor was qualified for this position, and, because he already had a free pass, he negotiated an agreement with the ski patrol director to receive daily ski passes for his girlfriend. He then fell while on ski patrol duty and injured his knees. His workers' compensation claim was contested on the ground that he was a volunteer and not entitled to benefits. An administrative law judge determined that he was an employee, and the court of appeals affirmed. The Supreme Court of Colorado agreed that the instructor was an employee. Here, the instructor negotiated with his employer and agreed to work only in exchange for the benefit of daily passes for his girlfriend. It did not matter that the instructor was not paid wages by the resort. **Because he specifically bargained for daily passes for his girlfriend, he was not a volunteer**, even if he would have been a volunteer had he only received ski passes for himself. The instructor was entitled to benefits. *Aspen Highlands Skiing Corp. v. Apostolou*, 866 P.2d 1384 (Colo. 1994).

◆   A South Carolina carpenter was hired by a subcontractor to work on a residential site. On his first day of work, he fell from a two-story high scaffold and was severely injured. He sought workers' compensation benefits from the contractor. The Workers' Compensation Commission awarded benefits, and the contractor appealed to the Supreme Court of South Carolina. The contractor contended that it was not the carpenter's statutory employer. However, the court noted that the contractor sent a letter to its insurer admitting the contractor-subcontractor relationship. Next, the contractor argued that the employee was required to establish that his immediate employer was financially irresponsible before bringing a claim against his statutory employer. However, the court noted that section 42-1-410 does not expressly require proof of the immediate employer's inability to pay. Rather, **the contractor was entitled to indemnity from the immediate employer (subcontractor)** and could either bring a separate action against him for indemnification or join him as a defendant in the action brought by the injured employee. Thus, the court upheld the decision of the Workers' Compensation Commission awarding benefits to the injured employee. *Long v. Atlantic Homes*, 428 S.E.2d 711 (S.C. 1993).

D. Other Issues

The following cases address various workers' compensation issues.

◆   Under Pennsylvania's Workers' Compensation Act, once an employer becomes liable for an employee's work-related injury, the employer or its insurer must pay for all reasonable and necessary medical treatment. The law was amended in 1993 to provide that where there is a disputed treatment, an insurer may withhold payment pending an independent "utilization review." A number of employees and employee representatives sued various insurers and self-insured entities under the Fourteenth Amendment and 42 U.S.C. § 1983, alleging that the withholding of payments without notice and an opportunity to be heard violated their due process rights. The case reached the U.S. Supreme Court, which stated that **the mere fact that a private business is subject to extensive state regulation does not by itself convert the business' actions into state action**. Here, the amendment to the workers' compensation statute allowing withholding and an independent review was not state authorization of insurers' actions. It was merely a decision not to intervene in disputes over whether particular treatments were reasonable and medically necessary. Further, even if there was state action, because the employees were not entitled to payment for medical treatment until the treatment at issue was found to be reasonable and necessary, there was no deprivation of their property rights under the Fourteenth Amendment. *American Manufacturers Mutual Insurance Co. v. Sullivan*, 526 U.S. 40, 119 S.Ct. 977, 143 L.Ed.2d 130 (1999).

◆   An Illinois company's policy allowed it to fire any employee seeking worker's compensation benefits if the employee refused to be tested for alcohol and drugs. An injured employee who wanted to file a workers' compensation claim was fired after he refused to take a drug test. He sued, claiming the company illegally retaliated against him for filing a workers' compensation claim. The court rejected the claim, reasoning that **the employee was fired because he refused to take the test and not because he filed a workers' compensation claim**. *Phillips v. Continental Tire The Americas, LLC*, 743 F.3d 475 (7th Cir. 2014).

◆   During his 90-day probationary period, a newly hired order selector for a New York employer injured himself while operating a machine. The employer had a policy that required it to fire any probationary employee who was injured and could have prevented the injury. It fired the employee pursuant to the policy. The employee filed for workers' compensation benefits. He also filed a discrimination claim against the employer under state workers' compensation law. A workers' compensation board determined that **the employer's policy was illegal because it dissuaded probationary employees from seeking workers' compensation benefits**, and a state appeals court upheld that determination. *Rodriguez v. C & S Wholesale Grocers, Inc.*, 968 N.Y.S.2d 728 (N.Y. App. Div. 2013).

◆   A maintenance mechanic for a Minnesota employer claimed he injured his back at work. He further claimed a manager told him he would be fired if he filed a claim for workers' compensation benefits. He filed a claim and underwent back surgery. When he was released to return, no position was found for him. He sued, claiming retaliatory discharge and unlawful refusal to offer continued employment. A state appeals court decided that **the state law provided a cause of action for threatening to discharge an employee because he seeks workers' compensation benefits**. It also found the retaliation claim should go to a jury. *Schmitz v. United States Steel Corp.*, 831 N.W.2d 656 (Minn. Ct. App. 2013).

◆   A hotel worker in Maryland was brutally assaulted during an attempted robbery on her shift. She was found unconscious in a pool of blood hours later. She was taken to a trauma center, where she was treated for a brain injury and multiple skull fractures. The hotel paid her medical expenses and workers' compensation benefits, but it balked at providing a home security system for her. **Her neuropsychologist explained that the home security system was necessary to make her feel safe and help her recover from the attack.** A trial court held that the security system wasn't a medical treatment as matter of law. However, the Maryland Court of Special Appeals found that the question was one of fact for a jury to decide. It reversed and remanded the case. *Simmons v. Comfort Suites Hotel*, 968 A.2d 1123 (Md. Ct. Spec. App. 2009).

◆   An undocumented worker in New York caught his right hand in a printing press and severed four fingers, two of which had to be amputated. The state workers' compensation board awarded him temporary disability benefits, and he interviewed with the board's office of rehabilitation regarding his return to work. He was referred to a vocational office for people with disabilities, but was ineligible for services because he was an illegal alien. After his temporary benefits ended, he sought additional disability benefits, but the New York Court of Appeals held that he was not entitled to them. One of the requirements for obtaining workers' compensation benefits beyond the initial award is that the worker participate in a board-approved work rehabilitation program. Since **the worker here was an illegal alien**, he could not do so. *Ramroop v. Flexo-Craft Printing, Inc.*, 896 N.E.2d 69 (N.Y. 2008).

◆   An illegal immigrant working for a company in Maryland injured his hand and required several surgeries. When he filed for workers' compensation, the company claimed that he did not qualify because of his resident status and the fact that he did not have a Social Security number. As such, he was not authorized to work in the U.S. under the Immigration Reform and Control Act. The case reached the Maryland Court of Appeals, which ruled that **the illegal immigrant was entitled to benefits**. The state's workers' compensation law only requires that an employee be "in the service of an employer" under "an express or implied contract of apprenticeship or hire." Because the employee met both of those conditions, it did not matter if he was unlawfully employed. *Design Kitchen and Baths v. Lagos*, 882 A.2d 817 (Md. 2005).

◆   An investment firm employee died in the terrorist attacks on 9/11. He had a fiancée and a 22-month-old daughter by a previous relationship. A dispute arose between the daughter and the fiancée over workers' compensation benefits. The case reached the New York Supreme Court, Appellate Division, which ruled that the daughter was entitled to $180 per week and the fiancée was entitled to $220. Workers' Compensation Law Section 4 provided that domestic partners of employees killed in the 9/11 terrorist attacks were eligible for the same benefits as surviving spouses. Even though the daughter would have received $400 per week if her father was killed at work on some other day, **the legislature permissibly created greater domestic partner rights for 9/11 victims' dependents**. *In re Novara*, 795 N.Y.S.2d 133 (N.Y. App. Div. 2005).

◆   A tool and die maker began experiencing pain in his forearms but did not report the problem to the shop foreman or complete an accident report until an incident of sharp pain occurred. After several months, the employee was diagnosed with carpal tunnel syndrome, and he filed for workers' compensation benefits. Between the time he had reported the pain and the diagnosis of carpal tunnel syndrome, the company had switched workers' compensation insurers. A question arose as to which of the two insurers was liable. The Pennsylvania

Commonwealth Court agreed with the Workers' Compensation Appeals Board that even though the injury was a cumulative one which developed over a period of time, **the date of injury for workers' compensation purposes was the date the injury was diagnosed**, making the second insurer liable. *Piad Corp. v. WCAB*, 761 A.2d 640 (Pa. Commw. Ct. 2000).

♦   A Texas staff leasing company chose not to provide workers' compensation insurance coverage to the employees it leased to other companies. When a corporation leased a number of workers from the leasing company, the state workers' compensation insurance fund sent it a premium, billing it for the workers as a co-employer. The Texas Supreme Court ruled that the corporation was not obligated to pay the premium. **The staff leasing company had the exclusive right to elect whether to obtain workers' compensation insurance coverage for its leased employees.** Because it had chosen not to do so, the corporation was not obligated to provide coverage either. *Texas Workers' Compensation Insurance Fund v. DEL Industrial, Inc.*, 35 S.W.3d 591 (Tex. 2000).

♦   A West Virginia truck driver submitted an accident report and claim for workers' compensation benefits after he was injured in a work-related incident. The employer's labor relations representative declared on the employer's portion of the form that there was no known job-related injury, and the employer denied the claim. The employee was subsequently awarded benefits by the state workers' compensation fund. He then sued the employer for fraud. The Supreme Court of Appeals of West Virginia held that an employee may maintain a private cause of action for fraud against an employer for the **employer's knowing and intentional filing of a false statement with the state workers' compensation fund**. The driver had described sufficient facts to support a claim for fraudulent misrepresentation by alleging that the employer had maliciously and knowingly filed a false report with the state. *Persinger v. Peabody Coal Co.*, 976 F.Supp. 1038 (S.D. W. Va. 1997).

♦   A clothing manufacturer operating plants throughout the U.S. contracted with an insurer to provide workers' compensation insurance at all its facilities. It gave notice to employees at an Oklahoma plant that it would close the following month, and 108 different employees submitted a total of 429 workers' compensation claims within the next few weeks. The insurer assigned reserve amounts for each claim and transferred claims data to the National Council on Compensation Insurance, resulting in a drastically increased experience rating modification and an increase in premiums from less than $800,000 to $6.8 million annually. The employer alleged that the insurer improperly agreed to settle claims totaling $4.8 million. It sued the insurer in a Kentucky court, alleging that excessive loss reserves, improper claim settlements and the increase in its insurance rating caused severe economic hardship. The employer later filed for bankruptcy. The Kentucky federal court granted the insurer pretrial judgment. The Sixth Circuit affirmed the findings that the insurer had not breached the insurance contract or failed to act in good faith by settling the claims. **Each of the actions by the insurer corresponded** to its **contractual rights or duties** and did not satisfy the standard for intentional wrongful conduct necessary to prevail in a bad faith insurance action. *Big Yank Corp. v. Liberty Mutual Fire Insurance Co.*, 125 F.3d 308 (6th Cir. 1997).

◆   A Maine employee became quadriplegic after a work-related incident and was unable to work. She required a specially adapted wheelchair and personal care assistants. The employer purchased a specially adapted van for her. Five years later, the former employee petitioned the Workers' Compensation Board for the cost of a replacement van. The employer agreed to pay for the cost of adapting a new van but refused to pay for the van itself or for the housekeeping activities of two part-time assistants employed by her. The board found that the van was not a physical aid under state law and that the employer did not have to purchase it. It also held that the claim for housekeeping expenses should be denied. The Supreme Judicial Court of Maine observed that **state law required the replacement or renewal of physical aids when necessary due to wear and tear**. Because of her severe disability and the absence of any other available transportation except an ambulance, the van should be considered a reasonable and proper mechanical aid under state law. Accordingly, the employer had to pay for the entire cost of the adapted van. The employee was also entitled to the amounts claimed for housekeeping performed by her personal assistants. *Brawn v. Gloria's Country Inn*, 698 A.2d 1067 (Me. 1997).

◆   In a case involving **sick building syndrome** and exposure to volatile organic compounds, the Supreme Court of Nebraska found that even though the employer had stipulated to partial liability, it had reserved the right to challenge the actual personal injury to the individual claimants, who bore the burden of proving their illnesses. *US West Communications, Inc. v. Taborski*, 253 Neb. 770, 572 N.W.2d 81 (Neb. 1998).

◆   A New Jersey man was shot and killed on the job by the mentally disabled boyfriend of a co-employee. His significant other filed for workers' compensation dependency benefits, contending that she was the **"de facto" wife of the decedent**. The Superior Court of New Jersey, Appellate Division, noted that "de facto" claims have only been sustained when "the surviving petitioner had entered into a ceremonial marriage unaware of any marital impediment on the part of the decedent employee." The parties here did not enter into a ceremonial marriage, and the woman was well aware of her single status. Thus, she was not entitled to dependency benefits. *Toms v. Dee Rose Furniture*, 621 A.2d 91 (N.J. Super. Ct. App. Div. 1993).

CHAPTER EIGHT

Unemployment Compensation

I. VOLUNTARY SEPARATION

Although the Federal Unemployment Tax Act establishes certain minimum federal standards that states must satisfy in order to participate in the program, the act leaves to state discretion the rules governing the administration of unemployment compensation programs.

Under state laws, there are three general requirements that must be satisfied for a claimant to be eligible for unemployment benefits:

1) A claimant must earn a specified amount of wages or work a specified number of weeks in covered employment during a one-year base period in order to be entitled to receive benefits,

2) A claimant must be able to work and be available for work in order to be eligible, and

3) A claimant must not be disqualified for the reasons set forth in the state's law.

The most common reasons for disqualification under state unemployment compensation laws are:

—voluntarily leaving the job without good cause attributable to the employer,

—participating in a strike,

—being discharged for misconduct, and

—refusing suitable work.

This first section deals with issues of voluntary separation.

A. Labor Stoppages

Many states have enacted unemployment compensation labor dispute disqualification statutes that prevent strikers from obtaining benefits.

Some statutes allow strikers to obtain benefits under certain circumstances, such as when the employer hires permanent replacement workers. However, other statutes require strikers to abandon the strike and put forth an unconditional offer to return to work.

1. Disqualification

If an employee is deemed to have caused his own unemployment by going out on strike, he generally will not be able to collect unemployment compensation.

◆ A Michigan statute made employees ineligible for unemployment compensation benefits if they provided "financing," by means other than the payment of regular union dues, for a strike that caused their unemployment. Employees of General Motors were required by their union to pay "emergency dues" to augment the union's strike insurance fund. Several local unions went on strike, curtailing operations at other plants. Strike fund benefits were paid to all the workers who were idle. They then sought unemployment compensation benefits but were denied such benefits by the Michigan Supreme Court. The U.S. Supreme Court agreed with the lower court that the employees' payment of emergency dues amounted to "financing" of the strikes that caused the unemployment. Even though federal labor law protects employee rights to authorize a strike, it does not prohibit a state from **disallowing unemployment benefits to employees who cause their own unemployment**. The decision to participate in the strike caused the unemployment in this case, making it voluntary rather than involuntary. The Court affirmed the Michigan Supreme Court's decision denying benefits. *Baker v. General Motors Corp.*, 478 U.S. 621, 106 S.Ct. 3129, 92 L.Ed.2d 504 (1986).

◆ The collective bargaining agreement between a union and a manufacturer in Indiana expired, and negotiations for a new agreement began. The manufacturer sought to include a provision on temporary workers, but the union objected. The union negotiator threatened to strike at 11:00 PM unless the manufacturer removed the temporary worker clause. The manufacturer's negotiator said he could not remove that clause but was willing to continue to negotiate. When the union negotiator refused to continue, the manufacturer began shutting down its operations. Employees who were willing to cross the picket line were allowed to work. Eventually a new agreement was reached, and the striking workers made an unconditional offer to return to work. A number of striking employees made a claim for unemployment benefits. That claim was ultimately denied. The Indiana Court of Appeals held that the employees were not locked out. Rather, **they were unemployed as a result of an impasse regarding the temporary employee clause**. Therefore, they were not entitled to benefits. *Lacher v. Review Board of Indiana Dep't of Workforce Development*, 954 N.E.2d 1098 (Ind. Ct. App. 2011).

◆ Employees of a nursing home in Pennsylvania went out on strike after the union was unable to negotiate a new collective bargaining agreement. The nursing home then hired replacement workers and sent letters to each striking employee, promising the increased wages and better benefits from its last offer to the union if they would return to work. Six weeks later, the nursing home rescinded its imposition of the new contract terms and invited the striking workers back to work under the terms of the expired bargaining agreement. The strike continued for several months until the union made an unconditional offer to return to work. A number of strikers sought unemployment compensation for the entire period of the strike. The question of whether the nursing home had converted the strike into a lockout reached the Commonwealth Court of Pennsylvania. It held that the letters to the striking employees and the hiring of replacement workers did not convert the strike into a lockout. **The union failed to prove that it was willing to return to work in accordance with the terms of the expired bargaining agreement during the strike.** The employees were not entitled to benefits. *Presbyterian SeniorCare v. Unemployment Compensation Board of Review*, 900 A.2d 967 (Pa. Commw. Ct. 2006).

◆ Honolulu contracted with a private nonprofit corporation to provide bus services for the city. After notifying the corporation that its budget would be reduced by $10 million, Honolulu entered into negotiations for a new labor agreement. When they failed to reach one, the union called a strike. The corporation then locked its gates for security reasons until a new agreement was reached five weeks later. When individual drivers filed for unemployment benefits for the five weeks they were off work, the unemployment commission denied them. The union appealed, but the Hawaii Supreme Court agreed with the decision to deny unemployment compensation benefits to the strikers. Even though Honolulu had not required transit services to be provided during the strike, **the strike caused "substantial curtailment of business activity" disqualifying the drivers from unemployment benefits**. This was not a lockout because the lack of work was caused by the labor dispute. The lockout was strictly for safety reasons. *Hawaii Teamsters and Allied Workers, Local 966 v. Dep't of Labor and Industrial Relations*, 132 P.3d 368 (Haw. 2006).

♦   The Supreme Court of Oregon affirmed the denial of unemployment compensation claims by a group of employees who were locked out of their workplaces during a labor dispute. Oregon law disqualifies employees from receiving unemployment compensation benefits because of a labor dispute with no exception for lockouts. The employers belonged to a multi-employer collective bargaining group, and not all of them had locked out their employees. Since this resulted in only a partial lockout, the employees argued that the work they had lost had not been as the result of a labor dispute. The court found no such distinction in state law even though not all of the employers had excluded employees from their workplaces. Since **the unemployment had resulted from a labor dispute**, the court affirmed the decision to deny benefits. *Abu-Adas v. Employment Dep't, Food Employers, Inc.*, 325 Or. 480, 940 P.2d 1219 (Or. 1997).

♦   Alabama aircraft employees called a strike after their union was unable to negotiate a new contract. Several weeks after the strike began, the employer hired permanent replacement employees. The union workers then filed claims for unemployment compensation that were denied because the unemployment was directly caused by a labor dispute. The Supreme Court of Alabama upheld the denial of benefits. Alabama was not a "stoppage of work" state like Michigan, Indiana, Ohio, Colorado, and California, where the mere hiring of permanent replacement workers lifted the statutory labor dispute disqualification. Instead, it was a "labor dispute in active progress" state like Wisconsin, Minnesota, Tennessee, Oregon and Arizona. In those states, replaced striking employees were required to show abandonment of the strike and an unconditional offer to return to work before the labor dispute disqualification could be lifted. Alabama followed the second type and its statute contained language that **a labor dispute could exist regardless of whether the disputants had an employer-employee relationship**. The use of replacement workers was not an event that ended the statutory disqualification for unemployment benefits. *Ex parte Williams*, 646 So.2d 22 (Ala. 1994).

2. Exceptions

Unemployment benefits can be awarded where:

—striking employees are permanently replaced (and thus no longer have jobs),
—employees are subjected to a lockout by the employer,
—the employer unilaterally imposes terms and conditions of employment on striking workers, and
—employees refuse to cross a picket line for safety reasons.

♦   Workers at a steel processing plant in Indiana went on strike after they failed to reach agreement on a new collective bargaining agreement. Four months later, even though no new agreement had been reached, a union official notified the company that the workers would return to work unconditionally effective at 3:00 p.m. that day. The company refused to reinstate the striking workers until a new agreement was reached. More than two weeks later a new agreement was reached, and the company then began rehiring workers in order of seniority. The workers filed for unemployment compensation, which the company fought. An administrative law judge (ALJ) held that **the workers were entitled to unemployment benefits after they unconditionally agreed to return to work**. The Court of Appeals of Indiana agreed that the offer to return to work ended the impasse because it showed that the employees were open to negotiations. Further, the ALJ did not err by failing to allot a start-up time for the company because the delay in rehiring workers was caused by the company's lockout. *Dietrich Industries, Inc. v. Teamsters Local Unit 142*, 880 N.E.2d 700 (Ind. Ct. App. 2008).

◆   After the union for 44 workers at an Ohio company failed to reach an agreement on a new bargaining agreement, its members voted to strike. The company then hired permanent replacement workers and three weeks later notified the strikers by letter that their positions had been permanently filled. When the strikers applied for unemployment benefits, a hearing officer determined that **they were entitled to benefits from the point of the letter informing them that their jobs were lost**. The company appealed. The case reached the Supreme Court of Ohio, which agreed that the strikers were entitled to unemployment benefits from the date of the letter. At that point, the labor dispute became a lockout. The company's actions permanently severed the employment relationship and removed the disqualification to benefits. *M. Conley Co. v. Anderson*, 842 N.E.2d 1037 (Ohio 2006).

◆   Approximately 650 employees of a tire factory in Iowa walked off the job, claiming the company was committing unfair labor practices. The company asserted that the real reason for the strike was economic such that replacement workers could be hired. Weeks later, the company sent out a final offer and notified employees their positions would be filled by permanent replacement workers if they failed to return to work. Most of the strikers stayed away. When they filed for unemployment compensation benefits, the Employment Appeal Board and the Supreme Court of Iowa ruled that they were entitled to them. Here, **the company had severed its relationship with the strikers, ending their disqualification for benefits**. It hired replacement workers, transferred production to Texas and failed to notify the union that jobs remained for those strikers who wished to return to work. *Titan Tire Corp. v. Employment Appeal Board*, 641 N.W.2d 752 (Iowa 2002).

◆   In anticipation of a labor dispute, a company issued a pamphlet entitled "Rules of Conduct for Striking Employees." The rules set forth grounds for discharge based on certain conduct. Its employees struck as a result of the dispute, and the company determined that six workers who were participating in the strike also engaged in misconduct prohibited by the rules. The company terminated the workers, and they sought unemployment benefits under Illinois law. A state claims adjudicator granted their requests for benefits, and the company appealed to the Appellate Court of Illinois. Under the relevant statute, a worker becomes ineligible for unemployment benefits if his unemployment "is due to a stoppage of work, which exists because of a labor dispute … [where] he was last employed." However, **once an employee on strike is discharged for misconduct, he or she no longer has an expectation to return to work and is no longer disqualified** by virtue of participating in the strike. The court rejected the argument that its ruling would encourage striking employees to engage in misconduct or violence to circumvent the statute's eligibility requirement. It noted that employees discharged for misconduct are ineligible to receive benefits. *Caterpillar, Inc. v. Dep't of Employment Security*, 710 N.E.2d 890 (Ill. App. Ct. 1999).

◆   Michigan's highest court consolidated appeals from the state Employment Security Board of Review involving claims by striking employees for unemployment compensation benefits where each of the employees accepted interim employment from at least one other employer after a labor dispute. Some of the employees, after first becoming ineligible for unemployment benefits during a labor dispute, requalified for benefits after obtaining interim employment for a combined period of two weeks through a union hiring hall. The hiring hall employment included jobs from more than one employer, and the struck employers argued that acceptance of work from multiple employers would encourage make-work employment and bad faith acceptance of interim employment. In another case, a number of employees appealed a decision reversing their awards on grounds that they had not acted in good faith in obtaining interim employment subsequent to a labor dispute. The supreme court found **no statutory requirement of good-faith acceptance of interim employment as a prerequisite to obtaining unemployment compensation benefits**. Also, the statute did not disallow requalification simply because employees accepted interim employment from more than one employer. The employees prevailed. *Empire Iron Mining Partnership v. Orhanen*, 565 N.W.2d 844 (Mich. 1997).

B. Discrimination and Harassment

Discrimination and harassment (e.g., sexual or racial) may constitute good cause for leaving employment, thereby entitling the employee to unemployment compensation benefits.

Some courts have also found that an employee who quits after failing to report workplace harassment to company officials is not disqualified from receiving benefits.

◆   An employee of a Washington, D.C., dry cleaning and laundry services company quit after her supervisor repeatedly screamed and cursed at her. An administrative judge awarded her unemployment benefits, finding she had good cause to leave the job. An appeals court agreed and upheld the award, deferring to the administrative judge's decision to discount the testimony of the employer. *Imperial Valet Services, Inc. v. Alvarado*, 72 A.3d 165 (D.C. Ct. App. 2013).

◆   A rural seafood production plant in Alaska announced employees' schedules on a hotline only a half-hour prior to their starting times. One employee biked to work, and bad weather made it difficult for her to get to the plant with only a half-hour notice. She also encountered perceived hostility from her supervisor because she didn't get along with the supervisor's girlfriend (also a plant employee). When she quit and filed for unemployment compensation benefits, the department of labor's claim center determined that she did not have good cause to quit. Thus, she was ineligible for benefits for the first six weeks, and her maximum potential benefits were reduced by three times the weekly benefit amount. The Supreme Court of Alaska upheld that determination. She never gave the company the chance to address her transportation problems, and **her supervisor's alleged hostility didn't rise to the level of a hostile work environment**. *Calvert v. State of Alaska*, 251 P.3d 990 (Alaska 2011).

◆   An employee of a company that sold caskets was subjected to repeated sexual comments by his supervisor, who at one point told the employee to "hold his dick." When he complained to the manager, he was told that his supervisor was just being himself. The employee was then placed on administrative leave. He returned to work for one day under the same supervisor before quitting and filing for unemployment compensation benefits. The company asserted that he was not entitled to them, but the Missouri Court of Appeals ruled in favor of the employee. **The supervisor's frequent sexual jokes gave the employee good cause to quit**, and he made good-faith attempts to resolve the issue before doing so. *Knobbe v. Artco Casket Co., Inc.*, 315 S.W.3d 735 (Mo. Ct. App. 2010).

◆   An Arkansas employee endured escalating sexual harassment at the hands of a co-worker, who happened to be related to the owner. She decided not to report the harassment to the owner, fearing that would lead to her firing. Instead, she waited for the owner to spot the behavior and told him about it only then. The owner gave her three weeks off and reassigned her to work in his office. However, the harasser still would have contact with her. She quit at that time and then filed for unemployment compensation. The unemployment compensation board denied her benefits, but the Arkansas Court of Appeals reversed that decision. It held that **she left her job for good cause after being repeatedly harassed by the co-worker**. Thus, she was entitled to benefits. *Relyea v. Director, Dep't of Workforce Services*, 290 S.W.3d 34 (Ark. Ct. App. 2008).

◆   A 28-year employee of a bank in Pennsylvania quit her job and applied for unemployment benefits, which the bank fought. She claimed that she was subjected to verbal abuse and harassment by a senior vice president and by the bank president, who also disciplined her unfairly after she spoke out about the harassment by the senior vice president. The unemployment compensation board of review reversed the hearing officer and found that the employee had a necessitous and compelling cause for voluntarily leaving her employment. The bank appealed. The Commonwealth Court of Pennsylvania affirmed the ruling in favor of the employee. Here, **the discipline, criticism and ridicule she was**

subjected to justified her action in quitting the job. *First Federal Savings Bank v. Unemployment Compensation Board of Review*, 957 A.2d 811 (Pa. Commw. Ct. 2008).

♦   A female employee complained that someone deliberately left pubic hair on the toilet seat in the restroom near her work station. The company discussed the matter with her and the co-worker she believed was responsible for the action. Shortly thereafter, she shouted at the co-worker, and when she was warned about her behavior, she stopped coming to work and informed the employer that she had no choice but to leave the job. When she filed a claim for unemployment compensation benefits, she was initially awarded $2,000. However, the labor department later found her ineligible and sought repayment of the money. The Supreme Court, Appellate Division, ruled that the employee's frustration with the situation did not constitute good cause to leave the job because **she did not show that her safety was ever compromised**. The employee had to repay the benefits she received. *In re Gully*, 778 N.Y.S.2d 212 (N.Y. App. Div. 2004).

♦   A human resources manager filed an employment discrimination complaint against her employer. The parties settled their dispute under an agreement that required the employee to resign. She negotiated language in the agreement that characterized her separation as voluntary retirement, in order to become eligible for certain retirement benefits. She then applied for unemployment compensation benefits and testified before an administrative appeals board that she had retired only because the settlement agreement required her to do so. The board awarded benefits, and the Court of Appeals of Arizona affirmed. Even though the employee had voluntarily entered into the settlement agreement, her primary reason for doing so was to settle her discrimination complaint and not to retire. Because she intended to continue working, the employer was the moving party in the termination. **Employment separation that results from an employer's intent and action is properly characterized as a discharge.** Since the employee had no independent desire to quit her job, but had been compelled to do so by the settlement agreement, she was entitled to benefits. *California Portland Cement Co. v. Arizona Dep't of Economic Security*, 960 P.2d 65 (Ariz. Ct. App. 1998).

♦   A North Carolina employee endured sexual harassment by her immediate supervisor for several years. Although she was offended and intimidated, she never told him to stop and failed to report the harassment to upper management as specified in her employer's anti-harassment policy. She felt that any report to management would not be believed. She eventually quit and applied for unemployment compensation benefits. An appeals referee determined that she had not left her work for good cause attributable to the employer because of her failure to abide by its anti-harassment policy. Because the employer was deprived of an opportunity to remedy the situation, she was not entitled to benefits. The state employment security commission affirmed the referee's decision. The case reached the Court of Appeals of North Carolina, which held that **sexual harassment constitutes good cause for quitting under the state**

unemployment compensation law. The failure to report sexual harassment according to the employer's policy did not disqualify the employee from receiving benefits. *Marlow v. North Carolina Employment Security Comm'n*, 493 S.E.2d 302 (N.C. Ct. App. 1997).

C. Layoffs and Transfers

Voluntary separations based on layoffs generally will not disqualify an employee from benefits. However, some courts have found that where the employer does not actually lay off any employees, and uncertainty about future employment does not establish good cause for quitting, benefits may be denied.

In other words, where an employee has notice that layoffs are likely to occur and decides to resign instead of being laid off, she may not be entitled to benefits if the layoffs do not in fact occur. However, if layoffs are announced and the employee volunteers to be laid off early, she may still be entitled to benefits.

Where an employee refuses a transfer to another work site or position, he may not be entitled to benefits where the transfer request was reasonable. However, where the requested transfer is to a distant location (e.g., another city) or to a position that is unreasonable (e.g., more dangerous but with less pay and seniority), the employee may be entitled to benefits.

♦   An employee of a social media site in New York received a negative performance review that included a plan to address his performance problems. It stated that failure to reach the stated goals could result in termination. The employee disagreed with the review and was reluctant to sign the plan. He was told that if he resigned he would get a positive reference and that he would be deemed "rehireable." He chose to resign immediately and then applied for unemployment benefits. After they were denied, he appealed, but the Supreme Court, Appellate Division, upheld the denial of benefits. **Neither criticism from a supervisor nor resignation in anticipation of discharge constitutes good cause for leaving employment.** Further, continued employment was available to the claimant. *Matter of Follett*, 87 A.D.3d 1233, 930 N.Y.S.2d 87 (N.Y. App. Div. 2011).

♦   A housekeeping supervisor at an Indiana hospital received three written warnings about his performance between April and August. He was also given performance improvement plans and daily assistance with his supervisory skills. In November, he received a final warning relating to scheduling problems. He then had another scheduling problem and was given yet another warning, after which he was demoted to housekeeping assistant, with an offer to start over at a new facility that was about to open. Instead, he quit and filed a claim for unemployment compensation benefits. After benefits were denied, the Indiana Court of Appeals affirmed. **The employee did not have good cause to quit his job because the demotion was not unreasonable.** *Davis v. Review Board of Indiana Dep't of Workplace Development*, 900 N.E.2d 488 (Ind. Ct. App. 2009).

♦   Verizon announced a voluntary buyout. **More than 200 employees in Washington accepted voluntary termination benefits and then filed for unemployment compensation.** After they were initially granted benefits, the Washington Supreme Court reversed, holding that they were not entitled to unemployment because they did not quit with "good cause." Verizon's offer did not include a provision reserving the right to reject any offer. Instead, it accepted every employee's offer to leave early. As a result, it took no "final action" with regard to the employees' offer – i.e., determining who would stay and who would be allowed to go. *Verizon Northwest, Inc. v. Washington Employment Security Dep't*, 194 P.3d 255 (Wash. 2008).

♦   A supervisor for a company that cleaned and maintained shopping carts drove his mobile maintenance unit to the customers' places of business to repair their shopping carts and also sell them carts and spare parts. His contract called for him to work a 260-day work year and awarded him compensatory time on a one-to-one basis for each day he worked over the 260 days. He was laid off for three months, and during that time he received compensatory pay for working Saturdays and Sundays during the prior year. He also obtained unemployment compensation benefits. The Nebraska Department of Labor determined that he had been overpaid unemployment benefits by $2,000 and sought to recover that amount. However, the Supreme Court of Nebraska ruled that **the deferred compensatory wages he received were actually earned during his time of employment, not while he was laid off**. As a result, the supervisor was not "employed" during his layoff and was thus entitled to the benefits. *Wadkins v. Lecuona*, 740 N.W.2d 34 (Neb. 2007).

♦   An Indiana bank restructured its loan department, eliminating some positions and moving others to another city. After an employee's position was eliminated, she signed a release, which stated that she had offered to resign and which provided for a severance payment in exchange. The agreement also stated that acceptance of the severance pay constituted an accord and satisfaction of all claims against the bank. The employee applied for and received unemployment compensation benefits, testifying in administrative proceedings that she had left the employment because her job had been eliminated and that she did not voluntarily resign. The bank appealed to the Court of Appeals of Indiana, which held that the employee had been laid off due to lack of work. The release she signed to obtain severance pay was ambiguous because it implied that she might receive additional pay and was therefore not the final resolution of all employment matters involving the parties. Because **the employee had not resigned but had voluntarily left for good cause**, the award of benefits was affirmed. *Salin Bank and Trust Co. v. Review Board of Indiana Dep't of Workforce Development*, 698 N.E.2d 1 (Ind. Ct. App. 1998).

♦   A Massachusetts electronic technician complained repeatedly to her supervisors about her job conditions, believing that male co-workers received better pay and advancement opportunities. The employer transferred her to the company's automotive products division, allegedly to accommodate her need for advancement. However, the new assignment was at the same level as her previous position, and the employee refused to report because of concerns about chemical exposure and possible allergic reactions. The employer fired her. The state commissioner of employment and training found that the employee had left her job voluntarily and was disqualified from receiving unemployment benefits. The Appeals Court of Massachusetts noted that both employer and employee stated that **the employee was discharged for failing to report to her new job assignment**. The record lacked substantial evidence that the employee had voluntarily quit. The commission had erroneously disqualified her from benefits on that basis. The court remanded the case for another hearing. *Potris v. Commissioner of Dep't of Employment and Training*, 679 N.E.2d 605 (Mass. App. Ct. 1997).

D. Medical and Personal Reasons

Certain medical and personal reasons may be deemed necessitous and compelling to allow the employee to recover unemployment benefits. If an employer offers the employee an alternative position to help alleviate the problems associated with the reason, however, the employee's refusal of the accommodation may result in a denial of benefits.

1. Medical Reasons

As a general rule, employees who quit their jobs for medical reasons will *not* be entitled to unemployment compensation benefits. However, if the medical condition is attributable to the employment or is somehow caused by the employment, benefits might be payable.

◆   A Missouri woman worked for a company for about three years and then requested a leave of absence due to pregnancy. The company granted her a "leave without guarantee of reinstatement," which meant that she would only be rehired if a position was available when she was ready to return to work. When she later notified the company of her willingness to return to work, no positions were available. She filed a claim for unemployment compensation benefits, which was denied. A trial court held that the statute – which disqualifies a claimant who has left work voluntarily without good cause attributable to the work or the employer – was inconsistent with the Federal Unemployment Tax Act (FUTA). The court of appeals affirmed, but the Missouri Supreme Court reversed. The U.S. Supreme Court held that the Missouri statute was consistent with the FUTA. Congress only intended to prohibit states from singling out pregnancy for unfavorable treatment when it decreed that no state could deny any compensation "solely on the basis of pregnancy or termination of pregnancy." Here, the Missouri statute was neutral toward pregnancy. Since **the employee had left work for a reason that had no causal connection to either her work or her employer**, she was not entitled to unemployment compensation benefits. She had not been denied benefits "solely" because of her pregnancy. The Court affirmed the decision against the employee. *Wimberly v. Labor and Industrial Relations Comm'n*, 479 U.S. 511, 107 S.Ct. 821, 93 L.Ed.2d 909 (1987).

♦   A Minnesota employee took a leave to visit his sick wife in Africa. While there, he contracted typhoid and gastritis, and he was hospitalized. He called his company's third-party administrator to request an extension, but the administrator failed to send the leave extension forms. He became too sick to call back, so someone called on his behalf, but again the administrator failed to send the forms. When the company fired him, he applied for unemployment compensation benefits. A hearing officer found that he quit and wasn't entitled to benefits, but the Minnesota Court of Appeals reversed. **The employee didn't engage in misconduct by failing to notify the company** because he contacted the administrator. Nor could he be deemed to have quit. *Abdi v. Electrolux Home Products, Inc.*, No. A11-1884, 2012 WL 3101285 (Minn. Ct. App. 7/30/12).

♦   A steel company in Pennsylvania negotiated a new collective bargaining agreement that included revisions to the company's health care plan. Under the new plan, costs increased substantially. A 59-year-old employee took two prescriptions that cost him $10 per month under the old plan but $140 per month under the new plan. He retired early and applied for unemployment compensation benefits, claiming that he had a compelling reason to leave his job. The company fought the claim and won. The Pennsylvania Commonwealth Court ruled that the employee failed to show the percentage by which the new plan would reduce his income. Therefore, **he didn't meet his burden of showing a compelling reason to leave the job**. *Elliott Company v. Unemployment Compensation Board of Review*, 29 A.3d 881 (Pa. Commw. Ct. 2011).

♦   An Ohio employee was involved in a car accident and missed a great deal of work due to medical problems. She exhausted her sick and personal time as well as her time under the FMLA. When her unexcused time went over 20 hours, she was fired. She applied for unemployment compensation benefits, which were granted. The unemployment compensation review commission found that she missed work because of medical problems beyond her control. Therefore, her termination was without just cause. Also, she could work full time. The employer argued on appeal that missing work for legitimate medical reasons was not a defense to repeated violations of a written absenteeism policy. However, the Ohio Court of Appeals disagreed. **Termination after repeated absenteeism for legitimate medical reasons does not disqualify an employee from unemployment benefits.** *Lorain County Auditor v. Ohio Unemployment Review Comm'n*, 185 Ohio App.3d 822, 925 N.E.2d 1038 (Ohio Ct. App. 2010).

♦   An Indiana employee with degenerative disc disease caused in part by military training was restricted by his physician to bed rest and limited home activity for at least one month. A week later, he was fired. He filed for unemployment benefits, and a hearing officer determined that **he was not eligible because he was not able, available and actively seeking work**. A review board affirmed that decision, as did the Indiana Court of Appeals. The employee could stand or sit for a maximum of 20 minutes at a time and reclined in a chair the majority of the day unless he had physical therapy or a doctor's appointment. Also, his doctor hadn't released him to return to work. Thus, he was not eligible for unemployment compensation. *M.M. v. Review Board of Indiana Dep't of Workforce Development*, 921 N.E.2d 16 (Ind. Ct. App. 2009).

◆   A front desk agent at a hotel in Florida contracted bronchitis and pneumonia as a result of mold and mildew in her work environment. When she notified her employer of her medical condition, he did nothing about the problem until after the Occupational Safety and Health Administration inspected the job site. Even then, he did not clean the air conditioner or ventilation systems, so the air continued to have contaminants. The employee became dissatisfied with the working conditions and quit her job, later filing for unemployment compensation benefits, which the Florida District Court of Appeal granted. The employee made reasonable efforts to preserve her employment, and quit only because the working conditions were so harsh as to require her separation. **Although the employer took some steps to remedy the problem, he failed to show that the problem was in fact remedied** by his efforts. *Kloepper v. Unemployment Appeals Comm'n*, 871 So.2d 997 (Fla. Dist. Ct. App. 2004).

2. Personal Reasons

Where an employee quits for personal reasons, unemployment compensation benefits generally are *not* payable. However, where the employer has caused, at least in part, the separation, the employee might be entitled to benefits.

◆   An administrative assistant in Minnesota scheduled drug screens for job applicants. When an applicant told her and a supervisor that he might fail a drug screen because he had used marijuana, the supervisor told the administrative assistant to "stretch out the time" for the appointment. The administrative assistant said the request made her uncomfortable, and she asked HR to put a note in her file about it. In a separate incident, an employee was paid for 90 minutes on a day that he was sent home for being drunk. The administrative assistant believed it was unethical to pay him. She resigned and applied for unemployment benefits. The court held she was not entitled to benefits because **she did not have good cause to quit**. She may have had good personal reasons for not wanting to work there anymore, but a reasonable employee would not have felt compelled to leave. *Grosland v. Smyth Companies LLC*, No. A13-0572, 2013 WL 6725764 (Minn. Ct. App. 12/23/13).

◆   A Pennsylvania man, having difficulty finding a job in the state, applied for a position in Oklahoma. Shortly thereafter, his son was killed in a car accident. He was offered a job in Oklahoma a month later and took it, leaving his wife and three surviving children behind in Pennsylvania. He attempted to work through his grief, but over a year later, he informed his boss that he could no longer handle being separated from his family. He offered to stay until a replacement could be found, then resigned and returned to Pennsylvania. When he applied for unemployment benefits, the Pennsylvania Commonwealth Court ultimately ruled that he was entitled to them. **His decision to leave his job was for a necessitous and compelling cause**, and he made a reasonable effort to preserve his employment by staying in Oklahoma for more than a year. *Fiedler v. Unemployment Compensation Board of Review*, 18 A.3d 459 (Pa. Commw. Ct. 2011).

◆   A telecommunications employee worked in Iraq. He took all his leave to return to Pennsylvania to help his fiancée, who was battling her abusive ex-boyfriend over the custody of their three-year-old son. The son had just been diagnosed with microcephaly and needed to see multiple specialists for treatment, and the fiancée had no family nearby who could help her. After returning to Iraq, the employee sought a transfer to the United States, but no jobs were available there. **The employee finally resigned and returned to Pennsylvania to marry his fiancée and help care for her son.** He applied for unemployment compensation benefits, which were initially denied. However, the Pennsylvania Commonwealth Court granted him benefits, finding that he quit for necessitous and compelling reasons. *Wagner v. Unemployment Compensation Board of Review*, 965 A.2d 323 (Pa. Commw. Ct. 2009).

◆   A New York employee visited his mother in Puerto Rico and learned that she had been diagnosed with lung cancer. He decided to relocate to care for her, and quit his job without notice. When he applied for unemployment compensation benefits, the Unemployment Insurance Appeal Board ruled that he was disqualified from receiving benefits because he voluntarily left his employment without good cause. The New York Supreme Court, Appellate Division, upheld that determination, finding **no evidence that the employee's relocation was medically necessary for the care of his mother**. Further, by neglecting to inform the employer of his departure or inquire about a leave of absence, he failed to take reasonable steps to protect his employment. *In re Soler*, 805 N.Y.S.2d 448 (N.Y. App. Div. 2005).

◆   A Florida employee claimed that her husband physically and mentally abused her and repeatedly threatened her life. She obtained a divorce and moved to California, believing that her life was in danger. She filed a claim for unemployment compensation benefits, asserting that she had not voluntarily left her employment. The state unemployment appeals commission held that the employee had not quit her job for good cause attributable to the employer and denied her claim. The District Court of Appeal of Florida observed that the legislature had amended the statute to allow benefits for a good cause separation only where the separation is attributable to the employer. There was **no evidence that the employee's separation from work had been caused by the employer**, and the court refused to extend an exception for domestic abuse cases. The employee was not entitled to benefits. *Hall v. Florida Unemployment Appeals Comm'n*, 697 So.2d 541 (Fla. Dist. Ct. App. 1997).

◆   A New Jersey appeals court affirmed a state administrative decision denying unemployment benefits to a legal secretary who quit her job due to domestic violence caused by her husband. She obtained a restraining order following a violent attack by her husband, who continued to harass her at work. Although she enjoyed her job and was good at it, she felt compelled to quit and move away to prevent a life-threatening situation that affected her job performance. The court observed that the state unemployment compensation law disqualifies claimants who voluntarily leave work without good cause attributable to work. Since the state agency had found that **the decision to leave work because of an abusive spouse was a personal reason that was not attributable to work**, the court affirmed the denial of benefits. *Pagan v. Board of Review*, 296 N.J.Super. 539, 687 A.2d 328 (N.J. Super. Ct. App. Div. 1997).

E. Other Circumstances

Many employees quit their jobs for reasons they believe are necessitous and compelling. However, unless the working conditions are so difficult that a reasonable person would be forced to quit, the employee will probably not be entitled to unemployment compensation benefits.

◆ A life insurance salesman in Missouri was told by his employer that he needed to sign a non-compete agreement. The agreement lasted for an initial period of three years, and it applied throughout the United States. It also broadly restricted his ability to work if he left. In addition, it made him liable for potential damages. In a meeting with management, the salesman expressed concerns about signing and said he wanted an attorney to review the agreement. He was told he had to sign it by the next day. He did not return the signed agreement the next day. The next business day after that, he went to work and was told to wait for HR staff to meet with him. **He left before they met with him, and he never went back.** He filed a claim for unemployment benefits, and the court said he was entitled to them. It said the agreement substantially constrained his future ability to earn a living and exposed him to significant liability. *Darr v. Roberts Marketing LLP*, 428 S.W.3d 717 (Mo. Ct. App. 2014).

◆ A company's owner told a project manager to let a dispatcher know that the project manager was on call. The project manager did not do so, but the dispatcher already knew he was on call. While on call, he was told to take some equipment to a work site. He did so and then left. When a supervisor called him to ask why he did not stay to manage the site, he said he was not paid to do so. In addition, the project manager failed to respond to a text he received relating to a fire. The text was received while he was on call. **The project manager was fired for insubordination, and he filed a claim for unemployment benefits.** A court held he was entitled to them. It failed to find he had a duty to respond to the text about the fire or stay at the job site after delivering the equipment. He did breach a duty to tell the dispatcher he was on call, but that was not enough to deny him unemployment benefits. *Phipps v. Unemployment Compensation Board of Review*, No. 1725 C.D. 2013, 2014 WL 2927192 (Pa. Commw. Ct. 6/26/14).

◆ A shipping clerk for a Pennsylvania company accepted early retirement when the company implemented a reduction in force. He then filed a claim for unemployment benefits. Under state law, benefits were available if the employee was otherwise eligible and exercised a voluntary layoff option. A lower court interpreted this rule to apply only in cases involving temporary layoffs, but the state's highest court reversed. It said that **for purposes of the rule, a layoff could be temporary or permanent**. The case was returned to a lower court for further consideration. *Diehl v. Unemployment Compensation Board of Review*, 57 A.3d 1209 (Pa. 2012).

♦   A Wal-Mart employee in Minnesota suffered a series of mini-strokes that affected his comprehension, concentration and his ability to multitask. His job was to stock various sections of the store. At one point he received an oral warning because he had difficulty completing his work. He told the store manager he thought his performance problems were related to his strokes. After his performance problems persisted, an assistant store manager gave him a final warning and told him to come up with a written plan on how to improve his performance. He was to bring that in the next time he worked. When he didn't show up for five shifts, he was fired. He filed for unemployment benefits, and the Minnesota Court of Appeals held that he was entitled to them. **He thought he wasn't supposed to return to work until he came up with a performance improvement plan**, which he wasn't able to do. *Cunningham v. Wal-Mart Associates, Inc.*, 809 N.W.2d 231 (Minn. Ct. App. 2011).

♦   On three occasions, the director of a child care center in Arizona threatened to quit by July 17 if she didn't get a bonus she believed the company had promised her. On the morning of July 17, while she was at work, a locksmith showed up to change the locks, and her supervisor told her to leave immediately. She filed a claim for unemployment compensation, which the company fought. It asserted that she had quit. However, the Arizona Court of Appeals disagreed. It noted that **threatening to quit is not the same thing as quitting**, and that the company took the final action in ending her employment. As a result, the director was entitled to unemployment compensation benefits. *Figueroa v. Arizona Dep't of Economic Security*, 260 P.3d 1113 (Ariz. Ct. App. 2011).

♦   A New Jersey sales rep with a poor attendance record received a written warning for being tardy. He later called in to work and explained that he was having personal problems that prevented him from working. Subsequently, he called in to work again and talked to a co-worker who told him that a rumor was circulating that he'd already been fired. He never checked with management to ascertain whether this was true. In fact, it was false. Instead, he filed for unemployment compensation benefits, which were denied. A state appeals court held that **he should not have relied on a co-worker's misinformed and unsubstantiated comment that he was fired**. Thus, he was deemed to have abandoned his job and was not entitled to unemployment benefits. *Pinto v. Board of Review, Dep't of Labor*, 2009 WL 3460726 (N.J. Super. App. Div. 10/23/09).

♦   A cook at a Florida children's center submitted a resignation letter effective two weeks later because things "just weren't going right." The center never formally accepted her resignation, but it advertised for a new cook, hired a replacement, and then told her to leave three days early because it couldn't afford to pay two cooks. She sought unemployment benefits, asserting that she hadn't voluntarily quit. After a denial of benefits by the unemployment appeals commission, the district court of appeal granted them, finding that **she did not quit voluntarily when the center fired her three days before the effective date of her resignation**. *Porter v. Florida Unemployment Appeals Comm'n*, 1 So.3d 1101 (Fla. Dist. Ct. App. 2009).

◆   A receptionist asked for a raise and was turned down. Shortly thereafter, she submitted a letter of resignation, giving 30 days' notice. However, with a little more than two weeks left in her tenure, the boss told her to leave. She filed a claim for unemployment compensation for the period between her termination and her resignation date. The Department of Employment Security held that she was not entitled to benefits for the time between the firing and the effective resignation date. However, the Missouri Court of Appeals reversed. **She did not agree to advance her resignation date. Thus, she did not voluntarily quit at that particular time.** The court remanded the case for a determination of whether she was otherwise eligible for benefits. *Fitzpatrick v. Don Brown Automotive Group*, 237 S.W.3d 595 (Mo. Ct. App. 2007).

◆   An employee with impaired vision took the bus to work every day. The company considered him a model employee. Years later, the company changed his shift so that he had to arrive at 3:30 p.m. and work until after midnight, when buses no longer ran. For nine months he tried to make the arrangement work, carpooling with a supervisor for a while and then carpooling with a co-worker who had slightly different hours. At times he was forced to leave at midnight to get a ride home. Fearing he would be fired for leaving early, he finally quit, then filed for unemployment compensation benefits. The case reached the New Jersey Supreme Court, which held that **he was entitled to benefits because he had "good cause" to quit**. The shift change altered the employee's working conditions, and he did all that was reasonable and necessary to stay employed. *Utley v. Board of Review, Dep't of Labor*, 946 A.2d 1039 (N.J. 2008).

◆   A truck driver for a transportation company in Florida got a ticket in Georgia and tried to arrange with the dispatcher to be given a route that would take him to Georgia during the time he was scheduled to be in court. The dispatcher did not do so, and the driver missed his court date. He managed to reschedule, but the dispatcher again refused to give him a route that would allow him to appear in court. After returning from that job, the driver waited at the facility for four days, hoping to speak with the owner to resolve the problem. When the owner refused to speak with him, he quit. He filed for unemployment compensation, and the Florida District Court of Appeal granted him benefits. There was clearly **good cause for the driver's resignation**. *Thomas v. Peoplease Corp.*, 877 So.2d 45 (Fla. Dist. Ct. App. 2004).

◆   An employee at a grocery store was accused of taking a missing bank deposit. She was told by the employer and a Division of Criminal Investigation agent that if she admitted to taking the money, she could keep her job, so she should either admit to taking the money or leave. She refused to admit to taking the money and left, believing she was fired. When she filed for unemployment compensation benefits, the Supreme Court of South Dakota determined that she had voluntarily left her job with good cause. Even though no one ever told her she was fired, she reasonably believed she had been. **Requiring an involuntary admission of guilt to theft changed the employment contract and gave her good cause to leave** her job. *Habben v. G.F. Buche Co., Inc.*, 677 N.W.2d 227 (S.D. 2004).

◆   An employee of a company in New York moved to Florida for personal reasons and was allowed to telecommute. The company paid for a computer, telephone line and other necessary items so she could perform her duties. Two years later, the company decided to end the telecommuting arrangement and offered the employee work in the New York office. She turned it down, and the company let her go. She applied for unemployment compensation benefits in Florida, but was turned down because she had voluntarily quit her job. The employee then filed an interstate claim for benefits under New York law. The case reached the Court of Appeals of New York, which ruled that **she was not entitled to benefits under New York law because she was regularly physically present in Florida** while she was working for the company. Thus, her work was "localized" in Florida. Benefits were denied. *Allen v. Commissioner of Labor*, 763 N.Y.S.2d 237, 794 N.E.2d 18 (N.Y. 2003).

II. RELIGIOUS BELIEF SEPARATION

The U.S. Supreme Court has recognized the right of employees to receive unemployment compensation benefits where continued employment interferes with a <u>sincerely held religious belief</u>. Denial of benefits in these cases has been held to violate the Free Exercise Clause of the First Amendment to the U.S. Constitution.

The most common scenario involves employees who are not willing to work on their religion's holy day (usually a Saturday or Sunday). Where possible, employers should be flexible and accommodating, not only to avoid paying unemployment compensation, but also to avoid claims of religious discrimination. For cases involving religious discrimination, please see Chapter One, Section V.

Where flexibility is not possible, note that employers can ask applicants if they are capable of performing the duties of the job, and if they need any accommodations to perform those duties.

If the applicant claims that he can perform the job's duties and later asserts that a religious belief prevents him from working on his holy day, you may then have to pay unemployment benefits if he quits rather than break a sincerely held religious belief.

◆   An Illinois man was offered a temporary retail position by a placement agency. He refused the position because the job would have required him to work on Sunday, a day he considered to be "the Lord's day." He applied for unemployment compensation benefits, claiming that there was good cause for his refusal to work on Sunday. The Illinois Department of Economic Security denied his application, and a board of review upheld that decision. It found that the applicant's refusal to work was based solely on an entirely personal belief that was not a tenet or dogma of a church, sect or denomination. The Illinois courts also upheld the denial of benefits, and appeal was taken to the U.S. Supreme Court. The applicant charged that the denial of benefits violated his free exercise of religion rights, as guaranteed by the First Amendment. The Court agreed. So long as the applicant had **a sincere belief that required him to refrain from the work offered**, it did not matter that the belief was not in response to the commands of a particular religious organization. Further, the state had not shown any justification for burdening the applicant's beliefs by denying unemployment benefits. Granting benefits was not likely to cause a mass movement away from Sunday employment by others. The Court reversed the lower courts and granted benefits to the applicant. *Frazee v. Illinois Dep't of Economic Security,* 489 U.S. 829, 109 S.Ct. 1514, 103 L.Ed.2d 914 (1989).

◆   A Florida jeweler hired a woman to work at a retail jewelry store. Subsequently, the woman became baptized in the Seventh-Day Adventist Church. She informed her supervisor that she could no longer work from sundown on Friday to sundown on Saturday due to her religious beliefs. After initially accommodating her, the jeweler discharged her. When she filed for unemployment compensation benefits, the jeweler contested payment, asserting that "misconduct" connected with her work was the reason for the discharge. Benefits were denied. The case reached the U.S. Supreme Court, which held that the denial of benefits violated the Free Exercise Clause of the First Amendment. Under a strict scrutiny analysis, the rejection of benefits failed. First, even though Florida law only disqualified applicants for a limited time, rather than making them completely ineligible, the denial could not be justified. Second, **it did not matter that the employer did not change the conditions of employment so as to conflict with the employee's religious beliefs**, or that the employee converted to the religion during the course of the employment. Benefits had to be paid. Finally, the Court noted that paying benefits here would not be a fostering of religion in violation of the Establishment Clause. *Hobbie v. Unemployment Appeals Comm'n of Florida,* 480 U.S. 136, 107 S.Ct. 1046, 94 L.Ed.2d 190 (1987).

◆   An employee of a foundry fabricated sheet steel for a variety of industrial uses. When the foundry closed, the company transferred him to a department that fabricated turrets for military tanks. The employee, a Jehovah's Witness, believed that working on weapons would violate the principles of his religion. Because there were no "nonweapons" jobs in the company and because the company refused to lay him off, he quit. He then applied for unemployment compensation, which was denied. The Indiana Court of Appeals awarded benefits, but the state supreme court reversed. On further appeal, the U.S. Supreme Court held that the denial of benefits violated the applicant's First Amendment right to the free exercise of his religion. **It did not matter that**

another Jehovah's Witness was willing to work on tank turrets. The religious belief in question need not be shared by all the members of a religious sect. Here, the important thing to consider was that the employee had quit for religious reasons. The Court stated that a person may not be compelled to choose between the exercise of a First Amendment right and participation in an otherwise available public program. It granted benefits to the applicant. *Thomas v. Review Board of Indiana Employment Security Division,* 450 U.S. 707, 101 S.Ct. 1425, 67 L.Ed.2d 624 (1981).

◆   A Jehovah's Witness at a jewelry repair store in Pennsylvania was asked to send birthday cards to clients inviting them in to have their jewelry cleaned. As a Jehovah's Witness, she believed that celebrating birthdays was the worshipping of false gods. She quit and filed for unemployment compensation benefits, which the Unemployment Compensation Board of Review granted. However, the commonwealth court reversed, finding that **the request to print messages on promotional birthday cards did not give her a "necessitous and compelling" religious reason to quit** so as to merit benefits. *Calhoun Jewelers v. Unemployment Compensation Board of Review*, No. 2081, 2010 WL 9514503 (Pa. Commw. Ct. 4/20/10).

◆   A part-time instructor at a college in Wisconsin sought unemployment compensation benefits when her job ended after the fall semester. The college then offered her work for the spring semester. **She rejected the job offer because she had to make a religious pilgrimage.** The Labor and Industrial Review Commission denied her benefits, finding that she did not have good cause to reject the job offer. However, it did not make factual findings as to whether she had to make the pilgrimage at the time she claimed she did. Nor did it address whether the "good cause" standard of Wisconsin law violated her religious free exercise rights. The case reached the Wisconsin Court of Appeals, which reversed the denial of benefits and remanded the case for further consideration. *Rashad v. LIRC*, 699 N.W.2d 254 (Wis. Ct. App. 2005).

III. MISCONDUCT

Employee misconduct often provides a valid reason for denying benefits, in whole or in part. Generally, misconduct entails a willful and wanton or intentional disregard of an employer's interests, a deliberate violation of rules or policies, or a disregard of behavioral standards that an employer has the right to expect. Incompetence or inability may not necessarily constitute misconduct.

A. Employer's Interests

Where an employee commits misconduct that is against the employer's business interests, he may be disqualified from benefits in whole or in part. Generally, employees commit such misconduct by ignoring or refusing orders, or by acts or omissions that harm the employer.

◆   An Idaho Wal-Mart employee was **fired after using foul language** and clocking out early. He had experienced problems with an assistant manager and stated that he was tired of the assistant manager's "F'ing BS" after the assistant manager told him he needed to step up his performance in front of customers and co-workers. Although he used profanity in the store, he spoke in the back room where other employees, but no customers, overheard him. He sought unemployment benefits, but the Idaho Supreme Court ruled that he wasn't entitled to them because he was fired for misconduct that fell below a standard of behavior the employer had a reasonable right to expect. *Rigoli v. Wal-Mart Associates, Inc.*, 263 P.3d 761 (Idaho 2011).

◆   A District of Columbia employee was fired for refusing to do work one day, apparently in retaliation for the company's refusal to consider giving him a raise or allowing him to work at home. When he filed for unemployment compensation, a hearing officer ruled that he had been fired for gross misconduct, thus disqualifying him from receiving benefits. The D.C. Court of Appeals reversed, finding that **the employee's refusal to work on the single day in question was simple misconduct rather than gross misconduct**. Gross misconduct is "an act which deliberately or willfully violates the employer's rules, deliberately or willfully threatens or violates the employer's interests, shows a repeated disregard for the employee's obligation to the employer, or disregards standards of behavior which an employer has a right to expect of its employee." Here, the employee's refusal to work on the day in question did not reach that level. *Odeniran v. Hanley Wood, LLC*, 985 A.2d 421 (D.C. Ct. App. 2009).

◆   A Pennsylvania software developer played games on his computer during work hours instead of working on a project to which he was assigned. He also tried to circumvent the computer security program and do consulting work for an outside client on his own. After he was fired, he sought unemployment compensation benefits. The case reached the Pennsylvania Commonwealth Court, which ruled against him. **His behavior reflected an unwillingness to work to the best of his ability and a conscious disregard for the standards his employer had a right to expect.** This was willful misconduct. *Hance v. Unemployment Compensation Board of Review*, No. 1920 C.D. 2008, 2009 WL 9097293 (Pa. Commw. Ct. 6/18/09).

◆   A car detailer at a Minnesota dealership was asked to pick up litter from the premises. He told his supervisor that he was busy and that the manager could go "f—— himself." He was then fired. He sought unemployment compensation benefits, which an administrative law judge denied. The Minnesota Court of Appeals reversed. It noted that misconduct occurs when an employee refuses to comply with a reasonable request by the employer. And the request here was reasonable. However, while misconduct such as what happened here could be a bar to receiving benefits, the state's unemployment compensation statute also provides that **a single incident of misconduct isn't a bar to benefits when the incident doesn't have a "significant adverse impact on the employer."** Here, there was no evidence that the employee's refusal to pick up trash had a significant impact on his job of detailing cars. *Williams v. Brooklyn Center Motors*, No. A06-1467, 2007 WL 1747125 (Minn. Ct. App. 6/19/07).

♦   After less than two months on the job, a paralegal at an Indianapolis law firm asked for the afternoon off to pick up her son, her car, and sign an apartment lease. What she didn't mention was that she was also going to attend Carburetion Day, the last day of practice before the Indianapolis 500. While she was there, someone used a cell phone to take a photo of her and emailed it to her at work. Her boss discovered the photo in her email and fired her. When she applied for unemployment benefits, she was initially awarded them. The law firm appealed and won. The Indiana Court of Appeals held that **she breached her duty of loyalty and that she was thus fired for just cause**. She was not entitled to benefits. *McHugh v. Review Board of the Indiana Dep't of Workforce Development*, 842 N.E.2d 436 (Ind. Ct. App. 2006).

♦   An employee at a store in New Hampshire with no warnings or disciplinary issues against her sold cigarettes to an underage customer in violation of store policy. In violation of store policy, she failed to verify the customer's age and used the override feature on the cash register to complete the sale without verifying the age. The customer was part of a sting operation, and the police issued her a summons for selling tobacco products to a minor. She was fired the next day and later applied for unemployment benefits. The case reached the Supreme Court of New Hampshire, which found that she was not entitled to benefits because she was fired for misconduct connected with her work. **She deliberately violated a company rule** reasonably designed to protect the legitimate business interests of the employer. *In re Riendeau*, 877 A.2d 207 (N.H. 2005).

♦   A manager at an Oregon retail automotive parts chain store conducted a training class for new employees and allegedly made racially and ethnically offensive statements during the class. After a new employee complained, his supervisor requested a written statement of what occurred, advising the manager that he should do this both as a subordinate and as the person being investigated. The manager was fired after he refused to submit a written statement. He sought unemployment benefits. An administrative law judge granted him benefits, but the Oregon Employment Appeals Board reversed. The Oregon Court of Appeals upheld the board's decision, finding substantial evidence that the manager engaged in misconduct when he **intentionally refused to provide his supervisor with a written statement of what he said during the class**. The court rejected the manager's argument that he was asked to voluntarily provide the statement, rather than directed to do so. The directive here came from the manager's supervisor, and he could expect the manager to comply. *Bingham v. Employment Dep't*, 987 P.2d 578 (Or. Ct. App. 1999).

♦   Beginning shortly after she was hired, a customer service representative constantly criticized her co-workers, yelling at them and sending them "nasty grams." After she initiated a hostile confrontation with a co-worker, she received a written warning that the company would no longer tolerate her conduct and that the next incident would result in her termination. In response, she wrote a letter to the company accusing management of having big egos and self-serving agendas. She was fired and sought unemployment compensation. An administrative law judge (ALJ) denied her benefits because **her conduct was done in willful disregard of the employer's interest and caused harm to the employer's business**. Both the state board and the Washington Court of Appeals affirmed the ALJ's findings. The representative argued that the court should consider principles enunciated under the National Labor Relations Act, which makes allowances for an employee's otherwise insubordinate behavior when it occurs during a disciplinary grievance procedure. The appeals court disagreed. This was not a collective bargaining situation. *Haney v. Employment Security Division*, 978 P.2d 543 (Wash. Ct. App. 1999).

◆   A Maryland nursing home discharged two nurses for failing to respond to a page requesting assistance for a patient who was experiencing chest pains. The facility then challenged their applications for unemployment benefits and produced witnesses who testified that they had left the building on a personal errand rather than assist the patient. A hearing officer found that the nurses had failed to assist the patient. The decision was affirmed by an appeals board, resulting in the denial of benefits for a nine-week period. The case reached the Court of Appeals of Maryland, which noted that there was substantial evidence of misconduct by the nurses. **Misconduct in an unemployment compensation claim need not be intentional to support temporary disqualification.** The statute that governed this case provided for disqualification for up to 10 weeks based on the seriousness of the misconduct. A separate statute governed cases of gross or aggravated misconduct. The court affirmed the temporary disqualification from unemployment benefits. *Dep't of Labor, Licensing and Regulation v. Hider*, 349 Md. 71, 706 A.2d 1073 (Md. 1998).

B. Rules or Policies

Violation of employer policies can result in denial of unemployment benefits. Common employer policies include <u>drug-free workplace</u> policies (for cases dealing with drug testing, please see Chapter Six, Section II) and <u>attendance</u> policies.

1. Drug Policies

Employees who violate drug policies can be fired even if they are recovering addicts who are in treatment. This does not violate the Americans with Disabilities Act because the employee is not being fired for what she is but for actions that violate a standard set forth by the employer.

When an employee fired for violating a drug policy seeks unemployment compensation, benefits generally will be denied either in whole or in part.

◆   A material handler in Michigan injured his ankle at work. He was sent to a medical center and was required to take a drug test. The employee tested positive for marijuana, and he revealed he had previously obtained a medical marijuana card. The card authorized him under state law to use marijuana for medical purposes, and he said he regularly used marijuana for his chronic back pain. The employer terminated his employment for violating its drug-free workplace policy. When the employee applied for unemployment benefits, a lower court found he was entitled to them because he did not engage in misconduct. On appeal, his case was joined with similar cases involving two other employees. The appeals court decided that **employees who possess medical marijuana cards, and are discharged for failing a drug test, cannot be denied unemployment benefits**. The denial of benefits would constitute an impermissible penalty under the state's medical marijuana law, which broadly provided that patients with the cards could not be penalized or denied any right or privilege because they used marijuana for medical purposes. *Braska v. Challenge Manufacturing Co.*, No. 313932, 2014 WL 5393501 (Mich. Ct. App. 10/23/14).

◆ A Pennsylvania employee signed a last-chance agreement in which he agreed not to have any marijuana in his possession. A year later, he was arrested for possessing marijuana. He admitted to an HR manager that he still had some marijuana that he planned to sell. After he was fired for violating the last-chance agreement and the company's drug policy, he sought unemployment compensation benefits. He claimed that the employer had to prove that his off-duty misconduct directly impacted his ability to perform his job. However, the Pennsylvania Commonwealth Court disagreed and denied him benefits. **The employee admittedly violated both the last-chance agreement and the company's drug policy.** *Maskerines v. Unemployment Compensation Board of Review*, 13 A.3d 553 (Pa. Commw. Ct. 2011).

◆ An employee of a window manufacturer was issued a reprimand for failing to call in on a day he was absent. Company policy required employees issued reprimands to submit to a drug test or be fired. He refused to take the test and left work without telling anyone of his decision. When he filed for unemployment compensation, the case reached the Missouri Court of Appeals. The court held that the employee left his job without good cause attributable to his employer, making him ineligible for unemployment compensation. **By refusing to take the drug test, he abandoned his job.** *Winco Manufacturing, Inc. v. Capone*, 133 S.W.3d 555 (Mo. Ct. App. 2004).

◆ A certified nurse's aide at a nursing home was treated for a workplace injury. Attached to the bill for services was her medical history, which indicated that she regularly used illegally obtained prescription medicine and marijuana. She admitted to her employer that she **used marijuana daily after work** but asserted that she did not report to work under its influence. She denied using illegal prescription drugs. The employer fired her, and she applied for unemployment compensation benefits, which were denied. On appeal, the Pennsylvania Supreme Court held that she was entitled to benefits. Here, the aide had not committed work-related misconduct. As for her off-duty misconduct, the employer failed to show both that her marijuana smoking was "inconsistent with acceptable standards of behavior" and that it directly affected her ability to perform her assigned duties. As a result, she was entitled to collect unemployment compensation. *Burger v. Pennsylvania Unemployment Compensation Board of Review*, 801 A.2d 487 (Pa. 2002).

◆   A trucking company installed a surveillance camera to try to determine whether marijuana was being sold on the premises. It recorded several people smoking a pipe. One of the individuals in the film identified a co-worker as the seller after he was promised that he would not be disciplined so long as he cooperated with the police. Another employee also implicated the co-worker as the seller in exchange for a promise of no adverse action. The co-worker denied selling drugs. When the company fired him, he filed for unemployment compensation benefits. His claim was denied, and he appealed to a court, which affirmed the denial. **The court noted that he had engaged in willful or deliberate misconduct**, and it found the testimony of the company's witnesses to be more credible than his. The company also did not treat him unfairly by firing him while retaining the two employees who had been caught smoking marijuana on the job, because by doing so, the company was able to rid itself of an undesirable and potentially dangerous element. *Daniels v. Unemployment Compensation Board of Review*, 755 A.2d 729 (Pa. Commw. Ct. 2000).

◆   An Oklahoma employer with a drug-free workplace policy fired an employee after learning that **she failed to report a guilty plea to a drug-related offense**. The employee had previously admitted having a substance abuse problem, for which the employer required her to seek treatment under an employer-sponsored program. She had instructed her attorney to contact the employer about the drug-related offense, but he failed to do so. Her claim for unemployment benefits was denied, based on evidence that the employer had adequately communicated its drug-free policy in employee handbooks. A trial court found no evidence that the employer had advised the employee of the drug-free policy. The Court of Civil Appeals of Oklahoma held that the employee had admitted knowledge of the workplace policy by revealing her abuse problem to a supervisor and directing her attorney to inform her supervisor of the guilty plea. Because there was substantial evidence of her misconduct, the trial court decision was reversed. *Davis v. Oklahoma Employment Security Comm'n*, 949 P.2d 683 (Okla. Ct. App. 1997).

◆   A Nevada hotel implemented a drug-free workplace policy and gave its employees 90 days advance notice of a drug test. An employee who often handled large amounts of cash and had access to the hotel computer system failed a radioimmunoassay hair analysis (RIA) for drug use, and a second test revealed cocaine use. The hotel fired her, and she filed for unemployment benefits. Her claim was denied. A trial court found that failure to pass a drug test without proof of drug-related activity was insufficient to show work-related misconduct sufficient to disqualify unemployment. The court also held that RIA was scientifically unreliable. The Supreme Court of Nevada observed that courts in New York and Florida have accepted RIA drug testing and that medical evidence indicated that this form of analysis was more accurate than urinalysis. The court also determined that **misconduct for unemployment purposes requires that the employer show a deliberate violation or disregard of employee standards of behavior** that the employer has the right to expect. The employer here had a sound reason for demanding compliance with the drug-free policy. It had also given the employee adequate notice to comply with the new policy, and her claim for benefits was properly denied. *Nevada Employment Security Dep't v. Holmes*, 914 P.2d 611 (Nev. 1996).

◆   An Indiana employer maintained a drug-free workplace policy making employees who were under the influence of alcohol or other drugs at work subject to discipline, which could include termination. The employer fired 16 employees for selling and distributing illegal drugs in violation of the policy, including one who had worked for the employer for 18 years. He obtained unemployment compensation benefits because a review board found that the employer had not uniformly enforced the drug-free workplace policy. The Court of Appeals of Indiana determined that the state unemployment compensation law, while requiring an employer to reasonably and uniformly enforce its rules, did not prohibit employers from creating **different categories of offenders within an employment policy**. While the employer had not previously fired employees for drug use, each of the 16 offenders in this case had been fired for the more serious offense of drug distribution, and this was sufficient uniformity for purposes of the statute. *General Motors Corp. v. Review Board of Indiana Dep't of Workforce Development*, 671 N.E.2d 493 (Ind. Ct. App. 1996).

2. Attendance Policies

Excessive <u>absenteeism</u> and <u>tardiness</u> can be construed as deliberate misconduct such that the employee will be denied benefits. Generally, there must be a pattern and practice of lateness or absenteeism for unemployment to be denied on grounds of misconduct. Attendance problems in and of themselves may not disqualify an employee from benefits, even though they justify the firing.

◆   A Minnesota employee was fired for excessive absenteeism and tardiness. His employer had given him oral and written warnings, and had even suspended him for two days, but failed to suspend him for 10 days per its progressive discipline policy before it eventually fired him. He applied for unemployment benefits, which a hearing officer denied. The court of appeals reversed, awarding benefits because the company had failed to follow its progressive discipline policy. On further appeal, the Minnesota Supreme Court reversed again, holding that **even though the employer failed to follow its progressive discipline policy, it had a reasonable expectation that the employee would show up for work and be on time**. The employee was not entitled to benefits. *Stagg v. Vintage Place Inc.*, 796 N.W.2d 312 (Minn. 2011).

◆   A New York machine operator was fired when she failed to return to work at the end of an authorized bereavement leave and also failed to notify the employer that her return would be delayed. She filed for unemployment compensation benefits, which were denied. The New York Supreme Court,

Appellate Division, upheld the denial of benefits, noting that **an employee's failure to return to work or contact the employer following an authorized leave of absence can constitute disqualifying misconduct**. Here, although the employee claimed she could not contact the employer because she was staying in a rural area that did not have phones, she had made several trips to a nearby city during her leave, where she had access to telephones. *In re Jimenez*, 811 N.Y.S.2d 481 (N.Y. App. Div. 2006).

◆   A Florida employer had a policy of progressive discipline that prohibited excessive absenteeism and tardiness. It applied a point system to each worker's attendance record. When a new employee was absent four times, late four times and left early on one occasion in his first four months, he was fired. He filed for unemployment benefits, claiming that his last tardiness (on the day he was fired) occurred because the person who was supposed to pick him up did not show up that day, forcing him to walk to work. Further, he had left work early a few days before that with the approval of his supervisor because he felt ill. As a result, he asserted that he had not committed misconduct under the statutory unemployment scheme. The case reached the Florida Supreme Court, which held that he had been properly denied benefits. **Even though his final two attendance problems might have been justified, they fit into the pattern of absenteeism and tardiness** that he had started. *Mason v. Load King Manufacturing Co.*, 758 So.2d 649 (Fla. 2000).

◆   A Florida employer discharged an employee for missing three consecutive workdays due to transportation problems. The state unemployment appeals commission affirmed an administrative decision disqualifying him from unemployment compensation benefits, finding that he had been discharged for misconduct connected with work. The District Court of Appeal of Florida held that the absences did not demonstrate willful or wanton disregard of the employer's interests through deliberate violation of standards of behavior that the employer had a right to expect, or demonstrate wrongful intent or substantial disregard of the employer's interests. **Although the absences might have justified discharge, they did not constitute misconduct** serious enough to deny unemployment benefits. The court reversed and remanded the decision, allowing the employee to claim benefits. *Roberts v. Diehl*, 707 So.2d 869 (Fla. Dist. Ct. App. 1998).

◆   A Rhode Island employer forced an employee to resign after an investigation disclosed the falsification of his time cards. The hearing referee determined that the employee had voluntarily left his job without good cause and was disqualified from receiving unemployment compensation benefits. The state board of review upheld that determination. A state court held that there was no evidence to support the board's decision based on the employee's exemplary work history and the employer's failure to warn him that he might be fired for falsifying time records. On appeal, the Supreme Court of Rhode Island agreed with the district court in reversing the review board's decision. **In two of the instances of time card falsification the difference in time reported was only a few minutes,** and the employer had failed to warn the employee that these discrepancies might result in firing. *Cardoza v. Dep't of Employment and Training Board of Review*, 669 A.2d 1165 (R.I. 1996).

◆   An Illinois computer attendant worked at a facility where employees were required to work eight-hour shifts including a 30-minute unpaid lunch break and two 15-minute paid breaks. Employees frequently asked for permission to combine lunch and break times at the end of the shift so they could leave early. These requests were usually denied, and the company circulated a memo stating that failure to fill out time sheets correctly would result in discipline. A company manager observed the attendant leaving at least one hour early on several occasions for which she submitted time sheets indicating that she had worked a full shift. The company fired her for falsifying time records, and she applied for unemployment benefits. A court held that the company had failed to follow its own progressive disciplinary policy. The Appellate Court of Illinois found **no requirement for compliance with progressive disciplinary policies in Illinois unemployment compensation law**. The statute provided for the denial of unemployment benefits to employees fired for misconduct, defined as the deliberate and willful violation of a reasonable rule or policy of the employer, where the violation harms the employer and the employee is explicitly warned to stop. The court denied benefits to the attendant. *DeBois v. Dep't of Employment Security*, 653 N.E.2d 1336 (Ill. App. Ct. 1995).

3. Other Policies

Where employers set reasonable workplace policies that are justified by a legitimate business reason, and where those policies are adequately communicated to the employees, the violation of those policies will not only justify discharge, but may also amount to misconduct that warrants the denial of unemployment compensation.

◆   A reservationist at a Florida hotel was fired for violating a company policy that barred employees from using work phones to make personal calls at work. When she filed for unemployment compensation, an appeals referee recommended that she be awarded benefits because the hotel did not show she knew about the policy. An appeals commission rejected the recommendation, finding that the reservationist should have known not to use a work phone to make personal calls because the hotel also banned employees from talking on their cell phones at work. However, a state appeals court decided she should be awarded benefits. **It was up to the appeals referee to make factual findings**, and he found that the hotel did not show the employee knew about the policy. *Cesar v. Reemployment Assistance Appeals Comm'n*, 121 So.3d 1181 (Fla. Dist. Ct. App. 2013).

◆   The husband of a warehouse associate in Louisiana got into a physical fight with a co-worker of the associate. When questioned by her employer, the associate initially denied knowing why the fight took place. It was later discovered that she knew the fight happened because the co-worker had sent her text messages. The employer fired the associate for violating **a company policy that required employees to be truthful during investigations**. When she filed for unemployment benefits, a state appeals court decided she was not entitled to them. The associate's misconduct disqualified her from receiving benefits. By being dishonest, she violated company policy and disregarded the company's behavior standards. *Williams v. Eysink*, No. 2012 CA 1821, 2013 WL 1791582 (La. Ct. App. 4/26/13).

♦   A 63-year-old Minnesota pizza delivery driver worked an overlapping shift with a 22-year-old. During an overlap, the younger driver grabbed the older driver's keys, threw them on a desk and told the older man to move aside. As the older driver did so, he poked the younger man in the side because he was "ticked off" at the younger man. The younger driver was suspended for his actions, but the older man was **fired under the company's no-violence policy**. He began drawing unemployment benefits from the state, but he was later deemed ineligible because of his misconduct. He was ordered to repay $1,207. He appealed, but the Minnesota Court of Appeals upheld the determination of ineligibility. *Potter v. Northern Empire Pizza*, 805 N.W.2d 872 (Minn. Ct. App. 2011).

♦   A Missouri employee sent sexual images to co-workers using the company's computer system. No one complained, but when the company monitored email usage, it discovered the inappropriate emails and fired him. He applied for unemployment compensation benefits, claiming that sending that type of email was common practice at the company and that even top managers did so. A hearing officer denied him benefits, but a review panel granted them. Ultimately, however, the Missouri Court of Appeals denied them. **It did not matter if there was a culture permitting inappropriate emails.** They violated company policy and as such amounted to misconduct connected with work. Therefore, he was not entitled to benefits. *Ernst v. Sumner Group, Inc.*, 264 S.W.3d 669 (Mo. Ct. App. 2008).

♦   While helping a new sales clerk look for a missing credit card receipt, a clerk for an adult novelty store opened the cash register using the emergency switch. However, the store had a policy requiring employees to open the cash register only by pressing the cash-total key or the no-sale key. Even though the clerk did not take any money from the register, he was fired after the manager reviewed security video while investigating the missing credit card receipt. He filed a claim for unemployment compensation, which the store fought. The Minnesota Court of Appeals ruled that he was entitled to benefits. **A single incident of misconduct that does not have a significant adverse impact on the employer does not disqualify a fired employee from receiving unemployment benefits.** *Pierce v. DiMa Corp.*, 721 N.W.2d 627 (Minn. Ct. App. 2006).

♦   After a kitchen worker at a Hawaii resort complained about a work scheduling policy, the food and beverage director changed the policy, resulting in numerous changes to employees' schedules. A hostess who had been with the resort for 22 years came up behind the worker and **jokingly choked her**, saying, "This is all because of you." The worker seemed to laugh it off, but reported it to the director after her shift. The resort then fired the hostess for violating its zero tolerance workplace violence policy. When she filed for unemployment compensation, she was denied benefits. The Supreme Court of Hawaii held that by pretending to choke her co-worker, the hostess showed a conscious disregard of the resort's zero-tolerance policy, which expressly prohibited talk of violence, including joking about violence. *Medeiros v. Hawaii Dep't of Labor and Industrial Relations*, 118 P.3d 1201 (Haw. 2005).

◆   A restaurant employee in Tennessee was given permission to wear her shirt untucked, even though the company's dress code said it should be tucked in. However, when a new manager arrived 11 months later, he told her to tuck in her shirt on several occasions. She refused to do so, became upset and used "foul language." She left work and was fired when she failed to return. When she filed for unemployment compensation benefits, her request was denied. The Court of Appeals of Tennessee held that **she engaged in misconduct by refusing to comply with the dress code**. *Hallowell v. Vestco, Inc.*, No. W2004-01322-COA-R3-CV, 2005 WL 1046795 (Tenn. Ct. App. 5/4/05).

◆   A Utah company issued an employee handbook, which provided that email was to be used for business purposes only. It later sent all employees an email reminding them that the policy was still in effect. After a former employee notified the company that she had received sexually offensive emails from current employees, the company fired two workers. One had sent 11 "clearly offensive" messages and the other had sent 25. When the two fired workers applied for unemployment benefits, the Utah Court of Appeals held that they were fired for just cause and that they were not eligible for benefits. The company did not have to warn them that their emails differed significantly from those of their co-workers. Here, the workers had **violated a universal standard of behavior by sending emails containing sexually explicit and offensive jokes, pictures and videos** (including videos depicting sexual acts). *Autoliv ASP, Inc. v. Dep't of Workforce Services*, 29 P.3d 7 (Utah App. 2001).

◆   A heavy equipment manufacturer suspended 19 union-affiliated employees for violation of a workplace rule forbidding T-shirts, buttons or other apparel containing messages that attacked or insulted co-workers. The employees had worn shirts referring to an unfair labor practices complaint against the employer based on the suspension of an employee who wore a shirt calling for the replacement of the company's chairman. The suspended employees applied for unemployment compensation benefits for the period of their suspension. In a separate action, the National Labor Relations Board (NLRB) made a finding of unfair labor practices by the employer. The employees obtained unemployment benefits, and the employer appealed.

The Supreme Court of Pennsylvania observed that unemployment benefits are not payable where an employee is discharged or suspended for willful misconduct connected with work. **Violation of an employer rule may constitute willful misconduct where the rule or policy is reasonable** under the circumstances. The employer's enforcement of the rule must also be reasonable. In this case, the NLRB had found that wearing the T-shirts was protected union activity. The employer's application of the rule did not support its goal of avoiding workplace confrontations, and the actions of the claimants did not constitute willful misconduct. The court affirmed the award of benefits. *Caterpillar, Inc. v. UCBR*, 703 A.2d 452 (Pa. 1997).

♦   An Illinois employee **refused to remove a pro-union sign from his personal vehicle that displayed the term "scab" in violation of an employer rule**. He was discharged for misconduct and applied for unemployment compensation benefits. The Appellate Court of Illinois agreed with the board's finding that the employer's rule was unreasonable. An employee may be disqualified on the basis of misconduct for violating only a reasonable employer rule, and the board was entitled to deference. The court also agreed with the employee that placing the sign in the window of his personal vehicle was not connected with work because it did not relate to the performance of his job duties as a lathe operator and did not govern his performance of work. The court reinstated the award of unemployment compensation benefits. *Caterpillar, Inc. v. Fehrenbacher*, 676 N.E.2d 710 (Ill. App. Ct. 1997).

♦   A Virginia sales rep worked for a security system installer under a commission agreement, which compensated him at a higher rate for equipment leases than for sales. He conducted extensive negotiations with a customer for a purchase agreement of equipment, which the employer later argued resulted in an overpayment to the representative of over $16,000. Even though the transaction had been closely monitored by his supervisors and a branch manager, the employer fired the sales rep for failing to follow company policy in structuring the transaction and failing to use a corporate-approved contract. The sales rep filed a claim for unemployment compensation, which was awarded. The employer appealed to the Court of Appeals of Virginia, asserting that the sales rep was guilty of misconduct connected with work and was therefore disqualified from receiving benefits. The court agreed with the sales rep that **his conduct had been authorized and directed by supervisors and** that his deviation from company rules had been approved by them. Because the supervisors had indicated their approval of the transaction, the court rejected the employer's claim that the sales rep had engaged in misconduct that disqualified him from benefits. *Wells Fargo Alarm Services, Inc. v. Virginia Employment Comm'n*, 24 Va. App. 377, 482 S.E.2d 841 (Va. Ct. App. 1997).

C. Behavioral Expectations

An employer can require employees to conform to reasonable standards of behavior. For example, an employer has the right to expect its employees will not engage in conduct that seriously endangers people's safety. Firing an employee who violates these expectations may result in the denial of unemployment benefits.

♦   An employee for a Kentucky water company accumulated three code of conduct violations within 24 months. The violations related to tardiness, inappropriate behavior in a meeting held to address her tardiness, and leaving work early. She also refused to sign written warnings. She was given the choice between resigning and signing a last chance agreement. When she refused to do either, her employment was terminated. The state unemployment insurance commission determined she was not entitled to unemployment benefits because she was fired for misconduct. A trial court affirmed that decision, but an intermediate appeals court reversed. The intermediate appeals court held it was not reasonable to force the employee to choose between being terminated and signing a statement including admissions she disputed. On further review, the state's highest court decided that the employee was not entitled to benefits because she was terminated for tardiness, which was included within a relevant state law definition of misconduct. The court further held that **a finding of willful or wanton misconduct was not a prerequisite to a denial of benefits**; it was enough that the employee's tardiness met the statutory definition of misconduct. *Kentucky Unemployment Insurance Comm'n v. Cecil*, 381 S.W.3d 238 (Ky. 2012).

◆   A temporary employee for a software company in Georgia knew that her job required her to travel a lot. On January 11, 2008, she received an email giving her a "heads-up" on an upcoming project in Kansas City. That email did not specify a start date, how long it would last, or even that the employee would be assigned to it. On Wednesday, January 23, she was told she was expected to travel to Kansas City on Monday, January 28. Having only two working days to get child care for when she was away, she failed to find anyone for that job. She was fired after she told the company she couldn't make the trip. When she filed for unemployment benefits, the company asserted that she had deliberately put off finding child care. The Georgia Court of Appeals disagreed. **She tried to find child care after receiving short notice of the out-of-town assignment but was unable to do so.** As a result, she was entitled to unemployment compensation. *Davane v. Thurmond*, 685 S.E.2d 446 (Ga. Ct. App. 2009).

◆   After a rude customer called a Macy's employee a "bitch," **the employee told the customer to get her "fat ass out of here."** She was then fired. When she applied for unemployment compensation benefits, they were denied. She appealed. At the hearing, Macy's was represented by a non-attorney employee of a company that specialized in unemployment matters. The hearing officer found for Macy's, but a court reversed on the grounds that Macy's wasn't represented by a lawyer. The Supreme Court of Pennsylvania eventually heard the case and decided that Macy's did not have to hire a lawyer to represent it at unemployment compensation hearings because such hearings were not trials and did not involve complex legal analysis. Macy's did not have to pay benefits to the fired employee. *Harkness v. Unemployment Compensation Board of Review*, 920 A.2d 162 (Pa. 2007).

◆   A spray painter worked for an Ohio company for 11 years, the last two of which were marred by harassing behavior from a co-worker who sabotaged his work. He complained repeatedly to management, but little was done. Finally, the painter saw the co-worker remove a lock from a box containing paint spray equipment, for which the painter was responsible. He told his supervisor he was going to "kill the f---ing son of a bitch, stab him in the heart with a screwdriver."

He was fired and applied for unemployment benefits. The Ohio Court of Appeals held that he was entitled to benefits. Here, the painter's inappropriate statement to his supervisor was predictable under the circumstances, and he never directly threatened the co-worker. The company was partly to blame for the incident because it failed to adequately address the earlier harassment. **Because the termination was not for just cause, benefits were awarded.** *Thompson v. Aeroquip Inoac Co.*, No. 5-02-022, 2003 WL 1861005 (Ohio Ct. App. 2003).

◆   A room service manager for a Missouri casino experienced substantial bleeding associated with her pregnancy, and on December 30, her physician advised her to stay off work for the next week. That night (her night off), she was observed at a rival casino with her husband. The casino determined that she had not conducted herself with the loyalty and integrity appropriate to a managerial employee and fired her. The casino believed that in light of her attendance at the rival casino, she could have worked New Years' Eve. The state employment security commission concluded that she had engaged in misconduct associated with her work and disqualified her from unemployment benefits for seven weeks. The Missouri Court of Appeals reversed. First, **even if the firing was justified because of poor judgment and irresponsible actions, those actions are generally not grounds for denying unemployment**. Second, the standard for denying benefits for off-duty conduct is whether the conduct is clearly egregious or illegal. Here, although irresponsible, the manager's conduct was neither. *Miller v. Kansas City Station Corp.*, 996 S.W.2d 120 (Mo. Ct. App. 1999).

◆   After being informed that he could not alter his schedule to make a scheduled court appearance that his immediate supervisor had previously authorized, an Ohio employee stated, "that's bullshit, ... that's f---ing bullshit," and left the office. After imposing a five-day suspension, the employer discharged th employee and opposed his subsequent application for unemployment compensation benefits. A state court reversed a final administrative decision in the employer's favor, finding that the expletives were not directed at any person and were of no relative severity or part of a pattern. An appeals court held that **profanity that was not directed toward anyone did not constitute misconduct** sufficient to disqualify a discharged employee from unemployment. Ohio courts have identified four factors when analyzing discharges based upon profanity, including the severity of the language used, whether the language is part of a pattern of behavior, and whether the outburst was provoked. In this case, each of the factors favored the employee, who had a good employment record and threatened no one. *Lombardo v. Ohio Bureau of Employment Services*, 119 Ohio App.3d 217, 695 N.E.2d 11 (Ohio Ct. App. 1997).

◆   A customer service representative at a Delaware bank made a sexually explicit proposition to another representative. The remark was overheard by another employee who monitored telephone calls for quality control purposes. The bank fired the rep for violation of its written sexual harassment policy, which had been published and distributed to all employees. The rep filed a claim for unemployment compensation benefits, which resulted in a determination that he had been dismissed for just cause. His administrative appeals were unsuccessful, and he appealed to the Delaware Superior Court. The court ruled that **an employee's sexually explicit proposition to a co-worker constituted misconduct** that justified the denial of unemployment benefits. It observed that a New York appellate division court had found similar conduct sufficient to justify the denial of an unemployment compensation claim even in the absence of a written sexual harassment policy. *Tuttle v. Mellon Bank of Delaware*, 659 A.2d 786 (Del. Super. Ct. 1995).

D. Incompetence or Inability

Generally, an employee's failure to perform as the result of inability or incapacity does not constitute misconduct sufficient to deny benefits. However, an employee's <u>lack of effort</u> or unwillingness to perform may result in the denial of unemployment.

♦   A dock worker and truck driver for a transportation company in North Carolina received several written warnings about his job performance. Eventually he was fired and filed for unemployment benefits. The Employment Security Commission determined that he was discharged for substantial fault not rising to the level of misconduct, and disqualified him from benefits for nine weeks. The case reached the Court of Appeals of North Carolina, which upheld that determination. The employee was careless in performing his job duties despite numerous written warnings. **His performance problems amounted to more than just inadvertent mistakes, minor rules infractions or insufficient skill.** The nine-week disqualification would stand. *Reeves v. Yellow Transportation, Inc.*, 613 S.E.2d 350 (N.C. Ct. App. 2005).

♦   The manager at a Mall of America store failed to perform up to the standards expected of her and was told that she would be fired if she did not improve. When she continued to have problems running the store, she was fired. She filed for unemployment compensation benefits and received them. The Minnesota Court of Appeals noted that under state law, **inefficiency, simple unsatisfactory conduct or poor performance due to inability or incapacity are not misconduct so as to deprive the claimant of unemployment benefits**. *Bray v. Dogs & Cats Limited (1997)*, 679 N.W.2d 182 (Minn. Ct. App. 2004).

♦   A typist employed by an Ohio law firm persistently made typing errors requiring three or four drafts to correct. The firm gave her two reprimands advising her that her job was in jeopardy if she failed to improve, then fired her. The state bureau of employment services allowed her claim for unemployment benefits, and an administrative referee affirmed, finding no just cause for the termination, since there was no evidence of willful or wanton misconduct. An appeals board found that the employee's inability, not her unwillingness, to improve her performance had resulted in the employment termination and that this did not constitute just cause for unemployment compensation purposes. The court of appeals reversed, and the employee appealed. The Ohio Supreme

Court stated that **unsuitability for a job position may constitute fault sufficient to support a just cause termination under the unemployment compensation act**. Employers may justifiably fire deficient employees who cannot perform required work. Because evidence indicated that the employee had made serious errors and could not do required work, the employment termination was supported by just cause, and the denial of benefits was affirmed. *Tzangas, Plakas & Mannos v. Administrator, Ohio Bureau of Employment Services*, 73 Ohio St.3d 694, 653 N.E.2d 1207 (Ohio 1995).

◆   A South Dakota truck driver was convicted of driving under the influence of alcohol. As a result, his driver's license was suspended for one year. He was granted a work permit; however, federal regulations require commercial truck drivers to possess a commercial driver's license (CDL). Because the employee could not obtain a CDL, the company offered him alternative continued employment operating a grinder. He experienced difficulties with the machine and was discharged. His claim for unemployment insurance benefits was denied, and a state court upheld that denial. The Supreme Court of South Dakota held that if the employee had been discharged for his off-duty traffic violation and consequent inability to obtain a CDL, the discharge would have been for work-connected misconduct that would disqualify him from receiving unemployment insurance benefits. The employee's voluntary conduct in driving drunk was a knowing and substantial disregard of an obligation he owed his employer. However, he had been discharged because of his inability to operate a grinder. South Dakota law states that the **failure to perform as the result of inability or incapacity is not misconduct**. Accordingly, the employee was entitled to unemployment benefits. *Rasmussen v. South Dakota Dep't of Labor*, 510 N.W.2d 655 (S.D. 1993).

◆   A man worked as a body shop painter in an Ohio automobile shop. He had a third-grade level of education and was functionally illiterate. As the state of technology of automobile paints advanced, his job required an ability to read in order to correctly blend and match the colors. On several occasions he mixed the wrong colors together, which resulted in costly corrections. The employer offered on numerous occasions to send him to school to learn to read, but he ignored the offers. Thereafter, he was issued repeated warnings for poor work performance, followed by a suspension and discharge. He filed a claim for unemployment compensation, which was denied. A board of review and the Court of Appeals of Ohio affirmed that decision. Discharge for just cause requires a finding that the employee was at fault in some way. The employee argued that the technological advances were beyond his control, and that he was therefore not at fault and should not be deprived of benefits. However, the court found that while inability to perform may not be just cause for discharge, **a lack of effort or unwillingness to perform is just cause for denial of benefits**. Here, the employee refused the help and assistance of his employer and co-workers. He did not demonstrate a good-faith effort to improve his performance. *Lee v. Nick Mayer Lincoln*, 598 N.E.2d 1238 (Ohio Ct. App. 1991).

IV. INDEPENDENT CONTRACTORS

In order to be eligible for unemployment compensation benefits, the separated worker must have been employed on terms that meet statutory definitions of employee. An independent contractor is not an employee and therefore receives no entitlement to unemployment compensation upon separation.

There can also be no employer liability for state unemployment compensation taxes where only independent contractors (and not employees) perform work for the "employer."

* A Minnesota laboratory hired "sensory assessors" to perform odor evaluations for clients. The lab maintained that the assessors were independent contractors rather than employees and paid them for each scheduled session, including sessions that were cancelled. After a routine audit, the state department of employment and economic development determined that the assessors were employees for unemployment compensation purposes and ordered the lab to pay unemployment taxes. The lab appealed, and the Minnesota Court of Appeals ruled in its favor. The assessors controlled the manner in which they performed the tests, they did not have fixed work schedules, and the lab would be liable for discharging them if they were performing according to their contract specifications. Thus, **the assessors were independent contractors and not employees**. *St. Croix Sensory, Inc. v. Dep't of Employment and Economic Development*, 785 N.W.2d 796 (Minn. Ct. App. 2010).

* A courier service in California paid drivers to pick up and deliver packages in a timely manner. It filed a complaint for a refund against the Director of the Employment Development Department to recover employment taxes it paid for the drivers. It argued that the drivers operated as independent contractors rather than employees, and that it should not have been assessed under the state's unemployment insurance code. A trial court ruled against the service, and it appealed. The California Court of Appeal held that **the drivers were employees. They worked a regular schedule, and many of those schedules involved regular daily routes.** They infrequently turned down jobs and were paid on a regular schedule. The evidence clearly permitted finding that the drivers were employees such that employment taxes had to be paid. *Air Couriers Int'l v. Employment Development Dep't*, 59 Cal.Rptr.3d 37 (Cal. Ct. App. 2007).

* The South Dakota Unemployment Insurance Division determined that **a flower dealer's rose peddlers were employees**. Thus, the dealer was responsible for paying unemployment insurance compensation taxes. The dealer contested the determination, asserting that the peddlers were independent contractors. The case reached the Supreme Court of South Dakota, which ruled against the dealer. The court noted that, first and foremost, the agreement signed by the peddlers contained a non-compete clause that prohibited them from selling flowers for any of the dealer's competitors for two years within a 70-mile radius of Sioux Falls, if they stopped selling for the dealer. Also, they were

not liable for unsold flowers; the dealer supplied the necessary items for them to sell the roses; the peddlers did not have their own offices; and they did not have sales tax licenses. Even if the non-compete clause was void as overreaching, it demonstrated an intent to keep the peddlers from engaging in independent work of the same nature if their relationship with the dealer ended. The dealer had to pay unemployment taxes. *Moonlight Rose Co. v. SDUID*, 668 N.W.2d 304 (S.D. 2003).

◆   The New York Supreme Court, Appellate Division, affirmed awards of unemployment compensation benefits in cases filed by drivers who owned their own vehicles and worked under contract for trucking and delivery companies. In the first case, an independent driver contracted with a transportation company to share revenues for loading and transporting freight. When he terminated his relationship with the company, the state labor department determined that he was not entitled to receive unemployment benefits. This decision was overturned in administrative appeals before reaching the appellate division, which observed that although the driver owned the vehicle, the company's name was painted on its doors and he responded to the company's instructions. The agreement required that he not work for another company without permission. There was substantial evidence that **the company exercised sufficient overall control over the driver to establish his status as an employee and his corresponding entitlement to benefits**. *Claim of Short*, 649 N.Y.S.2d 955 (N.Y. App. Div. 1996).

◆   In the second case, drivers who owned their own vehicles contracted with a delivery service to accept only deliveries authorized by the service. The service also required each vehicle to carry its emblem. Drivers were subject to a review process and responded only to service dispatch requests. Applying the rule of control to determine the existence of an employment relationship, the appellate court found that **the service maintained sufficient control over the drivers to establish their status as employees**. The service was liable for additional unemployment insurance contributions. *Claim of McKenna*, 649 N.Y.S.2d 953 (N.Y. App. Div. 1996).

V. SETOFF

State laws provide that unemployment compensation benefits can be offset by or can offset other awards. Disability benefits, vacation benefits, pension benefits and workers' compensation benefits may all allow a setoff in certain circumstances.

◆   A Minnesota bank employee with cancer was fired for excessive absenteeism. She asserted that the real reason was disability discrimination, and she sued under state law. The bank offered her a settlement of $50,000 – $18,423 for unspecified damages that was subject to withholding of taxes and issuance of a W-2; $18,423 for emotional injury damages that was subject to issuance of an IRS form 1099–MISC; and $13,154 for attorneys' fees. In the meantime, she began collecting unemployment benefits. The Minnesota Department of Employment and Economic Development determined that she was ineligible for unemployment benefits to the extent that she had received lost wages in the settlement. She appealed that ruling but lost. The Minnesota Court of Appeals held that **the $18,423 payment subject to the W-2 was compensation for lost wages that had to be offset by unemployment compensation benefits**. *Peterson v. Northeast Bank-Minneapolis*, 805 N.W.2d 878 (Minn. Ct. App. 2011).

◆   A Minnesota employee was discharged and received a final paycheck that included a bonus. When she applied for unemployment compensation, a judge determined that she was temporarily ineligible for benefits because of the bonus. She appealed. The Minnesota Court of Appeals noted that **the receipt of severance pay, bonus pay or sick pay made the recipient temporarily ineligible for benefits**. However, vacation pay does not affect eligibility. Here, the law judge had not correctly determined how much of the bonus should be attributed to vacation pay and how much should be attributed to severance, bonus or sick pay. The court remanded the case for further proceedings. *Larson v. Lakes & Prairies Community Action Partnership, Inc.*, No. A09-2081, 2010 WL 3119456 (Minn. Ct. App. 8/10/10).

◆   Ohio auto workers were laid off after a strike in Michigan caused a shortage of parts. When the strike ended, the automaker agreed to pay the Ohio employees a special one-time payment for the week of the Fourth of July, for which the employees would have been paid had they been able to work. The agreement stated that the payment might make the employees ineligible for unemployment compensation already received, and further stated that the employees would have to repay any overpayment. The employees asserted that the special payment should not prevent them from receiving unemployment compensation benefits for the week in question, but the Ohio Bureau of Employment Services ruled that the employees should not receive unemployment compensation for that week. The case reached the Ohio Court of Appeals, which held that **the special payment was "remuneration" such that the employees were not entitled to unemployment benefits for that week**. *Rodriguez v. Ohio Dep't of Job & Family Services*, 847 N.E.2d 458 (Ohio Ct. App. 2006).

◆   A Colorado worker with diabetes and other physical disabilities was laid off from the part-time job he held to supplement his Social Security Disability Insurance (SSDI) benefits. He applied for unemployment benefits, which he was initially awarded. However, when the Division of Employment learned that he was receiving SSDI benefits, it ruled that **because of the offset required by state law, he was not entitled to unemployment benefits**. State law provided for an offset of 50% of the prorated weekly social security benefit. In this case, the worker's weekly SSDI benefit was $311, more than twice his unemployment benefit of $108. Since half of $311 was still more than $108, he was ineligible for unemployment benefits. Further, there was no ADA violation because the offset did not discriminate against him on the basis of disability. He would also have been ineligible for unemployment if he were receiving retirement benefits. *Cericalo v. Industrial Claim Appeals Office of State of Colorado*, 114 P.3d 100 (Colo. Ct. App. 2005).

♦   A seaman worked under a collective bargaining agreement that compelled him to take vacation after 120 consecutive days aboard an employer's ship. Under the agreement, instead of paying the seaman for compelled vacation, the employer paid into a union trust fund, from which the seaman could apply for the benefits from the union. If he failed to do so within 15 months, he would lose the benefits. After 111 days aboard, the seaman began a period of unemployment and, rather than apply for the 56 days of union benefits he had coming, he sought unemployment benefits. The employer asserted that his unemployment benefits should be reduced by the amount of vacation pay it had paid into the union trust fund. The Oregon Court of Appeals disagreed. **The payment into the union trust fund did not entitle the employer to an offset.** *Alaska Tanker Co. v. Employment Dep't*, 61 P.3d 276 (Or. Ct. App. 2003).

♦   A Utah carpenter was laid off by two different employers in one year and received unemployment compensation benefits for parts of two years based on his employment with both employers. He then applied for social security benefits and received a retroactive award that encompassed some months during which he received unemployment compensation. He later filed a third claim for unemployment, which was denied. He appealed, and an administrative law judge ruled that he was ineligible for unemployment benefits and that the retroactive social security retirement income he received reduced his weekly benefit to zero. However, because the employee had notified the department of his social security application, the amount would only have to be repaid from any future unemployment compensation award. An appeal board affirmed the administrative decision, and the employee appealed to the Court of Appeals of Utah.

On appeal, the employee argued that it was improper to set off an unemployment compensation award with social security benefits because social security benefits are not retirement pay and the two programs have separate purposes. The board argued that the setoff was required by state law, which included social security in the definition of retirement benefits. The court agreed with the board, finding that Congress enacted the Unemployment Compensation Amendments of 1976 to **allow the states to reduce unemployment compensation awards by the amount of any public or private pensions received**, including social security retirement benefits. Since Utah's unemployment compensation code permitted a 100% reduction in benefits for retirement pay received, the court affirmed the decision. *Harrington v. Industrial Comm'n*, 942 P.2d 961 (Utah App. 1997).

APPENDIX A

UNITED STATES CONSTITUTION

[Relevant provisions with respect to employment law]

ARTICLE I

Section 1. All legislative Powers herein granted shall be vested in a Congress of the United States, which shall consist of a Senate and House of Representatives.

* * *

Section 8. The Congress shall have Power To lay and collect Taxes, Duties, Imposts and Excises, to pay the Debts and provide for the common Defence and general Welfare of the United States; but all Duties, Imposts and Excises shall be uniform throughout the United States;

To borrow money on the credit of the United States;

To regulate Commerce with foreign Nations, and among the several States, and with the Indian Tribes;

To establish an uniform Rule of Naturalization, and uniform Laws on the subject of Bankruptcies throughout the United States;

* * *

To promote the Progress of Science and useful Arts, by securing for limited Times to Authors and Inventors the exclusive Right to their respective Writings and Discoveries;

* * *

To make all Laws which shall be necessary and proper for carrying into Execution for the foregoing Powers, and all other Powers vested by this Constitution in the Government of the United States, or in any Department or Officer thereof.

* * *

Section 9. * * * No Bill of Attainder or ex post facto Law shall be passed.

* * *

Section 10. No State shall * * * pass any Bill of Attainder, ex post facto Law, or Law impairing the Obligation of Contracts, or grant any Title of Nobility.

ARTICLE II

Section 1. The executive Power shall be vested in a President of the United States of America.

* * *

ARTICLE III

Section 1. The judicial Power of the United States, shall be vested in one supreme Court, and in such inferior Courts as the Congress may from time to time ordain and establish. The Judges, both of the supreme and inferior courts, shall hold their Offices during good Behaviour, and shall, at stated Times, receive for their Services a Compensation, which shall not be diminished during their Continuance in Office.

Section 2. The judicial Power shall extend to all Cases, in Law and Equity, arising under this Constitution, the Laws of the United States, and Treaties made, or which shall be made, under their Authority; - to all Cases affecting Ambassadors, other public Ministers and Consuls; - to all Cases of admiralty and maritime Jurisdiction, - to Controversies to which the United States shall be a party; - to Controversies between two or more States; - between a State and Citizens of another State; - between Citizens of different States; - between Citizens of the same State claiming Lands under the Grants of different States, and between a State, or the Citizens thereof, and foreign States, Citizens or Subjects.

* * *

ARTICLE IV

Section 1. Full Faith and Credit shall be given in each State to the public Acts, Records and judicial Proceedings of every other State. * * *

Section 2. The Citizens of each State shall be entitled to all Privileges and Immunities of Citizens in the several States.

* * *

Section 4. The United States shall guarantee to every State in this Union a Republican Form of Government, and shall protect each of them against Invasion; and on Application of the Legislature, or of the Executive (when the Legislature cannot be convened) against domestic Violence.

ARTICLE V

The Congress, whenever two thirds of both Houses shall deem it necessary, shall propose Amendments to this Constitution, or, on the Application of the Legislatures of two thirds of the several States, shall call a Convention for proposing Amendments, which, in either Case, shall be valid to all Intents and Purposes, as part of this Constitution, when ratified by the Legislatures of three fourths of the several States, or by Conventions in three fourths thereof, as the one or the other Mode of Ratification may be proposed by the Congress; Provided that no Amendment which may be made prior to the Year One thousand eight hundred and eight shall in any Manner affect the first and fourth Clauses in the Ninth Section of the first Article; and that no State, without its Consent, shall be deprived of its equal Suffrage in the Senate.

ARTICLE VI

* * *

This Constitution, and the Laws of the United States which shall be made in Pursuance thereof; and all Treaties made, or which shall be made, under the Authority of the United States, shall be the supreme Law of the Land; and the Judges in every State shall be bound thereby, any Thing in the Constitution or Laws of any State to the Contrary notwithstanding.

The Senators and Representatives before mentioned, and the Members of the several State Legislatures, and all executive and judicial Officers, both of the United States and of the several States, shall be bound by Oath or Affirmation, to support this Constitution; but no religious Test shall ever be required as a Qualification to any Office or public Trust under the United States.

* * *

AMENDMENT I

Congress shall make no law respecting an establishment of religion, or prohibiting the free exercise thereof; or abridging the freedom of speech, or of the press; or the right of the people peaceably to assemble, and to petition the Government for a redress of grievances.

* * *

AMENDMENT IV

The right of the people to be secure in their persons, houses, papers, and effects, against unreasonable searches and seizures, shall not be violated, and no Warrants shall issue, but upon probable cause, supported by Oath or affirmation, and particularly describing the place to be searched, and the persons or things to be seized.

AMENDMENT V

No person shall be held to answer for a capital, or otherwise infamous crime, unless on a presentment or indictment of a Grand Jury, except in cases arising in the land or naval forces, or in the Militia, when in actual service in time of War or public danger; nor shall any person be subject for the same offence to be twice put in jeopardy of life or limb; nor shall be compelled in any criminal case to be a witness against himself, nor be deprived of life, liberty, or property, without due process of law; nor shall private property be taken for public use, without just compensation.

AMENDMENT VI

In all criminal prosecutions, the accused shall enjoy the right to a speedy and public trial, by an impartial jury of the State and district wherein the crime shall have been committed, which district shall have been previously ascertained by law, and to be informed of the nature and cause of the accusation; to be confronted with the witnesses against him; to have compulsory process for obtaining witnesses in his favor, and to have the Assistance of Counsel for his defense.

AMENDMENT VII

In Suits at common law, where the value in controversy shall exceed twenty dollars, the right of trial by jury shall be preserved, and no fact tried by jury, shall be otherwise re-examined in any Court of the United States, than according to the rules of the common law.

AMENDMENT VIII

Excessive bail shall not be required, nor excessive fines imposed, nor cruel and unusual punishments inflicted.

AMENDMENT IX

The enumeration in the Constitution, of certain rights, shall not be construed to deny or disparage others retained by the people.

AMENDMENT X

The powers not delegated to the United States by the Constitution, nor prohibited by it to the States, are reserved to the States respectively, or to the people.

AMENDMENT XI

The Judicial power of the United States shall not be construed to extend to any suit in law or equity, commenced or prosecuted against one of the United States by Citizens of another State, or by Citizens or Subjects of any Foreign State.

* * *

AMENDMENT XIII

Section 1. Neither slavery nor involuntary servitude, except as a punishment for crime whereof the party shall have been duly convicted, shall exist within the United States, or any place subject to their jurisdiction.

Section 2. Congress shall have power to enforce this article by appropriate legislation.

AMENDMENT XIV

Section 1. All persons born or naturalized in the United States, and subject to the jurisdiction thereof, are citizens of the United States and of the State wherein they reside. No State shall make or enforce any law which shall abridge the privileges or immunities of citizens of the United States; nor shall any State deprive any person of life, liberty, or property, without due process of law; nor deny to any person within its jurisdiction the equal protection of the laws.

* * *

Section 5. The Congress shall have power to enforce, by appropriate legislation, the provisions of this article.

APPENDIX B

TABLE OF RECENT AND IMPORTANT
UNITED STATES SUPREME COURT EMPLOYMENT CASES

Affirmative Action

Adarand Constructors, Inc. v. Pena, 515 U.S. 200, 115 S.Ct. 2097, 132 L.Ed.2d 158 (1995).

Martin v. Wilks, 490 U.S. 755, 109 S.Ct. 2180, 104 L.Ed.2d 835 (1989).

City of Richmond v. J.A. Croson Co., 488 U.S. 469, 109 S.Ct. 706, 102 L.Ed.2d 854 (1989).

Johnson v. Transportation Agency, Santa Clara County, 480 U.S. 616, 107 S.Ct. 1442, 94 L.Ed.2d 615 (1987).

U.S. v. Paradise, 480 U.S. 149, 107 S.Ct. 1053, 94 L.Ed.2d 203 (1987).

Wygant v. Jackson Board of Educ., 476 U.S. 267, 106 S.Ct. 1842, 90 L.Ed.2d 260 (1986).

Firefighters Local Union No. 1784 v. Stotts, 467 U.S. 561, 104 S.Ct. 2576, 81 L.Ed.2d 483 (1984).

County of Los Angeles v. Davis, 440 U.S. 625, 99 S.Ct. 1379, 59 L.Ed.2d 642 (1979).

Discrimination

Univ. of Texas Southwestern Medical Center v. Nassar, 133 S.Ct. 2517, 186 L.Ed.2d 503 (U.S. 2013).

Vance v. Ball State Univ., 133 S.Ct. 2434, 186 L.Ed.2d 565 (U.S. 2013).

Staub v. Proctor Hospital, 131 S.Ct. 1186, 179 L.Ed.2d 144 (U.S. 2011).

Thompson v. North American Stainless, LP, 131 S.Ct. 863, 178 L.Ed.2d 694 (U.S. 2011).

Wal-Mart Stores, Inc. v. Dukes, 131 S.Ct. 2541, 180 L.Ed.2d 374 (U.S. 2011).

14 Penn Plaza LLC v. Pyett, 129 S.Ct. 1456 (U.S. 2009).

Gross v. FBL Financial Services, Inc., 129 S.Ct. 2343, 174 L.Ed.2d 119 (U.S. 2009).

Crawford v. Metropolitan Government of Nashville and Davidson County, 129 S.Ct. 846, 172 L.Ed.2d 650 (U.S. 2009).

CBOCS West, Inc. v. Humphries, 553 U.S. 442, 128 S.Ct. 1951, 170 L.Ed.2d 864 (2008).

Meacham v. Knolls Atomic Power Laboratory, 554 U.S. 84, 128 S.Ct. 2395, 171 L.Ed.2d 283 (2008).

Sprint/United Management Co. v. Mendelsohn, 552 U.S. 379, 128 S.Ct. 1140, 170 L.Ed.2d 1 (2008).

Ledbetter v. Goodyear Tire & Rubber Co. Inc., 550 U.S. 618, 127 S.Ct. 2162, 167 L.Ed.2d 982 (2007).

Arbaugh v. Y&H Corp., 546 U.S. 500, 126 S.Ct. 1235, 163 L.Ed.2d 1097 (2006).

Ash v. Tyson Foods, Inc., 546 U.S. 454, 126 S.Ct. 1195, 163 L.Ed.2d 1053 (2006).

Burlington Northern and Santa Fe Railway Co. v. White, 548 U.S. 53, 126 S.Ct. 2405, 165 L.Ed.2d 345 (2006).

Smith v. City of Jackson, 544 U.S. 228, 125 S.Ct. 1536, 161 L.Ed.2d 410 (2005).

General Dynamics Land Systems, Inc. v. Cline, 540 U.S. 581, 124 S.Ct. 1236, 157 L.Ed.2d 1094 (2004).

Raytheon Co. v. Hernandez, 540 U.S. 44, 124 S.Ct. 513, 157 L.Ed.2d 357 (2003).

Clackamas Gastroenterology Associates, P.C. v. Wells, 538 U.S. 440, 123 S.Ct. 1673, 155 L.Ed.2d 615 (2003).

Desert Palace Inc. d/b/a Caesers Palace Hotel & Casino v. Costa, 539 U.S. 90, 123 S.Ct. 2148, 156 L.Ed.2d 84 (2003).

Chevron U.S.A. v. Echazabal, 536 U.S. 73, 122 S.Ct. 2045, 153 L.Ed.2d 82 (2002).

U.S. Airways, Inc. v. Barnett, 535 U.S. 391, 122 S.Ct. 1516, 152 L.Ed.2d 589 (2002).

Toyota Motor Manufacturing v. Williams, 534 U.S. 184, 122 S.Ct. 681, 151 L.Ed.2d 615 (2002).

Pollard v. E.I. du Pont de Nemours & Co., 532 U.S. 843, 121 S.Ct. 1946, 150 L.Ed.2d 62 (2001).

Reeves v. Sanderson Plumbing Products, 530 U.S. 133, 120 S.Ct. 2097, 147 L.Ed.2d 105 (2000).

Albertsons, Inc. v. Kirkingburg, 527 U.S. 555, 119 S.Ct. 2162, 144 L.Ed.2d 518 (1999).

Murphy v. United Parcel Service, Inc., 527 U.S. 516, 119 S.Ct. 2133, 144 L.Ed.2d 484 (1999).

Sutton v. United Air Lines, Inc., 527 U.S. 471, 119 S.Ct. 2139, 144 L.Ed.2d 450 (1999).

Cleveland v. Policy Management Systems Corp., 526 U.S. 795, 119 S.Ct. 1597, 143 L.Ed.2d 966 (1999).

Kolstad v. American Dental Ass'n, 527 U.S. 526, 119 S.Ct. 2118, 144 L.Ed.2d 494 (1999).

Faragher v. City of Boca Raton, 524 U.S. 775, 118 S.Ct. 2275, 141 L.Ed.2d 662 (1998).

Burlington Industries, Inc. v. Ellerth, 524 U.S. 742, 118 S.Ct. 2257, 141 L.Ed.2d 633 (1998).

Bragdon v. Abbott, 524 U.S. 624, 118 S.Ct. 2196, 141 L.Ed.2d 540 (1998).

Oncale v. Sundowner Offshore Services, Inc., 523 U.S. 75, 118 S.Ct. 998, 140 L.Ed.2d 201 (1998).

Oubre v. Entergy Operations, Inc., 522 U.S. 422, 118 S.Ct. 838, 139 L.Ed.2d 849 (1998).

Walters v. Metropolitan Educ. Enterprises, Inc., 519 U.S. 202, 117 S.Ct. 660, 136 L.Ed.2d 644 (1997).

Robinson v. Shell Oil Co., 519 U.S. 337, 117 S.Ct. 843, 136 L.Ed.2d 808 (1997).

O'Connor v. Consolidated Coin Caterers Corp., 517 U.S. 308, 116 S.Ct. 1307, 134 L.Ed.2d 433 (1996).

Commissioner of Internal Revenue v. Schleier, 515 U.S. 323, 115 S.Ct. 2159, 132 L.Ed.2d 294 (1995).

McKennon v. Nashville Banner Publishing Co., 513 U.S. 352, 115 S.Ct. 879, 130 L.Ed.2d 852 (1995).

Harris v. Forklift Systems, Inc., 510 U.S. 17, 114 S.Ct. 367, 126 L.Ed.2d 295 (1993).

Hazen Paper Co. v. Biggins, 507 U.S. 604, 113 S.Ct. 1701, 123 L.Ed.2d 338 (1993).

St. Mary's Honor Center v. Hicks, 509 U.S. 502, 113 S.Ct. 2742, 125 L.Ed.2d 407 (1993).

Astoria Federal Saving and Loan Ass'n v. Solimino, 501 U.S. 104, 111 S.Ct. 2166, 115 L.Ed.2d 96 (1991).

Gilmer v. Interstate/Johnson Lane Corp., 500 U.S. 20, 111 S.Ct. 1647, 114 L.Ed.2d 26 (1991).

Stevens v. Dep't of the Treasury, 500 U.S. 1, 111 S.Ct. 1562, 114 L.Ed.2d 1 (1991).

EEOC v. Arabian American Oil Co., 499 U.S. 244, 111 S.Ct. 1227, 113 L.Ed.2d 274 (1991).

Int'l Union, UAW v. Johnson Controls, 499 U.S. 187, 111 S.Ct. 1196, 113 L.Ed.2d 158 (1991).

Public Employees Retirement System of Ohio v. Betts, 492 U.S. 158, 109 S.Ct. 2854, 106 L.Ed.2d 134 (1989).

Jett v. Dallas Independent School Dist., 491 U.S. 701, 109 S.Ct. 2702, 105 L.Ed.2d 598 (1989).

Patterson v. McLean Credit Union, 491 U.S. 164, 109 S.Ct. 2363, 105 L.Ed.2d 132 (1989).

Lorance v. AT&T Technologies, Inc., 490 U.S. 900, 109 S.Ct. 2261, 104 L.Ed.2d 961 (1989).

Wards Cove Packing Co., Inc. v. Atonio, 490 U.S. 642, 109 S.Ct. 2115, 104 L.Ed.2d 733 (1989).

Price Waterhouse v. Hopkins, 490 U.S. 228, 109 S.Ct.1775, 104 L.Ed.2d 268 (1989).

Watson v. Fort Worth Bank and Trust, 487 U.S. 977, 108 S.Ct. 2777, 101 L.Ed.2d 827 (1988).

Goodman v. Lukens Steel Co., 482 U.S. 656, 107 S.Ct. 2617, 96 L.Ed.2d 572 (1987).

School Board of Nassau County, Fla. v. Arline, 480 U.S. 273, 107 S.Ct.1123, 94 L.Ed.2d 307 (1987).

Ansonia Board of Educ. v. Philbrook, 479 U.S. 60, 107 S.Ct. 367, 93 L.Ed.2d 305 (1986).

Local No. 93, Int'l Ass'n of Firefighters v. City of Cleveland, 478 U.S. 501, 106 S.Ct. 3063, 92 L.Ed.2d 405 (1986).

Local 28 of Sheet Metal Workers v. EEOC, 478 U.S. 421, 106 S.Ct. 3019, 92 L.Ed.2d 344 (1986).

Meritor Savings Bank, FSB v. Vinson, 477 U.S. 57, 106 S.Ct. 2399, 91 L.Ed.2d 49 (1986).

Western Air Lines, Inc. v. Criswell, 472 U.S. 400, 105 S.Ct. 2743, 86 L.Ed.2d 321 (1985).

Connecticut v. Teal, 457 U.S. 440, 102 S.Ct. 2525, 73 L.Ed.2d 130 (1982).

County of Washington v. Gunther, 452 U.S. 161, 101 S.Ct. 2242, 68 L.Ed.2d 751 (1981).

Texas Dep't of Community Affairs v. Burdine, 450 U.S. 248, 101 S.Ct. 1089, 67 L.Ed.2d 207 (1981).

Int'l Brotherhood of Teamsters v. U.S., 433 U.S. 324, 97 S.Ct. 1843, 52 L.Ed.2d 396 (1977).

Dothard v. Rawlinson, 433 U.S. 321, 97 S.Ct. 2720, 53 L.Ed.2d 786 (1977).

Trans World Airlines, Inc. v. Hardison, 432 U.S. 63, 97 S.Ct. 2264, 53 L.Ed.2d 113 (1977).

Massachusetts Board of Retirement v. Murgia, 427 U.S. 307, 96 S.Ct. 2562, 49 L.Ed.2d 520 (1976).

Albemarle Paper Co. v. Moody, 422 U.S. 405, 95 S.Ct. 2362, 45 L.Ed.2d 280 (1975).

Espinoza v. Farah Manufacturing Co., 414 U.S. 86, 96 S.Ct. 334, 38 L.Ed.2d 287 (1973).

McDonnell Douglas Corp. v. Green, 411 U.S. 792, 93 S.Ct. 1817, 36 L.Ed.2d 668 (1973).

Griggs v. Duke Power Co., 401 U.S. 424, 91 S.Ct. 849, 28 L.Ed.2d 158 (1971).

Employee Benefits

Burwell v. Hobby Lobby Stores, Inc., 134 S.Ct. 2751 (U.S. 2014).

Heimeshoff v. Hartford Life & Accident Insurance Co., 134 S.Ct. 604 (U.S. 2013).

U.S. Airways v. McCutchen, 133 S.Ct. 1537 (U.S. 2013).

Cigna Corp. v. Amara, 131 S.Ct. 1866, 179 L.Ed.2d 843 (U.S. 2011).

Kennedy v. Plan Administrator for DuPont Savings and Investment Plan, 129 S.Ct. 865, 172 L.Ed.2d 662 (U.S. 2009).

LaRue v. DeWolff, Boberg & Associates, 552 U.S. 248, 128 S.Ct. 1020, 169 L.Ed.2d 847 (2008).

Metropolitan Life Insurance Co. v. Glenn, Inc., 128 S.Ct. 2343, 171 L.Ed.2d 299 (U.S. 2008).

Beck v. PACE Int'l Union, 127 S.Ct. 2310, 168 L.Ed.2d 1 (U.S. 2007).

Sereboff v. Mid Atlantic Medical Services, Inc., 547 U.S. 356, 126 S.Ct. 1869, 164 L.Ed.2d 612 (2006).

Aetna Health Care v. Davila, 542 U.S. 200, 124 S.Ct. 2488, 159 L.Ed.2d 312 (2004).

Cent. Laborers' Pension Fund v. Heinz, 541 U.S. 739, 124 S.Ct. 2230, 159 L.Ed.2d 46 (2004).

Black & Decker Disability Plan v. Nord, 123 S.Ct. 1965, 155 L.Ed.2d 1034 (2003).

Great-West Life & Annuity Insurance Co. v. Knudson, 534 U.S. 204, 122 S.Ct. 708, 151 L.Ed.2d 635 (2002).

Egelhoff v. Egelhoff, 532 U.S. 141, 121 S.Ct. 1322, 149 L.Ed.2d 264 (2001).

Eastern Enterprises v. Apfel, 524 U.S. 498, 118 S.Ct. 2131, 141 L.Ed.2d 451 (1998).

Geissal v. Moore Medical Corp., 524 U.S. 74, 118 S.Ct. 1869, 141 L.Ed.2d 64 (1998).

Bay Area Laundry and Dry Cleaning Pension Trust Fund v. Ferbar Corp. of California, Inc., 522 U.S. 192, 118 S.Ct. 542, 139 L.Ed.2d 553 (1997).

California Division of Labor Standards Enforcement v. Dillingham Construction N.A., Inc., 519 U.S. 316, 117 S.Ct. 832, 136 L.Ed.2d 791 (1997).

Boggs v. Boggs, 520 U.S. 833, 117 S.Ct. 1754, 138 L.Ed.2d 45 (1997).

DeBuono v. NYSA-ILA Medical and Clinical Services Fund, 520 U.S. 806, 117 S.Ct. 1747, 138 L.Ed.2d 21 (1997).

Inter-Modal Rail Employees Ass'n v. Atchison, Topeka and Santa Fe Railway Co., 520 U.S. 510, 117 S.Ct. 1513, 137 L.Ed.2d 763 (1997).

Lockheed Corp. v. Spink, 517 U.S. 882, 116 S.Ct. 1783, 135 L.Ed.2d 153 (1996).

Varity Corp. v. Howe, 516 U.S. 489, 116 S.Ct. 1065, 134 L.Ed.2d 130 (1996).

Peacock v. Thomas, 516 U.S. 349, 116 S.Ct. 862, 133 L.Ed.2d 817 (1996).

Milwaukee Brewery Workers' Pension Plan v. Jos. Schlitz Brewing Co., 513 U.S. 414, 115 S.Ct. 981, 130 L.Ed.2d 932 (1995).

Curtiss-Wright Corp. v. Schoonejongen, 514 U.S. 73, 115 S.Ct. 1223, 131 L.Ed.2d 94 (1995).

John Hancock Mutual Life Insurance Co. v. Harris Trust and Savings Bank, 510 U.S. 86, 114 S.Ct. 517, 126 L.Ed.2d 524 (1993).

Mertens v. Hewitt Associates, 508 U.S. 248, 113 S.Ct. 2063, 124 L.Ed.2d 161 (1993).

Commissioner of Internal Revenue v. Keystone Consolidated Industries, Inc., 508 U.S. 152, 113 S.Ct. 2006, 124 L.Ed.2d 71 (1993).

Bath Iron Works v. Director, OWCP, 506 U.S. 153, 113 S.Ct. 692, 121 L.Ed.2d 619 (1993).

District of Columbia v. Greater Washington Board of Trade, 506 U.S. 125, 113 S.Ct. 580, 121 L.Ed.2d 513 (1992).

Nationwide Mutual Insurance Co. v. Darden, 503 U.S. 318, 112 S.Ct. 1344, 117 L.Ed.2d 581 (1992).

Ingersoll-Rand Co. v. McClendon, 498 U.S. 133, 111 S.Ct. 478, 112 L.Ed.2d 474 (1990).

FMC Corp. v. Holliday, 498 U.S. 52, 111 S.Ct. 403, 112 L.Ed.2d 356 (1990).

Mead Corp. v. Tilley, 490 U.S. 714, 109 S.Ct. 2156, 104 L.Ed.2d 796 (1989).

Massachusetts v. Morash, 490 U.S. 107, 109 S.Ct. 1668, 104 L.Ed.2d 98 (1989).

Firestone Tire and Rubber Co. v. Bruch, 489 U.S. 101, 109 S.Ct. 948, 103 L.Ed.2d 80 (1989).

Fort Halifax Packing Co. v. Coyne, 482 U.S. 1, 107 S.Ct. 2211, 96 L.Ed.2d 1 (1987).

Connolly v. Pension Benefit Guaranty Corp., 475 U.S. 211, 106 S.Ct. 1018, 89 L.Ed.2d 166 (1986).

Cent. States, Southeast and Southwest Areas Pension Fund v. Cent. Transport, Inc., 472 U.S. 559, 105 S.Ct. 2833, 86 L.Ed.2d 447 (1985).

Metropolitan Life Insurance Co. v. Massachusetts, 471 U.S. 724, 105 S.Ct. 2380, 85 L.Ed.2d 728 (1985).

City of Los Angeles Dep't of Water v. Manhart, 435 U.S. 702, 98 S.Ct. 1370, 55 L.Ed.2d 657 (1978).

Employer Liability

National Railroad Passenger Corp. v. Morgan, 536 U.S. 101, 122 S.Ct. 2061, 153 L.Ed.2d 106 (2002).

Haddle v. Garrison, 525 U.S. 121, 119 S.Ct. 489, 142 L.Ed.2d 502 (1998).

Metro-North Commuter Railroad Co. v. Buckley, 521 U.S. 424, 117 S.Ct. 2113, 138 L.Ed.2d 560 (1997).

Atchison, Topeka and Santa Fe Railway Co. v. Buell, 480 U.S. 557, 107 S.Ct. 1410, 94 L.Ed.2d 563 (1987).

Employment Practices

Integrity Staffing Solutions, Inc. v. Busk, 135 S.Ct. 513 (U.S. 2014).

Sandifer v. United States Steel Corp., 134 S.Ct. 870 (U.S. 2014).

Nitro-Lift Technologies v. Howard, 133 S.Ct. 500 (U.S. 2012).

National Aeronautics and Space Administration v. Nelson, 131 S.Ct. 746, 178 L.Ed.2d 667 (U.S. 2011).

Rent-A-Center, West, Inc. v. Jackson, 130 S.Ct. 2772 (U.S. 2010).

Ragsdale v. Wolverine World Wide Inc., 535 U.S. 81, 122 S.Ct. 1155, 152 L.Ed.2d 167 (2002).

EEOC v. Waffle House, Inc., 534 U.S. 279, 122 S.Ct. 754, 151 L.Ed.2d 755 (2002).

Circuit City Stores Inc. v. Adams, 532 U.S. 105, 121 S.Ct. 1302, 149 L.Ed.2d 234 (2001).

Eastern Associated Coal Corp. v. United Mine Workers of America, Dist. 17, 531 U.S. 57, 121 S.Ct. 462, 148 L.Ed.2d 354 (2000).

Brogan v. U.S., 522 U.S. 398, 118 S.Ct. 805, 139 L.Ed.2d 830 (1998).

California Federal Savings and Loan Ass'n v. Guerra, 479 U.S. 272, 107 S.Ct. 683, 93 L.Ed.2d 613 (1987).

Attorney General of New York v. Soto-Lopez, 476 U.S. 898, 106 S.Ct. 2317, 90 L.Ed.2d 899 (1986).

Free Speech

> *Dun & Bradstreet, Inc. v. Greenmoss Builders, Inc.,* 472 U.S. 749, 105 S.Ct. 2939, 86 L.Ed.2d 593 (1985).
> *Brockett v. Spokane Arcades, Inc.,* 472 U.S. 491, 105 S.Ct. 2794, 86 L.Ed.2d 394 (1985).
> *Connick v. Myers,* 461 U.S. 138, 103 S.Ct. 1684, 75 L.Ed.2d 708 (1983).

Labor Relations

> *Genesis Health Care Corp. v. Symczyk,* 133 S.Ct. 1523 (U.S. 2013).
> *Chamber of Commerce v. Whiting,* 131 S.Ct. 1968, 179 L.Ed.2d 1031 (U.S. 2011).
> *Kasten v. Saint-Gobain Performance Plastics Corp.,* 131 S.Ct. 1325, 179 L.Ed.2d 379 (U.S. 2011).
> *Chamber of Commerce of U.S. v. Brown,* 554 U.S. 60, 128 S.Ct. 2408, 171 L.Ed.2d 264 (2008).
> *IBP, Inc. v. Alvarez,* 546 U.S. 21, 126 S.Ct. 514, 163 L.Ed.2d 288 (2005).
> *Hoffman Plastic Compounds, Inc. v. NLRB,* 535 U.S. 137, 122 S.Ct. 1275, 152 L.Ed.2d 271 (2002).
> *Marquez v. Screen Actors Guild,* 525 U.S. 33, 119 S.Ct. 292, 142 L.Ed.2d 242 (1998).
> *Wright v. Universal Maritime Service Corp.,* 525 U.S. 70, 119 S.Ct. 391, 142 L.Ed.2d 361 (1998).
> *Air Line Pilots Ass'n v. Miller,* 523 U.S. 866, 118 S.Ct. 1761, 140 L.Ed.2d 1070 (1998).
> *Allentown Mack Sales and Service, Inc. v. NLRB,* 522 U.S. 359, 118 S.Ct. 818, 139 L.Ed.2d 797 (1998).
> *Textron Lycoming Reciprocating Engine Division, AVCO Corp. v. United Automobile, Aerospace and Agricultural Implement Workers of America, Int'l Union, Local 787,* 523 U.S. 653, 118 S.Ct. 1626, 140 L.Ed.2d 863 (1998).
> *Auciello Iron Works, Inc. v. NLRB,* 517 U.S. 781, 116 S.Ct. 1754, 135 L.Ed.2d 64 (1996).
> *United Food and Commercial Workers Union Local 751 v. Brown Group, Inc.,* 517 U.S. 544, 116 S.Ct. 1529, 134 L.Ed.2d 758 (1996).
> *Holly Farms Corp. v. NLRB,* 517 U.S. 392, 116 S.Ct. 1396, 134 L.Ed.2d 593 (1996).
> *Brotherhood of Locomotive Engineers v. Atchison, Topeka & Santa Fe Railroad Co.,* 516 U.S. 152, 116 S.Ct. 595, 133 L.Ed.2d 535 (1996).
> *NLRB v. Town & Country Electric, Inc.,* 516 U.S. 85, 116 S.Ct. 450, 133 L.Ed.2d 371 (1995).
> *North Star Steel Co. v. Thomas,* 515 U.S. 29, 115 S.Ct. 1927, 132 L.Ed.2d 27 (1995).
> *NLRB v. Health Care & Retirement Corp.,* 511 U.S. 571, 114 S.Ct. 1778, 128 L.Ed.2d 586 (1994).

ABF Freight System, Inc. v. NLRB, 510 U.S. 317, 114 S.Ct. 835, 127 L.Ed.2d 152 (1994).

Livadas v. Bradshaw, 512 U.S. 107, 114 S.Ct. 2068, 129 L.Ed.2d 93 (1994).

Hawaiian Airlines, Inc. v. Norris, 512 U.S. 246, 114 S.Ct. 2239, 129 L.Ed.2d 203 (1994).

Thunder Basin Coal Co. v. Reich, 510 U.S. 200, 114 S.Ct. 771, 127 L.Ed.2d 29 (1994).

Lechmere, Inc. v. NLRB, 502 U.S. 527, 112 S.Ct. 841, 117 L.Ed.2d 79 (1992).

Litton Financial Printing v. NLRB, 501 U.S. 190, 111 S.Ct. 2215, 115 L.Ed.2d 177 (1991).

Air Line Pilots Ass'n Int'l v. O'Neill, 499 U.S. 65, 111 S.Ct. 1127, 113 L.Ed.2d 51 (1991).

Martin v. OSHRC, 499 U.S. 144, 111 S.Ct. 1171, 113 L.Ed.2d 117 (1991).

Groves v. Ring Screw Works, 498 U.S. 168, 111 S.Ct. 498, 112 L.Ed.2d 508 (1990).

English v. General Electric Co., 496 U.S. 72, 110 S.Ct. 2270, 110 L.Ed.2d 65 (1990).

NLRB v. Curtin Matheson Scientific, Inc., 494 U.S. 775, 110 S.Ct. 1542, 108 L.Ed.2d 801 (1990).

Trans World Airlines v. Independent Federation of Flight Attendants, 489 U.S. 426, 109 S.Ct. 1225, 103 L.Ed.2d 456 (1989).

Communications Workers of America v. Beck, 487 U.S. 735, 108 S.Ct. 2641, 101 L.Ed.2d 634 (1988).

Fall River Dyeing & Finishing Corp. v. NLRB, 482 U.S. 27, 107 S.Ct. 2225, 96 L.Ed.2d 22 (1987).

Icicle Seafoods, Inc. v. Worthington, 475 U.S. 709, 106 S.Ct. 1527, 89 L.Ed.2d 739 (1986).

NLRB v. International Longshoremen's Ass'n, AFL-CIO, 473 U.S. 61, 105 S.Ct. 3045, 87 L.Ed.2d 47 (1985).

NLRB v. Action Automotive, Inc., 471 U.S. 1049, 105 S.Ct. 984, 83 L.Ed.2d 986 (1985).

Tony and Susan Alamo Foundation v. Secretary of Labor, 471 U.S. 290, 105 S.Ct. 1953, 85 L.Ed.2d 278 (1985).

Allis-Chalmers Corp. v. Lueck, 471 U.S. 202, 105 S.Ct. 1904, 85 L.Ed.2d 206 (1985).

Barrentine v. Arkansas-Best Freight System, 450 U.S. 728, 101 S.Ct. 1437, 67 L.Ed.2d 641 (1981).

Termination

Pennsylvania State Police v. Suders, 524 U.S. 129, 124 S.Ct. 2342, 159 L.Ed.2d 204 (2004).

Beck v. Prupis, 529 U.S. 494, 120 S. Ct. 1608, 146 L.Ed.2d 561 (2000).

Baker v. General Motors Corp., 522 U.S. 222, 118 S.Ct. 657, 139 L.Ed.2d 580 (1998).

Lingle v. Norge Division of Magic Chef, Inc., 486 U.S. 399, 108 S.Ct.
1877, 100 L.Ed.2d 410 (1988).

United Paperworkers Int'l Union v. Misco, Inc., 484 U.S. 29, 108 S.Ct.
364, 98 L.Ed.2d 286 (1987).

Caterpillar Inc. v. Williams, 482 U.S. 386, 107 S.Ct. 2425, 96 L.Ed.2d 318
(1987).

Unemployment Compensation

Frazee v. Illinois Dep't of Employment Security, 489 U.S. 829, 109 S.Ct.
1514, 103 L.Ed.2d 914 (1989).

Hobbie v. Unemployment Appeals Comm'n of Florida, 480 U.S. 136, 107
S.Ct. 1046, 94 L.Ed.2d 190 (1987).

Baker v. General Motors Corp., 478 U.S. 621, 106 S.Ct. 3129, 92 L.Ed.2d
504 (1986).

Thomas v. Review Board of Indiana Employment Security Division, 450
U.S. 707, 101 S.Ct. 1425, 67 L.Ed.2d 624 (1981).

Workers' Compensation

American Manufacturers Mutual Insurance Co. v. Sullivan, 526 U.S. 40,
119 S.Ct. 977, 143 L.Ed.2d 130 (1999).

Metropolitan Stevedore Co. v. Rambo (Rambo II), 521 U.S. 121, 117 S.Ct.
1953, 138 L.Ed.2d 327 (1997).

Ingalls Shipbuilding, Inc. v. Director, OWCP, 519 U.S. 248, 117 S.Ct. 796,
136 L.Ed.2d 736 (1997).

*Director, Office of Workers' Compensation Programs, Dep't of Labor v.
Newport News Shipbuilding and Dry Dock Co.,* 514 U.S. 122, 115 S.Ct.
1278, 131 L.Ed.2d 160 (1995).

Chandris, Inc. v. Latsis, 515 U.S. 347, 115 S.Ct. 2172, 132 L.Ed.2d 314
(1995).

Metropolitan Stevedore Co. v. Rambo, 515 U.S. 291, 115 S.Ct. 2144, 132
L.Ed.2d 226 (1995).

*Director, Office of Workers' Compensation Programs v. Greenwich
Collieries,* 512 U.S. 267, 114 S.Ct. 2251, 129 L.Ed.2d 221 (1994).

Thomas v. Washington Gas Light Co., 448 U.S. 261, 100 S.Ct. 2647, 65
L.Ed.2d 757 (1980).

Wengler v. Druggist Mutual Insurance Co., 446 U.S. 142, 100 S.Ct.
1540, 64 L.Ed.2d 107 (1980).

The Judicial System

To allow you to determine the relative importance of a judicial decision, the cases included in *Deskbook Encyclopedia of Employment Law* identify the particular court from which a decision has been issued. For example, a case decided by a state supreme court generally will be of greater significance than a state circuit court case. Hence a basic knowledge of the structure of our judicial system is important to an understanding of employment law.

Almost all the reports in this volume are taken from appellate court decisions. Although most employment law decisions occur at trial court and administrative levels, appellate court decisions have the effect of binding lower courts and administrators so that appellate court decisions have the effect of law within their court systems.

State and federal court systems generally function independently of each other. Each court system applies its own law according to statutes and the determinations of its highest court. However, judges at all levels often consider opinions from other court systems to settle issues that are new or arise under unique fact situations. Similarly, lawyers look at the opinions of many courts to locate authority that supports their clients' cases.

Once a lawsuit is filed in a particular court system, that system retains the matter until its conclusion. Unsuccessful parties at the administrative or trial court level generally have the right to appeal unfavorable determinations of law to appellate courts within the system. When federal law issues or constitutional grounds are present, lawsuits may be appropriately filed in the federal court system. In those cases, the lawsuit is filed initially in the federal district court for that area.

On rare occasions, the U.S. Supreme Court considers appeals from the highest courts of the states if a distinct federal question exists and at least four justices agree on the question's importance. The federal courts occasionally send cases to state courts for application of state law. These situations are infrequent and, in general, the state and federal court systems should be considered separate from each other.

The most common system, used by nearly all states and also the federal judiciary, is as follows: a legal action is commenced in district court (sometimes called trial court, county court, common pleas court or superior court) where a decision is initially reached. The case may then be appealed to the court of appeals (or appellate court), and in turn this decision may be appealed to the supreme court.

Several states, however, do not have a court of appeals; lower court decisions are appealed directly to the state's supreme court. Additionally, some states have labeled their courts in a nonstandard fashion.

In Maryland, the highest state court is called the Court of Appeals. In the state of New York, the trial court is called the Supreme Court. Decisions of this court may be appealed to the Supreme Court, Appellate Division. The highest court in New York is the Court of Appeals. Pennsylvania has perhaps the most complex court system. The lowest state court is the Court of Common Pleas. Depending on the circumstances of the case, appeals may be taken to either the Commonwealth Court or the Superior Court. In certain instances the Commonwealth Court functions as a trial court as well as an appellate court. The Superior Court, however, is strictly an intermediate appellate court. The highest court in Pennsylvania is the Supreme Court.

While supreme court decisions are generally regarded as the last word in legal matters, it is important to remember that trial and appeals court decisions also create important legal precedents. For the hierarchy of typical state and federal court systems, please see the diagram below.

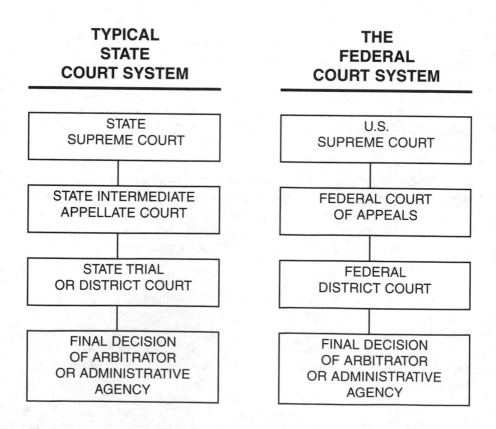

TYPICAL STATE COURT SYSTEM	**THE FEDERAL COURT SYSTEM**
STATE SUPREME COURT	U.S. SUPREME COURT
STATE INTERMEDIATE APPELLATE COURT	FEDERAL COURT OF APPEALS
STATE TRIAL OR DISTRICT COURT	FEDERAL DISTRICT COURT
FINAL DECISION OF ARBITRATOR OR ADMINISTRATIVE AGENCY	FINAL DECISION OF ARBITRATOR OR ADMINISTRATIVE AGENCY

Federal courts of appeals hear appeals from the district courts that are located in their circuits. Below is a list of states matched to the federal circuits in which they are located.

First Circuit — Maine, Massachusetts, New Hampshire, Puerto Rico, Rhode Island

Second Circuit — Connecticut, New York, Vermont

Third Circuit — Delaware, New Jersey, Pennsylvania, Virgin Islands

Fourth Circuit — Maryland, North Carolina, South Carolina, Virginia, West Virginia

Fifth Circuit — Louisiana, Mississippi, Texas

Sixth Circuit — Kentucky, Michigan, Ohio, Tennessee

Seventh Circuit — Illinois, Indiana, Wisconsin

Eighth Circuit — Arkansas, Iowa, Minnesota, Missouri, Nebraska, North Dakota, South Dakota

Ninth Circuit — Alaska, Arizona, California, Guam, Hawaii, Idaho, Montana, Nevada, Northern Mariana Islands, Oregon, Washington

Tenth Circuit — Colorado, Kansas, New Mexico, Oklahoma, Utah, Wyoming

Eleventh Circuit — Alabama, Florida, Georgia

District of Columbia — Hears cases from the U.S. District Court for the District of Columbia.

Federal Circuit — Sitting in Washington, D.C., the U.S. Court of Appeals, Federal Circuit, hears patent and trade appeals and certain appeals on claims brought against the federal government and its agencies.

How to Read a Case Citation

Generally, court decisions can be located in case reporters at law school or governmental law libraries. Some cases can also be located on the Internet through legal Web sites or official court Web sites.

Each case summary contains the citation, or legal reference, to the full text of the case. The diagram below illustrates how to read a case citation.

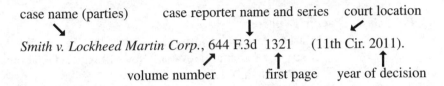

Some cases may have two or three reporter names, such as U.S. Supreme Court cases and cases reported in regional case reporters as well as state case reporters. For example, a U.S. Supreme Court case usually contains three case reporter citations.

The citations are still read in the same manner as if only one citation has been listed.

Occasionally, a case may contain a citation that does not reference a case reporter. For example, a citation may contain a reference such as:

The court file number indicates the specific number assigned to a case by the particular court system deciding the case. In our example, the Idaho Supreme

---

[1] Westlaw® is a computerized database of court cases available for a fee.

Court has assigned the case of *Watson v. Joslin Millwork, Inc.* the case number of "37166," which will serve as the reference number for the case and any matter relating to the case. Locating a case on the Internet generally requires either the case name and date of the decision, and/or the court file number.

Below, we have listed the full names of the regional reporters. As mentioned previously, many states have individual state reporters. The names of those reporters may be obtained from a reference law librarian.

P.   **Pacific Reporter**
               Alaska, Arizona, California, Colorado, Hawaii, Idaho, Kansas, Montana, Nevada, New Mexico, Oklahoma, Oregon, Utah, Washington, Wyoming

A.   **Atlantic Reporter**
               Connecticut, Delaware, District of Columbia, Maine, Maryland, New Hampshire, New Jersey, Pennsylvania, Rhode Island, Vermont

N.E.   **Northeastern Reporter**
               Illinois, Indiana, Massachusetts, New York, Ohio

N.W.   **Northwestern Reporter**
               Iowa, Michigan, Minnesota, Nebraska, North Dakota, South Dakota, Wisconsin

S.   **Southern Reporter**
               Alabama, Florida, Louisiana, Mississippi

S.E.   **Southeastern Reporter**
               Georgia, North Carolina, South Carolina, Virginia, West Virginia

S.W.   **Southwestern Reporter**
               Arkansas, Kentucky, Missouri, Tennessee, Texas

F.   **Federal Reporter**
               The thirteen federal judicial circuits courts of appeals decisions. See *The Judicial System, p. 555,* for specific state circuits.

F.Supp.   **Federal Supplement**
               The thirteen federal judicial circuits district court decisions. See *The Judicial System, p. 555,* for specific state circuits.

Fed. Appx. **Federal Appendix**
               Contains unpublished decisions of the U.S. Circuit Courts of Appeal.

U.S.   **United States Reports**
S.Ct.   **Supreme Court Reporter** ⟩ U.S. Supreme Court Decisions
L.Ed.   **Lawyers' Edition**

GLOSSARY

Administrative Law Judge (ALJ) - an officer who presides at administrative hearings. ALJs are empowered by employment and agency statutes to serve as initial fact finders in many employment cases, including workers' compensation and unemployment benefits claims and many labor disputes. Although courts must give ALJ findings of fact considerable weight, they are not bound by an ALJ's conclusions of law.

Age Discrimination in Employment Act (ADEA) - The ADEA, 29 U.S.C. § 621 *et seq.*, is part of the Fair Labor Standards Act. It prohibits discrimination against persons who are at least 40 years old, and it applies to employers that have 20 or more employees and affect interstate commerce.

Americans with Disabilities Act (ADA) - The provisions of the ADA, 42 U.S.C. § 12101 *et seq.*, specifically addressing employment discrimination went into effect on July 26, 1992. Among other things, the ADA prohibits discrimination against a qualified individual with a disability because of that person's disability with respect to job application procedures, the hiring, advancement or discharge of employees, employee compensation, job training, and other terms, conditions and privileges of employment.

Bona fide - Latin term meaning "good faith." Generally used to note a party's lack of bad intent or fraudulent purpose.

CBA - Collective bargaining agreement.

Class Action Suit - Federal Rule of Civil Procedure 23 allows members of a class to sue as representatives on behalf of the whole class provided that the class is so large that joinder of all parties is impractical, there are questions of law or fact common to the class, the claims or defenses of the representatives are typical of the claims or defenses of the class, and the representative parties will adequately protect the interests of the class. In addition, there must be some danger of inconsistent verdicts or adjudications if the class action were prosecuted as separate actions. Most states also allow class actions under the same or similar circumstances.

Collateral Estoppel - Also known as issue preclusion. The idea that once an issue has been litigated, it may not be re-tried. Similar to the doctrine of *res judicata* (see below).

Due Process Clause - The clauses of the Fifth and Fourteenth Amendments to the Constitution that guarantee the citizens of the United States *due process of law* (see below). The Fifth Amendment's Due Process Clause applies to the federal government, and the Fourteenth Amendment's Due Process Clause applies to the states.

Due Process of Law - The idea of "fair play" in the government's application of law to its citizens, guaranteed by the Fifth and Fourteenth Amendments. Substantive due process is just plain *fairness*, and procedural due process is accorded when the government utilizes adequate procedural safeguards for the protection of an individual's liberty or property interests.

Employee Retirement Income Security Act (ERISA) - Federal legislation that sets uniform standards for employee pension benefit plans and employee welfare benefit plans. It is codified at 29 U.S.C. § 1001 *et seq.*

Enjoin - (see Injunction).

Equal Pay Act - Federal legislation that is part of the Fair Labor Standards Act. It applies to discrimination in wages that is based on gender. For race discrimination, employees paid unequally must utilize Title VII or 42 U.S.C. § 1981. Unlike many labor statutes, there is no minimum number of employees necessary to invoke the act's protection.

Equal Protection Clause - The clause of the Fourteenth Amendment that prohibits a state from denying any person within its jurisdiction equal protection of its laws. Also, the Due Process Clause of the Fifth Amendment that pertains to the federal government. This has been interpreted by the Supreme Court to grant equal protection even though there is no explicit grant in the Constitution.

Establishment Clause - The clause of the First Amendment that prohibits Congress from making "any law respecting an establishment of religion." This clause has been interpreted as creating a "wall of separation" between church and state. The test now used to determine whether government action violates the Establishment Clause, referred to as the *Lemon* test, from *Lemon v. Kurtzman,* 403 U.S. 602, 91 S.Ct. 2105, 29 L.Ed.2d 745 (1971), asks whether the action has a secular purpose, whether its primary effect promotes or inhibits religion, and whether it requires excessive entanglement between church and state.

Ex Post Facto Law - A law that punishes as criminal any action that was not a crime at the time it was performed. Prohibited by Article I, Section 9, of the Constitution.

Exclusionary Rule - Constitutional limitation on the introduction of evidence that states that evidence derived from a constitutional violation must be excluded from trial.

Fair Labor Standards Act (FLSA) - Federal legislation that mandates the payment of minimum wages and overtime compensation to covered employees. The overtime provisions require employers to pay at least time-and-one-half to employees who work more than 40 hours per week.

Federal Employers' Liability Act (FELA) - Legislation enacted to provide a federal remedy for railroad workers who are injured as a result of employer or co-employee negligence. It expressly prohibits covered carriers from adopting any regulation, or entering into any contract, which limits their FELA liability.

Federal Tort Claims Act - Federal legislation that determines the circumstances under which the United States waives its *sovereign immunity* (see below) and agrees to be sued in court for money damages. The government retains its immunity in cases of intentional torts committed by its employees or agents, and where the tort is the result of a "discretionary function" of a federal employee or agency. Many states have similar acts.

42 U.S.C. §§ 1981, 1983 - Section 1983 of the federal Civil Rights Act prohibits any person acting under color of state law from depriving any other person of rights protected by the Constitution or by federal laws. A vast majority of lawsuits claiming constitutional violations are brought under Section 1983. Section 1981 provides that all persons enjoy the same right to make and enforce contracts as "white citizens." Section 1981 applies to employment contracts. Further, unlike Section 1983, Section 1981 applies even to private actors. It is not limited to those acting under color of state law. These sections do not apply to the federal government, though the government may be sued directly under the Constitution for any violations.

Free Exercise Clause - The clause of the First Amendment that prohibits Congress from interfering with citizens' rights to the free exercise of their religion. Through the Fourteenth Amendment, it has also been made applicable to the states and their sub-entities.

Incorporation Doctrine - By its own terms, the Bill of Rights applies only to the federal government. The Incorporation Doctrine states that the Fourteenth Amendment makes the Bill of Rights applicable to the states.

Injunction - An equitable remedy (see Remedies) wherein a court orders a party to do or refrain from doing some particular action.

Issue Preclusion - (see Collateral Estoppel).

Jurisdiction - The power of a court to determine cases and controversies. The Supreme Court's jurisdiction extends to cases arising under the Constitution and under federal law. Federal courts have the power to hear cases where there is diversity of citizenship or where a federal question is involved.

Labor Management Relations Act (LMRA) - Federal labor law that preempts state law with respect to controversies involving collective bargaining agreements. The most important provision of the LMRA is Section 301, which is codified at 29 U.S.C. § 185.

National Labor Relations Act (NLRA) - Federal legislation that guarantees to employees the right to form and participate in labor organizations. It prohibits employers from interfering with employees in the exercise of their rights under the NLRA.

Negligence per se - Negligence on its face. Usually, the violation of an ordinance or statute will be treated as negligence per se because no careful person would have been guilty of it.

Occupational Safety and Health Act (OSH Act) - Federal legislation that requires employers to provide a safe workplace. Employers have both general and specific duties under the OSH Act. The general duty is to provide a workplace that is free from recognized hazards that are likely to result in serious physical harm. The specific duty is to conform to the health and safety standards promulgated by the Secretary of Labor.

Overbroad - A government action is overbroad if, in an attempt to alleviate a specific evil, it impermissibly prohibits or chills a protected action. For example, attempting to deal with street litter by prohibiting the distribution of leaflets or handbills would be overboard.

Preemption Doctrine - Doctrine that states that when federal and state law attempts to regulate the same subject matter, federal law prevents the state law from operating. Based on the Supremacy Clause of Article VI, Clause 2, of the Constitution.

Prior Restraint - Restraining a publication before it is distributed. In general, constitutional law doctrine prohibits government from exercising prior restraint.

Pro Se - A party appearing in court, without the benefit of an attorney, is said to be appearing pro se.

Religious Freedom Restoration Act - Federal law that creates a statutory prohibition against governmental action that substantially burdens the exercise of religion, even if the burden results from a rule of general applicability, unless the government can show that the action is the least restrictive means of furthering a compelling governmental interest.

Remand - The act of an appellate court in returning a case to the court from which it came for further action.

Remedies - There are two general categories of remedies, or relief: legal remedies, which consist of money damages, and equitable remedies, which consist of a court mandate that a specific action be prohibited or required. For example, a claim for compensatory and punitive damages seeks a legal remedy; a claim for an injunction seeks an equitable remedy. Equitable remedies are generally unavailable unless legal remedies are inadequate to address the harm.

Res Judicata - The judicial notion that a claim or action may not be tried twice or re-litigated, or that all causes of action arising out of the same set of operative facts should be tried at one time. Also known as claim preclusion.

Section 504 of the Rehabilitation Act of 1973 - Section 504 applies to public or private institutions receiving federal financial assistance. It requires that, in the employment context, an otherwise qualified individual cannot be denied employment based on his or her handicap. An otherwise qualified individual is one who can perform the "essential functions" of the job with "reasonable accommodation."

Section 1981 & Section 1983 - (see 42 U.S.C. §§ 1981, 1983).

Sovereign Immunity - The idea that the government cannot be sued without its consent. It stems from the English notion that the "King can do no wrong." This immunity from suit has been abrogated in most states and by the federal government through legislative acts known as "tort claims acts."

Standing - The judicial doctrine that states that in order to maintain a lawsuit a party must have some real interest at stake in the outcome of the trial.

Statute of Limitations - A statute of limitation provides the time period in which a specific cause of action may be brought.

Summary Judgment - Also referred to as pretrial judgment. Similar to a dismissal. Where there is no genuine issue as to any material fact and all that remains is a question of law, a judge can rule in favor of one party or the other. In general, summary judgment is used to dispose of claims that do not support a legally recognized claim.

Supremacy Clause - Clause in Article VI of the Constitution that states that federal legislation is the supreme law of the land. This clause is used to support the *Preemption Doctrine* (see above).

Title VII, Civil Rights Act of 1964 (Title VII) - Title VII prohibits discrimination in employment based upon race, color, sex, national origin, or religion. It applies to any employer having 15 or more employees. Under Title VII, where an employer intentionally discriminates, employees may obtain money damages unless the claim is for race discrimination. For those claims, monetary relief is available under 42 U.S.C. § 1981.

U.S. Equal Employment Opportunity Commission (EEOC) - The EEOC is the government entity that is empowered to enforce Title VII (see above) through investigation and/or lawsuits. Private individuals alleging discrimination must pursue administrative remedies within the EEOC before they are allowed to file suit under Title VII.

Vacate - The act of annulling the judgment of a court either by an appellate court or by the court itself. The Supreme Court generally will vacate a lower court's judgment without deciding the case itself and remand the case to the lower court for further consideration in light of some recent controlling decision.

Void-for-Vagueness Doctrine - A judicial doctrine based on the Fourteenth Amendment's Due Process Clause. In order for a law that regulates speech, or any criminal statute, to pass muster under the doctrine, the law must make clear what actions are prohibited or made criminal. Under the principles of the Due Process Clause, people of average intelligence should not have to guess at the meaning of a law.

Writ of Certiorari - The device used by the Supreme Court to transfer cases from the appellate court's docket to its own. Since the Supreme Court's appellate jurisdiction is largely discretionary, it need only issue such a writ when it desires to rule in the case.

INDEX